The Essential
SHAKESPEARE

*An Annotated Bibliography
of Major Modern Studies*

A
Reference
Publication
in
Literature

James L. Harner
Editor

The Essential
SHAKESPEARE

An Annotated Bibliography
of Major Modern Studies

Second Edition

LARRY S. CHAMPION

G.K. Hall & Co.
An Imprint of Macmillan Publishing Company
New York

Maxwell Macmillan Canada
Toronto

Maxwell Macmillan International
New York Oxford Singapore Sydney

G.K. Hall & Co.   Maxwell Macmillan Canada, Inc.
An Imprint of   1200 Eglinton Avenue East
Macmillan Publishing Company   Suite 200
866 Third Avenue   Don Mills, Ontario M3C 3N1
New York, NY 10022

Macmillan Publishing Company is part of the Maxwell Communication Group of Companies.

Library of Congress Catalog Card Number: 92–39078

Printed in the United States of America

printing number
1 2 3 4 5 6 7 8 9 10

Library of Congress Cataloging-in-Publication Data

Champion, Larry S.
   The essential Shakespeare : an annotated bibliography of major
modern studies / Larry S. Champion. — 2nd ed.
     p. cm.
   Includes index.
   ISBN 0–8161–7332–X
   1. Shakespeare, William, 1564–1616—Bibliography. 2. Shakespeare,
William, 1564–1616—Criticism and interpretation—History—20th
century. I. Title.
Z8811.C53   1993
[PR2894]
016.8223′3—dc20   92–39078
                                          CIP

The paper used in this publication meets the minimum requirements of American
National Standard for Information Sciences—Permanence of Paper for Printed Library
Materials. ANSI Z39.48–1984. ⊚™

Contents

Contents

Contents

The Author

Educated at Davidson College, the University of Virginia, and the University of North Carolina, Larry S. Champion is currently professor of English at North Carolina State University, where he served as head of the department from 1971 to 1984. He has published numerous books on Shakespeare and Renaissance drama. An examination of Ben Jonson's late comedies (Kentucky, 1967) was followed by studies of Shakespeare's comedies (Harvard, 1970), Shakespeare's tragedies (Georgia, 1976), Shakespeare's histories (Georgia, 1980), Jacobean and Caroline tragedy (Tennessee, 1976), Thomas Dekker's dramatic works (Peter Lang, 1985), and of Shakespearean and non-Shakespearean chronicle plays (Delaware, 1990). He also compiled a two-volume annotated bibliography of *King Lear*, published in 1981 as number 1 in the ongoing Garland Shakespeare Bibliographies. His articles have appeared in such journals as *PMLA, Studies in Philology, Shakespeare Quarterly, Studies in English Literature, Modern Language Quarterly, Texas Studies in Literature and Language, English Studies,* and *Medieval and Renaissance Drama in England*.

Professor Champion's first edition of *The Essential Shakespeare*, published in 1986, covered items of significant Shakespearean scholarship through 1983. This second edition, enlarged from 1,511 to 1,807 entries and featuring over 650 new entries, provides coverage through 1991.

Preface

Far more is written about Shakespeare than about any other literary figure. Eight years ago I wrote that the *daily* rate of production varied from 1.5 to 8.8 articles/books, depending on which bibliography one uses for a point of reference. Despite recent attacks on the canon and on Shakespeare as its central icon, there has been no diminution in such interest. The *MLA International Bibliography* for 1990 cites 498 Shakespeare items, while the number in the more inclusive *World Shakespeare Bibliography*, covering such matters as reviews of recently published books, productions, and notices of conferences and colloquia, has risen steadily from 3,218 items in 1983 (8.8 per day), to 4,495 entries for 1989 (12.3 per day), and to 4,925 entries for 1990 (13.5 per day). Major plays like *Hamlet* and *King Lear* require literally hundreds of entries in each annual listing. For the Shakespeare specialist the task of covering this progressively burgeoning production is overwhelming. For the student and the more eclectic reader or scholar it is virtually impossible. Equally difficult—if for no other reason than the time required—is the selection of the most significant material from the hundreds of thousands of pages that each year appear in specialized journals, newspapers, and books both from university presses and commercial printing houses.

While this bibliography cannot address the difficulties of inclusiveness, it does aim to provide a convenient and annotated checklist of the most important criticism on Shakespeare in the twentieth century. Since the appearance of the first edition, with effective coverage extended through 1983, new critical methodologies have emerged, generating remarkably provocative perceptions. Formalist and New Critical studies have continued to appear, but the last eight years have clearly been dominated by structuralism, poststructuralism, deconstructionism, feminism, cultural materialism, and new historicism, along with renewed attention to Marxist and psychological criticism and a fresh interest in performance-oriented criticism. In many cases these new approaches have led to studies that interrogate and even repudiate more traditional views. In order to reflect the impact of these new methodologies on Shakespearean studies, this edition features more than 650 new entries representing coverage from 1984 through 1991. For practical purposes of manageability, over 350 entries from the earlier edition have been deleted (never an easy task), and many annotations have been slightly abbreviated. At the same time, for the sake of clarity and in order to make the material more readily accessible, analytic sections that appeared in the first edition, at the end of chapter one (general studies) and at the end of the general studies for each category (the poems, the English histories, the comedies, the tragedies, the romances), have in this edition been incorporated into a single index. Moreover, the entries covering such general sections and those under the individual titles of plays and poems have been increased and made more discursive in nature. This information will help to identify the focus of critical attention and will provide easy access to titles of interest and significance.

Obviously, any project limited to around eighteen hundred entries cannot pretend to include every item of merit, just as one person's list of inclusions will obviously differ in some detail from another's. The effort to cover the entire canon, moreover, imposes certain restrictions on the number of entries for any individual title or phase of the playwright's work. So, too, does the need to limit the number of books dealing with Shakespeare in broad and general terms in favor of a representative number of articles and chapters addressing individual plays, issues, or characters in order to make the bibliography as helpful as possible for users interested in investigating particular ideas in a given play or poem. Within such constraints this bibliography attempts to address the needs and interests both of the casual reader and the student with a specific and limited agenda. The entries as a body represent what is generally accepted as essential Shakespearean scholarship, and the annotations are developed in a manner that reflects the content in sufficient detail to provide helpful guidance for more selective reading.

The material of the bibliography, as suggested earlier, is organized in a relatively simple and straightforward manner. A major section on general studies is subdivided into the categories of greatest importance and interest—reference works, editions of the entire or major portions of the canon, biographies, history of criticism, dating and textual studies, general source studies, investigations of Shakespeare's language and style, discussions of the Elizabethan stage and of the stage history of Shakespearean productions and of the artistic development of Shakespeare on film, and a lengthy number of thematic and topical studies. By design, however, the chief focus is on the individual works—arranged under poems and the sonnets, the English histories, the comedies, the tragedies, and the romances. Each of these divisions includes a selected group of general studies followed by the individual titles and, for each, specific reference works, significant individual editions, critical studies of the individual work, and (for the plays) studies of the stage history.

The sections on critical studies of the individual works are intentionally reflective of the larger body of criticism they represent, both in quantity and in the variety of critical approaches. That for *Hamlet* there are 104 items and for *The Two Gentlemen of Verona* there are 17, for example, is not an inaccurate reflection of general critical interest and activity. Moreover, while the items representing an individual work have been chosen, first and foremost, for their significance, they at the same time are reasonably representative of the diversity of critical opinion and methodology. The *Hamlet* section, for instance, features those critics approaching the play through its language, whether the rhetoric (Maurice Charney—entry 1288, Madeleine Doran—entry 1294), the dramatic imagery (Alan Dessen—entry 1293), or the iconographic associations (Roland Frye—entry 1303, Bridget Gellert Lyons—entry 1334); those critics with psychoanalytic concerns (Avi Erlich—entry 1298, Ernest Jones—entry 1318); those who insist that the historical context provides a key for analysis, whether in the matter of Elizabethan pneumatology and the nature of the ghost (Robert West—entry 146, Geoffrey Hughes—entry 1314, Eleanor Prosser—entry 1347, Arthur McGee—entry 1337) or those concerned with the play as reflective of the profound philosophic transition occurring during the Renaissance (Maynard Mack—entry 1338, Walter King—entry 1324, Ruth Levitsky—entry 1331); those who focus on structural features of the play, whether its metadramatic qualities (James Calderwood—entry 1286, P. J. Aldus—entry 1281, Thomas Van Laan—entry 1359, Maurice Charney—entry 1287) or its relationship to conventions of popular revenge tragedy (Fredson Bowers—entry 1285, Charles and Elaine Hallett—entry 1309, Peter Mercer—entry 1341); those who view the play as fundamentally reflective of Christian precepts (Roy Battenhouse—entry 1284, Sister Miriam Joseph—entry 1342, S. F. Johnson—entry 1319); those whose concern is with the brooding closure (Richard Fly—entry 1302, Rudiger Imhof—entry 1316); those whose interest is in the developing Hamlet saga (Kemp Malone—entry 1340, William Hansen—entry 1310); those who insist on Hamlet's physical obesity (Laura Keyes—entry 1323); those who focus on textual matters, whether the first quarto is corrupt (G. I. Duthie—entry 1277), for example, or sound (Albert Weiner—entry 1276), or on the evolution of the received text (Barbara Mowat—entry 1278); those who focus on matters of political ideology, whether in the social makeup of Shakespeare's original audiences (Annabel Patterson—entry 1346), the text as a site for class conflict as reflected in burial rites (Michael Cohen—entry 1290, Michael MacDonald—entry 1336) or in the language (Oliver Grannis—entry 1307), or in the crisis of aristocratic corruption at the court (Terence Hawkes—entry 1311, John Turner—entry 1358); those with feminist concerns, whether the use of Ophelia to foreground the consequences of an oppressive patriarchal society (Elaine Showalter—entry 1353) or the play as a misogynistic condemnation of sexual activity (J. O'Meara—entry 1345); or those concerned primarily with performance, whether in the tremendous range of passages left open for the actor's interpretation (Michael Cohen—entry 1289), in the proper method for staging the duel between Hamlet and Laertes (James L. Jackson—entry 1318), or in film production (Bernice W. Kliman—entry 1327, Martin Brown—entry 1369, Rosamund Gilder—entry 1370, Alfred Rossi—entry 1373). In pursuing any investigation of critical method or concern with particular issues or structural components of the play, one should also be mindful of those studies cited by entry number at the end of the division that, by virtue of their larger focus, have been relegated to the section on general thematic and topical studies or the section of general studies of the particular genre.

Since the principal aim of this bibliography is to identify the specific essays and books of greatest significance and since limitations of space are so critical, I have not included, as individual entries, collections of essays such as Prentice-Hall's Twentieth Century Interpretations series (for instance, Ronald Berman's on *Henry V*, Hallett Smith's on *The Tempest*, Walter Davis's on *Much Ado About Nothing*, David Young's on *2 Henry IV*, Jay Halio's on *As You Like It*, Walter King's on *Twelfth Night*, Mark Rose's on *Antony and Cleopatra*, Terence Hawkes's on *Macbeth*); Crowell's Casebook series (for instance, Gerald Willen's and Victor Reed's on the sonnets, Leonard Dean's on *Othello*), Heath's Discussions of Literature series (for instance, J. C. Levenson's on *Hamlet*, Robert Ornstein's on the problem comedies, R. J. Dorius's on the histories, Maurice Charney's on the Roman plays, Herbert Weil's on the romantic comedies); the Norton Critical Edition series (for instance, Cyrus Hoy's on *Hamlet*, James Sanderson's on *1 Henry IV*) Scribner's Research Anthology series (for instance, Julian Markel's on *Julius Caesar*); Houghton Mifflin's Research Series (for instance, Rolf Soellner and Samuel Bertsche's on *Measure for Measure*); or individual collections like Laurence Lerner's on the comedies and on the tragedies for Penguin, Helmut Bonheim's on *King Lear* for Wadsworth, Clair Sacks and Edgar Wahn's on *Hamlet* for Appleton-Century-Crofts, Russell Leavenworth's on *Hamlet* for Chandler, Leonard Dean and James McPeek's on *Twelfth Night* for Allyn and Bacon, Leonard Dean's on modern essays for Oxford, or Clifford Leech's on the tragedies for Chicago. During the past few years, a number of commissioned anthologies have appeared, each committed exclusively to a particular methodology such as feminism (for instance, Carolyn Lenz, Gayle Greene, Carol Neely—entry 335) or cultural materialism (for instance, Jonathan Dollimore and Alan Sinfield—entry 264). Then, too, there has been a spate of volumes in honor or memory of individuals such as G. R. Hibbard, Harold Jenkins, Bernard Beckerman, Marvin Spevack, A. A. Ansari, Fitzroy Pyle, Richard Fogle, and Kenneth Muir. Harold Bloom has been indefatigable in producing collections of reprinted essays on both individual plays (for example, on *Julius Caesar* in 1988, *Hamlet* in 1986, *Antony and Cleopatra* in 1988) and the dramatic genres (for example, *William Shakespeare: Comedies and Romances* in 1986, *William Shakespeare: Histories and Poems* in 1986, William Shakespeare: The Tragedies in 1985). And the volumes in *Shakespearean Criticism*, edited by Laurie L. Harris and Mark W. Scott, continue to accrue (thirteen at last count, 1984–91), each providing critical excerpts on a particular play or plays "from the first published appraisals to current evaluations."

The list is only a small sampling of the numerous collections and study guides available on Shakespeare, and I cite them merely as reflective of this larger body of material. Any attempt to include information on every reprint of an article—with some appearing in four or five locations—or to indicate extensive reprint information on book–length studies would severely limit the space available for annotated entries and, since such information is readily available in libraries, would serve no particular need. Limitations of space also permit no attempt here to trace the major developments in Shakespearean criticism, but various entries indicate the availability of such studies (Augustus Ralli—entry 69, D. Nichol Smith—entries 72–73, Arthur Eastman—entry 64, Paul Siegel—entry 71, Paul Conklin—entry 1291, D. F. Bratchell—entry 63, Hugh Grady—entry 65, Terence Hawkes—entry 66, Raymond Powell—entry 68, the introductions to the Garland Shakespeare Bibliographies—entries 562, 588, 621, 658, 693, 804, 848, 919, 965, 1104, 1228, 1272, 1408, 1487, 1535, 1626, 1689, 1707.

This bibliography, more specifically, annotates the most significant items of Shakespeare scholarship from 1900 through 1991. The individual plays and poems are arranged alphabetically, as are the entries within each of the subsequent categories. While numerous individual bibliographies have been consulted, I have been primarily dependent, except for the most recent entries, on the annual listings in the World Shakespeare Bibliography (*Shakespeare Quarterly*), in the *MLA International Bibliography*, in the *Shakespeare Jahrbuch* (Weimar and Heidelberg), and in the Modern Humanities Research Association *Annual Bibliography of English Language and Literature*. The entries in this volume are limited to works published in English that are reasonably accessible in most libraries, either directly or through interlibrary loan. I am grateful to Garland Publishing for permission to reprint, with appropriate modifications, several of the *Lear* items from my *"King Lear": An Annotated Bibliography* (entry 1408).

A project of this nature would simply be impossible without the cooperation and support of numerous individuals. I am pleased to record my genuine appreciation to James L. Harner for his support and encouragement throughout the preparation of the manuscript, to David Covington and Gary Jones for providing technical electronic assistance, and to those members of the staff at the library of North Carolina State University who have been instrumental in locating books and materials both efficiently and courteously. I should also repeat my word of appreciation to the Department of English at North Carolina State University for support in the form of a semester's release from teaching duties so that the first edition could be brought to completion. Catherine Carter, Colby Stong, and Patterson Lamb have been helpful beyond measure in checking the accuracy of details at every stage of the project. Above all, I am grateful to my wife Nancy, whose patience and encouragement (to say nothing of the card filing, alphabetizing, and proofing) have been invaluable.

The Essential
SHAKESPEARE

An Annotated Bibliography
of Major Modern Studies

I.
General Studies

REFERENCE WORKS

1. ALEXANDER, MARGUERITE. *Shakespeare and His Contemporaries: Reader's Guide*. London: Heinemann; New York: Barnes & Noble, 1979, 386 pp.

   Provides a plot summary and a synopsis of critical commentary for each of Shakespeare's plays and poems, in addition to brief essays on comedy, dark comedy, poetry, the English history play, the Roman history play, tragedy, romance, and Shakespeare and his critics. Also discussed are twelve major Elizabethan-Jacobean tragedies (by Norton and Sackville, Kyd, Marlowe, Tourneur, Webster, Ford) and five comedies (by Jonson, Beaumont and Fletcher).

2. BERGERON, DAVID M., and DE SOUSA, GERALDO U. *Shakespeare: A Study and Research Guide*. 2d ed. Lawrence: University Press of Kansas, 1987, 202 pp.

   Represents a thoroughgoing revision of the first edition in 1975. The fundamental arrangement remains—a section on the broad outlines of scholarly commentary; a guide to resources covering bibliographies, editions, and studies of genres, groups, and movements; and a discussion that carries the student step by step through the preparation of a research paper. Additions to the first part include coverage of feminist and gender studies, poststructuralism, and new historicism.

3. BERMAN, RONALD. *A Reader's Guide to Shakespeare's Plays*. Rev. ed. Glenview: Scott, Foresman, 1973, 167 pp.

   Cites some three thousand books and articles on Shakespeare, with synoptic comment on many of them. A chapter is devoted to each play,

1

and the entries are divided into sections on texts, editions, sources, criticism, and staging.

4. CAHN, VICTOR L. *Shakespeare the Playwright: A Companion to the Complete Tragedies, Histories, Comedies, and Romances.* Westport: Greenwood Press, 1991, 888 pp.

Serves as a guide for the general reader. Following a brief introduction to Shakespeare's life and career, each play is discussed with interspersed quotations, analysis of historical settings, and descriptions of methods of staging. The focus of the study is to explain how the plays succeed as theater and how characterization, language, and theme contribute to this process. A list of suggested readings follows the treatment of each play.

5. CAMPBELL, OSCAR JAMES, ed., and QUINN, EDWARD G., assoc. ed. *The Reader's Encyclopedia of Shakespeare.* New York: Thomas Y. Crowell, 1966, 1014 pp.

Offers essential information on aspects of Shakespeare's life and works with entries arranged alphabetically. Material is included on individuals Shakespeare is thought to have known, on playwrights who influenced him or who have been influenced by him, on characters from the plays, and on notable actors, critics, and editors. A selected bibliography is also included.

6. CHARLTON, ANDREW. *Music in the Plays of Shakespeare.* Hamden: Garland Publishing, 1991, 440 pp.

Provides performance editions of the song arrangements, incidental music, and ceremonial music—along with play-by-play annotations—for all of Shakespeare's plays. Original melodies have been used for the songs where such evidence permits; otherwise, tunes existing at the time of Shakespeare have been adapted to the texts. These include instrumental settings of popular ballads, courtly and country dances, marches, processionals, and "mood" pieces.

7. DAVIS, J. MARION. *The Shakespeare Name Dictionary.* The Garland Reference Library of the Humanities, 976. Hamden: Garland Publishing, 1992, 400 pp.

Provides a guide to the historical, mythological, fictional, and geographic names that appear in Shakespeare's works, including the poems and the apocrypha. Entries offer likely sources for a name, briefly describe historical and mythological persons and places, and suggest various interpretations of a name. A general bibliography cites all sources for the volume.

8. DENT, R. W. *Shakespeare's Proverbial Language: An Index*. Berkeley: University of California Press, 1981, 289 pp.

Revises and expands the six-page "Shakespeare Index" appended to Morris P. Tilley's *A Dictionary of Proverbs in England in the Sixteenth and Seventeenth Centuries* (Ann Arbor: University of Michigan Press, 1950). The index itself cites 4,684 proverbs or proverbial references from the plays and poems and is followed by three interrelated appendices. "A" lists the citation for the great majority of references in the index; "B" provides for each the *Oxford English Dictionary* location and earliest date; "C" lists references excluded in "A" and explains the exclusion.

9. DORSCH, T. S. *"William Shakespeare."* In *The New Cambridge Bibliography of English Literature*. Edited by George Watson. Vol. 1, 600–1660. Cambridge: Cambridge University Press, 1974, columns 1473–1636.

Lists books and selected articles in Shakespearean scholarship under the following categories: general bibliographies, concordances, glossaries, dictionaries; Shakespeare societies and periodicals; collections; the quarto texts, the plays by individual titles; the poems by individual titles; Shakespeare's life; Shakespeare's personality and interests; technical criticism (sources; influences; transmission of the text; textual criticism; language, vocabulary, style, prosody); aesthetic criticism; Shakespeare's influence; and Shakespeare abroad (France, Germany, other countries). A rigorous compression of the material was edited by George Watson in "William Shakespeare," in *The Shorter New Cambridge Bibliography of English Literature* (Cambridge: Cambridge University Press, 1981), pp. 199–224.

10. EBISCH, WALTER, and SCHUCKING, LEVIN L. *A Shakespeare Bibliography*. Oxford: Clarendon Press, 1931, 294 pp.

Provides bibliographical listings for all titles considered to be "indispensable for scientific Shakespearean study." The section on general studies is divided into categories on bibliography, Elizabethan literature, Shakespeare's life, personality, text: transmission and emendation, sources, the art of Shakespeare, the stage and the production of his plays, literary taste in Shakespeare's time, aesthetic criticism, his influence through the centuries, civilization in Shakespeare's England, and the Shakespeare-Bacon controversy and similar theories. The section on the works themselves is divided into categories on the chronology of the dramas, the individual plays, the poems, and the apocrypha. An author index is included. See also *A Supplement for the Years 1930–1935* (Oxford: Clarendon Press, 1937), 104 pp.

Reference Works

11. ELTON, WILLIAM R. *Shakespeare's World: Renaissance Intellectual Contexts, 1966–1971*. Garland Reference Library of the Humanities, 83. New York: Garland Publishing, 1979, 464 pp.

Emphasizes contextual significances in the interpretation of Shakespeare's work. Although covering only a six-year period, the volume includes almost three thousand entries. The twenty divisions feature such categories as economic-social contexts, educational contexts, humanist-classical, iconographical, military, and musical. A final section on research tools extends the reader beyond the coverage of this single volume.

12. EVANS, GARETH LLOYD, and EVANS, BARBARA. *The Shakespeare Companion*. New York: Charles Scribner's Sons, 1978, 368 pp.

Features sections on Shakespeare and his times (the biographical record), Shakespeare in performance (the stage record through the centuries in England and North America), his works (commentaries on each of the plays and poems with discussion of the printing of the text), and Stratford (the town, Mary Arden's house, the birthplace, the grammar school, Anne Hathaway's cottage, New Place, Nash's house and Hall's Croft, and Holy Trinity Church). Also included is a review of the achievements of the major artists who have performed at Stratford.

13. FOAKES, R. A. *Illustrations of the English Stage 1580–1642*. Stanford: Stanford University Press, 1985, 180 pp.

Presents chronologically within specific groupings illustrations relating to the theaters, stages, and drama from 1580 to 1640. Of particular significance to Shakespeare studies are #5—Booth's view with the lone image of the Theatre, #16—Hollar's draft version for the "Long View" (West Part of the Southwarke) for a view of the second Globe and the Hope, #21—Hollar's "Long View" for the second Globe and the Hope, #22—Hollar's "London and Old St. Paul's" for a view of Blackfriars, #25—Peacham's scene from *Titus Andronicus*, as the earliest illustration to Shakespeare and for stage costume, and #26—Van Buchell's drawing of the Swan.

14. FRYE, ROLAND M. *Shakespeare: The Art of the Dramatist*. Rev. ed. London: George Allen & Unwin, 1982, 271 pp.

Features, in addition to extensive bibliographical guidance, sections on Shakespeare's life and work, the types of plays, the structure, the style, and the characterization. Concerning the comedies, for example, Frye investigates the atmosphere of optimism, the festive endings, the nonsatiric and genial tone, the predominance of young lovers and marriage, the background roles for older characters, the muting of evil, and the green–world environment. The discussion of "dramatic line" and "time line" provides a concept of structure that effectively moves beyond simplistic assumptions of plot summary.

15. GOOCH, BRYAN S., and THATCHER, DAVID. *Shakespeare's Music Catalogue*. 5 vols. Oxford: Oxford University Press, 1990, 4376 pp.

Provides comprehensive documentation of all the published and unpublished music related to Shakespeare's work. This collection incorporates music from many countries with the selections ranging from the sixteenth century to the present.

16. HALLIDAY, F. E. *A Shakespeare Companion 1550–1964*. Rev. ed. New York: Penguin Books, 1964, 565 pp.

Covers the major aspects of Shakespeare's work and the individuals who have been significantly associated with it, whether his contemporaries in the theater, printers and publishers, or later actors, editors, and critics. The material, with entries arranged alphabetically, falls into three general areas—Shakespeare's life and his most important associates; his works, considered as manuscripts and as printed books and their history; the theater, both the physical stages and the acting history of the plays.

17. HARBAGE, ALFRED. *William Shakespeare: A Reader's Guide*. New York: Noonday Press, 1963, 498 pp.

Includes a chapter on dramatic components followed by units on each of Shakespeare's three major periods—1587–96, 1597–1606, and 1607–13. Each unit describes Shakespeare's development in general terms and provides brief surveys of the plays in each period. Additionally, a separate section is devoted to the four major tragedies. Attention is focused on language, versification, prose style, implied stage business, developing characterizations, significant juxtapositions, structural devices, and technique.

18. KAWACHI, YOSHIKO. *Calendar of English Renaissance Drama 1558–1642*. Garland Reference Library of the Humanities, 661. New York and London: Garland Publishing, 1986, 351 pp.

Brings together a daily record of what is known about the plays, masques, royal and aristocratic entertainments, and other theatrical representations from 1558 to 1642. This compendium traces the activities of dramatic companies, indicating the relationship of their productions with each other; it reveals the extent of a play's popularity, and documents rivalries and amalgamations. Each entry is charted by date, di-

Reference Works

vision (whether acted, published, or cited by reference), dramatic company, place, type, author, earliest text, and source.

19. KÖKERITZ, HELGE. *Shakespeare's Names: A Pronouncing Dictionary*. New Haven: Yale University Press, 1959, 100 pp.

Features all proper names in Shakespeare's works, arranged alphabetically and through phonetic transcription indicating the proper English, American, and Elizabethan pronunciation, along with the metrical and phonological variants required by Shakespeare's rhythm. The work serves as a supplement to *Shakespeare's Pronunciation*.

20. ———. *Shakespeare's Pronunciation*. New Haven: Yale University Press, 1953, 516 pp.

Provides a comprehensive account of the playwright's pronunciation along with relevant phonological evidence. Section 1 describes the linguistic situation in Shakespeare's England and assesses the orthoepistic, orthographic, metrical, and rhyme evidence; section 2 discusses Shakespeare's homonymic puns; and section 3 presents the main body of material, the analysis of stressed vowels and diphthongs, of unstressed vowels, of consonants, of stress, and phonetic transcriptions of Shakespearean passages.

21. KOLIN, PHILIP C. *Shakespeare and Feminist Criticism: An Annotated Bibliography and Commentary*. Garland Reference Library of the Humanities, 1345. New York: Garland Publishing, 1991, 425 pp.

Covers feminist and gender criticism of Shakespeare's plays from 1975 through 1988. Over four hundred citations include topics dealing with Shakespeare's women, gender, androgyny, role playing, his own views of women, and his culture's response to them. Works critical of feminist criticism are also included to chart the influence of the movement on contemporary views. An introduction surveys the evolution of feminist analyses.

22. MCMANAWAY, JAMES G., and ROBERTS, JEANNE A. *A Selective Bibliography of Shakespeare: Editions, Textual Studies, Commentary*. Charlottesville: University Press of Virginia (for the Folger Shakespeare Library), 1975, 309 pp.

Includes 4,519 unannotated entries, with major emphasis on works since 1930 and, with few exceptions, a cutoff date of 1970. All items are arranged alphabetically within the major categories of general reference works, bibliographies, dictionaries and concordances, textual studies and critical bibliography, special collections, biographies, and the individual works. In addition to the commentaries, the section on the individual play or poem includes editions, adaptations, promptbooks, translations.

23. METZ, G. HAROLD, comp. *Four Plays Ascribed to Shakespeare: "The Reign of King Edward III," "Sir Thomas More," "The History of Cardenio," "The Two Noble Kinsmen": An Annotated Bibliography.* Garland Reference Library of the Humanities, 236: Garland Shakespeare Bibliographies, 2. New York: Garland Publishing, 1982, 193 pp.

Contains 208 entries representing virtually all publications on the plays from 1940 through 1980—books, chapters, articles, reviews, and notices of stage productions, along with the most significant scholarship prior to 1940. The categories for each play are criticisms, dates, sources, and texts and editions.

24. ONIONS, C. T. *A Shakespeare Glossary.* 3d ed. Revised by Robert D. Eagleton. Oxford: Clarendon Press, 1986, 360 pp.

Updates the 1911 edition and provides definitions of words in Shakespeare's canon now obsolete or surviving only in provincial or archaic use. An outgrowth of the analysis of Shakespeare's vocabulary conducted in the preparation of the *Oxford English Dictionary*, the work also supplies explanations of idiomatic usage, of words involving unfamiliar allusions, and of proper names with connotative significance. Some current words are included, primarily where there is textual obscurity or multiple ramifications of meaning.

25. QUINN, EDWARD G.; RUOFF, JAMES; and GRENNEN, JOSEPH. *The Major Shakespearean Tragedies: A Critical Bibliography.* New York: Free Press, 1973, 293 pp.

Provides a summary of major critical evaluations of *Hamlet* (101 items), *Othello* (153 items), *King Lear* (80 items), and *Macbeth* (82 items). An introductory essay for each play describes the significant approaches and places them in a chronological context. The annotated entries are also arranged chronologically, covering the years from the writing of the play to 1972. The material for each tragedy is divided under criticism, sources and date, textual criticism, editions, and staging.

26. ROTHWELL, KENNETH S., and MELZER, ANNABELLE HENKIN, eds. *Shakespeare on Screen: An International Filmography and Videography.* New York: Charles Schuman, 1990, 404 pp.

Includes 747 entries covering silent and sound films, television productions, Shakespeare offshoots, parodies and travesties, documentaries, operatic versions, and educational films. The entries provide critical commentary both through editorial analysis and through excerpts from a variety of reviews.

27. SAJDAK, BRUCE T. *Shakespeare Index: An Annotated Bibliography of Critical Articles on the Plays, 1959–1983*. 2 vols. Millwood, N.Y.: Kraus International Publishers, 1992, 2398 pp.

Includes citations to more than seven thousand English–language articles published from 1959 through 1983. Indexes are provided to characters and authors (volume 1) and to characters, scenes, and subjects (volume 2). A general introduction suggests major critical directions for the past thirty years and identifies major areas of disagreement.

28. SMITH, GORDAN ROSS. *A Classified Shakespeare Bibliography, 1936–1958*. University Park: Pennsylvania State University Press, 1963, 784 pp.

Cites 20,527 items covering all aspects of Shakespearean scholarship that would appear in standard bibliographies. The first section covers bibliographies, surveys of scholarship, textual studies, sources, Shakespeare's art and style, his stage and the production of his plays, aesthetic critism, his influence through the centures, the modern stage, and the authorship controversy. In the second section each individual play and poem has subdivisions for text, literary genesis, language, general criticism, characterization, miscellaneous, and history.

29. SPEVACK, MARVIN. *A Complete and Systematic Concordance to the Works of Shakespeare*. 9 vols. Hildesheim: Georg Olms Verlagsbuchhandlung, 1968–80, 11,302 pp.

Provides a comprehensive index to Shakespeare's vocabulary in a computer–generated word list. Volumes 1–3 comprise a series of interlocking concordances to the individual dramas and characters for the most part in the order of appearance in the folio, with general statistical information at the beginning of each play. Volumes 4–6 comprise a concordance of the complete works; and volumes 7–9, a concordance of additional specialized materials—stage directions, speech prefixes, bad quartos, variants.

30. ———. *The Harvard Concordance to Shakespeare*. Cambridge, Mass.: Belknap Press, Harvard University Press, 1973, 1600 pp.

Represents in substance if not in format volumes 4–6 of Spevack's *A Complete and Systematic Concordance* (entry 29). This single volume locates each appearance of the more than twenty-nine thousand different words used by Shakespeare, along with information on the frequency of each word, identification of the passage as prose or verse, and cross–references.

8

31. STOKES, FRANCIS GRIFFIN. *A Dictionary of the Characters and Proper Names in the Works of Shakespeare*. London: George C. Harrap, 1924, 360 pp.

    Consists of annotations, arranged alphabetically, of every proper name that appears in the First Folio, *Pericles*, and the poems attributed to Shakespeare. The subjects included are characters from medieval history, Greek and Roman historical and legendary characters, purely fictitious characters, persons alluded to or mentioned but not appearing in the dramatis personae, place names, and miscellaneous subjects such as festivals, seasons, planets, and the titles of books and songs.

32. SUGDEN, EDWARD H. *A Topographical Dictionary to the Works of Shakespeare and His Fellow Dramatists*. London and New York: Longmans, Green; Manchester: Manchester University Press, 1925, 580 pp.

    Provides information on all place names in Shakespeare's poems and plays, in the work of other English playwrights to 1660, and in Milton's works. The entry "East Cheap," for example, after indicating the precise location in London, traces each reference through the *Henry IV* plays, citing as well references in *The Famous Victories of Henry V* and in plays by Jonson, Dekker, Thomas Heywood, and Wager.

33. WELLS, STANLEY, ed. *The Cambridge Companion to Shakespeare Studies*. Cambridge: Cambridge University Press, 1986, 329 pp.

    Provides a revision of the *New Companion to Shakespeare Studies* published in 1971. Individual essays are included on Shakespeare's life, the thought of the age, the nondramatic works, playhouses and players, theatrical conventions, Shakespearean comedy, Shakespearean tragedy, Shakespeare's use of history, the transmission of the text, Shakespeare on stage: 1660–1900, critical approaches: 1660–1904, twentieth–century criticism, Shakespeare on the twentieth-century stage, Shakespeare on film and television, new critical approaches, and Shakespeare reference books.

34. ———, ed. *Shakespeare: A Bibliographical Guide*. Rev. ed. Oxford: Oxford University Press, 1990, 431 pp.

    Updates the earlier publication of 1973, providing a critically selective guide to Shakespeare studies. The opening section deals with bibliographies, periodicals, Shakespeare's life, general reference books, language, editions, reputation, sources and influences, and background. Individual chapters are devoted to the major tragedies and to genres. Later material deals with performance-oriented studies, Shakespeare on stage, film, television, and video. A separate entry features a discussion of recent critical approaches (cultural materialism, feminism and gender critique, new historicism).

COLLECTED EDITIONS

35. ALEXANDER, PETER, ed. *William Shakespeare: The Complete Works*. London: William Collins Sons, 1951, 1376 pp.

    Includes, without introductions, the thirty-seven plays, along with the poems and a transcript of Shakespeare's contribution to *Sir Thomas More*. The introductions to the individual plays may be found in *Introductions to Shakespeare* (New York: William Collins, 1964, 192 pp.). The general introduction describes Shakespeare's early life in Stratford and traces him in London through four periods of his active work as a playwright. A brief discussion of the publications is also included, as are reprints of the front matter of the First Folio and a glossary.

36. BARNET, SYLVAN, ed. *The Complete Signet Classic Shakespeare*. New York: Harcourt Brace Jovanovich, 1972, 1776 pp.

    Features in a single volume the material that appeared in forty volumes between 1963 and 1968. Critical and textual introductions are provided by individual editors for each play, the sonnets, and the nondramatic poems. The arrangement is generally chronological, and an extensive reading list is divided into thirteen categories. The general editor offers introductory comments on Shakespeare's life, the canon, the theaters and actors, the dramatic background, style and structure, Shakespeare's English, his intellectual background, the texts, Shakespeare's comedies, histories, and tragedies.

37. BEVINGTON, DAVID, ed. *Bantam Shakespeare: The Complete Works*. 29 vols. New York: Bantam Books, 1988, individual volumes.

    Represents an outgrowth and revision of Bevington's one–volume *Complete Works*. Assisting as associate editors are David Scott Kastan, James Hammersmith, and Robert K. Turner, with Richard Hosley involved with matters of staging and James Shapiro as co–editor (with Kastan) of the bibliographies. Each of these volumes features a general foreword by Joseph Papp, a section on plays in performance, and a section on the playhouse. The introductory essays to the particular plays are substantially unchanged.

38. ———, ed. *The Complete Works of Shakespeare*. 3d ed. Glenview: Scott, Foresman, 1980, 1745 pp.

    Abandons Hardin Craig's practice of chronological arrangement in favor of grouping by comedies, histories, tragedies, and romances. The text has been completely reset, with spelling modernized and speech prefixes normalized and expanded. In addition to interpretive introductions to each of the plays, a general introduction covers life in Shakespeare's England, the drama before Shakespeare, London theaters and companies, Shakespeare's life and work, his language, editions and editors, and a survey of criticism.

39. BROOKE, C. F. TUCKER, ed. *The Shakespeare Apocrypha: Being a Collection of Fourteen Plays Which Have Been Ascribed to Shakespeare.* Oxford: Clarendon Press, 1918, 456 pp.

Considers the doubtful plays in general and the history of their ascription; compares them in theme, style, and dramaturgic technique with those plays accepted as genuine. Specific comments are then provided on each of the apocryphal works, followed by the full text of *Arden of Feversham, Locrine, Edward III, Mucedorus, Sir John Oldcastle, Thomas Lord Cromwell, The Puritan, A Yorkshire Tragedy, The Merry Devil of Edmonton, Fair Em, The Two Noble Kinsmen, The Birth of Merlin,* and *Sir Thomas More.*

40. EVANS, G. BLAKEMORE, ed. *The Riverside Shakespeare.* Boston: Houghton Mifflin, 1974, 1902 pp.

Features an introduction to Shakespeare's life and to major critical opinions and salient existing problems by Harry Levin, an essay on the plays in performance since 1660 by Charles Shattuck, and a discussion of the text and a glossary of bibliographical terms by G. Blakemore Evans. A note at the end of each work explains the basis for selecting the copy text and lists all textual variants among quarto and folio publications. Introductions to the comedies are provided by Anne [Righter] Barton, to the histories by Herschel Baker, to the romances and poems by Hallett Smith, and to the tragedies by Frank Kermode.

41. HARBAGE, ALFRED, ed. *William Shakespeare: The Complete Works.* Baltimore: Penguin Books, 1969, 1481 pp.

Prints in a single volume the Pelican edition of the plays and poems that originally appeared in thirty-eight volumes between 1956 and 1967. Introductory material is provided on Shakespeare's intellectual and political background (Ernest Strathmann), his life and canon (Frank Wadsworth), his theater (Bernard Beckerman), his technique (Alfred Harbage), and his original texts (Cyrus Hoy). The material itself is divided into comedies, histories, tragedies, romances, and the nondramatic poetry. Each title represents the work of an individual editor who provides a critical introduction.

42. HINMAN, CHARLTON, ed. *The First Folio of Shakespeare.* New York: W. W. Norton, 1968, 928 pp.

Collected Editions

Reproduces a facsimile text from the corrected sheets of the First Folio. The corrected sheets were determined through a collation of the copies of the folio in the Folger Shakespeare Library. Included are an introduction (the value and authority of the First Folio, the printing and proofing, the facsimile) and two appendixes (on the variant states of the folio text and on the Folger copies used).

43. KÖKERITZ, HELGE, and PROUTY, CHARLES T., eds. *Mr. William Shakespeare's Comedies, Histories, and Tragedies*. New Haven: Yale University Press, 1954, 889 pp.

Features a preface by Kökeritz citing the copy text and explaining the reduction in size, an introduction by Prouty describing the nature and quality of the extant folios, and the general printing conditions of Shakespeare's day, and a facsimile edition of the First Folio.

44. RIBNER, IRVING, and KITTREDGE, GEORGE LYMAN, eds. *The Complete Works of Shakespeare*. Rev. ed. Waltham, Mass.: Ginn, 1971, 1743 pp.

Comprises a revision of Kittredge's 1936 edition, incorporating advances in the knowledge of Shakespeare's text, of dates, sources, and general historical background. Kittredge's text and many of his notes remain, though the general introduction and the critical introduction to each play have been written anew by Ribner. The introduction features discussion of Shakespeare and the English Renaissance, his life, life in Elizabethan England, the English drama before Shakespeare, Elizabethan theaters and companies, the publication of the plays, a general survey of criticism, a survey of plays in performance, and a bibliography.

45. WELLS, STANLEY, and TAYLOR, GARY, eds. *William Shakespeare: The Complete Works*. Oxford: Clarendon Press, 1986, 1432 pp.

Provides an introductory essay on Shakespeare's life and professional career as well as a description of the drama of his time. The plays, including *The Two Noble Kinsmen*, a brief assessment of *Cardenio*, and the parts of *Sir Thomas More* attributed to Shakespeare, are arranged in presumed chronological order. The full versions of both the quarto (1608) and the folio (1623) texts of *King Lear* are also included. The section of poems ascribes to Shakespeare the recently discovered "Shall I Die?" An electronic edition is now available in machine readable form (1989). Also published in conjunction with this edition was *William Shakespeare: The Complete Works, Original-Spelling Edition* (edited by Stanley Wells and Gary Taylor, Oxford: Clarendon Press, 1986, 1432 pp.) and *William Shakespeare: A Textual Companion* (by Stanley Wells and Gary Taylor with John Jowett and William Montgomery, Oxford: Clarendon Press, 1987, 671 pp.—see entry 97).

BIOGRAPHIES

46. ALEXANDER, PETER. *Shakespeare's Life and Art*. New York: New York University Press, 1961, 247 pp.

Provides a critical and biographical account of Shakespeare's life and work, with discussion of the plays and poems framed by chapters on his birth and youth in Stratford and on his retirement years. The critical analysis is divided chronologically into four sections: (1) from Shakespeare's arrival in London to his joining the Lord Chamberlain's Men in 1594, (2) from his association with Chamberlain's Men to the opening of the Globe in 1599, (3) from the Globe to the access to the Blackfriars Theatre in 1608, and (4) from the opening of Blackfriars to the burning of the Globe (1613).

47. BENTLEY, GERALD EADES. *Shakespeare: A Biographical Handbook*. New Haven: Yale University Press, 1961, 256 pp.

Depicts Shakespeare's life and artistic methods through the more than one hundred surviving Shakespearean documents. Following a description of the manner in which late seventeenth- and early eighteenth-century legends accrued detail by detail as they hardened into accepted fact and a discussion of the anti-Stratfordians, the study addresses the various phases of Shakespeare's professional career—the actor, the playwright, the nondramatic poet, his relationship with printers, and the contemporary publication of his poems and plays.

48. CHAMBERS, EDMUND KERCHEVER. *William Shakespeare: A Study of Facts and Problems*. 2 vols. Oxford: Clarendon Press, 1930. Reprinted 1989, 1062 pp.

Includes in volume 1 a biographical and textual study of Shakespeare covering his origin, the stage in 1592, his company of players, the book of the play, the quartos and First Folio, plays in the printing house, the problem of authenticity, the problem of chronology, and the plays of the First Folio. The last section provides a separate description of the publishing history of each play and the poems and sonnets. Volume 2 reprints all official contemporary documents relating to Shakespeare, all known contemporary allusions, materials documenting the development of the "Shakespeare–Mythos" from 1625 to 1862,

13

Biographies

and an extensive bibliography. An index is provided by Beatrice White in *An Index to "The Elizabethan Stage" and "William Shakespeare"* (Oxford: Oxford University Press, 1934, 161 pp.).

49. CHUTE, MARCHETTE. *Shakespeare of London*. New York: E. P. Dutton, 1949, 397 pp.

Focuses on Shakespeare as an actor, playwright, and theatrical entrepreneur and provides a wealth of detail about the country village of Stratford, Shakespeare's parents, his affiliation with the Lord Chamberlain's Men at the Theatre and the Globe, his relationships with fellow playwrights associated both with his own and other companies. Appendixes include a review of legends about Shakespeare that first became current during the Restoration and of the attacks on the authority of the First Folio editors that for a time earlier in this century led to a disintegration of the canon.

50. ECCLES, MARK. *Shakespeare in Warwickshire*. Madison: University of Wisconsin Press, 1961, 182 pp.

Recreates Shakespeare's immediate environment during his Stratford years through the court record of wills, lawsuits, property transactions, and miscellaneous letters and papers. In addition to providing a kind of social history of a prosperous country town, the study traces what is known of Shakespeare's ancestors and the career of his father as well as details from some of Shakespeare's boyhood neighbors on Henley Street. The emphasis throughout is not on legend and inference but on the evidence of archival records.

51. FRASER, RUSSELL. *Young Shakespeare*. New York: Columbia University Press, 1988, 247 pp.

Constitutes a biography of Shakespeare from his birth in 1564 until his establishment as a playwright in London in 1594. Known facts are relatively few, set out, for example, by Giles Dawson in sixteen pages in 1958 (*The Life of William Shakespeare*. Washington: Folger Shakespeare Library, 1958, 34 pp.). In this study the facts are fleshed out through Shakespeare's memory as recorded in his plays and poems and from the lives of his countrymen and patron and in the drama of his time. It is from both the public and private face that the portrait of the young artist emerges.

52. HALLIDAY, F. E. *The Life of Shakespeare*. London: Gerald Duckworth, 1961, 299 pp.

Purports to be neither a study of Shakespeare's art nor a fanciful reconstruction of his last years but an attempt to "fill in the gaps between the beads of biographical fact with as great a degree of probability as possible, yet without resorting to any extravagance of speculation" (p. 10). Following an introductory sketch of Restoration and eighteenth–century legends, Halliday chronologically divides the major sections of his narrative into the schoolboy, marriage, London, the Lord Chamberlain's servants, the death of Hamnet, the Globe, the man of property, the king's servant, a grandchild, and Stratford.

53. HONIGMANN, E. A. J. *Shakespeare: The "Lost Years."* Totowa: Barnes & Noble, 1985, 172 pp.

Investigates the so–called lost years, the time between Shakespeare's leaving school and his appearance in London as an actor and a playwright. Evidence suggests that he was probably raised as a Roman Catholic and that from about the age of sixteen he worked as a schoolmaster and player in the Catholic households of Alexander Hoghton and Sir Thomas Hesketh and later for the Earl of Derby. Apparently he secured his early teaching position with the help of the Stratford schoolmaster John Cottom. Composition of the early plays is pushed back to the mid to late 1580s. A chronological table charts the events described in the narrative.

54. QUENNELL, PETER. *Shakespeare: A Biography*. Cleveland and New York: World Publishing, 1963, 352 pp.

Notes that much factual information exists about Shakespeare, whether an attack by a fellow playwright, references to his increasing reputation, or allusions to his human qualities. When these facts are combined with the evidence provided in his plays and our general knowledge of the period, a clear portrait emerges. This study happily champions the ambitious Stratfordian as the author of the canon, tracing the various phases of his work and observing his ability to create onstage literary figures who reflect not only his own times but the universal condition of man.

55. REESE, M. M. *Shakespeare: His World and His Work*. Rev. ed. New York: St. Martin's Press, 1980, 422 pp.

Provides a full account of Shakespeare's life, age, and work through a topical rather than chronological approach. The basic divisions are Shakespeare's youth, his predecessors, the Elizabethan stage, the man as we know him, and his art. The inherited, traditional world picture, in the stages of dry rot just preceding fragmentation, formed the back-

Biographies

ground for Shakespeare's "artistic meditations about life" (p. 328); the age's alternating conception of humanity as at one moment an angel, at another a beast, was particularly well adapted to his dramatic vision of man.

56. ROWSE, A. L. *Shakespeare the Man*. New York: Harper & Row, 1973, 284 pp.

Proclaims itself the first three-dimensional biography of Shakespeare, revealing fully his personal life as recorded in the sonnets and placing his dramatic works in proper perspective. The sonnets can be dated 1592–95 with Southampton as the patron and Marlowe as the rival poet. The dark lady, whose identity was discovered in the manuscript casebooks of the London astrologer Simon Foreman, is Emilia Bassano, the daughter of Baptist Bassano, one of the well-known Italian musicians to the queen. Emilia, pregnant by Lord Hunsdon, the lord chamberlain, was married "for colour" to a minstrel, William Lanier.

57. ———. *William Shakespeare: A Biography*. New York: Harper & Row, 1963, 485 pp.

Claims with the methodology of historical research to have solved several basic issues that have confounded literary critics for countless decades—the problem of the sonnets, the date and occasion of *A Midsummer Night's Dream*, the significance of the Southampton circle to a full understanding of *Love's Labor's Lost* and *Romeo and Juliet*. Divided chronologically into seventeen sections moving from "Elizabethan Warwickshire" to "New Place," the account of Shakespeare's life and work includes many illustrations.

58. SCHMIDGALL, GARY. *Shakespeare and the Poet's Life*. Lexington: University Press of Kentucky, 1990, 368 pp.

Questions why Shakespeare chose to abandon the field of poetry after a signally successful period in the early 1590s. Images of the courtier poet "in waiting" are developed from *Venus and Adonis*, *Love's Labor's Lost*, the sonnets, and the dedicatory epistles. Similarly, the patron–client relationship and Renaissance attitudes toward the writer's profession are examined in *Love's Labor's Lost*, *Timon of Athens*, and *The Tempest*. The conclusion is that the ambitious young poet, "tired of the elaborate obliqueness and uncertain rewards of following in the trains of the powerful at Whitehall or Westminster" (p. 196), cast his lot with the playwrights in an effort to gain greater economic security.

59. SCHOENBAUM, SAMUEL. *Shakespeare's Lives*. 2d ed. Oxford and New York: Clarendon Press, 1991, 656 pp.

   Updates the 1970 edition and includes both a biographical account of Shakespeare and a history of the efforts to construct his biography from the seventeenth century to the present. The material is divided into eight major sections: materials for a life, Shakespeare of the legends, the first biographers, Edmond Malone, the earlier nineteenth century, the Victorians, deviations, and the twentieth century. Of special interest is the comprehensive account of the various Shakespeare claimants.

60. ———. *William Shakespeare: A Compact Documentary Life*. Rev. ed. Oxford: Oxford University Press, 1987, 416 pp.

   Updates the 1977 edition and includes a biographical sketch of Shakespeare, along with reproductions of over two hundred documents—records, public tracings in parish register entries, records of investment, litigation, and professional activity. Shakespeare's story, both in prose and in picture, unfolds against the backdrop of Stratford and London. A compact version of the book was published by the Oxford University Press in 1977. A companion volume, *William Shakespeare: Records and Images* (New York: Oxford University Press, 1981), reproduces and discusses more than 160 additional documents.

61. SPEAIGHT, ROBERT. *Shakespeare: The Man and His Achievement*. New York: Stein & Day, 1977, 384 pp.

   Sets a discussion of each of Shakespeare's poems and plays within the context of his life on the premise that his works constitute the best guide to his biography. If his dramas are not merely veiled accounts of his personal crises or mirrors of allegorical contemporary events, neither are they written in a vacuum; and to understand the subject matter, the perspective, and the level of achievement is in some measure to understand the man.

62. WILSON, JOHN DOVER. *The Essential Shakespeare: A Biographical Adventure*. Cambridge: Cambridge University Press, 1932, 148 pp.

   Believes that the essential Shakespeare is to be found in the relationship to his times, issues, and figures, and in his spiritual development as it can be traced in his poems and plays. Following a chapter on Elizabethan social and political conditions are four chapters intermingling biography with analysis of the plays. *The Tempest* is envisioned as the capstone of Shakespeare's career, achieving a dramatic and spiritual unity and reflecting much of Shakespeare in Prospero.

HISTORY OF CRITICISM

63. BRATCHELL, D. F. *Shakespearean Tragedy*. New York: Routledge, 1990, 224 pp.

Observes that Shakespearean tragedy continues to foster the reinterpretation generally agreed to be the mark of what we call "classic." No single definition of tragedy has gained anything like universal acceptance. Attempts to set Shakespeare's work against that of Aristotle, the Romantics, or Brecht merely give evidence that he wrote as a theatrical opportunist, not a literary theorist. Following a brief discussion of tragic theory from ancient Greek to modern, the focus is on the four major tragedies; for each, excerpts from discrete periods of tragic theory provide a chart of changing critical tastes.

64. EASTMAN, ARTHUR M. *A Short History of Shakespearean Criticism*. New York: Random House, 1968, 418 pp.

Studies the shifting currents of Shakespearean criticism through major critics reflective of the views of their age and of various critical methods of interpretation—Johnson, Lessing and Schlegel, Morgann and Coleridge, Goethe and Lamb and Hazlitt, Gervinus and Lowell, Dowden and Swinburne and Pater, Shaw and Tolstoy, Bradley, Bridges and Stoll and Schücking, Harris and Jones and Lewis, Knight, Murry and Armstrong, Spurgeon and Clemen, Spencer and Tillyard and Hubler, Granville-Barker and Harbage and Spivack, Barber and Holloway and Frye, and Sewall. The method throughout is to provide a framing commentary with liberal quotations from the critics themselves.

65. GRADY, HUGH. *The Modernist Shakespeare: Critical Texts in a Materialist World*. Oxford: Oxford University Press, 1991, 262 pp.

Asserts that Shakespearean critical discourse was formed through the interplay of the forces of scientific modernization and those of modernism that were culturally and aesthetically reactive to them. In other words, paradigms such as New Criticism and historical criticism (for example, the work of G. Wilson Knight, Cleanth Brooks, Robert Heilman, E. M. W. Tillyard) formed the cultural front line in a battle to preserve value and a sense of unity in the face of the dehumanizing, fragmenting tendencies of modernization. The poststructuralist plurality of critical discourses since about 1970 confronts the ideological blind spots and omissions of this cultural development in its own efforts "to rethink and refashion 'culture' for a postmodern era" (p. 245).

66. HAWKES, TERENCE, ed. *Coleridge's Writings on Shakespeare: A Selection of the Essays, Notes, and Lectures.* New York: Capricorn, 1959, 256 pp.

    Aims to provide a fair and accurate text of Coleridge's Shakespearean criticism, to overcome the occasional diffuseness by a reasonable and usable kind of order, to achieve a measure of conciseness and thus to be of value to the average student of Shakespeare. The material is organized into chapters on general principles regarding poetry and drama, Shakespeare as a poet, Shakespeare as a dramatist, the individual plays (extensive treatment for eight, less so for ten others). An essay on Coleridge as a critic by Alfred Harbage is included.

67. PARKER, G. F. *Johnson's Shakespeare.* Oxford: Oxford University Press, 1989, 232 pp.

    Contends that Johnson's criticism of Shakespeare is relatively radical, startling both to his contemporaries and to us as well. Whatever his reputation as a moralist, he in fact was more prone to face than to judge reality. Thus, his essay on Falstaff does not so much weigh the rogue's vices and virtues as it insists on the profound attraction of those vices. Concerning the quality of Shakespeare's tragedies, Johnson was alert to "what is shockingly unnatural" (p. 173) in them—the brutality of Othello's actions against Desdemona, the excruciating bleakness of the end of *Lear.*

68. POWELL, RAYMOND. *Shakespeare and the Critics' Debate.* Totowa: Rowman & Littlefield, 1980, 167 pp.

    Focuses on the "contradictoriness" of Shakespearean criticism as a reflection of the inexhaustibility of his plays, briefly explaining the concept of various critical approaches, then categorizing further discussion under language; topical meanings; source, Christian, and impressionistic criticism; ritual, myth, and archetype; thematic, structural, and Marxist criticism; and twentieth-century (contemporary) criticism. Plays examined in detail from this variety of approaches are *Love's Labor's Lost, Henry IV,* and *The Tempest;* glanced at more briefly are *The Merchant of Venice, Henry V, Measure for Measure,* and *Coriolanus.* The key to the richest criticism is the emphasis on Shakespeare's ambiguity.

69. RALLI, AUGUSTUS. *A History of Shakespearian Criticism.* 2 vols. Oxford: Oxford University Press, 1959, 1148 pp.

    Traces the course of selected criticism on Shakespeare from his own time to 1925 in England, France, and Germany. For each of the forty-two categories of critics, an introduction describes the individuals who make up the group, their distinctive methods, and the intrinsic worth of their views; a conclusion to each section considers those critics as a group to determine the major analytic directions. The study is not only a compendium of criticism on Shakespeare; it is also a partial aesthetic record of the European mind for three centuries.

70. RAYSOR, THOMAS MIDDLETON, ed. *Samuel Taylor Coleridge: Shakespearean Criticism*. 2 vols. London: J. M. Dent & Sons 1930, 506 pp.
    Aims to restore from the original manuscripts the exact words of Coleridge's Shakespeare criticism, which shortly after Coleridge's death was published in garbled form by his nephew. The influence of Goethe, Lessing, Schiller, Herder, Richter, and Schlegel is described in the introduction, as is Coleridge's general defense of the effectiveness of the comic scenes and his defense of Shakespeare's violation of the dramatic unities, and his psychological analyses of characters. In volume 1 the material is arranged in the first section by plays and in the second by topics. Volume 2 focuses on lectures between 1811 and 1819.

71. SIEGEL, PAUL N., ed. *His Infinite Variety: Major Shakespearean Criticism Since Johnson*. Philadelphia: J.B. Lippincott, 1964, 432 pp.
    Reflects Shakespearean criticism since the mid-eighteenth century. The selections, while representing all historical periods, have been chosen primarily on the basis of critical substance. The organization is, accordingly, by subject, with part 1 dealing with broad aspects of Shakespeare's dramatic art. Succeeding portions deal with the various genres—the history plays, the romantic comedies, the satiric comedies, the tragedies, the romances. Each section moves from a general discussion of the genre to treatment of particular plays and characters. A brief introductory sketch provides an overview of critical trends.

72. SMITH, D. NICHOL, ed. *Eighteenth-Century Essays on Shakespeare*. Glasgow: MacLehose, 1903, 340 pp.
    Provides a survey of eighteenth-century opinion of Shakespeare by Rowe, Dennis, Pope, Theobald, Hanmer, Warburton, Johnson, Farmer, and Morgann. The essays represent the chief critical phase between Dryden and Coleridge. The introduction analyzes both the salient points of the criticism itself—on such matters, for example, as the extent of Shakespeare's learning and his attitudes toward the dramatic unities—and also the critical methods brought to the editions. The third quarter of the century is described as one of major transition with emphasis on a return to Shakespeare's text itself and a critical interest in characterization.

73. ———. *Shakespeare Criticism: A Selection*. Oxford: Oxford University Press, 1916, 416 pp.

Includes selections representing the major movements in critical opinion and method from twenty-eight Shakespeare critics from John Heminge in 1623 to Thomas Carlyle in 1840. The early criticism consists of poems and comments comprising the prefatory materials of the First Folio, with the criticism dealing with principles and merits initiated some years later by Dryden. Johnson in the mid-eighteenth century provides a summary of major critical issues, and his judgments are marked by judiciousness and impartiality. Character criticism begins with Whatley, Richardson, and Morgann, culminating in the work of Hazlitt and Carlyle.

74. WILSON, EDWIN, ed. *Shaw on Shakespeare: An Anthology of Bernard Shaw's Writing on the Plays and Production of Shakespeare*. New York: E.P. Dutton, 1961, 284 pp.

Brings together from dozens of widely scattered sources all of Shaw's significant Shakespearean material. Included are over twenty reviews of Shakespearean productions along with letters to Ellen Terry, Mrs. Patrick Campbell, and John Barrymore on the playing of particular roles in the dramas. Matters of acting and production are also addressed. The material is arranged by plays in part 1; part 2 deals with aspects of the playwright—his philosophy, his dramaturgic techniques (weaknesses as well as skills), and his interpreters.

DATING AND TEXTUAL STUDIES

75. BLACK, MATTHEW W., and SHAABER, MATHIAS A. *Shakespeare's Seventeenth-Century Editors 1632–1685*. New York: Modern Language Association of America; London: Oxford University Press, 1937, 420 pp.

Comprises an examination of all variants in the folios of 1632, 1664, and 1685. Scholars have gradually come to realize that, excepting typographical errors, many of the changes in these folios are deliberate emendations meant to improve the text. The anonymous compositors and correctors engage in both acute, intelligent alterations and arbitrary, absurd ones. For each folio, analysis covers changes adopted by many or all subsequent editors, changes that restore the reading of an earlier text, superseded changes, intelligible changes not adopted by most modern editors, and mistaken and arbitrary changes.

76. BLAYNEY, PETER W. M. *The First Folio of Shakespeare*. Washington: Folger Library Publications, 1991, 46 pp.

Dating and Textual Studies

Carries the reader from initial negotiations about the publication of Shakespeare's plays in folio format between Shakespeare's fellow actors and publishers to changes in individual copies as they passed through the hands of binders, booksellers, and owners. New evidence is uncovered concerning the original price of the folio and the practice by at least one bookseller of renting a copy to customers. Discovered also are several leaves from a copy of *Hamlet* marked for use as a promptbook by a London company in the 1670s.

77. BOWERS, FREDSON T. *On Editing Shakespeare and the Elizabethan Dramatists*. Charlottesville: University Press of Virginia, 1966, 210 pp.

Asserts that textual editing is one of the significant aspects of modern scholarship. For Elizabethan drama the fundamental task is to determine the grounds for establishing the copy text—the text that most accurately represents the play as the author wrote it. An editor must also determine whether his edition is to be facsimile, diplomatic, or eclectic (critical). The editor of Shakespeare must make distinctions among foul papers, fair copy, prompt copy, transcriptions, and corrupt texts (bad quartos); must distinguish, as well, among textual variants in equally acceptable texts; and must have an understanding of the printing process and of the types of errors to which it is subject.

78. BURCKHARDT, ROBERT E. *Shakespeare's Bad Quartos: Deliberate Abridgments Designed for Performance by a Reduced Cast*. Studies in English Literature, 101. The Hague: Mouton, 1975, 124 pp.

Presents a detailed account of the nature of the abridgment in the "bad" quartos—*2,3 Henry VI, Romeo and Juliet, Henry V, The Merry Wives of Windsor*, and *Hamlet*. The study argues that the texts are not pirated in any fashion. Instead, they have been artistically and effectively shortened to reduce both playing time and the cast. Abridged good quartos for provincial performance by touring companies, these publications are not textually corrupt.

79. CRAIG, HARDIN. *A New Look at Shakespeare's Quartos*. Stanford: Stanford University Press, 1961, 134 pp.

Attempts through reexamination to simplify the history and classification of the Shakespeare quarto texts prior to the First Folio. In particular, the theory of memorial reconstruction as an explanation for the so-called bad quartos is ingenious but specious. Nor is the theory necessary since normal conditions—"namely, changes made by actors and managers in the texts of plays when they were acted on the stage" (p. 118)—fully account for alterations in the material. Other outmoded methods of textual criticism are also discussed.

Dating and Textual Studies

80. DE GRAZIA, MARGRETA. *Shakespeare Verbatim: The Reproduction of Authenticity and the 1790 Apparatus*. Oxford: Oxford University Press, 1991, 244 pp.

Investigates the emergence of the textual and critical imperatives of the late eighteenth century that motivated the creation of Shakespeare as a historical construct. The focal point is the ten-volume edition by Edmond Malone, published in 1790, revised and expanded to twenty-one volumes by James Boswell in 1821. This was the first edition to emphasize the principle of authenticity, to contain a "factual" biography, a chronological table, and full critical paraphernalia. A distinctly Enlightenment construct, Malone's work laid the foundation, not only for the enormous Shakespeare industry, but, more importantly, for the assumptions that underlie Shakespeare's canonicity.

81. FRANKLIN, COLIN. *Shakespeare Domesticated: The Eighteenth-Century Editions*. Brookfield, Vt.: Scolar Press, 1991, 246 pp.

Provides a general survey of Shakespeare's eighteenth-century editors and editions, including analysis of the debates engaged through prefaces and footnotes, as well as the textual emendations themselves. The discussion, more specifically, covers the editions of Rowe, Pope, Theobald, Warburton, Johnson, Capell, Malone, and the Boswell-Malone variorum, generally acknowledged as the foundation of modern Shakespeare scholarship. The vitriolic nature of the rivalry is aptly illustrated in the descriptive information in the front-matter of Warburton's 1747 edition: "The Genuine Text . . . is here settled: Being restored from the *Blunders* of the first two Editors, and the *Interpolations* of the two Last" (p. 25).

82. GREG, W. W. *The Editorial Problem in Shakespeare: A Survey of the Foundations of the Text*. Oxford: Clarendon Press, 1942, 210 pp.

Describes in the prolegomena the tenets basic to the study of Shakespeare's text concerning the aim of a critical edition and the significance of distinguishing between substantive and derivative editions in the selection of a copy text. Later chapters address the nature and types of theatrical manuscripts, the bad quartos (*2,3 Henry VI, Romeo and Juliet, Hamlet, The Merry Wives of Windsor, Henry V, The Taming of a Shrew, Pericles*) and the theory of memorial reconstruction, two doubtful quartos (*Richard III, King Lear*), the ten good quartos, and the First Folio and the nature of the text for the seventeen plays first printed in the folio.

83. ———. *The Shakespeare First Folio: Its Bibliographical and Textual History*. Oxford: Clarendon Press, 1955, 496 pp.

Dating and Textual Studies

Describes the planning and printing of Shakespeare's collected dramatic works in 1623. Individual chapters are devoted to those instrumental in the project (Heminge, Condell, Jaggard, Blount, the Lord Chamberlain) and to questions of copyright. The bulk of the volume discusses various editorial problems, both the nature of the copy text for each play and particular problematic features such as stage directions, irregular character designations, and indications of censorship or of contamination.

84. HART, ALFRED. *Stolne and Surreptitious Copies: A Comparative Study of Shakespeare's Bad Quartos.* Melbourne: Melbourne University Press, 1942, 478 pp.

Investigates the problems associated with the bad quartos (the "stolne and surreptitious copies"), concluding that all six are derivative texts. A principal form of evidence is Shakespeare's vocabulary. Each of the bad quartos displays "garbling, petty larceny, solecisms, anacoloutha, irrelevance, vulgarity, fustian, and nonsense" (p. 441). The study demonstrates that Shakespeare's version is the prior text and that the text of the bad quarto rests on the oral transmission of what an actor could remember of a part written out by a scribe from the acting version made officially from the author's manuscript.

85. HINMAN, CHARLTON. *The Printing and Proof-Reading of the First Folio of Shakespeare.* 2 vols. Oxford: Clarendon Press, 1963, 1067 pp.

Scrutinizes bibliographical evidence concerning the publication of the folio of 1623. Evidence suggests that about one-half of the plays were printed from manuscripts, and not all of them from Shakespeare's holograph. Others were set from earlier quartos and from a combination of materials, part manuscript and part printed. The cardinal aim of this study is to determine the nature of the copy used by the printer for a particular play or poem and the kinds and amount of modification to which the copy was subject during the printing process. Volume 1 surveys the kinds of evidence and their uses; volume 2, the sections of the histories, tragedies, and comedies.

86. HONINGMANN, E. A. J. *The Stability of Shakespeare's Text.* London: Edward Arnold, 1965, 212 pp.

Argues that editors have given too little thought to the vagaries of authors copying out their own work and that such attention in Shakespearean textual study would provoke a fundamental redirection of editorial policy. Whereas the tendency involving variants in Shakespeare is to assume that one or both must be corrupt, we must not in the name of a single copy text rule out the possibility that both may be

Dating and Textual Studies

Shakespeare's, especially where two authoritative texts exist as in *Othello* and *Troilus and Cressida*. A critical edition, by citing all variants in substantive texts, should make the reader aware of the full range of textual possibilities.

87. HOWARD-HILL, T. H. *Shakespearian Bibliography and Textual Criticism: A Bibliography*. Oxford: Clarendon Press, 1971, 177 pp.

Comprises volume 2 of the nine-volume *Index to British Literary Bibliography*. This volume covers both Shakespearean bibliographies and the literature devoted to the texts of Shakespeare's works, along with the circumstances of their production and distribution. The 1,981 items are categorized under general bibliographies and guides (periodicals, cumulative indexes, serial bibliographies), works (bibliographies, collections and libraries, general, quartos, folios), and textual studies (handwriting and paleography, collected emendations, individual plays and poems).

88. IOPPOLO, GRACE. *Revising Shakespeare*. Cambridge: Harvard University Press, 1991, 247 pp.

Discusses the textual revolution of Shakespeare within a broad historical, theatrical, textual, and literary context. The argument is that Shakespeare's "authoritative" text results from a writer who was constantly revising and rewriting his material (as creator and recreator, viewer and reviewer, writer and rewriter). Thus, the study challenges traditional views of the copy text for the printing of many of the plays.

89. MCKERROW, RONALD B. *Prolegomena for the Oxford Shakespeare: A Study in Editorial Method*. Oxford: Clarendon Press, 1939, 113 pp.

Represents a body of rules developed for an old-spelling edition of Shakespeare that itself never appeared. Individual chapters are devoted to the basis of the reprint (determination of the substantive text, derived texts), the degree of exactitude to be aimed at in reproducing the copy text (orthographical and grammatical irregularities, critical methods of earlier editors), and the recording of readings of other editions than the copy text (variant spellings, collation). Appendixes are included on typographical abnormalities and the descent of editions, along with two specimen pages of Shakespeare's text.

90. POLLARD, ALFRED W. *Shakespeare's Fight with the Pirates and the Problems of the Transmission of His Text*. London: A. Moring, 1917, 110 pp.

Describes the process by which Shakespeare's plays were pirated by journeymen actors hired for minor parts who acted in conjunction with printers willing to take the risk of running afoul of the law.

Dating and Textual Studies

Shakespeare's company responded to such pirates by entering a play in the Stationers' Register so that no pirate could obtain the copyright to it. Occasionally the company would authorize a better text. In several instances plays were sold directly to the printer to forestall piracy.

91. ———. *Shakespeare's Folios and Quartos: A Study in the Bibliography of Shakespeare's Plays 1594–1685*. London: Methuen, 1909, 176 pp.

Refutes Sidney Lee's theory of piracy as the cause of textual contamination in virtually all early Shakespearean quartos. The good quartos are not textually corrupt; they are regularly entered in the Stationers' Register, and the text generally agrees with that of the folio. The bad quartos (the first quarto of *Romeo and Juliet, Hamlet, The Merry Wives of Windsor, Henry V, Pericles*) are textually contaminated; they are not entered in the Stationers' Register or are irregularly entered, and the text differs substantially from that of the folio. The bad quartos probably result from pirated copy derived from a shorthand transcription.

92. ROBERTSON, J. M. *The Genuine in Shakespeare*. London: George Routledge & Sons, 1930, 170 pp.

Features a conspectus of the views contained in his multivolume *Shakespeare Canon*, arguing in general the presence of collaboration or alteration in most of Shakespeare's plays. At the beginning of his career Shakespeare notes that he invented no work in full prior to *Venus and Adonis* (1593); Heminge and Condell did not hesitate to include non–Shakespearean material in the First Folio. Shakespeare's hand in *1 Henry VI*, for example, is denied entirely, and it appears only briefly in *2 Henry VI*. Similarly, he wrote only parts of *The Comedy of Errors*. Individual chapters address the authorship of each play.

93. SEARY PETER. *Lewis Theobald and the Editing of Shakespeare*. Oxford: Oxford University Press, 1990, 248 pp.

Attempts to rehabilitate Theobald's tarnished reputation as an editor of Shakespeare by demonstrating that successive editions of the playwright flow from the canon of editorial principles that he established, principles based on fact and probability rather than taste. Theobald's approach to emendation "was far less arbitrary than that of the majority of his contemporaries in the eighteenth century and far more sophisticated than most twentieth-century scholars have realized" (p. 166), a fact attested by the more than 350 alterations by Theobald found in modern texts.

94. WALKER, ALICE. *Textual Problems of the First Folio: "Richard III," "King Lear," "Troilus and Cressida," "2 Henry IV," "Hamlet," "Othello."* Cambridge: Cambridge University Press, 1953, 170 pp.

Argues that the folio texts of the plays examined in this study were printed from corrected quarto copies. The principle is significant in light of the fact that modern editors still tend to mix texts in eclectic fashion as if they were independent prints. Such an argument generally asserts the quarto is the primary text; in *King Lear*, for instance, the quarto is much closer to Shakespeare than the First Folio even though in two scenes there is serious memorial contamination. The folio text of *Hamlet*, likewise, is edited; again the judgment and the accuracy of the collator or transcriber come between Shakespeare and the reader.

95. WALTON, JAMES KIRKWOOD. *The Quarto Copy for the First Folio of Shakespeare*. Dublin: Dublin University Press, 1971, 306 pp.

Investigates the nature of the copy used for the First Folio, specifically in cases where a prior good quarto exists—whether the copy text was quarto or manuscript and the nature of the collation where that occurred. Textual analysis based on the evaluation of substantive readings reveals which quarto served as copy (where there is more than one). It reveals, as well, that a manuscript, not a quarto, stands behind *2 Henry IV*, *Hamlet*, and *Othello*.

96. WELLS, STANLEY. *Re-Editing Shakespeare for the Modern Reader*. New York: Oxford University Press, 1984, 144 pp.

Discusses textual problems involved in a modern edition of Shakespeare, drawn from Wells's work as general editor of the Oxford Shakespeare. Particular topics include the advantages and disadvantages of modernized spelling and punctuation, the appropriate manner of amplification of stage directions, and the limits of editorial prerogative.

97. WELLS, STANLEY, and TAYLOR, GARY (with JOHN JOWETT and WILLIAM MONTGOMERY). *William Shakespeare: A Textual Companion*. Oxford: Clarendon Press, 1987, 671 pp.

Serves as a companion volume to the new Oxford Shakespeare published in both modern and old-spelling editions (*William Shakespeare: The Complete Works*. Ed. Stanley Wells and Gary Taylor. Oxford: Clarendon Press, 1986, 1482 pp.—see entry 45). A general introduction describes the various kinds of manuscripts that served as copy texts for the Elizabethan printer and the task of the modern editor in choosing among them; featured also are sections on the canon and chronology of Shakespeare's plays, a summary of control-texts, and editorial procedures. A chapter on each play provides a textual introduction, and textual notes indicate all variant quarto and folio readings along with significant emendations by Shakespeare's early editors.

Sources

98. WILLOUGHBY, EDWIN E. *The Printing of the First Folio*. Oxford: Oxford University Press (for the Bibliographical Society), 1932, 70 pp.

Traces the history of the First Folio, specifically attempting to identify the typographical habits of the two (or three) compositors. Individual chapters focus on the incidentals of publication (the price of the book, the size of the edition, the rate of printing), the printing process itself, and the composition and proofreading. Issued in an edition of one thousand copies, the folio was, except for twenty-two quires, printed on one press with work proceeding at the rate of two three-sheet quires per week. Orthographic analysis is the basis for identifying the work of the individual compositors.

SOURCES

99. BULLOUGH, GEOFFREY, ed. *Narrative and Dramatic Sources of Shakespeare*. 8 vols. London: Routledge & Kegan Paul; New York: Columbia University Press, 1957–75, 4252 pp.

Assembles the chief narrative and dramatic sources and analogues of Shakespeare's plays and poems. For each an introductory essay describes Shakespeare's use of source material; the texts of these sources then follow. Volume 1 includes the early comedies, the poems, and *Romeo and Juliet*; volume 2, the comedies (1597–1603); volume 3, the early English history plays; volume 4, the later English history plays; volume 5, the Roman plays; volume 6, the classical plays; volume 7, the major tragedies; and volume 8, the romances.

100. DESSEN, ALAN. *Shakespeare and the Late Moral Plays*. Lincoln: University of Nebraska Press, 1986, 196 pp.

Affirms that a knowledge of the conventions of the late moral plays often illumines Shakespeare's design. For instance, the pattern of the two-phased structure characteristic of the morals, in which a sinful world triumphs for a time but is eventually displaced by a social and ethical force, stands behind the structure of *Richard III*, in which Richard's evil is ultimately confronted by Richmond's unassailable goodness. So too, the pattern of the Vice carried off on the back of the devil helps to explain the significance of Falstaff's lugging Hotspur off stage. Moreover, to see Falstaff as a kind of public vice accounts well in *2 Henry IV* for his being old and diseased and for the need for a general restoration of public order.

Sources

101. DONALDSON, E. TALBOT. *The Swan at the Well: Shakespeare Reading Chaucer.* New Haven: Yale University Press, 1985, 165 pp.

Claims that Chaucer was a more pervasive influence on Shakespeare than has been previously recognized. After discussing Shakespeare's direct use of "The Knight's Tale" in *A Midsummer Night's Dream* and *The Two Noble Kinsmen*, the author argues the influence of *Troilus and Criseyde* in the writing of *Romeo and Juliet* and of the character of the Wife of Bath in the creation of Falstaff.

102. GUILFOYLE, CHERRELL. *Shakespeare's Play within Play: Medieval Imagery and Scenic Form in "Hamlet," "Othello," and "King Lear."* Edam Monograph Series, 12. Kalamazoo: Medieval Institute. Publications, Western Michigan University, 1990, 159 pp.

Argues that medieval mythic and religious structures stand behind key scenes in the tragedies. In the drunken porter scene, for example, Shakespeare intends for the spectators to recall a stage property, hell mouth, from the Harrowing and Doomsday plays of the miracle cycle. For another, the soldiers watching on a cold night in the opening scene in *Hamlet* are reminiscent of the men watching in the field on the night of Christ's birth. For yet another, the opening scene in *King Lear* can be viewed as an antithetical Fall of Lucifer play, with the wrong people being cast out of heaven.

103. GUTTMAN, SELMA. *The Foreign Sources of Shakespeare's Works: An Annotated Bibliography of the Commentary Written on This Subject Between 1904 and 1940 Together with Lists of Certain Translations Available to Shakespeare.* New York: King's Crown Press, 1947, 168 pp.

Cites items (many of them annotated) of English, French, and German commentary concerning Shakespeare's sources originally written in foreign languages—including 239 Latin sources, 117 Greek sources, 68 French sources, 91 Italian sources, and 41 Spanish sources. The entries cover scholarship from 1904 to 1940. Baconians, whatever their eccentricities, were among the first to awaken modern criticism to the significance of the classical influence on Shakespeare. Generally, critics now assume Shakespeare to have had a basic working knowledge of Latin, Greek, and French.

104. HART, ALFRED. *Shakespeare and the Homilies: And Other Pieces of Research into the Elizabethan drama.* Melbourne: Melbourne University Press, 1934, 262 pp.

Reveals that Shakespeare's views on divine right and on the relationship between monarch and subject are drawn essentially from *Certain Sermons or Homilies*, first published in 1547. It is here declared that

29

Sources

the king is God's immediate deputy on earth, not liable to deposition, that the subject's obedience is to be passive and without reservation, and that rebellion is a most heinous sin. These views permeate Shakespeare's work from early to late, and he appears to accept them uncritically.

105. HOSLEY, RICHARD, ed. *Shakespeare's Holinshed.* New York: Capricorn Books; Toronto: Longmans Canada, 1968, 346 pp.
    Reprints with modernized spelling and punctuation the material from Raphael Holinshed's *Chronicles of England, Scotland, and Ireland* (2d ed., 1587) that Shakespeare used as a principal source for thirteen of his plays. The material is presented in Holinshed's chronological order, organized separately by play; appendixes include an outline of English history (1154–1603), genealogical tables, and a bibliography.

106. JONES, EMRYS. *The Origins of Shakespeare.* Oxford: Clarendon Press, 1977, 290 pp.
    Focuses on the "archeology" of Shakespeare's contributions to the theater. Shakespeare's education was extensive and thorough. A familiarity with Euripides, for example, explains Shakespeare's overall conception of tragic form. The chief dramatic model for *Titus Andronicus* was *Hecuba*; the argument between Cassius and Brutus has its source in the argument between Agamemnon and Menelaus in *Iphigenia in Aulis*, *1,2,3 Henry VI* is a trilogy patterned after Thomas Legge's *Richardus Tertius*. *King John* is a paradigm of a morality like *Mundus et Infans*, in which the hero Faulconbridge encounters the baffling reality of worldly politics.

107. MARTINDALE, CHARLES, and MARTINDALE, MICHELLE. *Shakespeare and the Uses of Antiquity: An Introductory Essay on Shakespeare and on English Renaissance Classicism.* New York: Routledge, 1990, 256 pp.
    Maintains that, while he was not a learned writer by traditional standards, Shakespeare was profoundly influenced by classical literature. Again and again, he borrowed material and made it his own by individual treatment and assimilation to its new place and purpose. *Macbeth*, for example, is directly indebted to Seneca for its "heated rhetoric, the brooding sense of evil, the preoccupation with power, the obsessive introspection, the claustrophobic images of cosmic destruction" (p. 37). Ovid, likewise, informs *The Merchant of Venice*, *Titus Andronicus*, and *Cymbeline*. Ancient ideas become for Shakespeare "a means of creating and illuminating scenes and characters and controlling the audience's response toward them" (p. 167).

108. MILWARD, PETER. *Biblical Influences in Shakespeare's Great Tragedies*. Bloomington: Indiana University Press, 1987, 208 pp.

Argues that Shakespeare's single most significant source was the Bible.The playwright's avowed purpose is the "entertainment and instruction of his audience" (p. 205). By infusing the prosaic narrative of his plots with "deep Biblical resonances," he raises the plays "above their secularity and gives them a moral and religious dimension." These resonances consistently suggest parallels with the fall of man and the death of Christ. The tragedies, therefore, are simultaneously literal and figurative. Specific attention is directed to *Hamlet, Othello*, and *King Lear*.

109. MUIR, KENNETH. *The Sources of Shakespeare's Plays*. New Haven: Yale University Press, 1978, 320 pp.

Ascertains Shakespeare's sources for his plays and discusses how he used them. Shakespeare's method was to read all accessible works relevant to his theme and to utilize one source to amplify another, complicating his story by adding elements from a variety of places. In *King Lear*, for example, he combines an old chronicle play, at least one prose chronicle, two poems, and a pastoral romance. The chronological arrangement reveals his increasing skills in transmuting his materials for the stage.

110. NICOLL, ALLARDYCE, and NICOLL, JOSEPHINE, eds. *Holinshed's Chronicle as Used in Shakespeare's Plays*. London: Dent; New York: Dutton, 1927, 233 pp.

Presents selections of Raphael Holinshed's *Chronicles of England, Scotland, and Ireland* that Shakespeare drew upon in his plays. Contrary to the older view that he wrote upon whatever story came to hand, he apparently read widely—especially in North's Plutarch and Holinshed—seeking themes suitable for developing certain ideas or types of characters. Here the material is ordered by thirteen of Shakespeare's plays, with marginal notation of the volume and page of the *Chronicle* from which the passage is taken and with further notation, when appropriate, of the act and scene of the play.

111. NOBLE, RICHMOND. *Shakespeare's Biblical Knowledge: And Use of the Book of Common Prayer, as Exemplified in the Plays of the First Folio*. London: Society for Promoting Christian Knowledge, 1935, 303 pp.

Reveals Shakespeare's close knowledge of the Bible through listing identifiable quotations from and allusions to at least eighteen books of the Old and New Testaments and six from the Apocrypha. As Shakespeare matures as a playwright, such references—primarily from the

Sources

Geneva Bible and the Bishop's Bible—become more idiomatic, more closely woven into the text. For each of the plays, arranged in presumed chronological order, biblical quotations and allusions are identified and annotated.

112. ROOT, ROBERT KILBURN. *Classical Mythology in Shakespeare.* New Haven: Yale University Press, 1903, 134 pp.

Collects Shakespeare's allusions to classical mythology, examines their source, and describes their dramatic function. By far the greatest classical source is Ovid, followed by Virgil. As Shakespeare develops and his tragedy darkens, his mythology tends to disappear or, as in *Antony and Cleopatra*, to turn to jest. Part 1 consists of a dictionary of mythological characters with annotations indicating the Shakespearean play or poem in which they appear. Part 2 discusses Shakespeare's use of mythology.

113. SHAHEEN, NASEEB. *Biblical References in Shakespeare's Tragedies.* Newark: University of Delaware Press; London and Toronto: Associated University Presses, 1987, 245 pp.

Lists references to the scriptures in the tragedies, citing only those whose contexts support the validity of a biblical allusion. Such passages, keyed to the *Riverside Shakespeare* (see entry 40), include as well references to the *Book of Common Prayer* and the *Book of Homilies*. Individual chapters are included on the English Bible in Shakespeare's drama (the style, method of compilation, availability of Tudor and Stuart Bibles) and the Anglican liturgy (his familiarity with the church service and sermons other than those in the official *Book of Homilies*).

114. ———. *Biblical References in Shakespeare's History Plays.* Newark: University of Delaware Press; London and Toronto: Associated University Presses, 1989, 254 pp.

Lists references to the scriptures in each of Shakespeare's history plays, with all items keyed to the *Riverside Shakespeare* (see entry 40). A chapter on the English Bible in Shakespeare's day features sections on John Wycliffe, Miles Coverdale, Thomas Matthew, Richard Taverner, the Great Bible, the Geneva Bible, the Bishops' Bible, Tomson's New Testament, Franciscus Junius, and the Rheims New Testament. Appendixes include an index to Shakespeare's biblical references, references to the Book of Common Prayer, and references to the Homilies.

115. SPENCER, T. J. B. *Shakespeare's Plutarch.* Harmondsworth, Eng.: Penguin Books, 1964, 365 pp.

Includes North's translation of Plutarch's accounts of Julius Caesar, Marcus Brutus, Marcus Antonius, and Marcius Coriolanus. Plutarch's virtue was that he saw history in terms of human character, interpreting ambiguity as a "state of existence in which outstanding men molded events by their personal decisions and by the inevitable tendencies of their characters" (p. 7). The development of Enobarbus in *Antony and Cleopatra* reflects Shakespeare's later willingness to extend the material of his source. In *Coriolanus* the deviations from Plutarch are all in the direction of theatrical effectiveness, for example, the adding of Virgilia and the young son in the scene of supplication outside the walls of Rome.

116. THOMSON, J. A. K. *Shakespeare and the Classics*. London: George Allen & Unwin, 1952, 254 pp.
    Points to the danger of overestimating Shakespeare's obligation to classical authors in the original, given the relatively low standard of classical scholarship in Elizabethan England. After a general discussion of Shakespeare's education, the plays are individually examined for Shakespeare's use of classical material. *Macbeth* is considered the single work most heavily indebted to the classics, both in the use of the witches' prophecies to establish a pervasive sense of tragic irony and in the reflection of the direct influence of Seneca in Duncan's off-stage murder.

117. VELZ, JOHN W. *Shakespeare and the Classical Tradition: A Critical Guide to Commentary, 1600–1960*. Minneapolis: University of Minnesota Press, 1968, 459 pp.
    Includes 2,487 annotated entries covering relevant criticism in English, French, and German concerning Shakespeare's use of classical materials. Boethius (524 A.D.) is set as a forward limit, but Shakespeare's paths to the classics (Erasmus, Lyly, Susenbrotus, Palengenius, Mantuanus) are also included. Following a historical introduction to the topic, the material is classified under bibliographies, general works, the comedies, the histories, the plays on classical themes, the tragedies, the last plays, the poems and sonnets, and Shakespeare's classics (a section devoted to modern editions of the originals that Shakespeare probably used).

118. WALKER, LEWIS. *Shakespeare and the Classical Tradition*. Garland Reference Library of the Humanities, 1019. Hamden: Garland Publishing, 1992, 600 pp.
    Cites English-language books, articles, dissertations, bibliographies, surveys, and editions that concern Shakespeare's relationship to

Background Studies

the literature of ancient Greece and Rome. Coverage of such scholarly items through 1985 supplements the earlier work of John Velz (*Shakespeare and the Classical Tradition: A Critical Guide and Commentary, 1600–1900* [Minneapolis: University of Minnesota Press, 1968, 459 pp.—see entry 117). While noting briefly the general scholarship dealing with classical connections, the study annotates all significant work on those plays and poems based directly on classical sources (*Julius Caesar, Coriolanus, Antony and Cleopatra, The Rape of Lucrece*).

119. WHITAKER, VIRGIL K. *Shakespeare's Use of Learning: An Inquiry into the Growth of His Mind and Art.* San Marino: Huntington Library, 1953, 366 pp.

Charts Shakespeare's intellectual development through his use or adaptation of clearly defined sources and to allusions within the plays to contemporary learning. Generally, Shakespeare follows his sources faithfully in his early plays, adapting character to meet the demands of plot. From *Hamlet* forward, however, he freely reshapes material to illustrate or conform to philosophic concepts. Similarly, a mark of his intellectual progress is the substituting of the regular operation of the laws of nature as the moving force in events for a God who intervenes actively, an incalculable fortune, and erratic human behavior.

BACKGROUND STUDIES

120. BALDWIN, THOMAS WHITFIELD. *Shakspere's Five-Act Structure: Shakspere's Early Plays on the Background of Renaissance Theories of Five-Act Structure from 1470.* Urbana: University of Illinois Press, 1947, 848 pp.

Constructs through analysis of the body of critical commentary on classical writers, especially Plautus and Terence, the theory of dramatic structure as Shakespeare and other Renaissance dramatists would have understood it. Specifically, through Horace, Varro, Donatus, Servius, Landino, Latomus, Willichus, Melancthon, and Scaliger, Baldwin reveals the evolution of a five-act concept consisting of three basic movements—the protasis (1–2), the epitasis (3–4), the catastrophe (5). Shakespeare followed this structure closely in his early dramas, but by the mid-1590s and works such as *Romeo and Juliet* he outgrew strict adherence to these artistic constraints.

121. ———. *William Shakspere's Petty School.* Urbana: University of Illinois Press, 1943, 240 pp.

Describes the program of study in the petty school of Shakespeare's childhood. The early phases of study involved movement from the alphabet to the *Catechism* and thence to the *Primer, Psalter*, and perhaps the New Testament and movement generally from the English to the Latin. Essentially, the petty school aimed to teach reading, writing, and casting of accounts; clearly it stressed in its religious orientation the Reformation far more so than the Renaissance.

122. ————. *William Shakspere's Small Latine and Lesse Greeke*. 2 vols. Urbana: University of Illinois Press, 1944, 1525 pp.

Presents information on the kind of formal education Shakespeare is likely to have experienced in sixteenth-century Stratford. Chapters on the formulation of the tradition in the Restoration and eighteenth century that he had only a minimal education are followed by an investigation of the grammar school curricula and their content in the time of Edward VI and Elizabeth. Volume 2 analyzes the rhetorical training (Cicero, Erasmus, Quintilian) and describes study in the Latin poets (Ovid, Virgil, Horace), moral history, moral philosophy, and Greek. Jonson's phrase reflected in the title must be taken only in relative terms.

123. BERRY, RALPH. *Shakespeare and Social Class*. Atlantic Highlands: Humanities Press International, 1988, 198 pp.

Stresses Shakespeare's keen sense of social differentiation as reflected in the diverse range of classes from which his characters are drawn. These characters tend to behave in a way appropriate to their social ranks and occupations. Generally, the social classes recognized in Elizabethan England—the nobility, the gentry, citizens and burgesses, yeomen and laborers—are easily recognized in Shakespeare's plays, whether through their actions, their professions, or their language. The middle comedies and the second tetralogy of history plays test the assumptions of class in pressures of social competitiveness and war, the tragedies in issues of character and motivation, the problem comedies in relation to sexual affairs.

124. BRADBROOK, MURIEL C. *Shakespeare: The Poet in His World*. New York: Columbia University Press, 1978, 272 pp.

Places an account of Shakespeare's life and artistic growth in the wider context of the development of English theatrical history and of the spirit and major events of the Elizabethan-Jacobean period. Described as an "applied biography," the major focus is on the works themselves. Of particular interest is the identification of the rival poet in the sonnets as Marlowe and of Shakespeare's friend as Southampton,

Background Studies

the discussion of Falstaff as at once a dramatic success and a political blunder, of the influence of Jonson as friend and rival, and of the effects of the Gunpowder Plot on the later tragedies.

125. BRISTOL, MICHAEL D. *Carnival and Theater: Plebeian Culture and the Structure of Authority in Renaissance England.* New York: Methuen, 1985, 237 pp.

Observes that the theater is festive and political as well as literary, providing a privileged site for the celebration and critique of the needs and concerns of the *polis*. The spirit of "carnival" is a "second culture" sustained by the common people or the plebeian community that during the Renaissance, especially in drama, engages with and directly opposes the "official" culture. "The genres of literature become 'carnivalized,' their structures permeated with laughter, irony, humor, elements of self-parody" (p. 22). This element of carnival inserts into literature a quality of indeterminacy or open-endedness that reflects the political and social conditions of the real world.

126. BUSH, GEOFFREY. *Shakespeare and the Natural Condition.* Cambridge, Mass.: Harvard University Press, 1956, 135 pp.

Notes the essential duality of Shakespeare's view of nature as a philosophic doctrine of divine order and as the physical process of life and death. Ultimately his characters strike an attitude in the face of the world, not in a moment of certainty but in a doubt that a natural philosophy is sufficient to be the core of a view of life. If they must ask whether life may be explained by natural causes, they must also ask "what the consequence is to the human spirit of being compelled to ask this question" (p. 78). Shakespearean man is caught between the reality of surrender to time and the events of the world and the longing to be engaged in what is certain, absolute, and beyond the reach of time.

127. COX, JOHN D. *Shakespeare and the Dramaturgy of Power.* Princeton: Princeton University Press, 1989, 282 pp.

Suggests that in sixteenth-century England Christian idealism was the dominant cultural idea, in conflict both with the materialism of popular culture and the philosophic materialism implicit in the cosmology of Copernicus and Galileo and explicit in the theory of Machiavelli and Hobbes. Through the principles of Christian realism inherent in Augustine's *City of God*, Shakespeare qualifies Elizabethan concepts of political power and social privilege. In Shakespeare's mature tragedies, for example, the self-knowledge gained by the protagonist "is modelled in each case on the transforming self-discovery that usually distinguishes the powerless from the powerful in medieval religious drama" (p. 224).

128. DORAN, MADELEINE. *Endeavors of Art: A Study of Form in Elizabethan Drama*. Madison: University of Wisconsin Press, 1954, 482 pp.

Devotes considerable space to Shakespeare, who was the master of architectonic design, creating unity out of great diversity through syntax, diction, imagery, and prosody. More so than his contemporaries, he refused to be bound by traditional concepts of form; he seemed to understand, for example, the ethical basis of tragedy, focusing on man's responsibility for the effects of his action, no matter how little control can be exercised over his fate. Chapters are included on eloquence and "copy," verisimilitude, moral aim, dramatic forms, history and tragedy, comedy, tragicomedy, character, and complication and unraveling.

129. DRIVER, T. F. *The Sense of History in Greek and Shakespearean Drama*. New York: Columbia University Press, 1960, 231 pp.

Views Shakespeare's work as the fulfillment of the dramatic question of man's action in a historical situation. The Greek dramatists, on the other hand, raised questions about the relation of man to his world for which the Hellenic civilization had no satisfactory answers. Shakespeare, in addition to seeing man in a sequence of historical events, assumes these events to be controlled by and relating to a purposeful design. Whereas Greek action moves from the temporal to the non-temporal with a nonexistent or closed future, Shakespeare moves from event to knowledge to new event. Examined in detail are *Richard III*, *Hamlet*, *Macbeth*, and *The Winter's Tale*.

130. DUSINBERRE, JULIET. *Shakespeare and the Nature of Women*. London and Basingstoke: Macmillan, 1975, 329 pp.

Maintains that Shakespeare through the breeched heroines of romantic comedy and the gracious figures of forgiveness of the romances explores aspects of female emancipation. The Elizabethan-Jacobean society was basically sympathetic to the rights of women, in large part as a consequence of the Puritans' emphasis on the spiritual quality of Adam and Eve. The role of women was further enhanced by the presence of Queen Elizabeth on the throne and by humanistic educational doctrines. The nature of Shakespeare's women, in a word, is the result both of his own genius and the philosophic climate of the age.

131. FARNHAM, WILLARD. *The Medieval Heritage of Elizabethan Drama*. Oxford: Basil Blackwell, 1936, 487 pp.

Background Studies

> Argues that Shakespeare's tragedy is essentially a derivation of the medieval Gothic tradition. Whereas Greek tragedy limits its scope to the immediate events of the catastrophe, Gothic tragedy incorporates a more expansive view. The controlling *de casibus* narrative involves choric comment on the nature of the world and a conclusion in death (the *contemptus mundi* and the danse macabre). The tension between man's physical ignobilities and his spiritual nobilities takes effective shape in the morality play, with central emphasis on his freedom of choice; and in Shakespeare emerges the mature expression of "tragedy based upon inner struggle or spiritual civil war" (p. 51).

132. FRYE, ROLAND M. *Shakespeare and Christian Doctrine*. Princeton: Princeton University Press, 1963, 314 pp.

> Demonstrates that Shakespeare's personal beliefs cannot be deduced from the plays, that his drama is pervasively secular within its own structural constraints. Part 1 surveys the work of critics who have insisted on Christian archetypal interpretations of Shakespeare. Part 2 discusses the historical Reformation background, and part 3 provides a topical analysis and appraisal of Shakespeare's theological references. Unlike Milton's *Samson Agonistes* and Marlowe's *Dr. Faustus*, Shakespeare's plays are not patterned on a particular theological concept; to insist that they are is to engage in special pleading by distorting both the nature of drama and also the evidence.

133. HOENIGER, F. DAVID. *Medicine and Shakespeare in the English Renaissance*. Newark: University of Delaware Press: London and Toronto: Associated University Presses, 1991, 404 pp.

> Describes the background of various theoretical and practical aspects of medicine with which Shakespeare would have been familiar. Particular attention is addressed to fresh interpretations of *All's Well That Ends Well* and *King Lear* based on reference to this body of knowledge. An index provides ready access to the numerous Shakespeare references.

134. KEETON, GEORGE W. *Shakespeare's Legal and Political Background*. New York: Barnes & Noble, 1967, 417 pp.

> Explains the manner in which Shakespeare employed the language and content of the law in his plays and relates this information to the playwright's political ideas. Part 1 deals with the extent of Shakespeare's legal knowledge and particular legal questions concerning the law of nature, local justice, the law of debt, the legal basis of the pound of flesh, trial by battle, and Ophelia's burial. Part 2 places Shakespeare's political thought within the context of his age, covering such matters as his view of English kingship and the title to the crown, the political

background of *King John*, and the politics of the Greek and Roman plays.

135. KNIGHTS, L. C. *Drama and Society in the Age of Jonson.* New York: George W. Stewart, 1937, 347 pp.

Asserts that the prevailing mode of economic production and the social organization it fostered formed the basis of the political and intellectual history of the era. Shakespeare's period was one of great economic confusion in that there were large-scale capitalistic enterprises on the one hand and traditional forms of trade and industry (guilds) on the other. The dramatists directly reflect the society. Shakespeare's plays are referred to randomly throughout the study, especially concerning his topical satire and delineation of the trades.

136. MATUS, IRVIN LEIGH. *Shakespeare: The Living Record.* New York: St. Martin's Press, 1991, 174 pp.

Comprises a survey of the public and private buildings, the houses, the castles and ruins significant to a knowledge of where Shakespeare lived and worked. From an opening chapter on Stratford, the Guild Chapel and the house in the Chapel Quad that provided facilities for the Edward VI grammar school, nearby Charlecote, Warwick Castle, and Coventry, the study proceeds to London and such sites as the Tower, Shoreditch, Fleet Street, and Westminster Abbey. From thence the reader follows the Lord Chamberlain's Men on their 1597 provincial tour to the south, then to the east in 1603, and to the west in 1606.

137. MILWARD, PETER. *Shakespeare's Religious Background.* London: Sidgwick & Jackson, 1973, 312 pp.

Examines the major religious currents of the Elizabethan age and Shakespeare's response to them through his plays. Shakespeare as a deeply religious man was apparently grieved at the break with Rome and the resultant religious chaos. The plays, more specifically, are an analogical form of this religious situation—from the theme of mistaken identity in the comedies, to the schismatic strife threatening unity in the histories, to the sin and suffering consequent upon alienation in the tragedies, to the last plays with their hope of ultimate reunion. The theme of the last plays is the restoration of moral and social harmony possible only through forgiveness and love.

138. SIEGEL, PAUL N. *Shakespeare in His Time and Ours.* South Bend and London: Notre Dame University Press, 1968, 260 pp.

Argues that, while we respond in terms of our own experience, a full appreciation of Shakespeare requires some knowledge of Elizabe-

Background Studies

than culture as well. Just as Shakespeare's contemporaries could imaginatively accept Romeo and Juliet as achieving amoral bliss beyond the grave, so modern atheists can artistically conceptualize the afterlife adumbrated in Shakespeare's Christian tragedies. Cordelia's life and death, for example, assume greatest significance as the means by which Lear achieves spiritual salvation. Other essays consider the effects of honor without principle and the Elizabethan response to the stage Jew.

139. ———. *Shakespearean Tragedy and the Elizabethan Compromise*. New York: New York University Press, 1957, 243 pp.
   Observes that with the growth in the power of the bourgeoisie following the defeat of the Spanish Armada came new challenges to the Christian humanist worldview that provided rationalization for the dominant position of the new aristocracy. *Hamlet* depicts both ideal prince and malcontent with the prince torn between acceptance and rejection of the Christian humanist's view. Iago typifies the malcontent of low birth resentful of his superiors. Both *Macbeth* and *Lear* are based on a conflict of new and old views. Lear is saved by love, but the play reflects a degenerate society.

140. SPENCER, THEODORE. *Shakespeare and the Nature of Man*. New York: Macmillan, 1949, 233 pp.
   Explores Shakespeare's vision of life through an examination of the intellectual, social, and religious background. From the medieval period comes the belief in the three interrelated hierarchies—in the universe, in the ranks of created beings, and in the institution of government. In such a view nature is infused and controlled by God. On the other hand, a counterview was also developing, whether fostered by the Calvinistic assumption of the depravity of man or by attacks upon the received traditions by such men as Galileo, Machiavelli, Telesio, and Montaigne. Nature in this view is devoid of God and teleological design.

141. SPIVACK, BERNARD. *Shakespeare and the Allegory of Evil: The History of a Metaphor in Relation to His Major Villains*. New York: Columbia University Press, 1958, 508 pp.
   Maintains that Shakespeare wrote in a period of profound transition from one dramatic mode to another, specifically that some of our difficulties with Shakespeare's villains are the consequences of our attempts to impose a purely naturalistic view of evil on what for the playwright has allegorical dimensions. Figures like Iago, Richard, Aaron, and Don John may horrify, but the drapery of conventional humanity never fits them. The father of all such characters is the Morality Vice.

142. TILLYARD, E. M. W. *The Elizabethan World Picture: A Study of the Idea of Order in the Age of Shakespeare, Donne, and Milton.* London: Macmillan, 1946, 116 pp.

    Notes that the Elizabethans accepted a solidly theocentric concept of an ordered universe arranged in hierarchies and were obsessed with a fear of chaos and the fact of mutability. They pictured universal order in three major forms: the chain of being, which stretched from the foot of God's throne and linked all forms of created matter in its proper place and function; a series of corresponding planes—the divine and the angelic, the universe or macrocosm, the commonwealth or body politic, man or the microcosm, and the lower creation; and a dance, a vision of creation as music with the "static battalions of the earthly, celestial, and divine hierarchies . . . sped on a varied but controlled peregrination to the accompaniment of music" (p. 102).

143. WELLS, ROBIN H. *Shakespeare, Politics and the State.* London: Macmillan, 1986, 174 pp.

    Observes that the twenty-year period in which Shakespeare wrote was one of social unrest and political controversy. The combination of inflation, increased taxation necessitated by the war with Spain, a crippling series of bad harvests, and new outbreaks of plague had a devastating effect on the national morale. As society came gradually to be seen, not as a divinely sanctioned institution but as an aggregate of individuals united only by the principle of self-interest, kingship lost its special sanctity; and this fundamental political transition is registered in Shakespeare's plays.

144. WEIMANN, ROBERT. *Shakespeare and the Popular Tradition in the Theater: Studies in the Social Dimension of Dramatic Form and Function.* Edited by Robert Schwartz. Baltimore and London: Johns Hopkins University Press, 1978, 325 pp.

    Emphasizes Shakespearean drama as sociologically living theater. The governing literary trends (formalist, history of ideas) tend to remove Shakespeare from the theater and theater from society at large. By tracing the origins and values of Shakespearean drama from the mimes and mumming plays, one gains new insights into his stagecraft and its traditions, into the clowning conventions, for example, or into such figures as Richard III, Hamlet, and King Lear. Originally published in German (1967).

145. WICKHAM, GLYNNE. *Shakespeare's Dramatic Heritage: Collected Studies in Medieval, Tudor and Shakespearean Drama.* New York: Barnes & Noble, 1969, 277 pp.

Language and Style

>   Focuses on the concept of the tragic hero in Marlowe and Shake-
> speare. Early chapters trace how the subjects of the fall of man, the
> redemption, and the judgment day were developed by the church and
> by medieval drama and how the revival of classical learning affected
> these themes in the early sixteenth century. The heart of the study is an
> analysis of Shakespeare's *Richard III* and Marlowe's *Edward II* as artistic
> blendings of these dramatic traditions. Attention is also directed to *A
> Midsummer Night's Dream*, *Hamlet*, *Coriolanus*, and *The Winter's Tale*.

146. WEST, ROBERT H. *Shakespeare and the Outer Mystery*. Lexington: Uni-
     versity of Kentucky Press, 1968, 205 pp.

>   Explores the philosophical and supernatural elements in five
> plays—*Hamlet*, *Othello*, *King Lear*, *Macbeth*, and *The Tempest*. Since for
> reasons of art Shakespeare never "fixes the great surround" for any of
> his tragedies, critics are equally wrong to envision the plays as expres-
> sions of either the absurd or Christian parable. Instead, the metaphys-
> ical backdrop, visualized through the characters' perceptions that like
> the spectators are finite and limited, is ultimately ambiguous, maintain-
> ing a "vast reserve, a mysteriousness that should stop the critic from
> more than hesitant suggestions about how they may be read, or confine
> him to a modest statement of personal views" (p. 18).

LANGUAGE AND STYLE

147. BAXTER, JOHN. *Shakespeare's Poetic Styles: Verse Into Drama*. London
     and Boston: Routledge & Kegan Paul, 1980, 255 pp.

>   Perceives the power of Shakespearean drama to be the use of a
> multiplicity of styles to create effective individualization of character. In
> *Richard II* the playwright utilizes and at times intermingles four distinct
> styles—the golden, the moral, the metaphysical, and the Shakespearean.
> These styles are defined not by individual characters but by the rhetor-
> ical demands of the stage situation. York in act 2 uses the plain didactic
> style in citing Richard's exotic excesses while Gaunt's response, ringing
> with both disgust and patriotism, represents a mixture of the moral and
> the golden. Richard himself utilizes a plain style in moments of resig-
> nation bordering on despair but a golden Petrarchism in contemplating
> his religious seclusion.

148. BEVINGTON, DAVID. *Action Is Eloquence: Shakespeare's Language of Ges-
     ture*. Chicago: University of Chicago Press, 1984, 248 pp.

Focuses on gesture in Shakespeare's plays as a language in itself with its own vocabulary of signs and rich symbolic potential in staging. Nature, personality, social status, inner states of mind—such matters can be signaled to the spectators through a glance, a shrug, a turn of hand. In instances like Coriolanus's turning his back on Rome or Macbeth's start of fear at the sound of Macduff's knocking, the gesture reinforces a highly significant dramatic moment. Ceremonial posturing frequently also serves to clarify character or suggest conflicts.

149. BURCKHARDT, SIGURD. *Shakespearean Meanings*. Princeton: Princeton University Press, 1968, 317 pp.

Identifies key words, phrases, or sounds as those which, properly understood, can unlock a wealth of information about the meaning of the whole play. The striking clock in *Julius Caesar*, for example, far from being an error on Shakespeare's part, is his method of signaling as anachronistic Brutus's decision to kill Caesar in a classical, ritualistic manner. Similarly, the word *nothing* as diversely understood by Lear (who accepts it at face value) and Gloucester (who refuses to accept it and pursues the matter further) signals for both men the flaw that provokes their destruction—their unwillingness to gain truth by engaging in the mental struggle necessary to penetrate the veil of metaphor.

150. CERCIGNANI, FAUSTO. *Shakespeare's Works and Elizabethan Pronunciation*. Oxford: Clarendon Press, 1981, 432 pp.

Attempts to ascertain the extent to which Shakespeare's works afford reliable evidence of the types of speech then current in London and to discuss the information provided by rhymes, puns, spellings, and metrical peculiarities. The study investigates both passages from Shakespeare's plays and poems and contemporary writers on orthography and pronunciation. It aims further to correct Kökeritz's mistaken determination to prove Shakespeare's English virtually identical with that of present educated Southern English. The body of material analyzes accent, short vowels, long vowels, diphthongs, vowels in unaccented syllables, and consonants.

151. CLEMEN, WOLFGANG H. *The Development of Shakespeare's Imagery*. Cambridge, Mass.: Harvard University Press, 1951, 236 pp.

Pursues an analysis of Shakespeare's imagery in its dramatic context in order to discover relations and connections to the play as a whole. As Shakespeare's art develops, so does his ability to use imagery for multiple effects in expressing characterization and dramatic theme. In the early plays Shakespeare's imagery is largely decorative and unorganic; in *Richard II* he has learned to wed imagery and character; in

Language and Style

the major tragedies imagery has assumed manifold relevance in terms of mood, character, and theme. The emphasis throughout is on how the image patterns enhance the dramatic elements of style, diction, plot, and character.

152. ———. *Shakespeare's Soliloquies*. Cambridge: Cambridge University Press (for the Modern Humanities Research Association), 1964, 26 pp.

Stresses the variety, style, method, and function of Shakespeare's soliloquies. The test for the effectiveness of this dramatic convention is not one of psychological naturalistic analysis but one of its credibility in context, delivered on the platform stage by an isolated actor for whom the barren setting is transformed into a metaphor of inner experience. Often a symbolic partner (for example, sleep, a dagger, a personified idea such as honor or conspiracy) creates a dialogic rhythm.

153. COLMAN, E. A. M. *The Dramatic Use of Bawdy in Shakespeare*. London: Longman, 1974, 230 pp.

Emphasizes the dramatic function of Shakespeare's bawdy language. The simple farce of the Dromios in *The Comedy of Errors*, of Petruchio's household servants in *The Taming of the Shrew*, and of Romeo's foil Mercutio in *Romeo and Juliet* gives way to the sardonic jesting of Hamlet and the bitter raillery of Othello that directly reflect the state of the protagonist's mind and in turn to the grotesqueries of bestial figures in the late plays such as Cloten and Caliban. Also included is a glossary of Shakespeare's words and phrases with indecent connotations.

154. CRANE, MILTON. *Shakespeare's Prose*. Chicago: University of Chicago Press, 1951, 219 pp.

Describes Shakespeare's prose as the first body of prose in English that contributes both to the depiction of character and the creation of atmosphere. Shakespeare's delighted awareness of Elizabethan speech is reflected in the excellence of Falstaff's language. He follows tradition by using prose for comic characters, but he also utilizes it in the characterization of his tragic heroes. Almost from the beginning Shakespeare uses prose—for effective contrast—in *Romeo and Juliet* and *Henry IV*. Its excellence consists in its simplicity and naturalness and in the subtlety with which it contributes to creation of character.

155. DANSON, LAWRENCE N. *Tragic Alphabet: Shakespeare's Drama of Language*. New Haven: Yale University Press, 1974, 200 pp.

Concerns the tragic hero's difficulty in seeking for an adequate expressive mode—in a fully theatrical sense involving words, movement, costume, scenery—in the face of his dilemma. Traditional language fails, and he is forced to develop a new form of communication adequate to articulate his experience. In *Othello*, for example, the words of various worlds collide unintelligibly. When Othello succumbs to the Iago-world, he falls victim to perverted imagination masquerading as truth. Words of reality break through at the end, but Othello fears that Lodovico will never be able to speak of him as he really is.

156. DONAWORTH, JANE. *Shakespeare and the Sixteenth-Century Study of Language*. Urbana and Chicago: University of Illinois Press, 1984, 279 pp.

Explores the relationship between five Shakespearean plays and Renaissance pedagogical theory concerning language and the art of communication. *Love's Labor's Lost*, *King John*, *The Merchant of Venice*, *All's Well That Ends Well*, and *Hamlet* are examined as experimentations in the use and abuse of language for dramatic effect. *Hamlet*, for example, represents Shakespeare's consummate ability to render characters lifelike through language; in Hamlet's experience we come to realize that speech reflects the limitations as well as the transcendence of the human spirit.

157. ELAM, KEIR. *Shakespeare's Universe of Discourse: Language Games in the Comedies*. Cambridge: Cambridge University Press, 1984, 339 pp.

Explores the "self-consciousness" of Shakespeare's language, more specifically language in the comedies as a dynamic and active protagonist. Focusing primarily on *Love's Labor's Lost* as Shakespeare's most sophisticated play of words, the study examines the function of verbal activities and language games—those involving gesture, scenery, and physical property, the multiple meanings of words and the process of communication, and rhetorical figures. This analysis is framed by reference to sixteenth-century theories of meaning, language, decorum, and rhetoric.

158. FAAS, EKBERT. *Shakespeare's Poetics*. Cambridge and New York: Cambridge University Press, 1986, 263 pp.

Claims that, like Bacon and Montaigne but unlike most "Elizabethan aestheticians" (p. 78), Shakespeare gives preeminence to nature over art. Passages like Hamlet's advice to the players and Perdita's and Polixenes's art-nature debate in *The Winter's Tale* suggest that for Shakespeare poetry "no longer serves the bidding of metaphysics or theology in expressing absolute 'truths,' as it ought to do according to most Renaissance theorizing" (p. xxi). The grounding of that theory is explored in Lope de Vega, Castelvetro, Piccolomini, Buonamici, and Robertello.

Language and Style

159. GREENWOOD, JOHN. *Shifting Perspectives and the Spanish Style: Mannerism in Shakespeare and His Jacobean Contemporaries*. Toronto: University of Toronto Press, 1988, 227 pp.

Asserts that Jacobean drama, and English art in general, is more heavily mannerist than has been previously acknowledged. Though he may never have known the artist, Shakespeare was influenced by the illusionist art of Julio Romano. In drama this style is best reflected in abrupt juxtapositions, multiple asides, shifting points of view, and generally bizarre plotting. Such elements and their intentionally disorienting effect are discussed in a wide range of Shakespeare's late plays, culminating in the highly self-reflexive quality of Prospero's epilogue.

160. HALLIDAY, F. E. *The Poetry of Shakespeare's Plays*. London: Gerald Duckworth, 1954, 194 pp.

Argues that Shakespeare's superiority as a playwright results in large part from his superiority as a poet. The development of the three major contrapuntal elements in his poetry (the words themselves, the rhythmic relationship of the words, and the imagery and image patterns) can be traced through five distinct periods—the early histories and comedies (1590–94), the sonnets and lyrical plays (1594–97), the historical and romantic comedies (1597–1601), the tragedies (1601–08), and the romances (1608–13). A lyric poet before he was a dramatic poet, Shakespeare moves from a largely derivative ornamental, diffuse style to imagery "subdued to the action" and metaphor "stripped of its elaborations" (p. 40).

161. HANKINS, JOHN E. *Shakespeare's Derived Imagery*. Lawrence: University of Kansas Press, 1953, 289 pp.

Focuses on the sources of Shakespeare's imagery and their influences on his ideas, concluding that Shakespeare's genius was more adoptive and less inventive than has been commonly assumed. Almost inevitably the Shakespearean phrase is more concise and more intense than that of its source. The material is topically arranged—for example, the world as a stage, life as a brief candle, the internal struggle, love as a preserver, life as a dream, the golden world—and the major sources include the Bible, La Primaudaye's *The French Academy*, Montaigne, Aristotle, and Palengenius's *Zodiacus Vitae*.

162. HOUSTON, JOHN PORTER. *Shakespeare's Sentences: A Study in Style and Syntax*. Baton Rouge: Louisiana State University Press, 1988, 227 pp.

Aims to describe and chart the frequency of forms of sentence structure in Shakespeare's plays in order to describe their literary function in achieving a particular idiom for a given play. Coriolanus's fiercely asyndetic speech patterns, for example, modulate to softer syndetic patterns following his banishment and qualify our response to the character. *Hamlet* is characterized by a spate of "verbs positioned late in the sentence" and "formal periods of quite Latinate eloquence" (p. 87), along with a wide variety and unpredictability in clause length.

163. HULME, HILDA M. *Explorations in Shakespeare's Language: Some Problems of Word Meaning in the Dramatic Text.* London: Longmans, Green, 1962, 351 pp.

Explores the common currency in Elizabethan speech in an attempt to draw the modern reader and spectator closer to the original idiom of Shakespeare's words and phrases. An examination of manuscript local records of the sixteenth and seventeenth centuries often helps to clarify the meaning of troublesome words and phrases such as "aroint," "trammell," and "as thick as Tale / Can post with post" in the first act of *Macbeth*. Particular attention is directed to the proverb-idiom in Shakespeare's language, the vocabulary of Elizabethan bawdy, Latinate meanings, spelling habits, pronunciation variants, and provincialisms.

164. HUSSEY, S. S. *The Literary Language of Shakespeare.* London and New York: Longman Group, 1982, 214 pp.

Examines Shakespeare's various uses of language to demonstrate rank and to establish genre, along with his divergent styles—for example, the rational man, the language of invective, metadramatic language, affairs of state, a Roman style, and the language of ultimate integrity. Shakespeare utilizes the soliloquy from the beginning of his work, as in the expositional soliloquies of Richard III. The full possibilities are developed relatively slowly, however. Juliet's soliloquies introduce paradox; the Bastard's, mimicry; but it is Brutus who first articulates the psychological condition that points toward the major protagonists.

165. MAHOOD, M. M. *Shakespeare's Wordplay.* London and New York: Methuen, 1957, 192 pp.

Examines the central themes of five plays and the sonnets through the pervasive word play. Among the dominant patterns discussed are the *Liebestod* motif in *Romeo and Juliet*, the phrases of disquiet at all levels in *Hamlet*, the doubly and triply ironic meanings in *Macbeth*, and the variation on grace in *The Winter's Tale*. Poetic truth emerges through multiple meanings of words, and the richness of the dramatic experience results in part from the interplay of the various semantic levels.

Language and Style

166. MIRIAM JOSEPH, Sister. *Shakespeare's Use of the Arts of Language.* New York: Columbia University Press, 1947, 423 pp.

Presents in detail the theory of composition current during Shakespeare's time. Shakespeare would have learned the precepts in grammar school, then have employed them as a tool of analysis in reading, and finally have used them as a guide to composition. His early plays and poems are marked by an almost schematic use of rhetorical and logical devices; in his mature work his use of such devices is more subtle and dramatically refined. Part 3 presents a handbook of the general theory of composition and reading as defined and illustrated by Tudor logicians and rhetoricians. An abridged version—*Rhetoric in Shakespeare's Time* (New York: Harcourt Brace World)—was published in 1962.

167. NEWMAN, KAREN. *Shakespeare's Rhetoric of Comic Character.* New York: Methuen, 1985, 153 pp.

Insists that Shakespeare's comic characters possess a "rhetoric of inner life" (p. 5) that endows them with a remarkable "lifelikeness." The conventions of such characterization Shakespeare learned from his rhetorical training in the Elizabethan grammar schools; the schoolmasters, in turn, drew them from classical writers like Menander, Plautus, and Terence. Shakespeare, more particularly, "organizes soliloquies and monologic fragments as dialogue and complicates the relation of character to context by features of style like colloquial verse forms, [and by] caesuras and breaks in thought which counter end rhymes and iambic rhythm" (p. 93).

168. PARTRIDGE, ERIC. *Shakespeare's Bawdy: A Literary and Psycho-logical Essay and a Comprehensive Glossary.* 3d ed. New York: Routledge, 1991, 240 pp.

Examines the bawdy in Shakespeare's work from literary, psychological, and lexicographical angles. Part 1 is divided into a section on various kinds of bawdy—nonsexual, homosexual, sexual, general, and valedictory. Part 2 provides a glossary of some fifteen hundred words and phrases and briefly describes the bawdy connotations. Shakespeare is by turns witty, profound, idealistic, and cynical in his use of bawdiness. Only Jonson and Beaumont and Fletcher are as smutty, but their usage is not as straightforward, natural, and provocative as is Shakespeare's.

169. SHIRLEY, FRANCES A. *Swearing and Perjury in Shakespeare's Plays.* London: George Allen & Unwin, 1979, 174 pp.

Examines the dramatic function of swearing in Shakespeare's plays—as a device for increasing tension, for shock, for satiric attack, for delineation of character. The plays up to 1606 reflect his increasingly effective use of oaths. The self-excoriating attacks in Hamlet's soliloquies, for example, help to articulate his character and his inner tension. In act 5, though otherwise in self-control, he punctuates with an oath his forcing Claudius to drink from the poisoned cup. The antiblasphemy statute in 1606 limited Shakespeare's freedom with words and forced him to search for surrogate terms and expressions inoffensive to the censor.

170. SIPE, DOROTHY L. *Shakespeare's Metrics.* New Haven and London: Yale University Press, 1968, 266 pp.

Argues that Shakespeare, whatever the corrupting influences of Renaissance spelling and modern editing, wrote carefully constructed iambic verse, the normative line thus being a succession of two-syllable feet. Evidence demonstrates such regularity in 99.5 percent of the lines. In Shakespeare the metrical framework competes for predominance with the idea to be expressed and the semantic and morphological features of the language itself. Consistently he is able to make the constraints of and deviations from the meter enhance the power of his verse.

171. SPURGEON, CAROLINE F. E. *Shakespeare's Imagery and What It Tells Us.* Cambridge: Cambridge University Press, 1935, 425 pp.

Assembles, sorts, and examines on a systematic basis all of Shakespeare's images—sensory images, similes, metaphors—for what they can tell us about the man and about his plays. Following a comparison of Shakespeare's imagery with that of Bacon and other playwrights (especially Marlowe), the study discusses imagery under such categories as nature, indoor life and customs, and classes and types of men and then describes the personality of Shakespeare that emerges. Part 2 devotes individual chapters to the leading imagistic motives in the histories, comedies, romances, and tragedies. Charts visually demonstrate both the general predominant images and those for the individual plays.

172. STAUFFER, DONALD A. *Shakespeare's World of Images: The Development of His Moral Ideas.* New York: W. W. Norton, 1949, 393 pp.

Reveals Shakespeare's moral views through a consideration of his choice of subjects, alteration of sources, character analyses, plot structure, and images. *Measure for Measure* was written when his intellect was most active, but his ethical sense was not at its most certain; love in the play becomes an unweeded garden for desecration and monstrosities. *The Tempest,* on the other hand, champions the imagination as the

Language and Style

"servant of the 'nobler reason' in shaping images of natural beauty that vary from the delicate to the cosmic; and wondrous strange sea-music drifts through a life that is surrounded by sleep" (p. 302).

173. TARLINSKAJA, MARINA. *Shakespeare's Verse: Iambic Pentameter and the Poet's Idiosyncracies*. American University Studies Series 4: English Language and Literature, 41. New York and Bern: Peter Lang, 1987, 383 pp.

Analyzes the development of Shakespeare's blank verse line to trace the development of the playwright. A "stress profile" indicating variations within the pattern reveals that Shakespeare's metrical style evolved from strict to loose over the course of his career and that *Troilus and Cressida* is the play that divides such practice. Similarly, a study of accentual stress reveals where Othello's controlled language degenerates into choppy outbursts. So, too, an analysis of unstressed monosyllables in the final position of a line, from early to late Shakespeare, reveals a tenfold increase, thus illustrating the prevalence of enjambment in the second half of the canon.

174. THOMPSON, ANN, and THOMPSON, JOHN O. *Shakespeare: Meaning and Metaphor*. Iowa City: University of Iowa Press, 1987, 228 pp.

Calls attention to significant work being done on metaphors in linguistics, philosophy, and psychology in an effort to reinvigorate and enhance the study of Shakespeare's language. Theories of metaphor are linked to a "powerfully metaphoric text"—for example, *Troilus and Cressida* with George Lakoff and Mark Johnson's *Metaphors We Live By*, *King Lear* with Eva Kittay and Adrienne Lehrer's "Semantic Fields and the Structure of Metaphor," *Hamlet* with *A General Rhetoric*. This study is founded in speech-act theory, which argues a specificity of communication within a relatively stable context. Thus, it provides a theoretical base for confronting current critical theories that challenge the possibility of such definitive meaning.

175. VICKERS, BRIAN. *The Artistry of Shakespeare's Prose*. London: Methuen, 1968, 452 pp.

Traces the steady growth in Shakespeare's use of prose through the early comedies and histories, reaching a peak in the prose comedy *The Merry Wives of Windsor* but dominant as well in *Much Ado About Nothing*, *As You Like It*, and *Twelfth Night*. Of particular significance is Shakespeare's juxtaposition of prose and verse in a given play. Movement to prose can underscore sincerity as in Vincentio's conversation with Isabella or intensify parody as in *Troilus and Cressida*. It can also reflect a character's shifting moods as in Coriolanus or Timon. Its most profound use is in the madness of Lear and Othello.

176. WRIGHT, GEORGET. *Shakespeare's Metrical Art*. Berkeley: University of California Press, 1988, 349 pp.

Traces the development of the iambic pentameter line from Chaucer through Milton, with particular emphasis on Shakespeare's dramatic verse. Shakespeare cultivates contractions, elisions, and syncopations—syllabic and metrical conventions "aimed at making the verbal texture less obviously iambic" (p. 150). The tonal quality of *Twelfth Night*, for example, is achieved through liquids and sibilants, assonance, and alliteration. Likewise, the turbulence of Macbeth's mind is registered through metrical variations such as initial trochees, medial pyrrhics, and extra syllables. Shakespeare, throughout his plays, had the ability to develop metrical patterns that contribute to characterization, as in Polonius, Mercutio, Shylock, Juliet's nurse, and Pistol.

177. YODER, A. *Animal Analogy in Shakespeare's Character Portrayal: As Shown in His Reflection of the Aesopian Tradition and the Animal Aspect of Physiognomy*. New York: King's Crown Press, 1947, 150 pp.

Surveys and analyzes Shakespeare's use of more than four thousand animal comparisons in character portrayal either by delineating the foibles of man behind animal masks or judging men by attributes of animals they supposedly resemble. Generally, characters through such comparisons gain in intensity: villains, for instance, like Richard III (compared to a bottled spider) or Goneril (a gilded serpent); comic figures like Falstaff (a roasted Manningtree ox) or Malvolio (an affectioned ass); satiric figures like AJax (bitch-wolf's son) or Armado (a rabbit on a spit). Gentle souls like Henry VI (a deer whose skin's a keeper's fee) or Macduff's child (a poor monkey) gain in pathos. Shakespeare also uses animal analogies to heighten the tone or atmosphere.

STAGE, STAGE HISTORY, FILM

178. ADAMS, JOHN CRANFORD. *The Globe Playhouse: Its Design and Equipment*. Cambridge, Mass.: Harvard University Press, 1942, 435 pp.

Aims—with evidence from plays, dramatic entertainments, playhouse documents, letters, maps, pamphlets, and poems—to reconstruct as fully as possible the design and equipment of the Globe Playhouse. Sections of the theater discussed in detail include the frame, the audi-

Stage, Stage History, Film

torium (sign, yard, gallery subdivisions, gentlemen's rooms), the platform stage, the tiring house, and the superstructure.

179. ADAMS, JOSEPH QUINCY. *Shakespearean Playhouses: A History of English Theaters from the Beginnings to the Restoration.* Boston: Houghton Mifflin, 1917, 473 pp.
   Represents the first full attempt to provide a history of the playhouse in Shakespeare's time. Following a discussion of the inn yard as the forerunner of professional houses and of the general hostility of the city toward the players, individual chapters are devoted to seventeen regular theaters and to five temporary or projected theaters.

180. BALDWIN, THOMAS WHITFIELD. *The Organization and Personnel of the Shakespearean Company.* Princeton: Princeton University Press, 1927, 464 pp.
   Traces the development of Elizabethan acting companies as monopolies under license or patent, eventually limited to five companies of men in London at any one time. With the focus on the Lord Chamberlain's Men and the King's Men, individual chapters address membership in the Shakespearean company, the hired men and the permanent cadre, the economic operation and the division of labor, and the assignment of parts in Shakespeare's plays. The study reveals the considerable extent to which the development of Shakespeare's art was influenced by stage conditions (public and private) and by the strengths and ages of the principal actors.

181. BALL, ROBERT HAMILTON. *Shakespeare on Silent Film: A Strange Eventful History.* London: George Allen & Unwin, 1968, 403 pp.
   Discusses in part 1 the film productions of Shakespeare in chronological order from Herbert Beerbohm Tree's filming of *King John* in 1899 to an atrociously satiric German version of *A Midsummer Night's Dream* in 1928. Part 2 provides more specific details for each production treated in part 1. In a sense, silent Shakespeare is a contradiction; hearing the language is an indispensable part of the theatrical experience. Moreover the general public was not really ready for Shakespeare. Progress was made, though, in camera techniques and in gradually building a receptive public.

182. BENTLEY, GERALD EADES. *The Jacobean and Caroline Stage.* 7 vols. Oxford: Clarendon Press, 1941–68, 2903 pp.
   Provides information on all aspects of English drama from 1616 to 1642. Volume 1 discusses the acting companies, both adult and children; volume 2, the players; volumes 3–5, plays and playwrights (in-

cluding several plays attributed to Shakespeare in his own day); volume 6, private, public, and court theaters, along with two projected theaters; volume 7 reproduces pertinent theatrical documents and includes a general index. This study comprises an vast source of information on later Jacobean and Caroline drama.

183. ———. *The Profession of Player in Shakespeare's Time*. Princeton: Princeton University Press, 1984, 315 pp.

Provides a guide to the performer's professional life in Shakespeare's time. Following an opening chapter that describes general working conditions and employment patterns, attention turns to distinguishing among sharers (those who bore legal and financial responsibility and who shared debts or profits), hired men (those working for specific wages, from players and musicians to prompters and stagekeepers), and apprentices (boys recruited for female roles). Discussion of the duties of managers and of the challenges and opportunities of provincial touring concludes the study.

184. BERRY, HERBERT. *Shakespeare's Playhouses*. Illustrated by C. Walter Hodges. AMS Studies in the Renaissance, 19. New York: AMS Press, 1987, 260 pp.

Lays out what we know about the Theatre, hard information largely derived from lawsuits; we know that it was a large, expensive, timbered structure that frequently needed repair and cost around £700 to build. Another chapter relates the discovery of a lawsuit in 1635 involving the King's Men. This lawsuit reveals much about the cost, the expense of the lease to the property, and details about rebuilding in 1613; a second wave of litigation indicates that Burbage cleared £200 per year in clear profit from the Globe and that in 1635 it was worth 276 percent more in rent than in 1614.

185. BRENNAN, ANTHONY. *Onstage and Offstage Worlds in Shakespeare*. New York: Routledge, 1989, 321 pp.

Explores how Shakespeare distributes his material between onstage and offstage events to shape the responses of an audience. The structural complexity of offstage reporting is illustrated in *Richard II* (3.2) when Richard receives a series of reports (defecting troops, York's capitulation, the deaths of Bushy, Bagot, and Green) that focus our attention on his emotional roller-coaster reaction. Offstage reporting is also highly significant in Macbeth's receiving a report of his wife's death, as if to underscore their growing sense of separation. One chapter deals generally with Shakespeare's strategies for relating onstage and

Stage, Stage History, Film

offstage activities and another examines ways these strategies work in individual plays.

186. BROCKBANK, PHILIP, ed. *Players of Shakespeare: Essays in Shakespearean Performance by Twelve Players with the Royal Shakespeare Company.* Cambridge: Cambridge University Press, 1985, 179 pp. Jackson, Russell, and Smallwood, Robert, eds. *Players of Shakespeare 2: Further Essays in Shakespearean Performance by Players with the Royal Shakespeare Company.* Cambridge: Cambridge University Press, 1988, 203 pp.

Describes the preparation and performance of Shakespearean roles, concentrating on a single character on occasion played over a number of years in different productions. Volume 1 includes essays on Shylock, Portia, Malvolio, Orlando, Lavatch, the nurse, Polonius, Hamlet, Timon, Posthumous, Hermione, and Caliban. Volume 2 includes essays on Vincentio, Juliet, Ophelia, the fool, Othello, and Iago. An introductory essay in each volume discusses Shakespeare's general concept of characterization and describes matters of stage, periodization, stage design, and costume.

187. BUCHMAN, LORNE M. *Still in Movement: Shakespeare on Screen.* Oxford: Oxford University Press, 1991, 171 pp.

Focuses on the movie screen as the new medium in which Shakespeare production is realized. The concern is not so much with individual films, actors, or directors as with "central issues that illuminate how the plays are operating as products of cinematic technique" (p. 5). The process of film, for example, makes possible a multiplicity of perspectives, it provides a new freedom for space and locale, and the close shot thrusts the viewer into the prison of the mind or registers the full impact of reaction. In a word, film technique has the capacity to make of us a creative participant. Studied in some detail is the work of Orson Welles, Grigori Kozintsev, and Laurence Olivier.

188. BULMAN, J. C., AND COURSEN, H. R., eds. *Shakespeare on Television: An Anthology of Essays and Reviews.* Hanover and London: University Press of New England, 1988, 324 pp.

Focuses on Shakespeare on television, with essays divided into three sections: theoretical and ideological essays ("Wide Angles"), essays on particular plays or play-groups and particular directors ("Closeups"), and reviews ("Short Subjects"). Section one deals with the collision between an individual's mind-set toward Shakespeare and toward television; it explores also the difficulty in juxtaposing an essentially verbal form with an essentially visual medium. The second section deals with individual productions of *Much Ado About Nothing,*

The Merchant of Venice, As You Like It, Macbeth, and the first tetralogy of history plays.

189. BUZACOTT, MARTIN. *The Death of the Actor: Shakespearean Acting in the Age of Terror*. New York: Routledge, 1991, 180 pp.

Attacks contemporary theater practice and performance theory that identify the actor, rather than the director, as the key creative force in the performance of Shakespeare. Such contemporary theory and practice are based on a view of actors as respectable social and political figures, rather than as thieves and vagabonds, as they were considered in the Elizabethan age. The illusion of their centrality is sustained only by a rhetoric of heroism, violence, and imperialism.

190. CHAMBERS, EDMUND KERCHEVER. *The Elizabethan Stage*. 4 vols. Oxford: Clarendon Press, 1923, 1950 pp.

Provides information on all aspects of English drama during the reign of Elizabeth and during the first thirteen years of the reign of King James (1558–1616). Volume 1 discusses the historical period, the Revels Office, the Mask and the court play, the struggle between city and court, Puritanism and humanism, and the quality and economic conditions of the actors; volume 2, the history of the acting companies, both adult and children, and the actors; volume 3, the conditions of staging in the theaters and at court, the presenting of plays, and the actors; volume 4 offers reprints of various theatrical documents and a general index. An index is provided by Beatrice White in *An Index to "The Elizabethan Stage" and "William Shakespeare" by Sir Edmund Chambers* (Oxford: Oxford University Press, 1934, 161 pp.).

191. COHN, RUBY. *Modern Shakespeare Offshoots*. Princeton: Princeton University Press, 1976, 426 pp.

Concerns the manner in which Shakespeare's plays have been emended, adapted, and transformed for the modern theater in England, France, and Germany. Discussion covers modern adaptations of *Macbeth, Hamlet, King Lear*, and *The Tempest* as well as fiction stemming from *Hamlet* and essays inspired by *Lear*. Another section focuses on Shakespeare's influence on the creative work of Shaw, Brecht, and Beckett.

192. COLLICK, JOHN. *Shakespeare, Cinema and Society*. Manchester: Manchester University Press; New York: St. Martin's Press, 1989, 208 pp.

Argues that criticism of Shakespeare on film has generally supported "attempts from within Anglo-American culture to create a world-wide cultural hegemony based on the orthodoxy of New Criticism" (pp. 194–

95). Sponsorship of the BBC series in America by Time/Life and Morgan Guaranty illustrates the efforts by large corporations to subvert Shakespeare to the capitalist plans for cultural imperialism. Films afforded special attention include the 1935 *A Midsummer Night's Dream* with James Cagney and Mickey Rooney and the work of Laurence Olivier, Orson Welles, Celeotino Coronado, and Derek Jarman.

193. COOK, ANN JENNALIE. *The Privileged Playgoers of Shakespeare's London: 1576–1642*. Princeton: Princeton University Press, 1981, 316 pp.

Refutes Alfred Harbage's theory that England's "working class" comprised the majority of Shakespeare's audience in the public playhouses. To the contrary, evidence suggests that there was no appreciable difference between the audiences at the large public theaters and those at the smaller, more costly private ones. In both cases the great majority were those of wealth and substance. Seats in the galleries far outnumbered standing space, and the 2 pence charged for such seats would have been exorbitantly expensive for an apprentice or craftsman.

194. DAVID, RICHARD. *Shakespeare in the Theatre*. Cambridge: Cambridge University Press, 1978, 263 pp.

Provides detailed studies of the major English productions of Shakespeare during the 1970s, attempting not only to record those most strikingly successful individual moments but also to suggest the major trends in contemporary Shakespearean production. Twenty-two productions representing nineteen plays are discussed with *Hamlet*, *Romeo and Juliet*, and *Richard II* considered and compared in two productions. Shakespeare works in a wide range from the naturalistic to the surrealistic, from bare stage to full; but a play is generally most successful when presented on its own terms, "not rigidly or pedantically, but with an eye to avoiding anything that is counter to the peculiarities of its own nature" (p. 242).

195. DAVIES, ANTHONY. *Filming Shakespeare's Plays: The Adaptations of Laurence Olivier, Orson Welles, Peter Brook and Akira Kurosawa*. Cambridge: Cambridge University Press, 1988, 219 pp.

Asserts that "Shakespearean film continues to justify its place as a valid, vigorous and necessary dimension of the contemporary encounter with the world's greatest dramatist" (p. 187). To be sure, the Shakespeare we view on stage is not the one we encounter on film; the challenge is to develop a "spatial strategy that captures the theatricality" of the play rather than merely a group of actors/actresses in a highly restricted setting (p. 24). Individual chapters are devoted to Olivier's

Henry V, *Hamlet*, and *Richard III*, Welles's *Macbeth*, *Othello*, and *Chimes at Midnight*, Brook's *King Lear*, and Kurosawa's *Throne of Blood*.

196. DESSEN, ALAN C. *Elizabethan Stage Conventions and Modern Interpreters*. Cambridge: Cambridge University Press, 1984, 190 pp.

Focuses on an understanding of the conventions of acting and dramaturgy that can help us to reevaluate the reading and staging of Shakespearean plays. Such stage directions as enter "as from dinner," "as from play," "as from hunting," or "as rising from bed" were attended by particular conventions of dress and were often used symbolically to indicate a state of mind or psychological condition. Conventions of darkness (acted in full light but with a character carrying a lighted torch) would permit the spectators to perceive details often obscured in modern productions (like Iago's movements in the shadows under Brabantio's window).

197. FOAKES, R. A., and RICKERT, R. T., eds. *Henslowe's Diary*. Cambridge: Cambridge University Press, 1961, 368 pp.

Provides the text of the *Diary* of Philip Henslowe, the chief source for theatrical history between 1590 and 1604. Henslowe's account falls into two sections: (1) the names of the companies who performed at his theater (the Rose?), the plays, and the amount he received for rent (one-half of the gallery takings); (2) records of advances he made to the Admiral's Men (after 1597) for the purchase of plays and costumes and of advances to the players themselves. The introduction covers the history of the manuscript; and a general index, an index of plays, and an index of year-dates are included. This edition supersedes W. W. Greg's *Henslowe's Diary* (2 vols. London: A. H. Bullen, 1904, 640 pp.).

198. FROST, DAVID L. *The School of Shakespeare: The Influence of Shakespeare on English Drama, 1600–42*. Cambridge: Cambridge University Press, 1968, 304 pp.

Argues the pervasive influence of Shakespeare on English drama until the closing of the public theaters in 1642. Not only did his plays continue to hold the stage; their popularity is reflected also in the number to appear in print. Moreover, in numerous instances the popularity of a Shakespearean play forces the work of later playwrights into its mold. In particular, Shakespeare revived and redeemed both the romance and revenge tragedy; Marston, Massinger, Fletcher, and Middleton all produced imitations. The majority saw Shakespeare as a great repository of materials.

Stage, Stage History, Film

199. GOLDMAN, MICHAEL. *Acting and Action in Shakespearean Tragedy.*
Princeton: Princeton University Press, 1985, 182 pp.
    Asserts the centrality of the stage experience to any dramatic analysis
by focusing on the interdependency of the actor's ability (*poiesis*) and the
spectator's imaginative ability to compare the action on stage with that
in "real" life (*theoria*). *Hamlet*, for example, is a play about the problematics of action; the spectators are drawn into endless dubieties in the
"struggle to find a basis for action consonant with their sense of human
value and the dignity of the mind" (p. 26). *Othello*, on the other hand,
focuses on the manner in which perception is translated into deed.

200. GURR, ANDREW. *Playgoing in Shakespeare's London.* Cambridge: Cambridge University Press, 1987, 284 pp.
    Provides an analysis of Elizabethan theaters and the composition
of their audiences between 1567, when plays began to be performed at
the Red Lion, to the closing of the houses by the Puritans in 1642.
During this period "well over fifty million visits were made to the
playhouses" (p. 4), with the audience composed of nobles and gentlemen, citizens and burgesses, yeomen and rural smallholders, and artisans and laborers. The strongest evidence that the audience was socially
mixed was the graduated price of admission.

201. ———. *The Shakespearian Stage 1574–1642.* Cambridge: Cambridge
University Press, 1970, 192 pp.
    Comprises a conspectus of background material for Shakespearean
drama, the Elizabethan society, the acting companies, the theaters, the
mechanics of staging and acting, and the audience. One can trace a
shifting population among the companies as, dictated by financial circumstances, players moved from group to group. Traveling companies
generally were considerably smaller than those based in London. A
playwright was normally hired for a particular play or was paid for a
work he had for sale. Shakespeare, who wrote and acted for a single
company from 1594 to 1613, is an obvious exception.

202. GURR, ANDREW, with ORRELL, JOHN. *Rebuilding Shakespeare's Globe.*
New York: Routledge, 1989, 197 pp.
    Discusses the playgoers, the acting company, and the playhouse
that were intrinsic to Shakespeare's professional life. A historical sketch
of efforts since the nineteenth century to replicate the Globe concludes
with a description of London's projected International Shakespeare
Centre and the rebuilt Globe. Of particular interest concerning the
construction of the original Globe in 1599 is Burbage's selling shares to
five members of the company, Shakespeare included, to cover half the

considerable cost. After 1609 the company used the public theater during the warm months and Blackfriars from October to April.

203. HALIO, JAY L. *Understanding Shakespeare's Plays in Performance.* Manchester: Manchester University Press; New York: St. Martin's Press, 1988, 100 pp.

Serves as a theatergoer's guide, with chapters on "finding" the text, set design, characters, subtext, language, stage business, and coherence. Issues of concern include the legitimacy of adaptations and modernizations, the actor's search for motivation, and directorial intervention. Interwoven into the discussion are recollections of particular productions over the past thirty years, ranging from Stratford-upon-Avon to American theaters.

204. HARBAGE, ALFRED. *Shakespeare and the Rival Traditions.* New York: Macmillan, 1952, 393 pp.

Observes that the theatrical tradition is decidedly dualistic: the public houses and the adult companies evolving from the strolling players of the fifteenth century, the private or coterie houses from the boy choristers and grammar school troupes. The coterie theater, catering to a wealthier and more highly educated group, favored satiric comedy. The popular stage, operating within more traditional moral constraints, provided more varied fare, abounding in chronicle plays and romances. Writers for the private stage performed an important service in carrying on the earlier academic tendency to import and experiment, but most of the plays are overwritten and underimagined. To the contrary. Shakespeare's plays–written for the public stage–possess a broad appeal, establishing contact with significant numbers and kinds of people.

205. ⸺. *Shakespeare's Audience.* New York: Columbia University Press, 1941, 201 pp.

Refutes the popular misconception that the Elizabethan audience was rowdy and uncouth, ready at a moment's notice to be caught up in a passion in the pit at the expense of attention to the actor onstage. Crowds averaging some two thousand per day at the theaters are all too frequently attacked by disgruntled poets or actors. Evidence suggests that the patrons came in festive mood to mingle and to see a play; the "criminal or quarrelsome or persistently noisy were a threat to their enjoyment" (p. 113), and such trouble was relatively infrequent.

206. HILL, ERROL. *Shakespeare in Sable: A History of Black Shakespearean Actors.* Amherst: University of Massachusetts Press, 1984, 216 pp.

Stage, Stage History, Film

Charts the history of black Shakespearean actors from 1820 to 1970. The major focus is on Ira Aldridge and Paul Robeson, each in his own way an innovator in past years, and on the present work of Gloria Foster, Earle Hyman, James Earl Jones, and Jean White. Such a study inevitably deals with a significant social dimension, in this instance tracing the difficulty of blacks to gain recognition as serious dramatic actors. Especially supportive of black actors have been Joseph Papp and C. Bernard Jackson.

207. HODGES, C. WALTER. *The Globe Restored: A Study of the Elizabethan Theatre*. London: E. Benn, 1953, 190 pp.

Combines evidence and conjecture to present a general reconstruction of the Globe Playhouse. Most probably both the first Globe (burned 1613) and the second Globe (demolished in 1644) were polygonal in structure, a point clearly noted in Visscher's engraving of the Bankside around 1616. Seventy pages of plates include historical documents such as Visscher's View, Van Buchell's sketch of the Swan, and Hollar's engraving of the Bankside, along with eight reconstruction sketches.

208. HOTSON, LESLIE. *Shakespeare's Wooden O*. London: Rupert Hart-Davis, 1959, 335 pp.

Claims that Shakespeare was originally played in the round. The Globe resembled a tennis court with its blank fourth wall removed and the second long side opening to the yard below. Such an arrangement accommodated the essence of drama—contrast, antagonism, conflict—and it maintained a clarity of place, the significant location of heaven, the world, and hell enjoyed by the Middle Ages.

209. JORGENS, JACK J. *Shakespeare on Film*. Bloomington: Indiana University Press, 1977, 377 pp. Reprinted Lanham: University Press of America, 1991, 352 pp.

Deals with the art of film adaptation of Shakespeare, both literal and free, drawing from theater history, literary analysis, and film criticism to reveal relationships between Renaissance visions and modern re-visions. Individual chapters treat productions of *A Midsummer Night's Dream* by Max Reinhardt and Peter Hall, of *The Taming of the Shrew* and *Romeo and Juliet* by Zefferelli, of *Julius Caesar* by Mankiewicz, of *Henry V*, *Richard III*, and *Hamlet* by Olivier, of *Macbeth* by Polanski and Welles, of *Hamlet* by Kozintsev, and of *King Lear* by Brook and Kozintsev.

210. KING, T. J. *Shakespearean Staging, 1599–1642*. Cambridge, Mass.: Harvard University Press, 1971, 163 pp.

Surveys pre-Restoration staging techniques through an examination of 276 texts (promptbooks, printed plays with prompter's notations, playbooks printed from prompt copy) dating from 1599 to 1642. The aim is to reveal how the plays of Shakespeare and his contemporaries were staged, and the evidence, drawn from contemporary architecture and pictures of early English stages and from the texts themselves, suggests the use of unlocalized façades with commonplace stage properties. References to Shakespeare are pervasive, and a full chapter is devoted to the conjectural staging of *Twelfth Night* as performed during Candlemas Feast 1601/1602 at the Middle Temple.

211. KNUTSON, ROSLYN L. *The Repertory of Shakespeare's Company, 1594–1613*. Fayetteville: University of Arkansas Press, 1991, 252 pp.

Argues that Shakespeare's company should be viewed for what it is, a hard-nosed, highly competitive organization in an enterprise all the more economically precarious because it was socially marginalized. The study provides a clear vision of the dynamics of repertory management and the practice of playgoing in Shakespeare's day. Divisions include the repertory system and commercial tactics, the Chamberlain's Men (1594–99, 1599–1603), and the King's Men (1603–08, 1608–13).

212. MANVELL, ROGER. *Shakespeare and the Film*. New York and Washington: Praeger, 1971, 172 pp.

Examines the major films adapted from Shakespeare's plays during the period of sound film, from the early attempts of Douglas Fairbanks and Mary Pickford in *The Taming of the Shrew* and the Max Reinhardt production of *A Midsummer Night's Dream* to the achievements of Laurence Olivier, Orson Welles, Peter Brook, Sergei Yutkevich, Grigori Kozintsev, and Akira Kurosawa. Cinematic techniques can lend an excitement not unlike the appeal to Shakespeare's contemporary audiences. In particular, the heightened atmosphere and the visual imagery of film can enhance the play's poetic imagery.

213. MULLANEY, STEVEN. *The Place of the Stage: License, Play, and Power in Renaissance England*. Chicago: University of Chicago Press, 1988, 178 pp.

Asserts that popular Elizabethan drama, born of a contradiction between the court that in a limited way licensed and maintained it and a city that sought its prohibition, was viewed as potentially subversive, a distinct threat to civic and religious hierarchies. From the margins of society, its plays served to "define, articulate, and interpret both the social hierarchy and the communal landscape in which it was reflected" (p. 14). Chapters on *Measure for Measure*, *Macbeth*, and *Pericles* argue

Stage, Stage History, Film

that Shakespeare's plays, viewed from such a marginal perspective, constitute a critical attack on the cultural pretexts and practices that shaped Elizabethan society.

214. MURRAY, JOHN TUCKER. *English Dramatic Companies 1558–1642*. 2 vols. Boston: Houghton Mifflin, 1910, 804 pp.

Traces the history of English dramatic companies from the accession of Queen Elizabeth in 1558 to the closing of the theaters by the Puritans in 1642. Volume 1 covers the London companies (greater men's, lesser men's, children's), their affiliation with particular theaters along with court and provincial performances. Volume 2 covers the provincial companies, men's and children's under royal patronage, those under noblemen and commoners, those under players, and those under towns. Shakespeare's company (the Lord Chamberlain's) is treated at length.

215. NYBERG, LENNART. *The Shakespearean Ideal: Shakespeare Production and the Modern Theatre in Britain*. Acta Universitatis Upsaliensis: Studia Anglistica Upsaliensia, 66. Uppsala: Almqvist and Wiksell, 1988, 144 pp.

Traces the influence of modern drama and theatrical conventions on the production of Shakespeare's plays in the 1960s and 1970s, with emphasis on the development of the thrust stage, the relationship between the actors and spectators, and the acting style. The establishment of companies led to the emergence of innovative directors like Peter Hall, John Barton, Trevor Nunn, Terry Hands, Peter Brook, and Jonathan Miller. With experience in avant garde theater, they led the way in challenging traditional concepts of Shakespearean character and ideology.

216. ODELL, GEORGE C. D. *Shakespeare: From Betterton to Irving*. 2 vols. New York: Scribner, 1920, 954 pp.

Examines the stage history of Shakespeare's plays from 1660 to the early twentieth century with emphasis on major productions' alterations in dramatic representational technique, and alterations in the texts themselves. The material is divided into eight sections—in volume 1 the age of Betterton (1660–1710), the age of Cibber (1710–42), the age of Garrick (1742–76); in volume 2 the age of Kemble (1776–1817), the leaderless age (1817–37), the age of Macready (1837–43), the age of Phelps and Charles Kean (1843–79), and the age of Irving (1879–1902). A final chapter describes recent trends and actors (Bensen, Tree, Granville-Barker, Greet).

217. PILKINGTON, ACE G. *Screening Shakespeare from "Richard II" to "Henry V."* Newark: University of Delaware Press; London and Toronto Associated University Presses, 1991, 216 pp.

Treats the BBC film versions of the second tetralogy as texts for literary analysis. The emphasis on realism and historical accuracy in *Richard II*, for example, challenges Tillyard's worldview through a consistently tyrannical but subtly sympathetic portrayal of the monarch. *1,2 Henry IV* and *Henry V* are examined as a trilogy in which Hal the boy grows into the kingship physically, morally, and psychologically. Additional focus is on Olivier's *Henry V* and Welles's *Chimes at Midnight*. The final chapter concerns the impact of new technology and marketing strategies on Shakespeare films and film study.

218. SHATTUCK, CHARLES H. *Shakespeare on the American Stage: From the Hallams to Edwin Booth*. Washington: Folger Shakespeare Library, 1979, 170 pp.

Provides a historical sketch of Shakespeare in the American theater, noting that from 1752 (with Lewis Hallam's London company) until well into the 1820s Shakespeare was an entirely imported product both in the actors and in the eighteenth-century "improvements" on Shakespeare's plays. In the early nineteenth century a new wave of realistic characterization came in with George Frederick Cooke, Edmund Kean, and Junius Brutus Booth; and the first significant American actor emerged in Edwin Forrest. A more genteel tradition is found in the midcentury with William Burton, Edward Loomis Davenport, and John McCullough. American Shakespeare in the century climaxed in the work of Edwin Booth.

219. SMITH, IRWIN. *Shakespeare's Blackfriars Playhouse: Its History and Its Design*. New York: New York University Press, 1964, 577 pp.

Concerns a portion of Blackfriars on the north bank of the Thames (originally founded by the Black Friars in 1275) and its use for two theatrical ventures—the first commercial indoor theater for children's performance and later the indoor playhouse for Shakespeare's company. The particular focus is on the theater as used by the King's Men, with separate chapters on its auditorium, platform, rear stage, and upper stage.

220. ———. *Shakespeare's Globe Playhouse: A Modern Reconstruction in Text and Scale Drawings*. New York: Charles Scribner's Sons, 1956, 240 pp.

Results from the collaborative efforts with John Cranford Adams to construct a scale model of the Globe. The acceptance of the Elizabethan platform stage has freed actors and producers from the tyranny—both economic and artistic—of stage settings and has encouraged the current explosion of interest in Shakespeare festival theater. With information drawn from contemporary evidence, the

Stage, Stage History, Film

study concerns the site and shape of the Globe, its dimensions, fabric, auditorium, the stages (platform, inner, rear, and second-level), the music gallery, and the superstructure.

221. SPENCER, HAZELTON. *Shakespeare Improved: The Restoration Versions in Quarto and on the Stage*. Cambridge, Mass.: Harvard University Press, 1927, 406 pp.

Describes Shakespeare on the stage during the Restoration period from 1660 to 1710, the date that Betterton died and that (one year after the publication of Rowe's edition) essentially marks the end of a long sequence of altered independent quartos. Part 1 sketches the stage history of the two licensed companies at Drury Lane and Lincoln's Inn Fields and the first union in 1682. Part 2 deals with adaptations of Shakespeare—for example, Davenant's *Macbeth*, Dryden's *Tempest* and *All for Love*, Tate's *King Lear*, Shadwell's *Timon of Athens*, and Cibber's *Richard III*. Adapted versions greatly outnumber unaltered productions, many of them showing little regard for the nature of Shakespeare's plot, diction, or stage methods.

222. STYAN, J. L. *The Shakespeare Revolution: Criticism and Performance in the Twentieth Century*. Cambridge: Cambridge University Press, 1977, 292 pp.

Charts the movement of Shakespearean production from the late Victorian period to the present time, from the full-scene proscenium-arch stage to the empty stage and nonillusory presentations, from the experimental work of William Poel and Harley Granville-Barker to the revolutionary efforts of Jackson, Hall, Guthrie, and Brook. Also examined is academic influence on the stage (Bradley, Bradbrook, Knight, Knights, Leavis), especially of Jan Kott on Peter Brook's *King Lear*.

223. ———. *Shakespeare's Stagecraft*. Cambridge: Cambridge University Press, 1967, 244 pp.

Explores Shakespeare's stagecraft through the details of his work as a craftsman. Theatrical communication depends on a largely subconscious system of signals from actor to spectator through the script. Individual chapters address the Elizabethan stage (its flexibility, intimacy, and platform focus), staging and acting conventions (properties, symbols, the boy actor), the actor's movement (Shakespeare as director within the text, gesture, the soliloquy), grouping on the open stage (duologue, spatial distancing), the full stage (visual images, multiple entrances and groupings), speech (tones, rhythm), and orchestration (contrasting patterns of sound).

224. TREWIN, J. C. *Shakespeare on the English Stage, 1900–1964: A Survey of Productions*. London: Barrie and Rockliff, 1964, 328 pp.

Surveys productions of Shakespeare in the British theater since 1900, reflecting the theory and experimentation behind shifting representational fashions. While extensive discussion of individual performances is necessarily selective, an appendix cites a full list of West End, Old Vic, and Stratford-upon-Avon stagings. The general theatrical tendencies are suggested in the chapter headings—full dress (1900–l4), scene changing (1914–30), moving fast (1930–46), nothing barred (1946–64)

225. WILES, DAVID. *Shakespeare's Clown: Actor and Text in the Elizabethan Playhouse*. Cambridge: Cambridge University Press, 1987, 223 pp.

Focuses on the relationship between Shakespeare and William Kemp, clown of the Chamberlain's Men from 1594 to 1599. The first role constructed for Kemp was in all likelihood that of Launce in *The Two Gentlemen of Verona*, a role in which the clown might well improvise as he pleases. Other roles include the clown in *Titus Andronicus*, Bottom in *A Midsummer Night's Dream*, Launcelot Gobbo in *The Merchant of Venice*, Costard in *Love's Labor's Lost*, Peter in *Romeo and Juliet*, and Dogberry in *Much Ado About Nothing*. It may well be that Kemp also played the role of Falstaff in *1,2 Henry IV* and that he arranged to leave the company when Shakespeare decided to eliminate that character in *Henry V*.

226. WILLIS, SUSAN. *The BBC Shakespeare Plays: Making the Televised Canon*. Chapel Hill: University of North Carolina Press, 1991, 310 pp.

Chronicles the technical and dramatic accomplishments of the televising of the entire Shakespeare canon of thirty-seven plays by the British Broadcasting Company between 1978 and 1985. The study provides both a general history and analysis of the series and also an eyewitness account of the productions, from planning and rehearsal to taping and editing.

227. WOOD, LEIGH. *On Playing Shakespeare: Advice and Commentary from Actors and Actresses of the Past*. Westport: Greenwood Publishing Group, 1991, 256 pp.

Contains commentary from past Shakespearean players including such legendary figures as John Barrymore, Ellen Terry, Edwin Booth, and Helen Faucit. For easy reference and occasionally stark contrast, actors' differing reactions to specific roles are placed side by side. An early section deals with general stage matters like qualifications for acting, voice and diction, ease and polish.

THEMATIC AND TOPICAL STUDIES

228. ALLMAN, EILEEN JORGE. *Player-King and Adversary: Two Faces of Play in Shakespeare*. Baton Rouge and London: Louisiana State University Press, 1980, 347 pp.

   Asserts that Shakespeare employs the universality of human play as a mirror both for the character and the spectator in exploring, defining, and educating human nature. The pattern makers are of two generic types, the player-king and the adversary. In the educative process the player-king experiences a psychic shock—Richard II loses his name; Portia is bound by a casket; Hal mistrusts his political title; Vincentio fears his ability to rule; Prospero is stripped of authority and homeland. Whether in comic or tragic terms the characters and the spectators discover their true natures and regain psychic health.

229. ANDREWS, JOHN F., ed. *William Shakespeare: His World, His Work, and His Influence*. 3 vols. New York: Charles Scribner's Sons, 1985, 954 pp.

   Comprises a massive collection of sixty essays, each by an authority in the field, that is intended to offer a multifaceted survey of relevant information about Shakespeare. Proceeding from background essays on the Elizabethan-Jacobean state, the church, the law, and the society, the material moves to more specific topics such as economics, medicine, sanitation, warfare, patronage, the profession of dramatist, printing and publishing, and the theater audience. For Shakespeare, in particular, there are discussions of his language, his dramatic techniques and methods, and music. Individual plays are covered within their generic classifications, and essays on performance and a survey of criticism during the last twenty-five years are located in the final volumes.

230. ARTHOS, JOHN. *Shakespeare: The Early Writings*. Totowa: Rowman & Littlefield, 1972, 264 pp.

   Examines *Venus and Adonis*, *The Rape of Lucrece*, and the eight earliest plays in terms of Shakespeare's manipulation of humanistic dramatic conventions and the infusion of elements from the native tradition. Early in his career, for example, Shakespeare played with the platonic doctrine at the heart of Petrarchism, but the Platonism is matched and in some ways even confined by the common sense of a Launce, a Speed, or a Dogberry or by the conscious posing of a Feste. In his prodigality of language and action, the wide expanse of contrarieties and similarities, he enriches the limits of drama in a manner that will mature but not change.

231. BAMBER, LINDA. *Comic Women, Tragic Men: A Study of Gender and Genre in Shakespeare.* Stanford: Stanford University Press, 1982, 211 pp.

Maintains that Shakespeare inevitably writes from the masculine perspective (the self) and that the force that interacts with it (the other) is the feminine perspective. This interaction may involve genuine or apparent betrayal as in the tragedies, demolition of the social hierarchies as in the comedies, or spiritual fulfillment as in the romances. While Shakespeare is not a feminist, he does, except for the histories, associate the feminine with whatever man takes most seriously outside of himself.

232. BARROLL, J. LEEDS. *Artificial Persons: The Formation of Character in the Tragedies of Shakespeare.* Columbia: University of South Carolina Press, 1974, 267 pp.

Labels the theory of the humors an inadequate explanation for the dichotomy of passion and reason basic to the concept of character in the Renaissance. The duality is more effectively perceived as the conflict within one's "affections" (his natural yearnings) of love of self and love of God. The former is destructive when for reasons of lust, greed, or ambition it prevents proper fulfillment of the latter. Generally Shakespeare's protagonists can be envisioned as individuals whose attempt to establish their identity or personality is thwarted by such distorted values and whose sense of psychological wholeness is realized only through the insights concomitant with their final disastrous moments.

233. BARTHELEMY, ANTHONY GERARD. *Black Face, Maligned Race: The Representation of Blacks in English Drama from Shakespeare to Southerne.* Baton Rouge: Louisiana State University Press, 1987, 215 pp.

Considers the influence of English political, social, and theatrical history on the depiction of black characters on the English stage from 1589 to 1695. Almost without exception blackness was equated with treachery, evil, and ugliness. By far the most common black figure was the villainous Moor, as seen in Aaron in *Titus Andronicus*. In *Othello* stereotypical attitudes about blacks are initially reversed, but Othello is eventually trapped into acting in accordance with the stereotype.

234. BATE, JONATHAN. *Shakespeare and the English Romantic Tradition.* Oxford: Clarendon Press, 1986, 276 pp.

Gauges Shakespeare's impact on the major Romantic poets, not merely in specific, traceable borrowings but also in their theories of the imagination and their actual poetic practices. Coleridge, for example, is indebted to Shakespeare in his treatment of the supernatural in "The

Thematic and Topical Studies

Ancient Mariner" (images of sleeplessness and terror in *Macbeth*), and in "Dejection: An Ode" (Hamlet's ironic self-abnegation in his claim to have more offenses than he has imagination to give them scope). Similarly, Wordsworth draws upon Shakespeare in "An Evening Walk" (*The Tempest, Measure for Measure*), *The Borderers* (*Richard III, King Lear, Hamlet*), and "Tintern Abbey" (*King Lear, Macbeth*).

235. BERGERON, DAVID, ed. *Pageantry in the Shakespearean Theater*. Athens: University of Georgia Press, 1985, 251 pp.

Reveals, in essays focused on political, social, and aesthetic issues, the profound influence on Renaissance theater of events of spectacle and pageantry—tournaments, royal entries and progresses, Lord Mayor's shows, funeral processions, and court masques. Coverage includes a discussion of pageantry and the idea of civic triumph in *Richard II* (Gordon Kipling), the interlude of beggar and king in *Richard II* (James Black), civic pageantry in the second tetralogy (Barbara Palmer), funeral pageantry in Shakespeare (Michael Neill), and Shakespeare's problematizing of the heroic in Prince Hal (Gerard Cox).

236. BERRY, RALPH. *Shakespeare and the Awareness of the Audience*. New York: St. Martin's Press, 1985, 157 pp.

Analyzes the likely reaction of Shakespeare's audiences to his various plays. *Richard III*, for example, succeeds through a bonding effect upon the audience as English; right comes to be equated with the provinces. *Twelfth Night* incenses the spectators to a kind of blood sport, participation in the baiting of Malvolio. *Troilus and Cressida* combines irony and elegy in its treatment of chivalry, and *Julius Caesar* is a tragedy of communal violence stemming from a rigid enforcement of Roman identity.

237. BETHELL, S. L. *Shakespeare and the Popular Dramatic Tradition*. London: Staples Press, 1944, 164 pp.

Discusses a variety of aspects of Shakespearean drama, for example, the range of production and critical interpretation from the highly stylized to the realistic, the Elizabethans' heightened awareness of play as play as a consequence of the nature of Shakespeare's theater and the psychological impact of that awareness, and Shakespeare's use of anachronism. The use of dialogic conventions emphasizes the double nature of character, and the generic mixing of comedy and tragedy reflects the audience's familiarity with rapid modal shifts in early popular drama.

238. BILTON, PETER. *Commentary and Control in Shakespeare's Plays*. New York: Humanities Press, 1974, 247 pp.

Thematic and Topical Studies

Argues that the evolving sophistication of Shakespeare's drama-turgy is reflected in the changing nature of the "commenting charac-ters" who "keep us emotionally and imaginatively on the right track" (p. 15). The commentators of the early plays (Exeter and Lucy in *1 Henry VI*, Margaret in *Richard III*, Launce and Speed in *The Two Gentlemen of Verona*) are largely external to the action. Somewhat more integrated is the commentary of Feste and Touchstone in the mature comedies. The principal of the major tragedies is himself a commenta-tor, revealing in soliloquies the various stages of his spiritual explora-tion while surrounding characters establish tension through their sympathy, praise, or condemnation.

239. BIRNEY, ALICE LOTVIN. *Satiric Catharsis in Shakespeare: A Theory of Dramatic Structure*. Berkeley and London: University of California Press, 1973, 158 pp.

Focuses on five Shakespearean figures who function as satirists—Margaret of Anjou in the *Henry VI-Richard III* tetralogy, Falstaff in *1,2 Henry IV*, Jaques in *As You Like It*, Thersites in *Troilus and Cressida*, and Apemantus in *Timon of Athens*. Whereas Margaret employs the direct curse, Falstaff deals in witty invective and wordplay; Jaques is a fool-scapegoat whose rejection purges Arden of discordant emotions; Ther-sites infects his play with caustic views, transmitting his disease to others rather than purging; Apemantus drives Timon to rage, and in turn his death effects "a catharsis of such emotion of social censure that would have rocked the real world of 1609" (p. 17).

240. BRISSENDEN, ALAN. *Shakespeare and the Dance*. Atlantic Highlands: Humanities Press, 1981, 145 pp.

Concerns Shakespeare's use of dance, both literal and figurative, as a symbol of harmony throughout his plays. An opening chapter on the philosophic concept of dance in Renaissance thought and of the ubiq-uity of dance in Elizabethan society is followed by a discussion of dance in the plays themselves. Literal and celebrative in the comedies, largely ironic in the tragedies, dance in the romances is thematically related to the movement from psychic bondage to freedom.

241. BRISTOL, MICHAEL D. *Shakespeare's America, America's Shakespeare: Lit-erature, Institution, Ideology in the United States*. London and New York: Routledge, 1990, 237 pp.

Observes that Shakespeare in the United States "exists as a com-plex institutional reality that cuts across many different levels of culture and contrasting domains of social practice" (p. 2). The industry has formed part of a cultural policy to integrate the individual into a bour-

Thematic and Topical Studies

geois political economy. Current redefinitions of Shakespeare as pluralistic reflect the ideological dilemmas that characterize late twentieth-century American society. The image of Shakespeare in Emerson, Kittredge, Charles Mills Gayley, and Theodore Spencer has given way to new historicist investigations of how the plays mask state power and its strategies to contain subversion.

242. BROWER, REUBEN A. *Hero and Saint: Shakespeare and the Graeco-Roman Heroic Tradition.* Oxford: Clarendon Press, 1971, 424 pp.

Observes that the contrast between virtue in the sense of bravery and virtue in the sense of kindliness recurs constantly in the plays of Shakespeare's maturity from *Julius Caesar* to *The Tempest.* At times both virtues are depicted in the same play *(King Lear, Othello)*; at times the heroic predominates *(Antony and Cleopatra)* and at times the saintly *(The Winter's Tale).* They comprise for the morally sensitive and honest individual two metaphoric ways of facing life at its most terrible moments. The metaphors range from the Christ type to the Graeco-Roman type. No heroes in Shakespeare are absolute, but the image of the ideal is the source for measuring their grandeur and sense of failure.

243. BROWNLOW, FRANK WALSH. *Two Shakespearean Sequences: "Henry VI" to "Richard III" and "Pericles" to "Timon of Athens."* Pittsburgh: University of Pittsburgh Press; London: Macmillan, 1977, 245 pp.

Argues that Shakespeare's skeptical and analytical turn of mind led him to write at the beginning and at the end of his career genuinely experimental drama. Elizabethan plays are filled with figuratively topical allusions; and the organizing principle of Shakespeare's early histories, even while they pay tribute to the past, reflects the reality of contemporary political problems. The second sequence provides an answer to the corrosive evil of the tragedies and the problem comedies; the late plays depict evil contained and turned to good by time, nature, and patience.

244. BRYANT, JOSEPH A., Jr. *Hippolyta's View: Some Christian Aspects of Shakespeare's Plays.* Lexington: University of Kentucky Press, 1961, 239 pp.

Demonstrates through analysis of eleven plays that Shakespeare's view and practice of poetry derived from a Catholic Christian perspective. Hippolyta, like the Christian, "recreates the data of experience in a dream that is truth itself, or all we shall likely get of truth this side of paradise" (p. 4). From the literal tale the reader moves to the allegorical and from thence to the moral or spiritual insight that lies behind it. Shakespeare's plays, in a word, develop the great archetypal myths of the human race, in each case working by analogy or through transfiguration to embody and depict some aspect of the Christian faith.

245. CALDERWOOD, JAMES. *Shakespeare and the Denial of Death*. Amherst: University of Massachusetts Press, 1987, 233 pp.

Accepts as a cultural premise the fact that human beings contrive numerous strategies to deny death and examines such practices by the characters in Shakespeare's plays. These strategies include various ways of establishing the paradoxical oppositions of the flesh and the spirit, social cannibalism and money in *Timon of Athens*, *Coriolanus*, and *Henry IV*, disguise and role-playing in *Henry IV*, *Coriolanus*, and selected comedies, images of clothing in *Hamlet* and of imperishable money in *The Merchant of Venice*. *King Lear* is examined at some length as a drama "whose subject is uncreation" (p. 145).

246. ———. *Shakespearean Metadrama: The Argument of the Play in "Titus Andronicus," "Love's Labor's Lost," "Romeo and Juliet," "A Midsummer Night's Dream," and "Richard II."* Minneapolis: University of Minnesota Press, 1971, 192 pp.

Argues that dramatic art—its materials of language and theater, its generic forms and conventions, its relationships to society—is a dominant Shakespearean theme. Various interior playwrights like Aaron, Oberon, Iago, and Prospero underscore the illusion of dramatic art as do the illusions controlled by Poor Tom or Richard III or Hamlet. Each play generates its own dramatic tensions—the barbarism of poetic language in *Titus Andronicus*, the deposition of ceremonial language in *Richard II*, a language that can bind lovers to each other but not to society in *Romeo and Juliet*.

247. CAMPBELL, OSCAR JAMES. *Shakespeare's Satire*. Oxford: Oxford University Press, 1943, 227 pp.

Argues that Shakespeare in the first decade of the seventeenth century gave free rein to his satiric spirit. The mood darkens with Malvolio, and the spirit of derision fully controls *Troilus and Cressida*. While *Troilus* was designed for a private audience, *Measure for Measure* is a comical satire for the popular stage in which a conventional comic closure modifies and alters the derisive tone. Both *Timon of Athens* and *Coriolanus* are properly termed tragical satire. The heroes, as well as the surrounding figures, are hounded by caustic laughter, and a satiric ambiguity pervades both plays. The principles of sound polity and sane action must be inferred by the spectators.

248. CARTELLI, THOMAS. *Marlowe, Shakespeare, and the Economy of Theatrical Experience*. Philadelphia: University of Pennsylvania Press, 1991, 256 pp.

Thematic and Topical Studies

Explores the structure of psychological, social, and political exchanges negotiated between audiences and plays in the Elizabethan
public theaters. While the period was ostensibly dominated by Shakespeare, the roots are firmly grounded in Marlowe. Of special interest is
the discussion of the political significance of the public theater as a
marginal institution dealing with topics to which different social divisions of the audience would have remarkably diverse responses.

249. CHAMBERS, EDMUND KERCHEVER. *Shakespeare: A Survey*. London:
Sidgwick & Jackson, 1925, 325 pp.
Considers Shakespeare's treatment of generic objects and limitations, the shifting phases of pessimism and optimism, and the apparent
reflections of his personal experience upon the mirror of his art. The
keynote of *Hamlet* is the "tragic ineffectiveness of the speculative intellect in a world of action" (p. 189), and, as with Brutus, Hamlet gets the
worst of it and leaves us to wonder at the irony of why it must be so.
All's Well That Ends Well, like *Measure for Measure* and *Troilus and
Cressida*, is examined as a bitter comedy, Helena as degraded rather than
triumphant, womanly love rendered ignoble by the imperious instinct
of sex.

250. CLEMEN, WOLFGANG H. *Shakespeare's Dramatic Art*. London: Methuen, 1972, 236 pp.
Covers such topics as the art of Shakespeare's exposition, his soliloquies, devices of anticipation, the theme of appearance versus reality
in the plays, and Shakespeare in the modern world. Based on the assumption that a spectator's full experience involves his being drawn to
anticipate the action, Clemen notes that Shakespeare above all other
playwrights is skillful in forcing the spectator to "watch the development of the play, the delusions, hopes, discoveries, the 'false' and the
'right' actions of the characters on the stage with a mixture of pleasure,
apprehension, and critical detachment" (p. 5).

251. COHEN, DEREK. *Shakespearean Motives*. New York: St. Martin's Press,
1988, 142 pp.
Devotes individual chapters to seven plays, in which the focus is
upon the central character and his or her interaction with a basically
hostile environment. Isabella's final plea for Angelo in *Measure for Measure* is seen as "her most palpable defeat" (p. 51), a submission to the
male desire to mold her into a "bowed, supplicating, softly virtuous
individual." The Olivia-Malvolio relationship in *Twelfth Night* is a parody of that of Orsino-Olivia, the former socially weak but theatrically
strong and the latter just the reverse. *The Merchant of Venice* is a bla-

Thematic and Topical Studies

tantly antisemitic play; Shakespeare uses the cruel stereotype of the Jew "for mercenary and artistic purposes" (p. 118).

252. COLIE, ROSALIE L. *Shakespeare's Living Art*. Princeton: Princeton University Press, 1974, 370 pp.

Views Shakespeare's plays as explorations of his craft, as striking illustrations of an ability to interweave elements of farce, comedy, melodrama, and nightmarish tragedy. Such interaction is present in his expansion of the Senecan model in *Titus Andronicus*, his enrichment of the Plautine method in *The Comedy of Errors*, his exploitation of the range of language and his juxtaposition of mirth and sorrow in *Love's Labor's Lost*. This aspect of his artistry culminates in his merger of romance epic and derision in *Troilus and Cressida* and in the range of dramatic forms ("from interlude and morality to the most sophisticated forms of modern coterie plays" [p. 356]) in *King Lear*.

253. COOK, ALBERT. "Some Observations on Shakespeare and the Incommensurability of Interpretive Strategies." *New Literary History* 22 (1991):773–95.

Argues that many of the hermeneutic strategies involving Lacan, Freud, Derrida, Marx, and Foucault, so prominent in the past two decades, are based on philosophic reasonings that implicitly cut off other strategies and thus are ultimately reductionistic. Often they are treated as closed metasystems, and their inadequacy when utilized in a rigid and inflexible manner is reflected in their blatant contradictoriness.

254. COOK, ANN JENNALIE. *Making a Match: Courtship in Shakespeare and His Society*. Princeton: Princeton University Press, 1991, 273 pp.

Examines the nature and customs of courtship in Shakespeare's society and in his plays. This process, established as a practice by which to stabilize the commonwealth, is viewed from multiple angles—caricature, criticism, acceptance, subversion, indifference. The traditional assumption of patriarchal control, for example, is interrogated in Baptista and Petruchio in *The Taming of the Shrew*, that of female aggression in Helena in *All's Well That Ends Well*, that of rebellious youth in the doomed protagonists in *Romeo and Juliet* and in Florizel and Perdita in *The Winter's Tale*.

255. COUNCIL, NORMAN. *When Honour's at the Stake: Ideas of Honour in Shakespeare's Plays*. London: George Allen & Unwin, 1973, 165 pp.

Observes that honor in the Renaissance carried various meanings, ranging from the conferring of an external reward to a sense of obedi-

Thematic and Topical Studies

ence to what is due or right. In *1 Henry IV* the action of the major characters is defined in terms of honor with Hotspur embodying the principles of a rigorous code of honor and Falstaff consciously and explicitly rejecting it; Hal, neither accepting nor rejecting, exploits it for his pragmatic purposes. The search for honor forms the structural basis for *Lear* as well; the old king must endure the stripping away of the position and the possessions inherent to his false concept of value in order to experience the honor at the heart of humanity.

256. CRESSY, DAVID. "Foucault, Stone, Shakespeare and Social History." *English Literary Renaissance* 21 (1991):121–33.
　　　Maintains that the study of Shakespeare's plays has been radically refigured by "infusions of French historical theory" by Michel Foucault and the "application of social history" by Lawrence Stone. One should not "choose material to support pre-drawn conclusions": an argument must be "distilled from the sources" (p. 130). A greater knowledge of the history of literacy and of lay and clerical relations, for example, would help us make sense of Jack Cade's biases in *2 Henry VI*; Henry's speech before Agincourt could be enlightened by greater knowledge of "the cultivated anniversaries of Elizabeth's succession" (p. 133).

257. CRUTTWELL, PATRICK. *The Shakespearean Moment and Its Place in the Poetry of the Seventeenth Century*. New York: Columbia University Press, 1955, 262 pp.
　　　Examines the half-century from 1590 to 1640 that marks the social and cultural upheaval culminating in a transition from the medieval past to the essentially modern mentality. Shakespeare's tragedies lie artistically at the heart of this profound shift in thought and feeling, reflecting (like his sonnets before them) the currents and cross-currents of the age—"lost innocence, lost simplicity, lost certainty, all symbolized in a lost and regretted past" (p. 37).

258. CUTTS, JOHN P. *The Shattered Glass: A Dramatic Pattern in Shakespeare's Early Plays*. Detroit: Wayne State University Press, 1968, 153 pp.
　　　Suggests that Shakespeare in his early plays is moving through a series of experimentations in structure that culminate symbolically in the shattered glass in *Richard II*. It marks the point at which Shakespeare fully realizes a structure based on a dynamic figure who must shatter and be shattered, who must be broken into many people, and who must come to terms with the nature of his shattered personality. Earlier plays have dealt with mirror imagery (*The Comedy of Errors*), with shadow and substance (*Titus Andronicus, Richard III*), with fragmentation and synthesis (*A Midsummer Night's Dream*).

Thematic and Topical Studies

259. D'AMICO, JACK. *The Moor in English Renaissance Drama*. Tampa: University of South Florida Press; Gainesville: University of Florida Presses, 1991, 243 pp.

Concerns boundaries of perception set by race, religion, and custom in five plays of Shakespeare and others by Ben Jonson, Thomas Heywood, Christopher Marlowe, and Thomas Dekker. The Moor as a villain becomes a convenient focus for the darkly subversive forces that threaten European society. Major focus is on Shakespeare's *Othello* and *Titus Andronicus*.

260. DASH, IRENE G. *Wooing, Wedding and Power: Women in Shakespeare's Plays*. New York: Columbia University Press, 1981, 295 pp.

Asserts that Shakespeare's plays offer insights into women's self-perceptions in a patriarchal world. Drawn with neither anger nor condescension, these female figures challenge accepted patterns for female behavior. The right to make one's own choices, for example, is at the center of Kate's confrontation with Petruchio; so, too, in other plays are the rejection of the lovers' suits by the Princess of France and her attendants, Cleopatra's determination to live in adultery with Antony, and Isabella's unwillingness to sacrifice her virginity.

261. DAVIES, STEVIE. *The Feminine Reclaimed: The Idea of Woman in Spenser, Shakespeare, and Milton*. Lexington: University Press of Kentucky, 1986, 273 pp.

Describes the number, variety, and centrality of female figures in Spenser, Shakespeare, and Milton. Concerned with the idea of woman rather than with the female's actual condition in Renaissance England, this study demonstrates the influence of Orphic, Hermetic, and classical mythology in articulating the feminine. Viola, for example, is related to Hermes, Hermia to the Hermetic priestess of Isis, *Pericles* and *The Winter's Tale* to the Eleusian mysteries, and Paulina to a female magus.

262. DAWSON, ANTHONY B. *Indirections: Shakespeare and the Art of Illusion*. Toronto: University of Toronto Press, 1978, 194 pp.

Focuses on Shakespeare's uses of illusion, deceit, disguise, and manipulation not only to incite the movement of the plot itself but also to create a statement about the nature and function of the interaction between the character and the spectator. Disguise in the romantic comedies, for example, draws the characters into an illusion that is therapeutic for all the playgoers. Such comic manipulative devices are applied to morally ambivalent stage worlds in *Hamlet*, *All's Well*, and *Measure for Measure*. *The Tempest* is envisioned as Shakespeare's most stunning and most successful statement about theatrical artifice.

Thematic and Topical Studies

263. DESSEN, ALAN C. *Elizabethan Drama and the Viewer's Eye*. Chapel Hill: University of North Carolina Press, 1977, 176 pp.

Asserts that a full appreciation of an Elizabethan play requires a conjunction of the critic's interpretive perception, the director's theatrical insights, and the historian's contextual knowledge. Unity in a play frequently involves all three. The emphatic parallels between Hamlet and Pyrrhus as avengers, for example, lend structural coherence, as do the parallels between Hotspur's conspiracy and Falstaff's robbery at Gadshill. Also discussed are the significance of symbols or central images, the effect of metadramatic elements within the play, and the pattern of stage psychomachia.

264. DOLLIMORE, JONATHAN, and SINFIELD, ALAN, eds. *Political Shakespeare: New Essays in Cultural Materialism*. Ithaca: Cornell University Press, 1985, 244 pp.

Features revisionist readings of Shakespeare, including essays on Shakespeare, cultural materialism, and the new historicism (Dollimore), the subversion of authority in the *Henriad* (Stephen Greenblatt), *The Tempest* as a discourse of colonialism (Paul Brown), transgression and surveillance in *Measure for Measure* (Dollimore), the patriarchal bard in *King Lear* and *Measure for Measure* (Kathleen McLuskie), strategies of state in *A Midsummer Night's Dream*, *Henry IV*, and *Henry VIII* (Leonard Tennenhouse), the Royal Shakespeare Company and the making of ideology (Sinfield), Shakespeare on film and television (Graham Holderness), and Brecht's reading of Shakespeare (Margot Heinemann).

265. DRAKAKIS, JOHN, ed. *Alternative Shakespeares*. London: Methuen, 1985, 260 pp.

Features revisionist readings of Shakespeare including essays on poststructuralist Shakespeare (Christopher Norris), deconstructing Shakespeare's comedies (Malcolm Evans), sexuality in *Measure for Measure* (Jacqueline Rose), a semiotic reading of Shakespeare (Alessandro Serpieri), Shakespeare in ideology (James Kavanagh), meaning and gender in the comedies (Catherine Belsey), the discursive "con-texts" of *The Tempest* (Francis Barker and Peter Hulme), and ideology in *Henry V* (Jonathan Dollimore and Alan Sinfield).

266. DREHER, DIANE. *Domination and Defiance: Fathers and Daughters in Shakespeare*. Lexington: University Press of Kentucky, 1986, 204 pp.

Examines, through his characterization of the feminine, Shakespeare's perceptions of an androgynous ideal and, in particular, the psychological conflicts underlying the actions of Shakespeare's fathers and daughters. The greatest tension occurs at the point of the daughter's nubility, a moment when the father faces advancing mortality and the daughter a new set of loyalties. If either fails to accept individuation, domination or defiance will result, the former in Ophelia and Hero, the latter in Hermione, Imogen, Jessica, and Lear's daughters. The resolution of such a conflict is depicted in Prospero and Miranda.

267. DRISCOLL, JAMES P. *Identity in Shakespearean Drama.* Lewisburg: Bucknell University Press; London and Toronto: Associated University Presses, 1983, 202 pp.

Examines psychological, critical, and philosophical backgrounds of identity anxiety to probe the four aspects of identity found in Shakespeare—the conscious, the social, the real, and the ideal. Hamlet's quest for self-knowledge, for example, parallels in Jungian terms that of mythic heroes, whose dysfunctional view of society exposes the imbalance and the corruption. In *Othello* Iago cleverly manipulates the Moor's confusions about his social identity to produce a fundamental alteration in his conscious identity. Lear is viewed as a Jungian God-image whose Job-like experience forces him to recognize on a cosmic level the arbitrariness of his own will.

268. DUBROW, HEATHER, and STRIER, RICHARD, eds. *The Historical Renaissance: New Essays on Tudor and Stuart Literature and Culture.* Chicago: University of Chicago Press, 1988, 377 pp.

Provides an analysis both of the actual historical era of the Renaissance and of the proliferation of studies of English Renaissance culture. The aim is to reflect the variety of historical approaches on subjects ranging from Katherine Parr to Sidney and Spenser to Bacon and Donne. Shakespearean entries include essays on Richard III's deformity (Marjorie Garber), on servants whose disobedience deserves praise (Strier), and on topicality in *Cymbeline* (Leah Marcus).

269. EAGLETON, TERRY. *William Shakespeare.* Oxford: Basil Blackwell, 1986, 114 pp.

Views Shakespeare's plays as a constant exposure of the struggle between the privileged and the unprivileged, between the wealthy and the exploited or dispossessed. In *Macbeth*, for example, the witches are the heroines because it is they who expose the institution of kingship and the social hierarchical order for what it is—"the pious self-deception of a society based on routine oppression and incessant warfare" (p. 2). In the *Henry IV* plays Falstaff turns the "brute materiality of the body against the airy abstractions of ruling-class rhetoric" (p. 15). The ro-

Thematic and Topical Studies

mantic comedies present eros as a threat to established social order and marriage as a "ludicrously implausible" solution to the sexual and political dilemmas they pose.

270. EDWARDS, PHILIP. *Shakespeare and the Confines of Art*. London: Methuen, 1968, 170 pp.

Argues that Shakespeare consciously attempted to extend the boundaries of his generic form by subjugating nature to art and by creating an experience culminating in the reconciliation of contraries, in a word, by making art an effective model of the human experience. In his comedies Shakespeare seems to rewrite with variation something of the same play structured on the phases of separation, bewilderment, and harmony. The accumulation of irony in the middle comedies enables him to build in a dialectic that lends complexity to the form without repudiating it. *Hamlet* explores in depth the limits of what an individual with a sense of moral integrity can accomplish in a world of anarchy.

271. ———. *Shakespeare: A Writer's Progress*. Oxford: Oxford University Press, 1987, 204 pp.

Features a biographical sketch and an overview of the issue of human relationships in the plays followed by five chapters dealing with individual works, one chapter on the nondramatic poems, and one each on the comedies, the histories, the tragedies, and the last plays. In the section on the tragedies *Titus Andronicus* is viewed as an anticipation of *King Lear*, *Timon* as embryonic satire, and *Troilus and Cressida* as embryonic tragedy. The others are divided into tragedies of violence and tragedies of love. A single chapter on the "tragicomedies" combines coverage of the problem plays and the romances.

272. EGAN, ROBERT. *Drama Within Drama: Shakespeare's Sense of His Art in "King Lear," "The Winter's Tale," and "The Tempest."* New York and London: Columbia University Press, 1975, 128 pp.

Examines how Shakespeare establishes the theme of *Lear*, *The Winter's Tale*, and *The Tempest* through a character's effort to control and to alter reality through dramatic illusion. Prospero, Edgar and Lear, and Camillo and Paulina join the dramatic art within the play to that of the play itself. The pietà tableau of Lear and Cordelia, for example, sets artistic control against life's worst realities, enacted by Lear and observed and commented on by Edgar. *The Winter's Tale* depicts the fall of a cosmically ordered universe and, through the work of Paulina and Camillo, its regeneration through a renewed faith in essential human goodness.

Thematic and Topical Studies

273. ELLIS-FERMOR, UNA. *The Jacobean Drama: An Interpretation*. London: Methuen, 1936, 345 pp.

Surveys the range of moods and the dramatic technique that characterize English drama from 1598 to 1625. The heritage of this drama was spiritual uncertainty springing in part from the spread of Machiavellian materialism and fear of the impending destruction of a great civilization. After the spiritual nadir of the middle years of the period a slow return to a balanced view emerges. Shakespeare's transmutation of his sources in *Julius Caesar* and the *Henry IV-Henry V* plays signals this shift to a complex, ambivalent view of life; the full flood of Jacobean horror is reflected in the major tragedies and problem comedies, the return to balance in his romances.

274. ERICKSON, PETER. *Rewriting Shakespeare, Rewriting Ourselves*. Berkeley: University of California Press, 1991, 239 pp.

Participates in the current debate concerning the established literary canon, of which Shakespeare is the principal icon. In raising questions about the impact of multicultural studies on Shakespeare's status, the study engages as well the national debate concerning educational policies. A separate section deals with feminist approaches to Shakespeare, addressing both the playwright's ambivalence toward the female personality in his plays and providing views of several contemporary female Afro-American writers.

275. ERICKSON, PETER, and KAHN, COPPÉLIA, eds. *Shakespeare's "Rough Magic": Essays in Honor of C. L. Barber*. Newark: University of Delaware Press; London and Toronto: Associated University Presses, 1985, 322 pp.

Includes essays on tragedy (Norman Rabkin), *Troilus and Cressida* (Leslie Fiedler), broken nuptials (Carol Neely), male bonding (Janet Adelman), friendship in *The Merchant of Venice* (Kahn), *Love's Labor's Lost* (Harry Levin), Falstaff (Ann Barton), *Twelfth Night* (Stephen Booth), language in *Romeo and Juliet* (Edward Snow), the sonnets and *The Merchant of Venice* (Richard Wheeler), the Gloucester family romance (Harry Berger), a Jungian approach to *Macbeth* (H. R. Coursen), and on Renaissance authority and its subversion (Stephen Greenblatt).

276. EVANS, MALCOLM. *Signifying Nothing: Truth's True Contents in Shakespeare's Text*. Athens: University of Georgia Press; London: Harvester Press, 1986, 291 pp.

Attacks the fundamental assumptions of humanist criticism concerning the universality of Shakespeare's appeal, his ability to human-

Thematic and Topical Studies

ize, the plays' involvement with unchanging problems of human life, and their aesthetic capacity to "enrapture" (p. 7). Inevitably the plays come to mean for new generations what layers of encrusted criticism have proclaimed in the past. And such criticism, whether wittingly or unwittingly, endorses the capitalist status quo and promotes race, sex, and class conflict. *The Tempest* and *Love's Labor's Lost* are viewed as contests between book knowledge and speech knowledge at a time when England was moving from an oral-aural to a print culture.

277. FARLEY-HILLS, DAVID. *Shakespeare and the Rival Playwrights 1600–1606*. London and New York: Routledge, 1990, 226 pp.

Situates Shakespeare in 1600 within competition from children's companies whose venues threatened to divert the wealthier patrons from the public stage and argues that he confronted the new fashion with such plays as *Measure for Measure* while holding the favor of the outdoor stage with his major tragedies. *Hamlet* explores the drama of ambiguous personality, but the influence of other writers for the public stage was thereafter to draw Shakespeare to develop a central concern for action as the expression of moral pattern. *Troilus and Cressida*, apparently a failure on the public stage, is seen as an experimental response to the satiric work of Marston and Jonson.

278. FARNHAM, WILLARD. *The Shakespearean Grotesque: Its Genesis and Transformation*. Oxford: Clarendon Press, 1971, 175 pp.

Describes the grotesque spirit in literature and art as that which captures dramatically opposed forces in life. Falstaff is a generous fulfillment of that spirit, a monstrous body in the tradition of animal and man—an animal figure in whom "comicity" joins with "cosmicity" (p. 50). His tavern world of thievery joins with the political world of high endeavor. Hamlet's essential nature is invaded by the grotesque as he shares the role of court prince and court fool. He mocks the comic in mankind through Polonius and Osric, yet he in turn is ridiculed by the grave digger. Also discussed as grotesque are Thersites, Iago, and Caliban.

279. FARRELL, KIRBY. *Play, Death, and Heroism in Shakespeare*. Chapel Hill: University of North Carolina Press, 1989, 240 pp.

Relates fantasies of "play-death" in Shakespeare's plays to the Renaissance belief that through self-effacement an individual may achieve successful autonomy in the family and in society. Common to all of these play-deaths (Falstaff, Cleopatra, Hero, Lear, Gloucester, Pericles, Thaisa, Imogen, Hermione, Perdita, Vincentio, Helena) is the rhythm of resurrection or heroic apotheosis. Such activity is a means of engag-

Thematic and Topical Studies

ing death, forcing the threat of pollution to yield heroic meaning that could sustain society. In both *Antony and Cleopatra* and *Twelfth Night* the dread of annihilation inspires the creation of heroic significance. The histories explore the uses and misuses of prophecy to create visions of human empowerment or national destiny.

280. FIELDLER, LESLIE. *The Stranger in Shakespeare*. New York: Stein & Day, 1972, 263 pp.

Concerns the archetypal figure who, standing between "hero" and "villain," defines the limits of the human in representing that portion of life or culture that is seen as a threat and hence must be symbolically cast out. Whatever marginal ambivalence Shakespeare might have felt, he subscribed to the public mythology of his audience, and the "stranger" figure at various stages of his career appears as woman (Joan of Arc), as Jew (Shylock), as black (Othello), and as new world savage (Caliban).

281. FINEMAN, JOEL. *The Subjectivity Effect in Western Literary Tradition: Essays toward the Release of Shakespeare's Will*. Cambridge, Mass.: MIT Press, 1991, 234 pp.

Demonstrates how linguistic, visual, and architectural structures generate elaborate systems of meaning. More specifically, examples from Chaucer, Oscar Wilde, and especially Shakespeare are used to create parables of how language and narrative have come to constitute the present subject (the reader, the viewer) as one of their end products, how the literary construct along with its cultural biases becomes engrained in its recipients.

282. FLY, RICHARD. *Shakespeare's Mediated World*. Amherst: University of Massachusetts Press, 1976, 164 pp.

Isolates in five Shakespearean plays how "go-betweens" inadvertently distort communication and destroy both personal and social harmony. Such flawed mediation underscores the vulnerability of the human condition whether through the futile efforts of the nurse, Benvolio, and Friar Lawrence in *Romeo and Juliet* or the specious adulteration of the truth by Thersites and others in *Troilus and Cressida*. Also considered are Flavius's role and other disjunctive elements in *Timon of Athens* and the ineffectiveness of communication at various levels in *Measure for Measure* and *King Lear*.

283. FOAKES, R. A. *Shakespeare: The Dark Comedies to the Last Plays: From Satire to Celebration*. Charlottesville: University of Virginia Press, 1971, 186 pp.

Thematic and Topical Studies

Examines the last plays as structures designed for performance for which the vision is the result of new techniques and possibilities that arose in the dark comedies in connection with the revival of children's companies. Above all, the problem comedies exhibit a stubborn energy for life that incorporates the desires of the flesh into the basic movement of the play, a mingling of the satiric tone with the dramatic. The final plays exploit these techniques of distancing and disengagement that lead characters to accept and celebrate life on its own terms, unpredictable but wonderful.

284. FOULKES, RICHARD, ed. *Shakespeare and the Victorian Stage*. Cambridge: Cambridge University Press, 1986, 311 pp.

Features twenty essays that illustrate a variety both of Victorian attitudes toward Shakespeare and his work and also of critical approaches (performance-oriented, historical, sociological, psychological). The material is divided into six sections: Shakespeare and the picture frame (Moelwyn Merchant, James Fowler, Foulkes, Marion Jones), the Lyceum dynasty (Cary Mazer, Tracy Davis), Shakespeare as ancient and modern—the Renaissance heritage compared to his modernity and relevance (J. S. Bratton, Ralph Berry), Shakespeare as a contemporary (Arthur Jacobs), Shakespeare as a foreign dramatist (Simon Williams, Kenneth Richards), and Shakespeare in the provinces (Arnold Hare, Kathleen Barker, Jeremy Crump).

285. FRENCH, MARILYN. *Shakespeare's Division of Experience*. New York: Summit Books, 1981, 376 pp.

Insists on Shakespeare's primary concern with role-playing as a concept of cultural programming, society's assigning of certain roles on the basis of gender and obliging individuals to play them out, the relationship between political power and the "division" of experience according to gender principles. Man's role encompasses law, authority, and legitimacy, and he views the end of sexuality as ultimate control or possession. While Shakespeare's comedies and tragedies contain similar events, emphasis in the former is on man's deadly power, in the latter on women's ability to neutralize and negate that power in the interest of love and harmony.

286. FREY, CHARLES H. *Experiencing Shakespeare: Essays on Text, Classroom, and Performance*. Columbia: University of Missouri Press, 1988, 207 pp.

Consists of eleven chronologically arranged essays written between 1975 and 1985 that reflect stages in the development of the interpreter of Shakespeare and of fundamental changes in recent Shakespearean critical methodologies. The early essays, New Critical analyses, "feel to [the author] tied to a time past" in their concern with stability of meaning and fundamental truths (p. 164). The later essays experiment with new critical approaches, perceiving Shakespeare as "a scourge and skeptic against hierarchical and patriarchal views, a mind against itself, a playwright covertly subverting accepted denotation in language, thought, feeling, and art" (p. vii).

287. ———, ed. *Shakespeare, Fletcher, and "The Two Noble Kinsmen."* Columbia: University of Missouri Press, 1989, 222 pp.

Consists of essays by Frey, Paul Werstine, Donald Hedrick, Michael Bristol, Barry Weller, Susan Green, Jeanne Roberts, Richard Abrams, and Hugh Richmond on topics as varied as currents of sadness, harshness, and cynicism, authorial authority, mercantile metaphors, gender and generativity, patriarchy, social stereotyping, and the naivete of institutional scholarship. Of particular interest in several essays is the closure since it challenges our orthodox notions about the end of Shakespeare's playwriting career. Whereas the romance encapsulates tragedy within comedy, *The Two Noble Kinsmen* reintroduces a sense of pervasive tragic violence.

288. GARBER, MARJORIE B. *Coming of Age in Shakespeare.* London: Methuen, 1981, 248 pp.

Examines Shakespeare's characters in terms of the sociological concept of the rites of passage. The character in each case must change and adapt as the situation changes. Those who fail to do so are banished, rejected, or destroyed—Don John, for example, or Malvolio, or Falstaff. Against these characters can be measured the growth of Benedick and Beatrice, of Olivia and Orsino, and of Hal. As Cordelia's failure to respond to her father at the opening of *King Lear* provokes disaster, so her conciliatory posture in act 4 issues in reconciliation. Perhaps the quintessential rite of passage is that of the spectator, who in tragedy is "at once isolated and chosen, privileged and obligated" (p. 240).

289. ———. *Dream in Shakespeare: From Metaphor to Metamorphosis.* New Haven: Yale University Press, 1974, 226 pp.

Surveys the dominant Renaissance attitudes toward dreams and examines the use of the device in Shakespeare's work for architectonic structure—simultaneously foreshadowing events of the past and establishing an atmosphere of mystery and apprehension. Of ultimately more significance is Shakespeare's increasing ability to subsume the metaphoric sense of dream and the concomitant release of the imagination into the dynamics of the play. The process culminates in the romance,

Thematic and Topical Studies

in which the dream-state has become metaphorically synonymous with the created artifact of the stage world and the emphasis is directly upon the redemptive act of metamorphosis and transformation.

290. ———. *Shakespeare's Ghost Writers: Literature as Uncanny Causality*. London: Methuen, 1987, 203 pp.

Removes Shakespeare from the writing center, yet empowers him as a figure who haunts us through the pervasive textual effects on great minds who have followed and have fallen under his influence. Shakespeare, in a word, from the grave demonstrates a capacity to continue to rewrite us through the writing of others. *Richard III*, for example, as tragedy forever colors our present view with a skewed parodic self-consciousness. *Macbeth* in its questions of power and gender is replicated by those who seek to determine "the undecidability that may lie just beneath the surface of power—and perhaps of sexuality itself" (p. 119). *Hamlet*, above all, persists in its haunting—through Mozart, Lacan, Hegel, Derrida, Nietzsche, Freud.

291. GIRARD, RENÉ. *A Theater of Envy: William Shakespeare*. New York: Oxford University Press, 1991, 366 pp.

Examines desire as a rich source of paradox in Shakespeare's plays, a force by which envy subordinates "a desired *something* to the *someone* who enjoys a privileged relationship with it" (p. 4). Discussion ranges from the conflict between the erstwhile fast friends Valentine and Proteus (over Sylvia) in *The Two Gentlemen of Verona* to the struggle between the erstwhile cooperative Prospero and Caliban (over Miranda) in *The Tempest*. While fourteen plays are discussed, major emphasis is on *A Midsummer Night's Dream*, *Troilus and Cressida*, *Julius Caesar*, and *The Winter's Tale*. Concern often focuses on a crisis of degree and the practice of scapegoating that transforms the destructive force of rivalry into the constructive force of sacrificial mimesis.

292. GODDARD, HAROLD C. *The Meaning of Shakespeare*. Chicago: University of Chicago Press, 1951, 694 pp.

Considers Shakespeare whole, with each of the plays and poems envisioned as chapters of a single work. Each play is discussed in the presumable order of composition. *The Comedy of Errors* is drama in which the concept of character has not caught up with the dexterity of plotting; *Richard III* is exuberance of invention and excess of wit at its best; *Romeo and Juliet* champions a youthful passion searing enough to cut through the bonds of familial hatred. In *Antony and Cleopatra* Shakespeare is able to grasp the full range of love, containing both God

Thematic and Topical Studies

and the Devil. In the romances the focus is on some shock just short of death that awakens the full imagination of the personality.

293. GOLDMAN, MICHAEL. *Shakespeare and the Energies of Drama.* Princeton: Princeton University Press, 1972, 176 pp.

Seeks for the meaning of a Shakespeare play primarily in the response of the spectators and the manner in which it builds upon their awareness and exposes their "closed selves" to urgent and dangerous possibilities. We with the tragic protagonists must travel from one form of isolation to another, must share both the violence and the illumination of the love of Romeo and Juliet, must analyze like Hamlet the various roles (scholar, statesman, madman, critic, revenger) that he is forced to play, must admit the inadequacy of any single meaning in act 5 of *King Lear.* Shakespearean drama is a dynamic process binding both actor and spectator in an exchange of creative energies.

294. GOLDSMITH, ROBERT HILLIS. *Wise Fools in Shakespeare.* Liverpool: Liverpool University Press, 1955, 123 pp.

Focuses on Shakespeare's use and transcendence of the concept of the fool from popular and literary traditions. Shakespeare's various fools culminate in four complex and individual figures—Touchstone, a comic realist astray in the forest of romance; Lavache, a conscious and modish humorist who jokes about sex and chastity through innuendo; Feste, an artist who observes the golden mean in loving and laughing; and Lear's fool, who in following his sick king embodies the Christian doctrine of wise folly.

295. GRANVILLE-BARKER, HARLEY. *Prefaces to Shakespeare.* 4 vols. Princeton: Princeton University Press, 1946, 1026 pp.

Features analytic essays on *Hamlet* (1), *King Lear, Cymbeline,* and *Julius Caesar* (2), *Antony and Cleopatra* (3), *Love's Labor's Lost, Romeo and Juliet, The Merchant of Venice,* and *Othello* (4). The chief purpose of criticism is to serve the end of supporting the living play on stage. The character of Hamlet, for example, despite incongruities in personality, transports us into the "strange twilight regions of the soul" (1:131); the riches of his emotion and thought fall to those in the audience whose own are a touchstone for them, thus fulfilling the necessity of character in action. The text of Shakespeare's play is like a score awaiting performance.

296. GREENBLATT, STEPHEN. *Shakespearean Negotiations: The Circulation of Social Energy in Renaissance England.* Berkeley: University of California Press, 1988, 205 pp.

Thematic and Topical Studies

>Concerns the manner in which a text is created through "institutional negotiation and exchange of social energy" (p. 94). As Thomas Harriott tests on the Algonquin Indian society Machiavelli's theory that the primary function of religion is not spiritual but political, Shakespeare encodes in the moral values of the *Henry IV* plays a betrayal on both the political level (Prince John and the Archbishop of York) and on the personal level (Prince Hal and Falstaff). Other chapters cover the issue of cross-dressing as a means to gender clarification in the romantic comedies, Shakespeare's model for Edgar's histrionic disguise in *King Lear* (the church's effort to demystify exorcism), and the government's use of behavioral strategies as a process of containment in *Measure for Measure*.

297. ———, ed. *The Power of Forms in the English Renaissance* Norman: University of Oklahoma Press, 1982, 246 pp.

>Includes essays on text against performance in *Macbeth* (Harry Berger), the representation of power in *Measure for Measure* (Leonard Tennenhouse), the mixture of genres in *Much Ado About Nothing* (John Traugott), the rational playwright in *The Comedy of Errors* (Jonathan Crewe), and exorcism in *King Lear* (Greenblatt).

298. GREER, GERMAINE. *Shakespeare*. Oxford: Oxford University Press, 1986, 136 pp.

>Locates Shakespeare's peculiar effectiveness as a writer in his power to provoke the audience's imaginative response, in his appeal to the wisdom of the common folk. Falstaff, for example, because he preys upon the common people probably "excited not only laughter but jeering and cat calls" (p. 71) as well. Lear becomes heroic "when he is reduced to naked tramphood, . . . [the first in] a line of nobodies, simply struggling to survive" (p. 100). On marriage, Shakespeare viewed the institution as a "crucial and complex ideal"; women's "steadfastness is in direct relation to their aggressiveness" (p. 109).

299. GRUDIN, ROBERT. *Mighty Opposites: Shakespeare and Renaissance Contrariety*. Berkeley and London: University of California Press, 1979, 217 pp.

>Observes that Shakespeare's dramatic vision is grounded in paradox, from individual phrases such as Desdemona as an "excellent wretch" and Iago as a "precious villain" to concepts of character such as Prospero as at once God-like revenger and fallen man to concepts of an entire play such as Coriolanus as hideously heroic or *Antony and Cleopatra* as sublimely decadent. The interaction of contrarieties is one of the major philosophic traditions of the Renaissance; while Shakespeare

at first uses it within a moral and psychological perspective, it becomes the structural basis or the metaphysics of his great tragedies.

300. HAGAR, ALAN. *Shakespeare's Political Animal: Schema and Schemata in the Canon*. Newark: University of Delaware Press; London and Toronto: Associated University Presses, 1991, 164 pp.

Observes that Shakespeare was consistent in his depiction of the fundamental nature of politics and human interaction. In healthy societies he pictures people ruled by benevolent deception, whereas in diseased societies leadership collapses through a failure in self-fashioning and must be cured either by a comic ruse or by the tragic destruction of a victim. The necessary dissimulation in rule is analyzed in sonnet 94, *The Taming of the Shrew*, and the *Henriad*, oligarchic and monarchic disorder in *Much Ado About Nothing* and *Macbeth*, failed utopias in *As You Like It* and *The Winter's Tale*, reformed idealism in *The Tempest*.

301. HALLETT, CHARLES A., and HALLETT, ELAINE S. *Analyzing Shakespeare's Action: Scene Versus Sequence*. Cambridge: Cambridge University Press, 1991, 230 pp.

Argues for a distinction between "scene" and "action" in Shakespeare's plays, the latter normally occurring in a series or sequence of scenes. The penultimate sequence in *Macbeth*, for example, covers three scenes involving Macduff's killing of the protagonist. The scene, more precisely, is a unit of place, its boundary determined by a silence and a clearing of the stage. The sequence, on the other hand, is a unit of action, its boundary determined by the rising and falling rhythms of that action. So defined, it is the sequence that contains the dramatic structure and that is most significant in understanding Shakespeare's method for shaping and combining his units of action into the plot.

302. HAMILTON, A. C. *The Early Shakespeare*. San Marino: Huntington Library, 1967, 237 pp.

Examines the early plays and poems to illustrate that the subtleties and comprehensiveness of Shakespeare's dramatic genius are present from the first. As a sophisticated literary craftsman, he shares the wit and critical awareness of the Elizabethan poet. The *Henry VI* plays are explored as experiments in the history play, in which *3 Henry VI* moves very close to tragedy, while *Richard III* is indeed historical tragedy. The study contains individual chapters on each of the early works, concluding with sections on *Richard II*, *Romeo and Juliet*, and *A Midsummer Night's Dream* as the resolution of the early period.

Thematic and Topical Studies

303. HAPGOOD, ROBERT. *Shakespeare the Theatre-Poet*. Oxford: Clarendon Press, 1988, 267 pp.

Insists that Shakespeare builds into his plots a range of possible answers or reactions to key moments in the action, providing guidance through plots, choreography of gestures, and verbal kinetic imagery. To perceive a guiding principle in a play (for example, a movement toward ennoblement and community in *Henry V*, toward collective transfiguration in *A Midsummer Night's Dream*) does not limit these possibilities. In *Othello*, for instance, there are four moments in the temptation scene (3.3) when a given actor can choose to have the Moor become convinced of Desdemona's infidelity.

304. HARBAGE, ALFRED. *As They Liked It: A Study of Shakespeare's Moral Artistry*. New York: Macmillan, 1947, 234 pp.

Maintains that Shakespeare is moral without being a moralist, that his plays are designed to stimulate the imagination in a fundamentally positive manner. This focus can be gauged quickly by Shakespeare's modification of his sources and analogues—Lear's ferocious pride that must be purged through suffering, Hamlet's moral questions about revenge, Othello's agony concerning what he sees as the necessity of destroying Desdemona, the mitigation of Shylock's villainy. His plays stimulate the spectators' basic assumptions of man's moral nature and provide for continuing audiences the comforting reassurance that justice and harmony are both desirable and attainable despite their bleak existence outside the Globe.

305. HARTWIG, JOAN. *Shakespeare's Analogical Scene: Parody as Structural Syntax*. Lincoln and London: University of Nebraska Press, 1983, 243 pp.

Stresses the significance of small scenes in Shakespeare—usually dismissed as breathers or comic relief or tone setters—in reorienting the spectator's perspective through parallelism, antithesis, and verbal echo. Specific attention is focused on the scene with Cinna the poet in *Julius Caesar*, on Elbow's trial in *Measure for Measure*, on the apothecary's appearance in *Romeo and Juliet*, on York's determination to expose the treachery of his own son in *Richard II*, on scenes with the porter and the murderers and Malcolm in *Macbeth*, on the parodic subplot in *Twelfth Night*, on the parodic function of Polonius in *Hamlet*, on Cloten and Caliban as parodic villains.

306. HASSEL, R. CHRIS, JR. *Renaissance Drama and the English Church Year*. Lincoln and London: University of Nebraska Press, 1979, 215 pp.

Observes that 70 percent of all the court plays occur on one of the ten religious festival days and then investigates correlations between individual plays and the thematic, imagistic, and narrative facets of their festival occasion. *The Comedy of Errors*, for example, was performed on Innocents' Day, a feast day with biblical readings on the dispersal and reunion of families, and the celebration of human absurdity has liturgical overtones. Similarly, *Twelfth Night*, an epiphany play, shares extensive similarities with the religious service.

307. HAWKINS, HARRIETT. *The Devil's Party: Counter-Interpretations of Shakespearian Drama.* Oxford: Clarendon Press, 1985, 196 pp.

Grapples with questions about poetry at least as old as Plato's *Republic*, namely, in Shakespeare the glamor of evil, the moral dangers of vicarious identification with dramatic figures. Romantic and modernist critics are clearly demarcated, the one empathetic and tolerant to frailty and evil, the other detached and censorious. But the issue goes beyond such simplistic compartmentalization, to a need to distinguish between admiration and moral approval, between aesthetic and ethical pleasure, between shame and guilt.

308. HIRSH, JAMES E. *The Structure of Shakespearean Scenes.* New Haven and London: Yale University Press, 1981, 230 pp.

Maintains that the scene, the interval between one cleared stage and the next, is Shakespeare's fundamental artistic unit. These units can be solo, duet, unitary group, two part, or multipartite. Paradoxically, Shakespeare achieves unity of dramatic theme through a multiplicity of types of scenes. Frequently, the arrangement creates internal focus. In *As You Like It*, for example, juxtaposition of similar scenes indirectly produces conflict between Duke Senior and Duke Frederick although the two never meet. Similarly, the five unitary duets in *King Lear* form a symmetrical pattern that provides a skeleton of the action as a whole.

309. HOLDERNESS, GRAHAM, ed. *The Shakespeare Myth.* Manchester: Manchester University Press; New York: St. Martin's Press, 1988, 215 pp.

Consists of a series of essays treating ideology, popular culture, sexual politics, theater, education, and broadcasting in which the connecting thread is a cultural politics that "does not pretend to political neutrality. . . . On the contrary, it registers its commitment to the transformation of a social order that exploits people on grounds of race, gender, sexuality, and class" (p. x). Generally, Shakespeare's plays are viewed as an "antagonistic dialogue of class voices" (p. 36). In *Henry V*, for example, "Bare event makes Hal the hero of Agincourt, whereas the juxtaposition of scenes, and the play's failure to realise the rhetoric of

Thematic and Topical Studies

the Chorus, suggest he is a cynical, self-interested abuser of the commonweal" (p. 46).

310. HOLDERNESS, GRAHAM, POTTER, NICK, and TURNER, JOHN. *Shakespeare: Out of Court*. New York: St. Martin's Press, 1990, 266 pp.

Describes Shakespeare's dramatizations of an aristocratic society and patriarchal order that reached its culmination in Renaissance court life. Through the theater Shakespeare both celebrated and scrutinized such a society. In *Hamlet* and the problem plays, for example, he exposes key contradictions within the political structures and ideological self-understanding. James' Franco-Scottish ideas about royal absolutism inspired the critical readings of the feudal court in *King Lear* and *Macbeth*. And, the increasingly isolated court of James's later years inspired *The Winter's Tale* and *The Tempest* "when aging rulers cut off by personal weakness from the life of their court find themselves miraculously restored" (p. 8).

311. HOLLAND, NORMAN N. *Psychoanalysis and Shakespeare*. New York: McGraw-Hill, 1966, 412 pp.

Surveys major types of psychoanalytic criticism of Shakespeare's works, categorized by that which deals with the author's, with the character's, or with the audience's mind. In his endeavor to illumine either the creative or the responsive aspect of the drama, the psychoanalytic critic must concentrate on how the intellectual meaning of a play grows from its emotional content. In *The Tempest*, for example, Prospero can profitably be viewed as a character successfully mastering his oedipal attraction to his daughter, or the other characters can be investigated as projections of his own psyche.

312. ———. *The Shakespearean Imagination*. London: Macmillan, 1964, 338 pp.

Includes chapters on Shakespeare and his theater, shifting attitudes toward the playwright since 1616, and the textual studies and major critical methods of twentieth-century scholarship. Then follow analyses of sixteen plays, representing the most popular comedies, tragedies, and histories with emphasis on structure, parallelism, recurring images, themes, characterizations, and the particular quality of each individual play.

313. HOMAN, SIDNEY. *When the Theater Turns to Itself: The Aesthetic Metaphor in Shakespeare*. Lewisburg: Bucknell University Press; London and Toronto: Associated University Presses, 1981, 231 pp.

Thematic and Topical Studies

Concerns theatrical self-consciousness in nine Shakespearean plays, moving from early works in which Shakespeare comically celebrates the actor (the pageant of the Nine Worthies in *Love's Labor's Lost*, Bottom as actor, Puck and Oberon as controllers in *A Midsummer Night's Dream*); to controllers as playwright-surrogates in Rosalind, Iago, and Vincentio; to Hamlet, who is concerned at once with staging and play and manipulating the spectators' response and also with the artful progression of the entire tragedy. As *The Taming of the Shrew* is primarily concerned with the induction of the spectator into the dramatic experience, so *The Tempest* is concerned with his release or his departure.

314. ———, ed. *Shakespeare and the Triple Play: From Study to Stage to Classroom*. Lewisburg: Bucknell University Press; London and Toronto: Associated University Presses, 1988, 239 pp.

Divides material into three categories—the study, the stage, and the classroom. The first features essays on money in *The Merchant of Venice* (James Calderwood), magic and politics in *The Tempest* (Michael Payne), symbolic reality in *Richard II* (Harvey Birenbaum), Hamlet's melancholy (Zhang Siyang), and Hamlet's obesity (Laura Keyes). The second includes notes on playing Prospero (Sherman Hawkins) and *The Merry Wives of Windsor* in China (Homan). The third includes an exercise on Hamlet's first soliloquy (Robert Hapgood) and on Shakespeare on videotape (Roger Geimer).

315. HONIGMANN, E. A. J. *Myriad-Minded Shakespeare: Essays Chiefly on the Tragedies and Problem Comedies*. New York: St. Martin's, Press, 1989, 239 pp.

Encourages a diversity of critical methodology in exploring Shakespeare's plays rather than an interpretive straitjacket to prove mastery of some critical-ideological terminology. The analysis of particular plays illustrates such diversity with emphasis on character in *Othello*, on structure and a focus on key episodes in *King Lear*, on topicality in *Troilus and Cressida*, on Shakespeare's reactions to sexist platitudes about male authority and female obedience in *All's Well That Ends Well*, and on the playwright's conscious mixture of style, story, and genre in *Measure for Measure*.

316. ———. *Shakespeare's Impact on His Contemporaries*. London: Macmillan, 1982, 149 pp.

Challenges several traditional views concerning Shakespeare's life and work. What we know of his commercial transactions, for example, suggests that he was a hardheaded businessman, not "sweet" and "gentle." Also, rather than being indifferent to the publication of his plays,

Thematic and Topical Studies

he may well have requested the publication of good quartos to replace the garbled texts of the bad quartos. Other points of significance include a rebuttal of the idea that Shakespeare was a slow starter and a claim that Jonson was the rival poet of the sonnets and that *The Winter's Tale* was a response to Jonson's attacks upon his artistry.

317. ———, ed. *Shakespeare and His Contemporaries*. Manchester: Manchester University Press, 1986, 143 pp.
    Examines the technical inventiveness of the Elizabethan dramatists through a series of essays comparatively evaluating Shakespeare's work to that of his contemporaries. Included are discussions of bourgeoisie comedy in Shakespeare and Dekker (G. K. Hunter), Jonsonian satire and *Othello* (R. A. Foakes), scene patterns in *Faustus* and *Richard III* (Bernard Beckerman), the supernatural in *Faustus* and *Macbeth* (K. Tetzeli von Rosador), Roman politics in *Julius Caesar* and *Sejanus* (Edward Pechter), action and narration in *The Old Wives' Tale* and *The Winter's Tale* (Philip Edwards), corruption and retribution in *Measure for Measure* and *The Revenger's Tragedy* (Dieter Mehl), and the double reigns in *Richard II* and *Perkin Warbeck* (Alexander Leggatt).

318. HOWARD, JEAN. *Shakespeare's Art of Orchestration: Stage Technique and Audience Response*. Urbana: University of Illinois Press, 1984, 216 pp.
    Challenges the conception that Shakespeare's plays can be fully appreciated only through retrospective analysis of themes, imagery, and structure. To the contrary, drama means performance; and Shakespeare carefully controls the spectators' involvement with the play as it progressively unfolds, forcing them to imaginative participation in the events on stage. Specific attention is directed to visual, aural, and kinetic elements of performance by which Shakespeare creates this community of responses.

319. HOWARD, JEAN, AND O'CONNOR, MARION, eds. *Shakespeare Reproduced: The Text in History and Ideology*. New York: Methuen, 1987, 288 pp.
    Offers varying approaches to Shakespeare in history and ideology, but especially features feminism, new historicism, and cultural materialism. Essays cover political criticism of Shakespeare (Walter Cohen), power, politics, and the Shakespeare text (Don Wayne), *The Tempest* as colonialist text (Thomas Cartelli—see entry 1735), class-gender tensions in *The Merry Wives of Windsor* (Peter Erikson—see entry 957), femininity and the monstrous in *Othello* (Karen Newman—see entry 1577), the politics of gender and rank in *Much Ado About Nothing* (Jean Howard–see entry 1005), subversion and recuperation in *The*

Thematic and Topical Studies

Merchant of Venice (Thomas Moisan–see entry 942), legitimation crisis in *Coriolanus* (Michael Bristol–see entry 1233), the failure of orthodoxy in *Coriolanus* (Thomas Sorge–see entry 1263), the sources of *Macbeth* (Jonathan Goldberg), and a literary theory of ideology (Robert Weimann).

320. HUBERT, JUDD D. *Metatheater: The Example of Shakespeare*. Lincoln and London: University of Nebraska Press, 1991, 161 pp.

Notes that the printed text of a play provides a performative score through words, signs, images, and metaphors. Success on the stage depends directly on firm control exerted by such "rhetorical byplay" over "all forms of verisimilitude and mimesis" (p. 138). In *Much Ado About Nothing*, for example, nonverbal intrusions (music and dancing) effectively depict dramatic character reversals as dizzying permutations. Vincentio's leadership in *Measure for Measure* is measured in terms of his performance as actor, stage manager, and deus ex machina. Hamlet, reluctant to play a role to which he is solemnly sworn, is like an overly sophisticated actor constantly attempting to direct, if not rewrite, the plot.

321. HUNTER, ROBERT GRAMS. *Shakespeare and the Comedy of Forgiveness*. New York and London: Columbia University Press, 1965, 272 pp.

Investigates the denouement in forgiveness common to six of Shakespeare's plays—*Much Ado About Nothing*, *Measure for Measure*, *Cymbeline*, *The Winter's Tale*, *All's Well That Ends Well*, and *The Tempest*. The moment of forgiveness demands the approval and acquiescence of the spectators. That the issue is problematic for modern audiences and critics (with, for example, Bertram and Angelo) is a result of the fact that Shakespeare wrote in a now outmoded medieval and didactically Christian dramatic tradition inherited from the Middle Ages. A sympathetic understanding of the underlying doctrine is essential to a full appreciation of the plays.

322. JOCHUM, KLAUS PETER. *Discrepant Awareness: Studies in English Renaissance Drama*. Neue Studien zur Anglistik und Amerikanistik, 13. Frankfurt: Peter Lang, 1979, 310 pp.

Deals with the distribution of knowledge in Shakespeare's plays, the extent to which the spectator shares that knowledge, and the manner in which it determines or affects his attitude toward the characters and the action. Discrepant awareness in *Richard III*, for example, stems from the spectators" sharing both the private level of Richard's ambition and his devilish ability to dupe others and also the omniscient perspective on the fate of the last Yorkist king in the pattern of pre-

Thematic and Topical Studies

Tudor history. In *Romeo and Juliet* only the spectators are fully aware of what happens; the characters' lack of knowledge is the negative force leading to the catastrophe.

323. JONES, EMRYS. *Scenic Form in Shakespeare*. Oxford: Clarendon Press, 1971, 269 pp.
Claims that, quite apart from the verbal and poetic qualities, Shakespeare works with the structural unit of the scene. The rhythm within the scene can be one of repetition and accumulation or the character can be transformed from one polar extreme to another. The typical Shakespearean play has two units of action, with each comprising of a tonally and thematically related cluster of scenes. Discussed in the final half of the book is the scene structure of four tragedies—*Othello, King Lear, Macbeth*, and *Antony and Cleopatra*.

324. JORGENSEN, PAUL A. *Shakespeare's Military World*. Berkeley and London: University of California Press, 1956, 345 pp.
Views Shakespeare's concept of war and military personnel through Renaissance eyes. Disaster in war is traced strategically to discord, whether in lack of order in battle array and movements (*Cymbeline*), in dissension among the military personnel (*1 Henry IV, Julius Caesar*), or in insubordination (*Troilus and Cressida*). Generally, soldiership is depicted as an honorable occupation, though not infrequently military preeminence is no guarantee of success in a civilian context (*Coriolanus, Othello*).

325. KAHN, COPPÉLIA. *Man's Estate: Masculine Identity in Shakespeare*. Berkeley and London: University of California Press, 1981, 238 pp.
Questions the general critical posture that Shakespeare's plays present experiences identifiably equal with man and woman. To the contrary, the plays involve the masculine experience and perspective. The focus is on man's attempt to achieve social and psychological identity in a patriarchal world. The histories are viewed as a masculine world of war and politics in which man gains identity through relationships with other men; *Romeo and Juliet* and *The Taming of the Shrew* are tragic and comic versions of marriage as a passage to manhood; *Othello* features men uniting in cuckoldry against women as betrayers; and *Macbeth* and *Coriolanus* depict men who are "unfinished heroes" (p. 19) and who fight only because a woman has convinced them it will make them manly.

326. KAMPS, IVO, ed. *Shakespeare Left and Right*. New York: Routledge, 1991, 335 pp.

Includes essays representative of both radical and conservative views of the playwright and his works. Not surprisingly, the entries are markedly different both in politics and in literary methods. The study addresses such questions as whether feminism is best utilized as a hostile analytic tool with a political agenda or whether it can raise provocative and informative issues quite apart from any political overtones. Another question concerns whether Marxism as a literary tool continues to have validity in light of recent events in Eastern Europe.

327. KERNAN, ALVIN B. *The Playwright as Magician: Shakespeare's Image of the Poet in the English Public Theater.* New Haven and London: Yale University Press, 1979, 164 pp.

Focuses on Shakespeare's reflection in his poems and plays of the evolution of the poet-playwright from one supported by courtly patronage to one dependent upon commercial success. Through the various plays within plays, Shakespeare demonstrates the difficulties of communicating the theatrical intent to various kinds of audiences. The tensions between the poet's ideals and the nature of his marketplace are perhaps reflected most fully in Prospero as an exiled duke, practicing an illicit art on an isolated and barren island.

328. KERRIGAN, JOHN. *Motives of Woe: Shakespeare and "Female Complaint": A Critical Anthology.* Oxford: Clarendon Press, 1991, 310 pp.

Recovers a trend of writing to which some of the greatest medieval and Renaissance poets—women as well as men—contributed. Centering on Shakespeare's "A Lover's Complaint," it includes female-voiced lyrics, chronicle poems, and fictional letters by a range of authors from Chaucer to Aphra Behn and Henry Carey.

329. KIMBROUGH, ROBERT. *Shakespeare and the Art of Humankindness.* Atlantic Highlands and London: Humanities Press, 1990, 272 pp.

Defines androgyny as fully developed humanity and argues that Shakespeare's plays "are filled with signs of the androgynous vision which was slowly coming into focus during the high Renaissance in England" (p. 5). Cross-dressing in the romantic comedies provided a testing ground for exploring moments of androgynous awareness. *Macbeth* contains a "fierce war between gender concepts of manhood and womanhood played out upon the plain of humanity" (p. 12). Lear, with the dead Cordelia in his arms, is an emblem of androgyny. And the romances celebrate a kind of merger and synthesis of gender and generational differences.

330. KIRSCH, ARTHUR C. *Jacobean Dramatic Perspectives.* Charlottesville: University of Virginia Press, 1972, 134 pp.

Thematic and Topical Studies

Notes significant theatrical developments in the early Jacobean period—the rise of tragicomedy, satiric drama, and the private theater—occurring in part because of the decline of the aristocracy and the rise of economic individualism. *All's Well That Ends Well*, in particular, mixes the satiric with the romantic in a self-consciously paradoxical conception. The play celebrates the presence of grace in human life even while revealing the desperate need for it. *Cymbeline*, too, is a conscious exploration of the techniques and implications of tragicomic dramaturgy. Its providential pattern is a dramatic rendition of the *felix culpa*.

331. KIRSCHBAUM, LEO. *Character and Characterization in Shakespeare*. Detroit: Wayne State University Press, 1962, 168 pp.
Focuses on the dramatic function of Shylock, Albany, Edgar, Banquo, Othello, Hamlet, Ophelia, Cleopatra, Romeo, Angelo, Margaret, and Richard II. Angelo, for example, is described as two strikingly disparate characterizations; his importance to the plot is functional, a "pawn of theatricality" (p. 124). A Macbeth-like figure of conscience torn from within, he in the last part of the play is amorous, mean-spirited, and legalistic. To the contrary, Cleopatra is viewed as consistent in characterization, dazzling but a voluptuary to the end.

332. KNIGHT, G. WILSON. *The Shakespearian Tempest: With a Chart of Shakespeare's Dramatic Universe*. Oxford: Oxford University Press, 1932, 332 pp.
Asserts that the principle of Shakespearean unity throughout his plays is found in the opposition of tempest and music, that critics obsessed with character, psychology, and metrical tests have blinded themselves to this larger symbolic quality. Whether historical, comical, or tragical, all of his plays revolve on the axis of this imagistic tension. Analysis of the river, sea, tempest, and musical references throughout the canon reveals a movement from discord to harmony, whether in the pastoral idealism of romantic comedy or in the depths of the individual soul in the tragedies.

333. KNIGHTS, L. C. *Shakespeare's Politics: With Some Recollections on the Nature of Tradition*. Oxford: Oxford University Press, 1958, 18 pp.
Observes that Shakespeare always makes political issues subservient to the personal and the specific; he never, that is, writes a drama of ideas except as they are embedded in his characters and their actions. In *Julius Caesar* and *Henry V* he raises the question of what statesmen are liable to accept without question. *King Lear*, *Macbeth*, and *Coriolanus* explore in particular the nature of political order and its vulnerability to corruption. In effect, Shakespeare examines political conceptions such

Thematic and Topical Studies

as power, authority, honor, order, and freedom, but he forces us to view this examination in terms of the realities of human life and relationships.

334. KOTT, JAN. *Shakespeare Our Contemporary*. Translated by Boleslaw Taborski. Garden City: Doubleday, 1964, 372 pp.

Claims that today's spectator views the cruelty, the struggle for power, and the mutual slaughter in Shakespeare far more comprehendingly than did the nineteenth-century spectator. The histories, for example, chronicle the operation of the Grand Mechanism, the emergence of one king after another from the destruction of the previous ruler; every step of the way is marked by murder, violence, and treachery. *Hamlet* is paramountly a drama of political crime, *Troilus and Cressida* a sneering political pamphlet set in a world with no place for love, *Macbeth* a play without catharsis in which all the protagonist can do is "to drag with him into nothingness as many living beings as possible" (p. 97). *King Lear,* like Beckett's *Endgame*, mocks the absolute by transforming it into a blind mechanism.

335. LENTZ, CAROLYN R. S., GREENE, GAYLE, and NEELY, CAROL T., eds. *The Woman's Part: Feminist Criticism of Shakespeare*. Urbana: University of Illinois Press, 1980, 346 pp.

Seeks to liberate women from stereotypes through an examination of social patriarchal structures. Individual essays cover feminine sexuality as power (Paula Berggren), women in *Richard III* (Madonne Miner), the humanizing of Kate (John Bean), the distrust of women in *Much Ado About Nothing* (Janice Hays), Cressida's "self" (Greene), Gertrude's dilemma (Rebecca Smith), Lady Macbeth's infirm purpose (Joan Klein), Juliet's coming of age (Coppélia Kahn), and the Miranda trap (Lorie Leininger).

336. LEWIS, WYNDHAM. *The Lion and the Fox: The Role of the Hero in the Plays of Shakespeare*. London: Grant Richards, 1927, 326 pp.

Views the master-subject motif in Shakespeare as rooted in the Machiavellian obsession of his time. An anarchist in comedy, more the bolshevik than a figure of conservative romance, Shakespeare constantly mixes the humorous and the tragic, with one foot in the crude humility of medievalism and the other in the violent hubris of the Renaissance. The king in Shakespeare represents the personal ego, the object of jealous solicitude and disguised hatred from his subjects. Coriolanus—the lion—is the ornament of a strong aristocratic system set against the fox—the tribunes or Aufidius, as Othello is set against Iago.

Thematic and Topical Studies

337. LONG, JOHN H. *Shakespeare's Use of Music: A Study of the Music and Its Performance in the Original Production of Seven Comedies*. Gainesville: University of Florida Press, 1955, 213 pp.

Examines Shakespeare's use of choral and instrumental music in seven romantic comedies with the focus on how song intensifies the impact of the language and aids in developing the plot line and the character and in creating particular moods. The seventeen songs in these plays range in type from the elaborate song-dance-choral ayres of *A Midsummer Night's Dream* to the popular street song at the conclusion of *Twelfth Night*; and consort performances are featured in each play. The two art forms are fully integrated.

338. McGuire, Phillip C. *Speechless Dialect: Shakespeare's Open Silences*. Berkeley: University of California Press, 1985, 191 pp.

Insists that Shakespearean texts are subject to a multiplicity of readings based on performance history and infinite possibilities in performance. Precise meanings and effects are nonverbal, extratextual features (such as silences) that emerge only in performance. In *A Midsummer Night's Dream*, for example, the paucity of words assigned to Hippolyta in the opening scene leaves open the question of her amicability. In *Twelfth Night* the final silences of Antonio and Andrew challenge an actor to tease out meaning applicable to the individual performance, as do Antonio's silent response to Prospero's forgiveness in *The Tempest* and Isabella's to Vincentio's proposal in *Measure for Measure*.

339. MASEFIELD, JOHN. *William Shakespeare*. New York: Barnes & Noble, 1954, 227 pp.

Contains a biographical essay and brief analytic remarks on the sonnets and each of the poems and plays. Helena in *All's Well That Ends Well* is described as an ambitious vixen in a play "that cannot now be liked" (p. 96); Parolles, the play's only virtue, requires the kind of comic genius who can create Falstaff. *Hamlet* is a play dealing with a welter of promptings to kill and "seekings for a righter course than killing" (p. 107). In each of the tragedies the protagonist is destroyed in part by blindness in a noble nature but more significantly by a cool, resolute individual who takes advantage of this blindness.

340. MATTHEWS, HONOR. *Character and Symbol in Shakespeare's Plays: A Study of Certain Christian and Pre-Christian Elements in Their Structure and Allegory*. Cambridge: Cambridge University Press, 1962, 211 pp.

Argues that, since Elizabethan audiences were the direct inheritors of a drama reflecting a Christian unified view of life, symbolic elements recur persistently in Shakespeare's works. Their cumulative impact reveals something of Shakespeare's own values and provides a key to thematic interpretation. Progressively through his work can be traced a movement from the Luciferian sin of pride and the irreconcilability of justice and mercy to the difficulty of perceiving truth from the error with which evil powers in the universe attempt to destroy man and, finally, to the Christian archetype of redemption and of a new life in a new world.

341. MERCHANT, W. MOELWYN. *Shakespeare and the Artist*. London: Oxford University Press, 1959, 254 pp.
    Examines in part 1 the significance of a visual tradition in the interpretation of Shakespeare through the history of stage setting, the contributions of individual artists (whether working within the theater or simply painting Shakespeare's subjects), and the great mass of book illustration (especially engraved frontispieces). Stage history, more particularly, is considered in three phases—that of architectural setting (through Garrick), that of landscape setting, and that of topographical and historical accuracy (nineteenth century).

342. MIOLA, ROBERTS S. *Shakespeare's Rome*. Cambridge: Cambridge University Press, 1983, 244 pp.
    Examines Shakespeare's changing conception of Rome in *The Rape of Lucrece, Titus Andronicus, Julius Caesar, Antony and Cleopatra, Coriolanus,* and *Cymbeline*. The various transformations reflect Shakespeare's development as a playwright and the growth of his dramatic vision. In moving from a wilderness settlement (*Titus*) to a political arena (*Caesar*) to an empire (*Antony*), Shakespeare explores three basic Roman ideals—constancy, honor, and *pietas*.

343. MOISAN, THOMAS. " 'Knock Me Here Soundly': Comic Misprision and Class Consciousness in Shakespeare." *Shakespeare Quarterly* 42 (1991):276–90.
    Examines situations in three comedies—the exchange between Petruchio and Grumio in *The Taming of the Shrew*, between Lorenzo and Launcelot in *The Merchant of Venice*, and between Flavius and Murellus and the workmen in *Julius Caesar*—in which there is an altercation noticeably turning on distinctions of class. In each case the superior is temporarily thwarted and his authority called into question, but ultimately the inferior is dismissed from the stage with "the basis of his inferiority forcibly reaffirmed" (p. 276). In fact, however, such moments give voice to class discordances that challenge the assumptions of a benign social order.

99

Thematic and Topical Studies

344. MOONEY, MICHAEL E. *Shakespeare's Dramatic Transaction*. Durham and London: Duke University Press, 1990, 226 pp.

Observes that Shakespearean drama represents the fusion of *platea* (undifferentiated place) and *locus* (symbolic place), of the presentational and representational modes. In *Richard III*, for example, the power of the play arises from the fact that the spectator must mediate between two polarized opposites—a providential world and a teleologically undermining villain. The spectator's vicarious interest in *Richard II* develops as Shakespeare progressively divides the king's two bodies, the political and natural selves. In *Hamlet* the spectator, drawn to the experience of the play through the "gradation in illusionistic depth" (p. 93), at moments shares the level of Hamlet's perception and at other moments transcends it.

345. MORRIS, HARRY. *Last Things in Shakespeare*. Tallahassee: Gainesville: University of Florida Presses, Florida State University Press; 1985, 348 pp.

Focuses on Shakespeare's persistent concern with eschatological themes, viewing the four major tragedies as a tetralogy that investigates the theme of salvation or damnation from a variety of perspectives. Hamlet and Lear are ultimately saved, Hamlet by accepting his role as God's minister and Lear "through the absolution given by Christ himself in the symbolic figure of his daughter" (p. 162). Othello and Macbeth, to the contrary, lose their souls, Othello in a struggle with a literal devil Iago and Macbeth as a veritable antichrist.

346. MURRAY, JOHN MIDDLETON. *Shakespeare*. London: Jonathan Cape, 1936, 448 pp.

Describes Shakespeare as capable of shuffling off the mortal coil of moral judgment, of revealing that man—to be generous—must cease to be blind in any number of ways. His work transcends any rigorous critical method. Following a biographical essay, the study proceeds to examine Shakespeare's poems and plays in roughly chronological order. His early plays are viewed as experimental, to a degree imitative but also pieces in which he developed his individual style. Hamlet is described as a figure of the European consciousness; the final plays, defended against theories of boredom, are championed as dramatic portrayals of the miracles of nature.

347. NEELY, CAROL THOMAS. *Broken Nuptials in Shakespeare's Plays*. New Haven: Yale University Press, 1985, 261 pp.

Observes that marriage, whether harmoniously consummated or disrupted and thwarted, influences the themes and structures of the

Thematic and Topical Studies

plays and serves as a focus for the social and emotional relationship between the sexes. While movement toward marriage is the subject of the comedies, disrupted marital relationships loom large in the trage- dies. In the romances marriage or its reestablishment is a symbol of harmony. Shakespeare's various depictions of broken nuptials reflect the era's contradictory attitudes toward women and the complicated blend of power and subordination that characterized their status.

348. NEWMAN, KAREN. *Fashioning Femininity and English Renaissance Drama*. Chicago: University of Chicago Press, 1991, 182 pp.

Argues that "proliferating meanings in the discourses of femininity resist pat claims about patriarchal power and women's subject status" (p. xix). Following chapters on the age's concept of human anatomy, the Protestant concept of gender relations in marriage, and fundamen- tal assumptions concerning family politics, the study focuses on *The Taming of the Shrew, Othello, Henry V*, and Jonson's *Epicoene*. The effort is not merely to examine the role of women through literary analysis but to create a "textual intercourse" (p. 146) involving a variety of texts (theoretical, canonical, archival, historical) from Stowe, Shakespeare, Jonson, Elizabeth, and James to Marx, Derrida, and Foucault that yield a vision of gender based on shifting relations rather than on fixed categories and values.

349. NOBLE, RICHMOND. *Shakespeare's Use of Song: With the Text of the Principal Songs*. Oxford: Oxford University Press, 1923, 160 pp.

Observes that the brevity of expression and the rapidity of devel- opment distinguish Shakespeare's songs from those of his contempo- rary dramatists. He also is the first fully to integrate song into the dramatic action. "Who Is Sylvia?" for example, connects the two plots of *The Two Gentlemen of Verona*; and the songs in *Twelfth Night* char- acterize the discrepant moods of the play, as even more philosophically do the songs in *The Tempest*. Individual chapters for each play (or group of plays) present the text of the songs and discuss their lyric qualities and thematic relevance.

350. NOSWORTHY, J. M. *Shakespeare's Occasional Plays: Their Origin and Transmission*. New York: Barnes & Noble, 1965, 238 pp.

Suggests that *Hamlet, The Merry Wives of Windsor, Troilus and Cressida*, and *Macbeth* were originally designed for presentation before particular audiences on particular occasions (respectively, Oxford and Cambridge University, the Court of Elizabeth, one of the Inns of Court, and the Court of James) and that a wide range of problems for each (dating, collaboration, adaptation, revision, and textual variation) may

Thematic and Topical Studies

be largely resolved by this realization and close textual analysis. The plays were revised, most probably by Shakespeare himself, before they reached the public stage.

351. Novy, Marianne. *Love's Argument: Gender Relations in Shakespeare.* Chapel Hill: University of North Carolina Press, 1984, 237 pp.

Views Shakespeare's plays in their love relationships as moving beyond the conventional gender expectations of his age. In *The Taming of the Shrew* playfulness and festive disguise hold "elements of both patriarchy and mutuality in suspension" (p. 6), but in the mature comedies women's role-playing is a positive force, generating mutuality through a male participation and cooperation. In tragedy men relegate the women to an audience as they act out their aggressive masculine roles with disastrous consequences. The romances offer "transformed images of manhood" (p. 174) in which men become more amenable to the female experience of passivity, pregnancy, and childbirth.

352. Nuttall, A. D. *A New Mimesis: Shakespeare and the Representation of Reality.* London: Methuen, 1983, 209 pp.

Attacks modern critical obfuscation that stands between Shakespeare and his representation of reality—whether formalism, structuralism, or deconstructionism. The essence of Shakespeare's art is that he creates characters who demand to be viewed as possible human beings, not merely as functions in some formal system. While *The Merchant of Venice*, for example, sets Old Law against New, Jewish justice against Christian charity, Shakespeare transcends the archetypes and rigidly schematized methodology by imbuing each figure with an ambiguity that smacks of human nature as we know it.

353. Ornstein, Robert. *The Moral Vision of Jacobean Tragedy.* Madison: University of Wisconsin Press, 1960, 299 pp.

Considers the early years of the seventeenth century as a time in which the Elizabethan worldview of hierarchial providential control slowly defaults to a scientific, steady progress toward the secular. Whereas the tragic inspiration in Shakespeare's contemporaries is short-lived, with early scorn and indignation fading into philosophic or religious conviction, Shakespeare's vision persists; he "humanizes the categorical imperatives which the stern didacticist offers as the sense of ethical truth" (p. 223).

354. Paris, Bernard J. *Bargains with Fate: Psychological Crises and Conflicts in Shakespeare and His Plays.* New York: Insight Books, 1991, 303 pp.

Defines "bargain with fate" as one's assumption that he can "control fate by living up to its presumed dictates not after it grants [one's] wishes but before" (p. 2). Part 1 argues that the major tragedies focus on individuals who are in a state of psychological crisis resulting from the breakdown of such a bargain. Part 2 surveys the entire canon as a means by which one might infer the authorial personality. Shakespeare, more specifically, is viewed as a deeply divided man, one side of him vengeful, aggressive, and power hungry, the other forgiving, submissive, and idealistic.

355. PARKER, M. D. H. *The Slave of Life: A Study of Shakespeare and the Idea of Justice*. London: Chatto & Windus, 1955, 264 pp.

Observes that Shakespeare, while in the early plays working within the convention of justice in this world and mercy in the next, in the last plays transfers mercy from the heavenly to the earthly judge. *Measure for Measure*, *All's Well That Ends Well*, and *King Lear* are essays in redemption. In the tragedies Shakespeare's villains are consumed by pride, while the tragic heroes through suffering gain the self-knowledge that leads to redemption.

356. PARKER, PATRICIA, AND HARTMAN, GEOFFREY, eds. *Shakespeare and the Question of Theory*. New York: Methuen, 1985, 335 pp.

Includes essays on language, rhetoric, and deconstruction (Howard Felperin on *The Winter's Tale*, Elizabeth Freund on *Troilus and Cressida*, Hartman on *Twelfth Night*, Parker on *Othello*), the woman's part (Elaine Showalter on Ophelia, Nancy Vickers on *The Rape of Lucrece*, Joel Fineman on *The Taming of the Shrew*), politics, economy, and history (Stephen Greenblatt on *King Lear*, René Girard on *Troilus and Cressida*, Thomas Greene on the sonnets, Stanley Cavell on *Coriolanus*), and the question of Hamlet (Robert Weimann, Margaret Ferguson, Terence Hawkes).

357. PATTERSON, ANNABEL. *Shakespeare and the Popular Voice*. Cambridge, Mass.: Basil Blackwell, 1989, 195 pp.

Focuses on Shakespeare's profound and sympathetic interest in the common man, a "discourse of rural, artisanal, and peasant ideology" that he shares with Van Gogh. The aim is to uncover the social concerns of this glovemaker's son and to connect them with "today's thought about popular culture and popular protest" (p. 4). The anxiety that characterizes Elsinore reflects similar discontents perceived in London. The rebellion of the crazed prophet William Hackett is reflected in the Cade rebellion in *2 Henry VI*; repeated harvest failures are echoed in *A Midsummer Night's Dream* as are problems of Bedlam beggars in *King*

Thematic and Topical Studies

Lear or of the insurrection of the Midlands' farmers in *Coriolanus*.In such manner the theater of Shakespeare's day functioned as a powerful social construct.

358. PAULSON, RONALD. *Book and Painting: Shakespeare, Milton, and the Bible: Literary Texts and the Emergence of English Painting.* Knoxville: University of Tennessee Press, 1982, 236 pp.
    Suggests that the major influence on the emergence of English painting as it developed in the eighteenth century was neither a native graphic tradition nor a European tradition but English literature. Shakespeare to the eighteenth century represented a freedom from rules and restrictive classical imitation. Conventional Shakespearean illustrations tend to be constructed on visual oppositions of good and evil, light and dark, but his primary influence in art was the free interplay of individuals and of character. In Hogarth, especially, one views the Shakespearean copiousness, the psychological and moral complexity.

359. PYE, CHRISTOPHER. *The Regal Phantasm: Shakespeare and the Politics of Spectacle.* New York: Routledge, 1990, 198 pp.
    Explores the relationship between theatricality and power in Renaissance England in *Henry V*, *Richard II*, and *Macbeth*. The paradoxical manner in which Henry theatrically defers his mastery of kingship in itself is a remarkable strategy of political absolutism. Conversely, Richard II in his fall "plays out a form of excessive theatricality" (p. 11). The spectacle of the tyrant's head in the final scene of *Macbeth* engages the spectator in the "politics of rapture"; "political and theatrical power settle into the form of a specular trap" (p. 174). The spectator is simultaneously comforted and horrified; spectacle has served the purpose of political containment.

360. RABKIN, NORMAN. *Shakespeare and the Common Understanding.* New York: Free Press, 1967, 267 pp.
    Defines Shakespeare's method of depicting human conflict as "complementarity," a concept in physics in which one is forced to live with paradoxes and contrarieties incapable of solution. The plays present a universe in which we must make value judgments concerning the action and the characters, yet simultaneously we are forced to realize that any such judgment is reductionistic. Shakespeare structures his work in terms of polar opposites—reason versus passion in *Hamlet*, *realpolitik* and the traditional political order in *Richard II*, hedonism and responsibility in *Troilus and Cressida*, the world and the transcendent in *Antony and Cleopatra*, justice and mercy in *The Merchant of Venice* and *King Lear*.

Thematic and Topical Studies

361. ———. *Shakespeare and the Problem of Meaning*. Chicago: University of Chicago Press, 1981, 165 pp.

Extols the value of recent trends in Shakespearean criticism that stress contrarieties in the interpretation of the plays and the characters. The reductionistic quality of some critical approaches is illustrated in *The Merchant of Venice*, in which Shakespeare draws the spectators' response in contradiction to the overtly established movement of the theme, and in *Henry V*, which at one level directs an immediate response either favorable or unfavorable to Henry, but at another requires the simultaneous acceptance of both.

362. RIGHTER [BARTON], ANNE. *Shakespeare and the Idea of the Play*. London: Chatto & Windus, 1962, 200 pp.

Discusses Shakespeare's plays in relation to the sixteenth-century concept of drama and the evolution of a new relationship between actors and audience. The audience in medieval drama, which was poised between ritual and art, participated by attentive silence in the awful affirmation of theological absolutes. The influence of classical drama, in part, was to separate spectator and stage. In his early plays the metaphor of the stage as world is usually rhetorical flourish, but by the middle plays the player-king has become a central image.

363. ROBERTS, JEANNE A. *The Shakespearean Wild: Geography, Genus, and Gender*. Lincoln: University of Nebraska Press, 1991, 214 pp.

Examines the distinctions in various plays of Shakespeare between untamed nature and civilized settings and how gender stereotypes are affixed to those distinctions. Shakespeare's plays, more specifically, are products of a culture that regards women as peripheral and threatening. The "wild" of the title refers to the "female wild" often associated with malign and benign forces of nature. Attention is directed to how the male vision of culture exemplified in Shakespeare has reduced, distorted, and oversimplified the potentiality of women.

364. ROSE, MARK. *Shakespearean Design*. Cambridge, Mass.: Harvard University Press, 1972, 190 pp.

Focuses on major structural features of Shakespeare's dramaturgy. While Shakespeare draws on his predecessors, he is the first to apply principles of scene design to the play as a whole. A scene-by-scene analysis of *Hamlet* illustrates the method in detail; then follow briefer analyses of each play in roughly chronological order. Essentially Shakespeare's plays reveal "multiple unity" (p. 95); the scenic units may be relatively independent, but only in context do they assume full coloration and meaning.

Thematic and Topical Studies

365. ROSE, MARY BETH. "Where Are the Mothers in Shakespeare? Options for Gender Representation in the English Renaissance." *Shakespeare Quarterly* 42 (1991):291–314.

Argues that, even though the family in the Renaissance gradually changed from an institution that emphasized arranged marriages to one that emphasized the conjugal couple and the isolated nuclear family, Shakespeare's depiction of motherhood is "limited to the private realm, inscribed entirely in terms of early love and nurture" (p. 313). In his comedy the maternal role remains invisible; in his tragedy it is, if visible, dramatized and problematized—as in Gertrude or Volumnia. Similarly, it is only when Hermione's "represented maternal desire" (p. 306) is removed from the play that *The Winter's Tale* can be transformed into comedy.

366. RUTTER, CAROL. *Clamorous Voices: Shakespeare's Woman Today*. Edited by Faith Evans. New York: Routledge, 1989, 131 pp.

Traces the influence of the women's movement on the stage through interviews with actresses in Royal Shakespeare Company productions of the past decade (Sinead Cusack, Paola Dionisetti, Fiona Shaw, Juliet Stevenson, Harriet Walters). The struggle is often against directors and designers whose decisions sometimes trivialize the characters they play—for example, the insistence of a happy ending at the expense of Isabella's credibility in *Measure for Measure* or on utter stylization in the portrayal of Kate in *The Taming of the Shrew*. The actresses interviewed reveal an interesting cross-section of the feminist movement itself, with Sinead Cusack branding the charge that Shakespeare's roles are restrictive as "absolute balderdash" (p. xxv), while Juliet Stevenson regards Shakespeare's women as almost invariably supporting roles.

367. RYAN, KIERNAN. *Shakespeare*. Atlantic Highlands: Humanities Press International, 1989, 130 pp.

Views Shakespeare's plays as an indictment of a society that prevents men and women from realizing the full potential of humanity and destroys them by luring them into the very flaws on which it is constructed. The plays reflect the struggle between capitalism grounded in profit and the pursuit of an individualism that seeks to live more fully and more freely than the prevailing organization of life allows. Shakespeare's tragedies are tragedies of society, not of the individuals who are crushed by the social corruption into which they are born. Such revisionist readings are provided for each play in the canon.

368. SALINGER, LEO. *Dramatic Form in Shakespeare and the Jacobeans*. Cambridge: Cambridge University Press, 1986, 292 pp.

Thematic and Topical Studies

Features essays on Shakespeare's concept of art, *The Merchant of Venice* as a problem play, the structural design of *Twelfth Night*, the function of Falstaff, the romance elements in *King Lear*, and the influence of Montaigne and Harsnett on that tragedy. Falstaff, more specifically, is described as the "first major joke by the English against their class system" (p. 36); he shadows the false foundations of Henry's rule and the conflicting political interests that generated its momentum. The dark vision of life in *King Lear* is attributed in large part to Shakespeare's reading of Florio's translation of Montaigne, in particular the chapter "Of the Affection of Fathers to Their Children."

369. SANDERS, WILBUR. *The Dramatist and the Received Idea: Studies in the Plays of Marlowe and Shakespeare.* Cambridge: Cambridge University Press, 1968, 392 pp.

Attempts to examine the relationship between the playwright and his culture, the transformation of received ideas into dramatic conflict by setting the fixity of cultural tradition against the concept of the evolutionary process. *Richard III*, for instance, would hardly fully please either the Tudor propagandist or the monarchist; if Richard is the scourge of God, he is also a chilling study in Machiavellian political amorality. The play teems with the inextricability of justice as Richard's culpabilities excuse Bullingbrook no more than Richard can take refuge in the concept of divine right. *Macbeth* examines the inexorable relationship between the "overwhelming potency of evil" and the "concealed intention of nature" (p. 307).

370. SCHANZER, ERNEST. *The Problem Plays of Shakespeare: A Study of "Julius Caesar," "Measure for Measure," and "Antony and Cleopatra."* London: Routledge & Kegan Paul, 1963, 196 pp.

Defines a problem play as one in which the audience loses its moral bearing as the action unfolds. Shakespeare in these works demonstrably manipulates the spectators' angle of vision to the point that they perceive the futility of any attempt to assume an absolutist posture. In *Julius Caesar*, for example, he confronts the viewers with two essential problems—the psychological nature of the real Caesar and the justifiability of murder. Isabella in *Measure for Measure* must choose between the death of her brother and the sacrifice of her virginity; *Antony and Cleopatra*, the quintessential problem play, forces us to view Cleopatra in all her decadence and yet by act 5 to greet her death as somehow glorious.

371. SCHMIDGALL, GARY. *Shakespeare and Opera.* Oxford and New York: Oxford University Press, 1990, 394 pp.

Thematic and Topical Studies

Investigates Shakespeare's canon and the standard operatic repertory. The two genres are seen to be fundamentally akin in their shared
demand for virtuoso display, the similar functions of set speeches and
arias, and the similarities of verbal and musical rhetoric. The last section
of the study provides analysis of operatic versions of *Othello* (Verdi),
King Lear (Verdi), *Measure for Measure* (Wagner), *The Taming of the
Shrew* (Goetz, Gianni), *Much Ado About Nothing* (Berlioz), *The Tempest*
(Purcell), *A Midsummer Night's Dream* (Britten), *Antony and Cleopatra*
(Barber), *Romeo and Juliet* (Rossini, Bellini), *The Merry Wives of Wind-
sor* (Nicolai, Williams, Verdi).

372. SCHOENBAUM, SAMUEL. *Shakespeare and Others*. London: Scholar
Press; Washington: Folger Shakespeare Library Press, 1985, 285 pp.
Contains essays ranging from discussions of Shakespeare's learning
and the identity of the dark lady of the sonnets to the political realism
of the history plays, from the changing critical reception of Shakespeare
in England over the past two centuries and Shakespeare's plays in performance by the Royal Shakespeare Company to a contemporary account of William Henry Ireland's Shakespeare forgeries. There is a
lengthy refutation of William Rowse's claim that the dark lady is Emilia
Bassano, the daughter of Baptist Bassano, a well-known musician to the
queen.

373. SCRAGG, LEAH. *Discovering Shakespeare's Meaning*. Totowa: Barnes &
Noble, 1988, 234 pp.
Offers itself as a guide to the uninitiated, stressing the importance
of experiencing Shakespeare on the stage and cautioning to avoid generic definitions in approaching the plays. The focus is primarily on
technique, with chapters on verse and prose, expositions, plays within
plays, parallel action, characterization, and soliloquies. Shakespeare's
method of development is essentially by contrast, distinguishing, for
example, between the function of prose and poetry in depicting diverse
social layers or the differences in the use of the soliloquy by Richard III
and Macbeth.

374. SENG, PETER J. *The Vocal Songs in the Plays of Shakespeare: A Critical
History*. Cambridge, Mass.: Harvard University Press, 1967, 314 pp.
Includes an individual chapter on each play containing a vocal
song. The text of each song is collated with all sixteenth- and
seventeenth-century editions and with all major editions from Rowe
forward. The material for each song includes a headnote indicating its
source in the play, general and textual commentary arranged chronologically, information about the musical setting, information about

sources or analogues, and a discussion of the dramatic function of the song in the play.

375. SHAPIRO, JAMES S. *Rival Playwrights: Marlowe, Jonson, Shakespeare.* New York: Columbia University Press, 1991, 203 pp.

Explores the psychological dynamics, the commercial factors, and the historical milieu involved in the professional relationships of Marlowe, Jonson, and Shakespeare and how each influenced the plays and poems of the others. The range of intertextual concerns and strategies that came into play reveal rivalry and parody as social practice, "ways of leasing and building upon the intellectual and stylistic property of other writers" (p. viii). For Marlowe such parody was especially devastating; after the drama of Jonson and Shakespeare, his plays would not be taken seriously again for three centuries.

376. SKULSKY, HAROLD. *Spirits Finely Touched: The Testing of Value and Integrity in Four Shakespearean Plays.* Athens: University of Georgia Press, 1976, 288 pp.

Notes that Shakespeare forces a violent collision in his major work between cherished beliefs and the reality of human experience, as in Hamlet's nightmare about how God works and whether God's justice is merely an anthropomorphic extension of man's vengefulness, in Angelo's equation of the law and brute power in *Measure for Measure*, in Othello's disturbing sense of justice and the glimpse of man's limitless potential for bestiality, in the abolition of justice, human dignity, and love in *King Lear* to see whether intrinsic value remains.

377. SMITH, MARION B. *Dualities in Shakespeare.* Toronto: University of Toronto Press, 1966, 252 pp.

Examines the humanist's search for synthesis or order based on the reconciliation of opposition despite increasing philosophical disillusionment and social disruption. Tolerance, temperance, and charity manifest in the plays a harmonious ordering of differences in the personal and social spheres. The study specifically addresses the sonnets and six major plays, concentrating on the duality of love in the poems, the imagery of *Romeo and Juliet*, the inversions of *Twelfth Night* and *Macbeth*, the duality of order and justice in *Measure for Measure*, of structure in *Antony and Cleopatra*, and of intention in *The Tempest*.

378. SOELLNER, ROLF. *Shakespeare's Patterns of Self-Knowledge.* Columbus: Ohio State University Press, 1972, 454 pp.

Concerns what Elizabethans and Jacobeans thought self-knowledge to be and the dramatic patterns Shakespeare created from

Thematic and Topical Studies

this thought. Self-knowledge in some cases refers to the situation. Titus, for example, assumes a revenger's role in place of that of the suffering victim. Romeo enacts a Petrarchan love drama. Hamlet swirls with various roles ranging from that of lover to that of revenger; much of the play involves his search for a psychologically compatible posture. In *Antony and Cleopatra* a dream role triumphs, reducing history to insignificance. A final chapter focuses on the role of the internal dramatist, especially in *The Winter's Tale* and *The Tempest*.

379. STERNFIELD, FREDERICK W. *Music in Shakespearean Tragedy*. London: Routledge & Kegan Paul; New York: Dover, 1963., 334 pp.

Observes that tragedy uses far less music than comedy, both because of the Senecan influence and because of the nature of the tragic experience itself. Moreover, the use of instrumental music was greater than that of vocal music. Shakespeare uses lyrics to supplement tragic speech (for example, Desdemona's "Willow Song") and comic songs for particular effect (for example, the grave digger's song in *Hamlet*, Pandarus's song in *Troilus and Cressida*). Ophelia's mad songs, giving emphasis to her helplessness, become an integral part of the tragic scene itself. The fool in *King Lear* frequently mixes snatches of lyric and prose in his dialogue with the king.

380. STEWART, J. I. M. *Character and Motive in Shakespeare: Some Recent Appraisals Examined*. London: Longmans, Green, 1949, 147 pp.

Reacts to the critical overemphasis on "realistic" and "psychological" approaches to Shakespeare and the concomitant derogation of dramatic poetry and symbolic association. Pedestrian and unimaginative readings and performances with as much business and spectacle and as little poetry as possible depreciate Shakespeare's drama.

381. STIRLING, BRENTS. *The Populace in Shakespeare*. New York: Columbia University Press, 1949, 203 pp.

Illustrates through numerous documents of the period that the mob was viewed as a dangerous disintegrating and leveling force, illiterate, disorderly, vicious. This attitude is most clearly visible in the Jack Cade scenes in *Henry VI* and the mob scenes in *Julius Caesar* and *Coriolanus*. In large part this sharply satiric view of the masses was reinforced by the conservative reaction to growing political ferment in late Elizabethan England.

382. STOCKHOLDER, KAY. *Dreamworks: Lovers and Family in Shakespeare's Plays*. Toronto: University of Toronto Press, 1987, 281 pp.

Envisions the reader of Shakespeare as a protagonist in a dream and the characters and action as a means of working through psychic conflict. The emphasis is not on psychoanalyzing Shakespeare himself but on identifying—from an implicit feminist perspective—recurrent transformations of anxiety and desire. Since the choice of protagonist as dreamer is arbitrary, this study embraces the politics of textual indeterminacy. But in this study at least, the perspective is consistently male, both in the tragedies and the comedies; and the persistent theme is the male fear of female erotic power. In the figurations of women as corruption, betrayal, disease, decay, and death, this perspective examines the psychic structures of patriarchy.

383. STOLL, ELMER EDGAR. *Shakespeare Studies: Historical and Comparative in Method*. New York: Macmillan, 1927, 502 pp.

Collects the author's most significant articles and monographs on Shakespeare and the Elizabethan theater. General matters discussed include the folio; Shakespeare's life and the fallacy of viewing the periods of his work as reflections of his psychological state and of treating characters as extensions of his personality; Shakespeare's comic method; the ghosts in *Macbeth*, *Richard III*, and *Julius Caesar*, whether real or symbolic; and the criminals in the plays, especially the nature of the Elizabethan Machiavel. An individual chapter is devoted to Shylock, who is viewed as a purely comic villain.

384. SUMMERS, JOSEPH H. *Dreams of Love and Power*. New York: Oxford University Press, 1984, 176 pp.

Explores the primary concern with dreams in *A Midsummer Night's Dream*, *The Winter's Tale*, *Hamlet*, *Measure for Measure*, *King Lear*, *Antony and Cleopatra*, and *The Tempest*. At times the dream is literal, at times metaphoric; but in all cases it prefigures the dramatic character's desires, hopes, and fears. Shakespeare's use of dream is thematic as well as structural. While its vision transcends the actual in *Dream* and *Antony*, it confronts harsh reality in *Lear* and disturbing ambiguities in *Hamlet* and *Tempest*.

385. SINDELSON, DAVID. *Shakespeare's Restorations of the Father*. New Brunswick: Rutgers University Press, 1983, 165 pp.

Argues the centrality of Shakespeare's vision of the restored father to Shakespeare's vision of reconciliation, exploring both the presentation of patriarchy in specific plays and the larger psychological context of the father's return. The significance of the loss or the weakness of the father or surrogate father figure is examined in *Richard II, 1, 2 Henry*

Thematic and Topical Studies

> IV, Henry V, The Merchant of Venice, Measure for Measure, and The Tempest.

386. TALBERT, ERNEST. *Elizabethan Drama and Shakespeare's Early Plays: An Essay in Historical Criticism.* Chapel Hill: University of North Carolina Press, 1963, 410 pp.

Examines Shakespeare's early plays for methods by which he arouses and manipulates the spectators' response through familiarity with certain concepts such as multiplicity of plots, the use of rhetorical devices, the comedic element especially in the figure of the clown and courtly motifs, and through emotional biases such as national patriotism and animosity toward France and toward Roman Catholicism. Aspects of both native episodic structure and the classical concept of five-act structure figure in these early works.

387. TAYLOR, GARY. *Reinventing Shakespeare: A Cultural History, from the Restoration to the Present.* New York: Weidenfeld and Nicolson, 1989, 465 pp.

Surveys changing taste concerning Shakespeare in England and America from 1660 to 1986, noting fluctuating preferences for public reading and public production, shifting literary constructs of Shakespeare as a poet and a dramatist, and alternations that guide decisions in textual editing or period settings and stage designs. The fundamental view for the evaluation is the denunciation of the practice of valuing Shakespeare as supremely great. The study ridicules critics who make a living off the poet with yet another interpretation, through such a rhetorical process encouraging more serious consideration of his contemporaries in the theater.

388. TAYLOR, MARK. *Shakespeare's Darker Purpose: A Question of Incest.* AMS Studies in the Renaissance, 7. New York: AMS Press, 1982, 203 pp.

Observes that in no fewer than twenty-one of Shakespeare's plays does a young woman who marries or plans to marry find her father or the memory of her father an obstacle. In these interactions, a "degree of sublimated incestuous desire is nearly always present in the mixture of concern, possessiveness, and love that Shakespeare's fathers feel for their daughters" (p. 72). Dread of losing the daughter in marriage provokes acts that are arbitrary, selfish, irrational, violent, and cruel. *The Tempest* is considered the culmination of the incest motif. While Alonso forces his daughter into a transracial marriage, Prospero must overcome his own subliminal desires in emancipating Miranda.

389. TEAGUE, FRANCES. *Shakespeare's Speaking Properties.* Lewisburg: Bucknell University Press; London and Toronto: Associated University Presses, 1991, 222 pp.

Thematic and Topical Studies

Provides a systematic discussion of properties in Shakespeare's plays, focusing on their meaning within patterns of presentational imagery. Attention is also directed to significant image clusters that recur throughout the plays. Although the Elizabethan public theater featured a relatively barren stage, properties were still of vital importance in communicating meaning, both directly and symbolically.

390. TENNENHOUSE, LEONARD. *Power on Display: The Politics of Shakespeare's Genres*. New York: Methuen, 1986, 206 pp.

Observes that Shakespeare's plays function "as a forum for staging symbolic shows of power and as a vehicle for disseminating court ideology" (p. 39). In the romantic comedies, for instance, the transformation of the Petrarchan woman into a figure who is both pure and capable of desire formed a part of the courtly discourse surrounding Queen Elizabeth. The history plays develop a strategy to produce political order out of disorder by depicting competing hierarchies of power "which only the monarch can hold together in harmonious discord" (p. 73). The sensational features of Jacobean tragedy function as a kind of "political 'cosmography'" (p. 107) in which extravagant scenes of mutilation of the female display the legitimate exercise of patriarchal power. The romances serve to rewrite the political body of the monarch by viewing him as needed to "reform corrupt social practices" (p. 171).

391. THALER, ALWIN. *Shakespeare's Silences*. Cambridge, Mass.: Harvard University Press, 1929, 279 pp.

Focuses on Shakespeare's silences in characterization, at times calculated, at times oversights—for example, Sylvia's silence in *The Two Gentlemen of Verona* while being passed from Valentine to Proteus and back again, Isabella's silence to Vincentio's proposal in *Measure for Measure*, Hermione's silent forgiveness of Leontes in *The Winter's Tale*, Iago's refusal to speak further at the conclusion of *Othello*. Another form of silence is the mysterious disappearance of Rosaline in *Romeo and Juliet*, of the fool in *King Lear*, or the inconsistencies in Margaret's character in *Much Ado About Nothing*, or the unspoken details about Macbeth's children.

392. THAMPSON, MARVIN, and THOMPSON, RUTH, eds. *Shakespeare and the Sense of Performance: Essays in the Tradition of Performance Criticism in Honor of Bernard Beckerman*. Newark: University of Delaware Press; London and Toronto: Associated University Presses, 1989, 259 pp.

Provides a collection of essays focused on performance-centered criticism. Entries include discussion of Hamlet and the audience (Ralph Berry), language in *The Winter's Tale* (Inga-Stina Ewbank), silence in

113

Thematic and Topical Studies

> *A Midsummer Night's Dream* (Philip McGuire), offstage speech in *Hamlet* (Maurice Charney), stage images in *Troilus and Cressida* (R. A. Foakes), recent productions of *Love's Labor's Lost* and *As You Like It* (Glynne Wickham), speech in Shakespeare (John R. Brown), subtext in Shakespeare (Marvin Rosenberg), stage locales and modern interpretation (Alan Dessen), and Shakespeare's audiences (Andrew Gurr).

393. TILLYARD, E. M. W. *Shakespeare's Problem Plays*. Toronto: University of Toronto Press, 1950, 156 pp.

Views Shakespeare's problem plays as of two kinds—those that are genuinely abnormal like *All's Well That Ends Well* and *Measure for Measure* and those that deal with problems like *Hamlet* and *Troilus and Cressida*. They share a concern for religious dogma or abstract speculation, a serious but not pessimistic mood, realistic characterization, the common motif of a young man on the verge of adulthood receiving some form of traumatic shock, a nocturnal setting, and the juxtaposition of the old and new generations. The basic problem in both *All's Well* and *Measure for Measure* is an inability to fuse effectively romantic, fantastic plots with a vitality and realism of characterization.

394. TOLIVER, HAROLD. *Transported Styles in Shakespeare and Milton*. University Park: Pennsylvania State University Press, 1989, 276 pp.

Perceives a conflict between Shakespeare as playwright and poet. Poetry operates through an abundance of idea and emotion while drama through its specificity of context demands a shrinking of imaginative possibilities. Often, for example, the approach toward marriage in the plot has a flattening effect; the wedding match and the chess game in *The Tempest* lack poetic richness, and Hymen's song in *As You Like It* is something "Bottom might have extemporized" (p. 51). Generally, Shakespeare emerges as a more conservative writer than Milton, his characters always brought back within existing structures of authority whereas Milton more readily envisions a new world informed by transcendent values.

395. TOMARKEN, EDWARD. *Samuel Johnson on Shakespeare: The Discipline of Criticism*. Athens: University of Georgia Press, 1991, 205 pp.

Maintains that the notes in Johnson's edition of Shakespeare contain coherent interpretations of most of the plays and that many portions of the *Preface* are generalizations based on those specific comments. Focusing on eight plays (*Henry IV*, *Troilus and Cressida*, *Twelfth Night*, *The Taming of the Shrew*, *King Lear*, *The Tempest*, *Hamlet*, *Macbeth*), the study argues that moral aspects in Shakespeare can point the way to mediating ideological difficulties so divisive in modern criticism and theory.

396. TRAVERSI, DEREK. *An Approach to Shakespeare*. 3d ed., rev. and expanded. Garden City: Doubleday, 1969, 674 pp.

Observes that Shakespeare's early development takes place within dramatic conventions established by lesser artists—the revenge play, the chronicles, euphuistic or Plautine comedy. The mature tragedies, exhibiting a greater linguistic range and power, firmly trace the theme of passion's dominance through a clash between contrasted and opposed personalities and orders. The romances give artistic form to a new symbolic purpose focusing on the marvel of forgiveness and healing.

397. TURNER, FREDERICK. *Shakespeare and the Nature of Time: Moral and Philosophical Themes in Some Plays and Poems of William Shakespeare*. Oxford: Clarendon Press, 1971, 193 pp.

Stresses time in Shakespeare's plays as dynamic, a process and a becoming. Among the most significant aspects of time are the historical, the process of the personal experience, the natural or cyclic, and the secular. Whereas in the sonnets it is the great destroyer, destruction and restoration are juxtaposed in *The Winter's Tale*. With the appearance of the ghost from the outer world in *Hamlet*, the timeless world erupts ambiguously into the world of time; timeless forces also operate against Macbeth, but in that play they act as a kind of avenging angel. Shakespeare's interest is in time as a dramaturgical medium used for the development of character.

398. TURNER, ROBERT Y. *Shakespeare's Apprenticeship*. Chicago and London: University of Chicago Press, 1974, 293 pp.

Studies Shakespeare's development as a playwright, not in the manner in which he adapts source materials, but in the increasingly sophisticated utilization of dramatic technique—rhetoric, dialogue, scene division and emphasis, irony, staging, the generic mixture of comic and tragic. In the plays up to *A Midsummer Night's Dream*, Shakespeare's progress can be traced as a phylogenetic recapitulation of the "main historical movement in drama of the sixteenth century from the generalized didactic morality play to the relatively literal drama as a distinctive art form" (p. 5).

399. VAN DEN BERG, KENT T. *Playhouse and Cosmos: Shakespearean Theater as Metaphor*. Newark: University of Delaware Press; London and Toronto: Associated University Presses, 1985, 192 pp.

Thematic and Topical Studies

Explores Shakespeare's plays as a metaphoric experience, an imaginary world into which the spectator withdraws temporarily from actuality. The developing characterization prompts the spectator to participate emotionally in the activity shaped in the stage world, whether the progress of courtship, the heroic exploits on the battlefield, or the chilling isolation of selfhood in the alienation of the tragic protagonist. Shakespeare's overt attention to his theatrical medium ultimately discloses imaginative insights gained through this unique relationship between stage and actor.

400. VAN LAAN, THOMAS F. *Role-Playing in Shakespeare*. Toronto and London: University of Toronto Press, 1978, 267 pp.

Argues that role-playing through imagery or through actual misrepresentation abounds in Shakespeare's plays and forces the spectators to perceive a character's fulfillment or violation as a role through which he attempts to control his situation. Titus, for example, assumes a revenger's role in place of that of the suffering victim. Romeo enacts a Petrarchan love drama. Hamlet swirls with various roles ranging from that of lover to that of revenger; much of the play involves his search for a psychologically compatible posture. In *Antony and Cleopatra* a dream role triumphs, reducing history to insignificance. A final chapter focuses on the role of the internal dramatist, especially in *The Winter's Tale* and *The Tempest*.

401. VYVYAN, JOHN. *The Shakespearean Ethic*. London: Chatto & Windus, 1959, 208 pp.

Argues that ethical problems exercised an increasing fascination over Shakespeare and that frequently he deliberately sacrificed stage effect to pursue a question of human nature and human relationships. He, moreover, probably chose his plots carefully to permit analysis of the various stages in the tragic dilemma. *Macbeth*, for example, focuses on the aftermath of a deed of horror, while *Othello* examines the stages of temptation; *Hamlet* is concerned with the full impact of the inner conflict.

402. WAIN, JOHN. *The Living World of Shakespeare: A Playgoer's Guide*. London: Macmillan, 1964, 268 pp.

Aims to deepen the appreciation of theatergoers and amchair devotees of Shakespeare who lack a formal study of Elizabethan drama. Shakespeare had the advantage of working in an art form that had come to involve active mental and emotional participation on the part of the spectators. Then, too, he is the supreme artist in the use of the imaginative arts of language, poetry, and figurative prose, and he was fortunate to have a stage and a theater that could effectively accommodate this artistic flexibility. Such principles constitute the major focus in a series of essays on each of the plays, with emphasis constantly on the text and the performance.

403. WATKINS, W. B. C. *Shakespeare and Spenser*. Princeton: Princeton University Press, 1950, 339 pp.

Includes discussion of Shakespeare and Spenser who, as embodiments of the narrative traditions, demonstrate the achievement and potentiality of English poetry. The essays on Shakespeare cover his use of erotic verse ("spiritualized sensuality") in *Venus and Adonis*, *Troilus and Cressida*, *Othello*, and *Antony and Cleopatra* and, through a comparison of *Richard II* and *King Lear*, the evolution of his technique in the use of psychological realism and symbolic stylization and in the delineation of dualities both in matters transient and in matters universal. Yet another chapter compares Spenser's and Shakespeare's use of the concept of marriage.

404. WATSON, ROBERT N. *Shakespeare and the Hazards of Ambition*. Cambridge, Mass.: Harvard University Press, 1984, 360 pp.

Views ambition, in the context of human inherited limitations, as the force that both drives and destroys Shakespeare's tragic characters. The morally ambiguous quality of ambition, more specifically, is painfully apparent in such key scenes as Richard II's recollections of time wasted, Hal's rejection of Falstaff, Macbeth's realization of the equivocation of the witches, or Coriolanus's capitulation to his mother. Attention is also directed to the psychoanalytic implications of a character's efforts to remake his identity.

405. WAYNE, VALERIE, ed. *The Matter of Difference: Materialist Feminist Criticism of Shakespeare*. Ithaca: Cornell University Press, 1991, 348 pp.

Features ten essays investigating Shakespeare's plays in terms of the relations between material conditions of Renaissance culture and differences of gender, race, and ethnic practices. The assumption of these studies is that issues of gender, class, and ethnicity must be considered jointly if one is to achieve a clearer understanding of such concerns as social hierarchy and the law along with the strategies to constrain obedience. The volume includes three essays on the comedies (*Twelfth Night*, *The Merchant of Venice*), four on the tragedies (*Titus Andronicus*, *Othello*), and three on English Renaissance culture.

406. WEISS, THEODORE. *The Breath of Clowns and Kings: Shakespeare's Early Comedies and Histories*. New York: Atheneum, 1971, 339 pp.

Thematic and Topical Studies

Focuses on Shakespeare's ability in his early plays to utilize the stage to depict an expansive view of life. The persistent motif of the comedies is that love enlightens young men; the women are both stimulators to love and also sane educators. In the history plays a second theme emerges, the relationship between word and deed. Richard III is frenetically active as he hacks his way to the throne, delighting in words only as an expression of his egomania. Richard II, to the contrary, loses himself in a "regime of words" that becomes an occupation in itself. In *1,2 Henry IV* words felicitously join with action; Hal, like the young men of the comedies, must be educated—in part through his father, in part through his huge alcoholic companion.

407. WELSFORD, ENID. *The Fool: His Social and Literary History*. London: Faber & Faber, 1935, 381 pp.
    Examines the origins of the role of the fool as entertainer and the relationship of the fool to comedy. Part 3 deals, in part, with the court fool in Elizabethan drama, and part 4 with the stage clown. The principal English clown actors are Richard Tarleton, Will Kemp, and Robert Armin, transforming the type from the guild fool in motley into a mouthpiece for satire and topical allusion. Shakespeare develops the role far beyond that of his contemporaries with Touchstone as the authorized commentator in *As You Like It*, the merry critic of the would-be practitioners of the simple life; Feste as the sage fool who entertains with the truth; and the fool in *Lear* who cures with jest.

408. WILSON, FRANK PERCY. *Shakespearian and Other Studies*. Edited by Helen Gardner. Oxford: Clarendon Press, 1969, 345 pp.
    Includes, among others, essays on the English history play, Shakespeare's comedies, his diction, his reading, his proverbial wisdom, the Elizabethan theater, and memorial accounts of the Elizabethan scholars E. K. Chambers and W. W. Greg. The opening essay defines the history play as one in which character is revealed through politics and whose purpose is essentially instructive. A survey of the stage histories of the early 1590s suggests that Shakespeare's seriousness of purpose is in sharp contrast with the lighter purpose of his contemporaries. The comedies are examined primarily in terms of Shakespeare's working out of his own theories of comic drama.

409. YOUNG, DAVID. *The Heart's Forest: A Study of Shakespeare's Pastoral Plays*. New Haven and London: Yale University Press, 1972, 209 pp.
    Studies *As You Like It*, *King Lear*, *The Winter's Tale*, and *The Tempest* in terms of their stylistic, structural, and thematic relations both to each other and to the pastoral mode. Shakespeare utilizes the pastoral

to examine man's relationship to nature, in the alternate idealization of city and country, in the dream of an idyllic escape giving both sensual and spiritual gratification, in the relative good and evil in the civilized and the primitive worlds. The plays represent the great flexibility of the convention as well as the multiple meanings it can accommodate in the hands of a consummate artist.

410. ZEEVELD, W. GORDON. *The Temper of Shakespeare's Thought*. New Haven and London: Yale University Press, 1974, 266 pp.

Stresses the importance of historical context to the meaning of Shakespeare's plays—for example, the danger of the vestarian controversy in the sixteenth-century church and the English history plays, the topical implications of the differences between monarchy and commonwealth in the Roman histories, actual legal questions argued in the courts of equity, the central problems of *The Merchant of Venice* and *Measure for Measure*, and questions of civility and barbarism in the romances stimulated by the Jacobean brush with new and strange worlds.

II.

The Poems and Sonnets

REFERENCE WORK

411. TANNENBAUM, SAMUEL A., and TANNENBAUM, DOROTHY R. *William Shakespeare: "The Sonnets."* Elizabethan Bibliographies, 10. New York: Privately printed, 1940, 88 pp.

Cites 1,637 unannotated items covering major scholarship on the sonnets from the beginnings to 1938. The material is divided by the following categories and is arranged alphabetically by section—English editions, arrangements, anthologies; translations; musical settings; book titles from the sonnets; commentary. The majority of the material (1,197 items) is loosely classified under commentary.

EDITIONS

412. BOOTH, STEPHEN, ed. *Shakespeare's Sonnets: Edited with Analytic Commentary.* New Haven and London: Yale University Press, 1977, 578 pp.

Attempts through close analysis to resurrect the Renaissance reader's experience with the 1609 quarto, the only textual authority for all the sonnets except 138 and 144. A facsimile of the original publication and a modernized version are set on facing pages with the commentary on the individual sonnets following on pp. 135–538.Each commentary begins with general explicatory observations followed by specific notes

121

on individual lines. A brief section in the appendix reviews major critical theories on the sonnets.

413. CAMPBELL, S. C., ed. *Shakespeare's Sonnets: Edited as a Continuous Sequence*. London: Bell & Hyman; Totowa: Rowman & Littlefield, 1978, 177 pp.

Includes, in addition to the sonnets, introductory comment on the necessary rearrangement of the sonnet order, "A Lover's Complaint," and *The Phoenix and Turtle*. The principal argument of this edition is that the dark-lady sonnets describe a series of ailments—swallowing poison, fever, madness, perjury, danger of death—all of which the poet notes in the past tense as something from which he has recovered. Yet, in the 1609 quarto the latter sonnets precede the former. The rearrangement embeds the dark-lady group in the sonnets to the friend, from which the central theme emerges.

414. PRINCE, F. T., ed. *The Poems*. The Arden Shakespeare. London: Methuen; Cambridge, Mass.: Harvard University Press, 1960, 201 pp.

Includes discussion on the text and literary interpretations as well as appendixes featuring selections from Golding's translation of Ovid's *Metamorphoses*, Chaucer's *The Legend of Good Women*, Painter's *The Palace of Pleasure*, and Ovid's *Fasti*. The modernized texts of *Venus and Adonis* and *The Rape of Lucrece* are from the first quartos, for which the copy was probably Shakespeare's fair copies. The text of *The Passionate Pilgrim* is based on the first quarto for eight of the poems, the second quarto for the remainder. The text of *The Phoenix and Turtle* is from the edition of 1601.

415. ROLLINS, HYDER E., ed. *The Poems: "Venus and Adonis," "Lucrece," "The Passionate Pilgrim," "The Phoenix and Turtle," "A Lover's Complaint."* A New Variorum Edition of Shakespeare. Philadelphia: J. B. Lippincott, 1938, 667 pp.

Uses the first quarto as the copy text in each case. The texts of the poems themselves are printed on pp. 1–368. On each page, for that portion of the text, are cited variant readings, textual notes, and general critical commentary. Following the texts are sections on varying critical opinions, the diverse copies, the dates of composition, sources, general criticism, musical settings, and a list of works consulted.

416. ———. *The Sonnets*. 2 vols. A New Variorum Edition of Shakespeare. Philadelphia and London: J. B. Lippincott, 1944, 1010 pp.

Uses the First Folio as the copy text. The text of the sonnets is printed in volume 1. On each page, for that portion of the text, are cited variant readings, textual notes, and general critical commentary. Volume 2 includes sections on varying critical opinions, the texts of 1609 and 1640, the authenticity of the 1609 text, the date of composition, the arrangement, sources, questions of autobiography, the dedication and Master W. H., the friend, the dark lady, the rival poet, musical settings, general criticism, and a list of works consulted.

417. WELLS, STANLEY, ed. *"Shakespeare's Sonnets" and "A Lover's Complaint."* Oxford: Oxford University Press, 1986, 208 pp.

Features, in addition to the texts of the poems, a critical introduction, alternative versions of four sonnets, and textual notes. Whether urging a friend to marry, expressing jealousy with a friend's new acquaintance, vilifying a mistress who seduces his friend, or exulting in love's illusory triumph over time, Shakespeare's sonnets are "both an endorsement of a convention and a fierce reaction against it" (p. 2). Some, for instance, are irregular in form or meter, as if chafing against restrictive traditions; others transcend their ostensible subject and become "meditations on matters of universal importance" (p. 8).

418. WILSON, JOHN DOVER, ed. *The Sonnets.* 2d ed. The New Cambridge Shakespeare. Cambridge: Cambridge University Press, 1967, 273 pp.

Includes, in addition to the sonnets, introductory essays on the multiple critical theories about the sonnets, the quality of the Thorpe text, the friend and the poet, the identity of Mr. W. H., the themes and sources, and a table of sonnet order. The first quarto copy text, probably a transcript of Shakespeare's, is made up of two classes of sonnets—the framework sonnets described by Meres in 1598 as in circulation among his friends and the private sonnets concerning the young man's sexual misadventures probably secured by Thorpe from the dark lady. Authorities more than likely ordered Thorpe to discontinue further issues shortly after the 1609 quarto appeared in the bookshops.

CRITICISM

The Phoenix and Turtle

419. ARTHOS, JOHN. *Shakespeare's Use of Dream and Vision.* Totowa: Rowman & Littlefield, 1977, 208 pp.

Criticism

Considers the metaphysical dimensions of Shakespeare's work and the frequent use of dreams and visions to illumine the darkness of spirit. In *The Phoenix and Turtle* the poetic persona experiences a dream vision of love in which immortality is attained through sacrifice and resurrection; his friend appears as a phoenix, the turtle as her mate, and "their death through love becomes the means of entry into eternal life" (p. 64). This analysis of the significance of vision and allegory in Shakespeare's early work is used as a touchstone for exploring the use of dream in *A Midsummer Night's Dream*, *Julius Caesar*, *Hamlet*, and *The Tempest*.

420. BATES, RONALD. "Shakespeare's *The Phoenix and the Turtle*." *Shakespeare Quarterly* 6 (1955):19–30.

Examines *The Phoenix and Turtle* in relation to Shakespeare's work as a whole. Whereas the other poems in Chester's volume duly address the phoenix legend symbolizing union, love, and chastity, Shakespeare's approach is the opposite.In the plays of the period (*Hamlet, Troilus and Cressida*) Shakespeare is obsessed with inconstancy, unchastity, and lust; and he conveys something of the same spirit to the poem, denying both the sexual act and posterity. The poem reads like the outline of a drama. The first five stanzas form the dramatis personae, the anthem is the substance in intellectualized form, and the threnos is the epilogue.

421. COPLAND, MURRAY. "The Dead Phoenix." *Essays in Criticism* 15 (1965):279–87.

Views Shakespeare in *The Phoenix and Turtle* as lightly mocking the Platonic joining of the idea of female beauty and the idea of male fidelity. In praising male chastity Shakespeare is intending to shock in the fashionable metaphysical manner. The entire poem seems to be his half-humorous, half-affectionate "pastiche-tribute to the odd charm and elusive structure of the medieval dream-allegory form" (p. 283). The crowning metaphysical shock is to announce that the phoenix is indeed dead. The young are admonished to love and to be true and, above all, to relish this all-too-short human life.

422. CUNNINGHAM, JAMES V. " 'Essence' and *Phoenix and Turtle*." *ELH* 19 (1952):265–6.

Focuses on the statement of the relationship of the lovers in the central part of the poem as love and constancy, beauty and truth, the phoenix and the turtle. The beloved is the essence of the lover; they become one, yet neither annihilates the other. Consumed in flames, they have passed from mortal life into the real life of Ideas. The tradition from which this series of images derives is that of the Beatific

Vision, not that of the scholastic doctrine of love. The mystery confounds reason and finds its solution in love.

423. EMPSON, WILLIAM. *"The Phoenix and Turtle." Essays in Criticism* 16 (1966):147–53.

Finds the central problem to be locating the reason for Shakespeare's praise of the phoenix for extinguishing its breed through married chastity. The collection of poems in which it appears honors the knighthood of John Salisbury in 1601. While Shakespeare's poem expresses the martyrdom of chastity, it is joyously announced as a lie in the first line of the poem followed by Marston proclaiming a new heir. A new phoenix has arisen. The meaning of Shakespeare's poem is clear only when it is seen as a part of the movement of thought in the collection as a whole.

424. GARBER, MARJORIE. "Two Birds with One Stone: Lapidary Reinscription in *The Phoenix and Turtle.*" *Upstart Crow* 5 (1984):5–19.

Describes the poem as a juxtaposition of the elegy (or funerary inscription) and the epithalamium. The poem's curious diction underscores the paradox created by the union of inscription and wedding song. Three assumptions are basic to the progress of the poem: reason is useless in explaining the radical mysteries of love and death; the phoenix symbolizes a union of the temporal and the atemporal; the poem is about the condition of poetry. The love of the wedded pair is celebrated, but the actual event is a funeral. Shakespeare seizes in the phoenix the opportunity to fuse the two antithetical forms.

425. MATCHETT, WILLIAM H. *"The Phoenix and the Turtle": Shakespeare's Poem and Chester's "Loues Martyr."* Studies in English Literature, 1. The Hague: Mouton, 1965, 213 pp.

Argues that the poem, in the context of Chester's *Love's Martyr*, depicts Elizabeth and Essex as the phoenix and the turtle. The subject concerns not personal love but the mutual understanding that might have made Essex "the Queen's copartner in governing the country and determining the succession" (p. 194). A section of elaborate praise is countered by "Threnos," Reason's response in light of the sterile and tragic conclusion of the relationship. While Shakespeare was no doubt deeply shocked by Essex's disgrace, he uses Reason to mitigate and moderate this response; despite the magnitude of the loss, the world is not totally bereft of virtue and beauty.

426. UNDERWOOD, RICHARD A. *Shakespeare's "The Phoenix and Turtle": A Survey of Scholarship.* Elizabethan Studies, 15. Salzburg: Institut für englische Sprache und Literatur, Universität Salzburg, 1974, 366 pp.

The Sonnets

Systematically examines the history of previous scholarship. In general the critics speak for themselves as verbatim extracts make up virtually half the text. The chronological survey of scholarship is followed by the varying opinions concerning the authenticity of the text, the date of composition, the allegorical meaning, the sources, and the relationship of the poem to the plays. The poem is not an anomaly in Shakespeare's work; it provides a distinctive tone and theme for the Chester collection much as Shakespeare's songs make a functional tonal and thematic contribution to their stage worlds.

THE SONNETS

427. ACHESON, ARTHUR. *Shakespeare's Sonnet Story, 1592–1598*. New York: Edmond Byrne Hackett, 1933, 680 pp.

   Attempts to arrange the sonnets in chronological order by "books" (each with twenty sonnets) and to demonstrate their autobiographical nature, in part a comparison with similar personal phases in the plays. Anne Davenant, the first wife of John Davenant, is identified as the dark lady of the sonnets. The bulk of the sonnets were written to the Earl of Southampton between 1592 and 1599. In the publication, pursued by John Florio and George Chapman as an attack on Shakespeare, the sonnets were "disarranged both sequentially and chronologically" (p. 35).

428. BERG, SANDRA VAN DEN. " 'Mutual Ordering': Subjectivity and Language in Shakespeare's Sonnets." In *Contending Kingdoms: Historical, Psychological, and Feminist Approaches to the Literature of Sixteenth-Century England and France*. Edited by Marie-Rose Logan and Peter L. Rudnytsky. Detroit: Wayne State University Press, 1991, pp.173–201.

   Insists that the most significant trope in the sonnets is the mother/child bond that, "because it can attach to different characters and different aspects of erotic life, testifies to the enduring power of that bond in shaping the adult drama of desire" (p. 195). Shakespeare exploits this gendered role of mother at one moment to express his own feelings as subject to object, at another to suggest qualities within the young man, at another to indicate maternal absence in the dark lady. This "free-floating idea" is at the core of the sonnets' dramatic theme of merging and separation, of imaginary union and symbolic reunion.

429. BERMANN, SANDRA L. *The Sonnet over Time: A Study in the Sonnets of Petrarch, Shakespeare, and Baudelaire*. Chapel Hill: University of North Carolina Press, 1988, 174 pp.

Argues that lyric language reaches beyond ordinary assumptions and perceptions and that the sonnet, in its enforced brevity, leaves its fictions mysteriously inconclusive and indeterminate. The themes of Shakespeare's sonnets—time, death, the ambiguities of human relationships—are among the most powerful. His mental pictures derive in part from his vocabulary but above all from his vivid tropes. By distinguishing two sides of human love in contrasting figures of the male friend and the mistress, Shakespeare "effectively expands and humanizes the powerful psychological drama concealed within the Petrarchan tradition" (p. 85).

430. BOOTH, STEPHEN. *An Essay on Shakespeare's Sonnets*. New Haven and London: Yale University Press, 1969, 218 pp.

Demonstrates the organization of Shakespeare's sonnets as a multitude of coexistent and conflicting patterns—"formal, logical, ideological, syntactic, rhythmic, and phonetic" (p. ix). A part of the reader's pleasure derives from the movement of his ordered experience from one frame of reference to another. The sonnets depend upon a conflict in what is said and what the reader expects, the vocabulary of one kind of experience used to describe another. While the reader has the comfort of recognizing these rhetorical patterns, he also confronts exaggerated predictability and surprise, pertinence and impertinence, and the collision of value systems.

431. CROCKETT, BRYAN. "Word Boundary and Syntactic Line in Shakespeare's Sonnets." *Style* 24 (1990):600–10.

Concludes, through a stylistic analysis of the first one hundred sonnets, that syntactic structure contributes strongly to the sense of closure in the final couplet. The couplets have a higher proportion of phonetic words, a marked tendency to reinforce the iambic meter with syntactic breaks after the ictic positions, and a higher proportion of midline breaks.

432. DUBROW, HEATHER. *Captive Victors: Shakespeare's Narrative Poems and Sonnets*. Ithaca: Cornell University Press, 1987, 277 pp.

Treats systematically the connections between the sonnets and the narrative poems, maintaining that Shakespeare uses rhetoric to create characters as rich in philosophical and moral complexities as those found in his dramatic works. In each case the characters in the poems attempt to oppose change with an alternative ideal, whether in the elegiac vision of Lucrece or in the deification of constancy in the sonnets. Love for these characters is typically seen as a form of entrapment—Adonis caught in Venus's arms, Lucrece penned in by the bedclothes. Through

The Sonnets

the use of rhetorical power to deceive and dominate they become captive victors in an emotional relationship.

433. ENGLE, LARS. "Afloat in Thick Deeps: Shakespeare's Sonnets on Certainty." *PMLA* 104 (1989):832–3.

Believes that the sonnets, in which the theme is the achievement of a permanence or stability in beauty that opposes itself to death, are anti-essentialist or anti-Platonic in nature. This quality is what gives the poems a modernity, even a contemporaneity. By suggesting how love is fueled by social economics of human value, the poems reflect a deidealized concept of what makes things cohesive, "a world view in which 'truth' and lasting value are simply what a mutable community, for a variety of discussible reasons, chooses to regard as good for a long time" (p. 832).

434. FINEMAN, JOEL. *Shakespeare's Perjured Eye: The Invention of Poetic Subjectivity in the Sonnets*. Berkeley: University of California Press, 1986, 365 pp.

Accepts the traditional division of the sonnets, 1–127 addressed to a young man, 127–54 addressed to the dark lady. The first section represents the language of the eye, of affection that unites sign and signified, subject and object. The second section represents the language of the tongue, falsity that fractures former attachments. Moreover, the young man's infidelity is replicated by the dark lady's infidelity, and the betrayal is compounded by their own relationship. The sonnets themselves also become a point of departure for thoughts on larger issues such as the trappings of gender, the nature of modern subjectivity, and the function of literary history.

435. FOSTER, DONALD W. "Master W. H., R.I.P." *PMLA* 102 (1987):42–54.

Argues that "ever-living poet" in Thorpe's brief address to Master W. H. refers not to Shakespeare but to "our Lord," that "the only begetter" refers to Shakespeare the poet, and that "Master W. H." is a printer's misprint for what Thorpe actually wrote, "W. SH." All of this would suggest that the "notice" is an ordinary advertisement to the reader that all of the sonnets are by William Shakespeare.

436. FRASER, RUSSELL. "Shakespeare at Sonnets." *Sewanee Review* 97 (1989):408–27.

Takes John Crowe Ransom to task for his scarifying analysis of Shakespeare's sonnets, arguing that Shakespeare is voluntarily defective, working with a pattern to adjust or depart from in exploring a creative opposition. A master of dissemination, this poet is nonperspective. The questions he raises are answerable but only in their complexity. His is not a kernel of truth at the center, but multiple layers of thought from which the meaning is comprehensive.

437. GREENE, THOMAS M. "Pitiful Thrivers: Foiled Husbandry in the Sonnets." In *Shakespeare and the Question of Theory*. Edited by Patricia Parker and Geoffrey Hartman. New York and London: Methuen, 1985, pp. 230–44.

Reads the sonnets as attempts to cope with ever more "progressively powerful and painful forms of cost and expense" (p. 243), the conflict of values among a friend, a mistress, and a rival. Central to this concept is sonnet 125, which appears to offer the possibility of a "stable existential economics, a definitive end to penury, a compensation for the expense of living and feeling" (p. 240). The "pitiful thrivers" are those who attempt to profit emotionally from a relationship; the "mutual render" suggests an adequate economic system that avoids the wastes of excessive rent.

438. HAMMOND, GERALD. *The Reader and Shakespeare's Young Man Sonnets*. Totowa: Barnes & Noble, 1981, 247 pp.

Assumes that Thorpe's ordering of the sonnets in the 1609 quarto is essentially correct and examines the carefully designed sequence of sonnets dealing with the poet's need to function biologically and artistically. The general movement of the poems is from Shakespeare's almost total dependence on a human relationship to a realization of self-sufficiency in his verse. The reader is manipulated to a position of sympathy for the poet, disapproval of the young man, and scorn for the rival poet.

439. HOTSON, LESLIE. *Mr. W. H.* New York: Alfred A. Knopf, 1964, 328 pp.

Searches the sonnets themselves for identification of the "Mr. W. H." to whom the 1609 quarto is dedicated. The friend in the text is described as monarch, sovereign, prince, and king; his identity is William Hatfield of Lincolnshire, a noble youth of such beauty and character that he was chosen to be "TrueLove," Gray's Inn's Christmas King for 1588–1589. The dark lady was Luce Morgan; the rival poet, Marlowe. The order of the sonnets represents Shakespeare's own arrangement. The sonnets are poems of Shakespeare's youth; *Love's Labor's Lost* was written for the same Gray's Inn celebration.

440. ———. *Shakespeare's Sonnets Dated and Other Essays*. New York: Oxford University Press, 1949, 244 pp.

The Sonnets

Examines the topical sonnets against the principal events in England and Europe between 1585 and 1605. The "mortall Moone" sonnet (107) refers to the defeat of the Spanish Armada. The "pyramyds" of sonnet 123 refer to the re-creation of four obelisks from 1586 to 89. The "blow of thralled discontent" in sonnet 124 refers to the assassination of King Henri III of France in 1588. Such references confirm that Shakespeare completed the main group of his sonnets by 1589 and that he reached a remarkable stage of maturity by twenty-five in the l580s when the fad of the sonnet sequence was at its height.

441. HUBLER, EDWARD. *The Sense of Shakespeare's Sonnets*. Princeton: Princeton University Press, 1952, 169 pp.
    Observes that the sonnet, limited by its very form to the development of a single mood, image, or thought, provides a means for the expression of Shakespeare's major ideas before he was able to objectify and interweave them in the medium of drama—perceptions of friendship, the dynamics of personality in the experience of sin and expiation, the power of love and lust, the craft of the writer, the ultimate aims of poetry, the basis of reputation.

442. HUBLER, EDWARD, et al. *The Riddle of Shakespeare's Sonnets*. New York: Basic Books, 1962, 346 pp.
    Includes the text of the sonnets, introductory comments by Hubler, essays by Northrop Frye, Leslie Fiedler, Stephen Spender, and R. P. Blackmur, and the full text of Oscar Wilde's *The Portrait of Mr. W. H.* Hubler presents a chronological sketch of the critical history, noting the various putative identifications of the personae in the sequence. Frye describes the sonnets as a poetic realization of the whole range of love in the Western world, from the idealism of Petrarch to the disillusionment and frustrations of Proust. Fiedler focuses on the pure masculine principle corrupted by the female, Spender on Shakespeare's power to universalize the most fundamental human emotions, Blackmur on the duality of voices in love—the conscious and the unconscious.

443. JACKSON, MACDONALD P. "How Many Horses Has Sonnet 51? Textual and Literary Criticism in Shakespeare's Sonnets." *English Language Notes* 27, no. 3 (1989–90):10–19.
    Argues that overingenious poststructural criticism with its affinity for shaping perplexing readings rather than complex ones endangers our understanding and appreciation of Shakespeare's sonnets. For instance, in sonnet 51 emendation of "naigh" to "neigh" (l. 11) by virtually all modern critics creates a ludicrous, if perplexing, image of

neighing desire. The crux is either the consequence of compositor B's stupid misreading or, under the influence of the equestrian image being developed, turning "waigh noe" into "naigh noe," the verb then being "weigh," not "neigh." The caveat is to "sanction only puzzlements built in by the author" (p. 17).

444. KENNEDY, WILLIAM J. "Petrarchan Textuality: Commentaries and Gender Revisions." In *Discourse of Authority in Medieval and Renaissance Literature*. Edited by Kevin Brownlee and Walter Stephens. Hanover and London: University Press of New England for Dartmouth College, 1989, pp. 159–68.

Comments on the gender revision in Shakespeare's sonnet 8, with a male as speaker and another male as audience. The poem takes the form of a debate. Following a skeptical questioning of his friend's preference for loud music, the poet builds the second quatrain on the word *concord*, oxymoronic because the friend may not find it harmonious. The third quatrain poses a paradox, that the friend should cease being *one* and become *one* in marriage. In the abrupt conclusion he doubly mocks the friend through a pun; he will be *none* (nothing) unless he marries—and his celibacy will relegate him to the cloister of a *nun*.

445. KNIGHT, G. WILSON. *The Mutual Flame: On Shakespeare's Sonnets and "The Phoenix and the Turtle."* London: Methuen, 1955, 233 pp.

Attempts, not to settle the problems of the sonnets in factual and biographical terms, but to investigate these poems as the spiritual principle behind all Shakespeare's work. The sonnets deal with issues of time, death, and eternity in the context of sexual drive and human aspiration. The bisexuality reflected in them is a window to his dramas—the reconciliation of the sexes in the romantic comedies, the interweaving of Apollonian and Dionysian principles in the histories and tragedies, the address to the miraculous youth's eternal significance in the romances.

446. KRIEGER, MURRAY. *A Window to Criticism: Shakespeare's "Sonnets" and Modern Poetics*. Princeton: Princeton University Press, 1964, 224 pp.

Suggests that the miracle of poetry is the tension between the presence of moral contradictions and the power of order, for the sonnet the interworking of the Petrarchan convention, the Courtly Love convention, and the image of the individual poem. Shakespeare's sonnets comprise a "memorial tomb of love to which, as a womb, it gives eternal life" (p. 193). The paradoxical quality of his literal image (the transforming power of love, of youth, of spiritual union) functions as

The Sonnets

a mirror by which to assume universal qualities. Serving as the "typological figura," they are the microcosm explaining the macrocosm of poetry.

447. LANDRY, HILTON. *Interpretations in Shakespeare's Sonnets*. Berkeley and Los Angeles: University of California Press, 1963, 185 pp.

Reviews the major themes of the sonnets, concluding that the order in the 1609 quarto is essentially correct, that the surrounding sonnets serve as the best gloss for an individual poem, and that Shakespeare consciously works for ambiguity of feeling, syntax, and descriptive meaning. Unlike either the Elizabethans or Donne, Shakespeare frequently scatters his imagery, gaining unity through subtle associative processes. The structure is as varied as the imagery with grammatical, rhetorical, and logical patterns in evidence. The couplet may reiterate, supplement, contradict, qualify, or render ironic and humorous. Shakespeare's sonnets, in a sense, are both Elizabethan and metaphysical.

448. ———, ed. *New Essays on Shakespeare's Sonnets*. New York: AMS Press, 1976, 276 pp.

Contains essays on Shakespeare's sonnets by Rodney Poisson (on the theme of friendship in 18–26), Martin Seymour-Smith (a psychological reading of 1–42), W. G. Ingram (the quality of the Shakespearean sonnet as distinguished from the work of his contemporaries), Winifred Nowottny (form and style in 97–126), Anton M. Pirkhofer (the dramatic character), Hilton Landry (on Ivor Winters's and John Crowe Ransom's dislike of the sonnets), Marshall Lindsay (on French translations), Paul Ramsey (on syllabic structure), and Theodore Redpath (on the punctuation).

449. LEISHMAN, J. B. *Themes and Variations in Shakespeare's Sonnets*. London: Hutchinson, 1961, 254 pp.

Examines Shakespeare's sonnets within the context of the European poetic tradition. Part 1 surveys the dual themes of immortality through poetry for another and immortality for the poet himself as they appear in Horace, Ovid, Petrarch, Tasso, Ronsard, and the English sonneteers. Part 2 focuses on the theme of human transiency from classical times to Shakespeare; Shakespeare combines the theme of immortality with the theme of human transiency in a uniquely powerful manner. Part 3 concentrates on the use of hyperbole as a device for constructing a spiritual basis for evaluating the friend as the archetype of all beauty and excellence.

450. McGUIRE, PHILIP C. "Shakespeare's Non-Shakespearean Sonnets." *Shakespeare Quarterly* 38 (1987):304–19.

Urges scholars and readers, in order to appreciate more fully the variety and richness of the poems, to abandon the assumption that Shakespeare's sonnets invariably adhere to the so-called Shakespearean or English sonnet form—of three quatrains followed by a couplet. In number 29, for example, the sonnet (abab bcbc cdcd ee) breaks free of traditional form at the moment the poet breaks free from a state of self-despising. In number 21 (abab cdcd ecec ff), the moment of deviation authenticates the poet's abdication of traditional Petrarchan comparisons in order to "truly write" (l. 8). In number 3 (abab cdcd dede dd) the *d* rhymes embody a process of acoustic reproduction that reinforces the poet's call for his friend to marry and propagate.

451. MARTIN, PHILIP. *Shakespeare's Sonnets: Self, Love, and Art*. Cambridge: Cambridge University Press, 1972, 169 pp.

Believes that Shakespeare's feeling for selfhood underlies the whole body of the sonnets, interacting with poetry, with mutability, and with love for others. A discussion of the themes of destructive and constructive narcissism precedes a comparison of Shakespeare's love poetry with that of his contemporary sonneteers and that of Donne. Both Shakespeare and Donne transcend rather than work within the Petrarchan tradition, Donne primarily mocking and Shakespeare running the gamut from parody to a naturalistic revitalization of old themes. Both poets ultimately come to envision love itself as a power greater than the art that creates it.

452. MIZENER, ARTHUR. "The Structure of Figurative Language in Shakespeare's Sonnets." *Southern Review* 5 (1940):730–47.

Constitutes a defensive response to John Crowe Ransom's attack on Shakespeare's sonnets. Shakespeare's method is fundamentally different from that of the metaphysical poet; whereas Donne uses an illogical image that requires logical analysis, Shakespeare uses a logical image that requires figurative interpretation. The unique power of Shakespeare is in the intense metaphoric interaction—for example, love in sonnet 124 as time's blooming favorite, its hate, a worldly courtier, a house built in sand. His verbal construct requires a structure of figurative language that approaches the density and logical incompleteness of the mind itself.

453. MUIR, KENNETH. *Shakespeare's Sonnets*. London: George Allen & Unwin, 1979, 179 pp.

The Sonnets

Discusses the date, text, and order of the sonnets, then Shakespeare's greater indebtedness to Erasmus, Ovid, and Sidney than to Petrarch. In addition to extensive focus on the several groups of sonnets, individual chapters address the style, the poetic quality, the links with his other work, and a brief history of critical interpretation. One of the most significant features is Shakespeare's variety of structure within the three quatrain-couplet pattern—from the rhetorical structure of propositio, ratio, confirmatio, and conclusion to the couplet as summarial or paradoxical, the quatrains as cumulative or qualifying.

454. PARKER, DAVID. "Verbal Moods in Shakespeare's Sonnets." *Modern Language Quarterly* 30 (1969):331–39.
    Suggests that the sonnets be considered, not in biographical terms, but in terms of their rhetorical qualities. Virtually all of them are elaborate disguises of the imperative mood, and some play off one mood against another; in the first quatrain of sonnet 3, for example, the imperative mood ("Look in thy glass") turns to subjunctive ("that face should form another") and in turn shifts to the present indicative ("Thou dost beguile the world"). The important point is the dramatic quality. The sonnets, which are not static, register the mind in process.

455. PEQUIGNEY, JOSEPH. *Such Is My Love: A Study of Shakespeare's Sonnets.* Chicago: University of Chicago Press, 1985, 249 pp.
    Argues that the sonnet sequence constitutes "the grand masterpiece of homoerotic poetry" (p. 1), describing a complex and psychologically realistic story of the poet's erotic attachment to and sexual involvement with the fair young man of 1–126. Sonnets 127–54, dealing with the dark lady and the poet's lust for her, are read as a footnote to and elaboration of the crisis of jealousy described in 40–42. Such a reading suggests that the present order of the sonnets is essentially correct.

456. RAMSEY, PAUL. *The Fickle Glass: A Study of Shakespeare's Sonnets.* AMS Studies in the Renaissance, 4. New York: AMS Press, 1979, 242 pp.
    Focuses on the meter, rhetoric, structure, and major themes (negation and Neoplatonism) of Shakespeare's sonnets. Undeniably, critics unsympathetic with Elizabethan poetics can find faults. There is tautology because repetition of idea, sound, imagery, syntactical pattern, and rhythm is built into the form. There is metrical and rhetorical elaboration, in part reflecting the Renaissance love of artistic copiousness. There is at times obscurity, whether from vacillation, condensation, or abused metaphor. Above all, however, the sonnets tell of love in all its variations of ecstasy, grandeur, shame, and self-humiliation.

457. RANSOM, JOHN CROWE. "Shakespeare at Sonnets." *Southern Review* 3 (1938):531–53.

Describes Shakespeare's sonnets as generally ill constructed and metrically deficient, bound by a too arbitrary quatrain-couplet form. The imagery is often conventional or literary, shaped more by cliche than by genuine observation; the poetry is associative rather than behavioristic, filled with pretty words and indefinite analogies. The sonnets are mixed in effect. Some of the most successful are metaphysical in style; not even his later plays provide examples of better metaphysical effects. The lyric poem is the poet's microcosm whereas poetry in drama must serve the prior and peremptory claims of the stage.

458. ROSMARIN, ADENA. "Hermeneutics versus Erotics: Shakespeare's Sonnets and Interpretive History." *PMLA* 100 (1985):20–37.

Suggests that the problematic in Shakespeare's sonnets arises in large part from a disjunction between form and content. In form they are proffered by a poet who dexterously manipulates rhetorical devices to affirm his skills; in substance they are poems in which a love registers a sense of genuinely painful affection. Paradoxically, however, the power of the sonnets arises from this very struggle between *res* and *verba*.

459. STERNFIELD, F. W.; NEJGEBAUER, A.; AND LEVER, J. W. "Twentieth-Century Studies in Shakespeare's Songs, Sonnets, and Poems." *Shakespeare Survey* 15 (1962):1–30.

Surveys major work in the twentieth century on Shakespeare's music, sonnets, and poems. In music perhaps the most significant developments are the bibliographic and photographic facilities that make possible a fine degree of accuracy and detail. The amount of writing on the sonnets is second only to that on *Hamlet*; on the whole, criticism of the sonnets will not bear comparison with that of the plays, but there is a marked increase in sobriety. Among the poems *Venus and Adonis* has passed from virtual disregard to general acclaim, and interest in *The Phoenix and Turtle* has passed from identification of personae to themes.

460. STIRLING, BRENTS. *The Shakespeare Sonnet Order: Poems and Groups.* Berkeley and Los Angeles: University of California Press, 1968, 317 pp.

Argues that the extremely close linkages in several groups of Shakespeare's sonnets must be taken as Shakespeare's norm of cogency and that the place of thematic non sequiturs must be interpreted as a result of Thorpe's fragmentation. This reconstruction of the sonnet

The Sonnets

chronology is based less on the confused riddles of continuous narrative than on principles of multiple interconnections (theme, recurring metaphor or phrase) and the consequences on the surrounding sonnets (the standard of coherence).

461. WHEELER, RICHARD P. " 'And My Loud Crying Still': The *Sonnets, The Merchant of Venice*, and *Othello*." In *Shakespeare's "Rough Magic": Renaissance Essays in Honor of C. L. Barber*. Edited by Peter Erickson and Coppélia Kahn. Newark: University of Delaware Press; London and Toronto: Associated University Presses, 1985, pp. 193–200.

Observes that all three works focus on tensions that develop within and between a male bond of friendship and a sexual bond of man and woman. In the *Sonnets* the friendship is rendered increasingly unstable by a woman as an agent of sexual depletion and degradation for poet and friend. In *The Merchant of Venice* the threat of losing Bassanio's friendship casts Antonio into a melancholy exacerbated by the monetary bond that threatens his life. In *Othello*, the action drives the Moor into a symbolic male marriage between the undramatized marriage vows and the final consummation in death for both wife and husband. The unfocused verbal violence in the sonnets and *The Merchant of Venice* functions as a surrogate for death, and death in turn functions as a resolving agent in *Othello*.

462. WILSON, KATHERINE M. *Shakespeare's Sugared Sonnets*. London: George Allen & Unwin; New York: Barnes & Noble, 1974, 382 pp.

Traces the major attributes of the Elizabethan sonnet to primitive song, the chivalric convention, and Platonic theory. Shakespeare's use of and references to the sonnet in his early plays suggests that he considered the form puerile. In the context of writing his sonnet sequence he was consciously moving from the old sugared Petrarchan style to a plain speech of real love. The quality of style that seems to have impressed Shakespeare's contemporaries is his ability to catch "reality-experience in a verbal structure with layers of association" (p. 321), a quality resulting in rich polyphonic verbal tone.

463. WINNY, JAMES. *The Master-Mistress: A Study of Shakespeare's Sonnets*. London: Chatto & Windus, 1968, 216 pp.

Aims at an imaginative rather than biographical interpretation of Shakespeare's sonnets. An understanding of such poems can perhaps be achieved by investigating the nature of the particular imaginative experience that prompts him to write, "happenings inside the private world which is the field of his creative consciousness" (p. 22). The key appears to be in Shakespeare's dualistic nature, in a continuous self-destructive struggle within a body too deeply divided against itself to achieve unity, a theme traceable in the sonnets, narrative poems, and early history plays.

The Rape of Lucrece

464. DUBROW, HEATHER. "A Mirror for Complaints: Shakespeare's *Lucrece* and Generic Tradition." In *Renaissance Genres: Essays on Theory, History, and Interpretation*. Edited by Barbara Lewalski. Cambridge: Harvard University Press, 1986, pp. 399–417.

   Observes that Shakespeare's poem is written within the complaint tradition but that it also is crafted as a critique of that tradition. One significant feature that distinguishes it from other complaint poems is its attention to the psychological implications behind issues treated more uncritically elsewhere. As a member of a shame culture (one in which individuals primarily fear the disapproval of others), Lucrece is above all concerned with how the rape will affect her fame, her identity. By embedding her reaction within those of other figures, Shakespeare qualifies the Renaissance notion that language provides a useful purgation for one's emotions; carried to the extreme, language may even exacerbate the passions.

465. ———. "The Rape of Clio: Attitudes to History in Shakespeare's *Lucrece*." *English Literary Renaissance* 16 (1986):425–41.

   Maintains that *The Rape of Lucrece* implicitly comments on historiography and the nature of language. Renaissance historians were acutely aware of conditions that prevented their knowing the full truth. It is evident that Shakespeare in writing this poem confronted a number of different and even contradictory accounts. Ovid and Livy disagree, for instance, not only in facts but in tone as well. Shakespeare plays different methods of interpreting the past against each other by associating each of the principal characters with a distinctive approach to history. Ultimately, the poem encourages the reader to be circumspect, to evaluate history and its sources better than the characters within the narrative are able to do.

466. HYNES, SAM. "The Rape of Tarquin." *Shakespeare Quarterly* 10 (1959):451–53.

   Sees in the description of the tapestry depicting the fall of Troy an emblem of Lucrece's rape. Critics who have complained about its length and artificiality have failed to observe that the metaphor has shifted in

The Sonnets

l. 715 to Tarquin not as the besieger but as the besieged. We confront the rapist's soul torn with guilt, and in this moment we glimpse something of the vision Shakespeare was to develop in his great tragedies.

467. MAUS, KATHARINE EISAMAN. "Taking Tropes Seriously: Language and Violence in Shakespeare's *The Rape of Lucrece.*" *Shakespeare Quarterly* 37 (1986):66–82.

Observes that Shakespeare's poem concentrates not upon the action of the rape but upon Tarquin's frame of mind leading up to it and Lucrece's frame of mind after it. In both cases the tragedy arises from the individuals' being driven by a metaphor that they accept as literal and true. Tarquin, in his struggle between honor and desire, adopts a military metaphor in which he is a soldier commanded by affection. Lucrece subsequently determines to commit suicide because she metaphorically envisions herself as a fortress or a house that has been ransacked and its contents, however innocent of the event, mutilated and tainted.

468. VICKERS, NANCY. " 'The Blazon of Sweet Beauty's Best': Shakespeare's *Lucrece.*" In *Shakespeare and the Question of Theory.* Edited by Patricia Parker and Geoffrey Hartman. New York and London: Methuen, 1985, pp. 95–115.

Examines the poem in terms of the rhetorical tradition of blazon, a cataloguing of the beauties of separate parts of the female body. *Lucrece* is set in motion by a competition between husbands, each blazoning his wife's beauties. The poem reveals "the rhetorical strategies that descriptive occasions generate, and underline[s] the potential consequences of being female matter for male oratory" (p. 96). More specifically, Shakespeare locates the ultimate cause of Tarquin's desire for and rape of Lucrece in the excessive praise lavished upon her by the husband Collatine in a contest of epideictic oratory.

469. WADLEY, HAROLD R. *"The Rape of Lucrece* and Shakespearean Tragedy." *PMLA* 76 (1961):480–87.

Views the poem as an illuminating document concerning Shakespeare's development and his coming of age as an artist. One of the "most laborious and studied" of Shakespeare's works it is a revealing index to his mind. Significantly, the poem's narrative is a sequence of highly dramatic situations visualized as scenes to be staged. Major emphasis, though, is on the inner human conflict and the conditions and connotations of the physical action. The moral issue is presented in purely personal tragic terms.

138

470. WILSON, R. ROWDEN. "Shakespearean Narrative: *The Rape of Lucrece* Reconsidered." *Studies in English Literature 1500–1900* 28 (1988):39–59.

    Views the early poem as a "compendium" or "encyclopedia" of the narrative conventions that inform many of Shakespeare's plays. The characters in drama, for example, often relate the narrative as well as become centrally involved in it. Moreover, as is the case when Tarquin approaches Lucrece's bed with a divided mind, characters of split awareness appear throughout the dramatic canon. The deepening of Lucrece's characterization through the use of interior monologue is another obvious example, as is the technique of depicting the narrative from multiple points of view.

Venus and Adonis

471. BAUMLIN, TITA FRENCH. "The Birth of the Bard: *Venus and Adonis* and Poetic Apotheosis." *Papers on Language and Literature* 26 (1990):191–211.

    Claims that the poem is paradoxically most successful in its failure as an Ovidian love poem, in its rejection of its model. Whereas Adonis willingly submits to Venus's advances in Ovid, the goddess is unsuccessful in winning him as a paramour in Shakespeare's version. The emphasis is focused more on the poet's self-conscious attention to her language as she woos and fails. What begins in erotic, ironic comedy verbalized in ineffective, imitative Petrarchisms ends in a funeral elegy in which the elegiac poet eloquently mourns nature's own loss of Adonis.

472. FEINBERG, NONA. "Thematics of Value in *Venus and Adonis*." *Criticism* 31 (1989):21–32.

    Explores the view of the feminine in Shakespeare's early poem, noting that Venus's mutability and diversity contrast with Adonis's fixity and absoluteness. At times she represents the object of male misogyny—a threat to male potency, to patriarchy, to the structure of authority. A feminist reading of the poem suggests that Venus represents "a liberating reevaluation of the patriarchal world she both plays in and subverts, as she demonstrates the usefulness of a thematics of value to expose the limitation of absolutist perspectives" (p. 31).

473. KLAUSE, JOHN. "*Venus and Adonis*: Can We Forgive Them?" *Studies in Philology* 85 (1988):353–77.

The Sonnets

Maintains that only the perspective of forgiveness is sufficiently comprehensive to accommodate in a single response the need to scorn and admire, to condemn and bless. The idea of forgiving Venus and Adonis is a radical one since they do not confess and repent. Adonis remains stubborn, petulant, and shallow to the end; Venus never questions the legitimacy of her passions or the means by which she attempts to satisfy them. Shakespeare appears, nonetheless, to invite the reader to pardon them because they, like Falstaff, are "somehow too much a part of us to abandon to the strictures of principle" (p. 375).

474. LEECH, CLIFFORD. "Venus and Her Nun: Portraits of Women in Love by Shakespeare and Marlowe." *Studies in English Literature 1500–1900* 5 (1965):247–68.

Notes that, just as Shakespeare and Marlowe are instrumental in the development of English drama, so they are also pivotal in the popularization of Ovidian love poems in the 1590s. To read the mass of them is to recognize anew the creative talent of these two writers in *Venus and Adonis* and *Hero and Leander*. Their influence may go beyond the cult of the epyllion; it may well have set the conventions and the modes for the delineation of women in love in the plays of 1592 and thereafter.

475. LINDHEIM, NANCY. "The Shakespearean *Venus and Adonis*." *Shakespeare Quarterly* 37 (1986):190–203.

Views the poem as pivotal in Shakespeare's development. Coming between the apprentice comedies (like *The Comedy of Errors* and *The Two Gentlemen of Verona*) and those plays that represent the artistic maturation of his early period (like *A Midsummer Night's Dream* and *Romeo and Juliet*), *Venus and Adonis* is the playwright's earliest exploration of the nature of love. Here he begins to perceive love as an experience beyond sensual ecstasy, with a dark underside and the possibility of pain, and to explore it through a series of tonal shifts from the serious to the comic to the satiric. Thus, the poem's richest connections are not with Marlowe and Ovid but with his own subsequent plays.

476. MILLER, ROBERT P. "Venus, Adonis, and the Horses." *ELH* 19 (1952):249–64.

Defends the episode of the courser and the jennet as thematically significant to the work as a whole. Considered symbolically, it reflects a moral dimension in the poem and thus heightens and enhances Shakespeare's concept of love. When Adonis exhibits sound Renaissance morality in confronting Venus's advances, she—by praising the courser (the beast, animal man, conventional symbol of lust) as something for Adonis to emulate—makes her own passion unmistakable, namely, that she desires abandonment to sensual pleasure for its own sake.

477. PUTNEY, RUFUS. *"Venus and Adonis*: Amour with Humor." *Philological Quarterly* 20 (1974):533–48.

   Asserts that Elizabethan readers delighted in the rhetorical hyperboles of *Venus and Adonis* and that it is a sparkling and sophisticated comedy, not a lascivious and erotic narrative. Shakespeare's alterations of Ovid, such as the notion of a coy Adonis and the inability of the goddess of love to win her prey, are decidedly comic. So, too, is Adonis's exclamation that he is too young for an amorous encounter, a claim denied by his sweaty palm. Recognition of the demonstrably comic Ovidian tradition frees *Venus* from much of the critical attack to which it has been subjected.

III.

The English-History Plays

GENERAL STUDIES

478. BERRY, EDWARD I. *Patterns of Decay: Shakespeare's Early Histories*. Charlottesville: University Press of Virginia, 1975, 130 pp.

Focuses on a dominant theme in the *Henry VI-Richard III* sequence, expressed in language, character, and action, that both lends unity to the individual stage world and also marks a stage in the process of social and political organization that characterizes the entire series. The movement is generally away from the chivalric community idealized in Talbot in *1 Henry VI* to the maniacal tyranny represented in *Richard III*. The vision of history as process gives the series its meaning and form as distinct from the emphasis on personality that dominates the later histories.

479. BLANPIED, JOHN W. *Time and the Artist in Shakespeare's English Histories*. Newark: University of Delaware Press; London and Toronto: Associated University Presses, 1983, 278 pp.

Considers Shakespeare's English histories to be a nine-part sequence concerned with the evolving relationship between history and drama, the struggle between past facts and his creative imagination, which labors to cast the dramatic situation into compelling dramatic form. In the course of these plays Shakespeare moves from an objective, passive scrutiny of facts to energetic insights into relationships between the dead past and the seething present. This progress toward generative drama also involves a movement in delineating the king-figure from "antic" to "Machiavellian."

General Studies

480. BROMLEY, JOHN C. *The Shakespearean Kings*. Boulder: Colorado Associated University Presses, 1971, 138 pp.

Notes that, unlike the ethical reconstruction in personal terms of Shakespearean tragedy, the histories involve a political solution. The *Henry VI* plays, for example, exemplify man-made chaos in the absence of a forceful ruler and the succession of figures who pay the price for the anarchy—Talbot, Humphrey, Suffolk, York, Somerset, Clifford, and Henry VI. Richard III is a union of iron will and superb intellect but ultimately is "too moral to be a successful Machiavellian." Henry IV and Henry V are successful political animals without illusion, their remorse, nothing but the rhetorical posturing of individuals who are aware of the necessity of political performance.

481. CALDERWOOD, JAMES L. *Metadrama in Shakespeare's Henriad: "Richard II" to "Henry V."* Berkeley and London: University of California Press, 1979, 225 pp.

Focuses on the manner in which Shakespeare in the second tetralogy examines metaphorically the nature and materials of his art. The major metadramatic plot centers on the fall of a "language instinct with truth and value" (p. 179), the collapse of sacramental language associated with Divine Right in *Richard II*, the corrupt secular language of *Henry IV*, and the establishment of a pragmatic rhetoric in *Henry V*. Recognizing the frailties of his own dramatic office, Shakespeare admits that truth and value do not reside in theatrical presentation.

482. CAMPBELL, LILY BESS. *Shakespeare's "Histories": Mirrors of Elizabethan Policy*. San Marino: Huntington Library, 1947, 346 pp.

Argues that Shakespeare's history plays are best understood in relation to the methods of historiography current in sixteenth-century England. Specifically, there is in these plays a dominant political pattern characteristic of the political philosophy of Shakespeare's own age. While he does not produce polemical tracts, he is creating political mirrors, and each play "serves a special purpose of elucidating a political problem of Elizabeth's day and in bringing to bear upon this problem the accepted political philosophy of the Tudors" (p. 125). Individual chapters are devoted to *King John*, *Richard II*, *Henry IV*, and *Richard III*.

483. CHAMPION, LARRY S. *The Noise of Threatening Drum: Dramatic Strategy and Political Ideology in Shakespeare and the English Chronicle Plays*. Newark: University of Delaware Press; London and Toronto: Associated University Presses, 1990, 172 pp.

General Studies

Argues that the spectator's response to English chronicle plays depends on his political and social orientation. From one angle the actions appear to support the general aristocratic notions of absolutism. From another perspective, however, the plays counterpoint this view, either interrogating assumptions of power or reflecting the suffering and political dislocation of the nonprivileged. These plays begin to incorporate a view of history as a process of self-determined change, a struggle regarding matters of succession, inheritance, and power grounded in ideological confrontation. The plays discussed include *1,2,3 Henry VI*, *Richard II*, *1,2 Henry IV*, and *Henry V*.

484. ———. *Perspective in Shakespeare's English Histories*. Athens: University of Georgia Press, 1980, 226 pp.
Examines the structure of each of Shakespeare's English histories with major attention to the particular devices through which the playwright controls the audience's angle of vision and consequently its responses to the pattern of historical events. The constant experimentation from one stage world to the next, particularly in *King John* and the *Henry IV* plays, culminates in a dramatic technique distinct from that of the major tragedies. It is a structure combining the detachment of a documentary necessary for a broad intellectual view of history with the engagement between character and spectator essential to emotionally effective drama.

485. DEAN, LEONARD F. "From *Richard II* to *Henry V*: A Closer View." In *Studies in Honor of DeWitt T. Starnes*. Edited by Thomas P. Harrison and James H. Sledd. Austin: University of Texas Press, 1967, pp. 37–52.
Refutes the concept that Shakespeare's second tetralogy delineates the traditional Tudor party line. Richard II for all his decadence possesses a rhetorical brilliance that counters Bullingbrook's cold efficiency. Such counterpointing of mode and language continues in the *Henry IV* plays in the juxtaposition of court and tavern scenes. In *Henry V* Shakespeare balances the heroic mode with moments of irony; the consequence is not to negate dramatic power but to intensify "emotional sympathy for the heroic to the point of feeling it as near-tragedy" (p. 51).

486. DOBIN, HOWARD. *Merlin's Disciples: Prophecy, Poetry, and Power in Renaissance England*. Stanford: Stanford University Press, 1990, 257 pp.
Focuses on the use of prophecy in Shakespeare's histories as a political weapon to exalt or sustain monarchical authority. In one sense the prophecies serve to affirm the presence of God and the operation of

divine providence. On the other hand, many of the prophecies are "misnomers," that is, subject to diverse interpretation—like the prophecy that Henry IV will die in Jerusalem or Hume's revelation in *2 Henry VI* that he has been hired by Eleanor's rivals to "buzz [false] conjurations in her brain" (1.2.99). In that sense prophecies actually subvert the text, functioning not as strategies for containment but as devices for blurring the traditional moral constructs of the plays.

487. HART, JONATHAN. *Theater and World: The Problematics of Shakespeare's History*. Boston: Northeastern University Press, 1991, 224 pp.

Considers the theoretical and interpretive problems posed by the plays of Shakespeare's second tetralogy (*Richard II, 1 Henry IV, 2 Henry IV*, and *Henry V*). Special emphasis is on the complex relationship between history and drama. More specifically, each play is examined in terms of Shakespeare's adaptation of the historical record and the political dynamics of the Elizabethan public stage.

488. HAWKINS, SHERMAN. "Structural Pattern in Shakespeare's Histories." *Studies in Philology* 88 (1991):16–45.

Argues a comprehensive structural pattern for Shakespeare's eight histories dealing with the War of the Roses. Considered in the order of composition, the first tetralogy traces Gloucester's moral decline into a tyrant. By contrast, movement in the second tetralogy is upward, tracing Hal's development through repeated reformations into a true king. Shakespeare's argument turns on this contrast and opposition. Henry VI and Richard II are both weak kings who are deposed. The king who replaces each rules more effectively and dies repentant; the contrast comes, of course, in the next king in each sequence. The two tetralogies, in a word, form a "great diptych, shaped by parallel and contrast" (p. 25).

489. HODGDON, BARBARA. *The End Crowns All: Closure and Contradiction in Shakespeare's History*. Princeton: Princeton University Press, 1991, 309 pp.

Examines the pluralistic nature of closure in Shakespeare's history plays. The final scene of *King John*, for example, is packed with narrative and rhetorical signs of resolution but, in fact, is one of the bleakest succession scenes in Shakespeare. *Richard III* is securely enclosed in its establishment of Richmond and the House of Tudor, but it is undermined by Henry's "use" of Elizabeth to prop up his right just as flagrantly as Richard had intended to. With individual chapters on each play, this study points out that the histories in a sense "stop" rather than "close" because in their qualities of self-interrogation they "insist on opening onto future history" (p. 234).

General Studies

490. HOLDERNESS, GRAHAM; POTTER, NICK; and TURNER, JOHN. *Shakespeare: The Play of History*. Iowa City: University of Iowa Press, 1988, 240 pp.

Describes Shakespeare's view of history as an evolving process under human control, with change resulting primarily from the struggle for power within the patriarchal structures of family and state. In *Richard II*, for example, the conflict is between the monarchy and the aristocracy. When Bullingbrook and Mowbray insist on the baronial right of trial by combat, refusing Richard's admonitions to accept reconciliation, Richard's power is directly threatened. The residual feudal concept of the joint right of kings and barons held that dukes shared power with the king and could limit his rights. By refusing to allow the combat to proceed, Richard—albeit only temporarily—reasserts the absolute authority of the crown.

491. JONES, ROBERT C. *These Valiant Dead: Renewing the Past in Shakespeare's Histories*. Iowa City: University of Iowa Press, 1991, 172 pp.

Describes Shakespeare's use of evocations of the image of past warriors in the history plays as a device for enriching the perspective both for characters in the stage world and spectators in the audience. Recalling the heroic memory of Henry V in the opening lines of *1 Henry VI*, for example, ironically anticipates the bleak, negative scenes of national devastation that are to follow, just as York's recollection of the memory of Edward the Black Prince in *Richard II* inversely points up the wasteful king's responsibility for factionalism among his subjects. In an entirely different manner the memory of the Black Prince is evoked in *Henry V* as a pattern for Henry to emulate in his wars against the French.

492. KELLY, HENRY ANSGAR. *Divine Providence in the England of Shakespeare's Histories*. Cambridge, Mass.: Harvard University Press, 1970, 344 pp.

Analyzes Shakespeare's use of supernatural references in the historical writings covering his double tetralogy (1398–1485). These references are manifested primarily in the workings of providence in the lives and destinies of the kings. Whereas Tillyard's thesis is that the providential view extends through the plays to the glory of Henry VII, in fact the providential interpretations of the chronicles followed more immediate political lines. Thus, for a time a Lancastrian God developed, only in turn to give place to a Yorkist God. Shakespeare's characterizations and moral attitudes are consistent within a play, but they likewise shift from one play to another.

493. LEGGATT, ALEXANDER. *Shakespeare's Political Drama: The History Plays and the Roman Plays*. London: Routledge, 1988, 266 pp.

General Studies

Argues that the power of the playwright's vision lies in the interplay established between the model of a benevolent order imposed by an autocratic government, on the one hand, and the model of a constant struggle between the privileged and nonprivileged, on the other. Shakespeare's concern is not in how political structures do or do not serve the general good but in how people react to the quest for power in which they are caught up. The general movement of the discussion is from an obsession with the "appearance of power" in the early plays (the *Henry VI* plays, *Richard III*) to the realization of the "power of appearance" in the later (*Richard II*, the *Henriad*, *Coriolanus*, *Antony and Cleopatra*).

494. MANHEIM, MICHAEL. *The Weak King Dilemma in the Shakespearean History Play*. Syracuse: Syracuse University Press, 1973, 198 pp.

Observes that Shakespeare's history plays reveal a growing awareness that effective political rule encompasses a willingness to exercise devious and ruthless Machiavellian tactics. Henry VI fails, for example, because he is no match for the treacherous tactics of those around him. Henry V, on the other hand, if not devious, possesses the ability to deceive others about his true intentions and a willingness to threaten and use violence when necessary. The plays affect our own attitudes about political figures and represent a turning point in the public attitude toward the monarchic ideal.

495. ORNSTEIN, ROBERT. *A Kingdom for a Stage: The Achievement of Shakespeare's History Plays*. Cambridge, Mass.: Harvard University Press, 1972, 231 pp.

Asserts that Shakespeare created the history play virtually whole cloth. For him order depends not on abstract Tudor concepts of hierarchy and degree but on the "fabric of personal and social relationships which is woven by the ties of marriage, kingship, and friendship" (p. 222). The major foe to political order is the individualist who in his search for power defies kinship and affection. Chaos results not when one questions the doctrine of obedience but when brother turns on brother. *Henry V*, in part, celebrates military victory; more important, it celebrates the human bond between Henry and his soldiers.

496. PARIS, BERNARD J. *Character as a Subversive Force in Shakespeare: The Histories and Roman Plays*. Rutherford: Fairleigh Dickinson University Press; London and Toronto: Associated University Presses, 1991, 224 pp.

Notes that the powerful tension in Shakespeare's histories results in large part from a persuasive rhetoric designed to shape the responses of the spectators that is often undermined by characters who develop a life-style of their own. Rhetoric and mimesis, for example, are harmonious at the outset in the critical posture of Richard II and of Antony and Cleopatra, but the play in both cases ultimately glorifies them and romanticizes their fate. The view of Henry V as an exemplary monarch is eroded by inner conflict and glimpses of his darker side. Only in *Coriolanus* are rhetoric and mimesis consistent from beginning to end.

497. PIERCE, R. B. *Shakespeare's History Plays: The Family and the State.* Columbus: Ohio State University Press, 1971, 261 pp.

Observes that family life plays a prominent role in the language, characterization, and dramatic situation of Shakespeare's history plays, at times functioning as a microcosm of the state, at times as direct or ironic contrast. The analogy between kingdom and family, king and father, was commonplace. The whole concept of nobility rests on the concept that sons inherit from their father an inclination toward virtue. Especially notable is the chaos reflected in a father's discovering that he has killed a son and a son a father in *3 Henry VI*, the Gaunt-Bullingbrook relationship in *Richard II*, and the troubled relationships of Henry, Hal, and Hotspur in the Henry plays.

498. PORTER, JOSEPH A. *The Drama of Speech Acts: Shakespeare's Lancastrian Tetralogy.* Berkeley and London: University of California Press, 1979, 208 pp.

Traces Shakespeare's preoccupation with speech and language in *Richard II*, *1,2 Henry IV*, and *Henry V*, a time when Shakespeare was developing from his poetic phase into use of more dramatic dialogue. Richard's language is theatrical, placing him within an inner imaginative world from which he is unable to communicate with others. His language eventually becomes tedious prattle to others. Henry IV's language, and at times his silence, rings with verbal practicality. Hal ascends the stage as a princely polyglot, unifying a kingdom "in which men can, and must, talk to each other, and in which their speech is morally intelligible" (p. 187).

499. RACKIN, PHYLLIS. *Stages of History: Shakespeare's English Chronicles.* Ithaca: Cornell University Press, 1990, 256 pp.

Resituates Shakespeare's chronicle plays in terms of oppositional histories, reading them as a series of negotiations between separate, often opposed, discursive fields. In Renaissance England the theological concept of history was giving way to Machiavellian analyses of second causes, and Shakespeare for dramatic purposes endorses radically different notions of history and historiography. In *Richard II*, for

General Studies

example, the conflict between providential legitimacy and Machiavellian power is directly projected upon the two principal figures Richard and Bullingbrook. Again in *Henry V* the two views are "deliberately clashed" (p. 69), one in the chorus and one in the action itself.

500. REESE, M. M. *The Cease of Majesty*. London: Edward Arnold, 1961, 350 pp.

Surveys the development and artistry of Shakespeare's history plays. Shakespeare was able in the period of history stretching from Richard II to Richard III (ca. 1390–1485) to explore the relationships of ethics and power and also to mirror contemporary problems in the late Elizabethan period. Most striking is the identification between Shakespeare's queen and Richard II. While she was certainly her own person, it would seem that she could bring her country to the brink of disaster by whim. Serious political reflection occurs throughout Shakespeare's plays. Nowhere does he suggest that it is possible for a government to be sound without a leader who is dedicated, disciplined, and patriotic.

501. RIBNER, IRVING. *The English History Play in the Age of Shakespeare*. Rev. ed. London: Methuen; New York: Barnes & Noble, 1965, 356 pp.

Surveys the development of the English history play as a separate genre with chapters devoted to Shakespeare's first and second tetralogies and with *Henry VIII* included in a final section. The emergence and popularity of the genre is the dramatic reflection of the extreme popularity of history in all literary forms in the sixteenth century. More important is the playwright's intention to use the past for didactic purposes—the glorification of England and the Tudor humanistic doctrines. The *Henry VI* plays are a grim reminder of civil chaos; *Richard III* is testimony to the futility of self-sufficiency; the second tetralogy depicts the triumph of the House of Lancaster and the emergence and education of the ideal prince.

502. RICHMOND, HUGH M. *Shakespeare's Political Plays*. New York: Random House, 1967, 241 pp.

Observes that Shakespeare's history plays engage in a steadily evolving study of man as a political animal. Taken together, they represent a kind of epic statement of English experience, exerting an influence on the Englishman's political self-awareness. Chapters on each of the English histories and on *Julius Caesar* and *Coriolanus* trace the maturation of his art in using political themes; the distinctive cathartic function of the plays is the focus on man as a complex individual forced to learn how to manage his personal relationships, often at the cost of political success, and the refusal to accept simplifying political judgments.

503. SACCIO, PETER. *Shakespeare's English Kings: History, Chronicle, and Drama*. London and New York: Oxford University Press, 1977, 268 pp.

   Provides a historical guide to Shakespeare's ten plays on medieval history. For each of the plays the author interweaves discussion of the Tudor historiography concerning the particular ruler, the historical period as envisioned by modern scholarship, and the action as Shakespeare re-creates it on stage. Also included are genealogical and chronological charts and a compilation of names and titles. The series of plays has "high coherence" as a chronicle of fifteenth-century England; more than any other source, Shakespeare's plays are "responsible for whatever notions most of us possess about the period and its political leaders" (p. 4).

504. SIEGEL, PAUL N. *Shakespeare's English and Roman History Plays: A Marxist Approach*. Rutherford: Fairleigh Dickinson University Press; London and Toronto: Associated University Presses, 1986, 168 pp.

   Argues that Shakespeare in his English and Roman histories reflects the dominant Tudor ideology of Christian humanism being threatened by the most aggressive elements of the bourgeoisie, the moneylenders who were subjugating both impoverished landowners and craftsmen alike. Richard III is Shakespeare's incarnation of the supreme capitalist willing to destroy and exploit all for his personal gain. The playwright's depiction of the Roman republic in *Coriolanus* suggests comparison with bourgeoisie democracy, while his depiction of Julius Caesar suggests comparison with modern dictators.

505. THAYER, C. G. *Shakespearean Politics: Government and Misgovernment in the Great Histories*. Athens, Ohio, and London: Ohio University Press, 1983, 190 pp.

   Argues that Shakespeare in the second tetralogy is no spokesman for Tudor orthodoxy. *Richard II*, for example, undermines the political theology of passive obedience through the inept and unprincipled Richard, whose deposition is virtually required for the good of the kingdom. *Henry IV* depicts an era of just and effective rule with emphasis on a kingly dignity that prepares for the ideal ruler. These essays in statecraft have a particular relevance for the politically anxious years 1597–99, when all thoughts were focused on the question of Elizabeth's successor.

General Studies

506. TILLYARD, E. M. W. *Shakespeare's History Plays*. London: Macmillan, 1944, 383 pp.

Envisions Shakespeare's English history plays as a dramatic epic of England embodying the Elizabethan principles of world order and of God's retributive justice. Molding the chronicle play into authentic drama that is not merely ancillary to the form of tragedy, Shakespeare depicts a fundamentally religious scheme of history "by which events evolve under a law of justice and under the ruling of God's providence, and of which Elizabeth's England was the acknowledged outcome" (p. 362). Behind the disorder traced through the two tetralogies, *King John*, and *Macbeth* lies a macrocosmic principle of control that lends philosophic direction to the movement of the plays as a group and to the resolution of the conflict in the individual stage worlds.

507. TRAVERSI, DEREK A. *Shakespeare: From "Richard II" to "Henry V."* Stanford: Stanford University Press, 1957, 198 pp.

Describes Shakespeare's second historical tetralogy as a movement from the concept of the royal office as divinely instituted, to its interruption and disastrous consequences, and finally to the restoration of order on a more secure, if more limited, basis. Richard's failure to exercise his divinely sanctioned authority provokes Henry's usurpation, and Henry in turn is forced to rule without the support of traditional sanctions. Henry V, following his education, is able to consolidate a new political order combining his father's political capacities with an authority not flawed by dubious origins.

508. WATSON, DONALD G. *Shakespeare's Early History Plays: Politics at Play on the Elizabethan Stage*. Athens: University of Georgia Press, 1990, 192 pp.

Argues that Shakespeare, in dramatizing the past, exploits the paradoxes of politics to depict the irony and obliquity of what we call history. Characters like Richard of York and Richard of Gloucester manipulate the language and the appearances of corporate values, national interests, and divine justifications for their own purposes; those like the Bastard reconcile themselves to the imperfections and ironies of political life. Disjunctions of language and actions often reveal the inadequacy of isolated ideological constructs to encompass the complexity of history—Christian humanism in Henry VI, providentialism in Queen Margaret, chivalric loyalty in Clifford, the divinity of kings in Richard II, dynastic diplomacy in Lewis of France.

509. WINNY, JAMES. *The Player King: A Theme of Shakespeare's Histories*. New York: Barnes & Noble, 1968, 219 pp.

Insists that the history plays are essentially imaginative in character and that to read them as political statements is to distort their artistic design. While an imaginative view does not exclude moral awareness, Shakespeare's method is not one of homiletic commentary. The study traces the attempts of Richard II, Henry Bullingbrook, and Henry V to assume royal dignity, to deal with an identity larger than their own in a struggle to become the part they play—Richard as king in name, Bullingbrook as counterfeiter, Hal as true inheritor.

1,2 HENRY IV

Criticism

510. BARBER, C. L. "From Ritual to Comedy: An Examination of *Henry IV*." In *English Stage Comedy*. Edited by W. K. Wimsatt, Jr. English Institute Essays, 1954. New York: Columbia University Press, 1955, pp. 22–51.

   Develops the analogies between the comic elements of *1,2 Henry IV* and the misrule of traditional saturnalian holidays. The creation of Falstaff combines the clowning customary on stage and the folly customary on holiday. Through his relationship with Prince Hal, Shakespeare dramatizes both the need for and the necessity of limiting holiday; unrestrained, the Lord of Misrule might issue into the anarchic reign of a dissolute king. Ultimately Falstaff is rejected, like the scapegoat of saturnalian ritual, an event more logical in pattern than emotionally successful in drama.

511. BARISH, JONAS. "The Turning Away of Prince Hal." *Shakespeare Studies* 1 (1965):9–17.

   Notes that our attitude toward the rejection of Falstaff tends to reveal us as either moralists or sentimentalists. It is likely that Shakespeare intended to provoke the latter response since the sanctimonious and dishonest retrospective vision of Henry V imposes a sense of constriction rather than liberation upon our dramatic experience. Certainly by progressively depicting revelry as misrule Shakespeare renders inevitable the moral position and our transfer at the end from the spirit of comedy to the grim reality of history.

512. BERGER, HARRY, JR. "Psychoanalyzing the Shakespeare Text: The First Three Scenes of the *Henriad*." In *Shakespeare and the Question of Theory*.

1,2 Henry IV

Edited by Patricia Parker and Geoffrey Hartman. New York and London: Methuen, 1985, pp. 210–29.

Notes that patriarchal ideology supports itself through two forms of symbolic fatherhood—the Father (God) who distributes power through a hierarchical structure and a human father who does so through heraldic genealogy. The basis for successful transference of power is the development of a representational pattern or image of the son. In this regard, the relationship of Henry and Hal is tainted by a basic disorder in the mimetic principle itself. In *Richard II*, Gaunt's acquiescence in his son's banishment suppresses a fear that Bullingbrook's actions will bring disorder upon him. This scene adumbrates a textual dimension that is central to the *Henriad*, in which mechanisms of repression and displacement create similar tensions within the patriarchy.

513. BLACK, JAMES. "Henry IV's Pilgrimage." *Shakespeare Quarterly* 34 (1983):18–26.

Focuses on Henry IV's obsession with a voyage to the Holy Land as a pilgrimage neither of remorse nor of politics but of the heart. Bullingbrook speaks of his exile in *Richard II* as a long, weary, enforced pilgrimage; in the opening scene of *1 Henry IV* the theme begins anew with his pledge to march to Jerusalem to gain pardon for Richard's murder, and it continues until the final scene in the Jerusalem Chamber in which his speech to Hal is both confessional and advisory. With a wonderful irony this weary traveler finds his absolution in his own bed.

514. BOWERS, FREDSON T. "Shakespeare's Art: The Point of View." In *Literary Views*. Edited by Carroll Camden. Chicago: University of Chicago Press, 1964, pp. 45–58.

Maintains that drama is the most highly developed objective literary form in existence and that the plot—especially its climax—is the key to determining the dramatist's point of view. Perhaps the subtlest climax in drama occurs in *1 Henry IV*, in the king's apparent weaning of Hal from his dissolute life and setting him on the path to Shrewsbury and political glory. In fact, however, we have known how Hal would react since his soliloquy in act 1. Shakespeare deliberately undercuts the climax to give the initiative to Hal, who, instead of being acted upon, manipulates others to the goal of his self-education.

515. BRYANT, JOSEPH A., Jr. "Prince Hal and the Ephesians." *Sewanee Review* 67 (1959):204–19.

Asserts that Hal's reference to redeeming time in his "I know you all" soliloquy would remind Shakespeare's spectators of the command in Ephesians that Christians must walk circumspectly in evil, among fools, to redeem time. Throughout *1,2 Henry IV* Hal is attempting to define for himself the proper sphere of honor. In part 2 he must come to terms with Falstaff, the embodiment of time and common humanity. He fails, in casting his companion off completely, to redeem time, and this impulse to condemn rather than struggle through to redemption is a mark of his immaturity.

516. EVANS, GARETH LLOYD. "The Comical-Tragical-Historical Method–Henry IV." In *Early Shakespeare*. Edited by John Russell Brown and Bernard Harris. Stratford-upon-Avon Studies, 3. London: Edward Arnold, 1961, pp. 145–63.

Observes that the plot strands of *Henry IV* encompass both the world of ceremony and kingship and the world of nature. Hal confronts a father in each world—Henry IV and Falstaff—and both must perish before he comes into his kingdom. In Hal's educative process both Falstaff's hedonistic world and Hotspur's rebellious world slowly disintegrate. Through reflections of the natural and political, the comic and serious, the private and public, Hal emerges as representative of an order more inclusive than either of those he has rejected.

517. FISH, CHARLES. "*Henry IV*: Shakespeare and Holinshed." *Studies in Philology* 61 (1964):205–18.

Focuses on Shakespeare's intentions in the delineation of Henry Bullingbrook. Demonstrably he builds a sense of integrity into the character not found in Holinshed, for example in Henry's handling of the character of Edmund Mortimer. Also, unlike the situation in the *Chronicles*, Henry is never personally accused of usurpation until late in the action, when the rebels' denial of his offer of mercy justifies Henry's giving battle. Moreover, in Shakespeare the rebels are clearly planning war before they bring their demands to Henry. Shakespeare goes to some trouble to reflect Henry as worthy of his nation's respect.

518. HAPGOOD, ROBERT. "*Chimes at Midnight* from Stage to Screen: The Art of Adaptation." *Shakespeare Survey* 39 (1987):39–52.

Observes that Orson Welles's film, acclaimed a near masterpiece, was preceded by two stage versions that, while themselves unsuccessful, made important contributions to the movie version. *Five Kings*, for example, folded before reaching New York; and the stage play *Chimes at Midnight* was a critical success in London but a financial disaster. Nevertheless, successive versions reveal Welles's ability to sharpen focus and character. Eventually the dominant focus came to be upon the contrast between court and tavern, not upon the personal relationship

1,2 Henry IV

between Hal and the fat rogue; and the film also reveals Hal's motivations more clearly.

519. HAWKINS, SHERMAN H. *"Henry IV*: The Structural Problem Revisited." *Shakespeare Quarterly* 33 (1982):278–301.
Maintains that the two parts of *Henry IV* are too different for part 2 to be a carbon copy of part 1 added to capitalize on the dramatic success, but that they are too alike to fit the theory that the two parts form a single whole. The two parts do form a diptych, whether part 2 was conceived before or after part 1. The one moves from epic to tragedy, the other from tragedy to epic.

520. HEMINGWAY, SAMUEL B. "On Behalf of That Falstaff." *Shakespeare Quarterly* 3 (1952):307–11.
Observes that Falstaff accommodates controversy more than most Shakespearean characters because there are two figures, the Lancastrian Falstaff of *Henry IV* and the Tudor Falstaff of *The Merry Wives of Windsor*. While the latter is ignored, the former lives in books and articles because he is more than a synthetic character. To first-nighters he is a coward; later he is a huge foil that sets off the glory of Prince Hal. The real Falstaff is more than Morgann, Bradley, and Stoll suggest; he is visible in fresh nuances in every performance.

521. HUNTER, G. K. *"Henry IV* and the Elizabethan Two-Part Play." *Review of English Studies*, n.s. 5 (1954):236–48.
Calls the unity of *1,2 Henry IV* a diptych with the pattern of the shape and design of part 1 repeated in part 2. Chapman's two-part play *The Tragedy of Charles Duke of Byron* is organized by parallelism, as in a more rudimentary sense is Marlowe's *Tamburlaine* and Marston's *Antonio and Mellida*. In both parts of *Henry IV* the theme is rebellion leading to order, both in the state and in the mind of the prince. Whereas the emphasis is on the struggle of coming of age in part 1, it is on the evolving abstract view of kingship in part 2.

522. HUNTER, WILLIAM B., Jr. "Falstaff." *South Atlantic Quarterly* 50 (1951):86–95.
Perceives a pattern of moral allegory in the structure of *1,2 Henry IV*. Hal represents an Aristotelian mean between the extremes of Hotspur and Falstaff, the embodiment respectively of the excess and the deficiency of honor. Hal's full maturation as ideal king is signaled by his rejection of Falstaff and his ratification of the Lord Chief Justice.

523. JENKINS, HAROLD. *The Structural Problem in Shakespeare's "Henry the Fourth."* London: Methuen, 1956, 28 pp.

Maintains that Shakespeare at the outset did not envision *Henry IV* as a two-part play but that, in the course of composition, he determined that a sequel would be necessary. Shakespeare's original plan would have involved Hal's defeat of Hotspur at Shrewsbury, his rejection of Falstaff, and his subsequent assumption of the throne. The new pattern of action involves the delay of Falstaff's fate until a later play emerges in act 4. To fill out part 2 Shakespeare is forced to reduplicate Hal's display of physical valor as a parallel to his achievement of moral valor in the banishing of Falstaff.

524. KERNAN, ALVIN. "The Henriad: Shakespeare's Major History Plays." *Yale Review* 59 (1969–70):3–32.

Claims that Shakespeare's second tetralogy constitutes an epic—a large-scale heroic action involving the movement of a people or nation from one condition to another. In the movement from the rule of Richard II to that of Henry V Shakespeare traces England from the Middle Ages to the beginning of the Renaissance, from feudalism to the national state, from a closed world to an infinite universe. In the former Richard mistakes metaphor for science in his assumption of divine support; in the latter Hal banishes idealism and pleasure, losing his individual identity to assume the work that his role demands.

525. KERRIGAN, JOHN. "*Henry IV* and the Death of Old Double." *Essays in Criticism* 40 (1990):24–53.

Sees in the second tetralogy Shakespeare's examination of the "grotesquerie" of artful government. The playwright in *Henry IV* proliferates analogues that call attention to various aspects of the king. Consider, for example, the juxtaposition of the two scenes dealing with power and inheritance—one with a brooding king at Westminster who rehearses his isolation and failing support (pt. 2, 3.1), the other with warm reaffirmation in the conversation between Justice Shallow and Silence (3.2). Consider, too, the relationship of Falstaff's counterfeit death with the counterfeit death of the king in what might well be a trap for Prince Hal. And consider Hal's campaign as a brilliant form of counterfeiting, whether in the church's self-interested motive for supporting the war or in Hal's motive for using it to contain civil strife.

526. McLUHAN, HERBERT MARSHALL. "*Henry IV*: A Mirror For Magistrates." *University of Toronto Quarterly* 17 (1947):152–60.

Speaks of three themes and three groups in *1,2 Henry IV*—the court, the Boar's Head crowd, and the rebels. Since the court is corrupt, ruled not by principle but by policy, Hal takes refuge in the tavern. There the commoners reflect the corruption emanating from the court.

1,2 Henry IV

The rebels are also a part of that corruption, rendering Hotspur's honor ineffective. Henry, the source of evil, is finally poisoned by success. At his father's death it is perfectly natural for Hal to banish his erstwhile cronies and assert his true nature; the heroic mode has replaced the base.

527. NEWMAN, FRANKLIN B. "The Rejection of Falstaff and the Rigorous Charity of the King." *Shakespeare Studies* 2 (1966):153–61.

Examines the sermon on charity from the *Homilies* to determine that Henry in rejecting Falstaff reveals himself both as a devotee of sound government and of Christian virtue. The homily specifically charges one to rebuke and punish vice without regard to persons. Metaphorically Shakespeare is purging from the kingdom that which might corrupt others. This reading will obviously not remove all ambiguities from an act as important symbolically as it is physically, but it provides further evidence of the context within which Shakespeare conceived it.

528. PALMER, D. J. "Casting Off the Old Man: History and St. Paul in *Henry IV*." *Critical Quarterly* 12 (1970):267–83.

Observes that Hal's reference to redeeming time at the outset of *1 Henry IV* distinguishes the Prince in the spectators' eyes from the wild youth both Falstaff and the King thought him to be. Hal's allusion is to the admonition of St. Paul in Ephesians, who speaks of the old man as the unregenerate Adam who must be set aside. That Shakespeare consciously builds in the allusion is verified by the reference in *2 Henry IV* (2.2) to the Eastcheap community as Ephesians of the Old Church and to Hal's exclamation, "I know thee not, old man," at the point of his rejecting Falstaff.

529. SCOUFOS, ALICE-LYLE. *Shakespeare's Typological Satire: A Study of the Falstaff-Oldcastle Problem*. Athens, Ohio: Ohio University Press, 1979, 378 pp.

Argues that Shakespeare in his history plays inverts the medieval practice of typology and makes his characters "types" of contemporary Elizabethans, specifically in order to lampoon the Brooke family and Lord Cobham. The satire begins in *1 Henry VI*, continuing with the unfavorable depiction of Eleanor Cobham in *2 Henry VI*. The major focus is on the Falstaff and Percy satirical material in *1,2 Henry IV* and *The Merry Wives of Windsor*. Evidence of the attack shows up as late as *Macbeth* in reflections of the Gunpowder Plot involving the Ninth Earl of Northumberland (the "Wizard Earl").

530. SHIRLEY, JOHN W. "Falstaff, an Elizabethan Glutton." *Philological Quarterly* 17 (1938):271–87.

Observes that Falstaff has elicited diverse interpretations because he is essentially of a double nature, highly witty and also derisively obese. His physical characteristics are present in *Gula*, the Gluttony of the Seven Deadly Sins, while his mental characteristics are present in the Vice as it degenerates into a largely comic role and is merged with the character of the Glutton.

531. SPRAGUE, ARTHUR COLBY. "Gadshill Revisited." *Shakespeare Quarterly* 4 (1953):125–37.
    Maintains that Falstaff, notwithstanding the contrary arguments of Maurice Morgann in 1777, is a coward. Given his corpulence and his age, the spectators like him despite this lack of courage. His military reputation is sheer bogus, and Hal provides him a charge of foot both to watch his immediate reaction and to force him to lard the lean earth through a march of twelvescore. He is able to sleep behind the arras at the Boar's Head because he knows the Prince will protect him. Above all, his flight in the Gadshill robbery amounts to a dramatic demonstration of cowardice.

532. TENNENHOUSE, LEONARD. "Strategies of State and Political Plays: *A Midsummer Night's Dream, Henry IV, Henry V, Henry VIII*." In *Political Shakespeare: New Essays in Cultural Materialism*. Edited by Jonathan Dollimore and Alan Sinfield. Ithaca and London: Cornell University Press, 1985, pp. 109–28.
    Argues that both Shakespeare's romantic comedy and his chronicle histories depict disorder within patriarchal hierarchies that only a monarch can hold together harmoniously. Thus, the playwright utilizes drama to authorize political authority. For example, in *A Midsummer Night's Dream* elements of festival disrupt social hierarchical order and are eventually subsumed into a new form of political authority. *Henry V* depicts a monarch who can unify a heterogeneous body under his authority; in the *Henry IV* plays figures of carnival (especially Hal) play an instrumental role in the idealizing process. *Henry VIII*, conversely, compliments James by focusing on events that perpetuate the power of blood and of lineage.

533. TOLIVER, HAROLD E. "Falstaff, the Prince, and the History Play." *Shakespeare Quarterly* 16 (1965):63–80.
    Argues that Shakespeare involves the audience in a communal rhythm, integrating concepts of providential order and pragmatic political concerns with timeless human impulses. While Hal is able to perceive history as a continuous succession of events linking the present to past and future, Falstaff increasingly loses himself in the present

moment. In the course of the play Hal incorporates and transcends the characteristics of Hotspur, his father, and Falstaff. Falstaff's ultimate rejection coincides with and contributes to the anagnorisis in the audience.

534. TRAUB, VALERIE. "Prince Hal's Falstaff: Positioning Psychoanalysis and the Female Reproductive Body." *Shakespeare Quarterly* 40 (1989):456–74.

Argues that, in his development of the prototypical male figure in the *Henriad*, Shakespeare shares with psychoanalytic theory the need to repress the female reproductive body and its influence upon male subjectivity. The flawed father-son dynamic replicates the larger problems of patriarchy, and Falstaff represents "a projected fantasy of the preoedipal *maternal* whose rejection is the basis upon which patriarchal subjectivity is predicated" (p. 461). Both Falstaff (through banishment) and Katherine (through Hal's militaristic courtship) are female "Others" who must be repudiated in order for Hal to assume phallocentric control as Henry V.

535. WATSON, ROBERT N. "Horsemanship in Shakespeare's Second Tetralogy." *English Literary Renaissance* 13 (1983):274–300.

Views the literal and figurative equestrian references as highly controlled by Shakespeare to delineate in one's lack of mastery of horsemanship a failure of self-rule (for example, Hotspur, Falstaff) and in one's ability (Henry IV, Prince Hal) a political mastery of England. Specifically, Shakespeare transforms Plato's metaphor relating chariot driving with restraint of unruly passions into one relating horsemanship and rightful political authority. The king as horseman must restrain and guide an unruly state.

536. WEST, GILIAN. "Falstaff's Punning." *English Studies* 69 (1988):541–58.

Maintains that Falstaff's use of puns is more pervasive than has been previously recognized. Numerous examples are catalogued, for instance, "continence" for "countenance" when speaking of his "chaste mistress," the moon and "whoremaster" in his denial of promiscuity but admission of age ("hoar"). The tavern world's forthright abuse of language offers Hal an escape from the treacherous abuse of language in the political world.

537. WILLIAMS, PHILIP. "The Birth and Death of Falstaff Reconsidered." *Shakespeare Quarterly* 8 (1957):359–65.

Defends the theory that Hal figuratively kills Falstaff rather than kill his father. Falstaff becomes a father surrogate, sought out in part because of the antagonism between the prince and King Henry. Note also that in the tavern scene Falstaff in play actually assumes the paternal role. In part 2 Falstaff becomes old, and Hal is not comfortable as king so long as Falstaff is present.

538. WILSON, JOHN DOVER. *The Fortunes of Falstaff.* Cambridge: Cambridge University Press, 1943, 143 pp.

Insists that Falstaff is neither an unmitigated sinner nor a stage butt descended from the Plautine braggart. Instead he is a character who, as a mixture of moral abandon and spontaneity of wit, is riding for an inevitable fall. Such a vision of Falstaff also clears the focus on Hal, who is both generous and lovable, but also faulty. Hal, as he must, ultimately rejects Falstaff, but he provides well for him. The embodiment of liberty lives on but is replaced at center stage by the embodiment of order, with Hal representing the traditional ideals of public service.

539. YACHNIN, PAUL. "History, Theatricality, and the 'Structural Problem' in the *Henry IV* Plays." *Philological Quarterly* 70 (1991):163–79.

Argues that the assumption of a single, ten-act coherence in *1,2 Henry IV* arises from the "mistaken attempt to force the idea of aesthetic unity upon the genre of Shakespeare's histories" (p. 163). The question turns not so much on "structure" as on "sequence." To view the two as separate entities enacts the revisionist, open-ended nature of historical change. History in these plays is fluid and linear; it is the individuals who, in one way or another, attempt to reduce it to cyclic or providential meaning. Shakespeare, in a word, reveals that history becomes a "matter of interpretation" (p. 175).

1 HENRY IV

Reference Work

540. KIERNAN, MICHAEL, comp. *"Henry IV: Part I": A Bibliography to Supplement the New Variorum Edition of 1936 and the Supplement of 1956.* New York: Modern Language Association, 1977, 15 pp.

Includes 280 items representing scholarship on *1 Henry IV* from 1956 through 1972. The material is categorized alphabetically under editions, text, criticism, sources, commentary, music, and staging and stage history. Books with general focus are placed in the criticism sec-

1 Henry IV

tion; not included are collected editions and book reviews. Supplements entries 542–43.

Editions

541. BEVINGTON, DAVID, ed. *Henry IV, Part I.* The Oxford Shakespeare. Oxford and New York: Oxford University Press, 1987, 326 pp.

Includes an introductory essay addressing matters of date, reception, and reputation; sources (the chronicles, Daniel's *Civil Wars, The Famous Victories*) and the prince's wild youth; Falstaff and the Vice, Falstaff as soldier, other Falstaff antecedents; providential views of history versus Renaissance skepticism; the question of structural unity; a pattern of opposites: Hal and Hotspur on honor; from feudal chivalry to pragmatism, language and political change; father and son, role-playing and identity; Falstaff's cowardice, his playworld; the "education" of Prince Hal, the rejection of Falstaff; and the play in performance. Notes appear on individual pages of the text, and an appendix reprints the principal chronicle sources.

542. EVANS, G. BLAKEMORE, ed. *Supplement to "Henry IV, Part I."* A New Variorum Edition of Shakespeare. New York: Shakespeare Association of America, 1956, 121 pp.

Follows the same format as and provides a supplement to S. B. Hemingway's Variorum edition (entry 543). All significant items of scholarship from 1935 through July 1955 are included. Other than the main sections on textual notes and critical notes, material is categorized under the text, the date of composition, sources, general criticism, characters, style and language, and stage history.

543. HEMINGWAY, SAMUEL B., ed. *Henry the Fourth, Part I.* A New Variorum Edition of Shakespeare. Philadelphia: J. B. Lippincott, 1936, 554 pp.

Uses the first quarto (1598) as the copy text (pp. 3–341). On each page, for that portion of the text, are provided variant readings, textual notes, and general critical commentary. Following the text are sections on the text, the date of composition, sources, the individual characters, the stage history, stage versions, and a list of works consulted. Supplemented by entries 540 and 542.

544. HUMPHREYS, A. R., ed. *The First Part of King Henry IV.* The Arden Shakespeare. London: Methuen; Cambridge, Mass.: Harvard University Press, 1960, 202 pp.

Includes discussion of the text, date, questions of revision, sources, Falstaff, the unity of the play, the historical outlook, the spirit of the play, and the imaginative impact. The text is based on the first quarto (1598), for which the copy was probably a transcript of Shakespeare's foul papers. The date of composition is most likely 1596, with revisions of Falstaff's name occurring in 1597. Falstaff himself is a rich amalgam, a world of comic ingredients; although parasitical, he gives as much to life as he takes from it and, symbolically, is like life itself. The basic structure of the play is analogous to a morality—with vice and virtue contending for the soul of a prince.

545. WILSON, JOHN DOVER, ed. *The First Part of the History of Henry the Fourth*. Cambridge: Cambridge University Press, 1946, 210 pp.
    Provides extensive textual notes, a critical introduction, a discussion of the copy text, a section on stage history, and a glossary. This edition is based on the first quarto (1598), for which the copy was probably Shakespeare's foul papers. *1 Henry IV* is patently only a part of a whole dramatic conception in parts 1 and 2. The political and dynastic theme—the defeat of the rebels and the repentance of the prince—is only half concluded in this play. Moreover, to envision Hal as a cad or a hypocrite destroys the centerpiece of the Lancastrian trilogy, *Henry V*.

Criticism

546. BROOKS, CLEANTH, and HEILMAN, ROBERT B. "Notes on *Henry IV, Part I*." In *Understanding Drama*. New York: Holt, Rinehart & Winston, 1948, pp. 376–87.
    Envisions the question of unity as the central problem of *1 Henry IV* in that one must accommodate the fortunes of Falstaff to the resolution of the main plot at Shrewsbury. Falstaff on the battlefield strips the pretensions from honor and courage even as Hal displays those very qualities in confronting and defeating Hotspur. The strength of the play's conclusion lies in its rich ambivalence that forces the spectator to recognize with a touch of irony that we live in a fallen world demanding political compromises for survival.

547. COX, GERARD H. " 'Like a Prince Indeed': Hal's Triumph of Honor in *1 Henry IV*." In *Pageantry in the Shakespearean Theater*. Edited by David Bergeron. Athens: University of Georgia Press, 1988, pp. 130–49.
    Claims that we see more of the problematic in Hal than did those

in Shakespeare's audience. The heroic is stressed through the symbolic use of emblems, shows, and pageantry associated with chivalry. In the incident with Francis in the Boar's Head Tavern, Hal envisions himself in the place of the apprentice, conscious of the demands made upon him by both the court and the tavern. The episode functions as a kind of comic catharsis; "by laughing at Francis' predictably automatic responses, Hal could be said to purge himself of this 'base' association and thereby move himself to a better mood" (p. 138).

548. RENO, RAYMOND H. "Hotspur: The Integration of Character and Theme." *Renaissance Papers* (1962):17–25.

Notes that Hotspur, himself a figure of disorder in his inability to maintain self-control, reflects the play's major theme of disorder. For him honor is but rhetorical flourish without substance. This quality extends as well into the political center of the play, in which Henry IV, too, is obsessed with image and reputation rather than with actuality, and into the social center, in which Falstaff is a walking symbol of anarchy in the shape of appetite. The microcosmic disorder in Hotspur eventually extends into the larger pattern of the action and rends and deracinates the larger world of the state.

549. TRAVERSI, DEREK A. "*Henry IV*, Part I: History and the Artist's Vision." *Scrutiny* 15 (1947):24–35.

Argues that a significant part of Shakespeare's design in the second tetralogy is to trace a common destiny working itself out in the Lancastrian family. Whatever his desire for the general good, Henry IV—in calling for a crusade—is moved by motives essentially political. Hal in his opening soliloquy reveals himself as a true son of Lancaster. His false humility and amoral personality place him squarely in the service of political interests. Falstaff serves as a foil to Hal, in his human warmth, albeit sorely flawed, reflecting the cold, calculating nature of his royal companion.

2 HENRY IV

Reference Work

550. SHAABER, MATHIAS A., comp. *"Henry the Fourth, Part Two": A Bibliography to Supplement the New Variorum Edition of 1940*. New York: Modern Language Association, 1977, 18 pp.

Includes 398 items representing the scholarship on *2 Henry IV* from 1940 through 1975. The material is categorized alphabetically under editions, text, date, criticism, sources, commentary, music, and staging and stage history. Books with a general focus are placed in the criticism section, and book reviews are not included. Supplements entry 554.

Editions

551. BERGER, THOMAS L., ed. *The Second Part of Henry the Fourth*. The Malone Society Reprints. Oxford: Oxford University Press, 1990, 112 pp.

    Provides a photofacsimile edition of the Bridgewater copy of the quarto text in the Huntington Library. The introduction describes the publication in two issues in 1600, twenty-two copies of which are extant. Two copies from the British Library and one from Harvard were collated with the Bridgewater. Evidence suggests that the copy used by the single compositor was Shakespeare's foul papers. Differences with the folio text are highlighted, namely the presence of 160 unique lines in the folio.

552. HUMPHREYS, A. R., ed. *The Second Part of King Henry IV*. The Arden Shakespeare. London: Methuen; Cambridge, Mass.: Harvard University Press, 1966, 242 pp.

    Includes discussion of the text, date, the extent of revisions, the relationship to *1 Henry IV*, the sources, major themes, Falstaff and the rejection, and style, as well as appendixes featuring selections from Holinshed, Daniel, Stowe, Elyot, and *The Famous Victories of Henry V*. The date of composition was most likely late 1596 or early 1597, with revisions of the Falstaff name late in 1597 and of the epilogue by early 1599. One of the dominant themes of the play is miscalculation—rom the introduction by Rumor to the pervasive list of surmises, jealousies, and conjectures. Through the action Henry is deepened, not narrowed, as the play achieves a balanced complexity not inferior to part 1.

553. MELCHIORI, GIORGIO, ed. *The Second Part of King Henry IV*. The New Cambridge Shakespeare. Cambridge: Cambridge University Press, 1989, 242 pp.

    Features an introductory essay on publication and date, unconformities, the sources and *The Famous Victories*, the *Henriad* as remake, rewriting the remake, the morality structure, the comedy of humors, city and country comedy, language, history, psychodrama, time and disease, and *Part Two* on the stage. Extensive notes appear on individual pages of the text, and appendixes provide a textual analysis, discussions of Shakespeare's use of Holinshed, some historical and literary sources, portions of *The Famous Victories*, Tarleton and the Lord Chief Justice, and a list of suggested readings.

554. SHAABER, MATHIAS A., ed. *Henry the Fourth, Part 2.* A New Variorum Edition of Shakespeare. Philadelphia: J. B. Lippincott, 1940, 715 pp.
     Uses the first quarto (1600) as the copy text (pp. 1–460). On each page, for that portion of the text, are provided variant readings, textual notes, and general critical commentary. Following the text are sections on the text (the quarto, the folio, the copy text), the date of composition, the authenticity of the text, the sources, criticisms (the play as a whole, the rejection of Falstaff, local color, topical allusions, characters, identifications), the Dering Manuscript, acting versions, stage history, and a list of works consulted. Supplemented by entry 550.

Textual Studies

555. PROSSER, ELEANOR. *Shakespeare's Anonymous Editor: Scribe and Compositor in the Folio Text of "2 Henry IV."* Stanford: Stanford University Press, 1981, 219 pp.
     Argues for the rejection of eighty-six folio readings heretofore considered canonical. Instead of valid alterations reflecting stage practice, the first quarto (1600) represents changes made by the scribe and the compositor in Jaggard's printshop. Changes made by the scribe result from his own stylistic affinities; changes made by the compositor's deletions, insertions, and paraphrases were functional, resolving problems of page makeup. Other folio texts set from good quartos should be carefully examined for similar contaminations.

556. WALKER, ALICE. "Quarto 'Copy' and the 1623 Folio: *2 Henry IV.*" *Review of English Studies*, n.s. 2 (1951):217–25.
     Maintains that the first quarto (1600) was printed from foul papers and the 1623 folio text from a copy of the quarto that had been collated with a fair copy of the foul papers. Errors and anomalies common to both texts are the result of contamination of the quarto by the folio. The massed-entry stage directions, representing little more than bookkeeper's jottings, have been exaggerated. The elimination of oaths from the First Folio of *2 Henry IV* (but not, for example, from the First Folio of *Much Ado About Nothing*) suggests that, with the change of

command in the Office of the Revels during the printing process, Jaggard anticipated a more rigorous attitude toward profanity.

Criticism

557. ABRAMS, RICHARD. "Rumor's Reign in *2 Henry IV*: The Scope of a Personification." *English Literary Renaissance* 16 (1986):467–95.

Claims that the choric character of Rumor reflects a crisis in the kingmaking process, functioning as more than a narrative convenience and more than a device of dramatic irony to tie together the two parts of *Henry IV*. It is "England's emblazoned sinfulness–a nightmare apparition drawn from the king's and the people's guilty consciences" (p. 468).

558. BERGER, HARRY, *Jr*. "Sneak's Noise or Rumor and Detextualization in *2 Henry IV*." *Kenyon Review*, n.s. 6, no. 4 (1984):58–78.

Argues that "Sneak's noise" refers to a kind of "Punk Rock Antigua one might expect to hear in any big-town Renaissance tavern" (p. 62) and that their arrival moments before Hal comes in to spy in disguise on Falstaff and Doll Tearsheet has a distinct effect on the text. More specifically, the name "Sneak" drifts from bandleader to future king and aptly describes the entire game he has been playing with his London low-life companions. It also reflects the theme and tone of the action of the entire play from the conflicting half-truths of Rumor to the embodiment of deviousness in Falstaff.

559. BERGERON, DAVID. "Shakespeare Makes History: *2 Henry IV*." *Studies in English Literature 1500–1900* 31 (1991):231–46.

Notes the several versions of history operating in the play, all of which culminate in Falstaff. Shakespeare, in other words, makes history by shaping selected details of the past, along the way interrogating the various historical modes—the ahistorical, the political, the military, the literary. Falstaff wanders between narrative truth and narrative fiction as the playwright "'histories' the past to new remembrance, to new life" (pp. 240, 244).

560. KNIGHTS, L. C. "Time's Subjects: The Sonnets and *King Henry IV, Part II*." In *Some Shakespearean Themes*. Stanford: Stanford University Press, 1959, pp. 45–64.

Sees *2 Henry IV* as a transitional play, looking back to the sonnets and earlier history plays and forward to the great tragedies. Like the sonnets *2 Henry IV* is concerned with the theme of time and mutability

Henry V

and the various aspects of human frailty such as age, disappointment, and decay. The dying king, the repeated references to Northumberland's illness, the emphasis on Falstaff's age and diseases—all help to create the sense of a passing era that Hal must finally put behind him.

561. LEECH, CLIFFORD. "The Unity of *2 Henry IV.*" *Shakespeare Survey* 6 (1953):16–24.

Perceives in *2 Henry IV* a tone distinctly different from that of part 1. The overt morality pattern pitting the Lord Chief Justice against Falstaff, the preoccupation with the effects of time, the latent skepticism, and the striking objectivity in the presentation of the characters all contribute to a more somber quality that in itself creates a sense of dubiety concerning basic assumptions in the great historical scheme. The probing and ambiguous quality of the play is not unlike that of the dark comedies.

HENRY V

Reference Work

562. CANDIDO, JOSEPH, and FORKER, CHARLES R., comps. *"Henry V": An Annotated Bibliography.* Garland Reference Library of the Humanities, 281: Garland Shakespeare Bibliographies, 4. New York and London: Garland Publishing, 1983, 815 pp.

Contains 2,103 entries representing virtually all publications on the play from 1940 through 1981, along with the most significant items of scholarship prior to 1940. The categories, each arranged chronologically, are divided into criticism, individual editions, complete and collected editions, adaptations, textual and bibliographical studies, language, sources, influence, and staging. A brief introductory essay traces the history of recent criticism.

Editions

563. TAYLOR, GARY, ed. *Henry V.* The Oxford Shakespeare. Oxford and New York: Oxford University Press, 1984, 330 pp.

Includes an introductory essay addressing reception and reputation, the text and interpretation, sources and significances, Henry and historical romance; Chapman, epic, and the chorus, characters and roles, and will and achievement. Extensive notes on each page of the text identify specific problems of language and also provide background information. An appendix includes portions of Holinshed.

564. WALTER, J. H., ed. *King Henry V*. The Arden Shakespeare. London: Methuen; Cambridge, Mass.: Harvard University Press, 1954, 174 pp.

Includes discussion of the text, date, the epic nature of the play, the conversion of Hal, the spiritual significance of the play, other plays on Henry V, the rejection of Falstaff, and critical interpretations, as well as appendixes featuring selections from Holinshed and *The Famous Victories of Henry V*. The text of this edition is based on the First Folio, for which the copy was probably Shakespeare's foul papers. The earlier quarto versions are based on memorial reconstruction.

565. WILSON, JOHN DOVER, ed. *King Henry V*. Cambridge: Cambridge University Press, 1947, 201 pp.

Provides extensive textual notes and a discussion of the copy text (with sections on the first quarto [1600] and First Folio versions), the death of Falstaff, the origins of *Henry V*, a discussion of the stage history, and a glossary. The copy text is the First Folio, which probably represents Shakespeare's foul papers except for the act divisions and the purging of profanity. This frankly patriotic epic drama of Agincourt matches the national mood in the late sixteenth century.

Textual Studies

566. OKERLUND, GERDA. "The Quarto Version of *Henry V* as Stage Adaptation." *PMLA* 49 (1934):810–34.

Claims that the bad quarto of *Henry V* is an unauthorized stage adaptation from the theater manuscript pirated for provincial performance. Virtually all of the differences between quarto and folio texts are satisfactorily explained as the result of adaptation and errors of transcription. Both the length and the cast of characters are significantly reduced, and the style is compressed, made more simple and direct. The promptbook prepared for this production was the printer's copy for the First Folio.

567. PRICE, HEREWARD T. *The Text of "Henry V."* Newcastle-under-Lyme: Mandley and Unett, 1921, 55 pp.

Henry V

Examines the three quartos (1600, 1602, 1608) and the folio (1623) texts of *Henry V* to determine the proper copy text for modern editions. The conclusion is that the first quarto, from which the second and third quartos are derivative, is subsequent to the folio, that it is not a first sketch, and that the folio text is the work of Shakespeare alone.

Criticism

568. ALTMAN, JOEL B. "Vile Participation: The Amplification of Violence in the Theater of *Henry V.*" *Shakespeare Quarterly* 42 (1991):1–32.

Maintains that the play's power comes from "its crafted interaction with the needs of its players and its first audiences" (p. 3), by its evoking communal ritual and sacrifice, honoring the shame involved in such consummation, and providing a quality of reconciliation. The audience's response to England's struggle with France was likely to have been shaped by her contemporary struggle with Ireland. In its mixture of heroism, patriotism, violence, and political manipulation, *Henry V* spoke directly to an audience that felt vulnerable to princely calling, was uncertain of its response, and resistant to peremptory demands.

569. BATTENHOUSE, ROY W. "*Henry V* as Heroic Comedy." In *Essays on Shakespeare and Elizabethan Drama in Honor of Hardin Craig.* Edited by Richard Hosley. Columbia: University of Missouri Press, 1962, pp. 163–82.

Describes *Henry V* as pervaded with irony, not the irony of derisive subversion and derogation but the tolerant irony of that which is blandly content with itself and fails to perceive its monolithic vision. Shakespeare is portraying a Henry and an entire society as "admittedly illustrious but bounded within the limits of a sub-Christian virtue" (p. 168). Spectators and critics, blinded by the surface patriotism, admire the heroism, but the more discerning perceive an emptiness in the pageantry and a fulsomeness in the rhetoric. The crowning irony is that in act 5 Henry gains merely the title "heir" (not "king") of France.

570. BERGER, THOMAS L. "Casting *Henry V.*" *Shakespeare Studies* 20 (1988):89–104.

Reminds us that Shakespeare's audiences came to the playhouse steeped in the tradition of doubling and that he often depended on that mode of presentation to enhance their perception of a given characterization. In *Henry V*, for instance, the three traitors Cambridge, Scroop, and Grey reappear as the honest English soldiers Bates, Court, and

Williams; Bardolph and Nym ("sworn brothers in filching") appear first as the Archbishop of Canterbury and the Bishop of Ely (clerics not exactly disinterested in protecting their own property by encouraging Henry to pursue war against the French); the fustian-loving Pistol appears elsewhere as the rhetoric-drunk Chorus.

571. ———. "The Disappearance of McMorris in Shakespeare's *Henry V*." *Renaissance Papers* (1985):13–26.

Addresses enigmas of character that suggest Shakespearean slips or an unfinished condition in the text of *Henry V*. For instance, in 3.2 Fluellen and McMorris agree to settle their fight later, but McMorris never reappears because in act 4 the actor playing his part is doubling as Exeter. Verbal evidence suggests that McMorris was originally scripted into 4.7, but that the lines were assigned to Fluellen for the sake of doubling.

572. BERMAN, RONALD. "Shakespeare's Alexander: Henry V." *College English* 23 (1962):532–39.

Observes that in the sources Henry is both chivalric and patriotic and also ethical and Christian but that serious inconsistencies arise in the Henry of Shakespeare's play. The enigmatic tradition to which this Henry belongs is that of Alexander, whose account in Plutarch may well have served as an additional, albeit indirect, source. The life of Alexander is coupled with and immediately precedes that of Caesar, Shakespeare's source for *Julius Caesar* written in the same year 1599. Alexander, like Henry, comes to know both the world of ideals and that of practical reality. The death of each is a prelude to the rapid dissolution of their achievements.

573. CUBETA, PAUL M. "Falstaff and the Art of Dying." *Studies in English Literature 1500–1900* 27 (1987):197–211.

Observes that the mystery of Falstaff's death, in that we hear it only by report, binds comedy to tragedy in a manner "historically appropriate, morally satisfying, and psychologically dazzling" (p. 197). In this scene Shakespeare seems to be recalling the medieval and Renaissance tradition of *ars moriendi*. Whether this fat rogue who mocked repentance in the past indeed makes a good ending is an ambiguous point. But in his last moments, as reported by Mistress Quickly, he may engage in what Loyola calls "seeing the spot" (recalling a moment from the past) with a sense of moral or spiritual understanding.

574. DANSON, LAWRENCE N. "*Henry V*: King, Chorus, and Critics." *Shakespeare Quarterly* 34 (1983):27–43.

Suggests that *Henry V* was the first play at the Globe in the fall of 1599 and that the reference to Essex in the chorus of act 5 is a plucky

Henry V

defiance of temporary setbacks in Ireland. An English victory in late 1599 against the Irish would have been not unlike the victory at Agincourt. The interplay of the king as a representative of historical reality and of the chorus as a representative of theatrical reality creates a detached perspective that allows the spectator to view Henry as hero or scoundrel. Henry can control the course of history no more than Shakespeare can control the fate of his play.

575. DOLLIMORE, JONATHAN, and SINFIELD, ALAN. "History and Ideology: The Instance of *Henry V*." In *Alternative Shakespeares*. Edited by John Drakakis. London: Methuen, 1985, pp. 206–37.

Posits that, since the theater was a mode of cultural production especially exposed to the influence of subordinate and emergent classes, playwrights probably engaged topics in which ideology was under strain. For example, one can perceive the foreign war in *Henry V* as "a straightforward ground upon which to celebrate national unity" (p. 215). On the other hand, one also realizes that the obsessive preoccupation of the play is insurrection—treacherous factions within the nobility, a church deviously protective of its own interests, slandering subjects, soldiers who undermine the war or skeptically interrogate the king's motives.

576. GILBERT, ALLAN. "Patriotism and Satire in *Henry V*." In *Studies in Shakespeare*. Edited by Arthur D. Matthews and Clark M. Emery. Coral Gables: University of Miami Press, 1953, pp. 40–64.

Examines the three bodies of material that make up Henry V—*The Famous Victories of Henry V*, the *Chronicles*, and Shakespeare's additions—to determine why the play provokes such diversely opposed interpretations: Henry as ideal king or Henry as the exemplar of the blood-stained Machiavel. Whereas much of the action glorifies the pattern of princehood, Shakespeare deliberately undercuts it through emphasis on the horrors of war. Shakespeare also adds the third theme of the king worn with care as a consequence of his concern for his subjects.

577. HAWKINS, SHERMAN. "Aggression and the Project of the Histories." In *Shakespeare's Personality*. Edited by Norman N. Holland, Sidney Homan, and Bernard J. Paris. Berkeley and London: University of California Press, 1989, pp. 41–65.

Views rivalry, aspiration, and the will to power as fundamental motives in man and considers *Henry V* Shakespeare's effort to create an ideal of heroism and virtuous rule that fulfills and legitimates the energies of aggression. What in Marlowe's Tamburlaine is depicted as raw aggression has been carefully moralized in Henry V; the major battle itself at Agincourt is a kind of trial by combat in which God ratifies the winner. Nonetheless, *Henry V* is a problem play because, whatever Shakespeare's intention, his attitude toward aggression is deeply ambivalent, as is evident in the many strains, uncertainties, and skeptical undercurrents that run through the play.

578. HILLMAN, RICHARD. " 'Not Amurath an Amurath Succeeds': Playing Doubles in Shakespeare's *Henriad.*" *English Literary Renaissance* 21 (1991): 161–89.

Argues that the "Amurath factor" (the concept of Turkish tyranny) functions powerfully in the development of the character of Henry V. Fluellen's comparison of Henry and Alexander, for example, raises the specter of the hero's cruelty, linked as it is to the moment when the king orders the killing of all French prisoners. Henry also represents a stern disciplinarian in maintaining unity among ethnic divisions, a constantly recurring theme "in Renaissance explanations of Islamic military success" (p, 170). The Turkish analogue is woven intertextually, as a significant shadow, into the scene of Hal's succeeding his father.

579. HOBDAY, C. H. "Imagery and Irony in *Henry V.*" *Shakespeare Survey* 21 (1968):107–13.

Suggests that the major critical disagreements concerning *Henry V* reflect a division in Shakespeare's own mind in which his emotions rebelled against his conscious intentions. Image clusters afford an insight into Shakespeare's emotions, and a major cluster in *Henry V* is that associated with death. The fate of Bardolph comments ironically on the nature of war. Shakespeare's divided sympathies are most obvious at Agincourt where there is much that is patriotic and bright but where there is also Williams's moving indictment of Henry.

580. PATTERSON, ANNABEL. "Back by Popular Demand: The Two Versions of *Henry V.*" *Renaissance Drama*, n.s. 19 (1988):29–62.

Points out that analysis of *Henry V* requires a critic to address the concept of history that Shakespeare drew from Holinshed, the history in which the theater was environmentally situated in the 1590s, and the subsequent history of the play's reception and interpretation. Any attempt to "recuperate" Shakespeare's text must account for the sharp division among those who now view it as legitimation and those who view it as subversion. Perhaps it is best to see the play as "metacommentary," a self-conscious statement of how history can be manipulated for political purposes and of resistance to the authorities who "were dictating what forms the stories of English national experience, past and present, should take" (p. 57).

Henry V

581. SHAPIRO, JAMES. "Revisiting *Tamburlaine*: *Henry V* as Shakespeare's Belated Armada Play." *Criticism* 31 (1989):351–66.

Envisions *Henry V* as Shakespeare's response to Marlowe's *Tamburlaine* within the framework of the political climate in London during the spring and summer of 1599. Not only does the play reflect Shakespeare's debt to Marlowe as a point of departure in his other histories; it also represents the political changes that had occurred between 1588 and 1599 in representing national aspirations. Specifically, Shakespeare now found that Marlowe's deeply ironic view of heroical history was suitable for depicting, in equally ironic heroic terms, the severe cost England had paid since 1588 for its search for conquest and honor.

582. SMITH, WARREN D. "The *Henry V* Choruses in the First Folio." *Journal of English and Germanic Philology* 53 (1954):38–57.

Argues that the choruses were not a part of the play as performed at the Globe in 1599, that they were added—possibly after the quarto publication in 1600 and possibly by someone other than Shakespeare—especially for a private performance at court. In at least two places the choruses create unfortunate breaks in the plot (choruses 3 and 4). Specifically, the play was probably performed at the reconverted Cockpit at Whitehall, its dimensions justifying the apologetic tones for depicting mighty actions in such small places.

583. STOLL, ELMER EDGAR. *"Henry V."* In *Poets and Playwrights*. Minneapolis: University of Minnesota Press, 1930, pp. 31–54.

Views *Henry V* in the tradition not of Marlowe but of earlier popular tragicomedy. Depicting Henry's triumphal procession from Harfleur to Agincourt to the French crown and the princess's hand, the play gains unity through its patriotic passion. If the patriotism is not particularly enlightened, Shakespeare nonetheless sets forth the ideal of the practical leader, the country's notion of a hero-king. At the same time he manages to make this hero-king human with an individual voice that expresses both joy and grief, happiness and apprehension.

584. WALCH, GUNTER. *"Henry V* as Working-House of Ideology." *Shakespeare Survey* 40 (1988):63–68.

Argues that Shakespeare in *Henry V* turns the text into a "'quick forge and working-house' of ideology" (p. 64); more specifically, the play assumes meaning and directional style within the political and ideological contents of the age in which it is presented. The portrayal of a young king living in a world of history results in a complex character who, by highlighting discrepancies between orthodox historical legend (described in the Chorus) and actual history, reveals the official ideology as "an illusion effectively used as an instrument of power" (p. 68).

585. WILCOX, LANOR. "Katherine of France as Victim and Bride." *Shakespeare Studies* 17 (1985):61–75.

Focuses on the personality and situation of the French princess and how those elements help to illuminate the character of Henry. More precisely, Shakespeare's depiction of Katherine as a kind of stereotype of a French debutante mediates between Henry's twin roles as a good king and as a leader of an army that ravages the country of France. Her metamorphosis from victim to romantic partner helps to control our attitude toward Henry as aggressor.

586. WILLIAMS, CHARLES. *"Henry V."* In *Shakespeare Criticism 1919–35.* Edited by Anne Bradby Ridler. Oxford: Oxford University Press, 1936, pp. 180-88.

Notes the significance of the absence of Falstaff and Hotspur in *Henry V* so that Shakespeare through the protagonist can develop a new concept of honor as, in peace or war, the capacity to challenge the world and to endure the result of that challenge. Henry proves consistent whether in the brilliant light of victory, in the shadow of confronting conspirators, or in facing potential defeat in battle. His was the last "legerity of spirit" before the tragedies, the development of a capacity of spirit that "thrills through the already poring dusk" (p. 188).

587. WILLIAMSON, MARILYN L. "The Episode with Williams in *Henry V.*" *Studies in English Literature 1500–1900* 9 (1969):275–82.

Argues that Shakespeare does not suddenly transform the character of Hal into that of the ideal prince Henry V. In the Williams episode vestiges of the old Hal remain in his use of disguise to deceive those around him, in the soliloquy that recalls his planned reformation in *1 Henry IV*, in the exchange of gloves that travesties the chivalric values of *Richard II*, and in the attempt to pay off the common soldier. Clearly Henry is still learning to be a king and, thus, is a more complex figure than critics generally realize.

1,2,3 HENRY VI

Reference Work

588. HINCHCLIFFE, JUDITH, comp. *"King Henry VI, Parts 1, 2, and 3": An Annotated Bibliography.* Garland Reference Library of the Humanities, 422: Garland Shakespeare Bibliographies, 5. New York and London: Garland Publishing, 1984, 368 pp.

1,2,3 Henry VI

Contains 981 entries, representing virtually all publications on the plays from 1940 through 1982, along with the most significant items prior to 1940. The categories, each arranged chronologically, include criticism, authorship, textual studies, dating, sources, adaptations and influences, bibliographies, editions, and stage histories. A brief introductory essay traces the history of recent criticism and research.

Textual Study

589. ALEXANDER, PETER. *Shakespeare's "Henry VI" and "Richard III."* Cambridge: Cambridge University Press, 1929, 229 pp.

Establishes the first quarto (1594) of *The First Part of the Contention between the Two Famous Houses of York and Lancaster* and the first quarto (1595) of *The True Tragedy of Richard Duke of York* as bad quartos of *2,3 Henry VI*. The texts are memorial reconstructions by the actor playing Warwick and the actor doubling as Suffolk and Clifford. These actors were leading players in Pembroke's Company, which went bankrupt in 1593. Bibliographical and textual evidence suggests that *2,3 Henry VI* are entirely by Shakespeare and not works of collaboration.

Criticism

590. BERMAN, RONALD. "Fathers and Sons in the *Henry VI* Plays." *Shakespeare Quarterly* 13 (1962):487–97.

Suggests that a major unifying strand in the *Henry VI* plays is the relationship of fathers and sons reflecting tragically the refusal of the enlightenment of experience. Tainted by Richard II's murder, the royal family is deficient in the true qualities of kingship—the Lancastrians in political virtues, the Yorkists in moral virtues. In part 1 the death of the Talbots, father and son, contrasts nobly with bastardized royal kingship; the idea grows in parts 2 and 3 that blood relationships are inconveniences in the way of ambition. The idea of kingship is progressively debased both physically and spiritually.

591. BROCKBANK, J. P. "The Frame of Disorder—Henry VI." In *Early Shakespeare*. Edited by John Russell Brown and Bernard Harris. Stratford-upon-Avon Studies, 3. London: Edward Arnold, 1961, pp. 73–99.

Describes the *Henry VI* plays as a panoramic view of the "plight of individuals caught up in a cataclysmic movement of events for which responsibility is communal and historical, not personal and immediate" (p. 73). From this sweep of events emerge the two extremes of political man—the martyr Henry and the Machiavel Richard. Part 1 stresses the disastrous consequences upon the English forces in France of political dissension at home, part 2 the sacrifice of Gloucester and the dissolution of the law, and part 3 the triumph of soldierly and political anarchism and the creation of the power vacuum that will give rise to Richard.

592. CANDIDO, JOSEPH. "Getting Loose in the *Henry VI* Plays." *Shakespeare Quarterly* 35 (1984):392–406.

Suggests that through the large number of captures and attempted escapes (whether literal or metaphorical) Shakespeare was attempting to provide structural connections for disparate episodes in the *Henry VI* plays. Such a motif artistically binds the Talbot episodes, the relationship of Suffolk and Margaret, the fortunes of the Duke of York, and the connection between Henry VI and Edward IV. Increasingly the voice of the trapped animal or the sense of achievement crushed in these episodes underscores the cycle of brutality and anarchy that characterizes the trilogy.

593. DEAN, PAUL. "Shakespeare's *Henry VI* Trilogy and Elizabethan 'Romance' Histories: The Origins of a Genre." *Shakespeare Quarterly* 33 (1982):34–48.

Considers many of the puzzling features in the *Henry VI* plays to have their explanation in their indebtedness to romance history, a popular type of play when Shakespeare came to London that loosely incorporated historical personages within an imaginary and usually comic framework. Material of this flavor is not found in the chronicles—in part 1 the Temple Garden scene, Joan's scene with the devils, the wooing of Margaret and Suffolk; in part 2 the necromancy practiced by Eleanor, the Simpcox episode, the Jack Cade scenes. Such scenes constitute an ironic, grotesque, or farcical amplification of the major political themes and reveal the *Henry VI* plays to be among Shakespeare's most powerful and richly textured work.

594. PRICE, HEREWARD T. "Mirror-Scenes in Shakespeare." In *Joseph Quincy Adams Memorial Studies*. Edited by James G. McManaway, Giles E. Dawson, and Edwin E. Willoughby. Washington: Folger Shakespeare Library, 1948, pp. 101–13.

Describes Shakespeare's practice of inserting scenes that, while having little or no narrative value, enhance and clarify the emotional quality of the action. The fly scene in *Titus Andronicus*, for example, both reveals Titus's approaching madness and reflects his emotional extremes of love and hatred. The brief scene in *1 Henry VI* in which representatives of the houses of York and Lancaster pick white and red roses as emblems of their cause is another example. So, too, is the gardener scene in *Richard II*.

595. QUINN, MICHAEL. "Providence in Shakespeare's Yorkist Plays." *Shakespeare Quarterly* 10 (1959):45–52.

Suggests that Shakespeare's conception of providence as a controlling motif in the first tetralogy clearly marks his technical superiority over his contemporaries. Shakespeare received from the chronicles the narrative of the War of the Roses as controlled by the general providential view that crime is eventually punished and virtue triumphs. He was far more concerned, however, with cause and effect; by prophecies, explanation and judgment are wedded in the plays, and the spectators develop anticipatory judgments that the action then fulfills. Thus, the spectators see beyond a providential pattern to the individual human deeds and decisions that form the larger pattern.

596. RICKS, DON M. *Shakespeare's Emergent Form: A Study of the Structure of the "Henry VI" Plays.* Logan: Utah State University Press, 1968, 103 pp.

Observes that critics now view the *Henry VI* plays not as rude beginnings but as experimentation. *1 Henry VI*, for example, marks a revolutionary change in the nature of English drama in its blend of the medieval and the naturalistic and in the imposition of a single controlling idea. The emphasis on strands of action rather than on individual characters achieves a sense of the sweep of history, juxtaposing contrasting scenes in part 1, using a double plot to present the theme of dissolution of the law in part 2, and synthesizing plot and design for a greater organic focus in part 3.

597. RIGGS, DAVID. *Shakespeare's Heroical Histories: "Henry VI" and Its Literary Tradition.* Cambridge, Mass.: Harvard University Press, 1971, 194 pp.

Suggests that Shakespeare set out to imitate the heroical history play developed by Greene and his contemporaries, but that he quickly came to understand the humanistic tradition better than they. As he moves through the *Henry VI* trilogy, he progressively stresses the inherent anarchic elements in the tradition of history as "worthy and memorable deeds" in "lively and well-spirited action" (p. 14). Indeed, Richard III is the final distortion of heroic ideals. Hal, later, by insisting on his freedom from the heroic tradition in his repudiation of the style of Hotspur, frees himself to establish his own brand of heroism for national, not personal, glory.

1 HENRY VI

Editions

598. CAIRNCROSS, ANDREW S., ed. *The First Part of King Henry VI*. The Arden Shakespeare. London: Methuen; Cambridge, Mass.: Harvard University Press, 1962, 172 pp.

Includes discussion of the text and of historical and literary scholarship along with appendixes covering various source materials, a York-Lancaster genealogical table, and a list of "recollections" from *1 Henry VI* in bad quartos. Current appraisals, unlike those of the eighteenth and nineteenth centuries, view the play as the work of a single mind. Instead of what used to be considered a stringing together of episodes from various chronicle sources, the play implies a comprehensive world picture "embracing the deposition of Richard II and its consequences as far as the succession of Henry VII" (p. xxxix). The unifying theme of *1 Henry VI* is the breakdown of political order at home that in turn leads to the loss of France.

599. HATTAWAY, MICHAEL, ed. *The First Part of Henry VI*. The New Cambridge Shakespeare. Cambridge: Cambridge University Press, 1990, 210 pp.

Features an introductory essay on Henry VI's reign and the plays, the decay of empire, date and occasion, authorship, stage history, and sources. Extensive notes appear on individual pages of the text, and appendixes include a textual analysis, comments on Shakespeare's sources, genealogical tables, C. W. Hodges's sketch of a conjectural recreation of the stage of the Rose Theatre based on archeological excavation in 1989, and a reading list.

Criticism

600. BEVINGTON, DAVID. "The Domineering Female in *1 Henry VI*." *Shakespeare Studies* 2 (1966):51–58.

1 Henry VI

Observes that the theme of female domination in *1 Henry VI*—in Joan of Arc, the Countess of Auvergne, and Margaret of Anjou—echoes the larger theme of division and discord throughout the play and the tetralogy. That much of this material is not in the chronicles indicates that the playwright was consciously organizing his plot along these lines. The final seduction is that of Henry himself as he disregards wise advice and accepts a dowerless maiden sight unseen. It is the beginning of his self-indulgent withdrawal that characterizes his personality in *2 Henry VI*.

601. BOAS, FREDERICK S. "Joan of Arc in Shakespeare, Schiller and Shaw." *Shakespeare Quarterly* 2 (1951):35–45.

Notes that the image of Joan of Arc in *1 Henry VI* is inconsistent, reflecting her courage, shrewdness, and conviction of her divine mission to save France, on the one hand, and her lack of chastity, coarse mouth, and alliance with the devil on the other. Generally, though, Shakespeare does not distort the prejudicial view found in Holinshed. Joan in Schiller experiences a tragic purgation, but he falsifies history both in her love affair with an English soldier and in the manner of her death. Shaw announces her canonization and stresses the struggle of the church against national unity.

602. GREER, CLAYTON ALVIS. "The Place of *1 Henry VI* in the York-Lancaster Trilogy." *PMLA* 53 (1938):687–701.

Theorizes that there was a "Talbot" or "Harry the Sixth" play before *2,3 Henry VI* and that there was a later revised form of this play. Metrical tests suggest a much earlier revision, which probably took place immediately after *Richard III*.

603. GUTIERREZ, NANCY A. "Gender and Value in *1 Henry VI*: The Role of Joan de Pucelle." *Theatre Journal* 42 (1990):183–93.

Insists that in the depiction of Joan biological difference becomes the site for cultural conflict, that there is "a deliberate gendering that demonstrates the patriarchy's need to defuse and neutralize any female threat by transforming it into a reinforcement of the male prerogative" (p. 183). Shakespeare's dramatic technique of presenting her character largely through the perspective of other characters forces the audience into collusion with the patriarchal point of view. The power politics practiced by the English and French rests largely on gender ascription.

604. HARDIN, RICHARD F. "Chronicles and Mythmaking in Shakespeare's Joan of Arc." *Shakespeare Survey* 42 (1989):25–35.

Observes that Shakespeare inherited a mixed image of Joan from English chronicles, an image formed partly from historical account and partly from myth. Vilification increased with the Reformation and the accounts of John Bale, John Cooper, and John Stowe. Edward Halle was the first historian "to develop a full-scale assassination of Joan's character" (p. 27), an account repeated by Grafton and by Holinshed, who added (from earlier versions) the story of Joan's pregnancy. The second edition of Holinshed in 1587 fully developed this attack, and Shakespeare added the details of her witchcraft.

605. JACKSON, GABRIELE BERNHARD. "Topical Ideology: Witches, Amazons, and Shakespeare's Joan of Arc." *English Literary Renaissance* 18 (1988):40–65.

Argues that *1 Henry VI* situates itself in an area of conflict readily identifiable by the audience. At the time the play was composed (1591–92) England was back in France, but English policy was divided by the "war party" that cried for all-out aggression and the queen's favored policy of negotiation, delay, and minimal expenditure. The disjunctive presentation of Joan as numinous, subversively powerful, and demonized reflects Shakespeare's conscious development of a play in which ideologically opposed elements are found in coexistence.

606. KIRSCHBAUM, LEO. "The Authorship of *1 Henry VI*." *PMLA* 67 (1952):809–22.

Argues that the chief evidence for Shakespeare's authorship of *1 Henry VI* is its inclusion in the First Folio. Moreover, *1 Henry VI* was probably composed first, preparing the characters and the sequence of events for *2,3 Henry VI*. A careful analysis of the language, metrics, and structure indicates nothing to prevent claiming Shakespeare's sole authorship.

607. PRICE, HEREWARD T. *Construction in Shakespeare*. Ann Arbor: University of Michigan Press, 1951, 42 pp.

Derides the pervasive critical notion that Shakespeare was a child of nature and the manner in which it has for so long deterred attention from the artistry of his dramaturgy. Shakespeare, in fact, was a meticulous craftsman with a Gothic exuberance in intricate design. In *1 Henry VI*, for example, he imposes upon his material a controlling idea to which all directly or obliquely contributes—the effects arising from the strengths or weaknesses of the ruler. In scene 1 dissension breaks out even during the ritual of burying Henry V, and scene 2 offers a contrasting view in France. The play throughout exhibits a carefully controlled design in its rhythmic patterns of repetition.

608. RACKIN, PHYLLIS. "Anti-Historians: Women's Roles in Shakespeare's Histories." *Theatre Journal* 37 (1985):329–44.

Insists that, while Renaissance historiography constituted a masculine tradition, Shakespeare endows the women of his history plays with a voice that challenges the logocentric, masculine historical record. *1 Henry VI*, for example, can be seen as a series of attempts on the part of the English to write a history that will preserve Henry V's fame. All of the women—Joan of Arc, the Countess of Auvergne, Margaret of Anjou—are French and constitute a threat to the English protagonists and their heroic images. Such a gender struggle underlies each of the histories; the women "were anti-historians in . . . the story that the men had written" (p. 344).

2 HENRY VI

Editions

609. CAIRNCROSS, ANDREW S., ed. *The Second Part of King Henry VI*. The Arden Shakespeare. London: Methuen; Cambridge, Mass.: Harvard University Press, 1957, 197 pp.

Includes discussion of the text, the historical material, and literary interpretations, as well as appendixes covering source materials from Halle's *Chronicle* and Fox's *Acts and Monuments*, genealogical tables, and the relationship with the bad quarto, *The First Part of the Contention between the Two Famous Houses of York and Lancaster* (1594). The text is based on the First Folio, for which the copy was probably a theatrical manuscript. The likely date of composition was early 1590, and the current assumption is that Shakespeare was the sole author, having written the play for Pembroke's Men as part of a planned tetralogy.

610. HATTAWAY, MICHAEL, ed. *The Second Part of "Henry VI."* The New Cambridge Shakespeare. Cambridge: Cambridge University Press, 1991, 248 pp.

Features an introductory essay on Henry VI's reign and the plays, the political context, the stage history, the date and occasion, and the sources. Extensive notes appear on individual pages of the text, and a textual analysis, examples from Shakespeare's sources, selections from the *First Part of the Contention*, genealogical tables, and a reading list are appended.

Textual Studies

611. DORAN, MADELEINE. *"Henry VI, Parts II and III": Their Relation to "The Contention" and "The True Tragedy."* University of Iowa Humanistic Studies, vol. 4, no. 4. Iowa City: University of Iowa Press, 1928, 88 pp.

Reviews the three theories of the relationship of the First Folio *2,3 Henry VI* and *The First Part of the Contention between the Two Famous Houses of York and Lancaster* and *The True Tragedy of Richard Duke of York*, concluding that the only viable one is that the last two are bad quartos of the first. Abridgment of nondramatic material, occasional patching, and accretion of comic material suggest adaptation for acting purposes put together by memorial reconstruction. Probably a traveling group in 1592–93 included several who had played in the *Henry VI* plays and who communally reconstructed the texts, adding comic materials freely.

612. PROUTY, C. T. *"The Contention" and Shakespeare's "2 Henry VI": A Comparative Study.* New Haven: Yale University Press, 1954, 157 pp.

Concludes that the 1594 *The First Part of the Contention between the Two Famous Houses of York and Lancaster* cannot have been derived from the version of *2 Henry VI* in the 1623 folio. Thus, *The Contention* is not a bad quarto of *2 Henry VI*; instead, the style of the unique material in the First Folio suggests that *2 Henry VI* was a later revision. We can no longer assume that Shakespeare wrote original history plays early in his career. All that we can assume, based on the reference to Henry VI in the epilogue in *Henry V*, is that Shakespeare had revised the play *2 Henry VI* some time before 1599.

613. URKOWITZ, STEVEN. " 'If I Mistake in Those Foundations Which I Build Upon': Peter Alexander's Textual Analysis of *Henry VI Parts 2 and 3.*" *English Literary Renaissance* 18 (1988):230–56.

Denies the validity of the theory of memorial reconstruction as an explanation for the textual differences in the so-called bad quartos, suggesting instead that the two versions of the text represent stages of Shakespeare's work. Perhaps Shakespeare drafted a scene some distance away from his Holinshed and later revised it to straighten out particular

2 Henry VI

details of history. Indeed, Shakespeare's *Henry VI* and *Richard III* stumble through what elsewhere we would recognize as "authorial practices of composition and revision" (p. 255), Elizabethan dramatic scripts preserved in alternate texts.

Criticism

614. ALBERS, FRANK. "Utopia, Reality and Representation: The Case of Jack Cade." *Shakespeare Jahrbuch* 127 (1991):77–89.

Stresses the opposition between the utopian rebellion of Jack Cade and the reality of the courtly world in the play. Cade's model for reform (for example the abolishment of writing and of pecuniary exchange) is possible only through radically severing the ties with official discourse. Even though his goal of an egalitarian preliteral "otherworld" is safely encapsulated within the world it seeks to subvert (prompted and controlled by one powerful in that very society), it does serve to reflect "Elizabethan society's preoccupation with (re)organizing and (re)structuring an increasingly 'fluid' reality" (p. 86).

615. BERNTHAL, CRAIG A. "Treason in the Family: The Trial of Thump v. Horner." *Shakespeare Quarterly* 42 (1991):44–54.

Examines the master-apprentice relationship in the context of Tudor political and family structure in order to reveal the deeply divided response that Thump's killing of Horner would evoke in the Elizabethan audience. On the one hand, the victory of the weaker Peter over his master in a trial by combat exposes the latter's treason and provides support for the claim that Henry is King by divine sanction. On the other, for the victory to have been achieved by a servant's betrayal of his master would have been deeply disturbing to a society almost paranoid about the use of charges of treason as a strategy for political containment.

616. CALDERWOOD, JAMES L. "Shakespeare's Evolving Imagery: *2 Henry VI*." *English Studies* 48 (1967):481–93.

Notes that Shakespeare's imagery in this play begins to break its quality of set rhetorical speech and to acquire its own linear development in moving from the static and ornamental toward the active and functional. Four patterns of imagery are noteworthy, those dealing with trapping, sight, elevation, and hands. They are utilized to explore the kingly character of Henry himself and of two other regal figures, Gloucester the regent and York the claimant. Such imagistic patterns, while limited, suggest the texture of Shakespeare's rhetorical powers to come in the later plays.

617. LEE, PATRICIA-ANN. "Reflections of Power: Margaret of Anjou and the Dark Side of Queenship." *Renaissance Quarterly* 39 (1986):183–217.

Observes that Shakespeare's depiction of Margaret as pitiless, cruel, and energetic, a pattern of negative feminine power, was the end product of a lengthy period of development. Historically she was regarded as leader of the Lancastrian party during the final years of their struggle and decline, and the means by which the raw material of her life were turned into a literary image included both gossip and propaganda, material then finding its way into the chronicles of Edward's time. From Polydore Vergil forward, her story was more tragic than evil, but she still emerged as a manly, domineering figure. Shakespeare's dramatic portrayal was possible only because Elizabeth's position was so secure that the images of Margaret proved no threat.

3 HENRY VI

Editions

618. CAIRNCROSS, ANDREW S., ed. *The Third Part of King Henry VI*. The Arden Shakespeare. London: Methuen; Cambridge, Mass.: Harvard University Press, 1964, 187 pp.

Includes discussion of the text, date, company, sources, and critical interpretations, along with appendixes featuring selections from Halle's *Chronicle* and Brooke's *Romeus and Juliet*, genealogical tables, and alternative passages from the bad quarto, *The True Tragedy of Richard Duke of York* (1595). The text is from the First Folio, for which the copy was probably Shakespeare's manuscript annotated by the prompter. The play is now considered to be wholly Shakespeare's, the date late 1590 or early 1591. *3 Henry VI* is a study in anarchy—in the state, the family, and the individual mind as Richard develops into a living symbol of anarchy while Henry is a standing protest against the horrors of war.

619. WILSON, JOHN DOVER, ed. *3 Henry VI*. Cambridge: Cambridge University Press, 1952, 225 pp.

Provides extensive textual notes, a critical introduction (covering

Shakespeare's early dramatic style and a comparison of the theme of the War of the Roses as handled by Shakespeare and Holinshed), a discussion of the copy text, a section on stage history, and a glossary. This edition is based on the First Folio, for which the copy was probably a draft supplied to the prompter for the original performances. Most significant is the development of the character of Richard; he as a murderous Machiavel and Henry as a saintly hero reflect the two poles within which anarchy and chaos reigned in England between the battles of St. Albans and Tewkesbury.

Criticism

620. KERNAN, ALVIN. "A Comparison of the Imagery in *3 Henry VI* and *The True Tragedie of Richard Duke of York.*" *Studies in Philology* 51 (1954):431–42.

Observes that the imagery provides a striking contrast between *3 Henry VI* and *The True Tragedy*, although in both the imagery is more decorative than functional. Typically Shakespearean is the use of a comprehensive and recurrent central image, and such an image is the sea-wind-tide figure (the sea forcing against the land and blown back by the wind). Compared to the use of this image thirteen times in *3 Henry VI*, it appears only twice in *The True Tragedy*. Such facts pose difficulties for those who consider *The True Tragedy* to be a memorial reconstruction of *3 Henry VI*.

HENRY VIII

Reference Work

621. MICHELI, LINDA McJ., comp. *"Henry VIII": An Annotated Bibliography.* Garland Reference Library of the Humanities, 540: Garland Shakespeare Bibliographies, 15. New York and London: Garland Publishing, 1988, 444 pp.

Contains 969 items, representing virtually all publications on the play from 1940 to 1986, along with the most significant items prior to 1940. The categories, each arranged chronologically, include criticism, authorship, sources and background, dating, textual studies, editions and adaptations, translations, stage history, influences and analogues, and bibliographies. A brief introductory essay traces the history of recent criticism and research.

Editions

622. FOAKES, R. A., ed. *King Henry VIII*. The Arden Shakespeare. London: Methuen; Cambridge, Mass.: Harvard University Press, 1968, 215 pp.

Includes discussion of the text, authorship, date of composition, sources, critical interpretations, and stage history, as well as an appendix on *Henry VIII* and the burning of the Globe Theatre. The text is based on the First Folio, for which the copy was probably a fair copy of the author's manuscript by a meticulous scribe. Textual peculiarities suggest a single writer. The date of composition was 1613, and Shakespeare drew from a variety of historical sources. Structurally the play grows through a series of contrasts and oppositions, and its theme is "the promise of a golden future, after trials and sufferings, terminating in the attainment of self-knowledge, forgiveness, and reconciliation" (p. lviii).

623. MARGESON, JOHN. *King Henry VIII*. The New Cambridge Shakespeare. Cambridge: Cambridge University Press, 1990, 191 pp.

Features an introductory essay on date and occasion, authorship, sources, critical reception, the unity of the play, the verse, and stage history. Extensive notes appear on individual pages of the text, and appendixes include supplementary notes, a textual analysis, and a suggested reading list.

Criticism

624. BERMAN, RONALD. "*King Henry the Eighth*: History and Romance." *English Studies* 48 (1960):112–21.

Notes that *Henry VIII* is a symmetrical balance of themes and of modes of representation. It shares with the histories a concern for motive and heroic conflict while it shares with the romances a symbolic quality in which the principal figures are led to a new consciousness. The latter motif is greatly enhanced by the lavish quality of the staging; "full of state" and "noble scenes," the action involves twelve formal entrances, signs of power, music, and masquelike scenes. The final moments focus on Elizabeth as a child who will bring to the world a sense of blessedness.

Henry VIII

625. CESPEDES, FRANK V. " 'We Are One in Fortunes': The Sense of History in *Henry VIII*." *English Literary Renaissance* 10 (1980):413–38.

Argues that critics who attempt to minimize Henry's hypocrisy neglect the evidence that Shakespeare structures events to increase rather than to mitigate it. The final act does not vindicate Henry; to the end he is a thoroughly political self-aggrandizing monarch. The theme of the play is built on the conflict between the ends and means of history. The culminating irony is that events fall out beneficently, but not because men have done anything to guide them in that direction.

626. DEAN, PAUL. "Dramatic Mode and Historical Vision in *Henry VIII*." *Shakespeare Quarterly* 37 (1986):175–89.

Describes the structure of the play as a combination of chronicle and romance. As chronicle, the play, unlike Shakespeare's earlier *Henriad*, utilizes a single plot, a *de casibus* pattern of falls (Buckingham, Katherine, Wolsey), and a straightforward plot that refuses to be drawn into ethical, political, and religious controversies. Filtered into the chronicle pattern are elements of romance such as the Field of the Cloth of Gold (1.1), the banquet scene in which the king as a masquer is smitten by Anne Bullen (1.4), and the emphasis on the baby Elizabeth as a phoenix (5.4); the last lends a sense of closure to an open-ended chronicle.

627. FELPERIN, HOWARD. "Shakespeare's *Henry VIII*: History as Myth." *Studies in English Literature 1500–1900* 6 (1966):225–46.

Observes that critical attention to *Henry VIII* as drama, quite apart from the argument over who wrote it, has been patronizing and disappointing. In departing radically from his earlier uses of Holinshed and in subtitling the play "What Is Truth?" Shakespeare perhaps ironically hints that we should reconsider what historical truth is and what the truth of mimetic representation is. *Henry VIII*, more specifically, takes on the flavor of a myth. While the history plays set forth events for their own sake, *Henry VIII* is a metaphysical drama; the truth of the play resides in the eternal relevance of the Christian myth that the action re-creates.

628. HARRIS, BERNARD. "What's Past Is Prologue: *Cymbeline* and *Henry VIII*." In *Later Shakespeare*. Edited by John Russell Brown and Bernard Harris. Stratford-upon-Avon Studies, 8. London: Edward Arnold, 1966, pp. 203–34.

Notes Shakespeare's use of past events to reshape the present as a motif in all of the romances. *Cymbeline* employs historical legend, romance, and fairy tale to create a royal eulogy through a veiled reconstruction of the Tudor myth. *Henry VIII*, likewise, is historical romance, at once sympathetic, interesting, and instructive. Through pageant and ceremony it meditates upon the dangers of pride and the ambivalences of ambitious kingship, atoning for Katherine's wrongs through her private vision, humanizing Henry by treating his love as lust, and glorifying Elizabeth as a child designed by providence to lead England to greatness.

629. MOCHELI, LINDA McJ. " 'Sit by Us': Visual Imagery and the Two Queens in *Henry VIII*." *Shakespeare Quarterly* 38 (1987):452–66.
    Examines the visual imagery—the gestures, movements, and stage images—associated with Katherine and Anne, polar characters representing the old order and the new and opposing ideals of womanhood. In general, the visual imagery emphasizes the coherence and integrity of Katherine's character, whereas with Anne words and actions are on occasion at odds. This pattern reinforces the broadly sympathetic response to Katherine and the rather cool and reserved one to Anne. The conflicting qualities of opposing female archetypes, a love triangle, and a glimpse of the supernatural (in Katherine's vision) reinforce the romance features of the play, but they are also true to the chronicle record, itself deeply imbued with such elements.

630. NOLING, KIM H. "Grubbing Up the Stock: Dramatizing Queens in *Henry VIII*." *Shakespeare Quarterly* 39 (1988):291–306.
    Observes that, while he creates a dramaturgy of queens that admits dissent against the king's manipulation of women to produce a male heir, Shakespeare ultimately endorses Henry's patriarchal will. The playwright, more specifically, allows Katherine a generous and commanding exposure, but he denies Mary a stage presence at all and dramatizes Anne "just deeply enough to serve Henry's dynastic purposes" (p. 292). Moreover, Elizabeth, the fruit, is depicted as a "maiden Phoenix" from whose ashes will arise a new "heir [i.e., James] / As great in admiration as herself" (5.4.41–42). Thus, the threatening female body is transcended and queens are subverted into "no more than the means by which kings are produced" (p. 306).

631. RICHMOND, HUGH M. "Shakespeare's *Henry VIII*: Romance Redeemed by History." *Shakespeare Studies* 4 (1968):334–49.
    Points out the irony in the fact that charges of the flawed nature of *Henry VIII* coincide with assumptions in the second half of the nineteenth century that the play was a work of collaboration with Fletcher. The artistry of *Henry VIII* is best understood in light of the romances as a similar attempt to contrive events to reveal human fallibility overridden by providence. The action involves four successive trials of in-

timates of the king with Henry intervening to save the fourth, Archbishop Cranmer. This last episode is deliberately elevated to reflect Henry as a model magistrate.

632. RUDNYTSKY, PETER. *"Henry VIII* and the Deconstruction of History." *Shakespeare Survey* 43 (1990):43–57.

Asserts that like the second tetralogy *Henry VIII* is built on the tension of ambiguity, able to be viewed either as a celebration of royal power or an interrogation and demystification of it. The subtitle, "all is true," is not a promise of historical veracity but an indication that no single point of view is allowed to control or contain all others. The generic tension between history and romance is only one example of such pervasive ambiguity. A part of the historical context of the play is the marriage of James's daughter Elizabeth shortly after the death of his son Henry, as was James's order to exhume and rebury in Westminster Abbey the body of his mother Mary Queen of Scots, in whose judicial murder he years before had tacitly cooperated.

633. SCHREIBER-MCGEE, F. " 'The View of Earthly Glory': Visual Strategies and the Issue of Royal Prerogative in *Henry VIII.*" *Shakespeare Studies* 20 (1988):191–200.

Proposes that the discourse of power moves from the court to the stage to create a challenge to the legality of royal prerogative and that the play presents such discourse as an instrument for the exercise of power supporting the supremacy of the law over that of the crown. The issue is clearly one of royal prerogative; the "play literally gives a 'view of earthly glory' as broad patterns of political events are crystallized in costume, ceremony, and ritual" (pp. 192–93). If the spectacles of power manifested the supremacy of the crown at Whitehall, at the Globe they became a "subtle commentary on the inconsistencies in the nature and effects of this power" (p. 199).

634. TILLYARD, E. M. W. "Why Did Shakespeare Write *Henry VIII*?" *Critical Quarterly* 3 (1961):22–27.

Argues that Shakespeare's close familiarity in his early years as a dramatist with British history as recorded in Halle's *Chronicle* prepared him to write on the reign of Henry VIII. That reign was the culmination of Halle's account, and he spends virtually half of his book on it. Shakespeare probably stored in his mind the idea and details for a play that he was finally prompted to re-create in later life, whether by his conscience or by a request for a play suitable for royal celebration. The work reflects great technical skill but lacks the creative energy at the center of his greatest work.

KING JOHN

Editions

635. BEAURLINE, LESTER A., ed. *King John*. The New Cambridge Shakespeare. Cambridge: Cambridge University Press, 1990, 212 pp.

Features an introductory essay on stage history, dramatic speech, symmetries and design, politics and conscience. Extensive notes appear on individual pages of the text, and supplementary notes, a textual analysis, a discussion of the date, sources, and *The Troublesome Reign of King John*, and a list of suggested readings are appended.

636. BRAUNMULLER, A. R., ed. *King John*. The Oxford Shakespeare. Oxford and New York: Oxford University Press, 1989, 303 pp.

Includes an introductory essay addressing sources, the text (early records, folio copy, act/scene division, revision), political language and the language of *King John*, wills and the crown of England, monarchs—parents—the Bastard, patterns of action, early stage history, the text in the theater, and theatrical reputation and recent stage history. Extensive notes on each page of the text identify specific problems and provide background information.

637. FURNESS, HENRY HOWARD, Jr., ed. *The Life and Death of King John*. A New Variorum Edition of Shakespeare. Philadelphia: J. B. Lippincott, 1919, 728 pp.

Uses the First Folio as the copy text. On each page, for that portion of the text, are provided variant readings, textual notes, and general critical commentary. Following the text are sections on the nature of the copy, the date of composition, *The Troublesome Reign of King John*, Cibber's adaptation, the characters, criticisms, stage history, costumes, actors' interpretations, dramatic versions, and a list of works consulted.

638. HONIGMANN, E. A. J., ed. *King John*. The Arden Shakespeare. London: Methuen; Cambridge, Mass.: Harvard University Press, 1954, 176 pp.

Includes discussion of the text, sources, date, stage history, and critical interpretations, as well as appendixes featuring selections from Holinshed, consideration of the text of *The Troublesome Reign of King John*, and structural differences between that play and Shakespeare's. The text is based on the First Folio, for which the copy was probably Shakespeare's foul papers; and the likely date of composition is 1590–

King John

91. The play is a study in virtuoso politics. However shortsighted his strategy, John's tactics are brilliant; ultimately, though, the king collapses into ungovernable passion. Faulconbridge stands outside the inner framework as a commentator.

Criticism

639. BARISH, JONAS. *"King John* and Oath Breach." In *Shakespeare: Text, Language, Criticism: Essays in Honor of Marvin Spevack.* Edited by Bernard Fabian and Kurt Tetzeli von Rosador. Hildesheim and New York: Olms-Weidmann, 1987, pp. 1–18.

Views the play as virtually a disputation on the swearing and violating of oaths, with some breaches provoking respect and others disgust. The English lords, for instance, violate their pledge of loyalty to John out of a sense of moral outrage concerning what they presume to be the king's responsibility for Arthur's death. Quite different is the cold-blooded duplicity of Lewis, who trades in violated pledges as a kind of commodity. In effect, oaths in *King John* have meaning only to the degree that men are willing to invest them with meaning.

640. BONJOUR, ADRIEN. "The Road to Swinstead Abbey." *ELH* 18 (1951):253–74.

Notes that recent criticism has attacked the unity of the play in its lack of a central figure and a leading motive. To the contrary, Shakespeare achieves unity through a remarkable balancing of the development of two figures—John and the Bastard, their careers forming complementary panels of a diptych. Just as John's fall is epitomized in the scene in which he orders Hubert to murder Arthur, so the Bastard's rise is measured in terms of his reaction to this order. The scene measures his integrity in contrast to John's utter perfidy.

641. BRAUNMULLER, A. R. *"King John* and Historiography." *ELH* 55 (1988):309–27.

Points out that the chronicles are sources for Shakespeare in the same way *Menaechmi* is a source for *The Comedy of Errors.* In *King John,* more precisely, Shakespeare rewrites Holinshed, and from such an adaptation we can learn much about Elizabethan attitudes toward historical texts. His creation of the Bastard is a means of deflecting the censor's tendency to view with displeasure the dramatization of issues of legitimacy and rule. Similarly, he confuses the issue of responsibility for Arthur's death enough to escape political reprisal. Shakespeare, in other words, like others at the time, practiced an interpretation of history necessitated by "cultural constraints and threats of censorship or worse" (p. 327).

642. BURCKHARDT, SIGURD. *"King John*: The Ordering of This Present Time." *ELH* 33 (1966):133–53.

Argues that Shakespeare in writing *King John* became a modern in the sense that he no longer accepted order as defined by the Christian medieval worldview. In plot, style, and dialect the play directs attention to the falsity of this view. Arthur, for example, in pleading for Hubert to spare his life, never once mentions God; language must do its own work—and it works in that Hubert does not carry out the assassination. The Bastard's speech is another example, and John's counterclaim for the kingship strikes at a fundamental tenet of medieval divine sanction.

643. CALDERWOOD, JAMES L. "Commodity of Honour in *King John*." *University of Toronto Quarterly* 29 (1960):341–56.

Describes the Bastard's commodity speech as more than evidence that Shakespeare is progressing from rhetoric to a more trenchant style of utterance; it is in its extremity suggestive of the imbalance that runs throughout the action. Shakespeare, more precisely, tests the two antagonistic ethical principles of honor and commodity, and its application to John and to the Bastard gives the play a unity of structure not generally recognized. Appropriately the Bastard delivers the final speech, in which honor dictates to commodity in confirmation both of loyalty to England and to an ethical principle.

644. CARLISLE, CAROL J. "Constance: A Theatrical Trinity." In *"King John": New Perspectives*. Edited by Deborah T. Curren-Aquino. Newark: University of Delaware Press; London and Toronto: Associated University Presses, 1989, pp. 144–64.

Reviews the role of Constance as played by Sarah Siddons (late eighteenth through early nineteenth century), Helen Faucit (Victorian), and Clair Bloom (contemporary). All three have made maternal love, not personal ambition, the focal point of the characterization. The greatest challenge for the role is the proper modulation between poetry and frenzy. In general terms, Siddons's portrayal as a powerful and majestic woman dominated the stage, Faucit introduced a greater degree of tenderness and pathos, and Bloom stressed the gentle and quietly rational.

645. CURREN-AQUINO, DEBORAH T., ed. *"King John": New Perspectives*. Newark: University of Delaware Press; London and Toronto: Associated University Presses, 1989, 205 pp.

King John

>   Examines those aspects of *King John* that reveal, perhaps more
> than any other chronicle play, Shakespeare's notions of history and
> historiography. Essays cover issues of historiographic method (Marsha
> Robinson), *The Troublesome Reign* (Guy Hamel), subversion and con-
> tainment (Virginia M. Vaughan), staging (Barbara A. Traister, Ed-
> ward S. Brubaker), the role of the Bastard (Joseph A. Porter, Dorothea
> Kehler, Michael Manheim), politics and adultery (Joseph Candido),
> Constance (Carol J. Carlisle), female subversion (Phyllis Rackin), and
> the enigmatic closure (Larry S. Champion).

646. HAMEL, GUY. *"King John* and *The Troublesome Raigne*: A Reexamina-
      tion." In *"King John": New Perspectives*. Edited by Deborah T. Curren-
      Aquino. Newark: University of Delaware Press; London and Toronto:
      Associated University Presses, 1989, 41–61.

>   Defends *The Troublesome Reign* as "a remarkably advanced work"
> (p. 42). Most notably, the anonymous author creates the Bastard from
> slight and scattered hints in the chronicles. At the same time,
> Shakespeare's adaptation of this figure is a barometer of his more im-
> pressive effort. In *The Troublesome Reign* the Bastard is a figure of fable,
> a high adventurer who never escapes the limitations of his fictional
> context. In Shakespeare the Bastard soon outgrows such fantasy and, if
> as a fictional creation he cannot actually change the events of history,
> he, a candid figure of realpolitik, can serve as a commentator and guide
> for the spectators.

647. LEVIN, CAROLE. " 'I Trust I May Not Trust Thee': Women's Vision of
      the World in Shakespeare's *King John*." In *Ambiguous Realities: Women
      in the Middle Ages and the Renaissance*. Edited by Carole Levin and
      Jennie Watson. Detroit: Wayne State University Press, 1987, pp. 219–
      34.

>   Contends that the female characters in the play—Elinor, mother of
> John; Constance, widow of John's brother Geoffrey; and Blanche,
> John's niece—are more insightful and more honest about their corrupt
> political environment than their male counterparts. Elinor is the driving
> force, giving strength to John while she is alive; she is also more per-
> ceptive than her son concerning Constance's role. Had John followed
> her advice and come to terms with Constance, war might well have
> been averted. Ultimately, however, these characters are powerless to
> change the course of events, their influence fading as the corruption
> deepens.

648. MANHEIM, MICHAEL. "The Four Voices of the Bastard." In *"King
      John: New Perspectives*. Edited by Deborah T. Curren-Aquino. Newark:

University of Delaware Press; London and Toronto: Associated University Presses, 1989, pp. 126–35.

Perceives the Bastard as speaking in four distinctly different voices representing stages of his political coming of age. The first three reflect increasing degrees of worldly knowledge and the last how he uses such knowledge. His first stage is that of an Elizabethan soldier of fortune. By his "commodity" speech in act 2 he has been jolted into cynical manhood determined to become a part of the rotten system he has seen in operation. In acts 3–4 he says little or nothing, but he assumes a Machiavellian role in plundering abbeys and in intimidating lords of the realm. For his final stage in act 5 he finds the voice appropriate to the new state, "where brutalities and deceptions must take place beneath an attractive veneer" (p. 132).

649. MATCHETT, WILLIAM H. "Richard's Divided Heritage in *King John*." *Essays in Criticism* 12 (1962):231–53.

Envisions the plot of *King John* as built around the question of who should be the rightful king of England. Following Arthur's death and John's collapse, the Bastard seems to be moving toward a rightful position; but, when Henry emerges as a candidate in act 5, Faulconbridge kneels in obeisance to him. Honor in the play is finally seen, not as a matter of prestige and power, but as a matter of duty and responsibility. As a symbol of a true subject in a unified England, the Bastard is more important than the king himself.

650. PETTET, E. C. "Hot Irons and Fever: A Note on Some of the Imagery in *King John*." *Essays in Criticism* 4 (1954):128–44.

Notes that even the auditor in the playhouse can hardly miss the reiterated references to heat and fire. Shakespeare found no such imagistic predominance in his source play *The Troublesome Reign of King John* or in Holinshed. Central to the creative process is 4.1, which abounds with excruciating images of the hot irons with which Hubert threatens to blind Arthur, and 5.3, in which John in his last speech dies in burning agony from poison. Apparently these projected scenes exercised a compulsive force on Shakespeare's creativity throughout the play and are responsible for the pattern of associated images.

651. RACKIN, PHYLLISS. "Patriarchal History and Female Subversion in *King John*." In *"King John": New Perspectives*. Edited by Deborah T. Curren-Aquino. Newark: University of Delaware Press; London and Toronto: Associated University Presses, 1989, pp. 76–90.

Considers the patriarchal mythology inherent in Renaissance historiography and observes that Shakespeare's histories depict a world of male power. In *King John*, however, the playwright subjects the masculine voices of patriarchal authority to feminine interrogation. Driven by their hatred of each other, Elinor and Constance incite war between England and France. Elinor plays the role of soldier; and the two in their fury impugn the legitimacy of births (Arthur's, Geoffrey's) essential to patriarchal succession. Before the political factionalism can be resolved and the patriarchy restored in young Henry, the women's voices must be silenced.

652. STEVICK, R. "Repentant Ashes." *Shakespeare Quarterly* 13 (1962):366–70.

Describes 4.1 as an experimental scene in which Shakespeare fuses drama and imagery in a powerful manner suggestive of his later mature work. The scene involves Arthur's begging Hubert to spare his eyes, and the apogee of the appeal appears in Arthur's reference to repentant ashes. The iron has grown cold; and the breath of heaven, by strewing the repentant ashes on it, makes it incapable of reheating. The image functions synoptically for the language and action of the scene, while also describing the emotions imputed to Arthur and Hubert and directing the progress of emotions in the spectators.

653. VAUGHAN, VIRGINIA M. "Between Tetralogies: *King John* as Transition." *Shakespeare Quarterly* 35 (1984):407–20.

Asserts that *King John* is a vital transitional step between the first tetralogy, which focuses on a nexus of external actions to define the political process, and the second tetralogy, which probes the underlying causes of history in the political behavior of individual men. In its emphasis on the political present of decision making, this play marks a critical stage of development in its experimentation with techniques to convey political complexities rooted in character. Pretensions to majesty are undercut by commodity at every turn, juxtaposing the desire for the perfect ruler with the grim realities of guile and treachery.

654. ———. "*King John*: A Study in Subversion and Containment." In "*King John*": *New Perspectives*. Edited by Deborah T. Curren-Aquino. Newark: University of Delaware Press; London and Toronto: Associated University Presses, 1989, pp. 62–75.

Suggests that Shakespeare crafted John in part from the medieval villainous king and in part from the proto-Protestant hero. In this dual perspective the play also mirrors England in the 1590s—"at a crucial transition from the last vestiges of a medieval/feudal system to the modern age of individualism" (p. 63). The closure is far from convincing. The subversion of patrilineal inheritance still lingers, as does the fracture between England and the church, as does the conflict between lords and king. By refusing to privilege one ideology over another, however, Shakespeare depicts a disunity truer to life than he knew.

655. WIXSON, DOUGLAS C. " 'Calm Words Folded Up in Smoke': Propaganda and Spectator Response in *King John*." *Shakespeare Studies* 14 (1981):111–27.

Argues that *King John* deserves an interpretation that frees it from the bondage of a political morality play and allows us to see it frankly as characters playing political roles. The play's potential lies in such an open form, encouraging the spectator's response in a spirit of detachment and scrutiny, Elizabethan pamphleteering provided a model for this polemical rhetoric and debate structure; the dialectical structure tends to draw the spectator's own experience into the ideological context. *King John* has no hero, encouraging our engagement with no single figure so that our own views will remain free and active.

656. WOMERSLEY, DAVID. "The Politics of Shakespeare's *King John*." *Review of English Studies*, n.s. 40 (1989):497–515.

Suggests that the unalloyed patriotism at the end of the play is not orthodox, that instead it is "decisively shaped by our awareness of the route taken by the Bastard to reach the position from which he makes his final assertions" (p. 499). The play's studied reversals reveal that the political world is one without absolute values, one in which—as Elinor notes—possession is stronger than right. In "fitting" himself to the time, the Bastard is strongly reminiscent of the Vice character. If the play ends in an endorsement of the ideals or order and submission to monarchy, it is a highly qualified one, simply because the Bastard adopts this position of loyalty as the result of a conscious decision.

RICHARD II

Reference Works

657. BLACK, MATTHEW W., and METZ, G. HAROLD, comps. *"The Life and Death of King Richard II": A Bibliographical Supplement to the New Variorum Edition of 1955*. New York: Modern Language Association, 1977, 31 pp.

Includes 702 entries, representing the scholarship from 1955

Richard II

through 1973. The material is categorized alphabetically under editions, text, criticism, sources, commentary, music, and staging and stage history. Books with multiple focus are placed in the criticism section, and collected editions and book reviews are not included. Supplements entry 659.

658. ROBERTS, JOSEPHINE A., comp. *"Richard II": An Annotated Bibliography*. 2 vols. Garland Reference Library of the Humanities, 833: Garland Shakespeare Bibliographies, 14. New York and London: Garland Publishing, 1988, 1249 pp.

Contains 2,662 items representing virtually all publications on the play from 1940 to 1986 along with the most significant items prior to 1940. The categories, each arranged chronologically, include criticism, sources and historical background, dating, textual studies, individual editions, complete and collected editions, influence (adaptations, altered versions), staging and stage history, criticism of films and other media (films and film strips, phonographic records, audiocassettes). A brief introductory essay traces the history of recent criticism and research.

Editions

659. BLACK, MATTHEW W., ed. *The Life and Death of King Richard the Second*. A New Variorum Edition of Shakespeare. Philadelphia and London: J. B. Lippincott, 1955, 655 pp.

Uses the First Folio as the copy text. On each page, for that portion of the text, are provided variant readings, textual notes, and general critical commentary. Following the text are sections on the six quartos and the folio, the date of composition, the authenticity of the text, dramatic time, the sources, the play as a part of a series and as an individual entity, the influence of Lyly and Marlowe, style and imagery, the individual characters, stage history, the relationship to Elizabeth and Essex, and a list of works consulted. Supplemented by entry 657.

660. GURR, ALEXANDER, ed. *Richard II*. The New Cambridge Shakespeare. Cambridge: Cambridge University Press, 1984, 226 pp.

Features an introductory essay on date, history, sources, structure, imagery, language, setting, and stage history. Extensive notes appear on individual pages of the text, and appendices include comments on Shakespeare's use of Holinshed, extracts from Daniel's *The Civil Wars*, a reprint of "A Homily against Disobedience," extracts from *England's Parnassus*, and a list of suggested readings.

661. URE, PETER, ed. *King Richard II*. The Arden Shakespeare. London: Methuen; Cambridge, Mass.: Harvard University Press, 1956, 210 pp.

Includes discussion of the text, date, sources, the garden scene, the question of political allegory, and Richard's tragedy, as well as appendixes featuring selections from Holinshed, Daniel, John Eliot, and Sylvester. The text for this edition is based on the first quarto, for which the copy was probably Shakespeare's foul papers. The likely date of composition is 1595, and Shakespeare apparently drew on a variety of sources in addition to Holinshed. The dominant focus is on Richard's nature and behavior; the first phase of the action demonstrates his unfitness for kingly office, the second is concerned with the transference of power, and the third focuses on his human sufferings once he is deprived of political power and dignity.

Criticism

662. ALTICK, RICHARD D. "Symphonic Imagery in *Richard II*." *PMLA* 62 (1947):339–65.

Notes that certain words of multifold meanings recur throughout the play like a leitmotif in music, with language having become a willing servant of structure. Each word-theme—earth, land and ground, blood, sun, tears, tongues and words, plague and pestilence, a dark blot upon fair parchment, sweetness and sourness—symbolizes a fundamental idea of the narrative. Earth, for example, stands for England, also emblematizing the foundation of kingly pride, the vanity in human life, the untended garden, and the space one occupies at death. The iterative imagery lends the play a poetic unity unsurpassed in the major tragedies.

663. BERGER, HARRY, Jr. *Imaginary Audition: Shakespeare on Stage and Page*. Berkeley: University of California Press, 1989, 178 pp.

Maintains the inaccuracy of those who insist that Shakespeare in performance demands a simple, monolithic approach alien to the modern critical habit of disintegrating and recombining texts according to varied interpretive agendas. In an age of state censorship, Shakespeare's plays were anything but straightforward or direct. The multivalent qualities of contemporary criticism merely replicate what must have been

Richard II

the complexity of response among Shakespeare's own audiences. *Richard II* is explored at length to illustrate this assumption.

664. BERGERON, DAVID M. *"Richard II* and Carnival Politics." *Shakespeare Quarterly* 42 (1991):33–43.
Argues the centrality of carnival rhythms in the play—the tension between political stability and subversion—as a means of understanding its threatening qualities to Elizabethan authorities. In the deposition scene, more specifically, "the problem of misrule becomes explicit, prominent, theatrical, and carnivalesque" (p. 35) as the play moves from the misrule of the king to the King of Misrule. This scene, followed by the same piling up of gages that confronted Richard in the tournament scene, depicts one king replacing another and then himself falling victim to the same "carnival ephemerality. . . . What carnival raises up, it puts down" (p. 38).

665. BIRENBAUM, HARVEY. "Between the Mirror and the Face: Symbolic Reality in *Richard II*." In *Shakespeare and the Triple Play: From Study to Stage to Classroom.* Edited by Sidney Homan. Newark: University of Delaware Press; London and Toronto: Associated University Presses, 1988, pp. 58–75.
Addresses the tension in *Richard II* arising from the fact that Richard does indeed rule by divine right and yet deceives himself when he depends on divine sanction alone to keep him on the throne. As his tragedy unfolds, he probes the paradox of his situation through a series of myths or images—his personal salute to the earth of England, his visualization of the hollow crown, his explicit descent to the base court, his self-immolation with the mirror. Shakespeare, in effect, "re-creates a sacred king's ordeal in a world now grown skeptical of myth, even of art, and even of the human spirit" (p. 74).

666. BLACK, MATTHEW W. "The Source of Shakespeare's *Richard II*." In *Joseph Quincy Adams Memorial Studies.* Edited by James G. McManaway, Giles E. Dawson, and Edwin E. Willoughby. Washington: Folger Shakespeare Library, 1948, pp. 199–216.
Observes that in most instances Shakespeare prepared himself for writing a play by consulting a variety of sources. Various slips or inconsistencies in *Richard II* are best explained, not by the theory that Shakespeare was revising an old play, but by assuming that Shakespeare's mind was teeming with several accounts he had just been reading. He apparently worked directly from the chronicles, using Holinshed, Halle, *Chronique de la Traison et Mort de Richart Deux Roy*

Dengle-terre, and Creton. Such preparation, while wide-ranging, would not have required an inordinate amount of time.

667. BOGARD, TRAVIS. "Shakespeare's Second Richard." *PMLA* 70 (1955):192–209.

Envisions *Richard II* as a milestone in Shakespeare's tragic dramaturgy. Whereas in *Richard III* the drama is explicit, in that our understanding of the action depends largely on the actors' explanations of their goals and motivations and the character of Richard is essentially unpenetrated, *Richard II* is implicit drama. Richard's character grows out of the conflict with Bullingbrook. In the first three acts Richard is depicted as an actor-king fascinated with ritual, but in the last two acts human suffering becomes the material of tragedy.

668. BOLTON, W. F. "Ricardian Law Reports and *Richard II*." *Shakespeare Studies* 20 (1988):53–65.

Observes that the play abounds in legal procedures concerning property law. From a Ricardian standpoint, for example, the trial by combat was a matter of fourteenth-century law, not a "cult of honor." Also, Richard was well within the law when he seized the royalties and rights of Gaunt's estate, but he was outside the law in refusing to "accept Bullingbrook's homage and to permit him to sue his livery so as to regain seisen [possession]" (p. 59). In Richard's last long speech about his wasting time and being wasted by it, Shakespeare draws together strands of Ricardian law; legally Richard, as king, is no tenant and hence no such writ can be drawn against him, but figuratively he is indeed being brought to the bar.

669. CHAPMAN, RAYMOND. "The Wheel of Fortune in Shakespeare's Historical Plays." *Review of English Studies*, n.s. 1 (1950):1–7.

Notes that the tendency to regard Shakespeare's histories as politicosocial documents has obscured the fact that they are dramatic versions of the medieval theme of the fall of kings, a theme involving the goddess Fortuna and her ever-turning wheel. The pattern of a relentless alternation of rise and fall underlies the histories, especially as a linking theme of the tetralogies. The deposition scene in *Richard II* is perhaps the most striking example, with Fortune compared to two buckets in a well with the rabble holding on to the wheel at Bullingbrook's heels.

670. DEAN, LEONARD. "*Richard II*: The State and the Image of the Theater." *PMLA* 67 (1952):211–18.

Observes that *Richard II* is about a sick state while *Henry V* reflects a healthy state unified in terms of the Elizabethan ideal of monarchy. A key sign of the diseased kingdom in *Richard II* is found in the implicit and explicit comparison between the state and the theater, a comparison also found in More and Machiavelli. The theatricality of the opening scene reflects Richard's hypocrisy and his inability to handle dissension. Other examples include Richard's histrionic posturing, the comparison of the garden to an unruly kingdom, and Richard's theater-like analysis of his moral dilemma.

671. DORIUS, R. J. "A Little More Than a Little: Prudence and Excess in *Richard II* and the Histories." *Shakespeare Quarterly* 11 (1960):13–26.

Argues that Shakespeare's English history plays imply a standard of good kingship based on the virtues of kingly self-governance and political economy and prudence. Shakespeare broaches this theme in *Richard II* through image strands diametrically opposed to such a standard—carelessness, excess, waste, and disease. Richard through his imprudence creates a power vacuum that invites disaster. Falstaff in the later plays symbolizes both the sickness of the state and the caterpillars preying on the commonwealth. In banishing him Hal most nearly approaches the ideal of kingship; if he is not the kind of hero we would admire in the tragedies, he is clearly the hero-ruler postulated in the entire sequence of the history plays.

672. ELLIOTT, JOHN R., Jr. "History and Tragedy in *Richard II*." *Studies in English Literature 1500–1900* 8 (1968):253–71.

Defines *Richard II* as a history play rather than as a tragedy because of the manner in which its political purposes influence the dramatic structure. Shakespeare carefully selected his material from a wide range of sources in developing a primary focus on the successive stages by which Bullingbrook threatens, captures, and retains the crown. Gaunt's reaction to Richard's incompetence marks the first stage of the action, York's ambiguity the second, and his commitment to Bullingbrook the third.

673. GAUDET, PAUL. "The 'Parasitical' Counselors in Shakespeare's *Richard II*: A Problem in Dramatic Interpretation." *Shakespeare Quarterly* 33 (1982):142–54.

Notes that, whereas in Shakespeare's sources Richard's parasites (Bushy, Bagot, Greene) openly declare their villainy and thus their guilt, Shakespeare's technique is more allusive, representing a more complex experience for the audience. Clearly Shakespeare does not depict the parasites as totally responsible for Richard's decadence. Hence, there is an undeniable touch of the equivocal and self-righteous in Bullingbrook's pronouncements and actions. To continue to speak of the "parasitic" favorites is to load the dice against Richard and to fail to appreciate that Shakespeare's ambiguity extends even to these minor figures.

674. GOPEN, G. D. "Private Grief into Public Action: The Rhetoric of John of Gaunt in *Richard II*." *Studies in Philology* 84 (1987):338–62.

Focuses on the rhetoric of John of Gaunt's deathbed speech. In this passage Shakespeare simultaneously recognizes the greatness of England, the sanctity of royal government, and the legitimate need for Richard's deposition. Of the many rhetorical figures in the speech, a particularly important one is anaphora—namely, the repeated *this* that in each case introduces a new metaphor (twelve before England is named and for twenty lines before the verb). Clearly, in attacking the king for the very crime of which the duchess complained, Gaunt has found the courage she has accused him of lacking.

675. HAMILTON, DONNA B. "The State of Law in *Richard II*." *Shakespeare Quarterly* 34 (1983):5–17.

Asserts that *Richard II* on matters of kingship and its relationship to the law reflects the views of Shakespeare's, not Richard's, times. Specifically, Gaunt's charge that Richard is landlord rather than king does not question royal prerogative; it focuses on the well-being of those who are governed. It questions the wisdom of a king to act as if divine right gives him unlimited prerogative. The concepts that define the kingship and guide the spectators' response are precisely those that Shakespeare's contemporaries used to assess their own monarch; the careful design suggests that Shakespeare was not blind to the parallels between Richard and Elizabeth.

676. HARRIER, RICHARD. "Ceremony and Politics in *Richard II*." In *Shakespeare: Text, Language, Criticism: Essays in Honour of Marvin Spevack*. Edited by Bernard Fabian and Kurt Tetzeli von Rosador. Hildesheim and New York: Olms-Weidmann, 1987, pp. 80–97.

Argues that no one, Bullingbrook included, ever denies the validity of ceremonially constituted authority in the play and that Richard dooms himself by failing to complete a ritual act he has several opportunities to perform. Richard's words, upon returning from Ireland in 3.2, that he is like the sun rising to expose Bullingbrook's treasons may be vainglorious, but maintaining the show is all he needs to do to contain his enemy. By capitulating at Flint Castle and again at London, by not forcing the crown to be taken by an overt physical or verbal action, Richard never forces Bullingbrook to deny the king's royalty.

Richard II

677. HARRIS, KATHRYN M. "Sun and Water Imagery in *Richard II*: Its Dramatic Function." *Shakespeare Quarterly* 21 (1970):157–65.

Notes that the images of sun and water play an integral role in expressing the pattern of the action. In the development of their opposition emerges a metaphor of the play as a whole, of the political conflict of Richard and Bullingbrook, and of Richard's loss of royal identity concomitant with his self-discovery. Water and storm imagery, for example, are associated with Richard's arbitrary rule early in the play but come to symbolize Bullingbrook in the later action; conversely, the sun imagery used by Bullingbrook in act 1 to describe home and harmony becomes later the central symbol of Richard's divinity.

678. HENINGER, S. K., Jr. "The Sun-King Analogy in *Richard II*." *Shakespeare Quarterly* 11 (1960):319–27.

Notes that the tension between the actual and the ideal, both in Richard and Bullingbrook, is suggested in large part through cosmological imagery. The sun-king analogy at the end of act 3, for example, occurs at the moment this tension is most complete, restoring imagistically the political norm of natural order in that the king must maintain order among his subjects as the sun regulates the harmony of the planets. The image functions as a symbol of royal prerogative, as a mirror of the deficiencies in both principals, and as an instrument of the transition of power.

679. KANTORWICZ, ERNST H. "Shakespeare: *King Richard II*." In *The King's Two Bodies: A Study in Mediaeval Political Theology*. Princeton: Princeton University Press, 1957, pp. 24–41.

Describes the king as twin-born, with both greatness and humanity. Shakespeare may well have been familiar with the legal definition of the king as having two bodies. In any case it is the essence of his art in *Richard II* as he constantly plays the human aspect against the divine; indeed, *Richard II* could be described as the tragedy of the king's two bodies. Time and again Richard refers to the image of sacramental kingship, even as his corrupt mortal body undermines the concept. The mirror scene completes the act of splitting his personality and assuring his personal tragedy.

680. KLIGER, SAMUEL. "The Sun Imagery in *Richard II*." *Studies in Philology* 45 (1948):196–202.

Observes that the significance of Shakespeare's imagery is its function in the total design of the play. In this regard sun images are applied to Richard in the rising action—with the center of his kingdom like the center of the solar system. Quite different are the sun images in the falling action; here his kingship finds correlatives in an eclipse, the approaching night, and the cold and sunless climate. These image patterns contribute directly to the tragic form of the play.

681. MacDonald, Ronald R. "Uneasy Lies: Language and History in Shakespeare's Lancastrian Tetralogy." *Shakespeare Quarterly* 35 (1984): 22–39.

Reads Richard's attempts to employ the language of sacred kingship as a key to his failure as a ruler. Despite his mastery of a poetic verbal idiom, he finds it inadequate to deal with the human interactions that comprise realpolitik. Bullingbrook's usurpation brings an end to the language of divine kingship, demanding a language of agreement, trade-offs, and bargains to achieve political consensus. In the *Henriad*, Hal, who creates his own language after learning that of others, succeeds because he recognizes that verbal communication must change as events and contexts dictate.

682. MacKenzie, Clayton G. "Paradise and Paradise Lost in *Richard II*." *Shakespeare Quarterly* 37 (1986):318–39.

Observes that two mythological patterns are simultaneously at work in the structural fabric of the play, the mythology of England as a paradise and the opposite or antimythology of England as a fallen paradise. In the postlapsarian world of *Richard II* paradise is envisioned primarily as a physical and spiritual regeneration. it is to the iconographical traditions of this regeneration that Northumberland alludes in urging support of Harry Hereford: "Even through the hollow eyes of death / I spy life peering" (2.1.270–71). At the same time, the iconography of death shadowing life gathers force around Richard; in the battle for life in the cell at Pomfret Shakespeare's visual design becomes a theatrical emblem of England's paradise lost.

683. Merrix, Robert P. "The Character Allusion in *Richard II*: The Search for Identity." *English Literary Renaissance* 17 (1987):277–87.

Observes that, while the myth is used elsewhere in the canon, only Richard II directly compares himself with Phaeton. Inherent in Richard are the major traits exemplified in Phaeton—pride and a stubborn refusal to heed advice; moreover, since neither young man has ever known his father, neither has a role model to follow. In both cases the jades (whether horses or subjects) become unruly because they are given too much rein. In a word, Ovid's myth is an ideal vehicle for Shakespeare's immature youth searching for identity.

684. Pye, Christopher. "The Betrayal of the Gaze: Theatricality and Power in Shakespeare's *Richard II*." *ELH* 55 (1988):575–98.

Richard II

Asserts that the central question of the play is whether sovereignty can prove itself absolute by mastering its own subversion. In act 4, Richard, in seeking to deny the real condition of his recorded crimes against the state, unmasks a theatrical condition in which the performative effects weigh against him. Richard's shame is to be dispossessed of his shame; his "self-conquering act robs him even of the power to claim his guilt as his own" (p. 591). The anamorphic double perspective can at once create false shadows and take them for the truth.

685. QUINN, MICHAEL. " 'The King Is Not Himself': The Personal Tragedy of *Richard II.*" *Studies in Philology* 56 (1959):169–86.

Insists that to the Elizabethan Richard's tragedy is at once personal and political and that the issues of divine right, honor, and patience reflect the interaction of history and tragedy, politics and ethics. Richard, for example, uses the religiopolitical theory of divine right to cover his own ethical misconduct, provoking division both within himself and among his subjects. Honor is equally ambiguous, as reflected in Mowbray's and York's difficulty in distinguishing between proper conduct and political allegiance. Patience, too, is double edged, a virtue turned vice when the situation demands political and moral redress.

686. RACKIN, PHYLLIS. "The Role of the Audience in *Richard II.*" *Shakespeare Quarterly* 36 (1985):262–81.

Maintains that the play viscerally involves the audience, drawing them first to a painful dilemma concerning the divided loyalties of act 1, then to a wholehearted endorsement of the rebellion at the end of act 2, and finally to a repudiation of the rebellion and the deposition and murder of the king. The often deleted scene of York urging justice on his son's complicity while his mother pleads for Aumerle's forgiveness (5.2) is crucial in providing psychological relief for the spectators. With York reduced to a caricature in the lengths to which he carries his obedience to the new king, he loses his capacity to be a moral agent and becomes the spectators' scapegoat, drawing them to undivided sympathy for Richard.

687. ROSSITER, A. P. *Angel With Horns and Other Shakespeare Lectures.* Edited by Graham Storey. New York: Theatre Arts Books, 1961, 316 pp.

Examines Shakespeare's preoccupation throughout his plays with the equivocal nature of man. *Richard III*, for instance, juxtaposes a huge triumphant stage personality with a rigid Tudor schema of retributive justice; as the consummate actor and clown Richard draws us dangerously close to his side. *Richard II*, likewise, provokes an ambivalent response. In the half-fantasy world of the court, Richard's dream kingship reigns with angels at his command; in the world of curt reality he is a passive sufferer and king of woes. Whether in the characters who parade through history, the heroes and villains of tragedy, or the figures of comedy, Shakespeare's view is "double-eyed, ambivalent: it faces both ways" (p. 292).

688. SCHELL, EDGAR. "*Richard II* and Some Forms of Theatrical Time." *Comparative Drama* 24 (1990–91):255–69.

Argues against the realistic inference that Bullingbrook has already decided to return before Gaunt's death and that he uses the subsequent issue of his inheritance merely to give usurpation some color of justice. To the contrary, Shakespeare in dramatizing this scene shifts from one mode of time to another within the space of what is now designated 2.1. The second half is in a dramatic version of the summary rhetorical mode used by Holinshed in describing the sequence of events leading to Bullingbrook's invasion.

689. SCHOENBAUM, SAMUEL. "*Richard II* and the Realities of Power." *Shakespeare Survey* 28 (1975):1–13.

Maintains that Shakespeare does not strictly adhere to the Tudor myth in *Richard II*, that he incorporates his own insights into the delineation of men in dangerous situations. In part, the diversity of available source materials encouraged an artistic eclecticism—legends depicting Richard as virtually a saint, chronicle accounts treating him as a weak and moody individual who abdicated of his own free will. In act 1 Richard acts with political acumen, not vacillation and caprice, in handling the argument between Bullingbrook and Mowbray.

690. SIEMON, JAMES R. " 'Subjected Thus': Utterance, Character, and *Richard II.*" *Shakespeare Jahrbuch* 126 (1990):65–80.

Argues that Richard's soliloquy in act 5 following his deposition and imprisonment is charged with political topicality. More precisely, when he muses about his thoughts' being people, he suggests three recognizable social estates—the "better sort" of the religious, those who pursue "ambition" and "pride," and those who are "content" with subjection. None, however, is secure in position because all ultimately are discontented. Analogously, Bullingbrook has been "produced" as king within a social condition fraught with "inevitably discontented desire, since if a subject could be king, so could they always aspire to the 'next degree in hope'" (p. 78).

691. TALBERT, ERNEST W. *The Problem of Order: Elizabethan Commonplaces and an Example of Shakespeare's Art.* Chapel Hill: University of North Carolina Press, 1962, 244 pp.

Richard III

Demonstrates Shakespeare's use of current concepts and representational methods to achieve within the theater a highly charged ambivalent effect in the Flint Castle scene and the deposition scene in *Richard II*. Like the entire play these scenes briefly contrast Ricardian and Lancastrian interpretations of history. At one moment Richard is God's agent, at another the fallen ruler; at one moment Bullingbrook is the proud and ambitious usurper, at another a Lancastrian nobleman. The effect of the scenes is pervasively ambiguous. The deposition scene also plays upon a diversity of religious attitudes, including those in accordance with Aristotle's definition of the commonwealth.

692. ZITNER, S . P. "Aumerle's Conspiracy." *Studies in English Literature 1500–1900* 14 (1974):239–57.

Observes that, while the Aumerle scenes are not central to the development of the narrative, they function in several significant ways. They provide necessary filler material to separate Richard's pathetic farewell scene and Exton's intent to murder him; they serve to convey the message of political necessity that superior power must be obeyed; they furnish a commentary on the motifs of love, loyalty, treachery, and forgiveness. Possibly their comical nature reflects Shakespeare's disenchantment with the traditionally sober presentations of historical material.

RICHARD III

Reference Work

693. MOORE, JAMES A. *"Richard III: An Annotated Bibliography.* Garland Shakespeare Bibliographies, 11. New York and London: Garland Reference Library of the Humanities, 425: Garland Publishing, 1986, 867 pp.

Contains 1,914 items representing virtually all publications on the play from 1940 to 1984, along with the most significant items prior to 1940. The categories, each arranged chronologically, include criticism, editions, textual studies, bibliographies, sources and background, stage history, influence (adaptations, parodies, synopses), and media criticism (films, filmstrips, television, scripts, phonograph records, audiocassettes, published music). A brief introductory essay traces the history of recent criticism and research.

Editions

694. FURNESS, HENRY HOWARD, Jr., ed. *The Tragedy of Richard the Third: With the Landing of Earle Richmond and the Battle at Bosworth Field.* A New Variorum Edition of Shakespeare. Philadelphia:J. B. Lippincott, 1908, 641 pp.

Uses the First Folio as the copy text and on each page, for that portion of the text, provides variant readings, textual notes, and general critical commentary. Following the text are sections on the nature of the quarto and folio texts, the date of composition, the sources, the text of *The True Tragedy of Richard the Third*, the character of Richard, English and German criticisms, stage history, the principal actors, and a list of works consulted.

695. HAMMOND, ANTHONY, ed. *King Richard III*. The Arden Shakespeare. London and New York: Methuen, 1981, 382 pp.

Includes discussion of the publication, the text, and date of composition, *Richard III* in performance, the sources, and the play itself. Appendixes consider longer passages unique to the First Folio or the first quarto and reprint source materials from Halle's Chronicle and *The Mirror for Magistrates*. The text is based on the First Folio but readings from the first quarto are allowed when they seem to represent an authoritative later stage. The folio text was probably based on Shakespeare's foul papers collated with the third and sixth quartos; the first quarto represents a remarkably good memorial reconstruction.

696. SMIDT, KRISTIAN, ed. *William Shakespeare, "The Tragedy of Richard III": Parallel Texts of the First Quarto and the First Folio with Variants of the Early Quartos.* Oslo: Universitetsforlaget; New York: Humanities Press, 1969, 221 pp.

Describes the two substantive texts of *Richard III*, the first quarto of 1597 (with essentially derivative quartos in 1598, 1602, 1605, 1612, 1622, 1629, 1634) and the 1623 folio. The latter contains 212 unique lines while omitting 35 lines from the quarto. The quarto and folio texts are printed on facing pages, the former from a transcript of Greg's Shakespeare Quarto Facsimile collated with the Huth copy in the British Library, the latter from the Folger First Folio #42. Quarto variants are summarized on pp. 14–27.

697. WILSON, JOHN DOVER, ed. *Richard III*. Cambridge: Cambridge University Press, 1954, 280 pp.

Provides extensive textual notes, a critical introduction (covering

Richard III

the text and date of composition, the sources—the chronicles, More, *The Mirror for Magistrates, The True Tragedy of Richard the Third,* and other pre-Shakespearean drama—style, character, and plot), a discussion of the copy text, a section on stage history, a glossary, and a genealogical table. This edition is based on the First Folio, but readings from the first quarto—possibly a joint memorial reconstruction—are also admitted. The structural pattern centering on the villainous hero is serviceable because its very artificiality renders the character more credible and because the constant moral reiterations leave the audience comfortably free to enjoy his Machiavellian wickedness.

Textual Studies

698. PATRICK, DAVID LYALL. *The Textual History of "Richard III."* Stanford: Stanford University Press, 1936, 153 pp.
    Maintains that the first quarto and the First Folio do not represent two distinct texts. Instead, the quarto represents a piratical version of the play prior to 1597, incorporating deliberate alterations by the prompter or stage manager. The folio text represents essentially Shakespeare's original form. There is no indication that Shakespeare himself was involved in the variations preserved in the quarto. Hence, an editor is unjustified in producing an eclectic text based on both versions.

699. SMIDT, KRISTIAN. *Iniurious Impostors and "Richard III."* Oslo: Norwegian Universities Press; New York: Humanities Press, 1964, 213 pp.
    Maintains, through a study of transposition, anticipation and recollection, substitution, and omission—that the 1597 quarto text of *Richard III* is not a bad quarto based on memorial reporting by one or two actors or by the entire company, but that all evidence points to its authenticity. In all likelihood both the quarto and folio texts were set from an authoritative manuscript, with the quarto based on "a nontheatrical, or rather pretheatrical" version (p. 155).

700. WALTON, JAMES KIRKWOOD. *The Copy for the Folio Text of "Richard III": With a Note on the Copy for the Folio Text of "King Lear."* Auckland: Auckland University Press, 1955, 164 pp.
    Argues that the copy for the folio text of *Richard III* is not, as generally assumed, a corrected copy of the sixth quarto (1622) but a copy of the third quarto (1602) corrected with only sporadic accuracy by a collator. That the folio text of this play has the greatest number of

variants of all of Shakespeare's texts printed from corrected quartos is demonstrably not evidence of the accuracy and thoroughness of the collation. A similar situation appears to exist in the use of corrected quarto copy for the folio text of *King Lear*.

Criticism

701. BERMAN, RONALD. "Anarchy and Order in *Richard III* and *King John*." *Shakespeare Survey* 20 (1967):51–60.

Observes that, among the histories, *Richard III* and *King John* are distinguished by tough, cynical, and realistic wit. Their heroes are characterized by a skeptical attitude toward matters treated quite seriously in the other histories—legitimacy, honor, the sacredness of blood relationships. Richard's emancipation from morality is not unlike that of the Bastard's. Their minds are animated by a mixture of philosophical materialism and Machiavellianism. In both plays the egocentric, anarchic nature of the individual confronts and eventually succumbs to the ideals of order.

702. BROOKE, NICHOLAS. "Reflecting Gems and Dead Bones: Tragedy versus History in *Richard III*." *Critical Quarterly* 7 (1965):123–34.

Views the conflict in *Richard III* as the gigantic force and pattern of moral history set against the tragic concept of an individual struggling against overwhelming odds. Whereas the language of the one is highly structured and ritualized, Richard's language is sparkling as he shares with the spectator his determination to defy the force of history represented by Margaret. As Richard is defeated, so is the force of human free will, albeit perverted, and the world "is poorer for his loss" (p. 134).

703. BROOKS, H. F. "Richard III, Unhistorical Amplifications: The Women's Scenes and Seneca." *Modern Language Review* 75 (1980):721–37.

Finds Shakespeare's source for the women in *Richard III* in Seneca's *Troades* and, specifically, for the scene between Anne and Richard in act 1 in Seneca's *Hercules Furens* and *Hippolytus*. From *Troades* come the parallels of the Duchess of York and Hecuba, Elizabeth and Andromache, Anne and Polyxena, and Margaret and Helen. The hypnotizing of Anne by Richard corresponds to the wooing of Megara by Lycus and Richard's proffer of his sword by which Anne might kill him to Phaedra's similar offer to Hippolytus.

Richard III

704. CANDIDO, JOSEPH. "Thomas More, the Tudor Chroniclers, and Shakespeare's Altered Richard." *English Studies* 68 (1987):137–41.

Recalls that critics are in general agreement that there is a fundamental shift in Richard before and after he becomes king. His bustling energy is replaced with a sense of lethargy and uncertainty. His irony forsakes him, he cannot sleep, and even his powers of language fail. Since More's *History of King Richard III* depicts a zestful, witty Machiavellian and since it, unfinished, breaks off at the point he becomes king, Shakespeare probably began his drama "in Morean fashion" and ended it "under the shadow of Hall's heavy didacticism" (p. 141).

705. CARROLL, WILLIAM C. "Desacralization and Succession in *Richard III*." *Deutsche Shakespeare-Gesellschaft West Jahrbuch* (1991):82–96.

Suggests that Richard's failure to develop to some kind of emotional maturity is part of a larger pattern of desacralization of ritual evidenced in the transgression of specific cultural rites and in the violation of "form" itself in the world of the play. The law, for example, is violated in the illegality of the drafting of Hastings's indictment, as is the violation of family bonds in the murder of his brother and his nephews, and as is the violation of the rite of burial in his treatment of Henry's corpse. Only the principle of succession remains unblemished, but Richard's very actions overwhelm its "encompassing logic" and "annihilate his own claim" (p. 96).

706. CLEMEN, WOLFGANG H. "Anticipation and Foreboding in Shakespeare's Early Histories." *Shakespeare Survey* 6 (1953):25–35.

Views the element of anticipation and foreboding as an important feature of both Shakespeare's technique and his art of characterization. The *Henry VI* plays, much like pre-Shakespearean drama, use prophecies, omens, and dreams to establish patterns of anticipation for the spectators. More significant are the devices that structurally control the action in *Richard III*, whether the purely choric scenes for atmospheric effect such as the citizens discussing the dangers of a child king or the curses of Margaret remembered successively by each victim.

707. ———. *A Commentary on Shakespeare's "Richard III."* Translated by Joan Bonheim. London: Methuen, 1968, 247 pp.

Develops a scene-by-scene analysis drawing upon multiple critical approaches—stylistic, thematic, imagistic, dramaturgical. The interplay between tradition and originality is a major feature of the play, and from this interaction Shakespeare develops a bold, new dramatic form. The opening soliloquy announces the motivation for Richard's subsequent actions in nothing more or less than his aggressive will. With careful rhetorical modulation Richard draws our eyes to observe his deformity and his isolation. Throughout the play the spectator is made to fluctuate between disgust at the horror of Richard's machinations turned coldly and methodically into deeds and admiration for his fiery will and resourcefulness.

708. COLLEY, SCOTT. "Richard III and Herod." *Shakespeare Quarterly* 37 (1986):451–58.

Describes Shakespeare's Richard as a creation in part historical figure, Roman despot, tragic villain, and biblical archetype. The last, more particularly, involves characteristics drawn from the biblical Herod as depicted in medieval miracle plays. General parallels are numerous—malice of heart covered with false humility, apparent loyalty and piety that mask villainy. More telling are specific parallels such as the slaughter of the innocent children, the soldiers sent out to commit the murder confronted by a like number of grieving women, the fact that the tyrant's true rival resides elsewhere in safety, the crippled and twisted posture of the tyrant.

709. DOEBLER, BETTIE A. " 'Despaire and Dye': The Ultimate Temptation of Richard III." *Shakespeare Studies* 7 (1964):75–86.

Focuses on the relationship between Richard's death and the *ars moriendi* tradition. The appearance of the ghosts to Richard and Richmond in bed rings a variation on this iconographical tradition in that the spirits function like the good and evil angels to reenact the struggle for man's soul in life's final moments. Richard's cry about "coward conscience" is envisioned as a form of internalized struggle, and his despair in battle signifies the damnation of his soul.

710. ENDEL, PEGGY. "Profane Icon: The Throne Scene of Shakespeare's *Richard III*." *Comparative Drama* 20 (1986–87):115–23.

Notes that critics and theatergoers have been baffled at the actions of Richard, who in 4.2, on the throne and essentially in a public posture, conducts grimly private business—plotting the death of his nephews and brooding over the dangers posed by Richmond. The effect is apparently what Shakespeare intended, an unsettled response to the action and the context. More specifically, this image evidently grows out of a detail in More's *History* "in which King Richard and his page devise the death of the two princes in the tower while Richard sits not in pomp on England's throne, but on a 'draught' or privy" (p. 117).

711. FRENCH, A. L. "The World of Richard III." *Shakespeare Studies* 4 (1968):25–39.

Richard III

Considers Shakespeare's Richard III to be a more complex figure than the single-dimensional villain of Tudor propaganda. For one thing, Richmond is more a cipher than a Tudor hero; if he is morally without flaw, he is no emotional force in the play. For another, Stanley seems to point to the political climate of the play; a trimmer who does not openly oppose Richard, he plays both sides so as to be prepared for any political eventuality. Finally, Richard himself commands an almost perverse sympathy since the metaphysical dimension of the play seems so shallow and vindictive.

712. HAMMERSMITH, JAMES P. "The Melodrama of *Richard III*." *English Studies* 70 (1989):29–36.

Notes that the dramatic characterization of Richard is superior to its dramatic vehicle and suggests that the mixture of genres, especially tragedy and melodrama, is the inevitable consequence of this disjunction. Unarguably Richard is a melodramatic hero but arguably Richard can be both tragic hero or melodramatic villain. Shakespeare shapes the material around the character of Richard in tragic fashion, but the conclusion is sheer melodrama, a kind of trial by combat in which God takes the part of virtue and justice prevails.

713. JONES, ROBERT. *Engagement with Knavery: Point of View in "Richard III," "The Jew of Malta," and "The Revenger's Tragedy."* Durham: Duke University Press, 1986, 177 pp.

Focuses on the significance of the antic Vice figure who through soliloquies and asides enters into a private level of communication with the spectators and acts as a kind of guide to the action as he delights in his successes and shares his machinations regarding his future actions. With Richard III, for example, we "follow a neatly plotted course that takes us from engagement with his winning knavery to detachment from his cringing villainy" (p. 27). Increasingly, fear and frustration characterize Richard in the events concerning the murder of the young princes, and we gradually come to applaud the downfall of the villain who earlier had entertained us.

714. MCDONALD, RUSS. "*Richard III* and the Tropes of Treachery." *Philological Quarterly* 68 (1989):465–83.

Insists that this play, even more so than *Love's Labor's Lost*, reveals Shakespeare's awakening to the duplicity of words, a recognition that the weaknesses of words are encoded in the systems of rhetoric that the Renaissance inherited from the classics. His suspicions about language, however, developed faster than his suspicions about providential politics, and thus his rhetorical pattern in which a clever speaker wrests power from one not so verbally adept is at odds with the teleology implicit in the historical subject. "The historical victor is a rhetorical loser" (p. 466). It will be in the second tetralogy that these two elements are brought more nearly into balance.

715. McNEIR, WALDO. "The Masks of Richard III." *Studies in English Literature 1500–1900* 11 (1971):167–86.

Considers Richard's role-playing talents, a mode of characterization Shakespeare prepares in *3 Henry VI* in Richard's ability to manipulate others and in the soliloquies in which he shares his motives and ambitions with the spectators. In *Richard III* he continuously performs for two audiences—his auditors on stage, who are duped by his incessant references to piety, humility, and integrity and his auditors in the galleries, whose moral scruples are dulled by his wit and virtuosity. The disintegration of his character in act 5 is signaled by the three roles of self-accuser, self-defender, and conscience.

716. RICHMOND, HUGH M. "*Richard III* and the Reformation." *Journal of English and Germanic Philology* 83 (1984):509–21.

Comments on the appropriateness of the many allusions to medieval drama in *Richard III* since in York, the seat of Richard's power, the popularity of such drama continued well after the development of Protestant opposition. Indeed, the vocabulary of the play suggests that Shakespeare is giving new life to the old dramatic tradition in light of just such opposition, undercutting it with mocking irony and historical allusion generated by Puritan and humanist alike. Shakespeare's interest is not to discredit religion but to intensify it in Reformation terms; within Catholic terms it enhances the credibility of Richard's amorality.

717. SMITH, FRED MANNING. "The Relation of *Macbeth* to *Richard III*." *PMLA* 60 (1945):1003–20.

States that the parallels between *Macbeth* and *Richard III* are so numerous and so complex as to require an explanation other than that of coincidence. Both protagonists are called hellhounds, and the events in each play unfold as the fulfillment of prophecy. Moreover, the sequence of events and the general shape of the plot are strikingly similar. Shakespeare in writing *Macbeth* clearly turned to Holinshed, finding there the history and the outline of events; quite probably, he consciously was reminded of *Richard III* and drew from his own earlier play in matters of characterization, dialogue, and dramatic construction.

718. THOMAS, SIDNEY. *The Antic Hamlet and Richard III*. New York: King's Crown Press, 1943, 92 pp.

Richard III

Studies Richard III and Hamlet in relation to earlier dramatic types and to each other. Antic traditionally refers to a comic figure, a masked buffoon; and it is this figure to which Hamlet refers concerning his "antic disposition." As he is a mixture of the tragic and the comic, so Richard combines the villain and the comedian characteristic of the traditional vice character. Both are developments of these traditional roles in earlier native drama, not of Senecan influences as in *Titus Andronicus*.

719. WALLER, MARGUERITE. "Usurpation, Seduction, and the Problematics of the Proper: A 'Deconstructive,' 'Feminist' Rereading of the Seductions of Richard and Anne in Shakespeare's *Richard III*." In *Rewriting the Renaissance: The Discourses of Sexual Difference in Early Modern Europe*. Edited by Margaret W. Ferguson, Maureen Quilligan, and Nancy J. Vickers. Chicago: University of Chicago Press, 1986, pp. 159–74.

Notes that Anne, considering the recent deaths of her husband and father-in-law, is suffering from the "loss of her male points of reference and her role as a subjectivity that thinks of *itself* as authoritative" (p. 172). It is precisely when she asserts her autonomy through the Petrarchan stance assigned to her by Richard as wooer that Richard is able to visualize in her capitulation an objective, external indicator of his power.

Stage History

720. WOOD, ALICE I. P. *The Stage History of Shakespeare's "Richard III."* New York: Columbia University Press; Oxford: Oxford University Press, 1909, 186 pp.

Examines the stage history of *Richard III*, reconstructing the likely conditions in Shakespeare's day and basing later accounts on records of performances, conditions of staging, scenery, properties, costumes, and acting style. The productions of the early eighteenth century focus on the Cibber adaptation and those of the latter half on the acting style introduced by Garrick. Another chapter concerns the fortunes of the play in America. Combining elements of the chronicle, Marlovian tragedy, and Kydian revenge, Richard's perennial fascination is his reflection of that which in man is consummately evil.

IV.
The Comedies

GENERAL STUDIES

721. ADELMAN, JANET. "Male Bonding in Shakespeare's Comedies." In *Shakespeare's "Rough Magic": Essays in Honor of C. L. Barber*. Edited by Peter Erickson and Coppélia Kahn. Newark: University of Delaware Press; London and Toronto: Associated University Presses, 1985, pp. 73–103.

Views conflicting loyalty in Shakespeare's male protagonists between the bonds of male friendship and the commitment to heterosexual love as the central tension in the comedies. The paternal blocking figure of classical comedy is replaced by "an educative process which assumes that the most serious threats to a happy marriage are the internal ones" (p. 74). Bassanio, for example, must ultimately choose between love for Portia and friendship for Antonio. Similarly, Benedick's desire for Beatrice must grow more powerful than the attraction of his camaraderie with Claudio and Don Pedro.

722. ANDERSON, LINDA. *A Kind of Wild Justice: Revenge in Shakespeare's Comedies*. Newark: University of Delaware Press; London and Toronto: Associated University Presses, 1987, 195 pp.

Examines the devices of revenge central to the plots of Shakespeare's comedies and argues that such a conception of revenge constitutes an ethical social instrument. The comic revengers, more precisely, are admirable figures whose victims are either villains or potentially good people who need some form of therapeutic shock. Rosaline's imposition of a strong penance upon Berowne is an early

General Studies

example. In the middle comedies the action involves the thwarting of a harmful outsider by a comic revenger, such as Portia's against Shylock or Sir Toby's against Malvolio.

723. BARBER, C. L. *Shakespeare's Festive Comedy: A Study of Dramatic Form in Relation to Social Custom.* Princeton: Princeton University Press, 1959, 266 pp.

Asserts that the fundamental structure of Shakespeare's festive comedies (those through *Twelfth Night*) derives from the saturnalian pattern of Elizabethan holiday. Whatever the variation, this pattern involves inversion, statement and counterstatement, and a general movement leading through release to clarification. Both the holiday festivity and the comic form to which it gives rise are "parallel manifestations of the same pattern of culture, of a way that men can cope with their life" (p. 6). *A Midsummer Night's Dream*, for example, imaginatively recreates the experience of the traditional summer holidays. In Falstaff Shakespeare fuses the clown's part with that of the Lord of Misrule, a festive celebrant.

724. BAXTER, JOHN S. "Present Mirth: Shakespeare's Romantic Comedies." *Queen's Quarterly* 72 (1965):52–77.

Describes Shakespearean comedy as a form that appeals both to the intellect and the emotion. With its setting in the human spirit, it makes no attempt to criticize life through satirically mirroring the vices and abuses or by a Jonsonian stage figure who expresses the author's judgments. The function of Shakespeare's comedy is to enlarge the dimensions of the spirit and to comprehend life as it may be lived in rich fulfillment under the law of nature and the law of God.

725. BELSEY, CATHERINE. "Disrupting Sexual Difference: Meaning and Gender in the Comedies." In *Alternative Shakespeares.* Edited by John Drakakis. New Accents. London and New York: Methuen, 1985, pp. 166–90.

Insists that Shakespearean comedy can be read as disrupting sexual difference, challenging the traditional concept of defining women in relation to men and in terms of their relations with men. For one thing, the female disguised as a male can create situations that undermine assumptions of male superiority, as, for example, in Ganymed's negotiation with Corin for suitable accommodations and Viola's freedom as Cesario or Julia's as Sebastian. These heroines play the conventional role in the happy marriage that concludes the comedies, but they "become wives only after they have been shown to be something altogether more singular" (p. 188).

726. BERRY, RALPH. *Shakespeare's Comedies: Explorations in Form*. Princeton: Princeton University Press, 1972, 214 pp.

Investigates the ten comedies through *Twelfth Night*. The overriding theme is illusion, whether the consequences of simple error *(The Comedy of Errors)*, deception *(Much Ado About Nothing)* or self-deception *(Twelfth Night)*. Opposed to this illusion is reality, most often depicted in the clowns, servants, rustics—all in a sense extensions of the jester—who provide a commentary, often surprisingly tart, on the behavior of their social superiors. The closure is frequently more interrogatory than declarative, "clarifications" that must continue to be tested in the imagination extending beyond act 5.

727. BRADBROOK, MURIEL C. *The Growth and Structure of Elizabethan Comedy*. London: Chatto & Windus, 1955, 254 pp.

Traces Elizabethan comedy from its beginnings in medieval drama and the oral tradition to its fullest expression in Shakespeare, his contemporaries, and his immediate successors. Shakespeare's characterizations most successfully engaged the audiences of his own day. His use of disguise or the assumption of a conventional role as a means of indicating maturation of character is an extension of the method of contrasted plot and subplot. Especially significant is his development of the role of the heroine; his ladies sparkle with life, energy, and vitality compared with the stiff goddesses who stand to be wooed in duels of courtship or with the long-suffering "pieces of devotion" in sentimental comedy.

728. BROWN, JOHN RUSSELL. *Shakespeare and His Comedies*. London: Methuen, 1957.

Observes that, except for three early intrigue comedies, Shakespeare's plays follow the narrative tradition and are variations of the theme of true love. *The Merchant of Venice* reflects the theme of love's wealth (the manner in which love transcends mercantile values); *A Midsummer Night's Dream* and *Much Ado About Nothing*, love's truth (the complexity of the lover's truthful realization of beauty and the distinction between fancy and true affection); *As You Like It* and *Twelfth Night*, love's order (the power to infuse priorities issuing in harmony at both the social and the individual level); the problem comedies, love's ordeal (the conflict between the higher impulses of love and the instincts of man's corrupt nature).

729. BRYANT, JOSEPH A., Jr. *Shakespeare and the Uses of Comedy*. Lexington: University Press of Kentucky, 1986, 270 pp.

General Studies

Views the production of laughter, the presentation of young people in love, and the use of theatrical conventions of improbable plot and uncomplicated reconciliation as incidental to Shakespeare's major purpose in writing comedy, the search for meaning and the exploration of the human condition. *The Comedy of Errors*, for example, while filled with knockabout farce, is also about issues like love (both young and old), fidelity, and personal honor. Through all the romantic comedies a common thread is an agent of transformation (whether an eccentric male suitor or an aggressive female in disguise, or a seemingly innocuous flower) that effects or hastens "beneficent metamorphoses in men, women, or other sluggish creatures" (p. 67).

730. CARROLL, WILLIAM C. *The Metamorphoses of Shakespearean Comedy*. Princeton: Princeton University Press, 1985, 292 pp.
    Focuses on the recurrence of transformation in Shakespeare's comedies as a master trope encompassing the themes of identity, change, desire, marriage, and dramatic form. Each of Shakespeare's characters is transformed by love, whether erotic, Platonic, or carnal. The women often assume disguises for both practical and symbolic reasons. For the men, transformation is a necessary detour to marriage; "young love can only, should only, be consummated (in all senses) after some trial of the monstrous has been survived, some transformational stage passed through" (p. 147).

731. CHAMPION, LARRY S. *The Evolution of Shakespeare's Comedy*. Cambridge, Mass.: Harvard University Press, 1970, 241 pp.
    Views the development of Shakespeare's comedy as a movement toward progressively more complex characters and situations and the development of structural devices by which to maintain an effective comic perspective. The early works are essentially situation comedies with little significant development of character. The romantic comedies of the late 1590s establish plots in which characters who have assumed an unnatural or abnormal pose are forced to realize and to admit the ridiculousness of their position. In the final comedies character development turns on a fundamental transformation of values. The problem comedies are partially successful efforts to develop a comic perspective that can accommodate the fully delineated characterization.

732. CHARLTON, H. B. *Shakespearian Comedy*. London: Methuen, 1938, 303 pp.
    Maintains that Shakespeare elevated comedy to a mode of grandeur and full maturity that will probably never be equalled. Shakespeare's genius lies in the fusing of romance and comedy, thereby

enhancing both forms. From the early pieces that depict life as a comic game of youthful passion, the playwright moves to an examination of the enigmatic sources of true nobility and the complex nature of the joy in life; in *Much Ado About Nothing*, *As You Like It*, and *Twelfth Night* the heroine emerges in Beatrice, Rosalind, and Viola, "representations of the office of love to lift mankind to a richer life" (p. 283)

733. COGHILL, NEVILLE. "The Basis of Shakespearian Comedy." *Essays and Studies*, n.s. 3 (1950):1–28.
    Distinguishes Jonsonian satiric comedy from Shakespeare's romantic comedy with its roots in the Middle Ages and the belief that comedy, the reverse of tragedy, involved a story that starts in sorrow and danger and by a happy turn of fortune ends in felicity. As the medieval formula for comedy led through love to the Beatific Vision, so Shakespeare's comedies are built on love stories that, following a series of misadventures, firmly espouse social and personal harmony.

734. COX, ROGER L. *Shakespeare's Comic Changes: The Time-Lapse Metaphor as Plot Device*. Athens: University of Georgia Press, 1991, 205 pp.
    Argues that the thread connecting Shakespeare's comedies is a plot in which character change is presented metaphorically rather than realistically. Such change involves, not a gradual progression from one level of awareness to another, but a startling juxtaposition of radically different perspectives. The "time-lapse" metaphor is the chief device for depicting this change, with a view of a character as flawed and in conflict with society followed by an idealized view of the same character "reformed."

735. EVANS, BERTRAND. *Shakespeare's Comedies*. Oxford: Clarendon Press, 1960, 337 pp.
    Analyzes Shakespeare's comedies in terms of their levels of discrepant awareness, the gaps in knowledge that develop between character and spectator or character and character, the principal manner in which Shakespeare manipulates and controls his audience to achieve the maximum comic response. Of the 297 scenes in the seventeen comedies, the spectator holds the advantage in 177; of 277 named characters, 151 stand in a condition of exploitable ignorance by other characters. As the early comedies yield to the mature ones, the problem comedies, and finally to the romances, the nature of the spectator's higher level of awareness and the control of his response become more complex, more concerned with psychological principles than with comic practice for its own sake.

General Studies

736. FREEDMAN, BARBARA. *Staging the Gaze: Postmodernism, Psychoanalysis, and Shakespearean Comedy.* Ithaca: Cornell University Press, 1991, 244 pp.

Examines how *The Comedy of Errors, Twelfth Night, The Taming of the Shrew,* and *A Midsummer Night's Dream* play games with spectatorship that interrogate and reverse perspectives to such an extent that they question reading or viewing as mastery. Through what at first appears to be only broad farce they demonstrate "how gender, class, and ideology function as sites of misrecognition" (p. 3). Sly's displacement as a lord and his "madame wife" (a male servant disguised as a female) interrogate the spectator's view of class identity and constrictive gender relationships; Malvolio's attempts to reconstruct the "love letter" revealingly mock the reader's attempt to make sense of the play. The plays force him to consider how he constructs meaning in his own society.

737. FRYE, NORTHROP. "The Argument of Comedy." In *English Institute Essays 1948.* Edited by D. A. Robertson, Jr. New York: Columbia University Press, 1949, pp. 58–73.

Describes Shakespeare's comic form as a derivation of Menandrine New Comedy, with its material cause in a young man's sexual desire, a formal cause in the social order dramatized in the senex, and an efficient cause in the vice or clown (the Elizabethan version of the tricky slave). The final cause is the spectator, who through applause becomes a part of the comic resolution. Through a green-world experience a character gains release from the psychological strictures of his grey world, and society gains a renewed sense of social integration. Shakespeare's comic vision involves a "detachment of the spirit born of [the] reciprocal reflection of two illusory realities" (p. 51).

738. ———. "Characterization in Shakespeare's Comedies." *Shakespeare Quarterly* 4 (1953):271–77.

Views Shakespeare's comic characters, though seemingly unpredictable and lifelike, as derived basically from the three comic types described in the *Tractatus Coislinianus* of the third century B.C.—the alazon (a boaster or hypocrite), the eiron (a self-deprecator who exposes the alazon), and the buffoon (who amuses by his mannerism or rhetoric). Aristotle adds a fourth, the agroikoa or rustic. The eiron is the hero-heroine, who at the center of the plot is engaged in conflict with the alazon; the rustic and buffoon polarize the comic mood.

739. ———. *The Myth of Deliverance: Reflections on Shakespeare's Problem Comedies.* Toronto and Buffalo: University of Toronto Press, 1983, 90 pp.

Argues that the so-called problem plays are merely romantic comedies in which the chief magical device is a bed trick rather than an enchanted forest or identical twins. These comedies generally fuse the human concerns for survival and deliverance in a teleological plot moving through an end that through some form of anagnorisis incorporates its beginning. *Measure for Measure*, for example, is a dramatic diptych combining a tragic and ironic section with one of elaborate comic intrigue. Like the other problem plays, it has both a constricted meaning within its historic context and also a limitless meaning within the structure of literature itself.

740. GORDON, GEORGES S. *Shakespearian Comedy and Other Studies*. London and New York: Oxford University Press, 1944, 158 pp.

Observes that Shakespearean comedy juxtaposes two worlds, one occupied with those who play with words and the other with those who are played with by words. In another sense a world of poetic romance is countered by a world of comic realism, the two existing side by side without competing for attention. Characters at the conclusion must frequently move from the poetic to the real world. Normally young lovers populate the one, workaday people the other. Shakespeare's comedies excel in the power to alternate the action "between Nowhere and England" (p. 51).

741. HASSEL, R. CHRIS, JR. *Faith and Folly in Shakespeare's Romantic Comedies*. Athens: University of Georgia Press, 1980, 255 pp.

Claims that an understanding of the Pauline and Erasmian paradoxes concerning the nature of foolishness and wisdom enhances an appreciation of Shakespeare's comic artistry and enlarges our sense of the coherence of his comic vision. More specifically, the Pauline, liturgical, and Erasmian principle that one is wise only in realizing and admitting his stupidity underlies the roles of Bottom and Feste, the juxtaposition of Touchstone and Jaques, the romantic relationship of Benedick and Beatrice, and the theme of edification through humiliation in *Love's Labor's Lost*, *Twelfth Night*, and *The Merchant of Venice*.

742. HAWKINS, SHERMAN. "The Two Worlds of Shakespearean Comedy." *Shakespeare Studies* 3 (1967):62–80.

Observes in Shakespeare's comedies the recurrence of the two archetypal motifs of the journey or green world and the siege or closed world. The journey involves movement from a normal to a green world and back again, leading to self-knowledge and reconciliation (*The Two Gentlemen of Verona*, *A Midsummer Night's Dream*, *The Merchant of Venice*, *As You Like It*, *The Winter's Tale*). The siege deals with characters who are visited and changed by outside forces (*The Comedy of Errors, Love's Labor's Lost, Much Ado About Nothing, Twelfth Night*). The *Tempest* fuses the two; dream and reality are indistinguishable.

743. HERRICK, MARVIN T. "Shakespeare." In *Tragicomedy: Its Origin and Development in Italy, France, and England*. Illinois Studies in Language and Literature, vol. 39. Urbana: University of Illinois Press, 1955, pp. 249–60.

Traces the movement in Shakespeare from tragical comedy to a near-tragic tragicomedy. Most of the romantic comedies reflect tragi-comic qualities, but in *All's Well That Ends Well* and *Measure for Measure* Shakespeare breaks new ground in variety of incident, characterization, and diction. There is anxious suspense, more in the minds of the spectators than in the minds of the characters. *Cymbeline*, like Beaumont and Fletcher's *Philaster*, is more fully developed tragi-comedy, replete with surprising discoveries, romantic disguises, tragic complaints, and a happy ending.

744. JENSEN, EJNER J. *Shakespeare and the Ends of Comedy*. Bloomington: Indiana University Press, 1991, 158 pp.

Challenges the traditional view that the meaning of a Shakespear-ean comedy is to be found and determined by its closure. To the contrary, the comic vitality of Shakespeare's plays is in the experience of the narrative itself, the "moment-by-moment unfolding on the stage" (p. xii). Such a reading is unabashedly intended to restore a certain "joyousness" to plays like *The Merchant of Venice, Much Ado About Nothing, As You Like It, Twelfth Night*, and *Measure for Measure*, all of which receive individual attention in this study.

745. KIRSCH, ARTHUR C. *Shakespeare and the Experience of Love*. Cambridge: Cambridge University Press, 1981, 194 pp.

Focuses on the mystery and importance of love in forming the whole individual and a whole community, utilizing both Christian and Freudian analytic methods in five Shakespearean plays. *Othello*, for ex-ample, is highly resonant, representing a literal love story but also reflecting in its three central figures a single moral and psychic entity. Similarly, the multiple plots of *Much Ado about Nothing* have a symbi-otic relationship concerning the transforming power of love. While Posthumous's deception in *Cymbeline* provokes a virtual decomposition of his personality, the resolution of his inner guilt represents "a para-digm of spiritual and psychic transformation" (p. 176). Chapters are also devoted to *All's Well That Ends Well* and *Measure for Measure*.

746. LAWRENCE, WILLIAM W. *Shakespeare's Problem Comedies*. 2d ed. New York: Frederick Ungar, 1960, 259 pp.

Argues that the problematic issues in *All's Well That Ends Well*, *Measure for Measure*, and *Troilus and Cressida* must be viewed in the context of the early seventeenth century, when vestigial remnants of medieval standards still obtained. Of particular significance are the medieval analogues that form the basis of Shakespeare's plot and help to condition the response of the spectators. Helena, for example, must be seen in light of Boccaccio's tale of the clever wench, Giletta of Narbonne; and the basic outlines of Isabella's actions are drawn from a story common in the south of Europe. What the modern critic sees as psychological inconsistencies Shakespeare's spectators would accept without question as narrative convention.

747. LEECH, CLIFFORD. *"Twelfth Night" and Shakespearian Comedy*. Toronto: University of Toronto Press; Halifax: Dalhousie University Press, 1965, 88 pp.

Contrasts the comic formula of *The Comedy of Errors* (the Plautine single stage in which characters interact) with that of *The Two Gentlemen of Verona* (a journey with roots in the Hellenistic romance). The early years of festive comedy culminate in *Twelfth Night*. In those that follow, the darker tones suggested in Feste's epilogue prevail. Passing beyond the laughter of delight, Shakespeare depicts time's destruction in *Troilus and Cressida* and its reconstruction in *The Winter's Tale*, which insists that by control of conduct and manipulation of natural experience man can achieve a degree of control over the flux of things.

748. LEGGATT, ALEXANDER. *Shakespeare's Comedy of Love*. London: Methuen; New York: Harper & Row, 1974, 272 pp.

Seeks not the inner unity but the eternal variety of Shakespeare's comic artistry. At the center of the early plays is farcical comedy that, in turn, gives way to a more subtle humor based on the characters' response to their situation. Shakespeare sets the experience of being in love between contrasting poles of hostility and indifference and plays the theme off various perspectives, including that of the clown as parodic. The study discusses each of the comedies through *Twelfth Night*.

749. LEVIN, RICHARD A. *Love and Society in Shakespearean Comedy: A Study of Dramatic Form and Content*. Newark: University of Delaware Press; London and Toronto: Associated University Presses, 1985, 203 pp.

Asserts that the closure of Shakespeare's romantic comedy is just as significant for whom it excludes as for whom it includes. Characters who, because of "disadvantages of birth, the prejudices of society, lack of cunning, and one's unwillingness or inability to adapt to the prevailing winds" (p. 21), form no part of the final celebration. In *The Merchant of Venice*, for example, the "winners" watch Shylock's suffering as if he were not part of the human condition, and the happiness Bassanio finds in Belmont leaves his friend Antonio wretched and largely unnoticed. *Twelfth Night* best exemplifies the sinister qualities of romantic comedy; the cunning and intelligent succeed in a society that reflects "not a wholesome balance between idealism and practicality but a spiritual malaise" (p. 19).

750. MACCARY, W. THOMAS. *Friends and Lovers: The Phenomenology of Desire in Shakespearean Comedy*. New York: Columbia University Press, 1985, 264 pp.

Describes Shakespearean comedy as essentially an outgrowth from Menandrine barrier comedy, in which the young male overcomes various obstacles to satisfy his sexual desire. In Shakespeare, more precisely, the pattern of progression for the male protagonist is from narcissistic self-love, to love for his image of himself in a friend, to love for a young lady transvestized as a young man, and finally to love for a young woman fully revealed. The progression is satisfying and credible to the male viewer because it is the pattern of his own psychosexual development.

751. NEVO, RUTH. *Comic Transformations in Shakespeare*. London and New York: Methuen, 1980, 242 pp.

Observes that Shakespeare fused his comic form from the Donatan formula for plot and the battle of the sexes for motivation of the variegated romantic courtship stories. Since the journey toward self-knowledge and the reciprocal acceptance of love progresses at a slower pace for the character than for the spectator (whose perspective is at a higher level of awareness), the resolution is immediate for the one, holistic and integrative for the other. The characters in acting out their follies gain remediation, and the fools mediate through parody.

752. ORNSTEIN, ROBERT. *Shakespeare's Comedies: From Roman Farce to Romantic Mystery*. Newark: University of Delaware Press; London and Toronto: Associated University Presses, 1986, 265 pp.

Visualizes a continuum of theme and characterization throughout Shakespeare's comic canon that minimizes the validity of dividing the plays into groups such as "happy," "problem," and "romance." Primarily the comedies represent Shakespeare's attempt to dramatize his conception of the romantic, an exploration of romantic love as a joyous mutuality within parameters of social codes and convictions. The vanity of the courting male, the instinct to search out a rival, his vulnerability to the irrationalities of sexual jealousy are themes that connect his early work to his late.

753. PALMER, JOHN. *Comic Characters of Shakespeare*. London: Macmillan, 1946, 135 pp.

Includes chapters on Berowne, Touchstone, Shylock, Bottom, and Benedick and Beatrice. The key to Shakespeare's humor is his ability to delight in mocking the diverse misadventures of rascals at the same time he retains a kindred emotional fellowship with them. Berowne and Touchstone, foolish in their own right, share an ability to perceive the incongruities in the actions of those around them. Shylock is at once both comic villain and suffering human. Bottom for all his stupidity possesses a comic unflappability we all cherish. Sympathy, not satire, is the essence of Shakespeare's comic inspiration.

754. PARROTT, THOMAS MARC. *Shakespearean Comedy*. New York: Oxford University Press, 1949, 417 pp.

Surveys both the comedies themselves and the comic elements in the histories and tragedies. The comedy varies from the patterned structure of *Love's Labor's Lost* to the lively farce of *The Merry Wives of Windsor*, yet there is an element of realistic humor in both. From the exclusive use of verse in the early plays, Shakespeare moves to prose as the natural idiom of comedy. Advancement is also visible in his fool figures as the early clowns (Launce, Speed, Costard) become complacent citizens (Bottom, Dogberry) and, in turn, professional jesters (Touchstone, Feste). Comedy develops from action, language, and character, the latter being the most sophisticated form.

755. PETTET, E. C. *Shakespeare and the Romance Tradition*. London: Staples Press, 1949, 208 pp.

Views Shakespeare's romantic comedies as the assimilation into drama of the historical and aesthetic climax of the romantic heritage. Stories of farfetched adventures, they inevitably center on young lovers and their struggles against adverse circumstances. The narrative culminates in the triumph of an ideal poetic justice. The characters themselves are lightly sketched, but love is presented as a transcendent experience. Through overtly comic figures Shakespeare inserts a light antiromantic thread. *All's Well That Ends Well* and *Measure for Measure* mark his alienation from romance. He returns to romantic conventions in the final plays, but the tone is more discursive, evil more genuine, and the emphasis more sharply on reconciliation.

227

The Comedies

General Studies

756. PHILAS, PETER G. *Shakespeare's Romantic Comedies: The Development of Their Form and Meaning.* Chapel Hill: University of North Carolina Press, 1966, 314 pp.

Describes the goal of Shakespeare's romantic comedy as the achievement of an ideal attitude toward love. To this end characters must overcome not only primarily external obstacles but also a frustration or opposition to love from within—whether in the form of utter rejection of it or of an overly romantic or realistic view of it. Each comedy in its multiple plot strands juxtaposes divergent attitudes toward love, and the resolution builds toward a mutually qualifying relationship. The focus is on the comedies through *Twelfth Night*.

757. RACKIN, PHYLLIS. "Androgyny, Mimesis, and the Marriage of the Boy Actor on the English Renaissance Stage." *PMLA* 102 (1987):29–41.

Compares the role of transvestite heroines in five comedies including *The Merchant of Venice*, *As You Like It*, and *Twelfth Night*. In each play the ultimate bride of the plot wears male clothing, and the disguise is central to the development of the narrative. Each play, to be successful, must win both sexes in the audience with a playful androgynous appeal. The onstage marriage joins masculine and feminine qualities just as they had been joined in the androgynous boy heroines. Such plays provide a glimpse of "the liminal moment when gender definitions were open to play" (p. 38).

758. RICHMAN, DAVID. *Laughter, Pain, and Wonder: Shakespeare's Comedies and the Audience in the Theater.* Newark: University of Delaware Press; London and Toronto: Associated University Presses, 1990, 200 pp.

Maintains that our knowledge of Shakespeare is enriched through an examination of differences in the response to the play and to the page. Given the solitary activity of reading, comedy suffers most, since laughter flourishes most freely in communal settings. Readers only rarely are aware of how funny these plays are. Through reference to plays from the entire comic canon, distinctions are made as well between various kinds of humor—the aggressive and sorrowful, the sympathetic, the neutral and detached.

759. SALINGAR, LEO. *Shakespeare and the Traditions of Comedy.* Cambridge: Cambridge University Press, 1976, 356 pp.

Notes that Shakespeare's comedy represents a fusion of the native tradition—from which come the romantic elements in the plots, seasonal association, celebration, new beginnings—and the Roman tradition—from which stem his sense of comic irony, the trickster and clever servant, the deceptions. His comedies moreover, seem aware of their place in the life of the nation, featuring a panorama of the public aspect of the national monarchy in their emphases on aristocratic loyalty, good government, and proper education.

760. SMIDT, KRISTIAN. *Unconformities in Shakespeare's Early Comedies*. New York: St. Martin's Press, 1986, 235 pp.

Borrows the term *unconformities* from geology and, like Smidt's earlier study of Shakespeare's histories (*Unconformities in Shakespeare's History Plays*. Atlantic Highlands: Humanities Press, 1982, 207 pp.), investigates "breaks in narrative continuity, contradictions as to cause and effect, impossible or incredible sequences of events, or unexplained and surprising changes in the characters portrayed" (p. ix). The chapter on *The Taming of the Shrew* posits unconformities arising from Shakespeare's use of *The Taming of a Shrew* as his source. That on *The Merchant of Venice* sees the Bassanio-Antonio-Portia relationship as a homosexual reflection of the love triangle in the sonnets. *Love's Labor's Lost* begins as romance and concludes as satire with greatest censure falling on the women as teases and wantons.

761. SWINDEN, PATRICK. *Introduction to Shakespeare's Comedies*. London and Basingstoke: Macmillan, 1973, 188 pp.

Observes that Shakespearean comedy typically presents a medley of separate actions bearing on a central theme. Unlike Jonson's comedy, its intent is not to correct but to endorse a sentiment. In the course of the action, "Villainy and good sense manage to neutralize each other, leaving folly to blunder into a sort of happiness" (p. 21). Each of Shakespeare's comedies is discussed, and a chapter is devoted to the place of Falstaff in Shakespeare's comic development.

762. THOMPSON, KARL M. "Shakespeare's Romantic Comedies." *PMLA* 67 (1952):1079–93.

Finds the essence of Shakespeare's romantic comedy in the courtly love tradition involving several central characteristics: the feudal metaphor of the vassal lover and the lord mistress, the religion of love in which a youth must perform noble deeds for the goodwill of a lady fair, the punishment of scoffers at love, and the training of such scoffers in a school of love. Shakespeare added two distinct elements, a substitution of the romance of marriage for the romance of adultery and a humorous mockery of the conventions. The plays covered in greatest detail are *Love's Labor's Lost* and *The Two Gentlemen of Verona*, with briefer attention to *Much Ado About Nothing*, *As You Like It*, and *Twelfth Night*.

General Studies

763. TILLYARD, E. M. W. *Shakespeare's Early Comedies*. London: Chatto & Windus; New York: Barnes & Noble, 1965, 216 pp.

Describes Shakespeare's comedy as owing relatively little to classical theory. The range of background materials includes medieval romance, folk tales, the Bible, classical narrative (especially Ovid), and the Greek romance. While tragedy involves individual man's relation to the sum of things, comedy deals with man as a social creature, his relationship to his neighbor or to his society. Individual chapters discuss *The Comedy of Errors*, *The Taming of the Shrew*, *The Two Gentlemen of Verona*, *Love's Labor's Lost*, and *The Merchant of Venice*. Each play is discussed on its own terms with no overriding theme or motif.

764. VAUGHAN, JACK A. *Shakespeare's Comedies*. New York: Frederick Ungar, 1980, 249 pp.

Includes an introductory chapter on comedy in Shakespeare's time, followed by individual chapters on each of Shakespeare's seventeen comedies. *The Comedy of Errors* is described as fine farce in which characterization is subordinate to the intricacies of plot. This comedy is set apart from Shakespeare's other comedies of mistaken identity in that only the spectator's level of awareness comprehends the multiple confusions. And these confusions occur, unlike those in the later comedies, with no deceiver, no schemer. The denouement, with the appearance of the abbess, is sheer deus ex machina, but the framing device adds depth and resonance to the antics.

765. WESTLUND, JOSEPH. *Shakespeare's Reparative Comedies: A Psychoanalytic View of the Middle Plays*. Cambridge: Harvard University Press, 1984, 227 pp.

Maintains that Shakespeare's comedies from *The Merchant of Venice* to *Measure for Measure* transcend conflict and, in doing so, repair the spectators' sense of the dislocations in life and their nexus of hostile emotions. A Kleinian adaptation of Aristotle's catharsis, this reparation is achieved by arousing and then dispatching anger. Rosalind's autonomy and assurance, for example, "mirror and confirm our own independence and self-esteem" (p. 91). By frustrating our wish to idealize, *All's Well That Ends Well* tutors the spectators in the ways of the world, the reparative effect being that they are forced to accept the difference between conception and realization.

766. WHEELER, RICHARD P. *Shakespeare's Development and the Problem Comedies: Turn and Counter-Turn*. Berkeley: University of California Press, 1981, 229 pp.

Considers the problem comedies as a profound reorientation of Shakespeare's comedy from the festive plays to the later stage worlds. These plays are marked by psychological conditions central to the tragedies and a preoccupation with the place of sexuality in the social order. Helena extends the controlling female role of the earlier plays, but here it becomes threatening and ambiguous. The tension between the design of *All's Well* and its content is only intensified by the efforts to resolve it. Similarly, considering Angelo's sexual degradation, Isabella's frigidity, Claudio's fornication, and Vincentio's late-in-the-day proposal, the connecting theme in *Measure for Measure* is a degraded relationship forced to take the stamp of official respectability.

767. WHITE, R. S. *Let Wonder Seem Familiar: Ending in Shakespeare's Romance Vision*. London: Athlone Press; Atlantic Highlands: Humanities Press, 1985, 203 pp.

Traces Shakespeare's persistent effort to adapt the romantic conventions of closure to accommodate varying degrees of the realistic and the problematic. The series of overlapping endings in *A Midsummer Night's Dream*, for instance, both enhances the artifice and obviates a simplistic view of the powers of love. *The Winter's Tale* splices two dimensions of life; the long view of time that operates through memory and reconciliation is "slipped in to allow us to forget the explosive violence of a time that was too short for reflection, recollection, or forethought" (p. 149). Similarly, the closure of *The Tempest* is enigmatic with its grudging reconciliations looking toward the grave while its purged vision looks toward new life.

768. WILLIAMSON, MARILYN L. *The Patriarchy of Shakespeare's Comedies*. Detroit: Wayne State University Press, 1986, 207 pp.

Maintains that Shakespeare wrote for a changing audience throughout his career and that, in doing so, he provides differing representations of women and patriarchy. The romantic comedies of the 1590s focus on powerful women and profitable marriages, yet show that marriage for women is a subordinate state based on a double standard in which men may err with impunity but the erring wife brings opprobrium to her husband. The problem comedies depict marriage as a means of regulating the disruptive force of male desire. The romances mythologize patriarchal power in the father's natural authority and in the younger generation "whose succession to the power of the father is the lifestream of the patriarchy" (p. 157).

769. WILSON, JOHN DOVER. *Shakespeare's Happy Comedies*. Evanston: Northwestern University Press, 1962, 224 pp.

Notes that the critical neglect of Shakespeare's comedies not only has distorted our understanding of Shakespeare's artistic development but also has impaired our vision of the tragedies themselves. Unlike Jonson's, Shakespeare's comedy up to 1601 is not critical; his laughter is tolerant and delightful, and the clown is never far from the stage. In a word, his comedy is one of shared emotions. While each of the comedies through *Twelfth Night* has its distinct personality, they share a foreign setting with structured layers on domestic activities in the mercantile class and on the love affairs and friendship of the gentry in the class above.

ALL'S WELL THAT ENDS WELL

Editions

770. FRASER, RUSSELL, ed. *All's Well That Ends Well*. The New Cambridge Shakespeare. Cambridge: Cambridge University Press, 1985, 154 pp.

   Features an introductory essay on date, sources, the play, stage history, and the trends of recent years. Extensive notes appear on individual pages of the text, and appendixes include a textual analysis and a list of suggested readings.

771. HUNTER, G. K., ed. *All's Well That Ends Well*. The Arden Shakespeare. London: Methuen; Cambridge, Mass.: Harvard University Press, 1959, 152 pp.

   Includes discussion of the text, the source, critical interpretations, and the verse, as well as an appendix featuring selections from William Painter's *Palace of Pleasure*. The text is based on the First Folio, for which the copy was probably Shakespeare's foul papers. The theory that *Love's Labor's Won* was an earlier version of the play is now generally discounted. The ultimate source is "Giletta of Narbona" from Boccaccio's *Decameron*; Shakespeare's additions include the countess, the clown, Lafew, Parolles, and the subplot.

Criticism

772. ADAMS, JOHN F. "*All's Well That Ends Well*: The Paradox of Procreation." *Shakespeare Quarterly* 12 (1961):261–70.

Suggests that the play's title is not one of comic nonchalance but a kind of warning that an action can be judged right or wrong only if it is considered in its entirety and in relation to its consequences. The theme centers on how one is to know what constitutes right action in a world of deceitful and duplicitous ambiguities. The major themes are the problem of the nature of honor (which becomes synonymous with human worth), the problem of heritage (the responsibilities of youth to the past), and the problem of sex and procreation.

773. ADELMAN, JANET. "Bed Tricks: On Marriage as the End of Comedy in *All's Well That Ends Well* and *Measure for Measure*." In *Shakespeare's Personality*. Edited by Norman N. Holland, Sidney Homan, and Bernard J. Paris. Berkeley and London: University of California Press, 1989, pp. 151–74.

Views both Bertram and Angelo as psychological virgins about to experience sex for the first time. Both can desire only when the object is an illegitimate contamination of a pure woman. Since marriage is an institution for legitimizing sexual desire and since the bed trick is for the man a means of illicit gratification, there is little reason to believe that the physical pleasure derived from the latter can be translated into a meaningful spiritual relationship. *Measure for Measure* redoes the bed-trick and returns power to the male. Whereas in *All's Well* the trick is managed by a powerfully sexual woman, in *Measure for Measure* it is directed by an asexual father-figure in whose scheme the women are mere pawns.

774. ARTHOS, JOHN. "The Comedy of Generation." *Essays in Criticism* 5 (1955):97–117.

Argues that comedy means more than the spectator's response to humorous actions played out on a stage; it refers, as well, to the enjoyment of a detached intellectual concentration on the controlling idea of a play. One's enjoyment of the patterned action of *All's Well*, with its relation of love to conquest, to deceit, and to begetting, might be described as the comedy of generation. The whole of the action focuses on confusion at the very roots of love, and the conclusion is supported and given coherence by this mood; we call on comic faith to support our sympathies and hopes that Helena has achieved happiness.

775. ASP, CAROLYN. "Subjectivity, Desire and Female Friendship in *All's Well That Ends Well*." *Literature and Psychology* 32, no. 4 (1986):48–63.

Views Helena as coming to independent womanhood by surmounting attitudes and theories of female deprivation and inferiority.

Helena at first embodies conventional Renaissance psychoanalytic paradigms of female psychic masochism and powerlessness, but she ultimately is able to develop and accept an assertive desire of which she is the subject rather than object. "Fired by her desire, Helena refuses to submit to gender myths that link the female with loss unless that loss can be turned to gain" (p. 61).

776. BENNETT, JOSEPHINE WATERS. "New Techniques of Comedy in *All's Well That Ends Well*." *Shakespeare Quarterly* 18 (1967):337–62.
Argues that *All's Well* was composed after *Measure for Measure* and that it was consciously based upon the earlier play. Helena, perhaps the most subtle and intricate female character Shakespeare ever created, is consistent in her determination to do anything to satisfy her overwhelming passion. The play incorporates the romantic, the comic, the inexperienced, the mature, the theatrical, and the burlesque. The skillful intermingling is the key to the comic perspective.

777. BERKELEY, DAVID S., and KEESEE, DONALD. "Bertram's Blood-Consciousness in *All's Well That Ends Well*." *Studies in English Literature 1500–1900* 31 (1991):247–58.
Observes that the play is an oddity in that it presents an enforced marriage between armigerous persons, with Bertram of high nobility and Helena a "mean poor" gentlewoman. Bertram, in being blood-conscious, not wanting to debase his family, is realistic, whereas the king and the countess are romantic. Since the play reflects in Helena's situation that of Shakespeare himself, it is not surprising that it makes an appeal for "inferior blood to be accepted on the basis of supplicating merit" (p. 256).

778. BRADBROOK, MURIEL C. "Virtue Is the True Nobility." *Review of English Studies*, n.s. 1 (1950):289–301.
Contends that the leading question in *All's Well* is "Wherein lies true honor and nobility?" Whereas Bertram deems nobility the consequence of descent or birth, Helena considers it to issue from noble deeds. Bertram, in lying and disobedience to his mother and his king, squanders any claim to nobility. Helena and Parolles are arranged as his good and evil angels, and his conversion is a miracle of Helena's true virtue. The characters in this latter-day morality assume an extrapersonal significance.

779. COLE, HOWARD C. *The "All's Well" Story from Boccaccio to Shakespeare*. Urbana: University of Illinois Press, 1981, 145 pp.

Investigates pre-Shakespearean versions of the *All's Well* story in Boccaccio, an anonymous fifteenth-century French romance, Accolti's Italian play, sixteenth-century commentators on Boccaccio, and Painter's *The Palace of Pleasure*. Clearly Shakespeare did not inherit a monolithic and simplistic narrative; the main traditions had been characterized by wit, irony, cynicism, and, above all, intentional ambiguities. The ambiguity of Helena's motivation and our consequent inability to ascertain the precise nature of her character represent Shakespeare's determination to discover "new ways of capturing the old ironies" (p. 136).

780. COOK, DOROTHY. "Helena: The Will and the Way." *Upstart Crow* 10 (1990):14–31.

Asserts that Helena should not be sentimentalized, that instead she is a fully realized character who moves in a complex, realistic world. Shakespeare renders the heroine more sympathetic by disclosing with great charm both her weaknesses and her strengths. He explores the "power" of her love and its confident assumptions of eventual reciprocity. The major struggle in the play is a conflict of wills, and through resolving such a conflict she seems to solidify society and to affirm the "comic values of sympathetic tolerance . . . and gracious humility" (p. 28).

781. DENNIS, CARL. "*All's Well That Ends Well* and the Meaning of Agape." *Philological Quarterly* 50 (1971):75–84.

Views Helena's affection for Bertram as blind devotion to a man unworthy of her, as akin to agape in that it is given not in the expectation of reciprocation but in obedience to God's command. Bertram is depicted as totally unsympathetic until the very conclusion in order to emphasize the unconditional nature of this love. Agape stimulates moral growth in the recipient by encouraging a person to perceive his best self, and there is evidence in the final scene that such a change is occurring in Bertram.

782. ELLIS, DAVID. "Finding a Part for Parolles." *Essays in Criticism* 39 (1989):289–304.

Suggests an inherent contradiction between Parolles's character and his role in the play, namely that his lack of success in trying to hold his own with anyone (his exposure as a fool by Lafew, Helena, Diana, the countess, the lords in the army) makes it difficult to believe that he is capable of corrupting Bertram. This situation appears to illustrate a problem of casting that Shakespeare was struggling with throughout the early acts. Parolles finally sheds his pretensions and emerges as or finds his identity as a domestic fool. His reintegration into society "is no more unambiguously happy than the one which in the final scene unites the two protagonists" (p. 302).

783. HAPGOOD, ROBERT M. "The Life of Shame: Parolles and *All's Well*." *Essays in Criticism* 15 (1965):269–78.

Compares Parolles to Falstaff in his sheer zest for life and his unabashed acceptance of shame if necessary for life's continuance. His name suggests both word and verbal pledge, and indeed verbosity and empty promises bring him to his impasse. Other characters in the play also choose life before honor. Bertram, Helena, the king, and Diana all risk honor for life and love. If the result is not always "all's well" in the study, it is surely so in the theater where the sense of "felt life" prevails.

784. HODGDON, BARBARA. "The Making of Virgins and Mothers: Sexual Signs, Substitute Scenes, and Doubled Presences in *All's Well That Ends Well*." *Philological Quarterly* 66 (1987):47–71.

Addresses the play from Helena's point of view, examining Shakespeare's transformation of Boccaccio's tale, how sexual signs are articulated in character and event, and how substitute scenes and doubled presences function to sexualize its narrative structure. In changing the heroine's name from Boccaccio's Giletta, Shakespeare embraces a paradox, evoking connotations both of the adulterous Helen of Troy and of the lonely, virginal lass of *A Midsummer Night's Dream*. Helena talks openly with Parolles of losing her virginity, soliloquizes forlornly about her lower station, and suppresses both modes of speech with Bertram. The conditional closure signals compromise, a "real-izing of romance" (p. 68).

785. HUNT, MAURICE. "*All's Well That Ends Well* and the Triumph of the Word." *Texas Studies in Literature and Language* 30 (1988):388–411.

Relates speech-act theory to Christian doctrine to illuminate certain features of the play, for instance, the etymology of Parolles's name and the centrality of repeated riddles. Parolles (words) ironically registers truth when he speaks, whether in the scene of his hoodwinking or in his equivocating stance before the king in 5.3. But the words, as the surrounding characters only dimly begin to perceive, are capturing truths that can be expressed only in riddle or paradox. The gestures of affection in the play's concluding lines riddlingly reflect marvelously condensed words of love.

786. ———. "Words and Deeds in *All's Well That Ends Well*." *Modern Language Quarterly* 48 (1987):320–38.

Notes that the ideal of fitting the word to the deed, commented on in act 1 in the king's eulogistic remarks about Bertram's father, is a sign of what is lost in the remainder of the play. For one thing, the king himself in these early acts wavers between stressing words and recommending deeds as the means to virtue. For another, Helena's gracious speech persuades the king to try the cure, but her deed fails to achieve its goal, the winning of Bertram. Parolles, of course, in his pompous claims of courage notoriously divorces deeds from words. The play fittingly finds its closure in a riddle, a rhetorical device in which profound meaning arises from seemingly empty and nonsensical words.

787. HUSTON, J. DENNIS. " 'Some Stain of Soldier': The Function of Parolles in *All's Well That Ends Well*." *Shakespeare Quarterly* 21 (1970):431–38.

Considers Parolles a curious combination of the corrupt and the commendable. If he is vain, deceitful, and foolish, he is also possessed of a tremendous energy that infuses his world with dramatic life. When he comes on stage, the world is heavy with the atmosphere of death and decay. At his suggestion Bertram pursues his honor on the field of battle, and at his suggestion Helena pursues her honor in the form of union with Bertram.

788. KASTAN, DAVID SCOTT. "*All's Well That Ends Well* and the Limits of Comedy." *ELH* 52 (1985):575–89.

Notes that generic definitions of comedy derived from commentaries on Terence specify that comic action is to be feigned and shaped into comforting patterns of wish fulfillment. Shakespeare's comedies explore this freedom, and the problem comedies do not issue in comic celebration. In *All's Well That Ends Well*, for instance, fictive aspirations have been gratified, but we have been made suspicious of them. Moreover, the fragile and tentative nature of the closure is underscored through a litany of conditionals. The play, refusing to submit the show of things to the desires of our mind, explores and extends the limits of comedy.

789. KING, WALTER N. "Shakespeare's Mingled Yarn." *Modern Language Quarterly* 21 (1960):33–44.

Notes that critics who labor to explain away the moral and aesthetic lapses of *All's Well* ignore the possibility that Shakespeare is intending to depict individuals as they behave inconsistently in life as opposed to the way they behave consistently in traditional romantic story. The play may well be a psychological study of the responses of Helena, Bertram, the king, the countess, and Lafew to a love problem

All's Well That Ends Well

that forces to the surface the wavering balance between vice and virtue in ordinary human nature.

790. LAWRENCE, WILLIAM W. "The Meaning of *All's Well That Ends Well*." *PMLA* 37 (1922):418–69.

Cautions that we must temper our distaste for *All's Well* by attempting to understand how it was received in Shakespeare's day. Helena was meant to be wholly noble and heroic, fully justified in her actions; and Bertram's sudden conversion would have been accepted as a convention of medieval and Elizabethan storytelling. The study traces the clever wench story through numerous analogues to demonstrate the literary context in which Shakespeare worked and in which, while he was free to alter detail and emphasis, he was not free to change the basic direction and resolution.

791. LEECH, CLIFFORD. "The Theme of Ambition in *All's Well That Ends Well*." *ELH* 21 (1954):17–29.

Observes that each of the problem plays, establishing attitudes strangely at variance with traditional values, lacks emplastic power or a sense of fusion. Such a juxtaposition in *All's Well* is Helena's love for Bertram and her raw ambition. Together with old characters rebuking the young and sighing at the state of corruption is a young woman who loves a man but who is also determined to bring him to heel. As a result the spectator is forced to observe her analytically, and this ambivalence reflects the conception of love at once as grandly noble and as a sickness needing to be cured.

792. LEGGATT, ALEXANDER. "All's Well That Ends Well: The Testing of Romance." *Modern Language Quarterly* 32 (1971):21–41.

Proposes that two dramatic modes, romance and realism, are juxtaposed in such a manner that they test each other. The tension is genuine and the ending uncertain. The older aristocrats, Bertram, and Parolles are from a real and fallen world. Helena as the upholder of romance, cures the king; but realism intrudes when Bertram refuses to marry her. She, in turn, pursues and wins him on his own terms, and romance seems victorious in the end. His qualified acceptance, however, leaves the issue in doubt and reflects the continuing tensions between the two generic forms.

793. MAXWELL, J. C. "Helena's Pilgrimage." *Review of English Studies*, n.s. 20 (1969):189–93.

Believes that Helena, whatever her original intentions, never journeys to the shrine of St. Jaques, that she arrives in Florence by design, and that she is directly responsible for the report of her death by the rector of the shrine. Once the spectator or reader has a suspicion regarding Helena's motives, his imagination becomes a significant supplement to the plot structure of the play.

794. NAGARAJAN, S. "The Structure of *All's Well That Ends Well*." *Essays in Criticism* 10 (1960):24–31.

Argues that the love interest is the central focus, that the play follows the progress of a very young man who, subject to the base diversionary influence of Parolles, must come of age and accept the responsibilities of love and marriage. By refusing to consummate his marriage with Helena, Bertram makes the sexual act a symbol of marriage's meaning; and this meaning will be trivialized if he is allowed to have sex with Diana. Helena uses the bed-trick both to preserve the honor of the sexual act and to shock Bertram into recognizing its value as well.

795. PARKER, R. B. "War and Sex in *All's Well That Ends Well*." *Shakespeare Survey* 37 (1984):99–113.

Maintains that the play is built upon the concept of masculine honor in war and feminine honor in love and that the relationship wryly forces the abandonment of the purity of both ideals. As Bertram must learn to accept sexual love and its responsibilities, Helena must learn to abandon self-abnegation in love and bring it to fruition through deliberate aggression. These lessons learned, Bertram and Helena return to Rossillion to confirm and rejuvenate family and state; but the tone of the end is not without the shadow of uncertainty.

796. PRICE, JOSEPH G. *The Unfortunate Comedy: A Study of "All's Well That Ends Well."* Toronto: University of Toronto Press, 1968, 197 pp.

Reviews the stage history and surveys the criticism from the seventeenth century to the twentieth. Whereas English Romantic criticism blossomed into a panegyric for Helena, fantasy gave way to tragicomedy in the interpretations of the mid-nineteenth century. From the turn of the present century criticism generally condemned the play as a failure, whether the consequence of inconsistency of characterization, of demands upon the audience, or of the incapability of the author. Critics of the midcentury engaged in a gradual reappraisal, balancing weaknesses and merits with concepts of dark or satiric comedy, of high and serious romance, and of consistency of Shakespearean theme.

797. ROARK, CHRISTOPHER. "Lavatch and Service in *All's Well That Ends Well*." *Studies in English Literature* 28 (1988):241–58.

Maintains that Lavatch's role is useful in focusing the debate about the play's tone and its unsatisfying resolution. More specifically, the fool's proclamation to the countess, that his nonsensical "O Lord, sir" will serve as a response to all questions at court, parodies and points out the limitations of Helena's solution to how she will gain Bertram as a husband. Lavatch's remarks about cuckoldry also relate to Bertram, who in a sense cuckolds himself when he unwittingly copulates with his wife. His failure to serve, though a servant, parallels Bertram's inability to serve another through love and Helena's inability to serve except through manipulation and disguise.

798. SHAPIRO, MICHAEL. " 'The Web of Our Life': Human Frailty and Moral Redemption in *All's Well That Ends Well.*" *Journal of English and Germanic Philology* 71 (1972):514–26.

Views romantic love as the redemptive force that untangles the mingled yarn of life in the play. Both Bertram and Helena seek distinction, and the efforts of self-assertion produce disaster in both cases. The climax comes in 5.3 when Bertram begs forgiveness from a humble and contrite Helena. He implicitly forgives her attempt to claim her love by a kind of force, and she forgives him for his obstinate perversity. While Helena is responsible for his redemption, he is also the agent of hers.

799. SIMONDS, PEGGY MUÑOZ. "Sacred and Sexual Motifs in *All's Well That Ends Well.*" *Renaissance Quarterly* 42 (1989):33–59.

Concerns what Shakespeare's contemporary viewers thought about the subject of matrimony through references to Catullus, Erasmus, the text of the 1599 Anglican marriage liturgy, a scriptural use of the bed-trick to fulfill the obligations of the marriage contract, and a sermon by the Anglican divine Henry Smith. The point is not to claim these works as sources for Shakespeare but as a part of the common cultural context for a Renaissance viewer. Such a focus reveals that, while the "presence of sacred concerns . . . interpenetrating the lusty sexuality" (p. 34) might make the play "dark" to us, it would have ensured its commercial success in the early seventeenth century.

800. SNYDER, SUSAN. "*All's Well That Ends Well* and Shakespeare's Helena: Text and Subtext and Object." *English Literary Renaissance* 18 (1988):66–77.

Examines gaps and disjunctions in the speeches and actions of Helena, for instance whether she deliberately pursues Bertram to Florence or arrives there coincidentally. In any case, like Helena in *A Midsummer Night's Dream* she loves before she is loved and actively pursues her man, and in a sense the plot of the one play can function as a subtext for the other. In *A Midsummer Night's Dream* the friendship of Helena and Hermia is torn asunder; and, even though the play neatly sorts out its love tangles, it never reinstates that close bond when the ladies are inscribed within the patriarchal order. In *All's Well* to the contrary, a close friendship between Helena and Diana is of paramount significance in the success of a scheme that manipulates both king and husband.

801. TURNER, ROBERT Y. "Dramatic Conventions in *All's Well That Ends Well*." *PMLA* 75 (1960):497–502.

Describes *All's Well* as more of an age than for all time because in it Shakespeare adheres so closely to Elizabethan dramatic conventions. Shakespeare was adapting his material to the fashionable pattern of the prodigal son plays in which a hero undergoes a change of character preparing him, not for salvation, but for marriage. These plays do not normally test the heroine; *All's Well* is the only instance of a woman's being of lower social rank than the hero. Relating the play to terms of literary scholarship rather than of psychological consistency demonstrates that it is a failure of one kind but not of another.

802. WARREN, ROGER. "Why Does It End Well? Helena, Bertram, and the Sonnets." *Shakespeare Survey* 22 (1969):79–92.

Suggests that the relationship between Bertram and Helena reflects Shakespeare's personal relationship with the "friend" chronicled in many of the sonnets. Perhaps the saddest aspect is the sense of an inseparable difference in rank (especially sonnet 26) and the probability that Shakespeare himself had to endure and forgive slights and insults. While Shakespeare provides no reassuring speech for Helena at the conclusion, it is likely that he considered that her single-minded love assures that all ends well.

803. WILSON, HAROLD S. "Dramatic Emphasis in *All's Well That Ends Well*." *Huntington Library Quarterly* 13 (1950):222–40.

Argues that, for a modern audience unbiased by critical stricture, the play is skillfully contrived to render Helena appealing, Bertram's repentance credible, and the reconciliation of Bertram and Helena plausible. Shakespeare in making Helena more appealing at the outset than did Boccaccio runs the risk of her appearing conniving in the last half. Comic emphasis on the corruption of Parolles and on Bertram's recognizing his true nature, however, prepares the young count for his conversion and maintains the spectator's sympathy for Helena.

AS YOU LIKE IT

Reference Works

804. HALIO, JAY L., and MILLARD, BARBARA C., comps. *"As You Like It":
An Annotated Bibliography, 1940–1980*: Garland Reference Library of
the Humanities, 443: Garland Shakespeare Bibliographies, 8. New
York and London: Garland Publishing, 1985, 744 pp.

Contains 1,584 entries representing virtually all publications on
the play from 1940 through 1980, along with the most significant
items prior to 1940. The categories, each arranged chronologically, are
criticism, sources and background, dating, textual studies, texts and
editions, translations, stage history (performance criticism, films, television), influences (song collections, adaptations), and bibliographies.
A brief introductory essay traces the history of recent criticism and
research.

805. MARDER, LOUIS, comp. *"As You Like It": A Supplementary Bibliography
1890–1965*. The New Variorum Shakespeare. New York: American
Scholar Publications, 1965, 19 pp.

Includes representative scholarship on *As You Like It* from 1890 to
1965 and is intended to supplement H. H. Furness's Variorum edition
of 1890. The material is categorized under bibliographical sources,
modern editions, and critical studies (alphabetically arranged). While
not exhaustive, the material represents every major category of scholarship and criticism.

Editions

806. KNOWLES, RICHARD, ed. *As You Like It*. A New Variorum Edition of
Shakespeare. New York: Modern Language Association of America,
1977, 737 pp.

Uses the First Folio (1623) as the copy text (pp. 9–303), on each
page, for that portion of the text, providing variant readings, textual
notes, and general critical commentary. Following the text are sections
on the nature of the text (press variants, the copy for the First Folio, the
integrity of the text, theories of later revision, the staying entry of 4
August 1600), the date of composition, the sources—Lodge's *Rosalynde*, *Gamelyn*—a survey of criticism prepared by Evelyn Joseph Mat-

tern (the play as a whole, the tone, the technique, the characters, the stage history, the music), and a bibliography.

807. LATHAM, AGNES, ed. *As You Like It*. The Arden Shakespeare. London: Methuen; Cambridge, Mass.: Harvard University Press, 1975, 135 pp.

Includes discussion of the text, date, sources, critical interpretations, and stage history. The text is based on the First Folio, for which the copy was probably good prompt material transcribed for the press. The play is distinguished by a high proportion of prose, and the blank verse reflects considerable metrical freedom. Featuring more songs than any other Shakespearean play, *As You Like It* evokes a carefree mood and conjures up a woodland scene even on a bare stage. The date of composition was probably early 1599, and the primary source is Thomas Lodge's *Rosalynde*.

808. QUILLER-COUCH, ARTHUR, and WILSON, JOHN DOVER, eds. *As You Like It*. Cambridge: Cambridge University Press, 1926, 181 pp.

Provides extensive textual notes, a critical introduction, a discussion of the copy text, and a section on the stage history. There is a staying or blocking entry in the Stationers' Register on 4 August 1600; the only publication is that of the First Folio, and that text—apparently based on the promptbook—serves as copy for this edition. The play probably represents two strata, the second involving extensive revision of material composed around 1593. Touchstone and Jaques are deliberately opposed commentators on the romantic transformations that occur in Arden.

Criticism

809. BAKER, SUSAN. "Shakespeare and Ritual: The Example of *As You Like It*." *Upstart Crow* 9 (1989):9–23.

Maintains that Shakespeare in this play both presents and represents liminal experience. The spectator is separated from his normal routine when he enters the theater, and the recurrent pattern throughout the play is to show the characters confronting incongruities in their lives. Petrarchism is interrogated, and the pastoral is unmetaphored. The play, in a word, persistently calling attention to its fictive status, resembles a generic rite of passage. Unlike a tribal neophyte or a fictive character, however, the spectator can invoke, embrace, or repudiate the green world at will.

As You Like It

810. BARBER, C. L. "The Use of Comedy in *As You Like It*." *Philological Quarterly* 21 (1942):353–67.

Perceives Shakespeare's method as the interweaving of a serious theme (pastoral innocence, romantic love) with a layer of mocking accompaniment. The opposite of satire, which presents life and then ridicules its failures, Shakespeare presents ideal life and then mocks its shortcomings. Jaques and Touchstone are the principal figures in this comic machinery, which serves to reconcile the spectators to reality without cynicism or sentimentality.

811. BARNET, SYLVAN. " 'Strange Events': Improbability in *As You Like It*." *Shakespeare Studies* 4 (1968):119–31.

Believes that Shakespeare intentionally heightens the improbabilities at the end—the personality changes of Frederick and Oliver, the quickly established love relationships of Oliver and Celia and of Orlando and Rosalind. This interest in improbability for its own sake is a tenet of comedy, and to achieve this tone Shakespeare consciously departs from the carefully articulated motivation in his source, Lodge's *Rosalynde*. There is a return to the court at the end, but the characters, strangely transformed, will never be the same.

812. BENNETT, JOSEPHINE WATERS. "Jaques's Seven Ages." *Shakespeare Association Bulletin* 18 (1943):168–74.

Surveys the various attempts to find a source for Jaques's speech on the seven ages of man, noting that Shakespeare's account has little in common with medical and astrological convention, that he is satirically concerned with appearance and behavior. Not improbably Shakespeare has in mind Palengenius's *Zodiacus Vitae*, which describes the futility and folly of human life and places the idea of five ages in the context of life as a pageant. An associated source treating of seven ages and revealing numerous verbal parallels is the *Onomasticon* of Julius Pollux.

813. BONO, BARBARA J. "Mixed Gender, Mixed Genre in Shakespeare's *As You Like It*." In *Renaissance Genres: Essays on Theory, History, and Interpretation*. Edited by Barbara K. Lewalski. Cambridge: Harvard University Press, 1986, pp. 189–212.

Suggests that the patriarchal oedipal crisis in act 1 is "displaced back onto its preoedipal ground in the nature of the Forest of Arden" (p. 194). Orlando's masculine posturing and Petrarchism are subjected to a maturing process through Ganymed's tutoring. Rosalind, by virtue of her "double-voiced" discourse, is able both to play a role and to criticize it, acting out men's stereotypical expectations of women's fickleness and seeming cruelty and thereby creating an atmosphere for a companionate marriage in a world not deterministically bound by its cultural conventions.

814. BRACHER, MARK. "Contrary Notions of Identity in *As You Like It*." *Studies in English Literature 1500–1900* 24 (1984):225–40.

Notes that, of the two types of comedy, one emphasizes the blocking figure, exclusivity, and the satiric tone while the other emphasizes discovery and reconciliation, inclusivity, and the romantic tone. *As You Like It* depicts two such comic types—the inclusive (Celia, Rosalind) and the exclusive (Oliver, Duke Frederick)—gradually leading the audience toward full acceptance of the inclusive self. On another plane the play juxtaposes two types of comedy, the romantic and the satiric. The satiric vision is contrary to Shakespeare's both because it denies the ultimate value of love and because it reinforces the attitude of exclusivity.

815. CIRILLO, ALBERT R. *"As You Like It*: Pastoralism Gone Awry." *ELH* 38 (1971):19–39.

Suggests that, while the Forest of Arden is a pastoral retreat from life at court, the ideal must be tempered and in turn inform the world of the actual. Rejecting through irony the naive belief that the pastoral fiction is attainable in life, Shakespeare depicts Arden as able to correct the real world's problems involving young lovers and filial relationships. It is through Rosalind that the spectators come to realize the balance that must be established between ideal and actual.

816. DALEY, A. Stuart. "The Dispraise of the Country in *As You Like It*." *Shakespeare Quarterly* 36 (1985):300–14.

Insists that the antithesis established in *As You Like It* is not between country (new society) and city (old society) but between two political orders, that represented by Duke Senior and that represented by Duke Frederick. The former happens to reside in the Forest of Arden, but nowhere is that landscape idealized as pastoral. To the contrary, it is generally dispraised both by the courtiers in exile and residents like Corin who speak of the hardships of life there. Duke Senior and his followers learn that they must endure with patience the vicissitudes of providence, and they—the old society—return to the court (also a country setting) after the overthrow of the *new* duke and the *new* society.

817. ———. "Shakespeare's Corin, Almsgiver and Faithful Feeder." *English Language Notes* 27, no. 4 (1989–90):4–21.

As You Like It

Demonstrates that, whereas the Forest of Arden is in Lodge's *Rosalynde* an idyllic pastoral location, Shakespeare has transformed it into a stage image of wretchedness and of struggle for survival. So, too, Corin, a simple old farmer in the source, becomes one who in his comments delivers a kind of consolation of philosophy. In such a role Corin makes it clear that his circumstances are anything but idyllic, and Shakespeare reflects the conditions of the poor laborers in the English countryside in the 1590s. Corin's master is also an easily recognizable Elizabethan type, "the new avaricious landlord to whom a farm is primarily a property to be exploited for cash profit" (p. 8).

818. FRASER, RUSSELL. "Shakespeare's Book of Genesis." *Comparative Drama* 25 (1991):121–28.

Argues that the play "sponsors an eccentric version of the *Genesis* story" (p. 121). Oliver is a symbol of unregenerate man who resolves his crisis in the Garden. The "flood" at the end is one of projected weddings that will save the world when all is lost. The "vagabonds in the forest challenge the rest of us, who mean to pull ourselves up by our bootstraps" (p. 128).

819. GARBER, MARJORIE. "The Education of Orlando." In *Comedy from Shakespeare to Sheridan: Change and Continuity in the English and European Dramatic Tradition.* Edited by A. R. Braunmuller and J. C. Bulman. Newark: University of Delaware Press; London and Toronto: Associated University Presses, 1986, pp. 102–12.

Observes that Rosalind retains her disguise in the Forest of Arden in order to teach Orlando the substance of what it is to love. His education moves through three phases—the tongue-tied boy of the first shock of love, the psychologically self-absorbed author of lame love lyrics, and the articulate, knowledgeable husband.

820. GARDNER, HELEN. "*As You Like It*." In *More Talking of Shakespeare*. Edited by John Garrett. London: Longmans, Green; New York: Theatre Arts Books, 1959, pp. 17–32.

Views *As You Like It* as a play to please all tastes with its romance, *débat*, pastoral, and burlesque. Idealizing life's possibilities by means of fantasy, Arden is juxtaposed to a corrupt court ruled by a tyrant. Yet, even the forest is a variable place, where one can find love or learn a bitter lesson. In the ultimate reconciliations only Jaques opts out of the human condition. The imagery suggests that possibly Shakespeare intends to depict the Christian ideal of loving-kindness, gentleness, pity, and humanity.

821. HALIO, JAY. " 'No Clock in the Forest': Time in *As You Like It.*" *Studies in English Literature 1500–1900* 2 (1962):197–207.

Believes that Shakespeare exploits timelessness in Arden by juxtaposing it to the time consciousness of the court and city. Orlando, fleeing from his tyrannical brother, becomes enamored of the freedom of the forest; but he finds it to be a school in which he and others are prepared to discover their best selves by Rosalind, the agent for synthesizing the values of both worlds. The sense of timelessness in Arden links it with the sense of graciousness in the past that can serve to help regenerate a corrupt present.

822. JENKINS, HAROLD. *"As You Like It.*" *Shakespeare Survey* 8 (1955):40–51.

Views the structure of the play as basically a juxtaposition of the golden with the real world, of the simple life with the brittle refinements of the court. Each side, however, has its own dialectic. Of the immigrants to Arden, Rosalind, Orlando, Duke Senior, and Amiens praise the life of the green world, but Touchstone and Jaques humorously mock. Similarly, among the natives, Sylvius, Phoebe, and William may be poetic rustics, but Corin is a shepherd with rough and greasy hands. The constantly shifting valuations, with reality dissolving illusions but ideals ever newly creating, result in an all-embracing view of life richer and more satisfying than any fragmented perspective.

823. MINCOFF, MARCO. "What Shakespeare Did to *Rosalynde.*" *Shakespeare Jahrbuch* 96 (1960):78–89.

Argues that critics overly stress pastoralism in *As You Like It.* Indeed, the pastoral tone is muted considerably from that in Lodge's prose romance. Shakespeare's concern is primarily to achieve a harmonious fusion of two themes—love's foolishness and the clash between appearance and reality. The concern for balance is evident in his simultaneous development of the love affairs of his several couples whereas in *Rosalynde* the romantic liaisons constitute separate and distinct portions of the narrative.

824. ORKIN, MARTIN. "Touchstone's Swiftness and Sententiousness." *English Language Notes* 27, no. 1 (1989):42–47.

Develops a case for interpreting Duke Senior's comment that Touchstone is "swift and sententious"—in 5.4 when the fool appears before him prepared to wed Audrey—as meaning, not that he is clever and witty in conversation, but that he obviously is sexually eager to the point of being comic. Such a reading fits the context of a scene in which

As You Like It

Touchstone bawdily hints of premarital sex in the phrase "country copulatives" and also provides an ominous glance at future adultery in observing he is ready "to swear, and to forswear."

825. PALMER, D. J. *"As You Like It* and the Idea of Play." *Critical Quarterly* 13 (1971):234–41.

Observes that the minimal plot in the play is merely enough to move characters in and out of the Forest of Arden. Once in Arden the characters engage in a world of play reflecting the impulse to create a better world and the releasing of energies held in check by the real world. The game between Orlando and Rosalind is only the most significant of several activities and interrelationships designed to provoke self-awareness in preparation for encountering with resilience the challenges that lie outside the forest. Jaques and Touchstone are complementary figures, the one transparently foolish and the other wise in fooling.

826. PRIEST, DALE G. *"Oratio* and *Negotium*: Manipulative Modes in *As You Like It*." *Studies in English Literature 1500–1900* 28 (1988):273–86.

Observes that the characters in Arden comprise two camps, those like Corin, Orlando, and Duke Senior who as voices of accommodation promote integration and community and those like Jaques, Touchstone, and Rosalind who as oppositional voices seem to ridicule or reject the communal ideal. The character of Rosalind is depicted as balanced, in contrast to the antiromanticism of Phoebe, the pastoral fancifulness of Silvius, the witty if unfeeling Touchstone, the satiric melancholy of Jaques. It is she who uses the strategies of satire in the service of romance, and it is her benign manipulative powers and her balanced vision that produce harmony out of potential discord.

827. SHAW, JOHN. "Fortune and Nature in *As You Like It*." *Shakespeare Quarterly* 6 (1955):45–50.

Observes that behind the lighthearted actions of the play exists a fundamental philosophic strife between Nature and fortune that members of the Renaissance audience would quickly recognize. The rivalry is broached in Rosalind's witty repartee in act 1, epitomizing the situation in which fortune's benefits have gone awry with Duke Senior and Orlando (and shortly will go awry with Rosalind). Bearing their situation with patience and wisdom, they will receive their just reward at the end of the play. Comments throughout the play as well as the pastoral setting emphasize the struggle and the ultimate power of nature to counter fortune's mischief.

828. STAEBLER, WARREN. "Shakespeare's Play of Atonement." *Shakespeare Association Bulletin* 24 (1949):91–105.

Calls *As You Like It* a play of felicity, not because it is marked by rapture or lovers' ecstasy, but because of an evenhanded serenity resulting from a steady attitude toward life. The principal characters are at one with themselves and with each other. Orlando, for instance, despite the wrongdoings he has endured, has no malice for the world. The world of nature acts further to harmonize all who enter it. *As You Like It* is the most down to earth of Shakespeare's comedies, free of preciosity, fantasy, barbed wit, cruelty, and magic.

Stage History

829. SHATTUCK, CHARLES H. *Mr. Macready Produces "As You Like It": A Prompt-Book Study*. Urbana: Beta Phi Mu Chapbook Series, 1962, 105 pp.

Aims to provide in facsimile a significant specimen of a mid–nineteenth-century promptbook of a Shakespearean play. *As You Like It*, transcribed by the stage manager George Ellis for the instruction of a young actor, Hermann Vezin, is significant both by virtue of its completeness of record and of its being Macready's restoration of Shakespeare's text. It also reflects his continuing struggle to practice reasonable restraint in the face of the lavish stage designs of Charles Kean. The version contains 2,458 lines (cutting only 387), and the playing time was two hours, forty-nine minutes.

THE COMEDY OF ERRORS

Editions

830. DORSCH, T. S., ed. *The Comedy of Errors*. The New Cambridge Shakespeare. Cambridge: Cambridge University Press, 1988, 115 pp.

Features an introductory essay on the date of composition, sources, critical analysis of the play, presentation, staging, stage history, the nature and origin of the text. Extensive notes appear on individual pages of the text, and a reference to the performance of the play in 1594, source passages from the Bible, and a reading list are appended.

The Comedy of Errors

831. FOAKES, R. A. , ed. *The Comedy of Errors*. The Arden Shakespeare. London: Methuen; Cambridge, Mass.: Harvard University Press, 1962, 117 pp.

Includes discussion of the text, the date of composition, sources, staging, stage history, and literary interpretations, as well as an appendix on the Gray's Inn performance in 1594. The text is based on the First Folio, for which the copy was probably Shakespeare's foul papers. In the manner of indicating localities, *Errors* is unique among Shakespeare's plays, preserving a unity both of time and place and requiring only four playing areas.

Criticism

832. ARTHOS, JOHN. "Shakespeare's Transformation of Plautus." *Comparative Drama* 1 (1967):239–53.

Notes that Shakespeare in *The Comedy of Errors* warmly enriches the Roman stage world. Whereas Plautus depicts a man's world in which everyone's attempt to outwit another issues in rough humor and physical byplay, Shakespeare's world is that of a more highly organized social hierarchy, and women and the romantic experience emerge as significant elements. The reunion at all levels at the conclusion (parents, sons and proper mates, servants) humanizes the material and gives it greater depth.

833. BALDWIN, THOMAS WHITFIELD. *On the Compositional Genetics of "The Comedy of Errors."* Urbana: University of Illinois Press, 1965, 422 pp.

Reconstructs and describes the process by which Shakespeare must have composed *The Comedy of Errors*. As Stratford sheep become London sheep, Shakespeare like the twin Dromios finds himself much confused by the witchery of Ephesus-London. The political relations between Syracuse and Ephesus reflect those of England and Spain, and the setting of the play is demonstrably Hollywell Priory, where near the Theatre two priests had experienced what for Egeon is only threatened. Blended with these local elements is Plautus's plot, subjected to the Erasmian rhetorical device of analysis and synthesis and the additions of parody and doubling, and set within the obligatory five-act system.

834. ———. *William Shakespeare Adapts a Hanging*. Princeton: Princeton University Press, 1931, 202 pp.

Argues that Shakespeare transmitted in *The Comedy of Errors* impressions from his witnessing the execution of William Hartley, a seminary priest, in Finnsbury Fields on 5 October 1588. In depicting a priory or abbey ruled over by a lady abbess with the gate of the priory opening into a street that leads, behind the ditches of the abbey, to a place of execution, Shakespeare is shadowing the reality of his firsthand knowledge of Hollywell Priory. Such identification with place and event both give a glimpse into his creative method and aid in dating one of his earliest plays.

835. BARBER, C. L. "Shakespearian Comedy in *The Comedy of Errors*." *College English* 25 (1964):493–97.

Describes *The Comedy of Errors* as a dazzling display of dramatic control in the manipulation of characters whose language, albeit sometimes tedious, exhibits genuine verbal energy. Shakespeare feeds Elizabethan life into the Plautine farce, forcing it to reveal universal traits of human character, especially those arising from the tugs of marriage. The play also is filled with routine details of daily life. Shakespeare's sense of comedy as a moment in a large cycle leads him to frame the farce within action involving age and the threat of death.

836. BROOKS, C. "Shakespeare's Romantic Shrews." *Shakespeare Quarterly* 11 (1960):351–56.

Notes that, whereas traditional literary shrews are generally fools and monsters, Shakespeare's shrews (Adriana, Kate) are more humanly sketched as women unsure of their own hearts. Adriana, for example, has the will and the intelligence we admire in Shakespeare's heroines; she merely must learn to control these qualities more effectively. Both she and Kate in the course of the action come to realize that psychologically they have a need to submit, as a balance to their will to dominate.

837. CANDIDO, JOSEPH. "Dining Out in Ephesus: Food in *The Comedy of Errors*." *Studies in English Literature 1500–1900* 30 (1990):217–42.

Focuses on the centrality of food and dining in helping to define social relationships in the play. Antipholus of Ephesus's failure to come home to dinner signals a flouting of an accepted social ceremony by which he has achieved his identity as respected citizen and respectful husband. Both reputation and marriage are endangered when the wrong Antipholus dines with Adriana, and this mistake in turn leads Antipholus of Ephesus to a tryst with the courtesan that threatens to become a marital crisis. The comic banquet at the end celebrates the

clarification of identity and reestablishes a shared commitment to moral
and religious values inherent in the social act of familial dining.

838. COULTER, CORNELIA A. "The Plautine Tradition in Shakespeare."
Journal of English and Germanic Philology 19 (1920):66–83.
Concerns the influence of Plautus and Terence on English drama
in general and on Shakespeare in particular. The Plautine tradition
reached Shakespeare through both the classical revival itself and
through German education drama. Specifically, the influence is seen in
the stage setting of a street and three houses and the use of a prologue,
in plot elements and plot motifs such as mistaken identity, in stock
characters such as the clown servant and the amorous young man and
the braggart soldier, and in stage devices such as horseplay and satiric
asides. While Plautine elements are found throughout Shakespeare's
work, they are especially noticeable in *The Comedy of Errors*.

839. GRENNAN, EAMON. "Arm and Sleeve: Nature and Custom in *The Comedy of Errors*." *Philological Quarterly* 59 (1980):150–64.
Examines the dialectic of nature and custom that informs *The
Comedy of Errors* and points forward to a continuing concern throughout Shakespeare's career. Luciana, for example, when pacifying her
incensed sister, describes the traditional relationship of the superior
husband and the dutifully obedient wife; later, however, when lecturing
the person she assumes to be Adriana's husband, she describes marriage
as something that must be kept socially decorous at all costs. This
disparity between reality and appearance is central to every situation in
the play.

840. HENNINGS, THOMAS P. "The Anglican Doctrine of the Affectionate
Marriage in *The Comedy of Errors*." *Modern Language Quarterly* 47
(1986):91–107.
Maintains that the play is not so much an imitation of Plautus's
Menaechmi as it is a "deliberate Christian corrective of the Latin play
and its saturnalian themes" (p. 92). To side with Luciana's claim that a
wife should be obedient to her husband and against Adriana's claim for
conjugal affection is to disregard current marriage literature, especially
the officially sanctioned "Homilie of the State of Matrimony," which
asserts that a double standard is wrong and that "man and woman
should live lawfully in a perpetual friendship" (p. 96).

841. KINNEY, ARTHUR F. "Shakespeare's *The Comedy of Errors* and the Nature of Kinds." *Studies in Philology* 85 (1988):29–52.

Considers the play a combination of farce and comedy that gains enrichment through association with Holy Innocents' Day and through consistent Christian references. Such references shift our attention toward a sense of comedy as "providential confusion" (p. 33) that leads through bafflement to wonder, grace, rebirth, and a restructuring and reuniting. Egeon is the first of many innocents who would risk all to find his sons, and the ending is appropriately focused on the abbess, whose powers are sanctioned by religion and morality. At the end three united couples with their servants present onstage a living icon of Christian theology.

842. PARKER, PATRICIA. "Elder and Younger: The Opening Scene of *The Comedy of Errors*." *Shakespeare Quarterly* 34 (1983):325–27.
   Notes that Egeon's references in the opening scene to the positioning of the elder and younger sons, with each parent when the ship splits then being severed from the child he or she has been most careful for, is not a slip on Shakespeare's part and is significant to the structure of the entire play. The references echo the sibling rivalry between Jacob and Esau and make theatrically appropriate the conversation at the end between the Dromio twins as to who shall go through the door first and their decision to walk through together hand in hand.

843. SANDERSON, JAMES L. "Patience in *The Comedy of Errors*." *Texas Studies in Literature and Language* 16 (1974–75):603–18.
   Notes that *The Comedy of Errors*, like Shakespeare's later comedies, embodies a sense of ignorance of death that gives way to a resolution projecting a renewal of life. More important, it sets forth the theme of patience, a motif upon which Shakespeare elaborates in a number of his later and greatest plays. The "errors" arise from individuals whose impotence in the face of frustrating circumstances generates activities that deepen their confusion and multiply the misconceptions. Patience is counseled both literally and figuratively throughout the play, and only its cultivation provides the means by which the errors can be resolved.

844. TAYLOR, GARY. "Textual and Sexual Criticism: A Crux in *The Comedy of Errors*." *Renaissance Drama*, n.s. 19 (1988):195–225.
   Comments on the severe underrepresentation of women among Shakespeare's editors and notes that such male domination affects the nature of the text in ways large and small. A case in point is 2.1.109–13, a passage in which Adriana complains of her husband's failure to return home in timely fashion for dinner. The particular lines indicated make

little sense and thus diminish the intellectual quality of her indictment. Careful textual analysis, however, reveals the passage to be a powerful condemnation of the genderic double standard. Such attention to this crux reflects the greater sensitivity to gender resulting from two decades of feminist criticism.

845. WEST, GILIAN. "Lost Humor in *The Comedy of Errors* and *Twelfth Night.*" *English Studies* 71 (1990):6–15.
   Insists that much of the humor from these two acclaimed comedies now falls upon deaf ears. The first part of the article cites sixteen particular passages containing humor that will be missed by most modern-day audiences. The second part list two passages of long-lost ambiguity dependent upon textual emendation, and the third part discusses four passages of now-unnoticed cross-lingual puns. For example, when Antipholus of Syracuse swears he will leave Ephesus "lest myself be *guilty* to self wrong" (3.2.162), Shakespeare is punning on the now unfamiliar term "goety," witchcraft performed by the employment of evil spirits.

846. WILLIAMS, GWYN. "*The Comedy of Errors* Rescued from Tragedy." *Review of English Literature* 5, no. 4 (1964):63–71.
   Concentrates on the thin borderline between comedy and tragedy in *The Comedy of Errors.* Shakespeare's reason for duplicating Dromio was not merely to enhance the laughter but to save the play as comedy. The interaction of two Dromios not only provides farce; it also prevents either the apprehension of the one Antipholus or the violent temper of the other from becoming dominant. For the masters the confusion of identity is painful and potentially dangerous, as it also is for Egeon. The servants tip the balance toward humor.

847. WOOD, ROBERT E. "Cooling the Comedy: Television as a Medium for Shakespeare's *The Comedy of Errors.*" *Literature/Film Quarterly* 14, no. 4 (1986):195–202.
   Believes that the varied perspectives of the television camera offer new life to the joke arising from mistaken identity in the play. For one thing, the close-up camera allows us to look at the comic confusion through the eyes of the characters themselves, even while we remain emotionally distant from them. Moreover, since the audience within moments realizes that the same actor is playing the Dromios and another single actor the Antipholuses, the television production can enhance the element of play, of deliberate unreality, that is the essence of *The Comedy of Errors.*

LOVE'S LABOR'S LOST

Reference Works

848. HARVEY, NANCY LENZ, and CAREY, ANNA KIRWAN, comps. *"Love's Labor's Lost": An Annotated Bibliography*. Garland Reference Library of the Humanities, 365: Garland Shakespeare Bibliographies, 6. New York and London: Garland Publishing, 1984, 220 pp.

Contains 510 entries representing virtually all publications on the play from 1940 through 1982 along with the most significant items of scholarship prior to 1940. The categories, each arranged chronologically, are divided into criticism, sources, dating, textual studies, bibliographies and concordances, editions, stage history and recordings, and adaptations and synopses. A brief introductory essay traces the history of recent criticism and research.

849. MARDER, LOUIS, comp. *"Love's Labor's Lost": A Supplementary Bibliography 1904–1965*. The New Variorum Shakespeare. New York: American Scholar Publications, 1965, 19 pp.

Includes representative scholarship on *Love's Labor's Lost* from 1904 to 1965 and is intended to supplement H. H. Furness's Variorum edition of 1904 (entry 851). The material is categorized under reproductions of original folio editions of the play, bibliographical sources, and critical studies (arranged alphabetically). While not exhaustive, the material represents every major category of scholarship and criticism.

Editions

850. DAVID, RICHARD, ed. *Love's Labour's Lost*. The Arden Shakespeare. London: Methuen; Cambridge, Mass.: Harvard University Press, 1951, 196 pp.

Includes discussion of the text, date, sources, topical content, and the possible occasion for the play. The text is based on the first quarto (1598), for which the copy was probably Shakespeare's foul papers that had undergone revision at least once. The indication on the title page that the text is "newly corrected and augmented" suggests the earlier publication of a bad quarto. The date of composition of the play in its present form is probably the autumn of 1597, but the original draft must date from 1593–94. No source is known, but historical names, journeys, and visits are woven into the original narrative. In style it reflects the euphuistic language popularized by Lyly.

851. FURNESS, HENRY HOWARD, ed. *Love's Labour's Lost*. A New Variorum Edition of Shakespeare. Philadelphia: J. B. Lippincott, 1904, 401 pp.

Uses the first quarto (1598) as the copy text. On each page are included, for that portion of the text, variant readings, textual notes, and general critical commentary. Following the text are sections on the nature of the quarto and folio texts; the date of composition; the sources; English, German, and French criticisms; Shakespeare's word-play; imitations; and a list of works consulted. Supplemented by entry 849.

852. HIBBARD, GEORGE, ed. *Love's Labor's Lost*. The Oxford Shakespeare. Oxford and New York: Oxford University Press, 1990, 320 pp.

Includes an introductory essay featuring a discussion of the "reha-bilitation" of the play during the past several decades after three centuries of neglect and critical abuse. The copy text is the quarto of 1598, which probably was based on a now lost quarto by way of an authorial manuscript. Extensive notes on each page of the text identify specific problems of language and provide background material.

853. QUILLER-COUCH, ARTHUR, and WILSON, JOHN DOVER, eds. *Love's Labour's Lost*. Cambridge: Cambridge University Press, 1923, 213 pp.

Provides extensive textual notes, a critical introduction, a discussion of the copy text, a section on stage history, and a glossary. This edition is eclectic, based primarily on the first quarto but with readings also from the First Folio. In theme and phraseology the play is closely related to the sonnets; both include a concentration of light imagery, especially that comparing women's eyes to stars.

Criticism

854. ASP, CAROLYN. "*Love's Labor's Lost*: Language and the Deferral of De-sire." *Literature and Psychology* 35, no. 3 (1989):1–21.

Notes that Navarre and his courtiers attempt to exalt language at the expense of desire whether by fasting, studying, or prohibiting the presence of women. The princess and her attendants "decode" the nar-cissistic basis of such action. In this comedy Shakespeare establishes two separate yet equally powerful discursive groups. The men, in spite of their wit, lack humor and must be transformed into tolerant individuals "able to confront situations and mitigate them by compassion and the proper use of language" (p. 17). The songs at the end address the equilibrium of life in a kind of "natural" language.

855. BERMAN, RONALD. "Shakespearean Comedy and the Uses of Reason." *South Atlantic Quarterly* 63 (1964):1–9.

Views the play as a comic attack on the Platonic Academy. The Platonic ideal of solitary contemplation espoused by the King of Navarre would deny basic humanity, and the other characters continually assert the power of the senses. Berowne, Longaville, and Dumaine assume the role of courtly lovers; far more earthy is the relationship between Costard, Jaquenetta, and Armado. The play, in a word, sets body against mind, man against woman, folly against pedantry. Similarly, *The Taming of the Shrew* is discussed as a burlesque in its action of Platonic reason.

856. BERRY, RALPH. "The Words of Mercury." *Shakespeare Survey* (1969):69–77.

Describes the theme of the play as a delicate and controlled movement toward the acceptance of reality. If it opens with an assault upon Time/Death, it closes with the acknowledgment of Time's victory in Marcade's entry and the news of the death of the princess's father. As act 5 refutes act 1, so Winter's song refutes Summer's. Groups of characters use words in different ways—Navarre and his followers, the princess and her retinue, the clowns, the pedants—but Marcade-Mercury, bringing news of death, announces the presence of a reality that must be mediated by words.

857. BRADBROOK, MURIEL C. *The School of Night: A Study in the Literary Relationships of Sir Walter Raleigh*. Cambridge: Cambridge University Press, 1936, 190 pp.

Asserts that *Love's Labor's Lost* was Shakespeare's account of the "School of Night," Shakespeare's nickname for a group headed and patronized by Raleigh and including, among others, Thomas Harriott, the Earl of Northumberland, and Derby, Marlowe, and Chapman. This society studied theology, philosophy, astronomy, and chemistry, and various members were accused of atheism. The faction of Essex engaged in a literary skirmish with the faction of Raleigh. Shakespeare's comedy mocked Raleigh, who having been banished from court praised the solitary life of study and contemplation. Armado parodies Raleigh, but the satire is not sustained. On the whole the play is more concerned with theories of living than with personalities.

Love's Labor's Lost

858. CALDERWOOD, JAMES L. *"Love's Labor's Lost*: A Wantoning with Words." *Studies in English Literature 1500–1900* 5 (1965):317–32.

Speaks of *Love's Labor's Lost* as a play in which words become a fascination in themselves quite apart from their relevance to reality. Words function more to elicit aesthetic pleasure—through puns, metaphor, syntax, alliteration, coinage—than to express ideas or feelings. The academic society of Navarre ultimately breaks down because the language that creates it is divorced from the truth of human nature. The movement in the play is from self-aggrandizing and socially destructive uses of language to words that provoke genuine human interaction.

859. CARROLL, WILLIAM C. *The Great Feast of Language in "Love's Labor's Lost."* Princeton: Princeton University Press, 1976, 279 pp.

Focuses on *Love's Labor's Lost* as a debate concerning the proper uses of rhetoric, poetry, and the imagination, concluding not with rejection of art for life but with the reassertion of the need for sound art. Examples of rhetorical and theatrical excesses appear in the sonnet-reading scene, the Masque of Muscovites, the Pageant of the Nine Worthies, and in the six low characters who constitute a kind of commedia dell'arte troupe. The songs of spring and winter constitute an exemplum and model for the right use of language and art, highly structured yet direct in communication and functional in addressing time as cyclical and offering the capability of renewal for the characters in the play.

860. ELLIS, HERBERT A. *Shakespeare's Lusty Punning in "Love's Labour's Lost": With Contemporary Analogues.* Studies in English Literature, 81. The Hague and Paris: Mouton, 1973, 239 pp.

Examines the more than two hundred discernible semantic and homophonic puns in *Love's Labor's Lost* as one means of appreciating the dimensions of Shakespeare's comic artistry. Supporting evidence is drawn from dictionaries, works on Elizabethan pronunciation, and contemporary sources such as diaries, letters, broadside ballads, joke books, and the Bible. The study suggests that the humor of the play was intended for a more popular audience than critics have generally assumed and that Shakespeare's bawdiness is usually garbed in language that, through ambiguity, presents an outward semblance of innocence.

861. HOY, CYRUS. *"Love's Labor's Lost* and the Nature of Comedy." *Shakespeare Quarterly* 13 (1962):31–40.

Describes the play as a satire of fine manners, pedantry, disguised love, and the infirmity of the human purpose. Intended to enlighten without destroying, the comedy plays upon the incongruities inherent in the human condition—the spiritual and the material, the aspiration and the achievement. The basic pattern of Shakespearean comedy is a movement from the artificial to the natural, always with the object of finding oneself, a process achieved most effectively in a rural or natural setting.

862. KEHLER, DOROTHEA. "Jaquenetta's Baby's Father: Recovering Paternity in *Love's Labor's Lost*." *Renaissance Papers* (1990):45–54.

Suggests that Jaquenetta is pregnant not by the self-proclaimed aristocrat Armado but by the rustic Costard and that the play "insists that hierarchical and patrilinear systems remain vulnerable to female subversion due to the nature of the reproductive process" (p. 51). Jaquenetta is the only "maid" in Shakespeare to counter the patriarchal assumptions of proper female conduct and lose nothing by it. Since Armado is forced to accept the paternity, the play's subtext reverses male/female and menial/nonmenial binarisms.

863. KERRIGAN, JOHN. "Shakespeare at Work: The Katharine-Rosaline Tangle in *Love's Labor's Lost*." *Review of English Studies*, n.s. 33 (1982):129–36.

Explains the confusions between Katharine and Rosaline in act 2 as the consequence of Shakespeare's mind in the act of creation. In the quarto Berowne and Katharine converse apart, and later he and Rosaline flirt. The conclusion must be that Shakespeare wrote the act originally with only the vaguest conception of particular relationships and that specific pairings emerged only later—Katharine and Dumaine, Rosaline and Berowne. After having completed the play, he overlooked the inconsistency in his last-minute revisions.

864. LEVIN, HARRY. "Sitting in the Sky (*Love's Labor's Lost*, 4.3)." In *Shakespeare's "Rough Magic": Renaissance Essays in Honor of C. L. Barber*. Edited by Peter Erickson and Coppélia Kahn. Newark: University of Delaware Press; London and Toronto: Associated University Presses, 1985, pp. 113–30.

Comments on the remarkable title of *Love' Labor's Lost*, one that consciously forewarns the spectators that comedy's predestined happy ending in marriage will be violated. That which is to be overcome by the ladies in the king's academy is a "bookishness to the exclusion of experience to distinguish words from matter" (p. 116). What gets stripped away from the men is the linguistic excess; and what happens at the level of plot seems to be replicated at the level of composition. The labored, the laborious, and the overelaborate seem to be purged along with Navarre and his bookmen. "What Shakespeare won was his own courtship of the English language and his accession to artistic maturity" (p. 129).

865. McLAY, CATHERINE M. "The Dialogue of Spring and Winter: A Key to the Unity of *Love's Labor's Lost.*" *Shakespeare Quarterly* 18 (1967):119–27.

Maintains that the concluding songs or dialogue of Spring and Winter, although probably a part of the additions to the play in 1597, are functional, holding the key to interpreting the central theme of *Love's Labor's Lost.* The men and the ladies throughout the play represent the forces of art and nature; central to the action is the hunting scene in act 4, in which the women become the pursuers, leading to the men's subjugation by the force of nature. Opposite to the pole of nature, however, is death; and true wisdom can come only with the full realization of life's cycle, the theme of the concluding songs.

866. PARSONS, PHILLIP. "Shakespeare and the Mask." *Shakespeare Survey* 16 (1963):121–31.

Describes *Love's Labor's Lost* as, like *Romeo and Juliet*, a play unfolding personal destiny in the characters' coming to realize a deeper and more vital self-awareness. Both use the theatrical images of a black visor, in *Love's Labor's Lost* when it becomes clear to the lords that love demands more than the sugared sonnets and in *Romeo and Juliet* when Romeo first views Juliet. The lords bent on "finding themselves" put on a masque and are met by the ladies wearing black visors. The scene leads to the lords' acknowledgment of their true natures, a moment concomitant with the intrusion of darkness with news of the death of the King of France.

867. TAYLOR, RUPERT. *The Date of "Love's Labour's Lost."* New York: Columbia University Press, 1932, 134 pp.

Suggests a date of 1596 for the composition of *Love's Labor's Lost.* Individual chapters are devoted to the relationship between the masque of Muscovites and the Russian Episode presented at Gray's Inn in 1594–1595, to the significance of the presence of the Venus and Adonis stanza in the play, to the relationship of the plot to events in France and England between 1589 and 1596, and to references to the Thomas Nashe-Gabriel Harvey argument between 1592 and 1596.

868. YATES, FRANCES A. *A Study of "Love's Labour's Lost."* Cambridge: Cambridge University Press, 1936, 224 pp.

Views *Love's Labor's Lost* as a play bristling with allusions to contemporary events and to living persons; more specifically, the action reflects the struggle at court between the Essex-Southampton group and the Raleigh group. The core of the plot is drawn from the Gray's Inn Revels of 1594–95, and its mock speeches alternate in praise of study and of pleasure. John Florio, Gabriel Harvey, George Chapman, and the Earl of Northumberland make up Raleigh's "School of Night" group around which the topical satire is developed.

MEASURE FOR MEASURE

Editions

869. BAWCUTT, N. W., ed. *Measure for Measure*. The Oxford Shakespeare. Oxford: Oxford University Press, 1991, 255 pp.

Includes an introductory essay covering the Jacobean quality of the play, the sources, the play in performance, and textual problems. Extensive notes on each page of the text address specific matters of interpretation and provide background information. Appendixes provide longer textual notes and address alterations to lineation and John Wilson's setting of "Take, O Take."

870. ECCLES, MARK, ed. *Measure for Measure*. A New Variorum Edition of Shakespeare. New York: Modern Language Association, 1980, 555 pp.

Uses the First Folio as the copy text, on each page, for that portion of the text, providing variant readings, textual notes, and general critical commentary. Following the text are sections, citing varying critical opinion, on emendations; the text; the date of composition; sources, analogues, and influences; criticism—genre, character, style, technique, theme; stage history; music; and a list of works consulted.

871. GIBBONS, BRIAN, ed. *Measure for Measure*. The New Cambridge Shakespeare. Cambridge: Cambridge University Press, 1991, 213 pp.

Features an introductory essay on the date, Puritanism—political allusion and censorship, the sources and their shaping, a critique of the play, and the play on the stage. Extensive notes appear on individual pages of the text, and a textual analysis and a reading list are appended.

872. LEVER, J. W., ed. *Measure for Measure*. The Arden Shakespeare. London: Methuen; Cambridge, Mass.: Harvard University Press, 1965, 203 pp.

Includes discussion of the text, date, sources, and critical interpretations, along with appendixes on the songs and extracts from the source materials. The text is based on the First Folio, for which the copy was probably Ralph Crane's transcript of Shakespeare's foul papers contaminated by prompter's insertions and scribal idiosyncrasies. *Measure for Measure* is, in the broadest sense, a drama of ideas that transcends labels like "problem play," "allegory," "morality," or "satire" in dealing with the polarities of justice and mercy in a social setting with contemporary relevance. The tense antagonisms of the first half are woven into a texture of issues reconciled through a sense of painfully acquired self-knowledge.

Criticism

873. BACHE, WILLIAM B. *"Measure for Measure" as Dialectical Art*. Purdue University Studies. Lafayette: Purdue University Press, 1969, 66 pp.

Finds the key in a dialectical argument that runs throughout the play concerning man's proper behavior and the proper function of the law in that regard. Reflecting a realistic view of life as uncontrolled, devious, and disordered, the play forces choices in a context ambiguously defiant of absolutes. In the process Duke Vincentio and Isabella, forced in differing ways to extend themselves, realize their finest potential as human beings and enact the Shakespearean ethic of love and duty.

874. BAINES, BARBARA J. "Assaying the Power of Chastity in *Measure for Measure*." *Studies in English Literature 1500–1900* 30 (1990):283–302.

Maintains that for Isabella chastity is the definitive virtue precisely because it is a site and mode of secular power. It is a virtue within the social construct of Vienna because secular law mandates it as a remedy for the sexual license within the city. Indeed, her "power, place, and value in society are so determined by her chastity that its forfeiture would constitute for her a form of social and psychological suicide" (p. 288). In the duke's proposal at the end we see her final power since authority privileges chastity and in turn depends upon chastity to validate it.

875. BATTENHOUSE, ROY. *"Measure for Measure* and the Christian Doctrine of Atonement." *PMLA* 61 (1946):1029–59.

Sees the theme of the Atonement as the formal structuring principle of *Measure for Measure*. Vincentio (conqueror or God) reforms

Angelo (fallen angel), saves Claudio (lame one or sinful man), rights the wrong done to Mariana (combining the names of Mary the mother and Anne the immaculate mother), tempers justice with mercy, and reconciles Isabella (devoted to God) to himself when he proposes marriage. Christ the bridegroom woos the human heart and perfects it through suffering and sacrifice so that she may be his bride. Both the fishing metaphor (Christ as fisher of men) and the ransom metaphor (Christ as a ransom for man's soul) are prominent in the play.

876. BAWCUTT, N. W. " 'He Who the Sword Would Bear': The Duke versus Angelo in *Measure for Measure*." *Shakespeare Survey* 37 (1984):89–97.

Maintains that the words *law, mercy,* and *justice* are used throughout the play in an ambiguous and overlapping manner and that, therefore, it is impossible to assign one abstraction exclusively to a single character. Vincentio, for example, like Angelo, believes in the law, but his is a "personal or reflexive view" (p. 93). For him tyranny is not merely the infliction of harsh punishment but the infliction by one who is not in a moral position to do so.

877. BENNETT, JOSEPHINE WATERS. *"Measure for Measure" as Royal Entertainment*. New York and London: Columbia University Press, 1966, 208 pp.

Attempts to illumine Shakespeare's intentions by placing the play within the context of a single year and a single day. Chosen as the first play for performance before King James during the gala Christmas season of 1604, *Measure* models the role of Vincentio on the king's own account of his principles of government. Angelo is depicted in the guise in which James describes a tyrant, and Lucio provides a comic instance of James's complaints about being libeled. Stylized comedy from beginning to end, it invites its contemporary audience from a reasonable distance to perceive James's self-proclaimed image.

878. BRADBROOK, MURIEL C. "Authority and Justice in *Measure for Measure*." *Review of English Studies* 17 (1941):385–99.

Considers the leading quality of the play to be analytic, pitting justice against mercy or false authority against truth and humility. Angelo (authority) usurps the place of the duke (heavenly justice and humility); Claudio and Juliet stand for original sin, and Mariana for eros. The debate between justice and mercy occurs primarily in the struggle between Isabella and Angelo. While the duke is, in disguise, an external seemer, Angelo is a moral seemer. Ultimately, *Measure for Measure* is a problem play because its ethical values are controlled by doctrinaire imperatives.

Measure for Measure

879. BROWN, CAROLYN E. "Erotic Religious Flagellation and Shakespeare's *Measure for Measure*." *English Literary Renaissance* 16 (1986):139–65.

Observes that allusions to physical and mental abuse and to instruments for inflicting pain permeate the play and contribute to its morbid atmosphere. Through such references Shakespeare alludes to the historical and topical phenomenon of flagellation, accepted by the early church as the official form of penance and by Shakespeare's time reaching enough notoriety to appear in fictional literature. The play explores the psychological ramifications of such practice through the three principal characters who engage in abuse with a kind of religious glory and pleasure—Vincentio by practicing it, Angelo by inflicting it, Isabella by receiving it.

880. ———. "*Measure for Measure*: Duke Vincentio's 'Crabbed' Desires." *Literature and Psychology* 35, nos. 1–2 (1989):66–88.

Focuses on the conversation in 3.2, in which Lucio irreverently badgers Friar Lodowick (Vincentio in disguise) about Angelo's "crabbed" nature resulting from religious austerity and about how the duke would handle the issue of Claudio's fornication differently since he himself has "feeling of the sport." The friar-duke ignores Lucio's amiable tone, reacting excessively, like one guilty of the charge. Thereafter, Lucio becomes the victim of the duke's own insecurities stemming from his libidinous inclinations and prurient proclivities. His gratuitously punitive action against Lucio in the final scene seems to bring him pleasure.

881. CHAMBERS, R. W. *The Jacobean Shakespeare and "Measure for Measure."* London: Oxford University Press, 1938, 60 pp.

Asserts that Shakespeare has transformed the crudities of *Promos and Cassandra* into a "consistent tale of intercession of sin, repentance from and forgiveness of crime" (p. 54). With the Duke symbolizing something of the mystery of providence, the play focuses primarily on the spiritual alteration of Angelo's nature, but Claudio and Isabella are stretched and refined in the process as well. To argue that Shakespeare created these characters with irony and cynicism is to stand the play on its head. While it has affinities with the tragedies, it also points to the romances in its growth in faith in the power of goodness.

882. COGHILL, NEVILLE. "Comic Form in *Measure for Measure*." *Shakespeare Survey* 8 (1955):17–26.

Interprets *Measure for Measure* as an allegory in the tradition of the parables of Christ, reflecting a human world in an eternal situation. Vincentio, the *primum mobile* of the play, represents the anthropomorphic actions of God in effecting tests for Angelo, Isabella, and Claudio. Lucio, who through his unjust criticism of Vincentio functions as a device to retain the audience's sympathy for the duke even when this tester seems to be manipulative, is himself a form of Satan on the anagogical plane. *Measure for Measure*, in a word, is not a dark comedy; instead it resembles a medieval comedy of Christian joy.

883. COLE, HOWARD C. "The Christian Context of *Measure for Measure*." *Journal of English and Germanic Philology* 64 (1965):425–51.

Asserts the impossibility of explaining the tone of Vincentio's juggling of wrath and reconciliation that appears so at odds with our expectation of straightforwardness in such a morality framework. Bothersome, too, is the self-conscious staginess of his manipulations in the final act. In fact, Vincentio's actions merely reflect the larger theme of arbitrariness that unifies the plot and enforces the mood of general injustice. Perhaps the real difficulty lies in Shakespeare's having come to Cinthio's material through Whetstone the Puritan, who developed his characters along lines more divine than romantic.

884. COX, JOHN D. "The Medieval Background of *Measure for Measure*." *Modern Philology* 81 (1983):1–13.

Considers the medieval dramatic tradition to be in the broadest sense a source for *Measure for Measure*. In several miracle and morality plays dealing with sexual sin are found motifs not in *Promos and Cassandra*——the need to temper justice with mercy, the need for self-examination in accusing others, the problem of slander, the hypocritical abuse of authority, the contrast between the "old" and "new" laws, and the nature of sovereignty. The duke is humanized by being shown as less than divine while his opponents are humanized by being made more than abstractions.

885. DAWSON, ANTHONY B. "*Measure for Measure*, New Historicism, and Theatrical Power." *Shakespeare Quarterly* 39 (1988):328–41.

Cautions that new historicism is to a large extent an appropriation of Shakespeare's text for the contemporary purpose of reflecting upon late twentieth-century capitalism and its conditions of power. As such, for example, in its insisting that *Measure for Measure* be read as a legitimation of power, it runs the risk of imposing a new form of critical hegemony. Above all, *Measure for Measure* resists that kind of monolithic approach. The conclusion can just as readily be seen as a subversion of authority in which the duke's theatrical sense of power overdoes itself and is tripped up, in which "a mode of political power is deconstructed even as it is used and evoked" (p. 338).

Measure for Measure

886. DESMET, CHRISTY. "Speaking Sensibly: Feminine Rhetoric in *All's Well That Ends Well* and *Measure for Measure*." *Renaissance Papers* (1986):43–51.

Suggests that the ambiguous motives of Helena and Isabella reflect a Renaissance ambivalence about rhetoric and its relation to truth, the assumption that rhetoric can either perfect or degrade men. Both heroines are accomplished orators, yet both—for a good cause—flatter and lie for their own ends, manipulating others with the sophist's seductive charm. In the end, however, both are subordinated to a male world of law and judgment. And, ironically, both are "sentenced" to silence. Bertram retains the right to test Helena's improbable story, and Isabella loses her voice in not responding to Vincentio's abrupt proposal of marriage.

887. DOLLIMORE, JONATHAN. "Transgression and Surveillance in *Measure for Measure*." In *Political Shakespeare: New Essays in Cultural Materialism*. Edited by Jonathan Dollimore and Alan Sinfield. Manchester: Manchester University Press, 1985, pp. 72–87.

Rejects both the traditional reading that anarchy threatens to engulf the state unless sexuality is subjected to renewed and severe regulation and the oppositional reading that the social transgression reflects a subversion from below of a repressive official ideology of order. Instead, the play in its actions appropriates marginalized or subordinate aspects of Jacobean culture. As with any such practice in society, so in *Measure for Measure* "the more we attend to the supposed subversiveness of sexual license, and the authoritarian response to it, the more we are led away from the vice itself toward social tensions which intersect with it" (p. 76). Such tensions in the winter of 1604 included fear of a war with Spain, the plague, treason trials, and economic malaise in London.

888. DUNKEL, WILBUR. "Law and Equity in *Measure for Measure*." *Shakespeare Quarterly* 13 (1962):275–85.

Explores the temper of the times concerning the idea of justice with equity, especially James's actions involving the trial of Raleigh and others in 1603 in which mercy came as a climax to leading the defendants through agony and degradation to produce repentance and James's ideas an the dispensation of mercy in *Basilikon Doron*. Angelo's letter-of-the-law attitude and Vincentio's humanitarian actions both miss the mark, the one with severity and the other with lack of punishment. From their conflict arises the comedy in a theme dealing with the need for a ruler to recognize the necessity of justice with equity.

889. GLESS, DARRYL J. *"Measure for Measure," the Law and the Covenant.* Princeton: Princeton University Press, 1979, 280 pp.

Views the play as the movement of a series of flawed characters toward forgiveness, reconciliation, and renewal. Emphasis is on the elusive and problematic nature of morality and all the inherent imperfections of human knowledge by which one individual must judge another. These ambiguities arise from diverse conceptions of evil/sin in civil law and theological law and of society's appropriate response to it, from the ambivalent implications in the scriptural passage from which the title is drawn, and from the potential animosity of anti-Catholic sentiment in early seventeenth-century England. The complexity of the play is rooted in its cultural context.

890. HAMMOND, PAUL. "The Argument of *Measure for Measure*." *English Literary Renaissance* 16 (1986):496–519.

Maintains that, even though Vincentio promises "of government the properties to unfold" (1.1.3), what we actually confront is a series of incomplete and deceiving arguments. Having been introduced to Angelo's draconian defense of the law, Pompey's agility in circumventing it, and Isabella's plea for mercy along with its distortion on legal grounds, the spectator is in no mood to trust the duke's redemptive arguments in act 3. Moreover, the dominant images of coining, clothing, and evolution to describe the characters leave us equally mystified about an individual's true nature. The play almost methodically "takes apart the stability, equity and reciprocity epitomized in its own title" (p. 519).

891. HUBERT, JUDD D. "The Presence of Staging and Acting in *Measure for Measure*." *New Literary History* 18 (1987):583–96.

Sees Vincentio as the main dramatist, chief director, master of puppetry, and privileged spectator who, through a series of displacements, drives the action of the play. When the duke chooses Angelo to play the role of doctrinal rigorist without supplying a script, the latter composes a dubious play out of the texts of law and religion. Ultimately the duke verbalizes the displacement brought about by the Viennese public's false perceptions of those in the role of authority and the erotic displacement between love and death in terms of Elizabethan comic conventions.

892. HUNT, MAURICE. "Comfort in *Measure for Measure*." *Studies in English Literature 1500–1900* 27 (1987):213–32.

Maintains that comfort is a central idea in the play, that both Isabella and Vincentio have much to learn about love and comfort, and that insight is crystallized in the figure of Mariana. Neither the sister nor the duke can effectively provide solace to Claudio in act 3. The catalyst for true comfort is Mariana, in whom Isabella perceives a desire to embrace the man who has so basely wronged her. Speaking in the knowledge of forgiving love and offering to sacrifice oneself for another emerge as the source of true comfort in the play, and Isabella reiterates that truth when, kneeling in act 5 and having learned humility, she asks for Angelo's forgiveness.

893. IDE, RICHARD S. "Shakespeare's Revisionism: Homiletic Tragicomedy and the Ending of *Measure for Measure.*" *Shakespeare Studies* 20 (1988):105–27.

Suggests that Shakespeare's "experiment in tragicomedy" (p. 106) was influenced by Jean de Mairet's theory of tragicomedy predicated on the principle of distributive justice. Shakespeare, more precisely, uses visual tableaux for iconoclastic effect and naturalizes character in order to create an internal critique upon conventions. Each of Vincentio's judicial decisions in the play questions the possibility or even the desirability of distributive justice. The closure is open-ended, forcing the spectator to reevaluate both the ideals and the administration of justice on earth.

894. KNIGHTS, L. C. "The Ambiguity of *Measure for Measure.*" *Scrutiny* 10 (1942):222–33.

Observes that *Measure for Measure* is a disconcerting play because conflicting attitudes toward the characters are forced upon us. Isabella, for instance, is at one moment chaste serenity, at another frosty, self-regarding Puritanism. A major source of the spectator's uneasiness lies in the character of Claudio; he is not consistently created, living only in the intensity of his pleas to Isabella to be his savior. Admittedly in the later plays Shakespeare offers no solutions, but he does offer clarification and insight that are missing in *Measure for Measure.*

895. KRIEGER, MURRAY. "*Measure for Measure* and Elizabethan Comedy." *PMLA* 66 (1951):775–84.

Considers *Measure for Measure* an unsatisfactory blending of two comic fashions in dramatic construction. Whereas Shakespearean romantic comedy focuses on fanciful plot and demands from the spectators a sympathetic concern for the fortunes of the characters, Jonsonian comedy focuses on character types and demands an attitude of detachment and disdainful superiority. The opposed patterns are mixed in Angelo; in one plot he is the gull and Isabella the guller, and in the other he is the villain who repents after he is overcome. The spectator's response is simply unable to cope with such divergent demands.

896. LASCELLES, MARY. *Shakespeare's "Measure for Measure."* London: Athlone Press, 1953, 172 pp.

Describes *Measure for Measure* as bewildering in large part because critics have heightened our level of awareness of its numerous ambiguities. Shakespeare in this play has filled the vessel of tragicomedy "to capacity with thought and feeling" (p. 159), and it spills over; his thought transcends the bounds of his story. The characters refuse merely to play a role by coming to life as ambiguously human—the duke, powerfully involved with the problems of evil in Vienna but at times seemingly cold and dispassionate; Isabella, deeply angered in a moral crisis until she abdicates to the duke's manipulations; Angelo, pushed back from the threshold of tragic experience to two-dimensional stylization.

897. LEAVIS, F. R. "The Greatness of *Measure for Measure.*" *Scrutiny* 10 (1942):234–47.

Takes issue with the assertion that there is something distasteful about the play, an artistic uncertainty and confusion of feeling. Complexity of attitude does not necessarily mean conflict or confusion. Therein, in fact, lies the greatness of *Measure for Measure*. Shakespeare's approach requires subtler attitudes than those in the morality tradition when we approach Isabella, Angelo, and the duke. The resolution is artistically fitting, not hastily contrived. Angelo is stripped of his pretensions, but he is capable of his redemption because he is not basically the criminal type.

898. LEECH, CLIFFORD. "The Meaning of *Measure for Measure.*" *Shakespeare Survey* 3 (1950):66–73.

Argues that it is a gross oversimplification to view *Measure for Measure* as built on Christian views of justice and mercy. Whatever the Christian coloring it wells up sporadically from Shakespeare's unconscious inheritance; it does not determine the fundamental nature of the action. The overt theme is, indeed, the governor's duty to practice mercy and requite evil, but the play is far richer through its thematic undercurrents. In the morality framework is found satire, a psychological probing into the motives of the action, and a profound sympathy for the unfortunate and hard-pressed.

899. MACDONALD, RONALD R. "*Measure for Measure*: The Flesh Made Word." *Studies in English Literature 1500–1900* 30 (1990):265–82.

Measure for Measure

Argues that *Measure for Measure* pointedly departs from the traditional comic closure of romantic comedy in which sexual passion is aroused and then properly contained within the social institution of marriage. The strength of the play is that it leaves us pondering those reservations about living happily ever after that the earlier comedies encourage us to put aside. Justice and mercy are not mere abstractions but in the interactions of Isabella, Mariana, and Angelo take shape in the flesh in all its organic bluntness. The closure reflects "Shakespeare's fast ebbing faith in the ability of comic scheming to produce real solutions for the social malaise" (p. 280).

900. MacKay, Eileen. "*Measure for Measure*." *Shakespeare Quarterly* 14 (1963):109–13.

Asserts that the play comes into proper perspective only if we remember that the Catholic Church in England in the early seventeenth century stood in great disrepute. The play in its early stages exhibits a cynical attitude toward the church against which Isabella shines as an idealist in her integrity and humility. Her attitude toward seduction is no more priggish than her acceptance of the duke's offer of marriage is hypocritical. Once we perceive that her leaving the nunnery is to be seen as a pivotal act, we are free to envision her as a nubile young woman who rejects one man as a sinister and inhibited creature and accepts another as an individual motivated by a sincere affection for others.

901. Miles, Rosalind. *The Problem of "Measure for Measure": A Historical Investigation*. New York: Barnes & Noble, 1976, 349 pp.

Locates the central problem of the play in the linking of a basically comic plot to Vincentio as a disguised duke cult figure artistically related to James I and his self-image. The duke rules wisely but by stealth, and his concept of tempering justice with mercy in such a manner as to provoke a therapeutic response from his subjects is progressively revealed. The first half of the study comprises a critical and dramatic history of the play since its first production in 1604.

902. Mincoff, Marco. "*Measure for Measure*: A Question of Approach." *Shakespeare Studies* 2 (1966):141–52.

Decries those who pick out certain aspects of the plot, rearrange them, and then proclaim the result to be Shakespeare's intent—whether a satiric picture of a society under Puritan domination, the theme of justice versus mercy, the nature of law in an imperfect world, or a dramatization of the Christian atonement. We should accept the exciting story for what it is—the fall of a hypocritically proud man, a young girl whose hard choices suggest her initiation into full adulthood, and a brother whose idealistic vision of honor crumbles in the face of death.

903. NEVO, RUTH. *"Measure for Measure*: Mirror for Mirror." *Shakespeare Survey* 40 (1987):107–22.
    Challenges the trendy satiric reading of *Measure for Measure* as one in conflict with the engagement of our feelings in the first half. Given the psychological realism of the early acts, the "life drains out of the play with return of the fantastical Duke to take over the management of affairs" (p. 109). Perhaps, however, the psychological gap or incongruities can be addressed by reading the second half of the play as a replay—this time with escape possible—of the traumatic events that have trapped Isabella in her willingness to let her brother die and that have trapped Vincentio in his inability to rule with sufficient discipline.

904. NUTTALL, ANTHONY DAVID. *"Measure for Measure*: Quid pro Quo?" *Shakespeare Studies* 4 (1968):231–51.
    Points out the play's numerous "critical collisions"—Isabella's vowing chastity while condemning Mariana's sexual activity, the Duke's requirement both to love his subject and to punish him, his Machiavellian delegation of his punitive role, Angelo as both scapegoat and sinner, Vincentio as both heavenly and devilish in his methods. In these very collisions is the key to the ingenious structure, illustrating the Renaissance love of copiousness, of simultaneous multiplicity of seemingly paradoxical meanings. *Measure for Measure* is illusion at once provoking delight and shock, despair and consolation.

905. ORNSTEIN, ROBERT. "The Human Comedy: *Measure for Measure*." *University of Kansas City Review* 24 (1957):15–22.
    Describes *Measure for Measure* as a secular morality peopled with all-too-human figures; routine legality triumphs over compassion, and tragedy is averted by politic stratagems and unheroic compromises. Characters (ruler, virgin, judge) forever put themselves at the center of their moral universe but lack the self-knowledge vital to wise judgment. The conclusion is unsatisfactory because, while the resolution sustains communal life, it avoids the moral problems inherent in the plot. Echoes of the morality suggest a touch of grace beyond the reach of mortal man.

906. PRICE, JONATHAN R. *"Measure for Measure* and the Critics: Toward a New Approach." *Shakespeare Quarterly* 20 (1969):179–204.
    Argues that Shakespeare consciously works for diversity and complexity of response in *Measure for Measure*. Both Christian exegesis and

the Ibsenism inherent in the problem-play interpretation are ultimately reductionistic. By generic mixing and clever plotting Shakespeare forces us time and time again to shift our attention from one plane of reality to another. The progressive revelation of contradictory information is, in effect, a structural principle that defies simplistic analysis while it creates exciting theater.

907. ROSE, JACQUELINE. "Sexuality in the Reading of Shakespeare: *Hamlet* and *Measure for Measure*." In *Alternative Shakespeares*. Edited by John Drakakis. London and New York: Methuen, 1985, 95–118.

Sees charges of sexuality (an excess in Gertrude, a deficiency in Isabella) as a major focus of the plays. In both sexuality violates propriety, and in both a woman provokes the crisis that overturns the sexual identity of the central male figure. The fact that complexity of characterization, theme, structure, and ideology create tensions intractable to definitive analysis may explain why Gertrude and Isabella, in their own ways, have served as the critical focus. "Failing in a woman, whether aesthetic or moral, is always easier to point to than failure of integration within language and subjectivity itself" (p. 118).

908. SALE, ROGER. "The Comic Mode of *Measure for Measure*." *Shakespeare Quarterly* 19 (1968):551–61.

Considers *Measure for Measure* to be experimental in nature as Shakespeare comes to focus more directly on individual nature and motive in the face of social institutions. More specifically, he insists on the stubbornness of human folly and iniquity and on the inescapable necessity of authoritarian unscrupulousness if society is to enjoy even a modicum of order and well-being. The result is harsh comedy, strikingly different from Shakespeare's earlier romantic comedy; the ending is equivocal since Vincentio's methods are morally questionable.

909. SHELL, MARC. *The End of Kingship: "Measure for Measure," Incest, and the Ideal of Universal Siblinghood*. Stanford: Stanford University Press, 1988, 297 pp.

Views the exploration of the incest taboo and its relation to the conflict between nature and culture in the Western tradition as a central element in the structure of the play. The proposed marriage at the end between Isabella, a sister (nun), and Vincentio, a brother (friar) and father (priest), consciously blurs traditional lines of kinship and reflects the Christian ideal of universal siblinghood (brotherhood). Such sexual practice, by symbolic extension, blurs the rigid lines of parentage and undermines "the basis of political hierarchy and the ownership and transmission of property" (p. 70).

910. SIEGEL, PAUL N. *"Measure for Measure"*: The Significance of the Title. *Shakespeare Quarterly* 4 (1953):317–20.

States that Shakespeare's central problem is how to achieve dramatic justice and yet reflect Christian mercy, how to arouse derisive laughter at the same time he provokes a sense of moral elevation. The key is not the absence of retaliation but the careful working out of it. The title refers simultaneously to Angelo's method of dispensing justice in precise relation to the crime, to Isabella's and the duke's method of returning good for evil, and to the retribution visited upon the misdoers even though they are granted mercy.

911. STEVENSON, DAVID LLOYD. *The Achievement of "Measure for Measure."* Ithaca: Cornell University Press, 1966, 169 pp.

Refutes the concept that *Measure for Measure* is a flawed or obscure play penetrable only by a literary historian. Instead, it is a self-contained artistic achievement involving a complex set of ironies and reversals of both plot and character regarding moral behavior and human choice. A deliberately "uncomfortable" play compelling us to readjust our response to a greater level of apprehension than we are accustomed to, *Measure for Measure* forces the spectator to participate in a morally judgmental manner in its comic vision of the ineluctable evil in man.

912. TENNENHOUSE, LEONARD. "Representing Power: *Measure for Measure* and Its Time." In *The Power of Forms in the English Renaissance.* Edited by Stephen Greenblatt. Norman: University of Oklahoma Press, 1982, pp. 139–56.

Notes that "disguised ruler plays," popular in the early seventeenth century, depict a world in which prohibitions on desire have been ignored to the point that social order is threatened. Unregulated sexual desire, far from humanizing, is a destructive force that must be banned. Traditional family relationships can be restored only by a series of reversals accomplished through a series of substitutions made possible through Vincentio in disguise—the pirate's head for Claudio's, Mariana for Isabella.

913. VELZ, SARAH C. "Man's Need and God's Plan in *Measure for Measure* and 'Mark IV.' " *Shakespeare Survey* 25 (1972):37–44.

Measure for Measure

Asserts that Shakespeare's principal source for *Measure for Measure* was the fourth chapter of Mark in the Geneva Bible, specifically Christ's parable of the sower and the seeds. Angelo, Claudio, Lucio, and Mariana symbolize the various types of seeds; Angelo falls on stony ground, Claudio on shallow ground, Lucio is choked by thorns, and Mariana falls on fertile ground. Vincentio, like Christ asleep in the boat, is nearby to help his troubled followers, and both leaders trust subordinates who quickly prove unfaithful to the task.

914. WATSON, ROBERT N. "False Immorality in *Measure for Measure*: Comic Means, Tragic Ends." *Shakespeare Quarterly* 41 (1990):411–32.

Views the play as tragicomic in its abrupt and formulaic comic closure encouraging a suspicion that the aftermath of marriage is little more than an unpredictable biological process. Moreover, the comic design is consistently subverted by the action, harboring doubts and fear of death even as it points toward sexual union and procreation. With this twofold emphasis, perhaps *Measure for Measure*, as a product of the plague year, reflects the Weltanschauung of London in 1603. Perhaps Vincentio is allegorically an imitateo dei absconditi, Isabella is faith, Barnardine is the body, and Angelo is the angel of death.

915. WEIL, HERBERT, Jr. "Form and Contexts in *Measure for Measure*." *Critical Quarterly* 12 (1970):55–72.

Stresses the consistency of comic perspective in *Measure for Measure*. Shakespeare carefully prepares the spectator for the sudden reversal in tone when the duke emerges at the end of act 3 as an overt deus ex machina by allowing broad comedy again and again to undercut the serious theme in the early acts—the scene of comic gossip about venereal disease following Vincentio's delegation of power to Angelo, Lucio's interruption of Isabella's pious contemplation with "Hail virgin, if you be," Elbow and Pompey's interruption of the argument between Escalus and Angelo concerning the proper punishment for fornication. The energy of the early acts is thus transformed into joyous, mocking comedy.

916. WILSON, HAROLD S. "Action and Symbol in *Measure for Measure* and *The Tempest*." *Shakespeare Quarterly* 4 (1953):375–84.

Argues that both *Measure for Measure* and *The Tempest* employ a duke as a controlling figure but for different dramatic methods calculated for different dramatic effects. *Measure for Measure* presents a story ab ovo, and Vincentio's firm purpose becomes clear only at the end of the play when several characters—Angelo, Isabella, Claudio—are led to make choices that intensify and enrich their humanity. Prospero, by contrast, carefully explains his plan in advance, but here Shakespeare is presenting the end of a story; the question is not whether Alonso and Antonio will repent but whether Prospero will be able to exercise mercy instead of vengeance.

THE MERCHANT OF VENICE

Reference Works

917. MARDER, LOUIS, comp. *"The Merchant of Venice": A Supplementary Bibliography 1888–1965*. The New Variorum Shakespeare. New York: American Scholar Publications, 1965, 25 pp.

Includes representative scholarship on *The Merchant of Venice* from 1888 to 1965 and is intended to supplement H. H. Furness's Variorum edition of 1888. The material is categorized under reproductions and editions of *Merchant* quartos, bibliographical sources, modern editions, and critical studies (arranged alphabetically). While not exhaustive, the material represents every major category of scholarship and criticism.

918. TANNENBAUM, SAMUEL A., and TANNENBAUM, DOROTHY R., comps. *William Shakespeare: "The Merchant of Venice."* Elizabethan Bibliographies, 17. New York: Privately printed, 1941, 140 pp.

Cites 2,631 items covering major scholarship from the beginnings to 1939. The material is divided by the following categories and is arranged alphabetically by section—English texts, adaptations; translations; selections; abstracts, synopses; operas; songs; incidental music; commentary on music; parodies, burlesques; theatrical history; sources, analogues; law and *Merchant*; Jews and *Merchant*; Shylock; Portia, Nerissa, Jessica; general commentary; bibliographical notes; continuations, imitations; illustrations, costumes; book titles from *Merchant*; electrical recordings. The majority of the material (1,015 items) is loosely classified under general commentary.

919. WHEELER, THOMAS, comp. *"The Merchant of Venice": An Annotated Bibliography*. Garland Reference Library of the Humanities, 423: Garland Shakespeare Bibliographies, 9. New York and London: Garland Publishing, 1985, 386 pp.

Contains 1,144 items representing virtually all publications on the play from 1940 to 1983, along with the most significant items prior to

1940. The categories, each arranged chronologically, include criticism, sources, textual studies, bibliographies, editions and translations, stage history and productions, and films, music, and recordings. A brief introductory essay traces the history of recent scholarship and research.

Editions

920. BROWN, JOHN RUSSELL, ed. *The Merchant of Venice*. The Arden Shakespeare. London: Methuen; Cambridge, Mass.: Harvard University Press, 1955, 174 pp.

Includes discussion of the text, date, sources, stage history, and critical interpretations as well as appendixes featuring selections from Ser Giovanni, Anthony Munday, Alexander Silvayn, the ballad *Gernutus*, and the *Gesta Romanorum*. The text is based an the first quarto (1600), for which the copy was probably Shakespeare's foul papers; the second quarto, a Pavier forgery, was published in 1619 but falsely dated 1600. An introductory essay provides an analysis of the plot.

921. MAHOOD, M. M., ed. *The Merchant of Venice*. The New Cambridge Shakespeare. Cambridge: Cambridge University Press, 1987, 190 pp.

Features an introductory essay on date and source, attitudes and assumptions behind the play, experiencing the play, and the afterlife of *The Merchant of Venice*. Extensive notes appear on individual pages of the text, and appendixes include a textual analysis, comments on Shakespeare's use of the Bible in the play, and a list of suggested readings.

Criticism

922. AUDEN, W. H. "Brothers and Others." In *"The Dyer's Hand" and Other Selected Essays*. New York: Random House, 1948, pp. 218–37.

Describes Shylock and Antonio as two alien creatures unable to enter the Arcadian world of Belmont. Shylock is a usurer; and, while the immorality of usury was not a settled issue in Shakespeare's day, Shylock acts unprofessionally in his role and, as a Jew who defies the Christian society, is branded an alien. Antonio, likewise, is unable to experience the love of women, and his fanciful backing of Bassanio constitutes a form of idolatry. Their presence ultimately reminds us that Belmont is an illusion, that in the real world no hatred is totally without justification, no love totally innocent.

923. BEAUREGARD, RAPHAËLLE COSTA DE. "Interpreting *The Merchant of Venice*." *Cahiers Elisabéthains* No. 39 (1991):1–17.

Suggests that both exegesis and iconology are at work in the play in depicting the abstract and complex nature of justice. In exegetical terms, for example, Morocco and Arragon read the writing inscribed on the three caskets as allegorical, Morocco as an allegory of trade, Arragon as an allegory of heroism. Bassanio, on the other hand, reads them on the moral or ethical plane, in which lead is equated with humility. Portia functions as an emblem of justice in punishing greed and pride and leading Bassanio to a perception of true love.

924. BOOSE, LYNDA E. "The Comic Contract and Portia's Golden Ring." *Shakespeare Studies* 20 (1988):241–54.

Focuses on the role of Portia as mediator between play and audience. As Shakespeare develops his "comic bond" with the spectators, fulfilling their comic expectations in a formulaic closure of marriage, his development of the comic heroine (first fully realized in Portia) becomes the most significant device by which he can subvert and interrogate that form. Portia's manipulation of bonds (whether Antony's and Shylock's or the marital bond symbolized by the golden rings worn by Bassanio and Gratiano) suggests that "social contracts are merely patently insecure fictions that can always be invalidated, appropriated, read in new ways, rewritten, reassigned or even counter-fitted" (p. 252).

925. BROCKBANK, J. P. "Shakespeare and the Fashion of These Times." *Shakespeare Survey* 16 (1963):30–41.

Describes contemporary literary criticism as imaginatively exhausted, obsessed with objectively secured positions, and frequently overingeniously diverse. The trial scene of *The Merchant of Venice*, for example, has been the subject of flatly contradictory analyses. To the skeptical it is a magnificent exercise in law court virtuosity, a consummate piece of Jew-baiting. To the allegorist Portia is an analogue of Christ, and the action issues in divine mercy. We would do well to remember the various treatises that speak directly of admitting equity into law, that Portia remains far on this side of the magical, that the stereotyped Shylock is not tragically explored.

926. BURCKHARDT, SIGURD. "*The Merchant of Venice*: The Gentle Bond." *ELH* 29 (1962):239–62.

Perceives an exacting circular structure in that the bond, an instrument of destruction, becomes the source of deliverance. The circularity of the structure is reinforced by subsidiary metaphors of the bond and the ring. The ethic of the play is venture capitalism raised to a moral level; and Shylock, elevated by Shakespeare to a level of dignity, is the principal spokesman for this ethic. In order to gain, one must hazard one's possessions, material or emotional. The risks are genuine, and Shylock ultimately withdraws in the face of them.

927. DANSON, LAWRENCE. *The Harmonies of "The Merchant of Venice."* New Haven and London: Yale University Press, 1978, 202 pp.

Considers modern tendencies to play Shylock as a tragic figure or to read the play as an ironic attack upon uncharitable Christians a legacy of the Romantic and Victorian periods. The play must be interpreted in its particular theological context. The music as reflective of individual and cosmic harmony, the marriage of Jew and Gentile, the ring as physical and spiritual symbol—such elements in act 5 are merely the culmination of drama that is simultaneously sexual intrigue comedy and symbolic comedy suggesting that the dictates of charity can be fulfilled only through the mutuality of concern central to Christian doctrine.

928. DONOW, HERBERT S. "Shakespeare's Caskets: Unity in *The Merchant of Venice.*" *Shakespeare Studies* 4 (1968):86–93.

Claims that the main plot of *The Merchant of Venice* is not the bond motif but the courtship of Portia and her marriage to Bassanio, with the elopement of Jessica a parallel and related plot. Both women are subject to the will of a father, but the world of Shylock (by extension the Venetian world) is antithetical to that of Belmont. Portia's father has tendered love, and Portia accedes to his wishes; Shylock's failure as a father, in contrast, sets the stage for her repudiation of him. Portia's father in arranging the casket trial has inverted material value whereas Shylock pursues material wealth.

929. ENGLE, LARS. "Thrift Is Blessing: Exchange and Explanation in *The Merchant of Venice.*" *Shakespeare Quarterly* 37 (1986):20–37.

Maintains that bills and love letters are difficult to distinguish in *The Merchant of Venice* in the movement of cash, credit, and obligations. The erotic transactions link the play with other Shakespearean comedies, but here no such relationship is left as solely erotic or emotional; each has an explicit economic or legal analogue, whether Bassanio's love for Portia or his friendship with Antonio. In one sense the play is conservative; through Portia's manipulation the goods of a progressive commercial exchange system fall into the control of a landed aristocrat. In another sense, however, the play is radical in depicting a woman triumphing over men and male systems of exchange, both the homosexual desires of Antonio and the vengeful desires of Shylock.

930. FERBER, MICHAEL. "The Ideology of *The Merchant of Venice.*" *English Literary Renaissance* 20 (1990):431–64.

Claims that Shakespeare's elevation of a merchant to heroic status is a product of the cultural emergence of the bourgeois ideology in the late sixteenth century. This ideology of mercantile activity is imposed upon the aristocratic concepts of friendship and magnanimity as well as upon the privileging of Christianity. Shakespeare's audience would have felt a comfortable sympathy for the manner in which the themes of courtesy and social warmth are treated with such capitalistic bias.

931. FREUD, SIGMUND. "The Theme of the Three Caskets." In *Collected Papers*. Translated by Joan Riviere. Vol. 4. London: Hogarth Press and the Institute of Psycho–Analysis, 1949, pp. 244–56.

Analyzes the secret motives behind Bassanio's unconvincing argument that he prefers the baser metal lead. By symbolic substitution Bassanio, like Lear later, is choosing among three women. He prefers the third, who is silent and unobtrusive and who by ambiguous extension is both the Goddess of Love and Death herself. In Lear's case Cordelia is Death; in Bassanio's she is the fairest and wisest of women.

932. GARNER, SHIRLEY NELSON. "Shylock: 'His Stones, His Daughter, and His Ducats.'" *Upstart Crow* 5 (1984):35–49.

Concentrates on the impact of Jessica's elopement on Shylock—in his unwillingness to admit that she does not love him and in its place in his conflict with Antonio. Shylock's defeat strips him of his identity and darkens the play, reflecting the failure of humanity and love. Lorenzo and Jessica are reminiscent of tragic lovers; Portia must exorcise Antonio; and Gratiano distrusts Nerissa. Antonio strikes the final blow against Shylock by forcing him to become a Christian and thus isolating him from the Jewish community.

933. GEARY, KEITH. "The Nature of Portia's Victory: Turning to Men in *The Merchant of Venice*." *Shakespeare Survey* 37 (1984):55–68.

Observes that all the main characters in the play have double selves. Shylock is both a caricature and a human being; Bassanio is both a fortune hunter and a young man genuinely in love. So, too, action is often double. Antonio's financial bond with Shylock is also a personal bond with Bassanio; the ring is both a symbol of marriage and a comic sexual symbol. Portia assumes a masculine identity and, as such, at Antonio's urging, is given the ring by Bassanio. Through this stratagem she excludes Antonio in the relationship by fastening "the homoerotic tendency of Bassanio's sexuality to the obligations of masculine friendship on to herself" (p. 67).

934. GREBANIER, BERNARD. *The Truth about Shylock*. New York: Random House, 1962, 360 pp.

The Merchant of Venice

Examines the historical facts, sources, and primary themes of *The Merchant of Venice*, arguing that Shylock is paramountly a prototype of the banker whose only true god is money and, as such, is defeated by the comic forces of love and compassion. Repeatedly repudiating offers of mercy in the trial scene, he is ultimately banished as the exemplar of material as opposed to emotional value. The modern director and critic would do well to see beyond "the Jewish question" and to recognize that the play's real business is above distinction of race or creed.

935. KAHN, COPPÉLIA. "The Cuckoo's Note: Male Friendship and Cuckoldry in *The Merchant of Venice*." In *Shakespeare's "Rough Magic": Renaissance Essays in Honor of C. L. Barber*. Edited by Peter Erickson and Coppélia Kahn. Newark: University of Delaware Press; London and Toronto: Associated University Presses, 1985, pp. 104–12.

Observes that, while Shakespeare's comedy ends in merriment and marriage, the playwright never fails to undercut this ideal. In *The Merchant of Venice*, more specifically, the plot—even while it concludes with a double marriage—ends also with a flurry of accusations involving male friendship and the fear of cuckoldry. The ring theme provides the narrative means for resolving this conflict. Bassanio's final lines confirm his capitulation to marriage through an ironic reference to cuckoldry, and Gratiano's final lines "voice the homoerotic wish, succeeded by the heterosexual anxiety" (p. 111).

936. KUHNS, RICHARD, and TOVEY, BARBARA. "Portia's Suitors." *Philosophy and Literature* 13 (1989):325–31.

Suggests that Portia's suitors, as described by Nerissa, represent actual persons whose descriptions give clues to their real identities. More specifically, the suitors refer to writers from whom Shakespeare derived inspiration and plots—the Neapolitan prince, Boccaccio; the County Palatine, Spenser; Monsieur Le Bon, Montaigne; Falconbridge, Chaucer; the Scottish lord, Henryson; and the Duke of Saxony's nephew, Hans Sachs. In such an interpretation Bassanio stands for Shakespeare himself, heir to the tradition of those writers who have departed the scene.

937. LEVER, J. W. "Shylock, Portia, and the Values of Shakespearian Comedy." *Shakespeare Quarterly* 3 (1952):383–86.

Describes *The Merchant of Venice* as romantic comedy in which love is pitted against usury. Fittingly, the villain is a Jewish moneylender with a marriageable daughter. The bond plot transforms the Jewish usurer into a man challenging the pattern of recognized values, and Antonio's virtues have taken on harsh contours. When Jessica elopes, Shylock waives his final elements of Jewishness by calling for vengeance, not as an individual governed by the laws of the Old Testament but as a wronged man in Venetian society. He is ultimately defeated by commercial laws and customs that are hardly Christian. The struggle has totally transcended theological doctrine.

938. LEWALSKI, BARBARA. "Biblical Allusion and Allegory in *The Merchant of Venice.*" *Shakespeare Quarterly* 13 (1962):327–43.

Argues that patterns of Biblical allusion and imagery in *The Merchant of Venice* are too precise and pervasive not to be deliberate. At the moral level the play explores and defines Christian love and its various antitheses. Antonio's practice of Christian love is in his "venturing." At the allegorical level the Shylock-Antonio opposition symbolizes the confrontation of Judaism and Christianity. Antonio's trial scene suggests literary and iconographical presentations of the Parliament of Heaven in which fallen man was judged. Shylock, having refused the opportunity to embrace the principles of Christianity, must undergo "schoolmastership" to be saved.

939. LEWIS, CYNTHIA. "Antonio and Alienation in *The Merchant of Venice.*" *South Atlantic Review* 48 (1983):19–31.

Focuses on the ambiguous discomforts Antonio provokes in spectators and readers. Certainly from the moment of his introduction Antonio is strange or alien; he is obsessed with a deep melancholy he cannot explain. He also seems to lack a depth of perception in dealing with the dangers of the world; and his knowledge of Venetian law, when he is caught in Shylock's bond, is superficial. At the play's end he walks slowly off stage, his best friend now married. He reminds us that alienation and suppression are, for some, the consequence of social cohesion; and the truth of his predicament disturbs us.

940. LUCKING, DAVID. "Standing for Sacrifice: The Casket and Trial Scenes in *The Merchant of Venice.*" *University of Toronto Quarterly* 58 (1989):355–75.

Finds the heart of the play in the ethic of self-abnegation, as it manifests itself in the arena of practical conduct in two key scenes— Bassanio's solution of the casket riddle and Portia's intervention in Shylock's case against Antonio. In both of these scenes, "radically different value systems are . . . compelled to subject their most deeply held assumptions to the test of an alternative world view" (p. 356). These scenes reflect a conception of love with no expectation of reward in any currency of its own. It runs directly counter to the acquisitive spirit of Venice, so much so that the closure involves optimistic faith in the human spirit clouded with an ironic sense of human fallibility.

The Merchant of Venice

941. MIDGLEY, GRAHAM. "*The Merchant of Venice*: A Reconsideration."
     Essays in Criticism 10 (1960):119–33.
     Notes that any attempt to interpret *The Merchant of Venice* as either
     a love story or a study in the personality of the Jew is reductionistic. The
     two focal points of the play are Shylock and Antonio, and the two
     contrasting value structures are those of love and marriage and those of
     society, politics, and economics. As Shylock is an outsider to the social
     values, Antonio is an outsider to the love values. The play is a study in
     twin loneliness. As act 4 covers the defeat of Shylock, act 5 covers the
     defeat of Antonio. The last we see of each is a solitary figure walking
     disconsolately off stage.

942. MOISAN, THOMAS. " 'Which is the merchant here? And which the jew?'
     Subversion and Recuperation in *The Merchant of Venice*." In *Shakespeare
     Reproduced: The Text in History and Ideology*. Edited by Jean Howard
     and Marion F. O'Connor. New York and London: Methuen, 1987, pp.
     188–206.
     Questions whether the play actually produces a harmonious reso-
     lution and reconciliation or merely invokes them through the power of
     dramatic fiat and in the interest of ideological conformity. Central to
     the action are the economic discoveries of Shakespeare's day in the
     triumph over usury in the figure of Shylock, but Bassanio figures too,
     as middle borrower who seeks loans for conspicuous consumption.
     What we encounter in the play is a "mirroring both of the myths by
     which the age reads itself and of the anxieties those myths could not
     entirely dispel" (p. 197).

943. SHARP, RONALD A. "Gift Exchange and the Economics of Spirit in *The
     Merchant of Venice*." *Modern Philology* 83 (1986):250–65.
     Suggests that an examination of Shakespeare's elaborate treatment
     of gift exchange illumines the comic aspects of the play. Of particular
     significance is the distinction drawn between a gift freely given, such as
     Antonio's to Bassanio or Bassanio's to Portia, and usury, a commodity
     through which the giver intends to add to his own wealth and at no risk
     to himself, since he has security. Throughout the play it becomes in-
     creasingly apparent that nothing of value can be won without great
     risks. It becomes obvious, as well, that both marriages and friendships
     will decay from "lively bonding to sterile binding or bondage if the
     spirit of gift is not preserved" (p. 265).

944. SIEGEL, PAUL N. "Shylock and the Puritan Usurers." In *Studies in
     Shakespeare*. Edited by Arthur D. Matthews and Clark M. Emery. Coral
     Gables: University of Miami Press, 1953, pp. 129–38.

Argues that Elizabethan spectators would have seen in Shakespeare's depiction of the villainous moneylender of folk tradition reflections of contemporary Puritan usurers. Judaism, Puritanism, and usury were connected in the popular mind. Puritans, because of their emphasis on Old Testament law, were frequently charged with returning to Judaism. Shylock, like the Pharisaical Puritan, is intolerant of others, attributing his own spiritual defect to others. In the final act charity, friendship, and love triumph over the Puritan individualism and its "cash nexus."

945. SIEMON, JAMES E. "*The Merchant of Venice*: Act V as Ritual Reiteration." *Studies in Philology* 67 (1970):201–9.

Notes that *The Merchant of Venice* stands between the festive and the optimistic comedies and the problem plays or tragicomedies. The signal difference, first observed in Shylock, is the increased role of the villain and a greater focus on his motivation. Structurally the framing tale of Bassanio's wooing of Portia is raised to major prominence and becomes the efficient cause of the comic resolution. Act 5 recapitulates the action of acts 1–4 on a different level of awareness and meaning; in its comic lesson in the nature of harmony and the music of the spheres, it recapitulates Shylock's conversion in symbolic terms.

946. SMITH, JAMES H. "Shylock: 'Devil Incarnation' or 'Poor Man . . . Wronged?' " *Journal of English and Germanic Philology* 60 (1961):1–21.

Surveys the widely divergent interpretations of Shylock and proposes to explore Shakespeare's intentions through his arrangement of incidents. The first quarto describes Shylock's actions on the title page as "extreme cruelty"; and the resolution of the Shylock material at a relatively early stage makes certain that it will not cloud the romantic denouement. Shylock's bond motif becomes serious only after Jessica's elopement. He is neither comic butt nor tragic; he is a developing villain who progresses from human status in act 1 to that of savage monster in act 4.

947. STOLL, ELMER EDGAR. "Shylock." *Journal of English and Germanic Philology* 10 (1911):236–79.

Asserts that Shakespeare in his portrayal of Shylock depicts for the Elizabethan the prototypic Jew, moneylending, miserly, and hooknosed. Played in a red beard and embodying widely prevalent social antipathies, he is both villain and comic butt. Attempts to make him a martyr or a sympathetic rejected father are far afield. Any human traits are undercut by passages depicting his villainously comic nature. References to Jews elsewhere in Shakespeare's plays are consistent with this interpretation.

948. WERTHEIM, ALBERT. "The Treatment of Shylock and Thematic Integrity in *The Merchant of Venice.*" *Shakespeare Studies* 6 (1970):75–87.
    Asserts that Shylock's importance is primarily as a dramatic statement of a play involving the examination of certain values and morals. He epitomizes the disproportionate position of monetary over spiritual concerns. Portia counteracts his mercenary legalism, inculcating new values in Bassanio as well. The forced conversion of Shylock is an act of the highest mercy, the opportunity to find grace and Christian salvation. The characters are forced to realize that they cannot serve both God and Mammon.

Stage History

949. LELYVELD, TOBY. *Shylock on the Stage.* Cleveland: Western Reserve University Press, 1960, 149 pp.
    Traces the stage history of *The Merchant of Venice*, more particularly the characterization of Shylock with emphasis on those actors who have created significant changes in the role. Elizabethans viewed Shylock with comic opprobrium. George Granville in 1701 adapted Shylock's role in the vein of lowest comedy in *The Jew of Venice.* Charles Macklin in 1741 was the first to set the tragic tone so many later actors were to follow. Individual chapters are devoted to Edmund Kean, Edwin Booth, and Henry Irving, with some attention to the twentieth-century roles of George Arliss, John Gielgud, and John Carradine.

THE MERRY WIVES OF WINDSOR

Editions

950. CRAIK, T. W., ed. *The Merry Wives of Windsor.* The Oxford Shakespeare. Oxford and New York: Oxford University Press, 1989, 242 pp.
    Includes an introductory essay addressing Shakespeare's garter play: the occasion and the date, Shakespeare's English comedy: the substance and dramatic structure, critical and theatrical interpretations,

the quarto and folio texts. Extensive notes on each page of the text identify specific problems and provide background information. Appendixes discuss the textual crux at 1.1.19–20, Evans's song in 3.1, Falstaff's disguise as Herne the Hunter, and alterations to the folio lineation.

951. OLIVER, H. J., ed. *The Merry Wives of Windsor*. The Arden Shakespeare. London: Methuen; Cambridge, Mass.: Harvard University Press, 1971, 149 pp.

Includes discussion of the text, the relationship and printing of the quarto and folio, and the probable occasion of the play along with theories of personal satire, the relationship to Shakespeare's histories, and the literary sources or analogues. Theories have been advanced that *The Merry Wives of Windsor* was written to gratify Queen Elizabeth's desire to see Falstaff in love and that it was written for the Garter Feast in 1597. Similar attempts to relate the material to the history plays have focused on when the action occurs in relation to *Henry IV* and *Henry V*. The likely date of composition is 1597 after the production of *1 Henry IV* and before the completion of *2 Henry IV*.

952. QUILLER-COUCH, ARTHUR, and WILSON, JOHN DOVER, eds. *The Merry Wives of Windsor*. Cambridge: Cambridge University Press, 1921, 149 pp.

Provides extensive textual notes, a critical introduction, a discussion of the copy text, a section on stage history, and a glossary. This edition is based on the First Folio, for which the copy was "made up by standing together players' parts with the aid of the theatrical 'plot' of the play" (p. 93). While the main intrigue is handled effectively, the play abounds in loose ends and threads, and the quality of the small amount of verse is especially weak. These inconsistencies are possibly explained by the fact that Shakespeare, working under royal command to display Falstaff in love, was hastily reworking an old play now lost, *The Jealous Comedy*

Textual Study

953. BRACEY, WILLIAM. *"The Merry Wives of Windsor": The History and Transmission of Shakespeare's Text*. University of Missouri Studies, vol. 25, no. 1. Columbia: Curators of the University of Missouri, 1952, 154 pp.

Examines the quarto (1602) and folio (1623) texts of *The Merry Wives of Windsor*, focusing on the medium of transmission and the nature of the copy text for each. The theories of shorthand reporting, of a pirate-actor, and of memorial reconstruction are described as untenable, and the quarto text is considered an authorized stage version drastically abridged and adapted for special conditions of performance. The cutting is systematic—minor characters are eliminated, long speeches are reduced sharply, the plot is streamlined for effect—but it is dramatically consistent.

Criticism

954. BARTON, ANN. "Falstaff and the Comic Community." In *Shakespeare's "Rough Magic": Renaissance Essays in Honor of C. L. Barber.* Edited by Peter Erickson and Coppélia Kahn. Newark: University of Delaware Press; London and Toronto: Associated University Presses, 1985, pp. 131–45.

Views the delineation of Falstaff in *The Merry Wives of Windsor* as a painful confrontation between a larger-than-life comic figure and Shakespeare's own form of comedy, a form in which Shakespeare has consciously come to exclude just that kind of character. Falstaff descends from a long line of comic characters who, since Aristophanes, parade as shameless self-seekers, inordinate eaters and wenchers, and highly successful deceivers. Never again will a character like Falstaff occupy center stage in Shakespeare's comedy; such a figure will reappear in lesser roles as Sir Toby Belch in *Twelfth Night*, Lucio in *Measure for Measure*, and Autolycus in *The Winter's Tale*.

955. BENNETT, A. L. "The Sources of Shakespeare's *Merry Wives*." *Renaissance Quarterly* 23 (1970):429–33.

Surmises that Shakespeare felt compelled, because of Falstaff's popularity, to develop a domestic comedy with the fat clown as the butt of the jests and that he turned to *Ralph Roister Doister* for his principal source. Both plays place a braggart soldier center stage, and in both the soldier woos a citizen's wife, with money and not love as the prime motive. Both braggadocios are led to believe their passion is returned; and, following their comic exposure, both are forgiven.

956. COTTON, NANCY. "Castrating (W)itches: Impotence and Magic in *The Merry Wives of Windsor*." *Shakespeare Quarterly* 38 (1987):321–26.

Views the psychological core of the plot as Ford's sense of failure as husband and father because (unlike Page) he is childless. The result is a paranoia about female power that leads him unconsciously to equate his wife's power to cuckold or "unman" him with a witch's spell. Hence, his witch-beating of Mother Prat is a symbolic wife-beating, the one a surrogate for the woman he really wishes to beat. Falstaff's symbolic castration as a foiled suitor by the women at night in the forest again suggests their power as witches. Comically, when Ford's fears of betrayal are removed in the final scene, he speaks of again having the ability to "lie [tonight] with Mistress Ford" (5.5.245).

957. ERICKSON, PETER. "The Order of the Garter, the Cult of Elizabeth, and Class-Gender Tension in *The Merry Wives of Windsor.*" In *Shakespeare Reproduced: The Text in History and Ideology.* Edited by Jean Howard and Marion F. O'Connor. New York and London: Methuen, 1987, pp. 116–40.

Believes that *The Merry Wives of Windsor* grants superior power to women but is not progressive since the conservative treatment of both class and gender does not support an enlightened, egalitarian image of the play. The female-controlled plotting "parallels the Queen-dominated court politics and arouses a similar male uneasiness" (p. 119). Fenton's marrying Anne against her parents' wishes qualifies the woman's power. He is a crucial figure in marking the true nature of the play because of both his class and gender; the marriage transfers money from the bourgeoisie to the aristocracy and control into male hands.

958. GREEN, WILLIAM. *Shakespeare's "The Merry Wives of Windsor."* Princeton: Princeton University Press, 1962, 239 pp.

Examines the events surrounding the composition of *The Merry Wives of Windsor* and how these events shaped the text from its initial performance to the printing in the folio. The play was apparently written to order and was first performed at the Feast of the Garter on St. George's Day, 1597. At this time both Shakespeare's patron Lord Hunsdon and the German ruler the Duke of Wurttemberg were made Garter knights. Writing at Hunsdon's commission a comedy depicting Falstaff in love, Shakespeare also incorporated material that would serve as a tribute to the Order of the Garter. The folio represents the authentic text; the quarto text is a memorially reconstructed version for acting in the provinces.

959. GURR, ANDREW. "Intertextuality at Windsor." *Shakespeare Quarterly* 38 (1987):189–200.

Suggests that, when only two companies were competing for the playgoers between 1594 and 1600, they offered imitative rivals rather than radically different choices but that after the turn of the century there was a marked divergence. After 1600, more precisely, Henslowe's company tended to produce plays in which the conservative principal of parental authority was validated, whereas Chamberlain's continued the strain of validating the rebellion of young love set in motion by *Romeo and Juliet*, *A Midsummer Night's Dream*, and *Much Ado About Nothing*. That same rivalry may have prompted *The Merry Wives of Windsor*, in which Anne wins her victory for love over the wishes of her parents, as a response to the Admiral's production of *The Two Angry Women*, in which the father's wishes are sustained in two different weddings.

960. HUNTER, G. K. "Bourgeoisie Comedy: Shakespeare and Dekker." In *Shakespeare and His Contemporaries: Essays in Comparison*. Edited by E. A. J. Honigmann. Manchester: Manchester University Press, 1986, pp. 1–15.

Observes that both Dekker's *The Shoemaker's Holiday* and Shakespeare's *The Merry Wives of Windsor* combine aristocratic and bourgeoisie characters but that neither makes economic conflict the center of the action. In both plays the challenge to comic harmony disappears with the realization that class distinction is unimportant— the mistaken notions of aristocratic egocentricity in Falstaff and of aristocratic prodigality in Page. Both plays conclude with a large-scale action that reconfirms the representative value of the community.

961. OSBORNE, LAURIE E. "Play and Comic Creation in *The Merry Wives of Windsor*." *Michigan Academician* 22 (1990):143–52.

Addresses the metadramatic features of the play, focusing on figures who attempt to control their world through play. This playing takes a noticeably dramatic form, whether in the language Mistress Ford and Mistress Page use to describe their actions or in the elaborate staging they devise. The first trick, against both Falstaff and Ford, serves merely to produce comic humiliation; the second involves a comic education that issues in the reunion of marriage. The unexpected intervention of Fenton in the final trick unites the community by transforming all the player-dramatists to comic victims.

962. PARTEN, ANNE. "Falstaff's Horns: Masculine Inadequacy and Feminine Mirth in *The Merry Wives of Windsor*." *Studies in Philology* 82 (1985):184–99.

Views the significance of Falstaff, costumed as Herne the Hunter crowned with antlers, as Shakespeare's drawing upon the folk tradition of skimmington. This ceremony is a ritualized burlesque expression of a community's disapproval of sexual behavior and is frequently associated with feminine ascendancy and masculine subjugation. As ritual, it is both mock celebration and indirect exorcism. In a similar way, *The Merry Wives of Windsor* concerns "a situation in which a healthy marriage is threatened, in which women have gained the upper hand, and in which masculine ineffectuality is equated with cuckoldom" (p. 187).

963. ROBERTS, JEANNE ADDISON. *Shakespeare's English Comedy: "The Merry Wives of Windsor" in Context.* Lincoln and London: University of Nebraska Press, 1979, 169 pp.

Encourages a new evaluation of *The Merry Wives of Windsor* in its full context. Following individual chapters on the text, date, and sources, attention is directed to the generic form, and the play is set squarely within the tradition of Shakespearean comedy and of Shakespeare's work in the middle 1590s. *The Merry Wives*, more specifically, is experimental and transitional, coming between the histories and tragedies and sharing the bold comic developments of his finest romantic comedies. Of particular interest is the use of prose, the focus on married love, and the play within the play.

964. SCHELL, J. STEWART. "Shakespeare's Gulls." *Shakespeare Association Bulletin* 15 (1940):23–33.

Finds the precursor to Shakespeare's gulls in the epigram literature of the 1590s (Davies, Guilpin) in which the virtuoso touch was added to the standard characteristics of a foolish and credible simpleton. While Thurio in *The Two Gentlemen of Verona* is the first clear Shakespearean example, perhaps the most significant one is Abraham Slender in *The Merry Wives of Windsor*. The incompetent lover with "imperfect" speech, he boasts pridefully of family and status but melts into cowardice when confronted. Other gulls mentioned briefly are Aguecheek, Osric, Roderigo, and Cloten.

A MIDSUMMER NIGHT'S DREAM

Reference Works

965. CARROLL, D. ALLEN, and WILLIAMS, GARY J., comps. *"A Midsummer Night's Dream": An Annotated Bibliography.* Garland Reference Library of the Humanities, 440: Garland Shakespeare Bibliographies, 12. New York and London: Garland Publishing, 1986, 641 pp.

A Midsummer Night's Dream

Contains 1,528 items representing virtually all publications on the play from 1940 to 1984, along with the most significant items prior to 1940. The categories, each arranged chronologically, include criticism, sources (background, date), textual studies, bibliographies, editions and translations, adaptations (acting editions, synopses, influence), and stage history and the sister arts. A brief introductory essay traces the history of recent criticism and research.

966. MARDER, LOUIS, comp. *"A Midsummer Night's Dream": A Supplementary Bibliography 1895–1965*. The New Variorum Shakespeare. New York: American Scholar Publications, 1965, 18 pp.

Includes representative scholarship on *A Midsummer Night's Dream* from 1895 to 1965 and is intended to supplement H. H. Furness's Variorum edition of 1895. The material is categorized under bibliographical sources, modern editions, and critical studies (arranged alphabetically). While not exhaustive, the material represents every major category of scholarship and criticism.

Editions

967. BROOKS, HAROLD F., ed. *A Midsummer Night's Dream*. The Arden Shakespeare. London: Methuen; Cambridge, Mass.: Harvard University Press, 1979, 165 pp.

Includes discussion of the text, the date, the occasion of composition, the poetic style, the sources, and critical interpretations as well as appendixes on textual cruces, mislineation in the first quarto, and the proper punctuation of Quince's prologue. The text is based on the first quarto (1600), for which the copy was Shakespeare's foul papers, with occasional readings from the second quarto (a Pavier forgery printed from the first quarto in 1619 but falsely dated 1600) and from the First Folio (based on prompt copy). It is unlikely that there was any comprehensive source; instead, Shakespeare drew upon at least a dozen identifiable works.

968. FOAKES, R. A., ed. *A Midsummer Night's Dream*. The New Cambridge Shakespeare. Cambridge: Cambridge University Press, 1984, 148 pp.

Features an introductory essay on date and occasion, sources, the play on the stage, and the play in the mind. Extensive notes appear on individual pages of the text, and appendixes include a textual analysis, a further note on sources, and a list of suggested readings.

Criticism

969. ALLEN, JOHN A. "Bottom and Titania." *Shakespeare Quarterly* 18 (1967):107–17.

Focuses on the significance of the tableau scene in which the ass-headed Bottom lies in the arms of the fairy queen. Bottom is amusing in this situation both because it is a comedy of the grotesque and because he represents the universal combination of asshood and humanity. This quality for the spectators is represented in the chase taking place in the woods. Bottom's presence tends to short-circuit any attempt to moralize by choosing between the reasonable and the fanciful as a basis for everyday action.

970. BROWN, JANE K. "Discordia Concors: On the Order of *A Midsummer Night's Dream*." *Modern Language Quarterly* 48 (1987):20–41.

Explores the connection, in an allegorical reading of the play, between love and mental activity and locates it in popular Neoplatonist doctrine, specifically in the significance of love as a means of knowing higher truth. The plot establishes and develops a fundamental opposition between chaste and sexual love: Theseus and Hippolyta, the two pairs of young lovers, Titania and Oberon. The blatant burlesque in the mechanicals' performance in act 5 "frees us from the illusion of the world and thus reminds us of its—and the text's—allegorical nature" (p. 37).

971. DUNN, ALLEN. "The Indian Boy's Dream Wherein Every Mother's Son Rehearses His Part: Shakespeare's *A Midsummer Night's Dream*." *Shakespeare Studies* 20 (1988):15–32.

Proposes that both the romance and fairy plots of the play must be read from the perspective of their individual characters if we are fully to comprehend the fears and desires that animate the play. Both plots are about sexual conflict, the romance plot following that of Roman comedy with the blocking figure of the old father bested by the young man who pursues his daughter, the fairy plot reversing the movement toward satisfaction and social cohesion and operating on a psychological rather than realistic level. In the one plot the characters grow to maturation; in the other they regress to childhood. What joins the two is the complementary confrontation with parental authority; the violent quarrels of the forest are forgotten as the young Athenians watch such differences parodied on the stage by Bottom and his associates.

972. FABER, M. D. "Hermia's Dream: Royal Road to *A Midsummer Night's Dream*." *Literature and Psychology* 22 (1972):179–90.

A Midsummer Night's Dream

    Believes that Hermia's dream is the psychoanalytic center of *A Midsummer Night's Dream*. The theme, more specifically, concerns the movement of the various characters through dissociation to a new identity. Hermia's dream depicts classic characteristics of dissociation—with a snake (a phallic substitution for Lysander) attacking her breasts instead of her genitals. As a metaphor of the entire dramatic action, it realistically captures the "scope of unconscious causation in human experience" (p. 190).

973. FISHER, PETER F. "The Argument of *A Midsummer Night's Dream*." *Shakespeare Quarterly* 8 (1957):307–10.
    Views the major conflict of the play as the irrational force of sublunary passion (the four lovers) set against the rationally ordered world of Theseus and the Athenian court. Flanking each is the extreme of the grotesquely mundane world of Bottom and the fantastic world of Oberon. All four meet in the woods and through the action of the play are placed in proper perspective. The Theseus world is accepted as the controlling power; passion and desire are placed within the orbit of its control; the world of common life approvingly sports itself for their amusement; and the world of imagination provides impetus for the interplay.

974. HERBERT T. WALTER. *Oberon's Mazed World: A Judicious Young Elizabethan Contemplates "A Midsummer Night's Dream" with a Mind Shaped by the Learning of Christendom Modified by the New Naturalist Philosophy and Excited by the Vision of a Rich, Powerful England*. Baton Rouge: Louisiana State University Press, 1977, 200 pp.
    Applies Elizabethan dramatic, philosophical, and scientific issues to *A Midsummer Night's Dream* through the eyes of an informed sixteenth-century English theatergoer. This spectator discovers that the romantic comedy brings into focus diverse segments of society, diverse temperaments, and diverse ages of the world's history. His dramatic experience through the play's multiple worlds results in a sense of expansive love, "extending beyond the ignorant fictional Athenians to encompass his live, earnest, philosophic friends, himself, and even the world predicament they shared. He understood them with a new patience. He understood them with a newly compassionate heart" (p. 164).

975. HUSTON, J. DENNIS. "Bottom Waking: Shakespeare's 'Most Rare Vision.' " *Studies in English Literature 1500–1900* 13 (1973):208–22.
    Views Bottom's dream as reflective of both the theme of *A Midsummer Night's Dream* and of Shakespeare's art. The "dream" involves

love's tyranny in the form of Titania's enslaving Bottom and of his childlike acceptance of it. Love's tyranny is also the theme of the action involving the dominance of Egeus and the ruler Theseus in the romantic affairs of the confused Athenian youth. Bottom's dream also, however, is a liberation into self-knowledge and, as such, is a metaphor for the play as a whole.

976. KAVANAGH, JAMES H. "Shakespeare in Ideology." In *Alternative Shakespeares*. Edited by John Drakakis. London and New York: Methuen, 1985, pp. 144–65.

Maintains that Shakespeare's work constitutes a productive ideological practice, "the material means for provoking a specific imaginary experience, associated with specific ideas in unprecedented ways—ways that even the author 'himself' cannot anticipate" (p. 148). He was obliged to develop a language and a methodology that would satisfy a heterogeneous audience representing diverse social and political views. *A Midsummer Night's Dream* will serve to illustrate the typical Shakespearean landscape, with rebellious females, a challenge to authority, a hierarchical patriarchy, and a working class operating under the contradictory conditions of economic independence and political submission.

977. LEINWOLD, THEODORE B. " 'I Believe We Must Leave the Killing Out': Deference and Accommodation in *A Midsummer Night's Dream*." *Renaissance Papers* (1986):11–30.

Suggests that the artisans' play in *A Midsummer Night's Dream* provides significant social comment. The relationship of their play to its aristocratic audience reflects the same relationship between Shakespeare's company and the privileged class in England. The youths' confused marriage plans glance at marriage brokering in Elizabeth's court. The handicraftsmen's concern with offending the spectators embodies the players' efforts to accommodate themselves to numerous restrictions on playing. Shakespeare, in a word, "criticizes the relations of power in his culture, but does so with remarkable sensitivity to the nuances of threat and accommodations which animate their relations" (p. 30).

978. McGUIRE, PHILIP C. "Egeus and the Implications of Silence." In *Shakespeare and the Sense of Performance: Essays in the Tradition of Performance Criticism in Honor of Bernard Beckerman*. Edited by Marvin Thompson and Ruth Thompson. Newark: University of Delaware Press; London and Toronto: Associated University Presses, 1989, pp. 103–15.

A Midsummer Night's Dream

Probes how Shakespeare intended the moment of silence to be played when Theseus overbears Egeus's will concerning the marriage of Hermia (4.1.180). Contemporary productions range from Egeus's embracing his daughter to his stalking off stage in disgust. The text allows both reactions since the folio version mandates Egeus's willing participation in the wedding festivities while the quarto version notably excludes Egeus from act 5. Clearly, the actors must always come to terms with their characters in a process that is "collaborative, collective, and communal in nature" (p. 113).

979. MONTROSE, LOUIS. "*A Midsummer Night's Dream* and the Shaping Fantasies of Elizabethan Culture: Gender, Power, Form." In *Rewriting the Renaissance: The Discourse of Sexual Difference in Early Modern Europe*. Edited by Margaret W. Ferguson, Maureen Quilligan, and Nancy J. Vickers. Chicago: University of Chicago Press, 1986, pp. 65–87.

Observes that a concerted effort was made to foster an Elizabethan cult. Yet that female mystification, coupled with the fact that all other forms of public and domestic authority were vested in men, resulted in "peculiar tensions within an essentially patriarchal society" (p. 68). The "liaison between the fairy queen and the assified artisan is an outrageous theatrical realization" of male domination (p. 68). Indeed, the conclusion of the play, with its celebration of generative heterosexual union, "depends upon the success of a process whereby the female pride and power manifested in misanthropic warriors, possessive mothers, unruly wives, and wilful daughters are brought under the control of husbands and lords" (p. 76).

980. NEMEROV, HOWARD. "The Marriage of Theseus and Hippolyta." *Kenyon Review* 18 (1956):633–11.

Describes the marriage as a symbolic as well as physical union. The poetic style of Theseus is rational and discursive, frequently tending toward prose. Hippolyta's, to the contrary, is magical and highly musical, drawing constantly from the fabulous. Theseus tends to see the literal and the obvious, Hippolyta the imaginary and the allusive. Their wedded life metaphorically reflects the history of poetry in the English language.

981. OLSON, PAUL A. "*A Midsummer Night's Dream* and the Meaning of Court Marriage." *ELH* 24 (1957):95–119.

Describes *A Midsummer Night's Dream*, not merely as a shimmering fabric of moonlight, but as a carefully crafted work depicting the Renaissance philosophy of the nature of love in both its rational and irrational forms. Oberon's curing of Titania's obsession is central to the meaning of the play; similarly, through leading the Athenian youths alternately to mock and dote on each other, he purges their passionate view of love, freeing them from the fond fancy that misdirects the will.

982. PATTERSON, ANNABEL. "Bottoms Up: Festive Theory in *A Midsummer Night's Dream*." *Renaissance Papers* (1988):25–39.

Maintains that Bottom, as a visual pun and emblem, "stands at the fulcrum of Shakespeare's analysis of the festive impulse in human social structures" (p. 37). His name, in symbolic alliance with the ass's head, directs attention to the way the lower social orders as the lower body parts are undervalued for the services they perform. Moreover, the lower parts of the social body are invested with greater honor by affiliation with Bottom's dream, a utopian vision that he decides he cannot or will not put into words. The upshot is to reevaluate those unprivileged members normally mocked and burdened like asses, whose energies are indispensable to the social system.

983. RICHMOND, HUGH M. "Shaping a Dream." *Shakespeare Studies* 17 (1985):49–60.

Maintains, in the face of claims of myriad sources for the play, that Shakespeare characteristically preferred to work from some detailed source. *A Midsummer Night's Dream* offers a case in point, with the confused relationships among the young lovers probably deriving from Cinthio's *Hecatommithi* (the ninth novella of the second decade). Shakespeare's play clearly shares the source's underlying theme of an archaic, patriarchal approach to marriage being superseded with the help of a supernatural agent. Shared, too, is the assumption that "love though irrational is the least unsatisfactory basis for marriage" (p. 59).

984. ROBINSON, JAMES E. "The Ritual and Rhetoric of *A Midsummer Night's Dream*." *PMLA* 83 (1968):380–91.

Describes *A Midsummer Night's Dream* as a combination of realistic comedy, from both the primitive and medieval traditions, and of rhetorical comedy, from the Plautine-Terentian tradition. The one reaffirms the significance of a stable social order, while the other affirms a renewal of life by perceiving a reality beyond the physical world. While the humans with their concern for law, hierarchy, and authority represent the rhetorical world, the fairies represent the ritualistic world. The gods of nature become measure and mirror of human folly and love, and the result is both satiric and celebrative.

985. SCHANZER, ERNEST. "The Central Theme of *A Midsummer Night's Dream*." *University of Toronto Quarterly* 20 (1951):233–38.

A Midsummer Night's Dream

Notes that the events of the play take place not on Midsummer Night but on Walpurgisnight. Shakespeare probably used Midsummer Night in the title because of beliefs that flowers and herbs possess magical powers at that time and because of its association with madness. The theme involves a kind of love in which reason is subordinate to the senses, and Shakespeare's dramatic method is to parody it. In the relationship of Theseus and Hippolyta love and reason are reunited, and it is appropriate they should provide the resolving statements that give to these relationships a sense of permanence and sanity.

986. SCHLEINER, WINIFRIED. "Imaginative Sources for Shakespeare's Puck." *Shakespeare Quarterly* 36 (1985):65–68.

Observes that English folklore yields only the common noun form *pouk* (the Welch analogue is *pwyca*; the Irish, *pooka*), a knight with uncanny supernatural powers or an evil spirit. Shakespeare's idea to create the capital-letter individual spirit Puck may have come from the devil Pluck named by the confessed witch Alice Samuel in John Darrell's *Most Strange and Admirable Discovery of the Three Witches of Warboys* printed in 1593, two years before *A Midsummer Night's Dream*. To be sure, Shakespeare's Puck "is deeply imbued with dark conception of evil spirits" (p. 68); only Oberon refers to him as "gentle," and Shakespeare consciously plays against the older tradition in assuring the audience that he is "an honest Puck" (5.1.341).

987. SCHNEIDER, MICHAEL. "Bottom's Dream, the Lion's Roar, and Hostility of Class Difference in *A Midsummer Night's Dream*." University of Florida Department of Classics Comparative Drama Conference Papers, 7. In *From the Bard to Broadway*. Edited by Karelisa V. Hartigan. Lanham: University Press of America, 1987, pp. 191–212.

Studies the text for repressed signs of socio-political tension, specifically that of repressed class struggle. Repetitive word slips such as Bottom's "flowers of odious savors," considered laughable by the aristocrats, can be read as undercutting the seeming intent and obeisance of the mechanicals. Similarly, Quince's prologue, in fact, tells the aristocrats that the commoners offer intentionally to offend, that they come in spite, that true content is not their intent. In effect, the mechanicals "rule" the aristocracy in making them believe in their own superiority while actually telling them in a couched simplicity that the working class is not inferior.

988. WEINER, ANDREW D. " 'Multiformities Uniforme': *A Midsummer Night's Dream*." *ELH* 38 (1971):329–49.

Views the play as an ordered sequence of events by which to provoke emotional responses with the power to affect the will. As the scene shifts from city to wood, day to night, pragmatic to magical, the spectator moves "from joy to uncertainty to wonder and finally back to joy" (p. 340). In such a manner Shakespeare forces the audience to respond fully to the central theme—the mystery of God's grace in marriage, the culmination of the action in the union of the four sets of lovers who share a new perception of life's potential.

989. WELLER, BARRY. "Identity Dis-Figured: *A Midsummer Night's Dream*." *Kenyon Review* 7, no. 3 (1985):66–78.

Observes that the transforming power of theater depends upon the spectator's ability to distinguish between empirical reality and play. In *A Midsummer Night's Dream*, for example, characters exist primarily as metaphors and the fairies as tropes for both disruptive nature and the irrationality of love. Bottom's inability to distinguish between the literal and the figurative in his "rare vision" renders him immune to the transforming power of his experience. The other characters are dis-figured, through play undoing their fictive nature which "grows to something of great constancy in the mind and not the eye of the spectator" (p. 78).

990. WYRICK, DEBORAH BAKER. "The Ass Motif in *The Comedy of Errors* and *A Midsummer Night's Dream*." *Shakespeare Quarterly* 33 (1982):432–48.

Observes that the word *ass*, whether as simile, metaphor, or pun, frequently conveys connotations that radiate outward from speaker or hearer to subplot and to theme. *A Midsummer Night's Dream* provides the most striking example. Bottom, ass-headed, is a walking metaphor, the apotheosis of asininity; and his presence comments upon the interconnected themes of metamorphosis, imagination, and love. His hybrid nature (half-man/half-beast) symbolizes the basic pattern of the play— the Apollonian-Dionysian dialectic, Theseus's world representing the former and Oberon's the latter.

991. YOUNG DAVID P. *Something of Great Constancy: The Art of "A Midsummer Night's Dream."* New Haven and London: Yale University Press, 1966, 190 pp.

Views *A Midsummer Night's Dream* as a skillful synthesis of comic materials from courtly or coterie comedy and from popular comedy, as a structural blend of elements previously considered incompatible. The two worlds of the play—Theseus's orderly society and Oberon's confusing wilderness, with characters from each world discovering themselves temporarily lost in the fantastic one–correspond both to the moralities (the fall leading to reconciliation) and the romances (wandering in the grey-world leading to reunion in the green world).

992. ZITNER, S. P. "The Worlds of *A Midsummer Night's Dream*." *South Atlantic Quarterly* 59 (1960):397–403.

Identifies six different worlds in *A Midsummer Night's Dream* that coalesce to produce a comic inversion of the duties, responsibilities, and danger normally associated with them—the world of temporal power (Theseus and Hippolyta), the world of the lovers (Hermia, Helena, Lysander, Demetrius), the world of work (Bottom and his companions), the world of the fairies (Oberon and Titania), the world of illusion (the play within the play), and the world of nature (the elemental conditions). The interaction of these worlds recalls for the Elizabethans a delightful illusion of their rustic past.

MUCH ADO ABOUT NOTHING

Reference Work

993. MARDER, LOUIS, comp. *"Much Ado About Nothing": A Supplementary Bibliography 1899–1965*. The New Variorum Shakespeare. New York: American Scholar Publications, 1965, 19 pp.

Includes representative scholarship on *Much Ado About Nothing* from 1899 to 1965 and is intended to supplement H. H. Furness's Variorum edition of 1899. The material is categorized under reproductions of original folio editions, bibliographical sources, modern editions, and critical studies (arranged alphabetically). While not exhaustive, the material represents every major category of scholarship and criticism.

Editions

994. HUMPHREYS, A. R., ed. *Much Ado About Nothing*. The Arden Shakespeare. London and New York: Methuen, 1981, 237 pp.

Includes discussion of the publication, the date of composition, the significance of the title, the sources, the style, the stage history, the world of Messina, the form and structure, the text, and a critical resume.

Appendixes cover source analogues, the evolution of the style of wit, William Davenant's adaptation *The Law against Lovers*, the proxy wooings, and the songs. The text (with copious notes) is based on the first quarto (1600), for which the copy was apparently Shakespeare's foul papers.

995. MARES, F. H., ed. *Much Ado About Nothing*. The New Cambridge Shakespeare. Cambridge: Cambridge University Press, 1988, 162 pp.

Features an introductory essay on sources, the date of the play, stage history, and criticism. Extensive notes appear on individual pages of the text, and the appendixes include notes on the time scheme of the play, Lewis Carroll's letter to Ellen Terry, Benedick's song (5.2.18–22), and a list of suggested readings.

Criticism

996. ALLEN, JOHN A. "Dogberry." *Shakespeare Quarterly* 24 (1973):35–53.

Describes Dogberry as a comic Everyman in whom bland self-ignorance rules supreme. In his egotism he resembles Leonato, Don Pedro, and Claudio, whose pride blinds them to Borachio's villainy. He also parodies their excessive sense of self-esteem and reputation. His transformation into a vengeful fury at being called an ass parallels Leonato's all-too-tardy determination to defend Hero's wronged name. Dogberry is a comic deus ex machina who functions like Vincentio and Prospero as a moral philosopher and champion of justice.

997. BERGER, HARRY L. "Against the Sink-a-Pace: Sexual and Family Politics in *Much Ado About Nothing*." *Shakespeare Quarterly* 33 (1982):302–13.

Views *Much Ado About Nothing* as a play about two "wars," one between generations and one between genders. Hero, a male-dominated heroine, is a willing participant in the sexual politics of Messina, docile and submissive in her assumption that Don Pedro is to be her wooer and equally so when it turns out to be Claudio. Beatrice in this respect is her foil, continually mocking the norms of arranged marriage and parental authority that Hero has been trained to respect. The play celebrates the ending of bachelor happiness, the approach of the social tradition of marriage; as comedy it ends in the nick of time.

998. COOK, CAROL. " 'The Sign and Semblance of Her Honor': Reading Gender Difference in *Much Ado About Nothing*." *PMLA* 101 (1986):186–202.

Much Ado About Nothing

Argues that the play masks as well as expresses the mechanisms of power and that the explicit comic resolution is "something of an artful dodge" (p. 186). The persistent use of the cuckold joke among Messina's males reveals an anxiety about women's potential power over them. The society's repressed fear of the feminine is forced into the open by Don John's machinations. The play's ending engages in a ritual mode of comic closure that presents the fundamental structures of Messina's masculine ethos.

999. CRAIK, T. W. "Ado." *Scrutiny* 19 (1953):297–316.
Admits that there is some disharmony of tone in *Much Ado About Nothing* but challenges a critical misconception concerning acts 4–5. Virtually everyone condemns Claudio's cruelty and his public repudiation of Hero and proclaims the justice of Beatrice's vengeful move against Claudio. To the contrary, Claudio is exonerated both in that Don Pedro is also fooled and in that Don Pedro draws all censure upon himself; Friar Francis's plan establishes reason over passion. Beatrice's response, however correct about Hero's innocence, is mistaken about Claudio's guilt, and her mandate to Benedick to kill Claudio represents passion in ascendance over reason.

1000. CRICK, JOHN. "Much Ado About Nothing." *Use of English* 17 (1965):323–27.
Describes Messina as reflective of the shallowness, complacency, and inhumanity of a society that has turned upon itself in a stultifying manner. The evil in such a society lies, not in a cardboard villain like Don John, but within, in the "consuming egotism which expresses itself in a studied artificiality, and at times flippancy, of both language and attitude" (p. 227). Benedick and Beatrice, in their merry antagonisms and verbal bombardments, provide an outlet for the normal instincts that have been repressed in such an environment.

1001. EVERETT, BARBARA. *"Much Ado About Nothing."* *Critical Quarterly* 3 (1961):319–35.
Perceives *Much Ado About Nothing* as a less popular play than its predecessors in that it focuses on the mundane fact of life that men and women have different social planes, functions, loyalties, characters. It is the first play to treat the clash of these two worlds with a degree of seriousness and the first in which a woman dominates. The company of young bloods held together by a cheerful masculine solidarity is essentially displaced, a fact most clearly evident in Beatrice's mandate for Benedick to kill Claudio.

300

1002. GILBERT, ALLAN. "Two Margarets: The Composition of *Much Ado About Nothing.*" *Philological Quarterly* 41 (1962):61–71.

Proclaims that there are two Margarets in the play, the one of witty dialogue and unimportant to the plot, the other never on stage but essential to it. Shakespeare probably initially developed his plot and the role of the first Margaret from Bandello, later adding from *Orlando Furioso* or elsewhere the story of the disguised waiting woman. This latter function for simplicity's sake he gave to the Margaret of the former draft, but he failed to revise further and thus fully integrate the two. Thus arises the crux: why did Margaret not defend Hero against what she knows to be a false charge? If it is a flaw, it is bothersome only in the study, not in the theater.

1003. HOCKEY, DOROTHY C. "Notes, Notes, Forsooth. . . ." *Shakespeare Quarterly* 8 (1957):353–58.

Views *Much Ado About Nothing* as a dramatization of misnoting, a dramatized pun involving human frailty in observing, judging, and acting sensibly. The entire church scene, for example, turns on the idea that seeing is believing. Much is made also of the verbal pun on notes and noting or overhearing. To compound the confusion, Shakespeare places the principals behind masks. The Elizabethan pronunciation of "nothing" as "noting" reflects the centrality of this theme of misperception.

1004. HOROWITZ, DAVID. "Imagining the Real." In *Shakespeare: An Existential View.* New York: Hill & Wang, 1965, pp. 19–36.

Argues that *Much Ado About Nothing*, in its persistent pursuit of the question of appearances, reflects the multiplicity of human truth from an ontological perspective; that is, that phenomenal reality to any given individual is only what he apprehends. Reality is multiple and opalescent. The title of the play suggests the action that arises from different angles of seeing and understanding, whether at the level of Benedick and Beatrice in their wit combat, of Claudio in his manipulation by Don John, or Dogberry and Verges in their bumbling attempts to apply the law to villainy. Benedick and Beatrice, empowered by imagination, are ultimately able to move beyond appearances and to restore content to form.

1005. HOWARD, JEAN. "Renaissance Antitheatricality and the Politics of Gender and Rank in *Much Ado About Nothing.*" In *Shakespeare Reproduced: The Text in History and Ideology.* Edited by Jean Howard and Marion F. O'Connor. New York and London: Methuen, 1987, pp. 163–87.

Much Ado About Nothing

> Argues that *Much Ado About Nothing* in its theatrical practices deals with issues of patriarchal and hierarchical social order. For one thing, the success of Don John's trick depends on general male assumptions about women. For another, Dogberry and Verges operate virtually outside language and rationality; and for this reason these lower-class figures can solve society's problems without threatening its aristocratic power base. For yet another, Don Pedro's manipulation of Benedick and Beatrice reveals "how the investment of established authority in marriage is used to reproduce existing social relations (both gender and class relations) and to control threats to the social order" (p. 177).

1006. JENKINS, HAROLD. "The Ball Scene in *Much Ado About Nothing*." In *Shakespeare: Text, Language, Criticism: Essays in Honour of Marvin Spevack*. Edited by Bernard Fabian and Kurt Tetzeli von Rosador. Hildesheim and New York: Olms-Weidmann, 1987, pp. 98–117.

> Describes the ball scene (2.1) as a microcosm of the entire play. The couple who anticipate marriage is set off by a couple who scorn both marriage and one another. The arrangement of marriage is temporarily frustrated; the prospective groom despairs, believing his trust betrayed, but finally gains his bride. The dance symbolizes the play's larger actions with its disguisings and impersonations. Don Pedro is the matchmaker just as later he devises the stratagem to bring Benedick and Beatrice together; Don John is the matchbreaker who attempts both here and later to break off the affair.

1007. KING, WALTER N. "Much Ado About *Something*." *Shakespeare Quarterly* 15 (1964):143–55.

> Advocates the reading of *Much Ado About Nothing* as a comedy of manners, central to which is the critical inspection of a leisure class intellectually lethargic from long acceptance of an inherited social code. Shakespeare's two plot strands explore, more specifically, love and courtship as verbalized but not actually felt in such a society and the absurdity of elevating wit to the position of a primary value in life. The love that Benedick and Beatrice discover may be nothing, but it is the vital *something* that can give genuine meaning to a life otherwise stereotyped and impotent.

1008. LEWALSKI, BARBARA. "Love, Appearance and Reality: Much Ado About Something." *Studies in English Literature 1500–1900* 8 (1968):235–51.

> Argues that Bembo's Neoplatonic scale of love and knowledge provides a framework by which to gauge the development of Benedick

and Claudio. In moving from a position of love's scorner to one in which he perceives all excellencies in Beatrice, Benedick approximates movement through the ladder from the lowest rung involving mere physical attraction and the judgment of the senses to the highest involving an imaginative concept of love that transcends the physical and finds beauty in the mind's eye.

1009. McCOLLOM, WILLIAM C. "The Role of Wit in *Much Ado About Nothing*." *Shakespeare Quarterly* 19 (1968):165–74.

Asserts that the kind of wit a character possesses and the manner in which he employs it in *Much Ado About Nothing* are the means by which the audience comes to understand and judge him. Shakespeare employs four types of wit in the play—puns and quibbles, allusive understatement and sophistic logic, flights of fancy, and short parodies and burlesques. Generally, the theme is the triumph of true wit and harmless folly (Benedick, Beatrice, the friar) over false or pretentious "wisdom" (Don John, Don Pedro, Claudio, Leonato).

1010. McEACHERN, CLAIRE. "Fathering Herself: A Source Study of Shakespeare's Feminism." *Shakespeare Quarterly* 39 (1988):269–90.

Insists that a study of Shakespeare's use of sources finds him to be rewriting patriarchy, "resisting its conclusions, revealing its idealized images of fathers as fictions constructed against the complexities of human nature" (p. 290). Shakespeare, more specifically, questions the power of fathers that demands replication for the perpetuation of the patriarchal system. In *Much Ado About Nothing*, for example, Shakespeare's version of the slandered daughter is regulated not as in Bandello purely by public patriarchal concerns but by private and emotional ones as well. So, too, whereas *Leir* focuses on the question of political succession, *Lear* explores the consuming nature of patriarchy that the old king converts into "a tyrannical legislation of affective bonds" (p. 282).

1011. OSBORNE, LAURIE E. "Dramatic Play in *Much Ado About Nothing*: Wedding the Italian *Novella* and English Comedy." *Philological Quarterly* 69 (1990):167–88.

Claims that Shakespeare fashioned two plots from his source, the slandered maiden tale treated by both Ariosto and Bandello. In one, the story of Hero, he follows the traditional pattern of the Italian *novella*, but in the other, his own creation of the courtship of Benedick and Beatrice, he refashions the main plot according to comic principles. In doing so, he illustrates the utter dependence of the comic on the anti-comic. The closure can be perceived in three ways—through Dogberry's benevolent ineptitude, through the friar's production of Hero's death to reveal Claudius' true emotions, and through Leonato's insistence on expiation as a prerequisite for comic union.

1012. PAGE, NADINE. "The Public Repudiation of Hero." *PMLA* 50 (1935):739–44.

Argues that the repudiation of Hero at the altar is not morbid and distasteful but a reflection of Elizabethan social concepts and actualities. Woman was considered inferior to man intellectually and physically. The prevailing masculine attitude toward marriage was that it should be avoided as potentially destructive (Benedick) or that it should bring a wife with chaste reputation and a generous dowry (Claudio). Claudio's reaction was traditional, and Shakespeare carefully stresses the devices by which he later could be convinced of her innocence.

1013. PROUTY, CHARLES T. *The Sources of "Much Ado About Nothing": A Critical Study, Together with the Text of Peter Beverley's "Ariodanto and Ieneura."* New Haven and London: Yale University Press, 1950, 142 pp.

Maintains that Shakespeare's dramatic intentions can be determined by close examination of his modifications of his sources. Instead of the traditional romantic wooers, Claudio and Hero are realistic lovers following the way of the world with marriages arranged by parents or patrons. By adding Benedick and Beatrice, who search for emotion that is real, Shakespeare underscores his reaction against such social tradition. Through eavesdropping in both plots he achieves a unity of tone to match the unity of theme.

1014. ROBERTS, JEANNE ADDISON. "Strategies of Delay in Shakespeare: What the Much Ado Is Really About." *Renaissance Papers* (1987):95–102.

Insists that the true argument of comedy is not so much a movement toward sexual consummation as it is the elaboration of strategies to delay such closure. Typical strategies are parental opposition, death and threat of death, plays, games, and, above all, multiplication of lovers. In the case of *Much Ado About Nothing* the delay serves to integrate elements of Benedick's character through his association with and observance of other males, the youth and vulnerability of Claudio, the more sedate and parental Don Pedro, the villainous Don John, Dogberry's love of language. Once these aspects are properly united in Benedick, only a dance stands between him and matrimony.

1015. ROSE, STEPHEN. "Love and Self-Love in *Much Ado About Nothing*." *Essays in Criticism* 20 (1970):143–50.

Observes that the manner in which Claudio and Benedick respond to romantic hearsay is a measure of pride in one and essential humility in the other. Hearsay is at the narrative center of the play. It is what Hero is wooed by, what provokes suspicion in Claudio, what brings Benedick and Beatrice together, and what plays out and resolves the plot in the watch's overhearing the scheme against Hero and Benedick and Beatrice's overhearing their own stolen love poetry. Claudio's ready assumption of Hero's guilt reveals the very element of self-love that Benedick and Beatrice are able to repudiate in their declaration of love.

1016. STOREY, GRAHAM. "The Success of *Much Ado About Nothing.*" In *More Talking of Shakespeare.* Edited by John Garrett. London: Longmans, Green; New York: Theatre Arts Books, 1959, pp. 128–43.

Notes that, while some twentieth-century critics complain of an incongruous mixture of comedy, tragedy, and farce, Shakespeare's contemporaries viewed *Much Ado About Nothing* as an exciting Italianate melodrama enlivened by two variegated sets of humors in the wit combat of Benedick and Beatrice and the mental intoxication of Dogberry. Any attempt to force a concept of naturalistic realism upon the characters destroys the comedy, which finds its center not in character but in the theme of deception, miscomprehension, and man's "giddiness" at every level of society. The play's deliberate theatricality firmly establishes its comic perspective.

1017. WAIN, JOHN. "The Shakespearean Lie-Detector: Thoughts on *Much Ado About Nothing.*" *Critical Quarterly* 9 (1967):27–42.

Considers the play to be a brilliant failure in that Shakespeare is bored with the Hero-Claudio plot and thus is unable to give that strand of action consistent artistic attention. Shakespeare is at the point in his career at which he begins to develop three-dimensional characters, a quality evident in the dynamic figures of Benedick and Beatrice. On the other hand, the narrative requires a melodramatic Claudio who quickly falls victim to hearsay, deserts and denounces his bride at the altar, and shockingly agrees to a second marriage with wife unseen. Shakespeare finds himself creatively at odds with characters utterly devoid of psychological realism.

1018. WEY, JAMES J. " 'To Grace Harmony': Musical Design in *Much Ado About Nothing.*" *Boston University Studies in English* 4 (1960):181–88.

Discusses the manner in which actual onstage music and allusions to musical properties in the dialogue are incorporated thematically into the play's circle of meaning. Both music and musical allusions occur at moments of harmony and happiness in the action; conversely, they disappear at moments of disharmony and social disruption, even in the wooing scene itself. In the final movement the action swells to harmony through Benedick's love lament without accompaniment, Claudio's mournful dirge, and the full burst of pipers.

THE TAMING OF THE SHREW

Editions

1019. MORRIS, BRIAN, ed. *The Taming of the Shrew*. The Arden Shakespeare. London and New York: Methuen, 1981, 316 pp.

Includes discussion of the text, *The Shrew* compared to *A Shrew*, the date of composition, the authorship and sources, and the play itself (the stage history and adaptations). Appendixes cover the evidence to establish the relationship between *A Shrew* and *The Shrew*, the Sly scenes in *A Shrew*, and sources and analogues. The text, with copious notes, is based on the First Folio.

1020. OLIVER, H. J., ed. *The Taming of the Shrew*. The Oxford Shakespeare. Oxford and New York: Oxford University Press, 1982, 254 pp.

Includes an introductory essay on the folio text, the quarto text of *The Taming of a Shrew*, the relation of the two texts, the story of Christopher Sly, the Bianca subplot and the *Supposes*, Katherine and Petruchio, the style, and the play on stage. Extensive notes on each page of the text identify problems of language and provide background information. An appendix reprints the Christopher Sly scenes from *A Shrew* and discusses the song of 4.1.36.

1021. THOMPSON, ANN, ed. *The Taming of the Shrew*. The New Cambridge Shakespeare. Cambridge: Cambridge University Press, 1984, 190 pp.

Features an introductory essay on the date and theatrical context, *The Shrew* in the context of Shakespeare's work, sources, stage history, and critical approaches. Particular attention is addressed to the relationship of Shakespeare's play (especially the Sly scenes) to the anonymous *The Taming of a Shrew*, also to the fluctuating fortunes of the comedy in light of the evolution of feminist concerns. Extensive notes appear on individual pages of the text, addressing difficulties of language and providing background information. A list of suggested readings is appended.

Criticism

1022. ALEXANDER, PETER. "The Original Ending of *The Taming of the Shrew*." *Shakespeare Quarterly* 20 (1969):111–16.

Argues that the original ending of Shakespeare's play is not that found in the First Folio (spotlighting an obedient Katherine) but that of the 1594 quarto of *The Taming of a Shrew* (featuring a drunken Sly who prepares to go home, convinced that he now knows how to handle his shrewish wife). The quarto, pirated from Shakespeare's play, retains the final scene of what in *The Shrew* had been deleted by 1623. The importance of the scene is that those who have been carried away by Petruchio's triumph are returned to reality by the realization of what awaits Sly at home.

1023. BAUMLIN, TITA FRENCH. "Petruchio the Sophist and Language as Creation in *The Taming of the Shrew*." *Studies in English Literature 1500–1900* 29 (1989):237–57.

Views Petruchio as "a paradigm of the sophist rhetorician with a most successful and morally admirable stance" (p. 237), one who uses rhetoric to create for Kate a "new Reality" grounded in play, self-respect, and love. His goal is not material gain or masculine mastery but marital harmony. Their kiss is a symbol of compatibility, and the final scene displays Kate's newfound ability to use language for healing and edification, as therapy for the others.

1024. BOOSE, LYNDA E. "Scolding Brides and Bridling Scolds." *Shakespeare Quarterly* 42 (1991):179–213.

Asserts that the play registers both "women's abjected position in the social order of early modern England and the costs exacted for resistance" (p. 179). History yields records of numerous forms of punishment of the female during this time. Kate's final speech by "unspeaking" her rebellion repositions the female as subordinate. The female tongue, if it becomes unruly, "situates female speech as a symbolic relocation of the male organ, an unlawful appropriation of phallic authority in which the symbolics of male castration are ominously complicit" (p. 204).

1025. DUTHIE, GEORGE IAN. "*The Taming of a Shrew* and *The Taming of the Shrew*." *Review of English Studies* 19 (1943):337–56.

Analyzes the three major theories concerning the relationship of the anonymous *A Shrew* and Shakespeare's *The Shrew*—that the first is a source of the second, that the first is based on the second, that the two

The Taming of the Shrew

derive from a common source. Evidence suggests that *A Shrew* is memorially dependent on *The Shrew* as it stood in earlier form. The later revision of *A Shrew*, primarily in the full development of the subplot, resulted in *The Shrew* as we now have it. The main plot is almost entirely Shakespeare's work.

1026. FINEMAN, JOEL. "The Turn of the Shrew." In *Shakespeare and the Question of Theory*. Edited by Patricia Parker and Geoffrey Hartman. New York: Methuen, 1985, pp. 138–55.

Insists that the words and action of the play depict a battle between two types of language—"the determinate, literal language traditionally spoken by man and the figurative, indeterminate language traditionally spoken by woman" (p. 143). Petruchio uses "female" language to domesticate his wife, language that is erotic, enigmatic, scolding, excessive, and incessant; his plan is to overwhelm her with "hysterical tit for hysterical tat" (p. 143). The irony is that the play calls forth a closure it cannot produce; at the moment Kate is tamed, the subversive language of woman resurfaces in both Bianca and the widow.

1027. GREENFIELD, THELMA N. "The Transformation of Christopher Sly." *Philological Quarterly* 33 (1954):34–42.

Notes the multiple levels of dramatic irony operating in a production of *The Taming of the Shrew* as a play about Petruchio and Katherine on a public stage pretending to be the hall of a great house pretending to be performed for a drunken slob of whom it is pretended that he is a nobleman. The Sly material of the Induction has an organic relationship to the shrew story. In dropping the emphasis of *A Shrew*, in which Sly indicates that he has found the moral of the story for a married man, Shakespeare makes the Induction more than a farcical setting for a farce; it becomes part of a subtle comic juxtaposition of two contrasting worlds, the real and the imaginative.

1028. HOUK, RAYMOND A. "The Evolution of *The Taming of the Shrew*." *PMLA* 57 (1942):1009–38.

Asserts that both *The Taming of a Shrew* and *The Taming of the Shrew* derive from the same source. This earlier play had interludes and an epilogue, but no rival elopement or shortened chronology. Shakespeare's *The Shrew* makes full and direct use of Ariosto's *I Suppositi* in developing the rivalry for Bianca's hand, and this material in turn forces a shortening of the chronology of the latter part of the play. The earlier form may have been either a completed play or a set of sketches. If the former, *A Shrew* is probably a bad quarto. Shakespeare may possibly have authored this hypothetical common source.

1029. HUSTON, J. DENNIS. " 'To Make a Puppet': Play and Play-Making in *The Taming of the Shrew.*" *Shakespeare Studies* 9 (1967):73–88.

Asserts that Shakespeare, by thwarting our expectations with a series of false starts (the drunken Sly, the lord's practice through a troupe of players, Lucentio's pursuit of knowledge), jolts us into a fresh response to the theatrical experience of Kate's "Taming." She, like the audience, is transformed by a series of shocks, with Petruchio responding to each situation in a manner diametrically opposite to her expectations. Petruchio makes a puppet of her (as she claims), but it is so that she might lose her "woodenness of response."

1030. KEHLER, DOROTHEA. "Echoes of the Induction in *The Taming of the Shrew.*" *Renaissance Papers* (1986):31–42.

Questions how women in Shakespeare's audience would have reacted to the transparently obvious patriarchal assumptions at the core of *The Taming of the Shrew* and suggests that the play encodes a subversive subtext more reflective of the genuine sentiments of such viewers. The subtext is broached in the Induction when Sly's "page-wife" proves so attractive to him because of her humility and obedience. Similarly, Kate is acceptable to Petruchio only after she submits to him without response even though she has proven to be every bit his intellectual equal.

1031. NEWMAN, KAREN. "Renaissance Family Politics and Shakespeare's *The Taming of the Shrew.*" *English Literary Renaissance* 16 (1986):86–100.

Views the play as a theatrical realization of the tensions of the Elizabethan age concerning women who are rebellious in either deed or language. That patriarchal order was divinely ordained was emphasized in homilies and handbooks of behavior. The "tamed" Kate and the silent Bianca ostensibly capitulate to these constraints of behavior. Yet Kate, through sexual punning, maintains a kind of masculine exuberance while masquerading as an obedient wife, and, by insisting on having the last word, she contradicts the very sentiment she speaks.

1032. ROBERTS, JEANNE ADDISON. "Horses and Hermaphrodites: Metamorphoses in *The Taming of the Shrew.*" *Shakespeare Quarterly* 34 (1983):159–71.

Suggests that the Ovidian concept of metamorphosis underlies the surface of *The Taming of the Shrew* and helps to provide a subtle interaction of human and natural worlds. Whereas in Ovid people turn into animals, in Shakespeare's play metaphoric animals are turned into people. Sly is through allusion changed from a swinish beast into a happy and wealthy lord and husband. More important, Kate and Petruchio move through a series of animal metaphors before finding full human identity in marriage; especially significant is their development in the progressive image of the horse.

1033. SERONSY, CECIL C. " 'Supposes' as the Unifying Theme in *The Taming of the Shrew.*" *Shakespeare Quarterly* 14 (1963):15–30.

Maintains that the unity of *The Taming of the Shrew* involves far more than the mere fitting together of triple plots and that the subplot (the "supposes" plot) provides the material by which the organic inter-action is achieved in its theme of the suppositions or expectations con-cerning love. All three plots involve the interplay of love and illusion. In the Induction Sly's desire for his "boy wife" is pure illusion; in the sub-plot love is little more than infatuation; the shrew plot holds the possi-bility of happy wedded love because the love has grown from within.

1034. SLIGHTS, CAMILLE WELLS. "The Raw and the Cooked in *The Taming of the Shrew.*" *Journal of English and Germanic Philology* 88 (1989):168–89.

Suggests that Shakespeare in the play is less interested in the proper distribution between man and woman than he is in "exploring the comedy inherent in the human desire for both individual freedom and fulfillment as a social being" (p. 169), the contrast between civilized and uncivilized behavior. The Induction, more precisely, establishes a contrast between the cultivated and the brutish, and the contrast con-tinues with variations in the relationship of Petruchio and Kate. By transforming a shrew story about mastery into a process of domestica-tion, Shakespeare "manages to satirize the absurdities of social conven-tions while simultaneously celebrating the human capacity to shape society to express individual values" (p. 189).

1035. SOKOL, B. J. "A Spenserian Idea in *The Taming of the Shrew.*" *English Studies* 66 (1985):310–16.

Claims that evidence of language in Shakespeare's play indicates his close familiarity with *The Faerie Queene* and makes more likely the fact that Shakespeare in the relationship between Petruchio and Kate is mirroring the Spenserian concept that true temperance is the transcen-dence of dualism, the marriage of matter and spirit. The main plot is a kind of battle between Spenserian extremes. For the two characters, their "Prince Arthur, the source of their grace, is the *inter alia,* far from farcical, love that grows between them" (p. 315).

1036. STETNER, S. C. V. "Baptista and His Daughters." *Psychoanalytic Review* 60 (1973):223–38.

Maintains that Baptista is a recurring figure in Shakespeare's com-edies, the father who, ostensibly willing to allow his daughter's marriage, places obstacles in her way because of unacknowledged incestuous feelings. Variations on such a character occur in Antiochus in *Pericles*, Portia's dead father in *The Merchant of Venice*, the Duke of Milan in *The Two Gentlemen of Verona*, and Egeus in *A Midsummer Night's Dream*. Typically the father does not recognize his incestuous proclivities, and he is eventually reconciled with his son-in-law.

1037. WELLS, STANLEY. *"The Taming of the Shrew* and *King Lear*: A Structural Comparison." *Shakespeare Survey* 36 (1980):55–66.

Asserts that Shakespeare in writing a play must have been alert to both the complementary and opposing functions of the mind and the body in the layout of the overall narrative design, the characterizations, and the sentiments. In *The Taming of the Shrew* Petruchio determines to use his mind to suppress Kate, just as mind has confused Sly in the Induction. The taming of Kate involves both her mind and her body. The process serves to bring her to full realization of herself as a woman. Lear's mental process, though far more complex and tragic, is structurally similar.

TROILUS AND CRESSIDA

Reference Work

1038. TANNENBAUM, SAMUEL A., and TANNENBAUM, DOROTHY R., comps. *William Shakespeare: "Troilus and Cressida."* Elizabethan Bibliographies, 29. New York: Privately printed, 1943, 44 pp.

Cites 919 unannotated items covering major scholarship on *Troilus and Cressida* from the beginning to 1941. The material is divided by the following categories and is arranged alphabetically by section—editions, adaptations, abstracts, translations, theatrical history, commentary, bibliography, addenda. The majority of the material (669 items) is loosely classified under commentary.

Editions

1039. HILLEBRAND, HAROLD N., ed. *Troilus and Cressida*. A New Variorum Edition of Shakespeare. Philadelphia and London: J. B. Lippincott, 1953, 613 pp.

Uses the First Folio as the copy text. On each page, for that portion of the text, are provided variant readings, textual notes, and general critical commentary. Following the text are sections, citing varying critical opinions, on the printing of the two quartos and the folio; the early stage history; the date; authorship; *Troilus* and contemporary affairs; sources; structural analysis; *Troilus* on the modern stage; the individual characters; and a list of works consulted.

1040. MUIR, KENNETH, ed. *Troilus and Cressida*. The Oxford Shakespeare. Oxford and New York: Oxford University Press, 1982, 214 pp.

Includes an introductory essay addressing the text, the date, stage history, sources, and interpretation. Extensive notes on each page of the text identify specific problems of language and also provide background information. An appendix reprints the quarto epistle and describes alterations to the lineation.

1041. PALMER, KENNETH, ed. *Troilus and Cressida*. The Arden Shakespeare. London and New York: Methuen, 1982, 337 pp.

Includes discussion of the text, the date, sources, and the play itself (crucial scenes, time and time's subjects, treason and prophecy, identity and attributes, pride and envy, styles and methods) as well as appendices covering disturbances in sheet F in the First Folio, the possibility of the play's being written for a performance at one of the inns of court, a discussion of degree, and selections from the source materials. This edition is eclectic, based primarily on the first quarto (1609) but with readings also from the folio. *Troilus and Cressida* is, quite frankly, a generic anomaly—at once comedy, tragedy, satire, tragic farce. The men, while they await engagement in battle, question and argue; and it is the form of those questions that gives the play its peculiar dramatic idiom.

1042. WALKER, ALICE, ed. *Troilus and Cressida*. Cambridge: Cambridge University Press, 1957, 254 pp.

Provides extensive textual notes, a critical introduction (covering discussion of the generic confusion, Shakespeare and the Troy story, the audience, the satire, the integrity of the play, the date, and the sources), a discussion of the copy text, a section on stage history, and a glossary. This edition is eclectic, based primarily on the folio but with quarto readings allowed.

Criticism

1043. ADELMAN, JANET. " 'This Is and Is Not Cressid': The Characterization of Cressida." In *The (M)other Tongue: Essays in Feminist Psychoanalytic*

Interpretation. Edited by Shirley Nelson Garner, Claire Kahane, and Madelon Sprengnether. Ithaca and London: Cornell University Press, 1985, pp. 119–41.

Maintains that, when Troilus responds to Cressida with Diomed by proclaiming that it is not she, we regard him as near psychotic in his denial of reality, but that to some degree we as well are caught up in the psychosis because of a radical inconsistency in her characterization. Early in the play we are impressed with Cressida as a whole person, keenly aware that the world values something not for its intrinsic worth but for its market value. By the time she is transferred to the Greek camp, however, we see her only from the outside, as a stereotypical wanton, as a devalued object, and thus we too feel betrayed; not privileged, as earlier, to know her motives, we sense a radical loss of psychological character consistency.

1044. BAREFOOT, C. C. "*Troilus and Cressida*: 'Praise Us as We Are Tasted.' " *Shakespeare Quarterly* 39 (1988):45–57.

Argues that *Troilus and Cressida* depicts the instability of character, reputation, and indeed of truth itself. The imagery and action throughout the play remind us that "matters of life and death frequently hinge on what is perceived to be the market value of the person or the object that is being sought or sold or assessed in terms of a community price" (p. 48), whether Helen in her abduction by Paris, Achilles in his abstaining from battle to gain Polyxena's favor, Antenor as barter for Cressida, or Hector as chivalric honor betrayed. Ultimately we trade in selves as in words, and literature is perceived as inevitably both a transmitter and a transmuter of value and truth.

1045. BAYLEY, JOHN. "Time and the Trojans." *Essays in Criticism* 25 (1975):55–73.

Speaks of Shakespeare's ability to provoke a sense of compressed time that we bring to the play—our entire range of accumulated impressions of a character, his culture, and that which has made him what he is—as the playwright's most singular achievement. Anomalously, *Troilus and Cressida*, by disregarding the beginning and the ending of the war, creates an intensity of focus upon the present. The nightmarish world of the present is given no meaning by a context of time. Thersites speaks for the play in a kind of Brechtian way.

1046. CAMPBELL, OSCAR JAMES. *Comicall Satyre and Shakespeare's "Troilus and Cressida."* San Marino: Huntington Library, 1938, 246 pp.

Establishes a direct relationship between *Troilus and Cressida* and Jonson's "comicall satyres," by which comedy is converted into dramatic satire "devoted to the denunciation, exposure, or derision of some kind of folly and abuse" (p. viii). Probably written for a private audience at one of the inns of court, *Troilus* pictures social disintegration by combining the excoriation of sexual indulgence with the derisive delineation of the Homeric heroes. Both Thersites as railer and Pandarus as leering pimp function as choric figures to direct the spectators' caustic laughter, which in turn reflects a kind of moral enlightenment.

1047. CHARNES, LINDA. " 'So Unsecret to Ourselves': Notorious Identity and the Material Subject in *Troilus and Cressida*." *Shakespeare Quarterly* 40 (1989):413–40.

Insists that the power of the play stems from its very deformity as a play with neurotic characters that calls attention to its monstrosity at every turn. Specifically, Shakespeare here investigates the deeply conflicted relationship between absolutist and coercive forms and the fantasy of self-authored subjectivity. An ideology must be constructed to drive the story to completion and the characters to the fulfillment of their legendary status. The desire for Helen is such an ideology, underwriting the "actions that enable the male heroes . . . to generate reputations and renown among themselves" (p. 437).

1048. FIELDLER, LESLIE. "Shakespeare's Commodity-Comedy: A Meditation on the Preface to the 1609 Quarto of *Troilus and Cressida*." In *Shakespeare's "Rough Magic": Renaissance Essays in Honor of C. L. Barber*. Edited by Peter Erickson and Coppélia Kahn. Newark: University of Delaware Press; London and Toronto: Associated University Presses, 1985, pp. 50–60.

Maintains that Shakespeare himself authored the Preface to the first quarto and that it represents his frustrations concerning traditional forms of comedy and the audiences to whom they catered. Throughout his career he exploits the hackneyed forms of New Comedy with its "boy-gets-girl ending," pastoral comedy with its "cliche contrast of the Green World with Grey," and romance with its predictable lost child, sea storm, and long-delayed reunion (p. 57). Enough of a businessman to recognize that his plays were commodities, it was only in this Preface that he encoded his conviction that ordinary theatergoers deserved something better.

1049. GIRARD, RENÉ. "The Politics of Desire in *Troilus and Cressida*." In *Shakespeare and the Question of Theory*. Edited by Patricia Parker and Geoffrey Hartman. New York and London: Methuen, 1985, pp. 188–209.

Insists that the intensity and durability of a man's desire for a woman will prove inversely proportional to her willingness to satisfy it. While Troilus, in one sense, becomes indifferent to Cressida after she has succumbed to him, he fiercely desires her again when the Greeks are to possess her through an exchange for Antenor. Pandarus uses similar psychology in firing Cressida's initial interest in Troilus, dangling before her the bait of a Helen madly in love with the young Trojan. In such fashion, also, Ulysses attempts to prod the proud Achilles into military action by insinuating that Ajax has subsumed his image of the most valiant of the Greek warriors.

1050. GREENE, GAYLE. "Language and Value in Shakespeare's *Troilus and Cressida*." *Studies in English Literature 1500–1900* 21 (1982):271–85.
Calls attention to Ulysses's prophecy that in a world in anarchy the meaning of right and wrong in action and in word will be lost. Just such a situation has come to pass in the play's culminating action when Troilus perceives Cressida's vows to be meaningless and words to have become mere words without designation. While Ulysses sees the dissolution of language as consequence and Troilus as cause, they both believe that the validity of verbal communication depends upon a knowable reality. *Troilus and Cressida* reflects not only the crisis of values in the late Renaissance but also the linguistic revolution that it was precipitating.

1051. HOOKER, DEBORAH. "Coming to Cressida through Irigaray." *South Atlantic Quarterly* 88 (1989):899–932.
Argues that critical preoccupation with Cressida's sexual transgression has largely masked the fact that such figures as Troilus, Hector, and Ulysses are deeply implicated as well. To denigrate Cressida alone in the face of such flaws in male characters is to reveal the misogynist tradition that has informed readings of the love plot and to suggest "a certain phallogocentric bias at work in determining the philosophical parameters of honor and value debated in the play" (p. 900). For the modern reader who comes to her through Luce Irigaray's work, Cressida is a heroine "who outmaneuvers her own knowledge about her textual and literary damnation" (p. 929).

1052. KAUFMANN, R. J. " 'Ceremonies for Chaos': The Status of *Troilus and Cressida*." *ELH* 32 (1965):139–57.
Notes that great drama is philosophical in the sense that it constructs a dialectic for testing the utility and integrity of inherited, communal illusions. *Troilus and Cressida* is a play about competing modes of knowing, and the final view, instead of upholding any single mode, is

pluralistic. The organizing theme is the self-consuming nature of all forms called vice or virtue by one scale of value or another. It fails to provide a secure vantage from which to evaluate the action, whereas high tragedy focuses on the emotional cost of specific commitment.

1053. KAULA, DAVID. "Will and Reason in *Troilus and Cressida.*" *Shakespeare Quarterly* 10 (1961):272–76.

Speaks of Troilus as someone between a sensualist and an idealist. He appears to be moved by two wills, sexual passion and rational choice, and the word *will* as used in the play vacillates between these two senses. The religious quality of his imagery reveals his tendency to elevate his position of the moment to sacred and inviolable terms. This tendency to deification is fatal for him because it renders him incapable of dealing in war or sex with contingencies inherent in the human condition.

1054. KIMBROUGH, ROBERT. *Shakespeare's "Troilus and Cressida" and Its Setting.* Cambridge, Mass.: Harvard University Press, 1964, 208 pp.

Views *Troilus and Cressida* as Shakespeare's not wholly successful attempt to combine elements of the new drama of the private theaters with characteristics of popular drama as a means of offsetting the competition with the newly established chorister companies. Following a consideration of how the Trojan story would appear to an Elizabethan playwright, the study compares its major areas (the love story, the war as viewed from the opposing sides) to analogous aspects of the preceding Shakespeare canon. If the result is not cohesive, in part because of the attempt at inclusiveness of perspective, there are a dazzling variety of characters and a medley of profound themes.

1055. LYNCH, STEPHEN J. "The Idealism of Shakespeare's Troilus." *South Atlantic Review* 51 (1986):19–29.

Suggests that, while Troilus appears extraordinarily idealistic, he, in fact, is driven by "an egotism in a love affair pursued primarily for self-gratification" (p. 19). Caught up in a delusion of sanctity, simplicity, and truth, he during their parting scene seems totally oblivious to the fact that he is planting the seeds of suspicion in Cressida's mind. Later, in his profound anguish he struggles to sustain his pride through a vow of revenge first against Diomed for seducing Cressida and later against Achilles for murdering Hector. The bleak closure depicts a Troilus with no moment of penetrating self-analysis; he sees corruption everywhere but in himself.

1056. McALINDON, THOMAS. "Language, Style, and Meaning in *Troilus and Cressida.*" *PMLA* 84 (1969):29–41.

Views the disappointingly anticlimactic nature of the duel between Hector and Ajax (4.5), in which Hector's bombast and Latinized diction and neologisms appear utterly out of character, as a key to understanding the play as a whole. Throughout the action Shakespeare employs elements of stylistic dissonance to undermine the heroic and romantic characters, violations of decorum that reflect the graver maladies afflicting them. The aubade, for example, is evoked only to be degraded on the morning of the lovers' parting. Oaths and vows are spoken in one scene only to be broken in the next.

1057. MORRIS, BRIAN. "The Tragic Structure of *Troilus and Cressida*." *Shakespeare Quarterly* 10 (1959):481–91.

Observes that the failure to conform to traditional modes of tragedy has led *Troilus and Cressida* to be labeled some form of comedy. Shakespeare uses two relatively static plots to balance the climactic construction of the play; the monolithic war story forms the backdrop for a series of scenes revealing various stages of the love story. The conflict of honor and reason is focused on Troilus, whose passionate nature betrays him as surely as does Othello's. The peculiar tragic effect results from the use in the climactic scene of the comic device of multiple levels of perception—Diomedes and Cressida, Troilus and Ulysses, and Thersites.

1058. MUIR, KENNETH. "*Troilus and Cressida*." *Shakespeare Survey* 8 (1955):28–39.

Compares Shakespeare's delineation of Troy in *The Rape of Lucrece* and *Troilus and Cressida*. In both Shakespeare is sympathetic to the Trojans and critical of the Greeks, but in the latter both sides are presented more critically. Troilus is as unwise in idealizing Helen as in idealizing Cressida; his love is thwarted both by Cressida's wantonness and his environment. Hector is doomed in his failure to realize that the age of chivalry is dead. In general, the play deals with the foolishness of both war and love for unworthy purposes, an exposure of idealism from multiple perspectives.

1059. NOWOTTNY, WINIFRED M. T. " 'Opinion' and 'Value' in *Troilus and Cressida*." *Essays in Criticism* 4 (1954):282–96.

Views Ulysses, in his ability to preserve social stability among individuals intent on self-gratification, and Troilus, who espouses the view that a thing is valuable only as it is valued by others, as the polar thematic opposites in *Troilus and Cressida*. The idea is central both to the Trojan debate, in which Troilus argues the relative worth of Helen, and to the Greek debate, in which Ulysses argues that only fixed law prevents the collapse of society. The play is acted out against the back-drop of this antithesis between two worldviews, that of the statesman and that of the individual creative imagination.

1060. PRESSON, ROBERT K. *Shakespeare's "Troilus and Cressida" and the Legends of Troy*. Madison: University of Wisconsin Press, 1953, 165 pp.

Notes the continued popularity of the Troy legend in the reign of Elizabeth, but especially the intense interest that developed between 1598 and 1602 when a new interpretation was placed upon the material. Shakespeare drew his narrative from a variety of sources, in large part from Chapman's *Iliad*—for the characterization, the narrative flavor—but also from the *Recuyell*, Lydgate, and Chaucer. The theme is the destructive quality of passion: in Achilles, pride; in Hector, love of personal fame and glory; in Troilus, infatuation. It is reductionistic to call this "gateway to the later tragedies" (p. 142) a problem play, a dark comedy, or a comical satire.

1061. RABKIN, NORMAN. *"Troilus and Cressida*: The Uses of a Double Plot." *Shakespeare Studies* 1 (1965):265–82.

Maintains that a successful interpretation of *Troilus and Cressida* must come to grips with the underlying idea that relates its several discrete elements, the relationship between theme and plot. The play, more specifically, illustrates a double-plot structure (the affair between Troilus and Cressida and the Greek ruse to renew Achilles's participation in the Trojan War) to convey a complex theme implicitly through action and ironic language. As a symphonist sets theme against theme before resolving them in a stasis, so Shakespeare by developing the two plot strands forces upon us the theme of man's value and its relationship to time.

1062. RICHARDS, I. A. *"Troilus and Cressida* and Plato." *Hudson Review* 1 (1948):362–76.

Observes that *Troilus and Cressida* is not without power and that it in many ways reflects Plato at his height. Troilus is a young man who in the course of the play must confront his own mad idolatry, must watch the division within himself of will and reason. When he describes the gods as so angry that they will take Cressida from him, the reference is to Lachesis in *The Republic*, who sees to it that mortals reap the rewards of their choices. In more general terms, the central thought of the play accords closely with Plato.

1063. ROLLINS, HYDER E. "The Troilus-Cressida Story from Chaucer to Shakespeare." *PMLA* 32 (1917):383–429.

Notes that Shakespeare found the characters and incidents of the Troilus-Cressida legend far degraded from the Chaucerian treatment. The story is traced through Lydgate, Caxton's *Recuyell*, Elderton, Turberville, and Gascoigne. In Robert Henryson's *Testament of Creseyde* (1532), Creseyde is regarded as a wanton who ends in misery, struck down at the height of her folly by retribution. Subsequent authors (Howell, Whetstone Thomson, Heywood) follow Henryson in firmly establishing this literary tradition.

1064. SCHWARTZ, ELIAS. "Tonal Equivocation and the Meaning of *Troilus and Cressida*." *Studies in Philology* 69 (1972):304–19.

Maintains that disagreement concerning the theme of *Troilus and Cressida* stems from an intentional ambiguity as the tone changes abruptly from mock heroic to bathetic to farcical to pathetic to brutally satiric to near tragic. The result is a generic mixture envisioning the world as a meaningless chaos to which the characters (and the spectators) respond in various ways. Each in his own way attempts to create value where no value does or can exist; each realizes that time one day will end all.

1065. SOELLNER, ROLF. "Prudence and the Price of Helen: The Debate of the Trojans in *Troilus and Cressida*." *Shakespeare Quarterly* 20 (1969):255–63.

Maintains that the Trojan debate is of central significance to the theme of *Troilus and Cressida* and that the philosophic dialectic of the scene is not borrowed from Caxton or Lydgate but is original with Shakespeare. The voice of passion is pitted against the voice of prudence; Helena is only nominally the subject in a debate centering on the relevance of traditional morality. Hector argues from a traditional philosophic position, while Troilus reveals both contempt for reason and a skepticism that sees all values as subjective. Shakespeare uses the haunting figure of Cassandra to point up man's inability to foresee the tragic consequences of action based on passion.

1066. STEIN, ARNOLD. "*Troilus and Cressida*: The Disjunctive Imagination." *ELH* 36 (1969):147–67.

Describes Pandarus's cynical view of love in the opening scene of *Troilus and Cressida* as a countervoice that prevails over Troilus's exclamations. The second scene reinforces this mood in Cressida's lack of refinement in her conversation with Pandarus and her outright admission of fashionable reluctance aimed primarily at intensification of Troilus's lust. Similarly, the Greeks debate the grand mechanism of war but avoid mention of the rotten core of Helen that has produced it. The play engages our minds but deliberately keeps our sympathies at a

Troilus and Cressida

distance, thereby becoming "a dramatic form of the disjunctive imagination deploying mutually exclusive alternatives" (p. 167).

1067. STILLER, NIKKI. *The Figure of Cressida in British and American Literature: Transformation of a Literary Type.* Lewiston: Edwin Mellen Press, 1990, 193 pp.

Traces the character of Cressida from Boccaccio, to Chaucer, to Henryson, to Shakespeare, and into the twentieth century. The constant in the various portrayals is ambivalence; she is both the Madonna and the whore. In Shakespeare's redaction each character in the narrative is false to his or her legendary and heroic type. Love and war share the same human proclivity for falsehood and deception. Unlike her antecedents, Shakespeare's Cressida is primarily interested in power and domination. The "patrist, anticourtly force" (p. 72) and the bitter misogyny of Ulysses's reception of her in the Greek camp simultaneously presage her disappearance and the Puritan inroads into the English psyche.

1068. SUZUKI, MIHOKO. " 'Truth Tired with Iteration': Myth and Fiction in Shakespeare's *Troilus and Cressida.*" *Philological Quarterly* 66 (1987):153–74.

Focuses on how Shakespeare frees himself from merely repeating the story in both his classical and English sources by radically revising the myth of Troilus and Cressida through his own fiction. The tension generated by Troilus's self-serving mystification of Cressida finds its corollary in the war plot in Ulysses' speech on degree, which is borne out neither by the martial events in the play nor by Ulysses himself. In both plots Shakespeare, unlike Henryson, withholds judgment, even questions the possibility of rendering it. That is, the closure fails to provide a sense of finality from which judgments can be made.

1069. TAYLOR, GEORGE C. "Shakespeare's Attitude towards Love and Honor in *Troilus and Cressida.*" *PMLA* 45 (1930):781–86.

Observes that the theory that Shakespeare was working within a fixed literary tradition does not explain why one's reaction to the play involves a sense of revulsion. The problem centers on Shakespeare's untypical bitter and cynical treatment of love and honor. In all of his work the balance between romanticism and realism is delicately maintained. Characters like Berowne, Mercutio, Faulconbridge, Falstaff, Iago, and Enobarbus with slightly different emphasis might invoke a mood of cynicism and prurience. *Troilus and Cressida* is simply one play in which Shakespeare fails to maintain this balance.

1070. URE, PETER. "*Troilus and Cressida.*" In *William Shakespeare: The Problem Plays.* London: Longmans, Green, 1961, pp. 32–44.

Speaks of *Troilus and Cressida* as problem tragedy, noting structural peculiarities of the debate scenes and multiple principal characters. The interwoven war and love themes are given a sardonic tone by Thersites's crude commentary. The debate scenes provide the keys to the meaning and construction of the entire play. Typical is the irony inherent in Ulysses' emphasis on degree in his great speech coupled with his plan to invert rank for politico-military purposes in elevating Ajax over Achilles. The play ends in a minor key of melancholy with Hector's death and Troilus's meaningless commentary.

TWELFTH NIGHT

Reference Works

1071. McAvoy, William C., comp. *"Twelfth Night, or, What You Will": A Bibliography to Supplement the New Variorum Edition of 1901*. New York: Modern Language Association, 1984, 57 pp.

Supplements the Variorum edition (entry 1074), citing the most significant items published on the play between 1901 and 1981. The material is classified under editions, text, date, commentary, criticism, sources, music, staging, and stage history.

1072. Marder, Louis, comp. *"Twelfth Night": A Supplementary Bibliography 1901–1965*. The New Variorum Shakespeare. New York: American Scholar Publications, 1965, 22 pp.

Includes representative scholarship on *Twelfth Night* from 1901 to 1965 and is intended to supplement H. H. Furness's Variorum edition (entry 1074). The material is categorized under reproductions of original folio editions, bibliographical sources, modern editions, and critical studies (alphabetically arranged). While not exhaustive, the material represents every major category of scholarship and criticism.

Editions

1073. Donno, Elizabeth Story, ed. *Twelfth Night or What You Will*. The New Cambridge Shakespeare. Cambridge: Cambridge University Press, 1985, 158 pp.

Features an introductory essay on date and title, sources, critical commentary, and theatrical history (the Restoration, from Macklin to Olivier, recent years). Extensive notes appear on individual pages of the text, and a textual analysis and a reading list are appended.

1074. FURNESS, HENRY HOWARD., ed. *Twelfth Night, or, What You Will*. A New Variorum Edition of Shakespeare. Philadelphia: J. B. Lippincott, 1901, 434 pp.

Uses the First Folio as the copy text. On each page, for that potion of the text, are provided variant readings, textual notes, and a generous sampling of general critical commentary. Following the text are sections on the nature of the text, the date of composition, the sources, criticisms, the characters, stage history, costumes, and a list of works consulted. Supplemented by entries 1071–1072.

1075. LOTHIAN, JOHN M., and CRAIK, T. W., eds. *Twelfth Night*. The Arden Shakespeare. London: Methuen; Cambridge, Mass.: Harvard University Press, 1975, 188 pp.

Includes discussion of the text, sources, critical interpretations, and stage history, as well as appendixes on the songs and a selection from the source *Riche, His Farewell to the Military Profession* by Barnabe Riche. The text is based on the First Folio, for which the copy was probably a transcript of Shakespeare's foul papers. The date of composition is 1601, and Riche's source is the Italian play *Gl'Ingannati*.

Criticism

1076. BARNET, SYLVAN. "Charles Lamb and the Tragic Malvolio." *Philological Quarterly* 33 (1954):177–88.

Observes that the nineteenth-century conception of Malvolio as a tragic character is essentially the responsibility of Charles Lamb, who in recollecting in 1822 his memories of the role as played by Robert Bensley wrote of the "dignity" and "gravity" of the character: "I confess that I never saw the catastrophe of this character, while Bensley played it, without a kind of tragic interest." Not only is Lamb writing twenty-six years after Bensley retired; his recollection in no way agrees with contemporary accounts of the actor's role. Possibly Lamb's view was colored by the fact that his father was a kind of steward in the household of Samuel Salt.

1077. BERRY, RALPH. "*Twelfth Night*: The Experience of the Audience." *Shakespeare Survey* 34 (1981):111–19.

Argues that Shakespeare in the course of *Twelfth Night* forces the audience to reevaluate festive comedy itself, that the tensions between gulling and romantic action—between the joke gone too far and the sense of playful abandon—translate into the ideas of rain, aging, and labor in Feste's final song. The tension is best visualized in the characters of Sir Toby and Malvolio, polarized extremes. It is a critical mistake not to admit that the spectators with some degree of sympathy sense in Malvolio's dark-house experience a form of human debasement. His calling the group a "pack" is a key; we have unwittingly become involved in a kind of bearbaiting.

1078. BOOTH, STEPHEN. *"Twelfth Night* 1.1: The Audience as Malvolio." In *Shakespeare's "Rough Magic": Renaissance Essays in Honor of C. L. Barber.* Edited by Peter Erickson and Coppélia Kahn. Newark: University of Delaware Press; London and Toronto: Associated University Presses, 1985, pp. 149–67.

Suggests that the first scene of *Twelfth Night* is demonstrable nonsense, but a controlled nonsense that the audience understands and that functions as a metaphor by which the audience gains access to a metaphysical experience. Orsino's and Valentine's words about music, gluttony, disease, and hunting create syntactic sea-changes that translate into our ability to hear "what is silly as solemn, what is solemn as silly, what is base as noble, . . . to hear sense as nonsense" (p. 162). Much of our joy in *Twelfth Night* arises from the sense of a triumphant mental experience set free by the process of language in that brief scene.

1079. DICKEY, STEPHEN. "Shakespeare's Mastiff Comedy." *Shakespeare Quarterly* 42 (1991):255–75.

Notes that Shakespeare structures *Twelfth Night* on the Bear Garden spectacles, dramatizing the "human activity of indulging and restraining its own barbarity" (p. 275). Malvolio, especially, is subjected to pain in the service of the audience's pleasure. Goaded and baited and then subjected to insult and injury, he leaves the stage vowing to be revenged on the whole "pack." Other characters as well are subjected to pain for the sake of delight, and the imagery of bearbaiting is subtly woven into the language throughout the play.

1080. DOWNER, ALAN S. "Feste's Night." *College English* 13 (1952):258–65.

Notes that Feste's satiric jibes are both direct and indirect. In his first appearance, for instance, he overtly addresses Olivia as a fool. With Orsino in act 2, however, the mockery is subtle as—in response to a call for an old song that dallies with love—Feste sings of unrequited love in terms of the extravagant imagery of a mournful lover reduced to a thousand sighs searching for his grave. In both such cases, Feste's mocking function is central to the action, involving the exposure of hypocrisy and self-delusion.

1081. DRAPER, JOHN W. *The Twelfth Night of Shakespeare's Audience*. Stanford: Stanford University Press, 1950, 280 pp.

Insists on a thorough understanding of the characters—their inner psychology and outer social relationships—as the key to coming to terms with Shakespeare's structure and theme in *Twelfth Night*. Belch, for example, seems drawn from actual Elizabethan life, a younger son who could not hope to inherit lands and who became something of a soldier in his earlier years; of choleric humor, he has become a parasite in Olivia's household. Individual chapters are devoted, as well, to Aguecheek, Mary, Malvolio, Orsino, Olivia, and Feste. The episodes of the plot arise from the interactions of these personalities on their several social planes.

1082. EAGLETON, TERENCE. "Language and Reality in *Twelfth Night*." *Critical Quarterly* 9 (1967):217–28.

Stresses the power of language to shape reality in *Twelfth Night*. It can serve to clarify the truth as in the opening dialogue between Viola and the sea captain. It can distort reality as in the conversation between Maria and Sir Andrew. It can create an illusion as in Maria's forged letter to Malvolio. It can regulate reality as in Orsino's self-persuasion that he is deeply in love, or as in Belch's and Feste's practice upon others. Indeed, the entire play is an overlapping series of verbally created unrealities.

1083. EVERETT, BARBARA. "Or What You Will." *Essays in Criticism* 35 (1985):294–314.

Suggests that the late date of *Twelfth Night* is signally important in coming to terms with its autumnal tone. At the end there is a kind of content—arising from romantic comedy's traditional pairing off of lovers and repudiation of the blocking figure—but there is also a kind of sadness—in Olivia's acknowledging her interest in the living and fast-fading memory of a dead brother, in the shame of Orsino's acknowledgment of a greater interest in his page than in Olivia. This last of Shakespeare's romantic comedies "catches up into itself a great complex of human reactions to all our lighter but still serious attempts to shape time, to control our lives" (p. 303).

1084. FREUND, ELIZABETH. "*Twelfth Night* and the Tyranny of Interpretation." *ELH* 53 (1986):471–89.

Admits that the play evinces a narcissistic passion for rhetoricity. Viola, purveyor of texts, is a superb semiotic instrument, one who is and is not what mimesis claims her to be. Malvolio is a casualty of a carnival of letters. Feste as a "corrupter of words" deconstructs every discourse. More than the theatricality of spectacle, the play is a masquerade of language, creating and decreating fictions. Nonetheless, it is interpretation, despite its fragility and uncertainty, that as mediator confers recognition.

1085. GREIF, KAREN. "A Star Is Born: Feste on the Modern Stage." *Shakespeare Quarterly* 39 (1988):61–78.

Traces the role of Feste from a period of suppression when his lines were ruthlessly cut to our present age, in which his role has come to be featured as the veritable key to the play. An acting edition in the eighteenth century cuts both songs "O Mistress Mine" and "Come Away Death" and the accompanying dialogue. Further cuts throughout the nineteenth century essentially reduced the character to a sidekick of Sir Toby and Sir Andrew, an inconsequential zany. Productions in this century, beginning with Harley Granville-Barker's in 1912 and continuing through several in recent years at the Royal Shakespeare Theatre, have been concerned with capturing the tone of sadness as well as joy in the play, often portraying the fool as white-haired and wrinkled or as a ubiquitous chorus and critic.

1086. HARTMAN, GEOFFREY. "Shakespeare's Poetical Character in *Twelfth Night*." In *Shakespeare and the Question of Theory*. Edited by Patricia Parker and Geoffrey Hartman. New York and London: Methuen, 1985, pp. 37–53.

Considers the myriad interpretive views of the play and suggests that the evaluation tells as much about the critic as the literary work. Where J. M. Murry searches for the center of comprehension from which Shakespeare wrote, Empson and Leavis focus on language, Hotson on topical history, modern theorists on gender, hierarchy, and political ideology. The text by its very nature remains ultimately undeterminate. "The play . . . continues. There is always more to say" (p. 52).

1087. HOLLANDER, JOHN. "*Twelfth Night* and the Morality of Indulgence." *Sewanee Review* 68 (1959):220-38.

Maintains that *Twelfth Night* is consciously written as a counterpart to Jonsonian satiric comedy. Instead of merely presenting humor characters—static emblematic personality distortions—the play literally dramatizes the metaphor. The opening scenes introduce the characters and establish their active natures. Feste embodies not the spirit but the action of revelry as Malvolio does that of the scapegoat. The prank played on Malvoio is a condensed representation of the entire action, and the play—celebrating the Feast of the Epiphany—issues in the characters' realization of their true natures.

1088. HOTSON, LESLIE. *The First Night of "Twelfth Night."* London: Rupert Hart-Davis, 1955, 256 pp.

Asserts that *Twelfth Night* was first performed on Twelfth Night, 6 January 1601, for Queen Elizabeth at Whitehall where her guest of honor was Virginio Orsino, Duke of Bracciano. These festive events have been long obscured by the notoriety of Essex's rebellion a few weeks later. In this most musical of Shakespeare's plays, Lady Olivia is a shadow of the queen in her youth, Orsino a shadow of her courtly guest. Since it is a moment of licensed saturnalia, the play makes sport with William Knollys, the "sergeant major" of the household.

1089. HOWARD, JEAN. "Crossdressing, the Theatre, and Gender Struggle in Early Modern England." *Shakespeare Quarterly* 39 (1988):418–40.

Argues that cross-dressing was a site of social struggle, a practice condemned by the patriarchal society because it threatened male power by blurring gender distinctions. Within the theater, however, the extent to which cross-dressing constitutes hierarchical interrogation varies considerably. Viola in *Twelfth Night*, for example, uses masculine dress as a practical means of survival, and the whole thrust of the plot is to release her from the prison of male attire so that she can return to her proper and natural position as wife. Portia, on the other hand, assumes male disguise to appropriate power and to gain control of her sexuality while setting the terms for its use in marriage.

1090. HUSTON, J. DENNIS. " 'When I Came to Man's Estate': *Twelfth Night* and the Problems of Identity." *Modern Language Quarterly* 33 (1972):274–88.

Describes Viola's decision to disguise herself as a page rather than a eunuch as an indication of her gradual acceptance of the fact that her brother might be alive and of her search for identity through a borrowed masculinity. She must play out various roles to discover what she is not, attempting to integrate Sebastian's masculinity into her own personality. When Sebastian reappears, she puts aside her usurped masculine freedom and accepts her role as woman and wife.

1091. LEIMBERG, INGE. " 'M.O.A.I.': Trying to Share the Joke in *Twelfth Night* 2.5 (A Critical Hypothesis)." *Connotations* 1 (1991):78–95.

Observes that Malvolio is a victim of intellectual blindness and, as a self-loving man in love, is doubly blind. In the four-times repeated tetragrammatic pattern "M.O.A.I." Shakespeare is creating a clever parody of Revelations 1:8 and having this man who thinks he is a god say "I'm Alpha and Omega." The characters watching him furnish broad hints for the audience such as Fabian's "And 'o' shall end, I hope." Moreover, the order in which Malvolio repeats the letters provides a broad vocal imitation of an ass.

1092. LEWALSKI, BARBARA. "Thematic Patterns in *Twelfth Night*." *Shakespeare Studies* 1 (1965):168–81.

Asserts that *Twelfth Night*, reflecting the spirit and form of traditional Christmastide festivities at court and in the great houses of England, is informed as well by the religious significance associated with the Epiphany and the Christmas season. Typologically the story draws into itself and embodies larger meanings. Illyria is an Elysium-like setting of good will to which is opposed Malvolio or bad will, but it sorely needs the restoration and peace promised by the Christmas tidings. Maria and Feste are restorative forces of wit, while Viola and Sebastian function as restorative forces of love.

1093. LOGAN, THAD JENKINS. "*Twelfth Night*: The Limits of Festivity." *Studies in English Literature 1500–1900* 22 (1982):223–38.

Suggests that *Twelfth Night* is saturnalian comedy that calls the spectators' attention to the reasonable limits of festivity by abolishing those very limits in the stage world of Illyria. As such, the play merges the two major comic traditions, that of the celebration of festivity in which characters grow and discover more about their true nature and that of realistic didactic and satiric cast. The play discovers for us through its action the dangers of life without something of the principle for which Malvolio stands; Feste's concluding song is one last vivid reminder.

1094. MARKELS, JULIAN. "Shakespeare's Confluence of Tragedy and Comedy: *Twelfth Night* and *King Lear*." *Shakespeare Quarterly* 15 (1964):75–88.

Notes that the fool's function is in many ways similar in *Twelfth Night* and *King Lear*. Both perform a corrective social function for the characters who least know themselves—Malvolio and Lear; and in both instances the spiritual experience involves an obsession with the clothing they wear. Both at the outset are affected asses. In his tragic world Lear must actually be driven to madness by the fool, whereas Malvolio's refusal to yield to madness when prompted by Feste disguised as Sir

Topas signifies the opportunity for the continuation of a healthy society.

1095. MEUSCHKE, P., and FLEISHER, J. "Jonsonian Elements in the Comic Underplot of *Twelfth Night*." *PMLA* 48 (1933):722–40.

Focuses on the direct relationship between Jonson's humor characters in *Every Man in His Humor* and *Every Man out of His Humor* and the Shakespearean characters of Sir Toby and Sir Andrew (victimizer and gull) and Malvolio. Andrew, more particularly, is an unadulterated fool and gull, blindly imitating Toby, aping Viola's poetic speech, and claiming to be a great lover. Malvolio, a social pretender and hypocrite, is only incidentally a Puritan. Shakespeare in these figures adapts the Jonsonian humor character to his own larger dramatic purposes.

1096. OSBURNE, LAURIE E. "The Texts of *Twelfth Night*." *ELH* 57 (1990):37–62.

Notes that the work of new descriptive bibliographers implies a multiplicity of texts in the play. Once we accept the inaccessibility of an original, we must focus attention on the "series of copies," in this case, what "later performance editions can reveal about the folio editor's task and its ramifications for the relationship between the text and performance" (p. 41). Such exploration exposes the degree to which historical context determines what the text can be.

1097. PRESTON, DENNIS R. "The Minor Characters in *Twelfth Night*." *Shakespeare Quarterly* 21 (1970):167–76.

Views the minor characters in *Twelfth Night* as orchestral accompaniment to the solo passages, thereby preventing the principals from bogging down in tiring repartee. In the opening scene, for example, Curio and his prosaic nature and Valentine with his flourishing rhetoric verbally frame the pining Orsino in love with love. The sea captain and Antonio through their affection enhance the characters of Viola and Sebastian respectively. Fabian, a "well-born servant" useless in an overstaffed household, seems to be a social extension of Feste, reveling with Sir Toby and aiding in the tricks on both Sir Andrew and Malvolio.

1098. SCHWARTZ, ELIAS. "*Twelfth Night* and the Meaning of Shakespearean Comedy." *College English* 28 (1967):508–19.

Points out the differences between satiric comedy, which delineates characters who disobey the norms of social conduct and provoke a derisive laughter communally binding the spectators, and Shakespearean comedy, which sets forth characters with whom we identify and form a sympathetic bond because we recognize in them our own flaws, either actual or potential. Foolishness in the latter is not castigated but celebrated. In *Twelfth Night*, more specifically, all of the characters, save Sir Andrew and Malvolio, recognize their affectations; our response is "whole-souled" (p. 519) rather than merely intellectual.

1099. SEIDEN, MELVIN. "Malvolio Reconsidered." *University Review* 28 (1961):105–14.

Calls *Twelfth Night* a triumphant hoax. Shakespeare treats the confused and somewhat myopic lovers quite compassionately and without satire; they time and again escape involvements in embarrassment and humiliation. The playwright develops this tone for the romantic strain by diverting our derisive laughter to the figure of Malvolio. Moreover, Shakespeare carefully avoids a direct clash between Malvolio and the lovers, using, instead, secondary characters to bait the steward. Malvolio is a comic Coriolanus, goaded not only by his enemies but also by those who should, socially, be his friends.

1100. SUMMERS, JOSEPH H. "The Masks of *Twelfth Night*." *University Review* 22 (1952):25–32.

Notes that in *Twelfth Night* there is no conflict of generations; instead, the members of the younger generation create their own barriers through a lack of self-knowledge. Each character wears a mask—some unconsciously like Olivia (that of a grief-stricken lady) and Orsino (that of a literary lover), some consciously like Feste (that of a professional jester) and Viola (that of a young man). Generally we laugh at the former and with the latter. By the end of the play all save Feste are unmasked and comically forced to recognize their true identity.

1101. TILLEY, MORRIS P. "The Organic Unity of *Twelfth Night*." *PMLA* 29 (1914):550–56.

Argues that, beneath the romantic story of a love at cross purposes, Shakespeare sets forth an attack on the Puritan's tendency to denounce all forms of pleasure as sinful. Amid the Puritans' sweeping reforms and the follies engaged in by their opponents, Shakespeare composed *Twelfth Night* in praise of the much-needed well-balanced approach to life. Viola and Feste stand for such humane moderation while Malvolio, Sir Toby, and Sir Andrew represent the extremes on both sides.

1102. WIKANDER, MATTHEW H. "As Secret as Maidenhead: The Profession of the Boy-Actress in *Twelfth Night*." *Comparative Drama* 20 (1986–87):349–63.

Notes that Viola's comment that maids like roses die "even when they to perfection grow" (2.4.40) embodies the essential dilemma of the boy-actress, a marginal figure in an equally marginal institution. The boy on the threshold of masculinity, fully accomplished in the lady's role, might or might not survive beyond that threshold to assume masculine roles. Viola, who unlike Rosalind remains trapped in her cross-dressing at the end of the play, on several occasions reminds us of the duplicity and hypocrisy of her craft.

1103. WILLIAMS, PORTER. "Mistakes in *Twelfth Night* and Their Resolution: A Study in Some Relationships of Plot and Theme." *PMLA* 76 (1961):193–99.

Views the characters' mistakes, not merely as devices to incite superficial laughter, but as relations of subconscious patterns of human behavior. While the basic action moves through masking, the resulting deceptions and errors, and unmasking, the truly significant developments occur beneath the surface. The characters, wearing psychological masks that block their normal behavior and render them incapable of experiencing love, must be comically purged in order to achieve the richest fulfillment of both their physical and spiritual capacities.

THE TWO GENTLEMEN OF VERONA

Reference Work

1104. PEARSON, D'ORSAY W., comp. *"The Two Gentlemen of Verona": An Annotated Bibliography*. Garland Reference Library of the Humanities, 847: Garland Shakespeare Bibliographies, 16. New York and London: Garland Publishing, 1988, 265 pp.

Contains 841 items, representing virtually all publications on the play from 1940 to 1986, along with the most significant items prior to 1940. Material is categorized under such divisions as criticism, editions, textual studies, dating, sources and background, stage productions, and bibliographies. A brief introductory essay traces the history of recent criticism and research.

Editions

1105. LEECH, CLIFFORD, ed. *The Two Gentlemen of Verona*. The Arden Shakespeare. London: Methuen; Cambridge, Mass.: Harvard University Press, 1969, 122 pp.

Includes discussion of the text, date, sources, stage history, and critical interpretations. The text is based on the First Folio, for which the copy was probably a transcription of Shakespeare's foul papers. The material was apparently written in four stages with the earliest section dating from 1592 and the play in its present form from late 1593. It derives from the mass of friendship literature extending from the Middle Ages to the seventeenth century, especially *Damon and Pithias*, *Diana Enamorada*, and Brooke's *Romeus and Juliet*. *The Two Gentlemen of Verona* adheres closely to Terentian formula, making use of parody again and again in the juxtaposition of scenes.

1106. SCHLUETER, KURT, ed. *The Two Gentlemen of Verona*. The New Cambridge Shakespeare. Cambridge: Cambridge University Press, 1990, 156 pp.

Features an introductory essay on date, theme and criticism, structure and sources, Speed and Launce, the outlaws, and stage history. Extensive notes appear on individual pages of the text, and appendixes include a textual analysis, a note on stage directions, and a reading list.

Criticism

1107. ATKINSON, DOROTHY F. "The Source of *The Two Gentlemen of Verona*." *Studies in Philology* 41 (1944):223–34.

Claims that the major source of *The Two Gentlemen of Verona* is the fifth story of Henry Wotton's *A Courtly Controversy of Cupid's Cautels* (1578), a translation of Jacques d'Yver's *Le Printemps d'Yver*. Jorge de Montemayor's *Diana* provides the source for only the Julia parts of the plot that Shakespeare grafted onto Wotton. The numerous parallels in narrative and character reflect Shakespeare's tendency to use materials close at hand; he may well have been introduced to the volume by Thomas Kyd, who used the first story as the source for the play scene in *The Spanish Tragedy* and for the whole of *Soliman and Perseda*. This material has been supplemented by Jim C. Pogue, "*The Two Gentlemen of Verona* and Henry Wotton's *A Courtlie Controversie of Cupid's Cautels*" (*Emporia State Research Studies* 10, no. 4, 1962: 17–21).

1108. BROOKS, H. F. "Two Clowns in a Comedy (To Say Nothing of the Dog): Speed, Launce (and Crab) in *The Two Gentlemen of Verona*." *Essays and Studies*, n.s. 16 (1963):91–100.

Asserts that Speed and Launce contribute directly to the thematic unity of *The Two Gentlemen of Verona*. Launce, for example, in each of

his scenes burlesques the major themes; his monologue of imperson-
ation with the aid of props is far from irrelevant clownage in its un-
derlining of Proteus's love and friendship. Similarly, Speed, in having
to explain Sylvia's ruse in confessing her love for Valentine, underscores
the blind infatuation of his master. The subordinate characters are in no
way allegorical, but their actions contribute to and humorously reinforce Shakespeare's deliberate thematic design.

1109. COOK, ANN JENNALIE. "Shakespeare's Gentlemen." *Jahrbuch der
Deutschen Shakespeare-Gesellschaft West* (1985):9–27.
Observes that *The Two Gentlemen of Verona* presents a full panoply
of those considered by society as privileged. Valentine, it would appear,
is depicted as pursuing the path proper to such social station. By comparison to him, other figures lose their claim to the title: Proteus
through his attempted rape, Thurio through his cowardice, the bandits
through their crimes. In the final scenes, however, Valentine falls far
short as well in his projected disloyalty to the duke and his willingness
to hand over Sylvia to his friend. The driving force of the comedy is that
no one in the play behaves like a gentleman or lives up to his obligations
as a privileged member of society—and that fact calls into question the
validity of such social division. The discussion also covers Orlando of *As
You Like It*, Bertram of *All's Well That Ends Well*, and Leontes of *The
Winter's Tale*.

1110. DANBY, JOHN F. "Shakespeare Criticism and *The Two Gentlemen of
Verona*." *Critical Quarterly* 2 (1960):309–21.
Defends *The Two Gentlemen of Verona* as thematically a straightforward and serious dramatic treatment of the confrontation of love
and friendship, an issue popular in sixteenth-century literature. Our
modern lack of sympathy with issues in this debate has led to a wide
variety of distorted critical evaluations of the play.

1111. GIRARD, RENÉ. "Love Delights in Praises: A Reading of *The Two
Gentlemen of Verona*." *Philosophy and Literature* 13 (1989):231–47.
Observes that the principle of mimetic or mediated desire is at
work in the play. It is Valentine's desire for Sylvia that in turn makes her
the object of Proteus's intense desire. The experience is so shattering
that it permanently affects the relationship of these erstwhile fast friends.
The only cure for the situation is for Valentine to renounce his interest
in Sylvia and proffer her to Proteus in the name of friendship. While
this moment has been a crux for critics, it does function to purge
Proteus of his wild desire for Sylvia. The structure of conflict is similar

in comedy and tragedy; here the mode of resolution is a matter of dramatic convenience.

1112. GODSHALK, WILLIAM. "The Structural Unity of *The Two Gentlemen of Verona*." *Studies in Philology* 66 (1969):168–81.

Argues that, despite critical charges of structural flaws, *The Two Gentlemen of Verona* is firm in its construction. By utilizing three recurring elements—classical myths, letters, and journeys—Shakespeare initiates schemes of dramatic irony that mirror the action of previous events, thereby providing architectonic continuity of action and unity of purpose. The emphasis on classical myths with tragic outcomes and on the failure of communication in a series of letters adds psychological tension and suspense. Through the layered structure of the journeys, on the other hand, Shakespeare focuses on the theme of the educative process and points to a comic resolution.

1113. LINDENBAUM, PETER. "Education in *The Two Gentlemen of Verona*." *Studies in English Literature 1500–1900* 15 (1975):229–44.

Maintains that, despite an unevenness of tone, Shakespeare's intent in *The Two Gentlemen of Verona* is thematically serious—to dramatize man's moral education. Both Valentine and Proteus are adept in the social arts, but neither has experienced love. While romantic passion confuses Valentine, he never loses his nobility of character. Proteus, however, is transformed into a liar both to his mistress and to his friend. Valentine and Sylvia join in act 5 in revealing a truly noble pattern of conduct to him, thus producing a therapeutic shock of repentance.

1114. PERRY, THOMAS A. "*The Two Gentlemen of Verona* and the Spanish *Diana*." *Modern Philology* 87 (1989):73–76.

Maintains that Shakespeare's source for the play was not Young's translation but a Spanish version reinforced by a Spanish-English dictionary, Shakespeare's acquaintance with Latin, and the close similarity of many of the Spanish words to their Latin cognates. Several verbal echoes of *Diana* in *The Two Gentlemen of Verona* operate at the level of meanings and nuances present only in the original Spanish.

1115. SARGENT, RALPH M. "Sir Thomas Elyot and the Integrity of *The Two Gentlemen of Verona*." *PMLA* 65 (1950):1166–80.

Suggests that the flurry of action at the end of *The Two Gentlemen of Verona*—involving Proteus's repentance for attempting to rape Sylvia and, in turn, Valentine's offering her to his erstwhile friend—closely adheres to its source in Elyot's *The Book of the Governor*, which also juxtaposes the superior claim of friendship to love. Shakespeare focuses on Proteus's fall and Valentine's offer of salvation, an offer not without danger to Sylvia and to Valentine himself. The confidence in friendship and love provides the means by which the characters can achieve durable human relationships and by which Proteus is redeemed.

1116. SCOTT, WILLIAM O. "Proteus in Spenser and Shakespeare: The Lover's Identity." *Shakespeare Studies* 1 (1965):283–93.

Focuses on Shakespeare's intentions in the characterization of Proteus, tracing the significance of his name not only to the mythical god of shapes but also to another shape changer identified with him— Vertumnus, more flagrantly a wooer who utilizes lust, deceit, and trickery. The associations are implied by Spenser in the Proteus of book 3 of *The Faerie Queene*. The theme of identity with delineations of the true and false self, the subordinate theme of love and friendship, and the heroine who brings her man to a reconciliation with his true nature will be important elements of many Shakespearean comedies to come.

1117. SMALL, SAMUEL A. "The Ending of *The Two Gentlemen of Verona*." *PMLA* 48 (1933):767–76.

Views the conclusion of *The Two Gentlemen of Verona* as an artistic failure primarily because Shakespeare complicated the narrative by adding a new character, Valentine, and a new thematic motif, the conflict between love and friendship. Romantic love traditionally was regarded as superior to the bond of friendship. By offering Sylvia to Proteus and never acknowledging his affront to her, Valentine violates this primacy of love and distorts the conventional ending of romantic comedy.

1118. TETZELI VON ROSADOR, KURT. "Plotting the Early Comedies: *The Comedy of Errors, Love's Labor's Lost, The Two Gentlemen of Verona*." *Shakespeare Survey* 37 (1984):13–22.

Reaffirms the primacy of plot in Shakespeare's dramatic craftsmanship, especially the importance of precipitation or prefiguring both the middle and end of a play within its protasis. The protasis of *The Two Gentlemen of Verona* introduces the theme of love and two attitudes toward it in Valentine and Proteus, their reversal of attitude prefigured in their very names. So, too, honor is contrasted with love in the opening dialogue. The characters' attitudes will change as often as their locales. The protasis fails, however, to establish a meaningful relationship between plot, theme, and structure.

1119. WEIMANN, ROBERT. "Laughing With the Audience: *The Two Gentlemen of Verona* and the Popular Tradition of Comedy." *Shakespeare Survey* 22 (1969):35–42.

The Two Gentlemen of Verona

Analyzes the dramatic function of laughter in *The Two Gentlemen of Verona* as an essential means of organizing and evaluating through a larger comic vision. Control of the laughter rests primarily with the various levels of the awareness manipulated by Speed, Launce, and Julia in their role as a kind of comic chorus. Launce and Speed provide a burlesque parallelism with farce interwoven with the romantic scenes. In such a fashion the audience is drawn into and participates in the comic vision. Laughter is not so much a weapon of ridicule as it is an agent of communal ritual.

V.
The Tragedies

GENERAL STUDIES

1120. BARBER, C. L., and WHEELER, RICHARD P. *The Whole Journey: Shakespeare's Power of Development*. Berkeley: University of California Press, 1986, 354 pp.

Observes that the theater flourished in the generation after Protestantism replaced Catholicism as the state religion and argues that tragedy serves to address psychological needs no longer accommodated by Christian ritual. The tragedies, more specifically, "dramatize a series of failures to preserve or vindicate heritage by taking on the authority of the father or the figure of authority" (p. 11). Hamlet's tragedy, for example, results from "the destructive concentration of disabling bonds to a dead, exalted father, a murderous, hated stepfather, and a mother who is wife to both" (p. 238). Similarly Lear envisages a universe stripped of "love that has its roots in the nurturant and nurturing experience shared by child and parent" (p. 292).

1121. BATTENHOUSE, ROY W. *Shakespearean Tragedy: Its Art and Its Christian Premises*. Bloomington and London: Indiana University Press, 1969, 466 pp.

Believes that mainstream Christianity was the heritage that provided Shakespeare his fundamental premises concerning the value of life and the symbolism for signaling its meaning. *Romeo and Juliet*, for example, is envisioned as the tragic triumph of carnal love or eros leading both principals to suicide and damnation. The scene at the Capulet tomb, in particular, is developed as an upside-down analogy to

337

General Studies

the Easter story. Hamlet, too, is a story of damnation in which Hamlet wilfully chooses to pursue physical revenge and is in act 5 with Claudius a cocelebrant in a Black Mass. In a word, the tragedies can be more fully understood through a knowledge of Shakespeare's background in medieval Christian lore.

1122. BAYLEY, JOHN. *Shakespeare and Tragedy*. London: Routledge & Kegan Paul, 1981, 228 pp.

Argues that Shakespeare reveals the incompatibility of the protagonist with his situation in *Hamlet*, *King Lear*, and *Othello* by drawing the spectators as close as possible to the protagonists' consciousness and in *Julius Caesar*, *Antony and Cleopatra*, *Coriolanus*, and *Timon of Athens* by setting the central figure apart as "something from which a moral can be drawn, a case can be studied" (p. 73). *King Lear* achieves its supreme quality through the "free satisfactions both of delight and sorrow that seem unrelated to the tragic necessities" (p. 63). Similarly, *Hamlet* moves beyond a moralistic focus on the avenger's mission; here the paradox is "to find that life is too involved with [Hamlet's] own instincts and affections for him to be avenged on it" (p. 176).

1123. BOWERS, FREDSON T. *Elizabethan Revenge Tragedy 1587–1642*. Princeton: Princeton University Press, 1940, 288 pp.

Traces the background, origin, and chronological development of revenge tragedy as practiced in England between 1587 and 1642. The major classical motivation was Seneca, whose tragedy strongly emphasizes blood-revenge for murder or flagrant injury. Kyd's *The Spanish Tragedy* established the fundamental formula—the motive of revenge by a male blood relative, a ghost to incite the action, hesitation on the part of the hero, madness, and a Machiavellian villain. *Titus Andronicus* conforms closely to this Kydian formula. *Hamlet* is the supreme achievement in the form, differing from other revenge tragedies only because of Shakespeare's superior sense of dramaturgy; all of the elements are present, but the tragedy is made to turn upon the character of the revenger.

1124. BRADBROOK, MURIEL C. *Themes and Conventions of Elizabethan Tragedy*. Cambridge: Cambridge University Press, 1935, 275 pp.

Describes, in the first half, the assumptions that an Elizabethan would bring to a tragic performance based on the traditions and conventions of the public theater. The power of Elizabethan drama lies more in the words than in the action; the chief characteristics of the stage are its flexibility, its natural locale, its fast and slow time, its emotive gestures, and its symbolic groupings. The action, hovering between the realistic and the allegorical, is cumulative rather than logical, and the speech is frequently patterned. Part 2 focuses on the work of Shakespeare's major contemporaries.

1125. BRADLEY, A. C. *Shakespearean Tragedy*. New York: St. Martin's Press, 1904, 448 pp.

Describes Shakespearean tragedy as a story of exceptional calamity set in a world controlled by moral order. Hamlet is a figure whose love for Ophelia is weakened and deadened by melancholy; he returns from his sea voyage convinced that he is in the hands of providence. Othello, for all his poetry, is little experienced in the corrupt products of civilized life; he faces in Iago a creed that absolute egoism is the only rational and proper guide to action. *Lear* is Shakespeare's greatest achievement but, as a consequence of vagueness of scene and darkness of atmosphere, not his greatest play. *Macbeth* is a tragedy with characters almost superhuman in nature in which the protagonist is a soul "tortured by an agony which admits not a moment's repose" (p. 265).

1126. BROOKE, NICHOLAS. *Shakespeare's Early Tragedies*. London: Methuen, 1968, 214 pp.

Claims that the early tragedies have failed to receive their due share of estimation. The central theme in *Titus Andronicus* is the deterioration of individuals to bestial states under the dictates of vengeful passion. History in *Richard III* becomes imaginatively felt as a huge impersonal force against which Richard, despite his villainy, struggles with a strange degree of heroism. *Richard II* ambivalently sets Richard's rhetorical abilities against a new and calculating concept of divine order. *Julius Caesar* also manipulates the audience's sympathies by juxtaposing the roles of haughty conqueror, conscience-torn conspirator, and Machiavellian opportunist. *Hamlet* contrasts an honorable, active, and creative world with one that is negational, chaotic, and diseased.

1127. BUSHNELL, REBECCA W. *Tragedies of Tyrants: Political Thought and Theater in the English Renaissance*. Ithaca: Cornell University Press, 1990, 195 pp.

Explores the image of the tyrant in *Julius Caesar*, *Richard III*, and *Macbeth* measured against the language and idioms used to represent tyranny in the prose and drama of the Tudor-Stuart period. Richard III manipulates the traditional images of tyrannical lust and effeminacy, turning the charge against Edward, to consolidate his power. Macbeth's drive to the throne is compromised by uxoriousness, but his later separation from his wife and loss of passion and feeling challenge the conventional function of gender in political imagery. *Julius Caesar* ex-

General Studies

plores the power of ideology to shape the image of the ruler, with the words *king, tyrant,* and *caesar* circulating as tools used diversely by oppositional factions.

1128. CAMPBELL, LILY BESS. *Shakespeare's Heroes: Slaves of Passion.* Cambridge: Cambridge University Press, 1930, 296 pp.

Argues that Shakespearean tragedy is rooted in the Elizabethan psychological concepts of popular moral philosophy. Subjection of the vital moisture to excessive heat, the consequence of permitting passion to transcend reason, results in the excessive humor known as melancholy adust. All of Shakespeare's major protagonists suffer some form of such melancholy adust that transforms the healthy individual into one capable of evil action. Hamlet, for example, is a study in grief; Othello, in jealousy; Lear, in wrath in old age; Macbeth, in fear as it consumes both him and his wife. The lesson of these tragedies is that the protagonists, by failing to balance passion by reason, render themselves fortune's puppets.

1129. CANTOR, PAUL A. *Shakespeare's Rome: Republic and Empire.* Ithaca: Cornell University Press, 1976, 228 pp.

Views *Julius Casear* as central to a historical trilogy chronicling the tragedy of the fall of Rome, with *Coriolanus* as its historical antecedent and *Antony and Cleopatra* as its successor. The blending of aristocracy, monarchy, and democracy reflects the eclectic political situation in Rome, which never strictly epitomized one particular form. *Julius Caesar* explores prominent imperial heroes while *Coriolanus* focuses on Rome in its founding phase. *Antony* is a companion piece to *Coriolanus*; both protagonists are embodiments of the values of their times. The Rome of *Caesar* occupies a balance between the "spirited" and the "erotic" city of the other plays.

1130. CARLISLE, CAROL JONES. *Shakespeare from the Greenroom: Actor Criticisms of Four Major Tragedies.* Chapel Hill: University of North Carolina Press, 1969, 493 pp.

Presents comments on the playwright by English-speaking actors from the eighteenth century to the present. Chapters on *Hamlet, Othello, King Lear,* and *Macbeth* include actors' general views of the play; their consideration of particularly enigmatic aspects of the plot such as the question of Hamlet's age, or his madness, or his attitude toward his mother; the intensity of Othello's passion, the degree of his blackness; the question of the appropriate setting for *King Lear*, the shifting interpretations of the philosophic center; the nature of Macbeth's internal struggle as "demon incarnate" or "conscience in anguish," the method of presenting the supernatural machinery.

1131. CARTWRIGHT, KENT. *Shakespearean Tragedy and Its Double: The Rhythms of Audience Response.* University Park: Pennsylvania State University Press, 1991, 285 pp.

Examines Shakespeare's method of provoking both engagement and detachment in the spectators' relationship with the principals. In *Romeo and Juliet*, for example, while the young lovers themselves engage our emotions, the structure draws us back by exposing "causation and necessity as essentially 'poetic' manipulations" (p. 55). The spectators in *Hamlet* engage the protagonist at the outset because their spectatorship mimics his own view of the stage world, but later they grow detached when the play denies him a privileged point of view and when he denies his moral kinship with others. *Othello*, *King Lear*, and *Macbeth* are also discussed at length.

1132. CAVELL, STANLEY. *Disowning Knowledge in Six Plays of Shakespeare.* Cambridge: Cambridge University Press, 1987, 266 pp.

Investigates the consequence of skepticism in Shakespeare's plays. Because Othello has doubts, for example, he wants to believe Iago's insinuations about Desdemona's infidelity; ultimately, he is driven to kill both her and himself to create a kind of certitude and "ocular proof." Leontes's horror at Hermione's sexuality focuses not on her intercourse with Polixenes but on the visible pregnancy and child. Hamlet's fascination and disgust with sexuality express his inability to accept finitude as a condition of human life rather than death. Coriolanus, whose food is blood, is envisioned as not so much imitating Christ as competing with him. And Lear is propelled by a deep sense of human shame, driven mad by remembrance of what he has done to Cordelia.

1133. CHAMPION, LARRY S. *Shakespeare's Tragic Perspective.* Athens: University of Georgia Press, 1976, 279 pp.

Directs attention to the various structural devices by which Shakespeare creates and sustains in the spectators the necessary pattern of anticipation and double vision that provokes them simultaneously to participation in the protagonist's anguish and to judgment of his actions. The middle tragedies are envisioned as those in which the spectators most closely identify with the central figure, largely the consequence of soliloquies that reflect his spiritual experience. In the final tragedies Shakespeare seems deliberately to force the spectators to view the character from a greater distance and thus to recognize that the causes of tragedy exist not in isolation but as a combination of equally significant internal and external destructive forces.

1134. CHARLTON, H. B. *Shakespearian Tragedy*. Cambridge: Cambridge University Press, 1948, 246 pp.

Asserts that Shakespearean tragedy, while not religious, is intensely spiritual. In the early plays man accepts easily the laws of God; in the later, more vividly portraying his immeasurable spiritual potentiality, he must shape from within himself those values and relations that are "God-like." Man is a part of the animal kingdom; the beast is within, and the world often appears to be amoral; but the faith in man permeates the tragedies—faith in the vitalizing influence of human kindness, fellowship, and love despite the adversities and atrocities of life.

1135. CHARNEY, MAURICE. *Shakespeare's Roman Plays: The Function of Imagery in the Drama*. Cambridge, Mass.: Harvard University Press, 1961, 250 pp.

Investigates *Julius Caesar*, *Antony and Cleopatra*, and *Coriolanus* through verbal and nonverbal images that are set in a context not only of words but also of the dramatic situation, the interplay of characters, and the sequence of time. While *Caesar* illustrates a limited and controlled Roman style, *Antony* is characterized by hyperbolic and sensually evocative imagery. The imagery of *Coriolanus* depicts a cold and objective world with only Menenius comfortable with figurative language.

1136. COURSEN, HERBERT R., Jr. *Christian Ritual and the World of Shakespeare's Tragedies*. Lewisburg: Bucknell University Press, 1976, 441 pp.

Argues that the pattern of the Eucharist is seen in several tragedies; the movement from sin to reconciliation is aborted in each instance by a tragic hero, who through a flagrant act of defiant self-will drives himself away from the possibilities of communion. Hamlet, for instance, at the moment when Claudius might have confessed his murder, succumbs to a passion that preempts sacramental potentiality. Othello's critical moment is his parodic marriage with Iago, which reflects the discrepancy between what he believes he is doing and what he is actually doing. Lear's abdication parodically mirrors "God's giving the earth to unfallen man" (p. 212), and *Macbeth* imagistically reenacts the fall of man (Macbeth and Lady Macbeth) and the coming of the Messiah (Malcolm).

1137. DANSON, LAWRENCE. "Continuity and Character in Shakespeare and Marlowe." *Studies in English Literature 1500–1900* 26 (1986):217–34.

Asserts that Shakespeare's characters tend to develop, to undergo radical shifts in apparent identity, while Marlowe's figures "amaze or dismay us by the sheer tenacity of their will to be themselves" (p. 217). From his earliest plays Shakespeare toys with the concept of anagnorisis, which implies a character's self-discovery, whereas a Tamburlainean consistency marks each of Marlowe's central characters. Shakespeare's tragedies are driven by personal transformation as disaster, and his later comedies move toward problem plays, in which characters refuse to play the traditional festive roles, and toward romance, in which transformation is symbolically figured as a death and birth.

1138. DICKEY, FRANKLIN. *Not Wisely But Too Well: Shakespeare's Love Tragedies*. San Marino: Huntington Library, 1957, 205 pp.

Focuses on *Romeo and Juliet*, *Troilus and Cressida*, and *Antony and Cleopatra*, and the poems *Venus and Adonis* and *The Rape of Lucrece*. Shakespeare as a Renaissance playwright conceived of love as a rational force or a passionate force. The latter type upsets the balance of the body humors, producing a form of melancholia and leading in extreme cases to rash and bloody deeds. While *Romeo* utilizes many comic aspects of love, the protagonists themselves are morally responsible for their actions and ultimately for their suicides. Similarly, while Antony and Cleopatra provoke extreme terror and pity from the spectators, Shakespeare forces us to view their relationship, albeit glorious, as tarnished, "examples of rulers who threw away a kingdom for lust" (p. 179).

1139. DOLLIMORE, JONATHAN. *Radical Tragedy: Religion, Ideology and Power in the Drama of Shakespeare and His Contemporaries*. Chicago: University of Chicago Press, 1984, 312 pp.

Argues that the playwrights—actively subversive in their critique of ideology—developed a "subliteral encoding which bypasses the perfunctory surveillance of the censor" and is "reactivated in the performance" (p. 28). The dramas through the irony encoded in their closures defy the central assumption of a harmonious telos and a retributive providentialism. *King Lear* is, above all, a play about power, property, and inheritance, in its conclusion nullifying the humanist's vision of redemptive suffering. Both *Antony and Cleopatra* and *Coriolanus* "effect a skeptical interrogation of martial ideology and in doing so foreground the complex social and political relations which hitherto it tended to occlude" (p. 204).

1140. EVANS, BERTRAND. *Shakespeare's Tragic Practice*. Oxford: Clarendon Press, 1979, 327 pp.

General Studies

Analyzes the structure of Shakespeare's tragedies in terms of the varying levels of discrepant awareness, that is, the variation in the amount of knowledge the characters hold concerning themselves, their situation, and the other characters. Whereas exploitation of the gap in the characters' knowledge is the primary concern in comedy, the emphasis in tragedy is equally on the means by which the discrepancy is created and the disastrous consequences. In most instances, then, major emphasis is directed upon the villain and his practice. Interestingly, only in *Antony and Cleopatra* do the spectators fail to hold a significant information advantage over the principal figure.

1141. FARNHAM, WILLARD. *Shakespeare's Tragic Frontier: The World of His Final Tragedies*. Berkeley: University of California Press, 1950, 289 pp.
Examines the paradoxical nobility in the protagonists of Shakespeare's final tragedies—Timon, Macbeth, Antony, and Coriolanus. The world of these plays is carefully distinguished from that of the earlier tragic heroes in that these last figures are pervasively tainted but also possess a nobility that appears to emanate from their very ignobility. In a world devoid of conventional villains, these characters seem bent on destroying themselves, provoking simultaneous sympathy and antipathy. The tragic form is extended to its widest limits in these chilling analyses of deeply flawed human greatness.

1142. FELPERIN, HOWARD. *Shakespearean Representation: Mimesis and Modernity in Elizabethan Tragedy*. Princeton: Princeton University Press, 1977, 199 pp.
Asserts that Shakespeare, like other successful playwrights, subsumes within his work a "recognizably conventional model of life," then repudiates that model, and thereby creates the "illusion that he uses no art at all, that he is presenting life directly" (p. 66). Shakespeare's plays, in other words, burst the traditional mold and produce a startlingly naturalistic character or situation. Such a view accommodates the immediate response of the spectator or critic who brings no specialized historical knowledge to the playhouse as well as that of the scholar fully attuned to the literary tradition upon which the play is constructed.

1143. FOREMAN, WALTER C., Jr. *The Music of the Close: The Final Scenes of Shakespeare's Tragedies*. Lexington: University Press of Kentucky, 1978, 228 pp.
Examines the confrontation with death in Shakespeare's tragic heroes. Whether by suicide (Romeo and Juliet, Brutus, Othello, Antony and Cleopatra), murder (Titus, Coriolanus, Hamlet, Macbeth, Richard

II), or heartbreak (Lear), death is visualized by the spectators and in most instances by the characters themselves as either a rest from suffering or as the only possible outcome consistent with their integrity. The tragic figure is the play's "center of energy," and his actions disrupt the prevailing system of order and value. His death wish is a response to both specific and existential grief, to the inexorable limitations which in one way or another bind and restrict his aspirations.

1144. FRYE, NORTHROP. *Fools of Time: Studies in Shakespearean Tragedy*. Toronto: University of Toronto Press, 1967, 121 pp.

Observes that tragedy is the consequence of juxtaposing with the pattern of man's natural movement toward death a heroic movement involving a man's capacity for suffering that transcends the ordinary. In *Hamlet* the three concentric tragic spheres of Laertes, Fortinbras, and Hamlet interweave an ironic tragedy of blood and *de casibus* tragedy with the tragedy of moral imperative. In *Lear* Shakespeare interweaves a moral pattern with a pattern of the absurd. Lear's death parallels the absurdity of Christ's death and prompts a similar act of faith in the spectator.

1145. HALL, MICHAEL. *The Structure of Love: Representational Patterns and Shakespeare's Love Tragedies*. Charlottesville: University Press of Virginia, 1989, 224 pp.

Uses semiotic and reader response theory to demonstrate how a knowledge of such systems governs a reader's perceptions of sexual relationships in the plays. Specifically, exterior systems such as values, stereotypes, prejudices, and generic distinctions are manipulated to control our response to romantic love. For example, in *Love's Labor's Lost* the ascetic view (love as dangerous passion) is comically juxtaposed to Petrarchism (love as exalting and ennobling). In *Romeo and Juliet* Petrarchism is privileged by juxtaposition with the biases of oppressive patriarchy and social factionalism. *Troilus and Cressida* discredits both the epic and Petrarchan views, and *Antony and Cleopatra* ambiguously reflects the terrible price of ecstatic union.

1146. HONIGMANN, E. A. J. *Shakespeare: Seven Tragedies: The Dramatist's Manipulation of Response*. London: Macmillan, 1976, 215 pp.

Examines the structural features by which Shakespeare manipulates the spectator's response to achieve a profound sense of ambivalence. Brutus in *Julius Caesar* is the first clear example; the spectator, on the one hand forced to a detachment from which he judges the character in terms of his own and the play's value structures, is on the other hand drawn emotionally to the character and forced to share both the

General Studies

agony of his decisions and the insights that the tragic experience on occasion provokes. Cleopatra is a later example; critical attempts at overly neat clarification can only reduce the fascination of her character and minimize the profound mystery of the tragedy by forcing the spectator to a position not compatible with Antony's final vision.

1147. HUNTER, ROBERT GRAMS. *Shakespeare and the Mystery of God's Judgments*. Athens: University of Georgia Press, 1976, 208 pp.

Asserts that Elizabethan tragedy results in part from a "desire to embody in art the mysteries that were forced upon the consciousness of intelligent artists and their audiences by the controversies of the Reformation" (p. 18). Shakespeare's audiences were made up of semi-Pelegians, Augustinians, and Calvinists; and his tragedies reflect the various attitudes toward the nature of God's judgment. In *Richard III* the mystery of God's election is contained within the mystery of His providence. *Hamlet* represents God's artifice for catching consciences, both Claudius's and Hamlet's. *King Lear* dramatizes the final possibility that there is no God.

1148. IDE, RICHARD S. *Possessed with Greatness: The Heroic Tragedies of Shakespeare and Chapman*. Chapel Hill: University of North Carolina Press, 1980, 253 pp.

Centers on the "heroic tragedies" of Shakespeare and Chapman that in the early years of the seventeenth century address the tragic plight of the soldier-hero cast into a society that neither recognizes nor accommodates his heroic qualities. Both playwrights were deeply shocked by just such an event—Essex's fatal confrontation with society and with Queen Elizabeth in 1601—and their plays constitute a creative dialogue through which they examine from divergent points of view this disastrous conflict between martial conduct glorified in epic myth and that appropriate to social reality. Shakespeare's heroes gain tragic grandeur only through renouncing their idealism as a delusion and understanding their human frailties.

1149. KIEFER, FREDERICK. *Fortune and Elizabethan Tragedy*. San Marino: Huntington Library, 1983, 354 pp.

Insists that Shakespeare and his contemporaries reflect the profound fear that—whatever his degree of wisdom—man is subject to unexplainable and horrendous calamity. Richard II openly views himself as fortune's victim, for example; and Brutus unsuccessfully attempts to assert his individual will. If Hamlet succeeds in expunging fortune from his worldview, it reappears with a vengeance in the pattern of upheaval that characterizes *King Lear*. The societal implication of the final tragedies is that man's relationship to other men is a consequence of fortune's activity.

1150. KIRSCH, ARTHUR. *The Passions of Shakespeare's Tragic Heroes.* Charlottesville: University Press of Virginia, 1990, 163 pp.

Offers a rebuttal of contemporary criticism's fascination with man and woman as little more than cultural artifacts. The premise is that Shakespeare's plays represent enduring truths concerning our emotional and spiritual lives. Othello's tragedy may involve patriarchal sexual politics, for example, but it speaks afresh to each new generation because it dramatizes the fury of erotic discontent. If *King Lear* is a protest against social injustice and corruption, its more powerful theme is the deep and abiding rage against the conditions of human mortality. *Macbeth* may be a reflection of Jacobean capitalist individualism, but, more important, it traces the journey of an individual obsessed with self-sufficiency.

1151. KNIGHT, G. WILSON. *The Imperial Theme: Further Interpretations of Shakespeare's Tragedies Including the Roman Plays.* Oxford: Oxford University Press, 1931, 367 pp.

Focuses largely on the Roman tragedies with individual essays on *Hamlet* and *Macbeth*. The common thread is the search for "life themes," positive effects transmitted to the imaginative consciousness. The vision of *Julius Caesar*, for instance, is sensuous in the vivid apprehension of physical detail and spiritual in the sense of a dramatic energy in man that enriches the action from first to last. *Hamlet* is centered on a struggle of life and death forces; the prince becomes so obsessed with evil in himself and in others that he becomes a "death-force" (p. 123), and the play forces us to look for a solution outside the action in the gospel ethic of forgiveness. Both *Antony and Cleopatra* and *Coriolanus* are viewed as the opposition of war and love.

1152. ———. *The Wheel of Fire: Interpretations of Shakespearian Tragedy.* Oxford: Oxford University Press, 1930, 343 pp.

Stresses symbolic overtones and poetic atmosphere, the blend in Shakespeare of the temporal (individual plot) with the spatial (mysterious, universal reality). Hamlet, in "The Embassy of Death," is described as a sick soul suffering mental and spiritual death who brings death to all he touches. Othello ("The Othello Music") is set between the forces of divinity and hell. Two essays on *Lear*, "*King Lear* and the Comedy of the Grotesque" and "The *Lear* Universe," depict humanity as tortured and cruelly impaled; but suffering is also seen to be purga-

General Studies

torial; the good are sweetened by it while the evil are brutalized and demoralized by their success.

1153. LAWLOR, JOHN J. *The Tragic Sense in Shakespeare*. London: Chatto & Windus, 1960, 186 pp.

Asserts that the worlds of Shakespeare's tragic protagonists are in no sense mechanistic; to the contrary, once the tragic choices are made, events run to their natural conclusions despite any illumination that the central figure might experience. Lear, for example, is purged of his guilt by suffering; forgiveness is asked and freely given; yet utter disaster still occurs. Macbeth's awakening to life comes only as he becomes inalterably separated from it. The logic of tragic suffering escapes us, but the nature of tragic experience is not so much to reconcile as to reveal.

1154. McALINDON, THOMAS. *Shakespeare's Tragic Cosmos*. Cambridge: Cambridge University Press, 1991, 306 pp.

Examines Shakespeare's major tragedies from the perspective of duality and polarity—for example, justice and love, law and marriage, redemption and renewal, stoicism and Christianity, the symbolic uses of ritual and play. The basic assumption is that "the ancient model of natural order as a dynamic system of interacting opposites had a much more profound effect on the Renaissance interpretation and representation of tragic experience than did the related notion of universal hierarchy" (p. xiii). Such a model of world order encourages ambivalent, paradoxical, and occasionally subversive qualities in the various protagonists examined in their confrontation with tragedy.

1155. McCALLUM, M. W. *Shakespeare's Roman Plays and Their Background*. London: Macmillan, 1910, 666 pp.

Observes that Shakespeare in the Roman histories focuses on individuals caught up in the great mutations of state. Chapters on Shakespeare's treatment of history and on Plutarch, Amyot, and North are followed by individual sections on *Julius Caesar*, *Antony and Cleopatra*, and *Coriolanus* with emphasis on Shakespeare's alteration of his sources. *Caesar* is the first great tragedy; while Brutus is the central character, Caesar's spirit dominates the play. *Antony* is at once history, tragedy, and love poem; passion is the dominant force in Antony's character, and Cleopatra is ambiguously beauty without duty, impulse without principle. *Coriolanus* juxtaposes a depressed and famished populace with a prejudiced and unorganized aristocracy.

1156. MACFARLAND, THOMAS. *Tragic Meanings in Shakespeare*. New York: Random House, 1966, 179 pp.

Asserts that tragedy pushes us to the vicarious experience of death or nonbeing; its movement from disharmony to a transcendent affirmation parallels the movement of Christianity. The focus is on four major Shakespearean tragedies. Hamlet, by questioning the commandment to revenge, both fulfills and abolishes the Senecan revenge code. *Othello* transmutes to tragedy the comic possibilities of a social mismatch. The opposition of love and the world points early to the moral bankruptcy of Antony and Cleopatra, but the Machiavellian Octavius forces our sympathy back to those whose interests transcend the material. The theme of *Lear* is the search for a meaningful self by several major characters.

1157. MACK, MAYNARD, Jr. *Killing the King: Three Studies in Shakespeare's Tragic Structure*. New Haven and London: Yale University Press, 1973, 310 pp.

Observes that, as in Greek tragedy, the killing of a king is the central fact of several Shakespearean tragedies. Examination of *Richard II*, *Hamlet*, and *Macbeth* reveals a progressive movement from the literal to the symbolic significance of the act, the latter encompassing not only national politics and social consequences but also psychic tension, religious and metaphysical dimensions, and mythic structures. In each play the Tudor fiction of the king's two bodies collapses into a dramatic conflict of philosophic ideas and personal ambitions. Both the king killers and the audience are engaged in the common effort to achieve a balance between these forces of conflict.

1158. MASON, H. A. *Shakespeare's Tragedies of Love: An Examination of the Possibility of Common Readings of "Romeo and Juliet," "Othello," "King Lear," and "Antony and Cleopatra."* London: Chatto & Windus; New York: Barnes & Noble, 1970, 290 pp.

Examines the role of love in Shakespeare's plays and distinguishes those circumstances when the treatment can be considered tragic. In *Romeo and Juliet* love fails to make the young principals a cohesive whole; the nature of its passion is such that it isolates them from their society rather than enriching their function within it. In *Othello* the problem is one of balance; the passion of love is greater than the substance of character Shakespeare gives to either Othello or Desdemona. *King Lear* and *Antony and Cleopatra* explore variations of the paradoxicality of love in its ripest condition.

1159. MEHL, DIETER. *Shakespeare's Tragedies: An Introduction*. London: Cambridge University Press, 1987, 272 pp.

General Studies

Observes that Shakespeare's tragedies present "without mitigation the experienced reality of evil, the unpredictability of human nature, and man's helplessness in the face of a fate that seems indifferent if not hostile" (p. 5). A major source of his power is the plays' refusal to be bound by any kind of reductionism. The love relation in *Romeo and Juliet*, for example, cannot be exclusively viewed either as moralistic denunciation, unrestrained passion, or a glorification of *Liebestod*. Likewise, Hamlet's condition in act 5 can be variously explained as "resignation, irresponsibility, or confident reliance on God's providence" (p. 54). *King Lear* refuses to endorse either the hopes of Christian salvation or the despair of mute resignation.

1160. MORRIS, IVOR. *Shakespeare's God: The Role of Religion in the Tragedies*. New York: St. Martin's Press, 1972, 496 pp.

Argues that tragedy is most powerful, not when it is primarily concerned with abstract doctrine, but when metaphysical values must be inferred by the character and by the spectator from purely human disaster. Beneath the character's primary awareness, concerned with the operation of ambition and jealousy, the workings of passion and the grip of obsession, tragedy reveals a state of radical guilt—a pride or hubris that impels the hero to self-assertion. The catharsis is as much a liberation from the tyranny of emotion as it is a liberation from the tyranny of the self, the recognition that wisdom comes only through suffering.

1161. MUIR, KENNETH. *Shakespeare's Tragic Sequence*. London: Hutchinson University Library Press, 1972, 207 pp.

Observes that Shakespeare's tragedies defy generalizations despite the psychological efforts of Lily B. Campbell or the theological analysis of R. W. Battenhouse. If the governing principles are moral, each is its own unique world; and each is analyzed in a series of chapters. Hamlet's dilemma, for example, is the necessity of avoiding killing in haste lest it be revenge rather than justice coupled with his inability to kill in cold blood. In *Lear* questions concerning God's justice or the existence of an afterlife are irrelevant in the face of the nature of human behavior and the principles of a civilized society.

1162. NEVO, RUTH. *Tragic Form in Shakespeare*. Princeton: Princeton University Press, 1972, 412 pp.

Views Shakespearean tragedy as a five-phased sequence that is cumulative and consummatory and for which the tragic hero is the axis of development. The phases, correlating closely with the act divisions of the folio, are artistic extensions of the classical concept of five-act structure. The first phase—the "predicament"—forces the protagonist to confront an impossible choice. In phase two the terms of the conflict (the nature of the dilemma) become apparent. Phase three involves the psychomachia, and phase four the renunciation of values viewed ironically from outside the principal figure. In the final phase the protagonist through his dying mediates the survival of human value. Individual chapters pursue this structural pattern in each of the tragedies.

1163. PALMER, JOHN. *Political Characters of Shakespeare*. London: Macmillan, 1945, 335 pp.

Includes chapters on Brutus, Richard III, Richard II, Henry IV, and Coriolanus. The leading quality of the plays in which they appear is not the political issue but the character and his human responses to the motives and pressures that mold him—those qualities in Brutus, for instance, that have forever rendered the conscientious liberal ineffective in public life, the gesture and flourish in Richard III of an intellect untrammeled by conscience, the equally self-centered Richard II doomed to destruction by his withdrawal to a false world of his own creation, the fatal conflict in Coriolanus between personal pride and family affection.

1164. PHILLIPS, JAMES E. MERSON, Jr. *The State in Shakespeare's Greek and Roman Plays*. New York: Columbia University Press, 1940, 230 pp.

Examines Shakespeare's view of the nature and purpose of the commonwealth as described in the political action of the Greek and Roman plays. The idea of the state was a popular issue in Shakespeare's day largely because of Tudor dictatorial rule and the interpretation such a government imposed on earlier English history. In the Roman plays Shakespeare focuses on order, degree, vocation, and "specialty of rule." In *Coriolanus* democracy is found wanting, as is aristocracy in *Julius Caesar* and *Antony and Cleopatra*. In *Troilus and Cressida* and *Timon of Athens* society degenerates in its failure to recognize authority. The movement is slowly toward monarchy, the form of state considered by the Elizabethans to be divinely authorized.

1165. POOLE, ADRIAN. *Tragedy: Shakespeare and the Greek Example*. Oxford: Basil Blackwell, 1987, 265 pp.

Argues that genuine tragedy defies alliance either with ideology or with the didactic in its representation of the "unassimilability of pain, and the human qualities that survive through extreme suffering" (p. 10). A chapter on obsessive fear (Aeschylus's *Oresteia*, Shakespeare's

General Studies

Macbeth) is followed by discussions of man's insistent interrogation of his existence (Sophocles's *Oedipus Rex*, Shakespeare's *Hamlet*), and on the variety of man's confrontations with death (Sophocles's *Oedipus at Colonus*, Euripides's *Bacchae*, Shakespeare's *King Lear*).

1166. PRIOR, MOODY E. *The Language of Tragedy*. New York: Columbia University Press, 1947, 430 pp.

Devotes a large portion of chapter two, "The Elizabethan Tradition," to a discussion of Shakespeare's unequaled virtuosity in the use of language in tragedy. His development generally is toward a muted form of imagery in highly charged metaphorical language. *Romeo and Juliet* in its wide variety of styles characterizes Shakespeare's language at a fairly early state. The later *King Lear* in its metaphoric unity reflects the maturation of Shakespeare's power. The pervasive image of the play is nature and its derivative forms natural and unnatural as seen from such varying perspectives as Lear's, Gloucester's, and Edmund's. Other dominant image patterns are those of storm, of animals, of sharp bodily contact, and of the rending of an organic structure.

1167. PROSER, MATTHEW N. *The Heroic Image in Five Shakespearean Tragedies*. Princeton: Princeton University Press, 1965, 254 pp.

Examines *Julius Caesar*, *Macbeth*, *Othello*, *Coriolanus*, and *Antony and Cleopatra* as tragic studies in the discrepancy between a character's self-image and his social reality. Through his actions he attempts to sustain the heroic persona built on a mental allusion, and his ultimate death becomes symbolic of the nobility to which he unsuccessfully aspires. Macbeth's experience, for example, involves the progressive brutalization of soul and the suppression of prohibitive conscience, an enacting without moral reservation of the ethic of pure desire. The focus of delusion is in Brutus the image of the patriot, in Othello and Coriolanus the image of the warrior, and in Antony the image of the martial hero.

1168. RIBNER, IRVING. *Patterns in Shakespearian Tragedy*. London: Methuen, 1960, 205 pp.

Considers Shakespeare's growth in moral vision from the inherited dramatic forms with conventional morality to the successive visions of his major works that embody the emotional equivalent of an intellectual statement. Symbolic of human nature the tragic protagonists face critical choices arising from a condition of both faith and dubiety. Ultimately each tragedy explores man's place in the universe and implicitly affirms a metaphysical justice and benevolence. While *Hamlet, Othello,*

King Lear, and *Macbeth* end in a great affirmation, *Antony and Cleopatra* and *Coriolanus* end in paradox; but there is nonetheless an artistic sense of reconciliation, altruism, and self-sacrifice.

1169. ROSEN, WILLIAM. *Shakespeare and the Craft of Tragedy*. Cambridge, Mass.: Harvard University Press, 1960, 231 pp.

Investigates the dramatic techniques of point of view in *Lear, Macbeth, Coriolanus*, and *Antony and Cleopatra*. In each case Shakespeare clearly demonstrates the nature of the protagonist's personality before his world begins to crumble. Hamlet, Othello, and Macbeth fall away from an idea, whereas Lear grows to it. The spectators view the events of *Lear* and *Macbeth* from within the central figure's own conscience. Coriolanus, Antony, and Cleopatra, on the other hand, lack insight, and the values are imposed from without. For the former our concern is with the conditions of the spirit as a universal symbol; for the latter it is with public life and the world's opinion.

1170. ROZETT, MARTHA TUCK. *The Doctrine of Election and the Emergence of Elizabethan Tragedy*. Princeton: Princeton University Press, 1984, 329 pp.

Considers the Calvinist doctrine of election central to the mind-set of Elizabethan tragedy and focuses on the manner in which the best playwrights produce a compelling dualistic experience that provokes simultaneous engagement and detachment. Shakespeare's revenge tragedies, more specifically, force the spectator to come to emotional terms with a protagonist at once victim, villain, morality Vice, and hero. The tragic fate of Titus, who succumbs to the horrors of murdering his own children, "confirms the audience in their own sense of election by offering them a spectacle of the 'other' utterly removed from the realm of experience they inherit" (p. 199).

1171. SIMMONS, J. L. *Shakespeare's Pagan World: The Roman Tragedies*. Charlottesville: University Press of Virginia, 1973, 202 pp.

Contends that the essentially unique feature of Shakespeare's Roman tragedies is that they antedate Christian revelation, re-creating the historical reality of Rome's glory alongside the perception of the imperfection of that reality from a Christian perspective. The fully tragic experience that lends dignity to human suffering is impossible because man's struggle to endure in his allegiances to two worlds, the real and the ideal, has not yet been clarified by the Christian experience. Coriolanus, more specifically, represents the plight of man as a combination of artistic integrity, aristocratic inflexibility, and fatal hubris. *Antony*

General Studies

and Cleopatra captures the essential tension between Petrarchism and Neoplatonism.

1172. SMITH, MOLLY. *The Darker World Within: Evil in the Tragedies of Shakespeare and His Successors.* Newark: University of Delaware Press; London and Toronto: Associated University Presses, 1991, 195 pp.

Explores the early Stuart preoccupation with madness, violence, revenge, adultery, and incest and suggests that such an interest helped to create radical socio-political and cultural changes in the midcentury. Whether the Augustinian concept of evil as "nonbeing" depicted through stage representations of physical and mental fragmentation, the Ricoeurian sense of evil as corruption of what is healthy reflected in declining patriarchal systems, or Durkheimian evil as social deviation reflected in female domination, the plays of Shakespeare, Tourneur, Ford, Middleton, and Massinger functioned as a kind of social transformation ritual.

1173. SYNDER, SUSAN. *The Comic Matrix of Shakespeare's Tragedies: "Romeo and Juliet," "Hamlet," "Othello," and "King Lear."* Princeton: Princeton University Press, 1979, 185 pp.

Focuses on Shakespeare's use of comic conventions, structures, and assumptions in his major tragedies. Moving through three phases— the comic and tragic as polar opposites (*Romeo and Juliet*), as two sides of the same coin (*Hamlet*), and as two elements in the same compound (*King Lear*)—Shakespeare provokes comic expectations that, when proven false, reinforce the sense of tragic inevitability. The shadow side of comic events occasionally points toward the tragic; and, when comic elements threaten the hero with absurdity as in *King Lear*, the two have become generically fused into a single artistic force.

1174. STAMPFER, JUDAH. *The Tragic Engagement: A Study of Shakespeare's Classical Tragedies.* New York: Funk & Wagnalls, 1968, 336 pp.

Notes that, whereas the Christian tragedies involve a hero purged through pain, the classical tragedies (*Titus Andronicus, Julius Caesar, Troilus and Cressida, Antony and Cleopatra, Coriolanus*) depict a hero who loses his role or his identity or sense of equilibrium. In these plays the ability to adapt to the flow of politics counts more than moral depravity or redemption. *Julius Caesar* is the first play in which the "willful hero" (Octavius) wins rather than the "ethical hero" (Brutus). In later plays the ethical hero disappears, and the struggle is between the willful hero and the political hero (for example, Coriolanus and Aufidius).

1175. STIRLING, BRENTS. *Unity in Shakespearian Tragedy: The Interplay of Theme and Character*. New York: Columbia University Press, 1956, 212 pp.

Investigates for each tragedy the "state of mind" that governs both the principal figure and the play as a whole, the dominant motifs or themes and the selective use of materials, exposition, and cumulative repetitions by which they are established. In this relationship between the character and the larger action lie Shakespeare's principle of unity and the best evidence of his dramatic intention—for example, the variations of being played upon like a recorder in *Hamlet*, the theme of reputation in *Othello*, of ritual dedication in *Julius Caesar*, of "raptness" to evil in *Macbeth*.

1176. THOMAS, VIVIAN. *Shakespeare's Roman Worlds*. London: Routledge, 1989, 243 pp.

Examines the changing city of Rome in *Titus Andronicus, Julius Caesar, Antony and Cleopatra*, and *Coriolanus*, using the city-state as a locus for certain values—"service to the state, constancy, fortitude, valor, friendship, love of family and respect for the gods" (p. 1). By close analysis of Shakespeare's use and manipulation of his source, Plutarch, the study focuses fresh attention on the characterization and reassesses the political ideology of the plays.

1177. WATSON, CURTIS BROWN. *Shakespeare and the Renaissance Concept of Honor*. Princeton: Princeton University Press, 1960, 471 pp.

Discusses in part 1 the moral values and political convictions attached to honor by the Elizabethans and Jacobeans and in part 2 Shakespeare's use of these concepts in his poems and plays. Of major importance are the aristocratic ideals of glory, magnanimity, and heroic sacrifice that make honor and virtue virtually synonymous; but, relating both inwardly to moral rectitude and self-esteem and outwardly to reputation and public approbation, honor found at its center a fundamental pagan-humanist moral dualism. It is this ambivalence that Shakespeare capitalizes on in figures such as Brutus, Hamlet, Othello, Lear, Antony, and Coriolanus.

1178. WHITAKER, VIRGIL K. *The Mirror Up to Nature: The Technique of Shakespeare's Tragedies*. San Marino: Huntington Library, 1965, 332 pp.

Observes that only Shakespeare, in his "quasi-Aristotelian" tragedies, provides effective metaphysical depth by which aesthetically to accommodate a morality grounded in natural law and the psychology of human sin. In the early plays he is experimenting with established

General Studies

forms—revenge tragedy, *de casibus* tragedy, tragic romance. In *Julius Caesar* he moves toward his greatest plays by making moral choice central to the action. The tremendous ambiguities of *Hamlet* result from its being a pagan revenge play in a distinctly Christian setting. *Lear* is set in a pagan world, but peace comes only through a concept of patience and resignation originating in Christian doctrine.

1179. WHITE, R. S. *Innocent Victims: Poetic Injustice in Shakespeare's Tragedies.* London: Athlone Press, 1986, 149 pp.

Directs attention to the fate of tragedy's innocent victims, whether the young children or women physically mutilated or emotionally abused. Children destroyed as pawns in a political chess match brand Richard III, John, and Macbeth as cold-blooded creatures of monarchic convenience. Ophelia, manipulated by her father and driven by madness to a death condemned by the church as suicide is an "emblem of the victimization and official secrecy of a whole political world headed by a corrupt monarch" (p. 76). Both Desdemona and Cordelia are sacrificial victims, the one by her death liberating the remaining good impulses in her slayer, the other dying as a consequence of "civil disobedience against tyrannical exercise of authority" (p. 98).

1180. WILSON, HAROLD S. *On the Design of Shakespearian Tragedy.* Toronto: University of Toronto Press, 1957, 256 pp.

Divides Shakespeare's tragedies into those dealing with the "order of faith," in which the Christian conception of the significance of human actions is the governing principle, and those dealing with the "order of nature," in which the governing principle is man's relationship to a concept of natural order without reference to a supernatural force. In each play the structural pattern is thesis, antithesis, and synthesis. In the last movement the mystery of human love and magnanimity balances the mystery of human wickedness. The tragic vision of human love as the *summum bonum* is most profoundly expressed in *King Lear* and *Antony and Cleopatra*.

1181. YOUNG, DAVID. *The Action to the Word: Structure and Style in Shakespearean Tragedy.* New Haven: Yale University Press, 1990, 248 pp.

Explores the tension between dramatic action and expressive language in *Hamlet, Othello, King Lear,* and *Macbeth.* More precisely this study investigates how Shakespeare experimented with Hamlet's advice to the players to "suit the action to the word, the word to the action," creating multiple nuances of meaning through the interplay of structure and style, movement and speech, gesture and word.

ANTONY AND CLEOPATRA

Editions

1182. BEVINGTON, DAVID, ed. *Antony and Cleopatra*. The New Cambridge Shakespeare. Cambridge: Cambridge University Press, 1990, 274 pp.

Features an introductory essay on such matters as the date and sources, the contrarieties of critical response, the ironic gap between word and deed, transcending limits, genre and structure, style, stagecraft, and the play in performance. Particular attention is addressed to the place of the play in the canon and the relationship to the romances. Considered also are the significant alterations the playwright made in Plutarch's account. Extensive notes on each page of the text clarify specific problems of language and provide background information. A list of suggested readings is appended.

1183. RIDLEY, M. R., ed. *Antony and Cleopatra*. The Arden Shakespeare. London: Methuen; Cambridge, Mass.: Harvard University Press, 1954, 285 pp.

Includes discussion of the text and critical interpretations along with appendixes covering specific textual cruces and selections from North's Plutarch. The text is based on the First Folio, for which the copy was probably Shakespeare's foul papers. The date of composition was most likely 1607 or early 1608, and the major source was Plutarch by way of Sir Thomas North's translation. If *Antony and Cleopatra* is a lesser tragedy than *Othello* or *King Lear*, it is nonetheless highly successful, "a brilliant *tour de force*, perhaps Shakespeare's high-water mark of sheer technical brilliance" (p. 1). Ultimately, the peculiar glory of the play is not so much in its dramatic quality as in its poetry.

1184. SPEVACK, MARVIN, ed. *Antony and Cleopatra*. New Variorum Edition. New York: Modern Language Association, 1990, 886 pp.

Replaces the Variorum edition of 1907, providing the text of the play from the 1623 folio, textual notes indicating departures from that version in fifty-two other editions of the play, explanatory notes summarizing what a long succession of editors and scholars have written about the play, its theme, language, and characters, and an appendix featuring essays on the date, sources, critical heritage, and stage history. The volume also reprints the seven major source texts.

Antony and Cleopatra

Criticism

1185. ADELMAN, JANET. *The Common Liar: An Essay on "Antony and Cleopatra."* New Haven: Yale University Press, 1973, 235 pp.

Insists that multiplicity of perspective, forcing us to move simultaneously among the comic, the satiric, and the tragic, is the key to the structure of *Antony and Cleopatra*. A series of conflicting judgments by the protagonists themselves, the surrounding characters, and the spectators, the play forces us to judge and also to realize the foolishness of judging. *Antony and Cleopatra* stands between tragedy and romance; "poetry and action conflict, and each makes its own assertions and has its own validity" (p. 167).

1186. ALVIS, JOHN. "The Religion of Eros: A Re-Interpretation of *Antony and Cleopatra.*" *Renascence* 30 (1978):185–98.

Maintains that Antony and Cleopatra, in their ostentatious display of and argument for their love, make a religion of erotic passion. Their love grows monotonous in its very need constantly to be reaffirmed, not in privacy, but on the center stage of crowded events. *Antony and Cleopatra* is unique in the adulterous relationship of the protagonists. Whereas true love is the metaphoric killing of oneself in a new identification with the beloved in marriage, the love of Antony and Cleopatra leads to physical death and draws others after then.

1187. BARROLL, J. LEEDS. *"Antony and Cleopatra* and Pleasure." *Journal of English and Germanic Philology* 57 (1958):708–20.

Argues that in *Antony and Cleopatra*, as in his other tragedies, Shakespeare intends to depict the protagonist as flawed, as directly responsible for his tragedy because of a failure in reasoning and a moral weakness. The Renaissance was almost unanimous in condemning Antony and Cleopatra, and the imagery supports a similar view on Shakespeare's part. Antony was too much subject to the vices of fleshly pleasures. He is a figure loved by friends, feared by enemies, magnetic in personality, but he is destroyed by his passion and dies unreclaimed and deluded.

1188. ———. *Shakespearean Tragedy: Genre, Tradition, and Change in "Antony and Cleopatra."* Cranbury and Washington: Folger Shakespeare Library, 1984, 312 pp.

Focuses on the nature of tragic drama, the idea of the tragic hero and the problem of ethical argument in tragedy. Specifically, Shakespeare inherited from both classical and Christian nondramatic traditions the concept of tragedy as the representation of an individual who destroys himself by violating his society's highest moral values. While transplanting this concept to the stage is difficult because authorial commentary and guidance are removed, Shakespeare succeeds in depicting his tragic figures as responsible agents and in constricting the ethical framework by which their defeat must be measured. *Antony and Cleopatra* is analyzed in detail to illustrate the theory with greater specificity.

1189. BECKERMAN, BERNARD. "Past the Size of Dreaming." In *Twentieth Century Interpretations of "Antony and Cleopatra."* Edited by Mark Rose. Englewood Cliffs: Prentice-Hall, 1977, pp. 99–112.

Maintains that the sprawling spectacle belies the heart of the action, the development of thought and feeling between Antony and Cleopatra. This action falls into two halves—that in which Antony attempts to accommodate his amorous desires to his political world and that in which he attempts to accommodate his allegiance to Cleopatra. Only following his commitment to the East does Antony begin to display the first signs of tenderness rather than lust. Throughout act 4 he mounts in stature, not as a soldier, but as a man; and in act 5 Cleopatra achieves a state of spiritual identity with him.

1190. BEREK, PETER. "Doing and Undoing: The Value of Action in *Antony and Cleopatra.*" *Shakespeare Quarterly* 32 (1981):295–304.

Notes that the three uses of the verb "do" in the play (2.2.201–5, 4.14.47–49, 5.2.4–8) are paradoxical; a character in doing one action is undoing another. This paradoxical quality is central to the play's presentation of Cleopatra and the love relationship of Antony and Cleopatra. They embrace paradox in choosing life only to die; they simply discover that there are no successes worth having, and their deaths are rewards for this knowledge. In "undoing" their lives they "do" something better for their souls.

1191. BLISSITT, WILLIAM. "Dramatic Irony in *Antony and Cleopatra.*" *Shakespeare Quarterly* 18 (1967):151–66.

Argues that Shakespeare employs dramatic irony as a structural device to suggest the impression of two worlds, the cult of pleasure in the East and of Roman stoicism in the West. By discrediting that which represents Rome and enhancing that which represents Egypt, he draws the spectator to accept pleasure over duty. Actually Egypt comes to represent more than mere pleasure. While imagery of angels and stars clusters about Antony, Cleopatra is transmigrated from the harlot of the Apocalypse to the New Jerusalem.

Antony and Cleopatra

1192. BRADLEY, A. C. "Shakespeare's *Antony and Cleopatra*." In *Oxford Lectures on Poetry*. London: Macmillan, 1909, pp. 279–308.

Argues that *Antony and Cleopatra* in acts 3–4 is defective in its short, choppy scenes. More significantly, there is a difference in substance between this play and the great tragedies. The first half is not decisively tragic in tone, and it lacks both an explosion of passion and exciting bodily action. Shakespeare chooses not to portray either an inner struggle in Antony's attempt to break his bondage or the magnitude of the fatal step. A pervasive irony constantly undercuts any sense of tragic dignity. We do not, for example, consider Antony to be the noblest type like Brutus, Hamlet, and Othello. Cleopatra, in effect, destroys him, but she does attain tragic stature in act 5.

1193. COPPEDGE, WALTER R. "The Joy of the Worm: Dying in *Antony and Cleopatra*." *Renaissance Papers* (1988):41–50.

Examines the spiritual dimensions of the deaths of Antony and Cleopatra. Antony's death is sacrificial to the extent that it provokes a profound change in the queen. Her suicide by means of the asp, identified as it is with Egyptian religion, suggests divine instrumentality. The Eastern star noted by Charmian as her mistress dies may be Sires (associated with Isis) or Aphrodite, the star of the morning. "Cleopatra, radiant with love, firm in her resolve, takes the joy of the worm and becomes a dish for the gods" (p. 50).

1194. COUCHMAN, GORDON W. "*Antony and Cleopatra* and the Subjective Convention." *PMLA* 76 (1961):420–25.

Attacks Shaw's polemical pronouncements on *Antony and Cleopatra* as a play about a whore and without a moral. Seizing on Shakespeare's exaltation of the lovers as material for a Puritanical and antiromantic attack, Shaw totally misses the moral and the realism under his nose. Just as much as the play eulogizes love as the supreme emotion transcending time and death, it also is a tragic rendering of an individual incapacitated and destroyed by passion set against the backdrop of a society itself in the advanced stages of decay.

1195. DAICHES, DAVID. "Imagery and Meaning in *Antony and Cleopatra*." *English Studies* 43 (1962):343–58.

Observes that the brilliant power of the poetry in *Antony and Cleopatra* compels an intensity of attention and empathy that normally would be afforded only a play with a challenging moral pattern. The chain of events that drives Antony to suicide brings together, in terms of the poetic imagery, the man of action and the lover. Similarly, Cleopatra's development in the final act is viewed essentially through the imagery as Shakespeare combines the roles of mistress and wife, courtesan and queen, Egyptian and Roman. Ultimately we are left with the feeling that there is no known morality by which we can determine whether the play is about human frailty or human glory.

1196. DANBY, JOHN F. "*Antony and Cleopatra*: A Jacobean Adjustment." In *Poets on Fortune's Hill: Studies in Sidney, Shakespeare, and Beaumont and Fletcher*. London: Faber & Faber, 1952, pp. 227–33. Also published as *Elizabethan and Jacobean Poets: Studies in Sidney, Shakespeare, Beaumont and Fletcher*. London: Faber and Faber, 1964.

Argues that *Antony and Cleopatra* depicts neither the downfall of an infatuated soldier nor the epiphany of a soldier in love; instead the play's meaning is to be found in the Shakespearean dialectic, in the reality expressed through the contrarieties that are juxtaposed and mingled. Rome and Egypt, Cleopatra and Caesar, the soldier and lover—such opposites create for the spectator a swinging ambivalence as ultimately the ambiguous alternatives destroy each other. In a sense, this play, like *Timon of Athens*, appears to have been written in the aftermath of *King Lear* in that it is a deliberate construction of a world without a redeeming Cordelia-principle.

1197. DAVIES, H. NEVILLE. "Jacobean *Antony and Cleopatra*." *Shakespeare Studies* 17 (1985):123–58.

Notes that Shakespeare late in 1606 could not possibly have written about Caesar Augustus without associating him with James, whose propaganda was making just that connection. Moreover, the visit in the summer of 1606 by his brother, Christian IV of Denmark, brings James's character sharply into focus. Christian, like Antony, was a larger-than-life figure, immensely attractive, and a military man able to take pleasure in the company of all sorts. Above all, he was a drinker. How James reacted to "Shakespeare's opalescent fusion of ancient history and Jacobean observation " (p. 149) is a tantalizing question for which historical records provide no answer.

1198. DONNO, ELIZABETH STORY. "Cleopatra Again." *Shakespeare Quarterly* 7 (1956):227–33.

Asserts that the Christian readings of *Antony and Cleopatra* arise from injudicious suppressions or misinterpretations of certain portions of the text. It has been argued, for example, that Enobarbus repeatedly calls attention to Christian principles that inform the play. Such an argument distorts both what he says and what he does. An even greater distortion is to presume that Cleopatra's actions in act 5 are in their main outline comparable to the Christian penitent. Her shifting ideas, instead, reflect her psychological state, not her faith in anything beyond herself.

1199. FICHTER, ANDREW. "*Antony and Cleopatra*: The Time of Universal Peace." *Shakespeare Survey* 33 (1980):99–111.

Views *Antony and Cleopatra* as a fully conscious artifice that obliquely invokes a Christian vision chronologically and metaphysically uniting the quest traditions of Roman epic and Christianity. Because the play does not conform to the norms of tragedy, the spectators are encouraged to seek a vision of reference beyond the physical action itself. Enobarbus in such a vision suggests Judas, and Antony suggests John; Antony's struggle with death bears a metaphoric correspondence with Christ's struggle.

1200. FISCH, HAROLD. "*Antony and Cleopatra*: The Limits of Mythology." *Shakespeare Survey* 23 (1970):59–67.

Suggests that *Antony and Cleopatra* deals directly with myth, depicting Venus as the goddess of love and Mars as the god of war. This theme is merged later into the myth of Isis as goddess of fertility and Osiris as the sun god who dies and is resurrected. The Roman emphasis on history tends to reduce the tragedy of Antony and Cleopatra to an "incident," but their love grows to a point of transcending both the Roman and Egyptian worlds, indeed the entire pagan world, giving meaning not only to human relationships but to history itself.

1201. FITZ, L. T. "Egyptian Queens and Male Reviewers: Sexist Attitudes in *Antony and Cleopatra* Criticism." *Shakespeare Quarterly* 28 (1977):297–316.

Argues that almost all critical approaches to *Antony and Cleopatra* have been colored by chauvinistic assumptions made by male critics who feel threatened by Cleopatra. Response may take the form of disdain for a woman who attempts to rule and thus to usurp man's role or of distaste for the carnality of the play and Cleopatra's sexual frankness or of the assertion that Antony is the sole protagonist. Cleopatra's role and function as protagonist should be reassessed with greater fairness and objectivity.

1202. HALL, JOAN LORD. " 'To the Very Heart of Loss': Rival Constructs of 'Heart' in *Antony and Cleopatra*." *College Literature* 18 (1991):64–76.

Notes that of the many juxtaposed opposites in the play one of the most significant is "heart," which to the Romans denotes manly courage but to the Egyptians refers to the seat of love and affection. The play continually suggests that such a dichotomy cannot be rigidly maintained, a point best seen in the courageous Roman soldier Enobarbus, who dies of a broken heart out of affection to Antony. Antony's fragmentation ultimately "exposes the contradictions within any culture . . . that privileges combative heroics . . . above a wider nexus of human relationships" (p. 74).

1203. HARRIS, DUNCAN. " 'Again for Cydnus': The Dramaturgical Resolution of *Antony and Cleopatra.*" *Studies in English Literature 1500–1900* 17 (1977):219–31.

Claims that Shakespeare affirms the value of the lovers' relationship in life and in death through a technique called "framing" in which characters utter choric judgments that tend to focus attention more sharply on the action. Examples are the comments of Philo and Demetrius in 1.1, Enobarbus's observations about the doting Antony and his desertion, and Caesar's words following Cleopatra's suicide. While the first two prove to be largely inaccurate or inadequate observations, the audience suspends judgment in the final scene because the conflict between telling and showing is resolved in Caesar's reminiscent eulogy.

1204. HILLMAN, RICHARD. "Antony, Hercules, and Cleopatra: 'The Bidding of the Gods' and 'The Subtlest Maze of All.' " *Shakespeare Quarterly* 38 (1987):442–51.

Focuses on the scene in which Hercules deserts Antony as a shocking intrusion into what has been a play notably without reference to the supernatural, an intrusion that must point to some definite strategy since Shakespeare altered Plutarch both in the order of events and in context (music/Hercules instead of revelry/Bacchus). Whereas in Plutarch the god's departure precedes Antony's night of debauchery, in Shakespeare it precedes his military victory. The change signals Shakespeare's intention to subvert tragic form, to exploit the ambiguity of the scene in initiating a "countercurrent of triumph and beauty as the lovers go to their doom" (p. 450).

1205. HOOKS, R. "Shakespeare's *Antony and Cleopatra*: Power and Submission." *American Imago* 44 (1987):37–49.

Enhances the consideration of *Antony and Cleopatra* as a romance by viewing the "mother-child boundary dilemma as the model for the complications and unresolved tensions of adult sexuality in the play" (p. 37). The psychosis at the core of Antony's crisis is his inability to distinguish between a maternal environment and a reality-oriented perspective in his love. That is, an ability normally learned in the weaning process is absent in the dynamics of his relationship. As the "serpent of the Old Nile," Cleopatra represents a threat to patriarchal order and phallic dominance in both her public and private roles.

1206. JONES, GORDON P. "The 'Strumpet's Fool' in *Antony and Cleopatra*." *Shakespeare Quarterly* 34 (1984):62–68.

Suggests that Antony's transformation into the strumpet's fool possibly should be symbolized in the opening scene by Antony and Cleopatra wearing each other's clothes. Such a scene would emphasize both the sportiveness of the lovers and Antony's military and sexual degeneracy. It would also explain Enobarbus's comment that Antony is coming on stage in scene 2, when, according to the stage direction, Cleopatra enters first. The theme and the tone of the unmanning of Antony by the power of love would thus immediately take on the tone of heroic comedy so typical of the play throughout.

1207. LEAVIS, F. R. "*Antony and Cleopatra* and *All for Love*: A Critical Exercise." *Scrutiny* 5 (1936–1937):158–69.

Argues that *Antony and Cleopatra* is manifestly more powerful in poetry (metaphor, tone, movement) and tragic effect than *All for Love*. Shakespeare's verse enacts its meaning while Dryden's is merely descriptive eloquence. Moreover, Shakespeare's characters have a life corresponding to the verse, his overall drama a richness and depth that dwarf Dryden. In a word, *Antony and Cleopatra* is a very great dramatic poem and *All for Love* can be compared with it only in the sense of "setting off the character of the Shakespearean genius" (p. 168).

1208. MACDONALD, RONALD R. "Playing till Doomsday: Interpreting *Antony and Cleopatra*." *English Literary Renaissance* 15 (1985):78–99.

Maintains that Shakespeare in the play self-consciously interrogates the traditional notions of dramaturgy in order to suggest alternate modes of representation and that, moreover, in doing so he was also questioning classicism as a historical construct and interrogating its privileged position in Renaissance culture. Historical facts at times recede, and the histrionic control of imagination and language takes over. It is not an effort to make us replace one version with another but to see meanings of history as indeterminate, as a collection of meanings in competition.

1209. MARKELS, JULIAN. *The Pillar of the World: "Antony and Cleopatra" in Shakespeare's Development*. Columbus: Ohio State University Press, 1968, 191 pp.

Observes that Shakespeare, by forcing the spectator simultaneously to hold morally contradictory notions of both Antony and Cleopatra, slowly renders them amoral. Since the play has no villains, the evil that must be conquered is within the self, but it is irrevocably fused with the goodness as well. Both principals come to view death as not only a physical action but also an apotheosis in which vision moves beyond the naturalistic world of providential order. This is a key element of Shakespeare's romances, and in this sense Shakespeare in this play moves beyond (not above) *King Lear.*

1210. MOORE, JOHN REES. "The Enemies of Love: The Example of Antony and Cleopatra." *Kenyon Review* 31 (1969):646–74.

Defends the love of Antony and Cleopatra against the charges that they are too old, that they abandon religion and morality, and that they are too self-centered and worldly wise. Their theatricality masks genuine passion that becomes a gauntlet flung in the face of the Roman ideals of power and ambition. Throughout the play various forces tempt them to compromise their love; but the reverse occurs, and the affection is driven to greater heights.

1211. NEVO, RUTH. "The Masque of Greatness." *Shakespeare Studies* 4 (1968):111–28.

Views Cleopatra's final act as the dramatization of her imagination working toward its resolution. She dies neither as strumpet nor as ennobled queen but as the epitome of her own voluptuous Egyptian nature. Her reference to the "eloquence of Masques" is indirectly a reference to what she creates in "high Roman fashion." She removes herself physically from the possibility of being exhibited in Caesar's triumph by a grand spectacle of her own. The clown provides the antimasque and dramatizes Cleopatra's transcendence of a baser life.

1212. ORNSTEIN, ROBERT. "The Ethic of the Imagination: Love and Art in *Antony and Cleopatra.*" In *Later Shakespeare.* Edited by John Russell Brown and Bernard Harris. Stratford-upon-Avon Studies, 8. London: Edward Arnold, 1966, pp. 31–46.

Insists that the honesty of the imagination and its superiority to matters of political conquests demand our sympathetic perception of Cleopatra in the final act. Shakespeare faces full front the paradoxical ironies in the lovers, but their relationship is elevated in that it is juxtaposed to a sadly decayed Roman idealism in which treachery is ubiquitous. While morally there is little to choose between Rome and Egypt, they are polar opposites in matters of the heart.

1213. RACKIN, PHYLLIS. "Shakespeare's Boy Cleopatra, the Decorum of Nature, and the Golden World of Poetry." *PMLA* 87 (1972):201–12.

Antony and Cleopatra

Asserts that Shakespeare's strategy in writing *Antony and Cleopatra* is daring to the point of recklessness, a quality characteristic both of the love of the principals and also of the dramatic technique. The episodic structure shifting from continent to continent and leaping years directly defies the growing demands for neoclassical unities. The language, too, is reckless in its combination of Latinisms, slang, and mixed metaphors. Most daring of all is the inconsistency of Cleopatra as the heroine.

1214. ROSE, PAUL L. "The Politics of *Antony and Cleopatra*." *Shakespeare Quarterly* 20 (1969):379–89.

Notes that Caesar's triumph preserving society at the end of *Antony and Cleopatra* was reassuring to the Elizabethan spectator, while for modern audiences the emotional dislocation far outweighs political reassurance. In Shakespeare's day, with fear of anarchy at a fever pitch, Antony, Caesar, and Cleopatra were archetypes of conflicting views on kingship. Caesar is the ideal ruler, Antony exploits war for personal valor, and Cleopatra is a hereditary despotic power. The play, most assuredly, is not a political treatise; the dynamic of history is the human character torn between impulse and reason.

1215. SIMMONS, J. L. "The Comic Pattern and Vision in *Antony and Cleopatra*." *ELH* 36 (1969):493–510.

Asserts that *Antony and Cleopatra* is delightful tragedy in which death has lost its sting and the sense of triumph is overpowering in love's aspiration for a new heaven removed from imperfect realities. The play is structured more like romantic comedy than conventional tragedy; the worlds of Egypt and Rome function somewhat like the tavern and court of *Henry IV*, with Egypt having a quality of Saturnalia. Even without grace the play points upward, suggesting that death is not the final reality.

1216. SINGH, JYOTSNA. "Renaissance Antitheatricality, Antifeminism, and Shakespeare's *Antony and Cleopatra*." *Renaissance Drama*, n.s. 20 (1989):99–122.

Focuses on the theatrical function of Cleopatra in light of the ongoing debate in the sixteenth and seventeenth centuries about the theater and women in antitheatrical and antifeminist writings. More specifically, the play reproduces and contests the notion in such writings that women and actors duplicitously subvert the "natural" boundaries of social and sexual differences. Cleopatra's histrionic revisions repeatedly disrupt the orthodox impulse to fix identity and to secure the myth of the male hero against threats of demystification. "By conflating femininity and theatricality in such positive and powerful terms in the figure of Cleopatra, the playwright is identifying femininity as one of power's crucial modes" (p. 117).

1217. SPRENGNETHER, MADELON. "The Boy Actor and Femininity in *Antony and Cleopatra*." In *Shakespeare's Personality*. Edited by Norman N. Holland, Sidney Homan, and Bernard J. Paris. Berkeley and London: University of California Press, 1989, pp. 191–205.

Argues that the boy actor in Shakespeare is fundamental to the playwright's equivocal portrayal of femininity, functioning as a destabilizing element in the hierarchical order of gender and allowing him to present women as both "Other" and "not Other." More specifically, they portray on the one hand a loss of masculinity and male dominance, but on the other the possibility of a single-sex homosocial society. Cleopatra's allusion to the fact that she is male (her greatness being "boy-ed") allows Shakespeare to diminish her threat as woman, to represent female sexuality with less rigidity and greater gender tolerance, ultimately to equivocate and suspend questions of gender in a rich ambiguity.

1218. STEMPEL, DANIEL. "The Transmigration of the Crocodile." *Shakespeare Quarterly* 7 (1956):59–72.

Argues that *Antony and Cleopatra* is paramountly concerned with the restoration of health to a diseased state. Antony's domination by Cleopatra reverses the natural roles of male and female, corresponding on the psychological level to reason's domination by will in his character. The misogynistic hostility toward Cleopatra in the play is not playful but deadly serious. When Octavius successfully resists her in act 5 and Cleopatra commits suicide, the death scene is dominated by the theme of the nature of woman; her death is the transmigration of the crocodile, the death of the serpent of the old Nile.

1219. STEPPAT, MICHAEL. *The Critical Reception of Shakespeare's "Antony and Cleopatra" from 1607–1905*. Bochumer anglistische Studien, 9. Amsterdam: Grüner, 1980, 619 pp.

Surveys the criticism of *Antony and Cleopatra* from the beginning through Bradley in 1905 with the aim not only the elucidation of the play but also, through its impact on a wide range of critical expectation, the exploration of the transitoriness of critical taste and standards. Chapters focus on the seventeenth and eighteenth centuries (nature and art, dramatic structure, poetic justice, rhetoric and style) and the nineteenth century (the moral approach, the romantic view, continental criticism after the romantics). A concluding section contrasts Bradley's

emphasis on character and Schücking's emphasis on the ethical traditions and conventions.

1220. ——. "Shakespeare's Response to Dramatic Tradition in *Antony and
Cleopatra*." In *Shakespeare: Text, Language, Criticism: Essays in Honour of
Marvin Spevack*. Edited by Bernard Fabian and Kurt Tetzeli von Rosador. Hildesheim and New York: Olms-Weidmann, 1987, pp. 254–
79.

Examines Robert Garnier's *Marc Antoine* and Samuel Daniel's
Tragedy of Cleopatra as subtexts that "acted as stimuli for Shakespeare
during the development of thematic and verbal concepts, yet against
which he maintained his creative independence" (p. 255). From Garnier, for example, Shakespeare seems to have drawn the extended dramatic focus on Antony's inner suffering as well as moving Antony's
decision to kill himself to after (rather than before) he receives the false
report of Cleopatra's suicide. From Daniel Shakespeare apparently drew
the psychological insights in Cleopatra's response to the death of her
lover.

1221. Stoll, Elmer Edgar. "Cleopatra." *Modern Language Review* 23
(1928):145–63.

Describes Shakespeare's vision of Cleopatra as sympathetic but
austere; viewed from every angle, she both fascinates and bewitches.
Shakespeare's concern with character is its dramatic function; it must be
judged from what it says and does. Cleopatra is clearly a figure of vanity
and amorous indulgence, living for pleasure and neglecting her duties
of state. Shakespeare, though, holds the balance evenly; he disapproves
of the relationship of Antony and Cleopatra, but he does not refuse the
glorification of their love in poetry.

1222. Williamson, Marilyn L. "Patterns of Development in *Antony and
Cleopatra*." *Tennessee Studies in Literature* 14 (1969):129–39.

Argues for a design in Cleopatra's "infinite variety," perceptible
stages in her development that lend unity to the play as a whole. This
development is not so much basic changes in her personality as in her
moving, wavelike, through experiences of increasing intensity to the
final act of death. The mixture of her motives for suicide—love of
Antony and fear of Caesar's triumph—is only the culmination of other
motives we have seen in her earlier. She rises to death in the high
Roman fashion as she rose to parting with Antony in act 1.

1223. Wilson, Elkin Calhoun. "Enobarbus." In *Joseph Quincy Adams Memorial Studies*. Edited by James G. McManaway, Giles E. Dawson, and

Edwin E. Willoughby. Washington: Folger Shakespeare Library, 1948, pp. 391–408.

Describes Enobarbus as vital to the structure of *Antony and Cleopatra*. The privileged friend of Antony, a Roman at ease in the Egyptian world, Enobarbus with his realistic asides provides something of a choric function. As Antony's military fortunes wane, Enobarbus counsels his master as Antony's own better self would, finally deserting him as beyond hope. Like Lear's fool Enobarbus is a translation of the classical chorus into a human figure, a translation poignantly demonstrated by his remorse provoked by Antony's response to his desertion and by his own death of a broken heart.

1224. WIMSATT, W. K., Jr. "Poetry and Morals." *Thought* 23 (1948):81–99. Reprinted in *The Verbal Icon* (Lexington: University of Kentucky Press, 1954), pp. 85–100.

Distinguishes moral value from poetic value in that the business of poetry is not to think but to present the feelings connected with thinking. *Antony and Cleopatra*, for example, pleads for certain evil choices; it involves the victory of passionate, illicit love over practical political and moral concerns. These countervalues, on the other hand, are embodied in a corrupt, deceitful Roman world characterized by treachery and infidelity. In this instance the poetic value of love transcends narrowly defined moral values.

1225. WOLF, WILLIAM D. " 'New Heaven, New Earth': The Escape from Mutability in *Antony and Cleopatra*." *Shakespeare Quarterly* 33 (1982):328–35.

Traces Antony and Cleopatra's escape through suicide from a world of passion, turbulence, and change—a world of carnal love and lust—to a more lasting bond of love and affinity. With Egypt and Rome as the magnetic poles around which irreconcilable differences cluster, the love of Antony and Cleopatra develops to a point of rejecting both. Stripped of his armor, his suicide bungled, Antony responds to Cleopatra's trickery with a new patience and stoicism; Cleopatra, in turn, dons her robes for death, symbolizing her rejection of subjectivity to Caesar and her immortal longings for Antony.

1226. WORTHEN, W. B. "The Weight of Antony: Staging 'Character' in *Antony and Cleopatra*." *Studies in English Literature 1500–1900* 26 (1986):295–308.

Notes that, when he is hoisted up to Cleopatra's monument, Antony is momentarily suspended between legendary greatness and its tragic acting. Here Shakespeare calls the spectator's attention to the theatrical moment, and in doing so he dramatizes the duality in the idea of characterization, Antony as titan and Antony as mortally weighted human, Cleopatra as Queen of the Nile and Cleopatra as boy-actor. So, too, Cleopatra's physical enactment of death in the closing moments forces our attention to both the story and the acting, the myth and the physical reenactment.

Stage History

1227. LAMB, MARGARET. *"Antony and Cleopatra" on the English Stage*. Rutherford: Fairleigh Dickinson University Press; London and Toronto: Associated University Presses, 1980, 241 pp.

Covers forty-two productions of *Antony and Cleopatra* from the first performance at the Globe with Richard Burbage, probably in 1606, to the Peter Brook Royal Shakespeare Company production at Stratford in 1978 with Alan Howard and Glenda Jackson. Among the most revealing aspects of changing tastes, theatrical and ethical, are the difficulties of production during the "Age of Scenery" with the proscenium-arch stage and the disturbance at times of what appears to be the glorification of illicit love. Characterizations have ranged from the sexy to the cerebral, from the humanly weak to the regally strong.

CORIOLANUS

Reference Work

1228. LEGGATT, ALEXANDER, and LOIS, NOREM, comps. *"Coriolanus": An Annotated Bibliography*. Garland Reference Library of the Humanities, 483: Garland Shakespeare Bibliographies, 17. New York and London: Garland Publishing, 1989, 738 pp.

Contains 1,062 items representing virtually all publications on the play from 1940 to 1987, along with the most significant items prior to 1940. The categories, each arranged chronologically, include criticism, sources and background, textual studies, editions, adaptations and influence, translations, bibliographies and reference works, and staging and stage history. A brief introductory essay traces the history of recent criticism and research.

Editions

1229. BROCKBANK, PHILLIP, ed. *Coriolanus*. The Arden Shakespeare. London: Methuen; Cambridge, Mass.: Harvard University Press, 1976, 370 pp.

Includes discussion of the text, date, sources, language of the play, stage history, and critical interpretations, as well as appendixes featuring selections from North's Plutarch and Camden's *Remains*. The text is based on the First Folio, for which the copy was probably Shakespeare's foul papers, at least partly prepared by the playwright for the theater. The manifest maturity of the play's verse and its political insights suggest a date of 1607–1608. The tragedy is firmly established in the modern repertory, largely a consequence of an Old Vic production in 1938 with Laurence Olivier and Sybil Thorndike.

1230. FURNESS, HENRY HOWARD, Jr., ed. *The Tragedie of Coriolanus*. A New Variorum Edition of Shakespeare. Philadelphia: J.B. Lippincott, 1928, 762 pp.

Uses the First Folio as the copy text. On each page, for that portion of the text, are provided variant readings, textual notes, and general critical commentary. Following the text are sections on the nature of the text, Collier's trilogy, the date of composition, the source, criticisms, the characters, Shakespeare and the masses, dramatic versions, stage history, actors interpretations, and a list of works consulted.

1231. WILSON, JOHN DOVER, ed. *The Tragedy of Coriolanus*. Cambridge: Cambridge University Press, 1960, 274 pp.

Provides extensive textual notes, a critical introduction, a discussion of the copy text, a section on stage history, and a glossary. This edition is based on the First Folio, for which the copy was either Shakespeare's foul papers as touched up slightly by the prompter or bookholder or a transcript of the foul papers. Coriolanus, like Antony, is a soldier cast in the heroic mold and subject to vehement fits of passion that brought him to ruin. But, whereas Antony is a courteous, middle-aged sensualist, the other—little more than a boy in years—is a giant in strength, contemptuous of everything and everyone who fails to measure up to his idea of honor.

Criticism

1232. BEDFORD, KRISTINA. *"Coriolanus" at the National: "Th' Interpretation of the Time."* Selinsgrove, Pa.: Susquehanna University Press; London and Toronto: Associated University Presses, 1991, 300 pp.

Coriolanus

Provides a complete record of Peter Hall's 1984–85 production at the Olivier Theatre, tracing alterations in the text through rehearsal to the final production. The focus of the latter portion of the study is on how Hall's editorial changes were designed to capture the essence of the play's political vision within the context of the late twentieth century.

1233. BRISTOL, MICHAEL D. "Lenten Butchery: Legitimation Crisis in *Coriolanus*." In *Shakespeare Reproduced: The Text in History and Ideology*. Edited by Jean Howard and Marion F. O'Connor. New York and London: Methuen, 1987, pp. 207–24.

Views the play as an example of "legitimation crisis" with the central issue not the role of one individual within the political structure but the nature and purpose of that political structure itself. For Coriolanus the fundamental purpose of organized society is a state of readiness for war, a posture of aggression toward the geopolitical Other; the plebeians, on the other hand, view war as temporary. Any attempt to appropriate the play for an ideologically subversive discourse "remains bound up in the politically weak and practically insignificant corporate goal-values of pluralism" (p. 220). A more effective focus for revisionary activists would be on the history of the play itself and its previous use for ideological containment.

1234. BRITTIN, NORMAN A. "Coriolanus, Alceste, and Dramatic Genres." *PMLA* 71 (1956):799–807.

Observes that, just as a hair divides the comic character from the pathetic or tragic (Alceste in Molière's *Le Misanthrope*), certain characters have a tendency to cross over from the tragic to the comic (Coriolanus). Coriolanus's colossal egotism prevents our sympathetic engagement and retains a sense of intellectual detachment. More so than most Shakespearean protagonists, Coriolanus is unadaptable in a social sense. In his perversity at times almost approaching the level of caricature, he is diminished from tragic magnitude more nearly to comic size.

1235. BROWNING, I. R. "Boy of Tears." *Essays in Criticism* 5 (1955):18–31.

Notes that Plutarch provided Shakespeare the key to Coriolanus's character—his relationship with his mother. His sense of all Rome's having deserted him and his vicious verbal attacks upon the tribunes and the common people reflect his attempt, conscious or unconscious, to "censor and disguise his intense preoccupation with his own merits" (p. 24). This mind-set is the result of his upbringing, of Volumnia's determination to make him a man and to praise him only for martial exploits. When she begs him to spare Rome, she creates a dilemma that he is not trained to accommodate and destroys him as surely as she has created him.

1236. BURKE, KENNETH. "Coriolanus—and the Delights of Faction." *Arts in Society* 2, no. 3 (1963). Reprinted in *Hudson Review* 19 (1966):185–202.

Describes the moral problem or social tension of *Coriolanus* to be a discord intrinsic to the distinction between upper and lower classes. Coriolanus's frankness and courage reflect his nobility, but his hubris constantly aggravates the situation. Caught between the clash of motivations of nation, class, family, and individual, his natural prowess has been twisted by his mother's training. His tragedy is a consequence not only of his individual flaw but also of the events and persons who conspire to produce it.

1237. CARDUCCI, JANE. "Shakespeare's Coriolanus: 'Could I Find Out / The Woman's Part in Me.'" *Literature and Psychology* 33 (1987):11–20.

Maintains that Shakespeare in *Coriolanus* explores and finally rejects the Roman code of manliness, demonstrating the inadequacy and the artificiality of the predatory Roman ideal that denies the softer, feminine side. Fiercely independent, Coriolanus manifests his fear as anger, and he is triggered into furious rage when Aufidius calls him "boy" and thus strips him of his manhood. This "unfinished" character remains in perpetual adolescence, intolerant, vain, insolent, and aggressive. His failure to identify with his feminine side leads to his downfall.

1238. CAVELL, STANLEY. " 'Who Does the Wolf Love?': *Coriolanus* and the Interpretations of Politics." In *Shakespeare and the Question of Theory.* Edited by Patricia Parker and Geoffrey Hartman. New York and London: Methuen, 1985, pp. 245–72.

Asserts that the idea of cannibalization runs throughout the play, an imagistic theme established in the opening scene in the reference to the people as lambs to be devoured by the patrician wolves and in the final scenes in the image of Rome devouring itself. The fable of the belly acts as play within the play, and the spectator comes to realize that emotionally and politically he is "strung out on both sides of a belly" (p. 270). Coriolanus becomes a kind of sacrificial lamb butchered for the salvation of the city, an image fostered by his refusal to show his wounds (an inversion of Christ showing his wounds to prove His resurrection) and of the appearance of three women to Coriolanus before Rome (an analogue of the women who appear before Christ on the cross).

1239. CHAMBERS, R. W. "The Expression of Ideas—Particularly Political Ideas—in the Three Pages and in Shakespeare." In *Shakespeare's Hand*

Coriolanus

in the Play of "Sir Thomas More." Shakespeare Problem Series, 2. Cambridge: Cambridge University Press, 1923, pp. 142–87.

Points out parallels in the 147 lines of *Sir Thomas More* believed to be by Shakespeare and parts of *Coriolanus* and *Troilus and Cressida*. For one thing, there is an extraordinary likeness in the general outlook on state affairs, for example in the fear of anarchy and the insistence on social order. For another, there are numerous parallel images, phrases, and words. *More* and *Coriolanus* have scenes in which an individual is rescued from the mob with similar metaphors; the scenes also use similar metaphors in describing the sanctity of the state and the rioters' need for repentance.

1240. COLMAN, E. A. M. "The End of Coriolanus." *ELH* 34 (1967):1–20.

Asserts that *Coriolanus* illustrates a different kind of tragic technique from that of the major tragedies, that much is left unspoken but is established dramatically. Coriolanus's choice at the end is between his self-respect and his humanity. Given this choice earlier, there would have been no dilemma; now his mother's implorations confuse him, and he opts for humanity. His final outburst against Aufidius, however, gives evidence that he dies continuing to aspire to personal integrity.

1241. DAVIDSON, CLIFFORD. "*Coriolanus*: A Study in Political Dislocation." *Shakespeare Studies* 4 (1968):263–74.

Argues that *Coriolanus* remains unpopular because spectators prefer tragedy tinged with melodrama rather than a more complex resolution in which emotional identification with the protagonist is impossible. Shakespeare in all of his political plays encourages a peaceful balance between patricians and plebeians and places special emphasis on the moral responsibility of the leader. Coriolanus as a leader is a miserable failure, a choleric man guilty of such excessive pride that he considers the sacrifice of his country a viable option.

1242. ENRIGHT, D. J. "*Coriolanus*: Tragedy or Debate?" *Essays in Criticism* 4 (1954):1–19.

Notes that Coriolanus, a brilliant soldier but a disastrous politician, is the most talked about character in Shakespeare. The two sides of his personality are repeatedly discussed by those favoring and those opposing him, and the result is a cold accuracy that holds the spectators at emotional arm's length. In the final analysis, the tragedy is that of Rome, of the failure of self-understanding both in the people and in the leader. While it is a successful play, it is of a lower order than that of *Macbeth*.

1243. FABER, M. D. "Freud and Shakespeare's Mobs." *Literature and Psychology* 15 (1965):238–55.

Investigates the extent to which Shakespeare's description of mob behavior in *Julius Caesar* and *Coriolanus* accords with Freudian mob psychology. The erotic nature of group ties is central in *Coriolanus*, involving a mob that longs to be governed lovingly. Coriolanus loathes the people, denying them the very thing they desire. Brutus and Sicinius labor to prevent the formation of any such erotic ties. When Coriolanus finally agrees to woo the mob, the tribunes block it by whipping him into a prideful frenzy.

1244. FORTESCUE, JONATHAN. "The Folds in the Belly: A Parable of Taking Up Representation in *The Tragedy of Coriolanus*." *Shakespeare Jahrbuch* 127 (1991):106–20.

Maintains that the mutinous citizens who charge through the pit and rush upon the stage "foreground the divisive tension between a representable authority and the artisans who 'show forth' significant roles which are contiguous with the vulnerable mechanisms of theatre" (p. 108). Menenius's fable of the belly is intended through humor to contain the mob, with the role probably played by Robert Armin and the speech punctuated with belches where dashes appear in the text. Even so, from this point, Coriolanus is forced to contend with the multitude for "vocal control of Roman politics and, inevitably, of dramatic space" (p. 119).

1245. GAUDET, PAUL. "Gesture in *Coriolanus*: Textual Cues for Actor and Audience." *Upstart Crow* 8 (1988):77–92.

Comments on the profound implications of Coriolanus's moment of silence as he stands before his mother in act 5 of the play. To capitulate to her pleas to save Rome will mean his certain death, but the spectators are painfully aware that he will do so; they have been carefully prepared by clues placed into the text leading up to this moment. Coriolanus in 5.3 expresses affection for Menenius, thus increasing the emotional strain at the point his immediate family enters. The curtsying of Virgilia and the bowing of Volumnia precede his kneeling and then turning away in profound consternation. The culminating moment is when Volumnia reverses the gestural pattern of rejection, threatening to desert him.

1246. GOLDMAN, MICHAEL. "Characterizing Coriolanus." *Shakespeare Survey* 34 (1981):73–84.

Questions the validity of our expectations of novelistic characters, problematic and psychologically penetrable, in literary characters before

Coriolanus

the nineteenth century. Even so, *Coriolanus* offers in its protagonist a unique example in Shakespeare of distinctly modern characterization, with other characters constantly attempting to explain his actions and with the spectators growing increasingly aware of how inadequate their analyses are. Surely Shakespeare intends for Coriolanus to be viewed as a problematic figure, a reflection of the paradox of a distinctive individual "who is at once incommunicably private and unavoidably social" (p. 84).

1247. GURR, ANDREW. "*Coriolanus* and the Body Politic." *Shakespeare Survey* 28 (1975):63–69.

Attempts through *Coriolanus* to place in perspective the topical events of the Midlands riots of 1607 and the parliamentary quarrels of 1606. Specifically, Shakespeare exposes basic anomalies in the belly fable's concept of the body politic. The political realities of Rome constitute a parody of the concept, virtually a headless state. James, unlike Elizabeth, proclaimed that sovereignty rested in the king, not in the people; the play reflects the political realities, if not the popularity, of that tenet.

1248. JAGENDORF, ZVI. "*Coriolanus*: Body Politics and Private Parts." *Shakespeare Quarterly* 41 (1990):455–69.

Suggests that the driving force in the play is hatred between the ruling class and the common people in a time of war and questions why the trope of the body and body language are so prominent. The answer is that Shakespeare has depicted this conflict in terms of the body of the people against the body of the hero. Coriolanus views himself as autonomous, whole, and individual. Brought to the marketplace, he refuses to exchange wounds for voices and turn his reputation into liquid assets. The crowning irony is that this "whole" man is torn to pieces by the people in what amounts to a victory of number over singularity.

1249. HALIO, JAY L. "*Coriolanus*: Shakespeare's 'Drama of Reconciliation.' " *Shakespeare Studies* 6 (1970):289–303.

Claims that in Coriolanus's reconciliation with his own inner conflicts, with his family, and with Rome's structured society we see his growth from a flat, arrogant soldier to a complex and frustrated individual. This growth inevitably plays him into the hands of his manipulators. The tribunes abuse him by drawing a false antithesis between gods and men, and Aufidius does so by drawing an equally false distinction between man and boy. Ironically, Coriolanus makes the right decision—to spare Rome—but Aufidius provokes an immediate and fatal regression.

1250. HILL, R. F. *"Coriolanus*: Violentest Contrariety." *Essays and Studies*, n.s. 17 (1964):12–23.

Notes that Menenius's description of the opposition between Coriolanus and Aufidius as one of "violentest contrariety" aptly describes the structure of the play, a series of contrarieties both moral and physical. The knot of moral conflict is in Coriolanus himself, in whom pride is in conflict with duty and honor is set against policy. So, too, the plebeians are characterized by ambiguity in their vacillation between extremes in opinion and in action. Coriolanus's intransigence, compounded of folly and integrity, issues in both his failure and his nobility.

1251. HUFFMAN, CLIFFORD CHALMERS. *"Coriolanus" in Context*. Lewisburg: Bucknell University Press, 1971, 260 pp.

Stresses the significance of the time of composition for *Coriolanus*, a period under James I in which the argument was intense between royal absolutism and limited monarchical power. The Jacobean age inherited from sixteenth-century discussions of the nature of English government an actively debated legal and political issue, and many in Shakespeare's audience would have had either theoretical or practical political experience. Shakespeare's position in *Coriolanus* is that both the immoral tribunes and the proudly intransigent Coriolanus are tyrannic extremes for a commonwealth desperately in need of an ethically temperate aristocracy.

1252. HUNT, MAURICE. " 'Violent'st' Complementarity: The Double Warriors of *Coriolanus*." *Studies in English Literature 1500–1900* 31 (1991):309–25.

Notes that Coriolanus and Aufidius, despite their apparent differences, are alike, "virtual alter egos" (p. 309). Their military union forges a complementarity of separate characters, a variation upon the kind of symbolic union found in that of Othello and Iago. In this manner Shakespeare portrays "in two warriors the disastrous melding of traits previously synthesized with relative success by single individuals" (p. 322).

1253. HUTCHINGS, W. "Beast or God: The *Coriolanus* Controversy." *Critical Quarterly* 24 (1982):35–50.

Focuses on the perverted relationship between word and subject, man and fellow man, that characterizes the civil life of Coriolanus. Menenius fails to respond meaningfully to the people's needs, just as the citizens fail to respond correctly to Caius's heroic deeds. When Coriolanus desires to befriend a citizen, he forgets the man's name. He dies with language at its lowest form, a base repetition of bestial noise,

Coriolanus

"Kill." The play reflects Aristotle's assertion in the *Politics* that man is meant for political association, that he is little more than an animal if isolated from law and justice, and that the isolated man is either a beast or a god.

1254. KNIGHTS, L. C. "Shakespeare and Political Wisdom: A Note on the Personalism of *Julius Caesar* and *Coriolanus*." *Sewanee Review* 61 (1953):43–55.

Illustrates through *Julius Caesar* and *Coriolanus* how Shakespeare can enrich one's perceptions of perennial political issues. The value of *Julius Caesar*, for example, is to heighten our awareness of the potential conflict between public and private life. *Coriolanus*, on the other hand, insists on the human dimension of politics. Both Volumnia and Coriolanus view the masses as an inanimate force unworthy of serious concern. Their inability to relate to the plebeians as human beings produces disruption in the state. Public crisis, in a word, is rooted in one's personal orientation to the human condition.

1255. LOWE, LISA. " 'Shall I Play the Man I Am': Gender and Politics in *Coriolanus*." *Kenyon Review* 8, no. 4 (1986):86–95.

Argues that social and political conflicts are reflected in, and informed by, gender conflict within the family. Coriolanus's struggle with his mother and his constant search for male companionship, for example, have analogues in his battle with the Roman crowds and his alliance with the Volsces, as do the civil strife in the city and the enmity between Rome and Antium with Coriolanus's separation from his mother and his fratricidal rivalry with Aufidius. Matters of language, metaphor, and rhetoric press the reader to consider the significance of political conflicts within the family and the inscription of gender upon civic activities.

1256. LUCKYJ, CHRISTINA. "Volumnia's Silence." *Studies in English Literature 1500–1900* 31 (1991):327–42.

Focuses on the significance of Volumnia's silence and the nature of her unspoken response at the moment of her son's capitulation to her plea to spare Rome. Even though Shakespeare leaves her motivation open-ended, he employs two dramatic strategies to deflect her guilt—the fact that she is a spokeswoman for a humane cause and the fact that she is immediately supplanted by Aufidius as the agent of Coriolanus's destruction.

1257. McCANLES, MICHAEL. "The Dialectic of Transcendence in Shakespeare's *Coriolanus*." *PMLA* 82 (1967):44–53.

States that one attempts to transcend something in order to escape it, to dominate it, to make it one's slave. In any attempt to transcend, ambiguity exists since positions are defined against and thus tied to each other. In *Coriolanus* praise and power are the controlling values, and the action depicts Coriolanus in a dialectical, and therefore ambiguous, relation with both friends and enemies. Coriolanus offers respect to Aufidius through a hatred that maintains his drive for superiority, and he is unable to accept the praise of the citizens because to do so would represent a concession.

1258. MacLure, Millar. "Shakespeare and the Lonely Dragon." *University of Toronto Quarterly* 24 (1955):109–20.

Notes that Shakespeare's delineation of the hero in a political situation almost inevitably opens the plane between the private and the public consciousness of the leader. The intervention of the private self into the political arena produces sloth in Achilles, treason in Coriolanus, and apotheosis in Antony. Coriolanus loves to play his star role, but he refuses to join the company; he can bear neither blame nor praise because either suggests a kind of equality between him and other people. His pride may have an austere and monolithic beauty, but it is fatal to society.

1259. Marcus, Leah. *Puzzling Shakespeare: Local Reading and Its Discontents*. Berkeley: University of California Press, 1988, 267 pp.

Provides a local reading of Shakespeare, that is, a repositioning of the play text within the framework of specific current events and public debate. Anxieties of Elizabeth, for example, are perceived in the figure of Joan la Pucelle in *1 Henry VI* and in Lady Macbeth. *Measure for Measure* is read as a reflection of the struggle in 1603 between Protestant Stuarts and Hapsburg Catholics. A major focus is on *Coriolanus*, which, read topically, reenacts the civic victory of London in extending its authority over certain liberties by virtue of a new charter granted by James I. Coriolanus's banishment from Rome and the "victory" of the plebeians can be perceived as the banishing by the London citizens of one who symbolizes the arbitrary claims of absolutism.

1260. Oliver, H. J. "Coriolanus as a Tragic Hero." *Shakespeare Quarterly* 10 (1959):53–60.

Describes as fallacious the charge that *Coriolanus* is an unsatisfactory play because the central figure is unsympathetic. The play focuses on the place in a would-be democratic society of a pure aristocrat who refuses to compromise and who thus falls where a lesser person would survive. Both the tribunes' duplicity and Coriolanus's shock that his mother advises him to play the politician develop the spectators fundamental sympathy for Coriolanus. Shakespeare's late tragic vision is that there are certain kinds of goodness that themselves lead to tragedy because they cannot adapt themselves to hard reality.

1261. PETTET, E. C. "*Coriolanus* and the Midlands Insurrection of 1607." *Shakespeare Survey* 3 (1950):34–42.

Notes that 7 May 1607 witnessed an outburst of desperate, ill-organized peasants in Northamptonshire that quickly spilled over into adjacent counties and just as quickly was brutally extinguished. The uprising, a marked demand for economic redress, was a struggle against enclosures. Something of this revolt is reflected in *Coriolanus*; as a landowner Shakespeare must have been confirmed in his attitude against the mob. The number of images of country life in an urban and political play not otherwise rich in imagery strongly suggest the correlation.

1262. RABKIN, NORMAN. "*Coriolanus*: The Tragedy of Politics." *Shakespeare Quarterly* 17 (1966):195–212.

Notes that *Coriolanus* and *Antony and Cleopatra* appear to be polar opposites, the one expansive in scope and championing the transcendent quality of romantic love, the other narrow in focus and cold in the utter absence of romantic passion. Yet, paradoxically, the plays create almost identical visions of life; both create worlds in which we are forced to judge man's actions within the context of two opposing value systems. Coriolanus's virtue, for example, is also his vice; he is incomparably better and worse than anyone else in the play. Like *Antony and Cleopatra* the play rejects the optimism of the early tragedies in its vision of the impossibility of heroism in a corrupt society.

1263. SICHERMAN, CAROL M. "*Coriolanus*: The Failure of Words." *ELH* 39 (1972):189–207.

Views the central problem as the relation between word and meaning. Specifically, Coriolanus is incapable of wedding word and meaning in his communication with citizens, with his mother, and even with himself—as indicated in the awkward soliloquies. Not merely inarticulate, Coriolanus appears to have a defect in hearing as well. His language is either rampantly uncontrolled or uncommonly rigid. His speech is continually out of tune with his feeling, and the play ends in disharmony—"no common values, no common language, no consolation" (p. 207).

1264. SIMMONS, J. L. "*Antony and Cleopatra* and *Coriolanus*, Shakespeare's Heroic Tragedies: A Jacobean Adjustment." *Shakespeare Survey* 26 (1973):95–101.

Notes that of all Shakespeare's plays only *Coriolanus* and *Antony and Cleopatra* are distinguished by definitively aristocratic appeals. Coriolanus's disgust at being displayed in the marketplace is not unlike Cleopatra's attitude toward being impersonated by mechanic slaves. This new set of appeals indicates a different kind of audience from those of his earlier plays, an audience becoming increasingly unsettled with social and moral fragmentation. To transcend this diversity Shakespeare incorporates the popular, didactic morality of the people with a heroic aspiration beyond that moralism.

1265. SLIGHTS, WILLIAM E. "Bodies of Text and Textualized Body in *Sejanus* and *Coriolanus.*" *Medieval and Renaissance Drama in England* 5 (1991):181–94.

Observes that in the play the process of translating the physical body into the text reflects Jacobean techniques for dealing with rebellion and subversion. Menenius, for example, relates the time-worn fable of the belly to distract a rebellious mob by textualizing it; Coriolanus does the same thing when he asserts that he would fill a quarry with pieces of quartered slaves. Just as the citizens are written into the patrician's text, so in act 5 is Coriolanus contained by being written into Volumnia's. When she threatens to depart (while pleading with him to spare Rome), he is transferred to the margins of power, and the warrior-hero is subsumed in the "notion of a family politic, dominated in this case by a strong mother" (p. 191).

1266. SORGE, THOMAS. "The Failure of Orthodoxy in *Coriolanus.*" In *Shakespeare Reproduced: The Text in History and Ideology.* Edited by Jean Howard and Marion F. O'Connor. New York and London: Methuen, 1986, 225–41.

Suggests that by presenting three models of government—rule by one, by few, and by many—*Coriolanus* "challenges authority's representation of monarchy as the only form of rule beneficial to England" (p. 232). Just as Coriolanus fails, as chief representative of the oligarchy, to make himself acceptable to the people, the fable of the belly fails to persuade the people to obedience. By mid-play, with the emergence of a new plebeian political force, the belly fable is turned against the patricians.

1267. STOCKHOLDER, KATHERINE. "The Other Coriolanus." *PMLA* 85 (1970):228–36.

Coriolanus, like Lear, is flawed by a blindness that renders him ridiculous as well as awesome. Both devote themselves to creating an image of virile masculinity that makes them dependent on the choric response of their following for ratification of that image. Ironically, Coriolanus's braggardism reveals his amoral separation of valor and virtue. The play needs a scene of anagnorisis between his leaving Rome and arriving at Corioles. While Volumnia taught her son the qualities of strength essential to a well-balanced leader, she failed to teach him the counterbalance of humanity.

1268. WAITH, EUGENE M. *The Herculean Hero in Marlowe, Chapman, Shakespeare, and Dryden.* New York: Columbia University Press; London: Chatto & Windus, 1962, 224 pp.

Examines the concept of the classical heroic image in the protagonist of seven plays including Shakespeare's *Antony and Cleopatra* and *Coriolanus*. Both plays set the hero against society but in different ways. Antony is a man of Herculean excess, whether in battlefield achievements or in sensuality; much of the play concentrates on his efforts to regain his heroic image of the past. Shakespeare uses a dialectic method of contrasts (choric conversations, parallelisms with other individuals) to develop the character of Coriolanus. His greatness lies in his rejection of anything contrary to his personal ideal of honor, including his homeland itself; his tragedy lies in the fact that, in despising a corrupt and petty world, he denies nature.

1269. WECKERMANN, HANS-JÜRGEN. "*Coriolanus*: The Failure of the Autonomous Individual." In *Shakespeare: Text, Language, Criticism: Essays in Honour of Marvin Spevack*. Edited by Bernard Fabian and Kurt Tetzeli von Rosador. Hildesheim and New York: Olms-Weidmann, 1987, pp. 334–50.

Observes that Shakespeare must have had Coriolanus in mind at the beginning of his career since the situation with Lucius in *Titus Andronicus* is that one intends to attack his homeland and is meant to be dissuaded by a parent and since nothing of that is in Shakespeare's source for the early tragedy. In any case, the political focus of the two plays is entirely different. *Coriolanus* explores one's need for human society for meaningful existence, and tragedy results "when the community is not able to offer its outstanding individual an appropriate place within its structure and when the individual is not willing to make any concessions in order to fit into that community" (p. 336).

HAMLET

Reference Works

1270. MARDER, LOUIS, comp. "*Hamlet*": A Supplementary Bibliography 1867–1964. The New Variorum Shakespeare. New York: American Scholar Publications, 1965, 46 pp.

Includes representative scholarship on *Hamlet* from 1877 to 1964 and is intended to supplement H. H. Furness's Variorum edition of 1877. The material is categorized under bibliographical sources, reproductions of original folio editions, reproductions and editions of *Hamlet* quartos, modern editions, and critical studies (alphabetically arranged). While not exhaustive, the material represents every major category of scholarship and criticism.

1271. RAVEN, ANTON ADOLPH, comp. *A "Hamlet" Bibliography and Reference Guide: 1877–1935*. Chicago: University of Chicago Press, 1936, 292 pp.

Includes 2,167 entries representing *Hamlet* scholarship from 1877 through 1935. The material is categorized under *Hamlet* and Hamlet; sources, early texts, and date; textual comments; characters (other than Hamlet); editions; *Hamlet* on the stage, fiction (music, opera, burlesques, poems, novels); the influence of *Hamlet*; *Hamlet* and Elsinore; and miscellaneous. The first category covers items on Hamlet's character and on specialized topics such as his madness and his relationship with Ophelia.

1272. ROBINSON, RANDAL F. comp. *"Hamlet" in the 1950s: An Annotated Bibliography*. Garland Reference Library of the Humanities, 417: Garland Shakespeare Bibliographies, 7. New York and London: Garland Publishing, 1984, 383 pp.

Contains 1,115 citations, representing virtually all publications on the play from 1950 through 1959—books, chapters, articles, reviews, notices of stage production, accounts of writers and works directly influenced by the tragedy. The categories, each arranged alphabetically, are divided into criticism, sources, dating, textual studies, bibliographies, editions, stage history, and adaptations and synopses. A brief introductory essay traces the most significant aspects of criticism during the decade.

Editions

1273. EDWARDS, PHILIP, ed. *Hamlet*. The New Cambridge Shakespeare. Cambridge: Cambridge University Press, 1985, 245 pp.

Features an introductory essay on source and date, the play's shape, the play and its critics, the action of the play, and Hamlet and the actors. Extensive notes appear on individual pages of the text, and a reading list is appended.

Hamlet

1274. HIBBARD, GEORGE, ed. *Hamlet*. The Oxford Shakespeare. Oxford and New York: Oxford University Press, 1987, 416 pp.

Includes an introductory essay on date, sources, from stage to study, and a textual introduction: the first quarto (1603), the second quarto (1604), and the First Folio (1623). Extensive notes on each page of the text identify particular problems of language and also provide background information. An appendix reprints *Der Berstrafte Brudermord*.

1275. JENKINS, HAROLD, ed. *Hamlet*. The Arden Shakespeare. London and New York: Methuen, 1982, 574 pp.

Includes discussion of the date, the publication, the texts (the first quarto, 1603; the second quarto, 1604; the First Folio, 1623), the editorial problem and the present text, the sources, a discussion of *Der Bestrafte Brudermord*, and a critical introduction. This edition is based primarily on the second quarto, but independent folio readings are allowed. The play is unique in having three substantive texts; the first quarto has its greatest value in suggesting the source of corruption where the other two texts vary.

1276. WEINER, ALBERT B., ed. *"Hamlet": The First Quarto 1603*. Great Neck: Baron's Educational Series, 1962, 176 pp.

Argues that the first quarto, the first of three significantly different texts of *Hamlet*, is neither a reported (memorial reconstruction) text nor a pirated shorthand text, that, in fact, it is not a bad quarto at all. Purged almost entirely of poetry and rhetoric, it is consistently and methodically cut with none of the action missing. Four characters— Hamlet, Corambis, the king, and Horatio—speak about 70 percent of the sixteen hundred lines, and the play could easily be produced by no more than twelve actors. This cut version was required for a touring performance by the Lord Chamberlain's Men during the summer of 1600, 1601, or 1602.

Textual Studies

1277. DUTHIE, GEORGE IAN. *The Bad Quarto of "Hamlet": A Critical Edition*. Shakespeare Problems, 6. Cambridge: Cambridge University Press, 1941, 279 pp.

Argues that the quarto printed in 1603 is a memorial reconstruction for a provincial performance by an actor who had played the role of Marcellus (and perhaps others) in a full performance. While this version is dependent primarily on the text represented in the second quarto, printed in 1604, it also contains reminiscences of the pre-Shakespearean *Ur-Hamlet*. A similar conglomerate type of memorial reconstruction is represented by *Der Bestrafte Brudermord*.

1278. MOWAT, BARBARA. "The Form of *Hamlet*'s Fortunes." *Renaissance Drama,* n.s. 19 (1988):97–126.

Observes that critical preference for a version conflating the second quarto and First Folio texts is under attack and that re-formation of the text is, in fact, nothing new. Except for the period of slightly more than a century (1866–1980), the text has been radically unstable and multiform. Even so, editors like Rowe, Pope, and Theobald all created their individual texts by weaving together portions of the two versions; and the tendency of present-day revisionists like G. R. Hibbard and Stanley Wells to insist on exclusively privileging the folio text "seems a bit provincial—but understandable" (p. 119).

1279. WALKER, ALICE. "The Textual Problem of *Hamlet*: A Reconsideration." *Review of English Studies,* n.s. 2 (1951):328–38.

Argues that since the first quarto was consulted where autograph copy was illegible and since we have no idea how frequently that occurred, all readings where the second quarto agrees with the first are suspect. If the folio was printed from a transcript of the promptbook, at least four agents are postulated—the compositors of the second quarto and the folio, the scribe who prepared the promptbook, and the copyist who transcribed it for the folio. Only the assumption that a corrected quarto was used as copy for the folio provides an adequate explanation for the textual situation.

1280. WILSON, JOHN DOVER. *The Manuscript of Shakespeare's "Hamlet" and the Problems of Its Transmission.* Cambridge: Cambridge University Press, 1934, 437 pp.

Examines the kind of manuscripts used for the printing of the second quarto and the First Folio and then attempts to reconstruct Shakespeare's autograph manuscript. Playhouse cuts and revised stage directions in the folio point to a text corrupted by playhouse interference and suggest that the printer's copy was closely associated with, if not identical to, the Globe promptbook. Copy for the quarto was either Shakespeare's foul papers or a faithful copy of them. In determining Shakespeare's original text, the second quarto must be granted authority; readings from the folio can be allowed only in clearly justified instances.

Criticism

1281. ALDUS, P. J. *Mousetrap: Structure and Meaning in "Hamlet."* Toronto and Buffalo: University of Toronto Press, 1976, 235 pp.

Argues that our response to *Hamlet* comes ultimately not from the surface plot or some assumption about the poet's psyche but from some mysterious power in the structure itself that stirs our imagination at the subliminal level, "a controlling and unifying metaphor on the grandest scale that embodies a heritage of literary myths" (p. 20). The literal becomes figurative in a mythic sense; two mythic patterns are entwined: one Greek, ending in death, and the other Christian, ending in Doomsday. At the center of both are the metaphorical implications of the mousetrap dumb shows, prologue, and play.

1282. ALEXANDER, NIGEL. *Poison, Play, and Duel: A Study in "Hamlet."* Lincoln: University of Nebraska Press; London: Routledge & Kegan Paul, 1971, 212 pp.

Suggests that the action of poisoning, playing, and dueling, recurring at the beginning, middle, and end, forms the structure of the play. The inner play, for example, represents the past in such a way as to determine the future act. It forces the members of the on stage audience to reveal the roles they intend to play in the future, ironically posing the question of the relationship of Lucianus as murderer and Hamlet in his determination to assassinate Claudius. The play, in a word, functions as a complex moral reference for both the prince and the king.

1283. ALTICK, RICHARD D. *"Hamlet and the Odor of Mortality." Shakespeare Quarterly* 5 (1954):167–76.

Describes *Hamlet* as a play enveloped in an atmosphere of stench and a preoccupation with the corruption of mortal flesh. Hamlet gives the generalized sense of sickness a specific connection with his second line, stating that he is too much in the sun; so, too, the ghost relates his tale in language dominated by images of rottenness and disease. The motif reaches its climax in the graveyard scene. The sense of evil permeating the play is a result not only of iterated allusions to corruption but also of association with the most unpleasant of man's sensory perceptions.

1284. BATTENHOUSE, ROY W. "Hamlet's Apostrophe on Man: Clue to the Tragedy." *PMLA* 66 (1951):1073–1113.

Describes Hamlet's noblest gift as the ability for speculation, even though his reason is flawed, as evidenced in its continually defeating his actions as a man. His apostrophe on man is noticeably lacking in reference to the supernatural; it, rather, is grounded in natural reasoning. Since he sees nothing for man beyond the natural condition, he is a man "deprived of the light of grace" (p. 1081). The passage is a touchstone to the entire play both in its mood and in its theme. It reflects the psychology of frustration in man cut off from the Christian faith.

1285. BOWERS, FREDSON T. "Hamlet as Minister and Scourge." *PMLA* 70 (1955):740–49.

Investigates Hamlet through the Elizabethan concept of how God intervened externally in human affairs to punish crime—either through an act of destruction committed by one already damned (a scourge) or through a constructive act by one who is spiritually healthy (a minister). Hamlet considers the ghost's mandate to be a divine command to set right the disjointed times. As a minister of God, however, he must act to secure a public vengeance; unable to do so and at the point of committing himself to private vengeance, he describes himself in 3.4 as scourge as well as minister.

1286. CALDERWOOD, JAMES L. *To Be and Not to Be: Negation and Metadrama in "Hamlet."* New York: Columbia University Press, 1983, 222 pp.

Examines the structure of *Hamlet* as a movement through deconstruction to reconstruction that occurs simultaneously on several levels. Hamlet is compelled to seek his individual identity apart from his filial role as filial-avenger; by determining his own path of action instead of sweeping to his revenge, he "denames" himself as son and namesake and thereby "names" himself as his own distinct personality. At the same time, Shakespeare—by allowing his protagonist to assume this greater role than that of a Kydian revenger—"de-names" the strictures of traditional revenge tragedy and creates an individually identifiable and highly ambiguous dramatic form for himself, the spectators at the Globe, and all future actor-Hamlets and spectators.

1287. CHARNEY, MAURICE. *Hamlet's Fictions.* New York: Routledge, 1988, 163 pp.

Observes that, within the larger fiction of the play, Hamlet creates other "fictions" for himself as strategies to avoid or engage his mandate to revenge. At one point or another, for example, he contemplates revenge in the style of Pyrrhus, Fortinbras, and Laertes; in the final act he transfers his need for personal revenge to the workings of providential wisdom. Polonius, Rosencrantz, Guildenstern, and Osric act as surrogates for Claudius, and Hamlet must confront each of them in a kind of comic fiction before he can address his usurping uncle in the serious action.

1288. ———. *Style in "Hamlet."* Princeton: Princeton University Press, 1969, 333 pp.

Explores the style of *Hamlet*—puns, particular Elizabethan connotations, the imaginative embodiment of a theme, the contrapuntal quality of the various dramatic voices. The book is divided into three parts—imagery, staging and structure, and dramatic character. The first part focuses on the recurrent images of war, weapons, explosives, secrecy, poison, corruption, and limits. The middle section deals with imagery in nonverbal presentational terms (gesture, music, sound effects, costumes, stage properties), and the final section is concerned with the specific nature of the rhetorical roles that interact with Hamlet and the rhetorical complexity of the protagonist.

1289. COHEN, MICHAEL. *"Hamlet" in My Mind's Eye.* Athens: University of Georgia Press, 1989, 173 pp.

Asserts that *Hamlet* is "a play of choices" that can legitimately be played/read any number of ways. Through references to nine productions and nine Hamlets (Edwin Booth, John Gielgud, Maurice Evans, Laurence Olivier, George Grizzard, Inokenti Smotunovski, Richard Burton, Nichol Williamson, Derek Jacobi), this discussion provides "a kind of performance variorum *Hamlet*" (p. 8). The actors' diverse interpretation of key moments in the action attest to the imaginative richness of the plot, most especially to that of the protagonist's role.

1290. ———. " 'To What Base Uses We May Return': Class and Mortality in *Hamlet.*" *Hamlet Studies* 9 (1987):78–85.

Asserts that class considerations are no less important in 5.1 than the discussion of death. The clowns "see the suborned coroner and priest as agents of an upper class conspiracy to make sure that the rich and privileged are treated with class distinctions even after death" (p. 80). Similarly, the ensuing conversation between the grave-digger and Hamlet can be perceived as the game of "getting the best of the gentlemen" and can momentarily shift the sympathy of our perspective to the commoner.

1291. CONKLIN, PAUL S. *A History of "Hamlet" Criticism 1601–1821.* New York: King's Crown Press, 1947, 176 pp.

Chronicles the growth of *Hamlet* criticism from its beginnings to 1821 and the manner in which this criticism reflects the climate of the times in the dominant trends of thought. The material is basically of three types—allusions to Hamlet, primarily imaginative reflections by some later writer; theatrical comments concerning actual stage productions; and critical analysis involving an attempt to establish some sort of philosophic context for interpretation. Individual chapters address French and German criticism. Of special interest is the sharp dualism that develops in the late eighteenth century between the theatrical tradition and that of the closet or study.

1292. Cox, Lee Sheridan. *Figurative Design in "Hamlet": The Significance of the Dumb Show.* Columbus: Ohio State University Press, 1973, 184 pp.
    Argues that Shakespeare intends the dumb show to function as an intrinsic component of the whole figurative and structural pattern. This dumb show, occupying a central structural position, is also thematically central; the symbolic importance of the mime provides an essential code for comprehending the entire play. Significant parallels exist between the "puppets" in the court entertainment and the characters in *Hamlet*, between the reiterated allusions to "dumbness" throughout the play and the muteness of the scene.

1293. Dessen, Alan C. "Hamlet's Poisoned Sword: A Study in Dramatic Imagery." *Shakespeare Studies* 5 (1969):53–69.
    Maintains that the visual image of Hamlet's poisoned sword is symbolic of his role as the tainted hero in a corrupt world. The sword appears throughout the play, in the cellarage scene, in the description of Priam's death, in the duel of the final scene. Its use, crossed, to ward off blasts from hell as an instrument of justice contrasts with its later use, poisoned, to corrupt. Hamlet's tragedy is that he is unable to achieve his ends in a corrupt world without himself partaking of that corruption.

1294. Doran, Madeleine. "The Language of *Hamlet.*" *Huntington Library Quarterly* 27 (1964):259–78.
    Examines Shakespeare's use of rhetoric for dramatic purposes in *Hamlet*. The conceits in the speeches in *The Murder of Gonzago*, for example, are formed and labored, the sententious passages commonplace and old-fashioned. Such language tends not to call attention to itself, allowing interest to focus on how Hamlet, Claudius, and Gertrude are reacting. Similarly, the turgidly rhetorical speech of the player about Hecuba provokes a naturalistic response in Hamlet and thus furthers our identification with the prince as a real character. The cadences and imagery of his soliloquies help us to track his emotional progress through the play.

Hamlet

1295. DRAPER, JOHN W. *The "Hamlet" of Shakespeare's Audience*. Durham: Duke University Press, 1939, 254 pp.

Attempts to set *Hamlet* within its literary and historical context, examining the minor figures as individuals in a contemporary court. The play is envisioned as "a microcosm of the Renaissance state and of Renaissance society" (p. 229). In its cross-currents of action it illustrates current political, religious, and social themes—the inescapable consequences of sin, the consequences of the blind pursuit of duty, the loyalty to elders, the struggle between church and state, the problem of regicide, the struggle of the individual in a highly organized social structure.

1296. ELIOT, T. S. "Hamlet and His Problems." In *The Sacred Wood*. London: Methuen, 1920, pp. 95–103. Reprinted in *Selected Essays: 1917–1932* (New York: Harcourt, Brace, 1932), pp. 121–26.

Asserts that since *Hamlet* represents a stratification, the efforts of a series of men, we should treat it as Shakespeare's design superimposed upon much cruder material. The simple revenge motive, the difficulty of assassinating a monarch, and madness feigned for protection came from previous layers. While complicating these factors in terms of his protagonist, Shakespeare adds the principal motive of the effect of a mother's guilt upon her son. The play in failing to bring coherence to these varied elements is an artistic failure. To comprehend *Hamlet* completely we would "have to understand things which Shakespeare did not understand himself" (p. 126).

1297. EMPSON, WILLIAM. "*Hamlet* When New." *Sewanee Review* 61 (1953):15–42.

Notes that there was no *Hamlet* problem until the eighteenth century. Critics would have us believe that Shakespeare wrote an extremely popular play that held the stage for nearly two hundred years before anyone perceived its essential enigmatic quality. Shakespeare's task was to capitalize on the popularity of the revenge play but to do so in a way that would be intriguing and exciting and not a laughingstock like the older *Hamlet*. Possibly our text represents two Shakespearean versions, with the play evolving into its present shape.

1298. ERLICH, AVI. *Hamlet's Absent Father*. Princeton: Princeton University Press, 1977, 319 pp.

Views Hamlet's problem as stemming in large part from the elder Hamlet's physical or emotional absence and thus the father's failure to provide an adequate role model for masculine identity in the crucial formative years. His obsessive desire is to prove his father (now the ghost figure) to be strong and dominant by discovering some means by which the spirit might exact his own revenge, hence the son's refusal or inability to accept the adult responsibility inherent in the mandate to kill and the rationalization for inactivity sought in near madness.

1299. FISCH, HAROLD. *Hamlet and the Word: The Covenant Pattern in Shakespeare*. New York: Frederick Ungar, 1971, 248 pp.

Considers Hamlet's confrontation with the ghost in act 1 a conventional encounter in which he is elected to a unique responsibility. His soliloquies throughout the middle acts reveal his "intestinal warfare," character defining itself in relation to destiny. Acting without soliloquy in the final act, he is rewarded with the recovery of a "faint but perceptible degree of faith in man and his future" (p. 75). In the tradition of Hellenic tragedy he is swept to his doom, but in the Hebraic tradition he has also become the divine instrument of a moral purging.

1300. FISCHER, SANDRA K. "Hearing Ophelia: Gender and Tragic Discourse in *Hamlet*." *Renaissance and Reformation*, n.s. 14 (1990):1–10.

Sees Ophelia as the "Other" in the play. One senses in her personality a "continual psycholinguistic frustration" resulting from her inability to "allow language either a cognitive or a therapeutic function" (p. 3). Her role is that of an object to men, whether Polonius, Laertes, or Hamlet; and her language is an index to her enforced silence. "The textual politics of Ophelia's rhetoric offer a feminine counterpoint to Hamlet's tragedy as well as a devastating commentary on it" (p. 9).

1301. FLATTER, RICHARD. *Hamlet's Father*. New Haven: Yale University Press, 1949, 207 pp.

Asserts that the ghost of Hamlet's father is the true protagonist of the play. As the motivating force, he sets the action in motion by directing his son to avenge his murder, intervening in person in act 4 when the son appears to be seriously digressing from his aim. Eventually the ghost succeeds through Hamlet's execution of Claudius as justice is victorious over covert evil. A key moment in the play is the spirit's forgiveness of Gertrude in the closet scene and his instructing the son to do likewise and to direct all vengeance against the usurping king as the source of corruption.

1302. FLY, RICHARD. "Accommodating Death: The Ending of *Hamlet*." *Studies in English Literature 1500–1900* 24 (1984):257–74.

Argues that tragedy forces us to rethink the meaning of death for a particular individual, a death for which the traditional cultural tropes of its being a common fate or its being a passageway into another life are not sufficient. *Hamlet*, more specifically, questions the validity of the nontragic response to death. The contrast between the two is most vividly seen in the juxtaposition of Hamlet's sharp encounter with death both in his own words and in Horatio's response and Fortinbras's alien and impersonal view of death as he arrives upon the scene.

1303. FRYE, ROLAND M. *The Renaissance "Hamlet": Issues and Responses in 1600*. Princeton: Princeton University Press, 1984, 398 pp.
Investigates the climate of opinion in which *Hamlet* took shape by analyzing contemporary response to events resembling those in the tragedy—for example, the Elizabethan response to death and funerals, to spiritual hauntings, to sexual misconduct. A king's untimely death and a queen's incest would be seen as sufficient to motivate Hamlet's distress; similarly, Catholics and Protestants alike shared an ambivalence toward the supernatural that would lend credibility to Hamlet's tyrannicide. Such problems of the play are examined and defined in historical terms.

1304. GOLDBERG, JONATHAN. "Hamlet's Hand." *Shakespeare Quarterly* 39 (1988):307–27.
Argues that the hand (writing) is a social manifestation of empowerment. Hamlet's career, for example, is continually affected by the power of the written word. He receives the ghost's mandate as a scriptive command, implanting it within "the book and value" of his brain (1.5.103). He scripts certain lines in *The Murder of Gonzago*, and their power is visibly evidenced in Claudius' reaction. Claudius sends dispatches throughout the play, and Hamlet's forging of that hand bests Rosencrantz and Guildenstern at their own game. In a sense that mystifies literacy as ensuring a kind of immortality, "Hamlet's character is—literally—the character" (p. 324).

1305. GORFAIN, PHYLLIS. "Toward a Theory of Play and the Carnivalesque in *Hamlet*." *Hamlet Studies* 13 (1991):25–49.
Observes that *Hamlet*, with its "amalgam of genres and voices in its riddling tests, tricky deceptions, grotesque revenges, and cyclical saga of deaths, near-deaths, and returns" (p. 26) is Shakespeare's most ludic and metatheatrical tragedy. More than a mere ingredient, the carnivalesque represents the fundamental prevailing attitude in the play. This atmosphere tends to break down barriers between performer and audience and thus contributes to the spectator's profound sense of vicarious involvement in the dilemmas of the protagonist.

1306. GOTTSCHALK, PAUL. *The Meanings of "Hamlet": Modes of Literary Interpretation since Bradley*. Albuquerque: University of New Mexico Press, 1972, 197 pp.

Notes the immense variety of interpretations of *Hamlet*, especially in the post-Bradleyan era. Emphasis is on the evolutionist critics who explain problems and inconsistencies in terms of Shakespeare's adaptations of his sources; the psychological critics, both those who analyze the prince in terms of Elizabethan psychology and those who apply post-Freudian tactics; the Christian and archetypal critics whose concern is with Hamlet's accommodation to the moral imperatives of his world; and the anagogical critics, who examine the play and the protagonist as archetypes of human experience. In each case the focus is either on the external struggle of hero and villain or on the struggle within Hamlet's soul.

1307. GRANNIS, OLIVER. "The Social Relevance of Grammatical Style in Shakespeare." *Jahrbuch der Deutschen Shakespeare-Gesellschaft West* (1990):105–18.

Points out that Shakespeare was acutely aware of the social relevance of particular forms and lexical items in his day. The use of "shall," for example, when present in the second and third persons is a clear indicator of personal volition or power. In *Hamlet* the word is so used 114 times, with a relative frequency of O.385. Claudius, the figure with most authority, uses it with a relative frequency of O.759, Horatio only O.196. Similarly, Claudius's use of "we" forms is four times that of Hamlet, another signal indication of his obsession with power.

1308. GREBANIER, BERNARD. *The Heart of "Hamlet."* New York: Thomas Y. Crowell, 1960, 301 pp.

Interprets *Hamlet* in its Elizabethan context, abjuring the adaptation and attempts at modernity or peculiar contemporaneity that have characterized so many recent productions. The weight of criticism notwithstanding, Hamlet is perfectly sane, and never pretends to be otherwise. His delay is attributable, not to some quirk of personality, but solely to the conventions of the revenge play. His tragedy results from defeated thought, not excessive thought, and it is a tragedy only because Hamlet in a rash moment kills Polonius and sets destruction in motion. Critics and actors alike would do well to allow the play to speak for itself and to avoid the labyrinthine bypaths of sheer speculation.

1309. HALLETT, CHARLES A., and HALLETT, ELAINE S. *The Revenger's Madness: A Study of Revenge Tragedy Motifs*. Lincoln: University of Nebraska Press, 1980, 349 pp.

Hamlet

Claims that Shakespeare in *Hamlet* significantly enhances several of the basic revenge play motifs established by Kyd. For one thing, the ghost, though presumably an embodiment of the spirit of revenge, epitomizes human dignity and majesty as well. Horatio's and Hamlet's reminiscences about the elder Hamlet's nobility and integrity, the ghost's solicitude for Gertrude, the fact that the ghost does not appear directly responsible for the multiple deaths in act 5—such touches lend the ghost a dimension of personality quite absent in Andrea and Andrugio. For another thing, Shakespeare, through the protagonist's declared intention of assuming an antic disposition, is able to present Hamlet's madness without degrading his character.

1310. HANSEN, WILLIAM F. *Saxo Grammaticus and the Life of Hamlet: A Translation, History, and Commentary*. Lincoln and London: University of Nebraska Press, 1983, 202 pp.

Examines our knowledge of the tradition of Hamlet before and after Saxo, specifically how Saxo transforms the oral legend into a literary text and how the literary figure evolves from Danish to Latin to French. Considered also are Scandinavian and Roman legends as analogues of the Hamlet story and Shakespeare's transformation of the material for the stage in Renaissance England. Saxo's life of Hamlet from his *History of the Danes* is translated into idiomatic English prose.

1311. HAWKES, TERENCE. "Telmah." In *That Shakespeherian Rag: Essays on a Critical Process*. London: Methuen, 1986, 92–119.

Argues that *Hamlet*, like any text, is a site of conflicting potential interpretations, none of which has authority. Any such interpretation is subject to intrinsic political and economic determinants. A text, like jazz, is a means; interpretation is symbiotic. John Dover Wilson's fervid denunciation in 1917 of the claim that the play affords Claudius tragic potential is cited as an example; Wilson's convictions grew in part out of his antipathy toward the Bolshevik revolution.

1312. HOFF, LINDA KAY. *Hamlet's Choice: "Hamlet"—A Reformation Allegory*. Lewiston and New York: Mellen Press, 1988, 383 pp.

Argues that the play first and foremost is a reflection of sociotheological controversies of Shakespeare's age. It is a "'typal' allegory of the Reformation itself, informed by a biblical book that was considered to present 'history': Revelation, the Elizabethan 'book of times'" (p. 17). The well-trained spectators in Shakespeare's audience would perceive the pro-Calvinist ecclesiastical allegory, more precisely the Apocalypse and the demise of Roman Catholicism. Denmark represents the

Holy Roman Empire, Ophelia the Virgin Mary, Fortinbras the arrival of Calvinism.

1313. HOLLERAN, JAMES V. "Maimed Funeral Rites in *Hamlet*." *English Literary Renaissance* 19 (1989):65–93.

Observes that of all the characters who die in the play none (most obviously Ophelia) is given a full and proper burial and suggests that this is merely one example of a general breakdown of ceremony signaling the corruption at Elsinore. In a healthy kingdom a secret murderer would not strut as king, his chief counselor would not be an eavesdropper, a sweetheart and old friends would not be employed as spies, a queen would mourn for a proper space the death of her husband, a play would not be used to trap a killer, and a family duel would not be a sinister assassination plot.

1314. HUGHES, GEOFFREY. "The Tragedy of a Revenger's Loss of Conscience: A Study of *Hamlet*." *English Studies* 57 (1976):395–409.

Argues that Hamlet, instigated by a supernatural agency whose moral nature is highly suspect, damns himself by anticipating Heaven and assuming he is God's agent. Accepting the ghost's integrity on nothing more than his own intuition, he displays a blasphemous arrogance in refusing to kill Claudius at prayer. The final proof of his damnation is his refusal to take the opportunity to remain with pirates and thus escape the necessity of murder.

1315. HUNT, MAURICE. "Art of Judgment, Art of Compassion: The Two Arts of *Hamlet*." *Essays in Literature* 18 (1991):3–20.

Notes that Shakespeare utilizes two plays within the play—*The Murder of Gonzago* and the nameless narrative of the Fall of Troy—to stress the need for a compassionate rather than judgmental response to human failings. Hamlet, bent on revenge, ignores the message in both instances. These inner dramas replicate Shakespeare's method within the larger play of inviting the playgoer to formulate either a sympathetic or judgmental response to principal figures like Hamlet, Ophelia, and Gertrude.

1316. IMHOF, RUDIGER. "Fortinbras *Ante Portas*: The Role and Significance of Fortinbras in *Hamlet*." *Hamlet Studies* 8 (1986):8–29.

Suggests that, despite his alleged marginality, Fortinbras serves a significant function in the tragedy. For one thing, he serves as a foil to the Dane. Both have lost their fathers, both have been robbed by their uncles of their rightful claim, and both in their own ways make it their business to avenge their father's death. For another, he serves as a delicate prince for Hamlet to apotheosize in order to shame himself in his "How all occasions do inform against me" soliloquy. Finally, as a rash individual with no just claim upon the throne who marches in with sounds of war even before realizing that Claudius is dead, he offers dark and brooding closure to this stage strewn with corpses.

1317. JACK, ADOLPHUS ALFRED. *Young Hamlet: A Conjectural Resolution of Some of the Difficulties in the Plotting of Shakespeare's Play.* Aberdeen: Aberdeen University Press, 1950, 176 pp.

Asserts that Hamlet is not a Goethe-like prince too gentle for his task or a Coleridge-like contemplative soul but a man who sweeps to his revenge as readily and as entertainingly as obstacles will allow. In the first quarto, Shakespeare's first version, Hamlet is about nineteen, and the lines of action are much clearer than in the second quarto, in which much speculation is added. *Hamlet* is a highly theatrical play of action; the spectator observes without identifying, and the "slaughter at the end is exciting but not moving" (p. 175).

1318. JACKSON, JAMES L. "'They Catch One Another's Rapiers': The Exchange of Weapons in *Hamlet.*" *Shakespeare Quarterly* 41 (1990):281–98.

Insists that the exchange of weapons is a crucial moment in *Hamlet* and that the action as conceived by Shakespeare can be reconstructed and made historically sound. More specifically, the exchange was to be effected through a method of disarm known as the "left-hand seizure," a move in which the fencer, "after discarding the dagger, takes his opponent's rapier hilt with his left hand and twists the weapon outward from his grasp" (p. 281–82). The defendant then responds with a similar action, and the two actions result in an exchange of rapiers. Laertes engages in the exchange in part because it is the only mode of defense and in part because he wants to maintain the fiction of a friendly match as long as possible.

1319. JOHNSON, S. F. "The Regeneration of Hamlet: A Reply to E.M.W. Tillyard with a Counter-Proposal." *Shakespeare Quarterly* 3 (1952): 187–207.

Asserts that Hamlet, by accepting and obeying the dictates of providence in act 5, experiences a regeneration that is the counterpart to the antic disposition he portrays earlier. As in the morality play the conflict between divine and bestial nature brings Hamlet to the verge of despair. This conflict he transcends when he goes beyond reason in depending on providence to provide the necessary opportunities for action. His spiritual renewal does not mitigate the tragedy; instead, it increases the spectator's sense of waste and heroic sacrifice.

1320. JONES, ERNEST. *Hamlet and Oedipus*. New York: W. W. Norton, 1949, 194 pp.

Locates Hamlet's problem in the sphere of unconscious conflicts known to Freudian psychologists as psychoneurosis; he suffers from an internal struggle inaccessible to his introspection. As a child he viewed his father as a rival for his mother's affection. These repressed memories are revived by the realization of his father's death and his mother's remarriage. The more vigorously he berates his uncle, the more fully does he stimulate his own latent complexes. "In reality his uncle incorporates the deepest and most buried part of his own personality, so that he cannot kill him without also killing himself" (p. 100). Only when he has received his own death wound from Laertes is he able to avenge his father's murder.

1321. JOSEPH, BERTRAM L. *Conscience and the King: A Study of "Hamlet."* London: Chatto & Windus, 1953, 176 pp.

Insists that *Hamlet,* in its language and plot, be seen as an Elizabethan play, of which the elements (Hamlet's melancholy, his character, his relationship with his mother, his delay) become clear so long as we do not read it as a forerunner of modern sensibility. He does not delay, for example, because he examines the revenge code in the abstract and exposes its flaws; he delays for fear of damnation and constantly excoriates himself for doing so. He eventually becomes passive, an instrument of God, and is able to act, not fearing death but viewing it as a consummation.

1322. KERRIGAN, JOHN. "Heironimo, Hamlet and Remembrance." *Essays in Criticism* 31 (1981):105–26.

Draws parallels among *Hamlet*, Kyd's *The Spanish Tragedy*, and Aeschylus's *Orestes* concerning remembrance and revenge, tracing the evolution of the motivation for revenge and noting how retrospection or remembrance draws the revenger back from his task or drives him toward it. Whereas in Greek tragedy, one either remembers or satisfies his vengeance, the Elizabethan has the third choice based on belief in God's providence. The last choice confounds Hamlet because the patience central to it fails to provide the catharsis achieved more easily through physical action.

1323. KEYES, LAURA. "Hamlet's Fat." In *Shakespeare and the Triple Play: From Study to Stage to Classroom*. Edited by Sidney Homan. Newark:

University of Delaware Press; London and Toronto: Associated University Presses, 1988, pp. 89–104.

Argues that a fat Hamlet makes both poetic and dramatic sense. For one thing, being overweight correlates well with his lethargy, irresolution, and passivity. For another, since fatness might mirror an identification with women, it could help explain his "conflicted identification" (p. 195) with his mother and his unwillingness to assume his father's throne. Fatness, moreover, accords with dominant image patterns in the play of disease, food as poison, and sacrifice for which one is fatted.

1324. KING, WALTER N. *Hamlet's Search for Meaning*. Athens: University of Georgia Press, 1982, 180 pp.

Claims that Christian thought is fraught with ambiguities, that it is far less rational than we normally tend to assume. Hamlet finally pursues his problem to the point of Christian certitude, but for the spectator with an omniscient perspective the fundamental ambivalences remain. In a real sense Hamlet's search for meaning ramifies outward and becomes the spectator's search as well. If it is enough in the play for Hamlet to reconcile himself with himself, for us the rest is silence.

1325. KIRSCH, ARTHUR C. *"Hamlet's Grief."* ELH 48 (1981):17–36.

Views *Hamlet,* not only as a study in revenge, but also as a study in grief. Hamlet's vow to the ghost intensifies his mourning and leads to pathological depression, preventing the ego to heal by emotionally coming to terms with the fact of the father's death; and he is deprived of sympathy from his mother, Ophelia, and Rosencrantz and Guildenstern. In act 5 Hamlet's state of mind changes as he completes the act of mourning by accepting his losses as an inevitable part of his own condition.

1326. KITTO, H. D. F. "Hamlet." In *Form and Meaning in Drama: A Study of Six Greek Plays and of "Hamlet."* London: Methuen, 1956, pp. 246–337.

Argues that *Hamlet,* like *Oedipus,* must be considered, not as an individual tragedy of character, but as a religious drama involving the all-pervading evil in Denmark. The individual tragedies of Hamlet, Laertes, and Ophelia emanate from the murder of a king and the corruption of his wife. Hamlet in a sense is humanity itself; and, as in Greek tragedy, evil, "once it has broken loose, will feed on itself and on anything else that it can find until it reaches its natural end" (p. 337).

1327. KLIMAN, BERNICE W. *"Hamlet": Film, Television, and Audio Performances.* Rutherford: Fairleigh Dickinson University Press; London and Toronto: Associated University Presses, 1988, 344 pp.

Concentrates on media productions of *Hamlet*, including those featuring Maurice Evans (1953), John Neville (1959), Christopher Plummer (1964), Nicol Williamson (1969), Richard Chamberlain (1970), Ian McKellan (1971), and Derek Jacobi (1980). Also covered are the German version with Maximilian Schell (1984) and a Swedish version of 1984. The principal points of concern are the effectiveness of the setting for the media productions and the continuing heavy influence of the Olivier film. A substantial section also discusses silent films, and yet another focuses on sound recordings, especially those of Orson Welles (1936), John Barrymore (1937), and Richard Burton (1964).

1328. KNIGHTS, L. C. *An Approach to "Hamlet."* Stanford: Stanford University Press, 1961, 107 pp.

Asserts that *Julius Caesar, Hamlet,* and *Othello* were written at a time Shakespeare was growing concerned with the relationship between the mind and the world, more specifically with various distortions in man's way of looking at the world. In such plays the spectators are not required to take sides but to observe the distortion of actuality by an abstracting, simplifying habit of mind. In *Hamlet* we are drawn to look more closely at the attitudes with which Hamlet confronts his world than the actual evil in it. He represents a fixation of consciousness.

1329. LAWLOR, JOHN J. "The Tragic Conflict in *Hamlet*." *Review of English Studies*, n.s. 1 (1950):97–113.

Asserts that Hamlet delays simply because his nature is such that he cannot perform the deed demanded of him; he is reluctant to act on the grounds of moral scruples about the justice of revenge. He endlessly seeks the cause of his aversion, calling it by every other name, and never actually knows it for what it is. The true tragedy of Hamlet is that he is a man condemned to do what he has no assurance is right. He is able to act only when responding to immediate and personal issues, not to the original mandate.

1330. LEVIN, HARRY. *The Question of "Hamlet."* New York: Oxford University Press, 1959, 178 pp.

Emphasizes the universality of Hamlet, who—as a "man in a plight, a mind resisting its body's destiny, a fighter against cosmic odds" (p. 7)—commands our identification. The play like life is founded in mystery and question, and the protagonist is committed to a rite of initiation, hemmed in on all sides. Any attempt to locate and delimit his experience is at his peril because, when will confronts fate, the odds confound his best-laid plans. The deflating tool in the play turns out to be Yorick, who beyond the grave mocks Hamlet's mortality at the same time he prompts in the prince a sense of compassion for man's plight.

1331. LEVITSKY, RUTH M. "Rightly to Be Great." *Shakespeare Studies* 1 (1965):142–67.

Observes that Hamlet's problem of how to behave with honor and dignity in an intolerable situation was especially critical to Elizabethans at the turn of the seventeenth century. His dilemma is occasioned by the fact that to members of the contemporary audience the sometimes contradictory philosophies of Aristotelianism, Stoicism, and Christianity all held partial validity. Shakespeare dramatizes this dilemma by setting Hamlet within a Christian context but having him motivated to action by characters (the ghost, Horatio, Claudius, Laertes) who find their sanctions in the pagan philosophies of Greece or Rome. In gaining his revenge he transcends the received traditions by combining passion and reason, faith in divine providence and in himself.

1332. LEWIS, C. S. *Hamlet: The Prince or the Poem?* London: Oxford University Press, 1942, 18 pp.

Finds the power of *Hamlet,* not in character and motive, the essence of which has boggled critical minds for three centuries, but in the play itself as mysterious, fascinating, at times even terrifying. Hamlet's speeches are spellbinding because they describe spiritual regions through which most spectators themselves have passed. In a sense the play's subject is death; it is kept constantly before us, whether in terms of the soul's destiny or the body's. The ghost, like its play and like its chief character, is permanently ambiguous.

1333. LISZ, THEODORE. *Hamlet's Enemy: Madness and Myth in "Hamlet."* New York: Basic Books, 1975, 258 pp.

Examines Hamlet's madness both as a literal phenomenon within Shakespeare's play and as a symbolic phenomenon that sets off resonances within the audience about man's eternal struggle to tame his passion and to control human nature. Central issues include the corrupting nature of disillusionment, its preoccupation with death and its destruction of the ability to love, and the ultimate loss of the human soul in passionate isolation. The tragedy in *Hamlet* stems from infractions of cardinal rules of family life blocking the normal development of both Hamlet and Ophelia, whose deaths are attributable to the transgressions of prior generations.

1334. LYONS BRIDGET GELLERT. "The Iconography of Ophelia." *ELH* 44 (1977):60–74.

Observes that the ambiguity of Ophelia's character is reflected in the ambivalence of her iconographic associations. As she stands reading a book, she symbolizes devoutness, but the appearance is hypocritical since she is being used as a spy by her father and Claudius. Also, in the flower scene she reverberates both with positive associations with Flora, goddess of spring and love, and with Plutarch's Roman prostitute won for a night by Hercules in a wager. Her sexual confusion is seen in the contrast of her courtly language and her bawdy songs.

1335. ———. "Melancholy and Hamlet." In *Voices of Melancholy: Studies in Literary Treatments of Melancholy in Renaissance England.* London: Routledge & Kegan Paul, 1971, pp. 77–112.

Notes that melancholy is central to *Hamlet*, not only in the images of disease and the graveyard scene, which in imagery and symbols support Hamlet's view of the world, but more functionally as a source of his superior imagination and in his role playing of a series of stereotyped melancholy parts (the political malcontent, the scholar and satirist, the madman). His role playing is expressive of his unwillingness to trust and communicate with others, and it is justified by the diseased world to which it is a response.

1336. MacDonald, Michael. "Ophelia's Maimed Rites." *Shakespeare Quarterly* 37 (1986):309–17.

Maintains that burial customs were in a state of transition in Renaissance England and that the various attitudes toward Ophelia's burial reflect the degree of ambiguity. As a rule only raving lunatics were excused for suicide and provided full burial. At the other extreme suicides without such an excuse were denied Christian burial, interred at night with a stake through the body. A middle ground, apparently employed primarily for aristocrats, was a ruling of accidental death that permitted limited Christian rites. Laertes, the grave digger, and the priest reflect the full range of such views.

1337. McGee, Arthur. *The Elizabethan Hamlet.* New Haven: Yale University Press, 1987, 208 pp.

Asserts that to Shakespeare's Protestant spectators there would have been no question concerning the nature of the ghost from Catholic purgatory. "In the symbolic terms which they were familiar with Hamlet has let himself become the tool of the Devil and a modern approach which does not appreciate this misunderstands the diabolic role of the ghost in the play" (p. 103). The extent of the spirit's manipulation is reflected in Hamlet's mad role, and his soliloquies reveal the ambition, conscience, and suicidal despair that damn him.

Hamlet

1338. MACK, MAYNARD. "The World of *Hamlet*." *Yale Review* 41 (1952):502–23.

Focuses on the interrogative mood of the *Hamlet* world, a mysteriousness characterized by riddles of language and action and by the problematic nature of reality and the relation of reality to appearance. The nature of the ghost, Hamlet's madness, Ophelia's innocence, Gertrude's guilt, the enigma of Claudius—all are essentially indeterminate matters to characters and spectators alike. Reinforcing these ambiguities are the frequent uses of "assume," "put on," "shape," "show," "act," and "play," and the verbal imagery of theatricality and painting. By the final act Hamlet has come to accept the ambivalence of the world and of life itself, and he is prepared for "the final conflict of mighty opposites" (p. 523).

1339. MALONE, CYNTHIA NORTHCUTT. "Framing in *Hamlet*." *College Literature* 18 (1991):50–63.

Observes that Hamlet frames a theatrical mousetrap to demonstrate Claudius's guilt and that he surrounds this play within a play with a framing discourse. As the players enact *The Murder of Gonzago*, the boundaries between elements within the spectacle and those in the outside court become increasingly blurred. Both the preceding dumb show and Hamlet's running commentary during the subsequent performance mediate between the inner and outer forms. In the violent closure of the playlet, the ghost is absorbed into the central action and Hamlet himself is absorbed into the revenger.

1340. MALONE, KEMP. *The Literary History of Hamlet: The Early Tradition.* Anglistische Forschungen, 59. Heidelberg: C. Winter, 1923, 268 pp.

Explores the literary history of Hamlet and the Hamlet saga, dealing with the origin and development of the hero and tale before the twelfth-century version in the *Historia Danica*. The origins probably lie in the Swedish king Onela, whom scops variously fashioned as a Danish, Norwegian, and Geatish folk hero. The major aspects of the legend—the mistreatment of Amleth's mother, Amleth's apparent acquiescence, and his attack on Fjalkar-Feng—are traced through several Scandinavian tribes; and the hypothetical primitive plot, in its fullest form before Saxo, is constructed in the final chapter.

1341. MERCER, PETER. *"Hamlet" and the Acting of Revenge.* Iowa City: University of Iowa Press, 1987, 269 pp.

Focuses on Hamlet's difference as a revenger from the central figures in other Elizabethan revenge plays. Hamlet is an individual whose moral sensibilities could never accommodate "the bloody inhumanity of revenge" (p. 217). This fact is nowhere clearer than in the comparison with figures like Heironimo, Antonio, and Vindice. From such a contrast can be constructed a fundamental difference between the hero and the revenger, the one human, the other a monster of guile and blood.

1342. MIRIAM JOSEPH, SISTER. *"Hamlet:* A Christian Tragedy." *Studies in Philology* 59 (1962):119–40.

Defines a Christian tragedy as one in which the hero's flaw and catharsis have explicitly Christian significance. The ghost, a soul from purgatory acting as God's agent, orders Hamlet to dispatch Claudius but, in doing so, not to taint his mind with hatred. Hamlet does just that, however, in refusing to kill Claudius at prayer for fear of the king's repentant state. The result is a chain of deaths for which he is ultimately responsible—those of Polonius, Ophelia, Laertes, Gertrude, Rosencrantz and Guildenstern.

1343. MORRIS, HARRY. *"Hamlet* as a *Memento Mori* Poem." *PMLA* 85 (1970):1035–40.

Considers the similarity of the structure of *Hamlet* and that of the *timor mortis—memento mori* lyric. The grave diggers' scene in *Hamlet* (5.1) is a set piece involving three skulls and imagery of the instruments and furniture of burial and of flesh-stripped bones. Shakespeare's main source is Thomas Lord Vaux's *memento mori* lyric, but he also apparently uses St. Bernard's poem. The entire play is structured around this motif of remembering and preparing for death, both in Hamlet's desire for death and in his attempts to accomplish his duty without endangering his soul.

1344. NEWELL, ALEX. "The Dramatic Context and Meaning of Hamlet's 'To Be or Not to Be' Soliloquy." *PMLA* 80 (1965):38–50.

Insists on interpreting Hamlet's "To Be or Not to Be" soliloquy within its dramatic context. Specifically, this soliloquy involves his grappling with the idea of the presentation of the mousetrap play that he has just previously discussed with the players. The opening question accrues meaning as Hamlet thinks through the situation, but it clearly concerns whether to act against Claudius or to suffer. By the time he comes to sense that thought may be a symptom of fear, he sees more deeply into the complexity of the human personality. The soliloquy moves from specific to general considerations.

1345. O'MEARA, J. "Hamlet and the Tragedy of Sexuality." *Hamlet Studies* 10 (1988):117–25.

Hamlet

Argues that Hamlet's melancholia at the outset of the play arises not from his preoccupation with his mother's overhasty marriage but simply from profound grief over the death of a father whose final judgment, he assumes, contrasts signally with the present ignoble life of his mother. The true shock comes with the ghost's revelation that his judgment was not favorable and that Hamlet, if he has "nature" in him, must "bear it not." Hamlet takes this pronouncement as a condemnation of sexual activity itself, and his subsequent outbursts against both his mother and against Ophelia are evidence of his "new sense of the sexual paradox" (p. 122).

1346. PATTERSON, ANNABEL. " 'The Very Age of the Time His Form and Pressure': Rehistoricizing Shakespeare's Theater." *New Literary History* 20 (1988):83–104.

Considers various problems of the text that move beyond analysis of the play as literature, namely the social structure of the original audiences and how that relates to interpretive competence, the socioeconomic and political environment of the theaters, and the status of plays as cultural representations of contemporary events and issues. *Hamlet*—and more precisely the conditions under which it was first produced—bears rethinking as a play of political usurpation in the aftermath of Essex's failed rebellion and for an age apprehensive about new rulership.

1347. PROSSER, ELEANOR. *"Hamlet" and Revenge.* Stanford: Stanford University Press, 1967, 304 pp.

Argues that Hamlet is the only revenger who seeks the damnation of his victim, that something is fundamentally wrong with the play if the protagonist is morally obligated to kill Claudius. Numerous stage cuts and critical treatises have attempted to explain away the difficulty. In truth, Shakespeare intends the spectator to be appalled by the savage course on which Hamlet embarks. The ghost, in a word, is a demonic spirit, appearing at midnight to a melancholic thirsting for revenge and presenting a temptation to Hamlet to resort to blood revenge at the expense of his own spiritual health.

1348. QUILLIAN, WILLIAM H. *"Hamlet" and the New Poetic: James Joyce and T. S. Eliot.* Studies in Modern Literature, 13. Ann Arbor: UMI Research Press, 1983, 171 pp.

Examines the literary response to *Hamlet* in the decade from 1911 to 1922 when the so-called new poetic was being forged in the work of Eliot and Joyce. Whereas the nineteenth century was fascinated with unraveling the heart of Hamlet's mystery, the present age focuses more frequently on the artistic techniques and the conditions of the age. So deeply has *Hamlet* become a part of Western consciousness that every new interpretation echoes the past and prefigures the future. Though ultimately not successful, both Joyce and Eliot attempted to free *Hamlet* from the vagaries of historical relativism, to see it as a play in its own historical context.

1349. REPLOGLE, CAROL. "Not Parody, Not Burlesque: The Play Within the Play in *Hamlet.*" *Modern Philology* 67 (1969):150–59.

Argues that the play within the play in *Hamlet*, far from being burlesque and parody either stylistically or thematically, has a climactic function and that it is a serious and successful stylistic experiment. For one thing, *The Murder of Gonzago* is filled with sententiae that deal with love and loyalty, marriage and remarriage, and vacillations of purpose, thus reiterating the major themes of the play. For another, with its abundance of monosyllabic words and closed couplets the action slows the pace and suggests the passage of time.

1350. ROSE, MARK. "*Hamlet* and the Shape of Revenge." *English Literary Renaissance* 1 (1971):132–43.

Views Hamlet as an individual whose freedom is sorely restrained. Mentally and physically "tethered" in the play, he has come to envision Denmark as a prison. Claudius's refusal to permit him to return to Wittenberg prevents his leaving a court he now abhors, and God's decree against suicide blocks yet another avenue of escape. His major problem is to find a satisfactory shape for his revenge. Unlike Laertes, he refuses to be played upon; he must take the vulgar concept and refine it so that it no longer offends the modesty of nature or the dignity of man.

1351. ROWE, ELEANORE. "*Hamlet*": *A Window on Russia*. New York: New York University Press, 1976, 186 pp.

Examines the impact of *Hamlet* on Russian life and literature from 1748 to 1970. Used as a window to life's meaning, the play has shifted in focus from one age to another. Lermontov, Turgenev, Chekhov, and Pasternak, for example, attribute qualities of Hamlet to their own heroes, but the hero's plight and search for truth vary widely. Current Marxist interpretations generally stress Hamlet's victimization by two clashing ideologies. For the very reason that Russians have consistently assigned to the play and its hero immediately applicable moral and social values, their critical and creative commentary provides a significant insight into the Russian mind.

Hamlet

1352. SHARMA, GRANSHIAM. "The Function of Horatio in *Hamlet*." *Hamlet Studies* 8 (1986):30–39.

Focuses on the significance of Horatio's function in the play—to serve as the audience's spokesman to interrogate and then to establish the presence of the ghost, to interpret its intentions, to act as co-judge with Hamlet of Claudius' guilt during the play within the play, to receive privileged information concerning what has happened to Hamlet during his abortive voyage, and, most important, to serve as a positive "foil" to the hero throughout the tragedy. What Hamlet admires most lives on in Horatio and proffers some hope for the future.

1353. SHOWALTER, ELAINE. "Representing Ophelia: Women, Madness, and Responsibilities of Feminist Criticism." In *Shakespeare and the Question of Theory*. Edited by Patricia Parker and Geoffrey Hartman. New York: Methuen, 1985, pp. 77–94.

Surveys portrayals of Ophelia in English and French painting, photography, psychiatry, literature, and theatrical productions as a reflection of attitudes toward women from the past to the present day. For the Elizabethans, Ophelia's madness was presented as a predictable outcome of erotomania. For the Romantics her derangement resulted from an excess of "feeling." Ellen Terry in the nineteenth century led the way in depicting Ophelia as a victim of sexual intimidation, a girl terrified of her father, her lover, and life itself. Freudian studies produced a figure with unresolved oedipal attachment to her father, and since the 1970s feminist discourse has proclaimed her madness a powerful protest against family and social order.

1354. SKULSKY, HAROLD. "Revenge, Honor, and Conscience in Hamlet." *PMLA* 85 (1970):78–87.

Views *Hamlet* as a tragedy of spiritual decline caused by pride. Hamlet must choose between the law of the talon (the lustful determination to murder) and the code of honor (the desire through the duello to inflict injury). While Hamlet chooses the latter, both are motivated by the will; and Hamlet's linking of conscience to cowardice is an indication of his moral deterioration. He resolves his scruples by speciously determining that he is God's scourge and minister.

1355. SPENCER, THEODORE. "Hamlet and the Nature of Reality." *ELH* 5 (1938):255–71.

Notes that the sense of enlargement in scope and dimension in Shakespeare's major tragedies has its origin in *Hamlet* in the playwright's sophisticated utilization of the difference between appearance and reality in the creation of dramatic character and situation. This motif capitalized on the implicit conflict between man's dignity and his wretchedness in the inherited Christian view of man and his universe. In Hamlet's soliloquies Shakespeare weaves into the character a dialectical tension regarding morality and social duty based on this philosophic dualism. His discovery of the differences between appearance and reality is so disillusioning that it paralyzes the sources of deliberate action.

1356. STOLL, ELMER EDGAR. *"Hamlet": An Historical and Comparative Study.* Minneapolis: University of Minnesota Press, 1919, 76 pp.

Aims to discover Shakespeare's intentions by analyzing the techniques, characters, and sentiments of the play and by describing modifications Shakespeare makes in his source materials. Above all, Shakespeare shifts the revenge itself into the background and labors to make the revenger a sympathetic figure, a heroic—not pathetic—individual. The point of confusion is the numerous transformations of Hamlet in later times that have obscured his character, as each age attempts to remake him in its own fashion.

1357. TAYLOR, MYRON. "Tragic Justice and the House of Polonius." *Studies in English Literature 1500–1900* 8 (1968):273–81.

Views Polonius as the purest symbol of all that is rotten in Denmark, a Machiavellian villain consumed by deceit whose main function is to act as Claudius's spy and who dies serving that purpose. Laertes, like his father, also engages in deceitful villainy, and Ophelia allows herself to be used for similar ends. In the deaths of Polonius and his children the clear hand of providence is at work. The activities of the household underscore the motif of appearance versus reality in the play.

1358. TURNER, JOHN *"Hamlet*: The Court in Transition." In *Shakespeare Out of Court.* By John Turner, Graham Holderness, and Nick Potter. New York: St. Martin's Press, 1990, pp. 49–79.

Suggests that Horatio, in considering suicide by drinking from the poisoned cup, forces a philosophic choice between abandoning himself to baleful, nihilistic destiny or asserting a "faith in the power of human rationality to understand, and perhaps also to control, [his] destiny" (p. 52). The play captures the crisis in moral and political authority within the new Renaissance states—whether in the Machiavellianism of Claudius and Fortinbras or the Platonic idealism of Hamlet. The destruction of his "aristocratic idealism . . . enables us to judge the meanness of what survives" (p. 78), a concept that sets the pattern for the great tragedies still to come.

Hamlet

1359. VAN LAAN, THOMAS F. "Ironic Reversal in *Hamlet*." *Studies in English Literature 1500–1900* 6 (1966):247–62.
Observes that the primary conflict in *Hamlet* is the tension created by the view, on the one hand, that asserts a ubiquitous evil in a corrupt and fallen world and, on the other, that proclaims a world controlled by a just and benevolent God. The tension is for many critics resolved in act 5 with Hamlet's vision of the fallen sparrow and the purgation of evil through his self-sacrifice. But ironic reversal has operated throughout the play, and in the announced deaths of Rosencrantz and Guildenstern and the fact that Fortinbras arrives on the scene, having escaped all consequences of his actions, a dark ambiguity reasserts itself.

1360. WADDINGTON, RAYMOND. "Lutheran Hamlet." *English Language Notes* 27, no.2 (1989–90):27–42.
Suggests that Hamlet's line "Your worm is your only emperor for diet" (4.3.20) alludes to the Diet of Worms presided over by the emperor that in 1521 pronounced its ban on Luther for refusing to recant. Such an allusion, more precisely, casts Claudius into the role of Charles V, Holy Roman Emperor, and himself into the role of Martin Luther. The association helps to illuminate Hamlet's severe melancholia and contempt for the world, as well as distinctions between the temporal and spiritual kingdoms. Like Luther, Hamlet following his sea voyage is "an entirely new man who thinks differently, wills differently" (p. 39).

1361. WALDOCK, ARTHUR J. A. *"Hamlet": A Study in Critical Method.* Cambridge: Cambridge University Press, 1931, 94 pp.
Argues that Hamlet's so-called delay and all its ramifications concerning the protagonist's personality are essentially fabrications of critical minds. Taken at a glance, or as the play is experienced in the theater, Hamlet's action occurs in a reasonable continuum. Problems of delay and motivations for delay aside, the play gives evidence of a fine harmony in "the portrait of a man who seems to express (and the more in his sufferings and his disasters) all that Shakespeare found of greatest beauty and worth in the human spirit" (p. 94).

1362. WALKER, ROY. *The Time Is Out of Joint: A Study of "Hamlet."* London: Andrew Dakers, 1948, 157 pp.
Asserts that it is disastrously erroneous to envision Hamlet as a maladjusted, obstinate, and self-centered individual. To the contrary, he has a transfiguring view of the decadent world, and his soul fights against time for immortality. Scene 1 establishes the ghost as an objective phenomenon, and in the ensuing action we witness the crucifixion

of the godlike in man, the pride in suffering man must pay for his idealism and his imagination. Hamlet does not delay; only in his weaker moments does he conceive his duty to be merely the murder of his uncle. His task is to await the proper moment to purge the entire kingdom of evil.

1363. WARHAFT, SIDNEY. "The Mystery of *Hamlet*." *ELH* 30 (1963): 193.

Questions how *Hamlet* can provoke such a wide range of critical opinion, much of it flatly contradictory in nature, and suggests that the play was intended to comprehend such diversity. *Hamlet*, more specifically, might well have been intended as an inscrutable mystery dealing with the ambiguous predicament of a sensitive and intelligent individual caught in the providential workings of history. Heaven is ordinate in the fall of a corrupt dynasty, and this providential hand is dramatized in the actions of a baffled and tormented young prince.

1364. WEITZ, MORRIS. *"Hamlet" and the Philosophy of Literary Criticism*. Chicago and London: University of Chicago Press, 1964, 335 pp.

Investigates the meaning of criticism by focusing on the critical paraphernalia surrounding *Hamlet*. Major attention is directed to the nature and the function, the relationship of poetics to aesthetics, the nature of disagreement, the conflict between schools or methods, and the problem of standards. The first part establishes the major critical approaches, while the second part attempts to articulate the twenty-four areas or issues of critical analysis. The multiple views complement rather than discredit one another because the realm of literary interpretation defies all absolutist approach.

1365. WEST, REBECCA. *The Court and the Castle: Some Treatments of a Recurrent Theme*. New Haven: Yale University Press, 1957, 319 pp.

Bemoans the tendency to read *Hamlet* as an inscrutable and mysterious drama with an equally enigmatic protagonist. Hamlet is, quite frankly, an exceptionally callous murderer. But he can kill only on his own behalf; he refuses the mandate of the ghost, who represents the values of tradition, preferring individual impulse as his motivation. Shakespeare's focus is also on the corruption of the entire court and of society. Calvinistic in its image of total depravity, *Hamlet* illustrates the impossibility of escape from the guilt of society and the human race.

1366. WILLIAMSON, CLAUDE C. H. *Readings on the Character of Hamlet 1661–1947*. London: George Allen & Unwin, 1950, 783 pp.

Hamlet

Provides representative criticism of Hamlet, through selected passages, for almost three hundred years. The items are arranged chronologically and comprise 332 entries by 264 different critics. While the study provides critical appraisal, a postscript also describes the major subjects of critical disparity (for example, Hamlet's madness, his religion, his causes for delay). The material obviously illustrates shifting critical fashions, representing English, American, and European authors. The entries range in length from a single sentence to ten pages.

1367. WILSON, JOHN DOVER. *What Happens in "Hamlet."* Cambridge: Cambridge University Press, 1935, 357 pp.

Provides a close and extensive analysis of *Hamlet* along with the background of Elizabethan beliefs. Hamlet's task is a family affair involving the honor of the entire family. That the ghost itself is seen by four persons nullifies the possibility of melancholic illusion though it does not remove the mystery concerning its nature. The four (Bernardo, Marcellus, Horatio, Hamlet) represent the various contemporary assumptions about spirits—that they might be spirits of the departed, angels, or devils. Of special interest is the discussion of the dumb show, which Claudius simply was not observing and which—since it threatened to warn the king of the impending trap—sorely annoyed Hamlet.

1368. WOOD, ROBERT E. "Space and Scrutiny in *Hamlet*." *South Atlantic Review* 52 (1987):25–42.

Suggests that the modernity of *Hamlet* arises in large part from the severely restricted use of space in the play. Shakespeare's Elsinore has no real significance in the play; instead, the locus of the action is a confined area in which characters always have easy access to each other, eavesdropping, observing each other to determine intention, creating scenarios to observe reaction. The text is written with the limited space of the stage in mind and draws its major force from interactions arising from such close proximity.

Stage History

1369. BROWN, MARTIN E. "English Hamlets of the Twentieth Century." *Shakespeare Survey* 9 (1956): 16–23.

Highlights some of the significant trends in *Hamlet* productions in the twentieth century. The descriptive sketch covers the Forbes-

Robertson staging at Drury Lane in 1913, a reading by H. B. Irving (son of Henry Irving), Brown's production in Sussex in 1923 with Robert Speaight as Hamlet, versions in 1925 in London with Ernest Milton, John Barrymore, and Barry Jackson, John Gielgud's in 1930, Robert Helpmann's in 1948, and Alec Guiness's in 1951. Most memorable are Gielgud and Forbes-Robertson, those who have most fully interpreted the part.

1370. GILDER, ROSAMUND. *John Gielgud's "Hamlet."* New York and Toronto: Oxford University Press, 1937, 233 pp.

Compares John Gielgud with Burbage, Betterton, Garrick, Kean, and Booth in having the power to articulate a Hamlet that is both true to Shakespeare and pertinent to their own times. Complex, moody, by turns furious and dejected, Gielgud's Hamlet focuses on the conflict of the driving force of emotion neutralized by a contemplative, questioning, rational mind. Included are Gielgud's notes on costume, scenery, and stage business, along with—on pages facing the text—a scene-by-scene description of his performance at the New Theatre, London, 1934–35, and at the St. James Theatre, New York, 1936–37.

1371. KLIMAN, BERNICE. "Olivier's *Hamlet*: A Film-Infused Play." *Literature/Film Quarterly* 5 (1977):305–14.

Observes that Olivier, by deciding not simply to film Shakespeare's play, gained freedom both of space and of perspective. By using a flexible stage set (with movable stairways, pillars, and halls), a traveling camera to move from one angle to another, fade-outs, music, close-ups (at times several in rapid succession), and aural and visual transitions, Olivier achieves startling effects. His intent was to create, not a hybrid of film and stage, but a film-infused experience.

1372. REYNOLDS, GEORGE. "*Hamlet* at the Globe." *Shakespeare Survey* 9 (1956):49–53.

Notes that actors and directors are increasingly realizing that the absence of specific demands in the original text permits a wide latitude in the manner of staging *Hamlet*. It can, in fact, be played entirely on an arena stage without distortion. The difficulty of seeing and hearing when scenes are recessed and the question of whether there was even an inner, curtained stage at the Globe suggest that the action should be pulled forward on the stage as far as practicable. The play-within-the-play scene, for example, requires that Hamlet and Claudius be on opposite sides of the main stage so that the spectators might watch both the king's and the prince's reaction to the playlet.

Julius Caesar

1373. ROSSI, ALFRED. *Minneapolis Rehearsals: Tyrone Guthrie Directs "Hamlet."* Berkeley: University of California Press, 1970, 236 pp.

Charts Tyrone Guthrie's direction of the Minnesota Theatre Company's production of *Hamlet* at the Tyrone Guthrie Theatre in Minneapolis in 1963. Prepared by a member of the company and the assistant to the director for this production, the study includes a *Hamlet* log written during rehearsals and the postscript by Edward Payson Call, whose tendency to verbalize the action results in a record of stage directions, not merely of stage movements. This production was in modern dress, with scenic and costume design by Tanya Moiseiwitsch, whose sketches are also included.

JULIUS CAESAR

Reference Work

1374. VELZ, JOHN W., comp. *"The Tragedy of Julius Caesar": A Bibliography to Supplement the New Variorum Shakespeare Edition of 1913.* New York: Modern Language Association, 1977, 58 pp.

Includes 1,252 entries representing the scholarship on *Julius Caesar* from 1913 through 1972. The material is categorized alphabetically under editions, commentary, text, date, sources, criticism, and stage and stage history. Books with multiple focus are included in the criticism section; editions and book reviews are not included. Supplements entry 1376.

Editions

1375. DORSCH, T. S., ed. *Julius Caesar.* The Arden Shakespeare. London: Methuen; Cambridge, Mass.: Harvard University Press, 1955, 166 pp.

Includes discussion of the text, date, contemporary allusions, Shakespeare's treatment of the sources, other Caesar plays, the language and imagery, and the characterization, as well as an appendix featuring a selection from Thomas Platter's account of his visit to England. The text is based on the First Folio, for which the copy was probably the promptbook. Apparently one of the first plays performed at the Globe in 1599, *Julius Caesar* is effectively constructed with the balance of power divided among the conflicting parties.

1376. FURNESS, HENRY HOWARD, Jr., ed. *The Tragedie of Julius Caesar*. A New Variorum Edition of Shakespeare. Philadelphia: J. B. Lippincott, 1913, 482 pp.

Uses the First Folio as the copy text. On each page, for that portion of the text, are provided variant readings, textual notes, and general critical commentary. Following the text are sections on the nature of the text, the date of composition, the text of William Alexander's *Julius Caesar*, the individual characters, criticisms, stage history, the principal actors, dramatic versions, and a list of works consulted. Supplemented by entry 1374.

1377. HUMPHREYS, ARTHUR, ed. *Julius Caesar*. The Oxford Shakespeare. Oxford and New York: Oxford University Press, 1984, 264 pp.

Includes an introductory essay on date, sources and their shape, Shakespeare's Roman values, politics and morality, style, the play in performance, and the folio text. Extensive notes on each page of the text identify problems of language and provide background information. An appendix reprints apposite passages from North's Plutarch.

1378. SPEVACK, MARVIN, ed. *Julius Caesar*. The New Cambridge Shakespeare. Cambridge: Cambridge University Press, 1988, 184 pp.

Features an introductory essay on the date of composition, the play-frame, structure, theme, persons and politics, and the stage history. Extensive notes appear on individual pages of the text, and supplementary notes, a textual analysis, excerpts from Plutarch, and a reading list are appended.

Criticism

1379. ANSON, JOHN S. "*Julius Caesar*: The Politics of the Hardened Heart." *Shakespeare Studies* 2 (1966):11–33.

Argues that Shakespeare in *Julius Caesar* develops the image of Rome as a body, an organism in which all parts have a necessary and significant function. Gradually this body, governed by a repressive ethic, loses its sensibility, and head is separated from hand. The contagion spreads from Caesar to the conspirators to the populace at large. Corporately the body loses compassion and the heart hardens, a political

Julius Caesar

situation dramatized in the play. *Julius Caesar* is a drama of rivalries, of "culture purchased at the price of perpetual suffering" (p. 30).

1380. BONJOUR, ADRIEN. *The Structure of "Julius Caesar."* Liverpool: Liverpool University Press, 1958, 81 pp.
Observes that—unlike the conscience-stricken criminal Henry IV or the repentant King John or the satanic slaughterer Richard III, all of whom commit murder for political ambition—Brutus is an intrinsically noble individual whose aims are politically disinterested. He determines to sacrifice Caesar to a higher political imperative, but in that very act of subordinating the human level to that of abstraction lie the seeds of his own destruction. Shakespeare forces the spectators' sympathies to fluctuate toward and away from Brutus as he focuses on certain ramifications of the political act.

1381. BOWDEN, WILLIAM R. "The Mind of Brutus." *Shakespeare Quarterly* 17 (1966):57–67.
Maintains that deromanticizing Brutus yields a more realistic figure consistent with the text. Brutus, for one thing, is not an intellectual; he is seduced by Cassius into joining the conspiracy, and his independent decisions are blunders. For another, it is impossible to focus on precisely the nature of Brutus's inner conflict, if indeed there is one. Finally, he experiences no anagnorisis, persisting to the point of death in refusal to admit moral culpability. He is a self-righteous do-gooder who is always wrong.

1382. BURKE, KENNETH. "Antony in Behalf of the Play." *Southern Review* 1 (1935):308–19.
Imagines Antony just after the murder addressing the spectators rather than the mob, explaining Shakespeare's method as variously stressing the Caesar principle and the Brutus principle. In Antony the Caesar principle is continued, and it continues to be problematic in the spectators' eyes through Antony's inciting the mob to riotous and destructive action. Even so, the Brutus principle degenerates even more strikingly through the quarrel between Cassius and Brutus, his "descent to soft tearfulness" (p. 290), and the prophetic appearance of Caesar's ghost as Brutus's "evil spirit."

1383. BURT, RICHARD A. " 'A Dangerous Rome': Shakespeare's *Julius Caesar* and the Discursive Determinism of Cultural Politics." In *Contending Kingdoms: Historical, Psychological, and Feminist Approaches to the Literature of Sixteenth-Century England and France.* Edited by Marie-Rose Logan and Peter L. Rudnytsky. Detroit: Wayne State University Press, 1991, pp. 109–27.

Argues that discourse determines politics. In *Julius Caesar* persuasion is necessary because characters are positioned within a discourse. The initial effect of the assassination, for example, is neither pro- nor antirepublican. Brutus, in speaking to the plebeians, attempts to interpret Caesar as enemy to Rome and thus win the crowd's acceptance; Antony in his subsequent populist discourse succeeds because Brutus has positioned the plebeians as subjects rather than citizens. In Renaissance England *Julius Caesar* does not prescribe a particular ideological position; the political effect is determined by how the play is articulated and received.

1384. FORTIN, RENÉ. "*Julius Caesar*: An Experiment in Point of View." *Shakespeare Quarterly* 19 (1968):341–47.

Believes *Julius Caesar* is a deliberate experiment in point of view to reveal the limitations of human knowledge. Truth is at least partially subjective, modified by the individual's perspective. The theme of misconstruing permeates the play. Each principal character has his own view of Caesar; but Brutus because of his patrician pride allows himself to be seduced by Cassius, and his deception persists until the end of the play.

1385. GREENE, GAYLE. " 'The Power of Speech to Stir Men's Blood': The Language of Tragedy in Shakespeare's *Julius Caesar*." *Renaissance Drama*, n.s. 11 (1980):67–83.

Suggests that the rhetorical style of *Julius Caesar* is central to its tragic meaning, that the depiction of Rome as a society filled with speakers whose rhetorical skills mask moral and political truth demonstrates the use of language to pervert, conceal, and misconstrue. Particular focus is on Cassius's success in persuading Brutus to join the conspiracy, Brutus's self-justifying soliloquy, Brutus's funeral oration, and Antony's counteroration. Language, man's medium for coming to terms with his objective world, is turned inwardly and destructively back upon itself.

1386. HAGAR, ALAN. " 'The Teeth of Emulation': Failed Sacrifice in Shakespeare's *Julius Caesar*." *Upstart Crow* 8 (1988):54–68.

Asserts that Shakespeare schematizes the dangers of man's reversion to the savage in a time of crisis, yielding to group violence that triumphs over conciliation and communion. The ritual sacrifice of Caesar fails because it lacks general sanction. Such "'bad-blood' augments vendetta arithmetically until, in this play, we seem to be concerned only with numbers" (p. 60).

1387. HARTSOCK, MILDRED. "The Complexity of *Julius Caesar*." *PMLA* 81 (1966):56–62.

Julius Caesar

Claims that a study of Shakespeare's use of sources in *Julius Caesar* reveals that he intends the play to be problematic and that any attempt to tilt the moral balance to a particular critical posture is false to the dramaturgical design. Alterations from Plutarch, more precisely, render ambiguous Caesar, Brutus, Cassius, and the Roman people. In such a manner Shakespeare effectively dramatizes the dilemma of being forced to act on what is inevitably a partial view and stimulates consideration of the nature of political realities.

1388. KIRSCHBAUM, LEO. "Shakespeare's Stage Blood and Its Critical Significance." *PMLA* 64 (1949):517–29.

Observes that spectacular blood effects through concealed bladders, sponges, and animal entrails were relatively common on the Elizabethan stage. The bloody sergeant in *Macbeth* and the bleeding Coriolanus after the battle at Corioli are merely two examples. One of the most striking is in *Julius Caesar* where the assassination actualizes Calpurnia's dream that Caesar was a fountain spouting blood from many holes in which the conspirators bathe their hands. Shakespeare not only excites the spectators by such a scene; he also reflects the bloodthirstiness of the conspirators.

1389. MCALINDON, THOMAS. "The Numbering of Men and Days: Symbolic Design in *The Tragedy of Julius Caesar.*" *Studies in Philology* 81 (1984):372–93.

Suggests that *mean* in the sense of both significance and intention is the key word in *Julius Caesar*. The most remarkable feature of the play is that Shakespeare involves the spectators in the hermeneutic problems, why Caesar pushed back the crown, why Brutus could join the conspiracy. Number symbolism also engages the spectators in a search for meaning, specifically the Pythagorean four (amity, justice) and eight (justice, regeneration). The numbers become reverberative through reiteration both verbal and visual. The observant minority in Shakespeare's audience would note that the characters in the play blandly disregard the signs of fate around them and that meaning is mockingly allusive.

1390. MARSHALL, CYNTHIA. "Totem, Taboo, and *Julius Caesar.*" *Literature and Psychology* 37 (1991):11–33.

Observes that *Julius Caesar*, written a year or so before *Hamlet*, "rehearses some of the attitudes familiar from the more notably Oedipal play" (p. 11). Brutus, cast as a symbolic son, participates in the killing of Caesar, who is traditionally identified as Rome's *pater patriae*. According to Freud, a primitive society performs actions that would be sublimated in a later civilized society. The story of Julius Caesar "exists on the cusp of civilization" (p. 28). Brutus's willingness to sacrifice himself for the sake of the state signals his attempt to become the father through reenactment.

1391. MILES, GARY B. "How Roman Are Shakespeare's Romans?" *Shakespeare Quarterly* 40 (1989):257–83.

Points out the radical difference between the concept of character in ancient Rome and in Elizabethan England. Shakespeare conceived of character as an essentially private, internal struggle. Brutus, for instance, is an idealist struggling with his conscience and deceived about his own nature and the nature of man himself. To the Romans, to Plutarch, on the other hand, character is developed and expressed through public action, which provided the standard for judging the personal character and questions of value. Brutus's uncompromising political action formed his character; certainly he experienced internal struggle, but that was insignificant to the public standards by which worth was ultimately measured—and ultimately rewarded for posterity.

1392. MIOLA, ROBERT S. "*Julius Caesar* and the Tyrannicide Debate." *Renaissance Quarterly* 38 (1985):271–89.

Notes that the England of Shakespeare's time was preoccupied with the question of tyrannicide and that a significant point in the debate was the controversial assassination of Julius Caesar. Such a debate contributes much to the form of Shakespeare's play; the playwright, more specifically, "transformed a confused welter of historical fact and legend into taut, balanced, and supremely ambivalent drama" (p. 273). The play dramatizes the differences between human history and political theory. Theoretical logic is shot through with the temptation of self-interest and the inevitable eruptions of deceit and demagoguery that can transform an ideal into political Machiavellianism.

1393. MOONEY, MICHAEL E. " 'Passion, I See, Is Catching': The Rhetoric of *Julius Caesar.*" *Journal of English and Germanic Philology* 90 (1991):31–50.

Notes that in this play Shakespeare dramatizes the way individuals may be moved by others, fashioned to conform to another's will. He focuses, as well, on the degree to which men may deceive themselves. He does so, at first, by alternately privileging and deceiving the spectators. Later, however, he increasingly "distances the spectators from their offstage counterparts, so much so that the rhetoric found *in* the play is ultimately opposed to the rhetoric *of* the play" (p. 32). The perspective continually shifts and collapses, no sooner formulated than subject to revision.

Julius Caesar

1394. PASTER, GAIL KERN. " 'In the Spirit of Blood There Is No Blood': Blood as Trope in *Julius Caesar*." *Shakespeare Quarterly* 40 (1989):284–98.

Interrogates the bodily signs of blood and bleeding in the play as "historically specific attributes of gender, as important tropes of patriarchal discourse . . . [in which] the bleeding body signifies a shameful token of uncontrol . . . particularly associated with women" (p. 284). The conspirators stab and display Caesar's body, revealing its womanly inability to stop bleeding. Antony in the funeral oration consciously redirects the political valences of this rhetoric, acknowledging femaleness as a source of differentiation in Caesar but refiguring it as an affective power to heal and transform.

1395. PETERSON, DOUGLAS L. " 'Wisdom Consumed in Confidence': An Examination of Shakespeare's *Julius Caesar*." *Shakespeare Quarterly* 16 (1965):19–28.

States that Caesar's indifference to the omens and to Artemidorus's letter is not evidence of his contempt for superstition or of his nobly placing matters of state above personal issues but of a character flaw invented by Shakespeare to account for his vulnerability to the conspirators' plot. While such a flaw explains how Caesar is manipulated into a situation culminating in his assassination, it in no way justifies his murder as a political tyrant. There is no trace of Plutarch's suggestion that Caesar's death is caused by an angry god in retribution for past crimes.

1396. PRIOR, MOODY E. "The Search for a Hero in *Julius Caesar*." *Renaissance Drama*, n.s. 2 (1969):81–101.

Argues that Brutus should not be viewed as an introspective tragic hero like Hamlet or Macbeth and that *Julius Caesar* should be considered as structurally akin to the history plays, which maintain a political theme while dividing the interest among the characters. Brutus and Cassius are the only figures of continual interest. While Brutus attempts to maintain his moral integrity as he confronts the issues raised by the conspiracy, Cassius acts as a political realist who attempts to guide the course of the rebellion by political consideration alone.

1397. PUGHE, THOMAS. "What Should the Wars Do with These Juggling Fools?: The Poets in Shakespeare's *Julius Caesar*." *English Studies* 69 (1988):313–22.

Suggests that the two poets (Cinna the poet and the camp poet) represent a type of discourse—imaginative—that is avoided by the main characters. More specifically, their fate represents the conflict between the prevailing power politics and the suppressed discourse of emotion and intuition. These poets "establish a metalevel of criticism on which the discourse of reason can be seen to deconstruct itself" (p. 313). Antony, the only character who freely admits this quality, is less liable to lose control of his discourse, though his lack of moral sense destroys his credibility for the spectators.

1398. REBHORN, WAYNE A. "The Crisis of the Aristocracy in *Julius Caesar*." *Renaissance Quarterly* 43 (1990):75–111.

Reads the killing of Caesar as the consequence of a struggle among "aristocrats—senators—aimed at preventing one of their number from transcending his place and destroying the system in which they all ruled as a class" (p. 78). In such a view the assassination is not a matter of regicide but of restoring the original political status quo. The play also holds a mirror up to the state of Shakespeare's England, suggesting that there, too, the aristocrats as a class are losing power and influence through factionalism and their marginalization by increasingly absolutist monarchs.

1399. RIBNER, IRVING. "Political Issues in *Julius Caesar*." *Journal of English and Germanic Philology* 56 (1957):10–22.

Focuses on two fundamental political issues—the chaos that results when a tyrant overthrows long-established governmental institutions and the equally destructive consequences of noble men violating their own natures to engage in political action for what they assume will be the greater good. Caesar exemplifies the first, claiming the prerogative of kingship with no legal right; Brutus typifies the second, the inevitable failure of a virtuous murderer. Shakespeare may well have been reflecting anxieties about political succession in England.

1400. SCHANZER, ERNEST. "The Tragedy of Shakespeare's Brutus." *ELH* 22 (1955):1–15.

Observes that the conception of Brutus's divided mind, self-deception, and tragic disillusion are original with Shakespeare. Following his agreement to participate in the assassination, Brutus is subject to nightmarish doubt as his "whole instinctive emotional and imaginative being rises in revulsion against the decision which his intellect has made" (p. 5). His later quarrel with Cassius reflects the tragic disillusionment of a man who, by basing his rationale for acting

Julius Caesar

on what Caesar might have been, commits himself to the mercy of events.

1401. SMITH, GORDON ROSS. "Brutus, Virtue, and Will." *Shakespeare Quarterly* 10 (1959):367–79.

Views Brutus as a character of internal psychological consistency. Brutus's central quality is not his virtue but his thoroughly egotistic will for which virtue serves as a splendid muffling of self-justification. His insistence that the conspirators not swear an oath, that Cicero not be included, that Antony not be slain, that Metullus Cimber be included, that Antony be permitted to speak over Caesar's body, that Cassius provide money for his troops, and that he and Cassius attack the enemy at Phillipi—all such instances reveal a relentless willfulness. To the very end Brutus conceives of himself as capable of mistake but not of fault.

1402. Smith, Warren D. "The Duplicate Revelation of Portia's Death." *Shakespeare Quarterly* 4 (1953):153–61.

Claims that the duplicate passages involving the revelation of Portia's death in 4.3 are textually authentic and are intended by Shakespeare to bear "unmistakable witness to the unselfishness, fortitude, and able generalship characteristic of Brutus in other parts of the play" (p. 154). Capitalizing on the variance of proscription figures and of the names of those slain in Rome as reported to Brutus, Shakespeare intends Messala's question about Portia to give Brutus desperate hope that she still lives. The remarkable manner in which he holds up under the double blow renders him highly heroic in the eyes of both the spectators and Cassius.

1403. VELZ, JOHN W. "Clemency, Will, and Just Cause in *Julius Caesar*." *Shakespeare Survey* 22 (1969):109–18.

Notes that Caesar has a radically different conception of himself than do the conspirators, who brand him a present tyrant likely to grow far worse if allowed to assume the power of kingship. According to Renaissance political thought (Pierre Charon, La Primaudaye) this view was essentially correct, and Brutus is thus neither hypocrite nor self-deceiver in his reasoning. That Brutus and his fellow conspirators fail exemplifies the tragic paradox that those who cleanse the body politic must sacrifice themselves in the holocaust.

1404. WELSH, ALEXANDER. "Brutus Is an Honorable Man." *Yale Review* 64 (1975):496–513.

Notes that honor is closely associated with one's identity as defined by what others think of him. Cassius, in this sense, convinces Brutus that his identity is being threatened by Caesar's putative ambition, that Caesar is bypassing the system of judgment by which social being is produced—ancestry and noble deeds. Brutus in turn acts purely from (and to protect) his code of honor, and the result is politically and humanly disastrous. Such autonomous action is revealed as a luxury society as a whole will not tolerate.

1405. WILSON, RICHARD. "Is This a Holiday? Shakespeare's Roman Holiday." *ELH* 54 (1987):31–44.

Observes that the first scene of the play, in which the Roman tribune Flavius urges the plebeians to get home since this is no holiday, can be seen "as a manoeuvre in the campaign to legitimize the Shakespearean stage and dissociate it from the subversiveness of artisan culture" (p. 33). The text recognizes drama's appropriation of carnival but also seems to mediate upon its sublimation and control. The play itself represents a world turned upside-down to be restored, and victory goes to those who administer and distribute the access to discourse. Coming at a point when the English bourgeoisie were asserting themselves, the text "discloses the materiality of power with self-important openness" (p. 41).

1406. ZANDVOORT, R. W. "Brutus's Forum Speech in *Julius Caesar.*" *Review of English Studies* 16 (1940):62–66.

Describes the style of Brutus's speech as euphuistic in its deliberate elaboration and repetition of a number of stylistic patterns (schemata such as *isocolon*, *parison*, and *paromion*). Shakespeare probably assigned Brutus this highly rhetorical speech to mark it off from Antony's. Certainly, whereas Brutus's speech appeals to the intellect, Antony's appeals to the emotions. The speech is the most pronounced example in Shakespeare of the sustained use of rhetorical schemes.

Stage History

1407. RIPLEY, JOHN. *"Julius Caesar" on the Stage in England and America 1599–1973.* Cambridge: Cambridge University Press, 1980, 370 pp.

Works from promptbooks, dramaturgical sketches, letters, diaries, biographies, reviews, and interviews to construct a stage history of *Julius Caesar.* The study focuses on four major areas—the texts and information they provide concerning the age's taste and sensibility; the stagings, involving matters such as sets, costumes, lighting, and crowd scenes; the interpretation of the four major roles, Caesar, Brutus, Cassius, Antony; and the extent to which academic theory and analysis have influenced the production.

KING LEAR

Reference Works

1408. CHAMPION, LARRY S., comp. *"King Lear": An Annotated Bibliography.* 2 vols. Garland Reference Library of the Humanities, 230: Garland Shakespeare Bibliographies, 1. New York and London: Garland Publishing, 1980, 909 pp.

Contains 2,532 entries, representing virtually all publications on *King Lear* from 1940 through 1978, along with the most significant items of scholarship prior to 1940. The categories, each arranged chronologically, are divided into criticism, sources, dating, textual studies, bibliographies, editions, stage history, and adaptations, influence, and synopses. An introductory essay briefly traces the history of recent criticism and research.

1409. MARDER, LOUIS, comp. *"King Lear": A Supplementary Bibliography 1880–1965.* The New Variorum Shakespeare. New York: American Scholar Publications, 1965, 30 pp.

Includes representative scholarship on *King Lear* from 1880 to 1965 and is intended to supplement H. H. Furness's Variorum edition of 1880. The material is categorized under reproductions of original folio editions, reproductions of original quarto editions, bibliographical sources, modern editions, *King Lear* bibliography, and critical studies (alphabetically arranged). While not exhaustive, the material represents every major category of scholarship and criticism.

1410. TANNENBAUM, SAMUEL A., and TANNENBAUM, DOROTHY R., comps. *William Shakespeare: "King Lear."* Elizabethan Bibliographies, 16. New York: Privately printed, 1940, 101 pp.

Cites 1,934 unannotated items covering major scholarship on *King Lear* from the beginnings to 1938. The material is divided into the following categories and is arranged alphabetically by section—editions, adaptations; translations; music, songs, operas; commentary on music; illustrations, costumes; parodies, burlesques; old *King Leir*; *King Lear* in the theater; commentary on *King Lear*; book titles; addenda. The majority of the material (1,254 items) is loosely classified under commentary on the play.

Editions

1411. DUTHIE, GEORGE IAN, ed. *Shakespeare's "King Lear": A Critical Edition*. Oxford: Basil Blackwell, 1949, 425 pp.
Uses the First Folio as the principal copy text, but allows readings from the first quarto. In addition to a textual introduction, textual variants at the bottom of the page and textual notes are provided. The aim of this old-spelling edition is to establish a text "as near to what Shakespeare wrote as it is possible to get" (p. 3). The folio text is a copy of the first quarto brought by an editor into general agreement with a theatrical manuscript containing a shortened version of the play, probably the promptbook; the quarto text is a reported version by the entire company when the King's Men were on tour in 1606.

1412. DUTHIE, GEORGE IAN, and WILSON, JOHN DOVER, eds. *King Lear*. Cambridge: Cambridge University Press, 1960, 300 pp.
Provides extensive notes, a discussion of the copy text, a critical introduction, sections on sources and date, Lear, Cordelia, Kent, the fool, Lear's suffering, the subplot, nature, man's double nature, the play's "pessimism," and a glossary; C. B. Young provides notes on the stage history. Duthie abandons his earlier assumption that the first quarto is a memorial text reconstruction by an entire company in favor of a modified view that the source is two boy actors who played Goneril and Regan. The copy for this edition is eclectic, with the folio as a base text.

1413. MUIR, KENNETH, ed. *King Lear*. The Arden Shakespeare. London: Methuen; Cambridge, Mass.: Harvard University Press, 1952, 259 pp.
Includes discussion of the text, date, sources, stage history, and critical interpretation, as well as appendixes featuring selections from *King Leir*, Holinshed's *Chronicles*, Spenser's *The Faerie Queene*, *The Mirror for Magistrates*, and Sidney's *Arcadia*. The text is based on the First Folio, with quarto readings allowed where the folio text is corrupt. Current criticism fully accepts the tragic quality of the play, though opinions range from one polarity that it is set in a teleological

universe in which suffering is redemptive to the other that Shakespeare is delineating the ultimate horror of an absurdist universe.

Textual Studies

1414. DORAN, MADELEINE. *The Text of "King Lear."* Stanford: Stanford University Press, 1931, 148 pp.

Notes that the order of the quartos is now settled, with the first quarto printed in 1608 and the second quarto printed in 1619 but falsely dated 1608; the precise nature of the texts is, however, still a matter of debate. The first quarto is not a reported text but Shakespeare's original version considerably revised. The folio text, omitting three hundred lines from the quarto, is more regular and satisfactory; it is divided into acts and scenes, and the stage directions are more complete and precise. The copy text for the folio was the promptbook, a transcript revised and shortened by Shakespeare himself.

1415. DUTHIE, GEORGE IAN. *Elizabethan Shorthand and the First Quarto of "King Lear."* Oxford: Basil Blackwell, 1949, 82 pp.

Argues that the folio text of *King Lear* was printed from a copy of the first quarto that had been brought by a scribe into general agreement with an authentic playhouse text, probably the promptbook. The quarto text bears the marks of memorial reconstruction. Theories that it was based on a shorthand account are not valid. A careful analysis of the three systems of shorthand available in 1608 reveals conclusively that none was sufficiently sophisticated to produce the text. A person might capture the essence or summary through these systems, but nothing approaching the verbal detail.

1416. KIRSCHBAUM, LEO. *The True Text of "King Lear."* Baltimore: Johns Hopkins University Press, 1945, 81 pp.

Views the quarto text of *King Lear* as a memorial reconstruction, while the folio text was printed from a copy of the quarto emended by reference to a transcript that derived from Shakespeare's associates. Any substantive difference between the quarto and the folio indicates a change deliberately introduced by someone directly connected with the company; hence, where the two texts differ, the folio reading must be adapted. A careful analysis of the two texts reveals that the quarto text is thoroughly undependable, plagued by omission, anticipation, recollection, assimilation, vulgarization, substitution, misunderstanding, and misinterpretation.

1417. STONE, P. W. K. *The Textual History of "King Lear."* London: Scholar Press, 1980, 280 pp.

Argues that the first quarto is a reported text based on a longhand account developed during visits to several performances and that the folio is a refurbished version of the same report. It is impossible safely to select either the quarto or folio as the basis for a modern edition. Instead, a modern text must be "a judiciously compiled amalgam of selections from each, . . . an independent entity, the hypothetical reconstruction of a text which does not in fact exist, but which once did as the ancestor of the editions still surviving" (p. 163).

1418. TAYLOR, GARY, and WARREN, MICHAEL, eds. *The Division of the Kingdom: Shakespeare's Two Versions of "King Lear."* New York: Oxford University Press, 1984, 320 pp.

Includes twelve original essays dealing with the current theories concerning the textual status of *King Lear*. The tragedy exists in two versions, the first quarto (1608) and the 1623 folio, and virtually all editions are eclectic, conflating the two into a single text. Recent criticism has begun to challenge this view, arguing that the two versions represent different stages in Shakespeare's composition and that the folio text represents the form he finally intended.

1419. URKOWITZ, STEVEN. *Shakespeare's Revision of "King Lear."* Princeton: Princeton University Press, 1980, 184 pp.

Challenges the assumption that the first quarto and the folio are blemished variations of the now lost text of *King Lear* and that an eclectic, inclusive modern text best approximates that original version. Instead, the quarto and folio texts represent two stages of Shakespeare's composition, an early draft and a final revision. Theatrical variants in the texts reveal much about Shakespeare's sense of dramatic movement, rhythm, and character development. The folio is clearly the superior text.

1420. WARREN, MICHAEL. *The Complete "King Lear," 1608–1623.* 4 Pts. Berkeley: University of California Press, 1989, 420 pp.

Contains facsimiles of the first quarto (1608), the second quarto (1619), and the First Folio (1623). Also, a parallel-text section juxtaposes photographs of the 1608 and 1623 versions to permit close scrutiny of the variants between the two texts. A general introduction describes the textual and editorial history of the play and contains a selective annotated bibliography of bibliographical and textual studies. Part 1 is separately published under the title *The Parallel "King Lear," 1608–1623* (Berkeley: University of California Press, 1989, 120 pp.).

Criticism

1421. BAUER, ROBERT J. " 'Despite of Mine Own Nature': Edmund and the Orders, Cosmic and Moral." *Texas Studies in Literature and Language* 10 (1968–69):359–66.

Observes that Edmund, in the light of nominalism, skepticism, and moral empiricism, exemplifies Renaissance individualism defiant of all that would negate the primacy of self-interest in legal, moral, or ethical circumstances. The dual concept of nature—*nomos*, nature as law, and *physis*, nature as vital force—is as old as the pre-Socratics, and the concept of nature as a goddess exempt from moral law (*physis*) runs throughout the literature of the Middle Ages. For Montaigne, Machiavelli, and William of Ockham society thrives by competition and contention rather than by harmony and cooperation. Edmund, a stark individualist whose relation to society has been severed by society's brand of bastard, strives to prove his superior physical and intellectual prowess.

1422. BERGER, HARRY, Jr. "Text Against Performance: The Gloucester Family Romance." In *Shakespeare's "Rough Magic": Renaissance Essays in Honor of C. L. Barber.* Edited by Peter Erickson and Coppélia Kahn. Newark: University of Delaware Press; London and Toronto: Associated University Presses, 1985, pp. 210–29.

Argues that a lawful heir prescribes the power of the father by binding him psychologically to his son's future lordship. As potential enemy and competitor, the son raises anxieties and a subliminal desire for aggression in the father. When Gloucester discovers that his fears are groundless, his aggression turns against himself in remorse and guilt. When Edgar, in turn, learns the truth, his impulse to forgive and seek reconciliation coincides with a desire to administer justice. His comments as Poor Tom during Lear's mad trial scene suggest that he is conducting his own trial of his father. His later explanation to Albany "edits out all his darker moments, and stresses his devoted tendance" (9. 223).

1423. BICKERSTETH, GEOFFREY LANGDALE. *The Golden World of "King Lear."* Oxford: Oxford University Press, 1946, 24 pp.

Argues that Shakespeare's purpose in *King Lear* is essentially didactic, to reveal that morally evil elements and the suffering they provoke ultimately work for the cause of good. What we slowly realize is that all suffering, when accepted and patiently endured for another's sake and not for self-advantage, is sacrificial and redemptive. Cordelia's actions, more specifically, suggest Christ's Harrowing of Hell. Divine love enters a kingdom already divided, operating first as a disruptive force before restoring all things to order. It is Lear's conviction that she does live that causes his heart to break, not from sorrow, but "in an ecstasy of joy" (p. 25).

1424. BLECHNER, M. J. *"King Lear, King Leir,* and the Incest Wishes." *American Imago* 45 (1988):309–25.

Observes a crux in that individuals often condemn the seeming irrationality of *Lear* and yet admit its profound psychological power. Much of the difficulty centers on the seeming contradictions in Lear's actions in the opening scene. His true motive appears to be to keep Cordelia from marrying and thus to keep her for himself. He assumes that by establishing a flattery contest in which she will refuse to participate he will be able to disinherit her in a fit of wrath and thereby make her undesirable to France and Burgundy as a wife. This subliminal desire he accomplishes in his final lines, best described as a *Liebestod* or love-death.

1425. BOOTH, STEPHEN. *"King Lear," "Macbeth": Indefinition and Tragedy.* New Haven: Yale University Press, 1983, 183 pp.

Finds the key to Shakespeare's tragic power in the play's confrontation with inconclusiveness. By constantly sending false generic signals in *King Lear*, Shakespeare establishes expectations only to dash them and thus to stretch the audience out on the rack of this tough world. The Cinderella-like story of the banished younger daughter promises a happy ending; Gloucester's whorish boasting suggests a story in which he will be chastened and his illegitimate son morally enhanced; Lear's division of the kingdom points to a play about political folly. The sudden intrusion of tragic events aborts the play's suggested directions, and the spectators' response arises in part from the realization of the "folly of relying on artificial, arbitrary limits" (p. 61).

1426. BROOKE, NICHOLAS. "The Ending of *King Lear.*" In *Shakespeare 1564– 1964: A Collection of Modern Essays by Various Hands.* Edited by E. A. Bloom. Providence: Brown University Press, 1964, pp. 71–87.

Asserts that the ending of play, specifically Cordelia's death, is as unbearable as Johnson claimed it to be. The pagans on stage suggest no

King Lear

benignity in the gods, and Lear hints at no further life for Cordelia either in heaven or on earth. Nor is there any profound wisdom in Lear's dying deluded. Every positive act or assertion in the play is followed ironically by one that modifies or negates it. Lear's impassioned howls at the end are clearsighted. There is no affirmation in the final undoing of the order implicit in repentance, forgiveness, redemption, and regeneration, in the negation of all forms of hope.

1427. CALDERWOOD, JAMES L. "Creative Uncreation in *King Lear*." *Shakespeare Quarterly* 37 (1986):5–19.

Maintains that Shakespeare in this tragedy engages in a kind of creative uncreation. Beginning with a state of order in which a kingdom subsumes its differences into a hierarchical social chain under the unified rule of a king, Shakespeare moves the characters from the state of "it is" to another more searing in nature; the characters' responses constitute moments of arrest within a current of worsening. The audience is forced to become an onlooker trying to make sense of what ends without formal closure, a kind of un-end in which Edgar's "speak what we feel" means what fails to make sense within known frames of reference.

1428. CALLAGHAN, DYMPNA. *Women and Gender in Renaissance Tragedy: A Study of "King Lear," "Othello," "The Duchess of Malfi," and "The White Devil."* Atlantic Highlands: Humanities Press, 1989, 187 pp.

Maintains that tragedy places gender issues center stage and in doing so proclaims the precarious state of phallic power, which encodes the disruptions it seeks to forestall. Female transgression is the catalyst for the four tragedies examined; the women act autonomously and thus become "unruly." In both *King Lear* and *Othello* there is a sense of lost masculinity that must be reasserted through symbolic union with a lead female figure. Voracious sexual desire is the single most conspicuous sign of gender difference, noted in Goneril's and Regan's lust for Edmund and in Othello's conception of the adulterous Desdemona.

1429. CAMPBELL, OSCAR JAMES. "*The Salvation of Lear*." *ELH* 15 (1948):93–109.

Describes *King Lear* as a sublime morality play involving man's finding true and eternal spiritual values at the very moment of death. Like the central figure in the moralities, Lear must discover his true friends who will face death with him without fear; he must come to repudiate his kingdom, his retainers, and his creature comforts. Above all, he must master his passion of wrath. On his pilgrimage he is accompanied by two faithful companions, Kent and the fool, both of whom are cynic-stoic commentators. Lear's suffering is purgatorial and allows him to realize the full dimensions of his own humanity. His moment of true redemption, when he awakens in Cordelia's arms, renders him forever independent of material circumstances.

1430. CARROLL, WILLIAM C. " 'The Base Shall Top the Legitimate': The Bedlam Beggar and the Role of Edgar in *King Lear*." *Shakespeare Quarterly* 38 (1987):426–41.

Traces Edgar's passage through *King Lear* from naive legitimate son to outcast beggar to peasant to unknown soldier to restored son and finally, perhaps, to king. His experience of dispossession embitters him, but it also allows him to develop a deeper vision of the world. If, as the folio attribution of the last four lines suggests, Edgar is to become king, he has earned the right to assume such responsibilities.

1431. ———. " 'When Beggars Die, There Are No Comets Seen': The Discourse of Poverty and the Shakespearean Beggar." *Shakespeare Jahrbuch* 126 (1990):96–104.

Notes that Shakespeare, by fusing the beggar and the madman in Edgar's disguise, presents a figure doubly marginalized. To a remarkable extent the real suffering of the beggar emanates from this role, in part as a depiction of the personal pain of Edgar's disposition but also in part as an authentic voice of social dispossession and human suffering. Edgar's literal descent from privilege to persecution establishes the role both Lear and Gloucester must play out on the emotional plane, a situation through which Shakespeare interrogates the beggar's cultural status as dispossessed sufferer within an affluent society.

1432. CHAMBERS, R. W. *"King Lear."* Glasgow *University Publications* 54 (1940):20–52.

Observes that Shakespeare remodels his sources to save Cordelia from despair and suicide. What really matters in the play is what is happening to Lear's soul under Cordelia's influence and to Gloucester's soul under Edgar's influence. *Lear* is, like the *Paradiso*, a vast poem on the victory of true love. The old king ultimately dies in a moment of ecstasy, believing that Cordelia is alive; Gloucester also dies in the joy of the knowledge that his child lives, and Kent's strings of life begin to crack as he witnesses the death of Gloucester between joy and grief.

1433. DANBY, JOHN F. *Shakespeare's Doctrine of Nature: A Study of "King Lear."* London: Faber & Faber, 1949, 234 pp.

Envisions in *King Lear* a dramatization of the two fundamental meanings of nature in Shakespeare's day—the orderly, rational, and benevolent arrangement of the universe under God's control and the Hobbesian manifesto of superior enlightenment with man as king of the beasts and with Machiavelli's self-interest as the operable force. Lear must make his way through a conflict in nature that his own actions have instigated, and at the point of his greatest horror he achieves something of a religious insight. The fool is a synthesis; his heart is with Lear, but his head recognizes the logic by which Edmund, Goneril, and Regan operate. Cordelia represents the kind of nature Edmund denies to exist and which Lear is unable to perceive until the final moments of his life.

1434. DELANEY, PAUL. "*King Lear* and the Decline of Feudalism." *PMLA* 92 (1977):429–40.

Views the conflict as between the values of feudal aristocracy and those of an acquisitive and irreverent bourgeois class, reflecting the Tudor monarch's determination to establish central power in the throne by abolishing the right of the aristocracy to maintain an armed retinue. Shakespeare, fundamentally unable to reconcile himself with these emerging forces, equates their predominance with the decay of feudal-heroic values. Lear must tragically realize the horrible injustices of his earlier aristocratic views, but the sinister and avaricious schemes of Edmund, Goneril, and Regan offer no viable alternative. The humanism of the play reflects the idealization of the glories of the old regime.

1435. DOWNS, WILLIAM. "Discourse and Drama: King Lear's Question to His Daughters." In *The Taming of the Text: Explorations in Language, Literature, and Culture.* Edited by Willie Van Peer. London and New York: Routledge, 1988, pp. 225–57.

Observes that Lear's question as to which of his daughters loves him most is a grammatical imperative. Moreover, the "felicity conditions" are absent because the daughters are constrained to answer in only one way. Lear's game is teleological with each utterance controlled by his power. His wish to renounce his power as king but retain it as father shatters his identity. Most disastrously, he has attempted to institutionalize love in a context of hierarchies of authority, while, in reality, genuine love is "outside verbal and social structures" (p. 254).

1436. ELLIS, JOHN. "The Gulling of Gloucester: Credibility in the Subplot of *King Lear.*" *Studies in English Literature 1500–1900* 12 (1972):275–89.

Observes that Gloucester serves as a foil to Lear, emphasizing the latter's titanic power and passion and making the old king's action more profoundly tragic. The action of the subplot is credibly motivated. Certainly Edmund's bastardy and Gloucester's discussion of it in his presence in the opening scene provide adequate motivation for his villainy. Gloucester, moreover, is psychologically an ideal victim for slanderous intrigue because his world has suddenly become chaotic, inverted, and preposterous as a consequence of Lear's actions and the disarray of the royal family. His later defiant move against Edgar is credible, considering what he believes to be the serious domestic crisis that confronts him at the very moment when he as a host must receive his feudal lord.

1437. ELTON, WILLIAM R. *"King Lear" and the Gods*. San Marino: Huntington Library, 1966. Reprint: Lexington: University Press of Kentucky, 1988, 374 pp.

Notes that the contention that *King Lear* is an optimistically Christian drama is not supported by an examination of the intellectual milieu of the early seventeenth century in England. The four major pagan attitudes toward providence prevalent in the Renaissance are present both in Sidney's *Arcadia* and in *Lear*. The *prisca theologica*, reflected in Cordelia and Edgar, anticipates the higher values of faith, hope, and charity through combining wisdom, knowledge, and understanding. Goneril, Regan, and Edmund adumbrate pagan atheism. Gloucester embodies pagan superstition, and Lear represents the human reaction to the effects of a hidden providence, the *deus absconditus*. Shakespeare places before his spectators a wide spectrum of contemporary pagan beliefs.

1438. EVERETT, BARBARA. "The New King Lear." *Critical Quarterly* 2 (1960):325–39.

Counters those critics who insist upon the profoundly Christian nature of Lear's experience, those who in effect are creating a new *Lear* whole cloth for the twentieth century. Lear's greatness emerges not from his choice of any moral quality but rather from the transformation of his suffering into something vital and strong. This vitality is overwhelmed, however, by a sense of nihilism. The drama does not juxtapose the world against the spirit, but instead it mixes the two inextricably.

1439. FLAHIFF, F. T. "Edgar: Once and Future King." In *Some Facets of "King Lear": Essays in Prismatic Criticism*. Edited by Rosalie L. Colie and F. T. Flahiff. Toronto: University of Toronto Press, 1974, pp. 221–37.

Observes that Thomas Elyot in *The Book of the Governor* describes King Edgar as one who, like Moses, Agamemnon, and Augustus, imposed order and rule upon an "odiouse and uncomly" society. While

King Lear

Shakespeare's Edgar is not Elyot's Edgar, the playwright may well have been concerned with delineating that period in prehistory of the erosion of a primitive and paternalistic social order and concomitantly the development of a concept of kingship involving a larger vision of social responsibility. Edgar alone survives as one capable of assuming such a responsibility.

1440. FRASER, RUSSELL A. *Shakespeare's Poetics in Relation to "King Lear."* London: Routledge & Kegan Paul, 1962, 184 pp.

Argues that stage characters in the Renaissance assumed life to a large degree through association with a stereotyped iconographical figure. The iconology in *Lear* is examined in the motifs of providence, kind, fortune, anarchy and order, reason and will, show against substance, and redemption. Evil consuming itself is emblematic of the destruction of Edmund, Goneril, and Regan, just as the role of time in the revelation of truth and the function of humility and affliction in the achievement of redemption are pictorial representations of Lear's experience. The spate of bestial images reflects the consequences of will's ascendancy over reason.

1441. FRENCH, CAROLYN. "Shakespeare's 'Folly': *King Lear.*" *Shakespeare Quarterly* 10 (1959):523–29.

Argues that the intellectual orientation for *King Lear* is derived for the original audiences from Christian theology, which orders the action upon a spiritual as well as an intellectual plane. Specifically, the play is about Christian folly; one achieves true wisdom and self-knowledge through actions the world considers foolish, through overcoming one's physical and emotional dependence on material values and objects. The fool's function is to bring Lear to spiritual wisdom by deflating his pride with the bitter truth. Cordelia replaces the fool when Lear is able to acknowledge the truth with his sanity restored.

1442. FRYE, DEAN. "The Context of Lear's Unbuttoning." *ELH* 32 (1965):17–31.

Argues that the moment Lear sees Poor Tom, identifies with him, and begins to pull off his own clothes is fraught with significance because the gesture of undressing is related to the clothes imagery that runs throughout the play. This imagery functions as a kind of abstract language that lends universality to the situation. Dress in Elizabethan England had became a symbol of an ordered society, readily reflecting one's position and social rank. Lear must learn the extent to which his identity is dependent upon the external symbol of clothing, his lowest point being his rejection of all artifice in his denial of any difference between man and the beast, a point from which he must reconstruct a human perspective.

1443. GARDNER, HELEN. *"King Lear."* Oxford: Oxford University Press, 1967, 28 pp.

Describes the integration of language, character, and action in *King Lear*. The opening scene is critical both in establishing a stylized tone and at the same time a powerfully destructive force in the central figure. The character of the fool and the nature of the integration of the double plot, which both parallels and counterpoints, contribute to the dramatic effect. There is no blenching from the essential mystery of the play's conclusion. The *Lear* world can offer no consolation for the image of the old king holding the dead Cordelia in his arms. This secular pietà constitutes one of the most profound artistic visions of human suffering.

1444. GOLDBERG, SAMUEL LOUIS. *An Essay on "King Lear."* Cambridge: Cambridge University Press, 1974, 192 pp.

States that the experience of *King Lear* refuses to be contained in a single interpretation, whether that of idealism, moralism, absurdism, or redemptionist sentimentality. For the spectator the play becomes all of these things as he is forced to observe the various characters attempting to come to terms intellectually and emotionally with the welter of events. Ultimately what the spectator must acknowledge is that his response is not merely a matter of ambiguity, a concept suggesting multiple meanings within a coherent whole, but rather of divergent and contradictory realities, each of which he experiences.

1445. GREENFIELD, THELMA. "The Clothing Motif in *King Lear*." *Shakespeare Quarterly* 5 (1954):281–86.

Notes that, while in medieval art the clothed figure—set against a naked figure—represents the superior value, Renaissance iconography reverses this symbolism as nudity becomes the conventional representation of virtues such as temperance, fortitude, truth, and chastity. Lear comes to the perception that Tom represents the poor naked wretches oppressed and destroyed by society, and he deliberately assumes the role of nakedness in recognition of his kinship with "unaccommodated man." This symbolic condition signals his self-recognition and points the way to his salvation.

1446. HARRIS, DUNCAN. "The End of *Lear* and a Shape for Shakespearean Tragedy." *Shakespeare Studies* 9 (1976):253–68.

King Lear

Claims the closure of *Lear* is basically Christian, depending for its astonishing effect upon the Christian notion of man's role in life and the meaning of death. Four resolutions make up this closure—a resolution of justice (a meting out of reward and punishment according to merit), a resolution negating the first (through the suffering deaths of Cordelia, Lear, and Gloucester), a resolution returning those who have survived to a perilous and provisional order (in which Kent and Edgar, both annealed by their experiences, resume their own identities), and a resolution involving a catharsis of clarity in which audience and survivors share.

1447. HEILMAN, ROBERT B. *This Great Stage: Image and Structure in "King Lear."* Baton Rouge: Louisiana State University Press, 1948, 339 pp.

Sees in the play two types of human nature, the traditional or religious and the rationalistic, individualistic, or opportunistic. These types of human nature also represent an age in turmoil and transition. The struggle focuses on Lear and Gloucester, who as representatives of the old order must come to realize that the egocentric values of the new generation actually are rooted in the arrogance, the indiscriminate action, the complacency, and the loss of equilibrium of the old. Both old men are spiritually blind at the outset of the play; and Gloucester's physical blinding, which leads to genuine perception, is but the culminating physical moment of a multitude of images of sight and blindness through which this theme has been developing since the first scene.

1448. JAFFA, HARRY V. "The Limits of Politics: An Interpretation of *King Lear*, Act I, Scene i." *American Political Science Review* 51 (1957):405–27.

Views Lear's decision to divide his kingdom as politically prudent. Cornwall (in the south) and Albany (in the North) represent the geographic extremities of the land, and English kings found it impossible to rule the entire land without the support of powerful nobles. Lear's intention was to gain support of those nobles through a gift of land and to give Cordelia the middle portion following her marriage to Burgundy. He would live with her, continuing to reign with his one hundred knights, which would have been a majority, not a minority, in a land maintained by a foreigner who would have only a limited number of troops.

1449. JAMES, DAVID GWILYM. *The Dream of Learning: An Essay on "The Advancement of Learning" and "King Lear."* Oxford: Clarendon Press, 1951, 126 pp.

Claims that Bacon and Shakespeare, writing in an age of uncertainty and philosophic barrenness, set forth divergent visions of life that are equally a repudiation of the theodicy of medieval Christianity. Hamlet's mind falters before the wickedness of man and its implications; Lear is overwhelmed by it. Struggling between "blood" and "judgment," Hamlet is paralyzed by doubt in the face of life's awesome ambiguities; in Lear evil is the dominant force, and, though its vision is dark, suffering is a kind of proof against overwhelming odds.

1450. JAYNE, SEARS. "Charity in *King Lear.*" *Shakespeare Quarterly* 15 (1964):277–88.

Views *Lear* as a scathingly pessimistic statement of man's desperate need for love, but his inability to give it. While Cordelia's actions at the outset are immature, Lear's love could lead him through the crisis if it were sufficiently selfless. Kent, like Cordelia, defends truth over love and promptly inherits a period of pain only his death will alleviate. Like Lear's, Gloucester's experience is a slow awakening to sensitivity and love, partly under loving and partly under brutal tutelage. But every character fails to reestablish social bonds based on charity.

1451. JORGENSEN, PAUL A. *Lear's Self-Discovery.* Berkeley: University of California Press, 1966, 154 pp.

Discusses the centrality of the concept of self-knowledge in contemporary philosophic treatises to Shakespeare's concept of the anagnorisis in the tragic hero. Pride and self-love are obstacles to such knowledge, and affliction is the purest guide to achieving it. As Lear progresses from arrogance, to rage, to self-pity, and to humble questioning, he must come to perceive the necessity for and true meaning of love. These perceptions he eventually gains through his own suffering, his reduction in status, and his philosophic acceptance of unaccommodated man in the naked Edgar. Having journeyed through the purgatory of self-discovery, he returns to full sanity moments before his defiance in the final enigmatic scene.

1452. KAHN, COPPÉLIA. "The Absent Mother in *King Lear.*" In *Rewriting the Renaissance: The Discourses of Sexual Difference in Early Modern Europe.* Edited by Margaret W. Ferguson, Maureen Quilligan, and Nancy J. Vickers. Chicago: University of Chicago Press, 1986, pp. 33–49.

Observes that the play depicts the failure of a father's power to command love in a patriarchal world and that the "absence of the mother points to her hidden presence" (p. 36). Lear in his emotional reference to hysteria in 2.4.52–58, a female disease also known as "the mother," is reflecting a male anxiety in his inability to keep in check the feminine, both within himself and within his family unit. His scheme for parceling out the kingdom reflects a child's image of being mothered—the desire for absolute control and absolute dependence; his madness "is essentially his rage at being deprived of the maternal presence" (p. 41).

1453. KIRSCHBAUM, LEO. "Banquo and Edgar: Character or Function?" *Essays in Criticism* 7 (1957):1–21.

Views Edgar as a multifunctional character without psychological mimetic unity. His various roles contribute to Shakespeare's overall psychological unity, but as an individual he is a theatrical convention, a puppet manipulated in accordance with dramatic need. His roles include those of an incredibly naive son, the Bedlam beggar Tom, a peasant ministering to his blind father, the unknown and helmeted knight, and finally the son who reappears and stands ready to serve in the new day.

1454. KOZINTSEV, GRIGORI. *"King Lear."* In *Shakespeare: Time and Conscience*. Translated by Joyce Vining. New York: Hill & Wang, 1966, pp. 47–102.

Considers words all-important to Shakespeare since his plays were presented on nonrepresentational platforms. Imagery transferred the action into the midst of life, and the possibilities extended the limits of the theater into infinity. The storm is the key symbol in *Lear*, raging through the whole imagistic fabric of the tragedy. The events of the play occur in a real world of tyranny; indeed, additional emphasis is gained through the placement of a legendary hero into a society of contemporary processes, a world in which feudalism is passing into a new era governed by avarice and the cash nexus.

1455. KREIDER, PAUL V. "Gloucester's Eyes." In *Repetition in Shakespeare's Plays*. Princeton: Princeton University Press, 1941, pp. 194–214.

Considers the sight and blindness imagery central to the emotional pitch and harmony of the parallel Lear and Gloucester plots. The congestion of tone or theme words involving blindness is evident in key scenes in the drama. In the final scene Lear's faulty material vision fails him just as his moral vision has failed him throughout the play. His mad speeches constitute a veritable fanfare of references to sight. Through such a verbal and physical pattern Shakespeare creates a highly unified tragedy of moral and physical blindness.

1456. LARNER, DANIEL. "The Image and the Thing Itself: Reflections on Musical Form in *King Lear*." *Shakespeare Jahrbuch* 127 (1991):31–38.

Suggests that the structure of *King Lear* is "something like musical phrases shaped into overarching structures and vertical harmonies" (p. 31), its line weaving an ironic counterpoint of dissonance and harmony. The action, more specifically, resembles a sonata allegro, with three themes moving from development, to change, to a return to the tonic key, and to recapitulation or climax. The horizontal structure of parallel journies to the heath, to Dover, and to death is vertically intersected by movements of suddenness of decision and action, of ominous stillness on the heath, of the consequences of war, of a false sense of security, and finally of a hideous silence.

1457. LASCELLES, MARY. *"King Lear* and Doomsday." *Shakespeare Survey* 26 (1973):69–79.
    Surmises that Shakespeare chose the figure of a Bedlamite for Edgar's disguise in order to provoke terror in the spectators through allusion to the commonplace Doomsday paintings dealing with the final judgment and also using the image of nakedness and defenselessness. Lear's calling on the gods to disclose the guilty, his awakening in Cordelia's arms and describing her as a "soul in bliss," his reference to the wheel of fire, and Kent's references to the "promis'd end" are further choric and allusive iconographical images.

1458. LINDHEIM, NANCY. "King Lear as Pastoral Tragedy." In *Some Facets of "King Lear": Essays in Prismatic Criticism.* Edited by Rosalie Colie and F. T. Flahiff. Toronto: University of Toronto Press, 1974, pp. 169–84.
    Views *Lear* as related to pastoral literature in its basic concerns—the necessity of stripping man of all the accouterments of society, the perception of the decadence and corruption of that society once the detachment has been achieved, and a determination of the minimal conditions conducive to a genuinely human existence. Once the play has utilized the pastoral structure to develop the theme of man naturally purified and socially purged, it tragically forces the characters and the spectators beyond that point to the apocalyptic horror of act 5. There is no perception in that final scene of the pastoral's emphasis an cyclic rebirth.

1459. LUSARDI, JAMES P., and SCHLUETER, JUNE. *Reading Shakespeare in Performance: "King Lear."* Rutherford: Fairleigh Dickinson University Press; London and Toronto: Associated University Presses, 1991, 248 pp.
    Aims to scrutinize the text for signals that guide production, to identify those moments in the text that constitute performance cruces, and to examine those occasions when performance has generated in-

terpretation of the text. The opening scene is explored for motivation, for instance what is meant by Lear's hoping to set his rest in Cordelia. Other principal points of focus are the mock trial scene and the cliff scene, which are directed respectively by a madman and a man pretending to be mad. Throughout the study, "seeing" becomes the focus, the interplay between language and stage.

1460. McLuskie, Kathleen. "The Patriarchal Bard: Feminist Criticism and Shakespeare: *King Lear* and *Measure for Measure*." In *Political Shakespeare: New Essays in Cultural Materialism*. Edited by Jonathan Dollimore and Alan Sinfield. Manchester: Manchester University Press, 1985, pp. 88–108.

Demands a radical feminist oppositional reading of Shakespeare's plays. Whereas, for example, the traditional interpretations of *King Lear* establish a connection between sexual subordination and anarchy and privilege a social order based on fixed and determined patriarchal authority in which woman's lust is the center and source of the corruption, feminists should focus on society's responsibility to provide an individual a sense of personal autonomy, the conflict between affective relations and contractual obligations, the connection between loving harmony and economic justice, and the fool as a means of comically undermining the traditional focus on Lear.

1461. McNeir, Waldo. "The Role of Edmund in *King Lear*." *Studies in English Literature 1500–1900* 8 (1968):187–216.

Views Edmund at the outset as an Iago-like manipulator with only the limited objective of gaining Edgar's lands. As opportunity easily comes his way, he broadens his scope to include his father's title and eventually the crown. When Goneril collapses in the final act, he confesses his sins and appears duly remorseful; but his repentance is aborted in the final stage. This failure to achieve repentance is in stark contrast with the full development in Lear and Gloucester; indeed, his moral vacillation is directly responsible for the deaths of both Cordelia and Lear.

1462. Mack, Maynard. *"King Lear" in Our Time*. Berkeley: University of California Press, 1965, 126 pp.

Addresses the play's compelling contemporaneity. Since in many ways our age (especially from 1930 to the present) is able to respond more fully to the jagged violence of the tragedy, we are not surprised that these years have been a period rich in notable Lears—Gielgud, Devlin, Ayrton, Wolfit, Olivier, Murray, Redgrave, Laughton, Scofield. Its current fascination is due in part to our interest in the antiheroism in which the capacity to endure is admired more than the ability to act, our casual attitude toward death, and the play's apocalyptic implications and its shattering experience of violence and pain. The closure of the tragedy should be faced squarely as victory and defeat ambiguously simultaneous and inseparable.

1463. MILLARD, BARBARA C. "Virago with a Soft Voice: Cordelia's Tragic Rebellion in *King Lear.*" *Philological Quarterly* 68 (1989):143–65.

Insists on the centrality of Cordelia's role in the political structure of the play. In an attempt to reverse the effects of her personal rebellion in act 1, she chooses in act 4 to transfer the action to a political plane through leading a French invasion of the island. In doing so, she prevents Lear from receiving the serenity he needs to survive. Such action casts her into the role of the doomed *Virago* of Renaissance legend and into the role of a tragic hero who has mistaken the nature of things and the proper way to achieve the desired end. Paradoxically, she rejects the self-obliterating role of daughter and then is killed in an attempt to assume the role of the heroic militant normally reserved for the son/ father.

1464. MUIR, KENNETH. *The Politics of "King Lear."* Glasgow University Publications, 72. Glasgow: Jackson, Son, 1947, 24 pp.

Views the theme as a confrontation between two social orders, that of medieval communal values and that of modern individualism. Goneril and Regan are exemplars of the new order, soulless and amoral and driven by a lust for power that reduces them to the level of animals; Edmund's ominous emergence foreshadows the rise of fascism in later European history. The old order, characterized by morality, duty, and responsibility, possesses the capacity for compassion, pity, and humanitarian concerns.

1465. MURPHY, JOHN L. *Darkness and Devils: Exorcism in "King Lear."* Athens: Ohio University Press, 1984, 267 pp.

Examines the detailed connections between the world of *King Lear* and the Papist exorcisms of the mid-1580s, the trial and execution of Mary Queen of Scots, and Samuel Harsnett's antipapal satire in *A Declaration of Egregious Popish Impostures.* Behind the play lies the bitter rivalry among religious factions as to the reality of spirits and demonic possession, specifically the dramatic qualities of the Roman Catholic service of exorcism and Harsnett's fierce attack on that practice. Many of the fool's and of Tom o'Bedlam's comments directly relate to the issue, the most important of the "levels of intertextuality."

King Lear

1466. NOVY, MARIANNE. "Patriarchy, Mutuality, and Forgiveness in *King Lear*." *Southern Humanities Review* 13 (1979):281–92.

Considers the violation of the bonds of mutuality between father and daughter central to Lear's tragic experience. Lear's misuse of power provokes diverse reactions from Goneril and Regan, who use deception to survive, and Cordelia, who attempts to maintain her integrity in a patriarchal world. The father's denunciation of womankind in act 4 is in reality an acknowledgment of his own guilt as well; and his reconciliation with Cordelia, visualized in a parent's kneeling before the child, "suggests that in a patriarchal society mutuality between man and woman must include the mutuality of forgiveness and repentance" (p. 288).

1467. OATES JOYCE CAROL. "Is This the Promised End? The Tragedy of *King Lear*." *Journal of Aesthetics and Art Criticism* 33 (1974–75):19–32.

Insists that *King Lear* is profoundly pessimistic, with Shakespeare altering the conclusion to defeat the very forces of salvation at work in the story. In one sense the tragedy results from the lack of proper male-female balance in Lear and in his society. In another it poses a vision of life related to the social and political milieu of the times. In yet another sense it dramatizes the soul's yearning for infinity, man's desire to reach to a higher form of himself.

1468. ORWELL, GEORGE. "Lear, Tolstoy, and the Fool." In *Shooting an Elephant and Other Essays*. New York: Harcourt, Brace, 1945, pp. 32–52.

Notes that Tolstoy's bitterly negative response to *King Lear* was probably occasioned by the resemblance between Lear's story and his own. Like Lear, Tolstoy renounced his estate in order to live like a peasant. He, too, acted on mistaken motives and was persecuted because of this renunciation. He, too, lacked humility and the ability to judge character. He, too, was inclined to revert to his earlier aristocratic attitudes and had two children who ultimately turned against him. Moreover, he shared Lear's revulsion toward sexuality. Tolstoy's examination of the play, in brief, is far from impartial; indeed, it is an exercise in misrepresentation.

1469. PARKER, DOUGLAS H. "The Third Suitor in *King Lear* Act 1, Scene 1." *English Studies* 72 (1991):136–45.

Maintains that the opening scene of the play depicts neither an old man in his dotage nor an emblematic ritual of self-deposition. Instead Lear dangles the "largest bounty," the most opulent third, before Cordelia to win the hand of his daughter and consequently defeat the rivals for her hand, France and Burgundy. Failing to win her in that manner, he curses her and strips away her dowry in an attempt to make the other two reject her. He assumes that, if he does so, she will have no one to turn to except her father.

1470. PECHTER, EDWARD. "On the Blinding of Gloucester." *ELH* 45 (1978):181–200.
    Sees the basic pattern of the tragedy as the provocation of a passionately direct response, the need to justify that response through some form of philosophic assumption, and finally the painful realization of the deep-seated error in that assumption. The spectator, time and again, is made to pay for his attempts to escape suffering through rationalization. It is Gloucester's blinding that so painfully commits us to develop this pattern of anticipation. We like Gloucester must smell our way to Dover (our own assumptions that the action of the play will issue into a sense imposed by teleological control) only once again to be punished for our response.

1471. PECK, RUSSELL A. "Edgar's Pilgrimage: High Comedy in *King Lear*." *Studies in English Literature 1500–1900* 7 (1967):219–37.
    Views Edgar as a significant dynamic figure in the play, developing—through his various disguises as bedlamite, incognito stranger, Somersetshire peasant, and divine avenger—into "the Christian ideal in his large capacity to empathize with and take upon himself the afflictions of his fellow men" (p. 226). Through Christian analogues Edgar's journey lends a universality to that of Lear, and it serves a specifically choric function at the end of the play. By the conclusion of his pilgrimage, he among those remaining alive is most fit to rule.

1472. RAY, ROBERT H., ed. *Approaches to Teaching "King Lear."* New York: Modern Language Association of America, 1986, 166 pp.
    Provides, in addition to sixteen essays that form the core of the book, an annotated bibliography of critical analyses and editions and also a survey of slides, records, films, and film studies. The essays, consciously varied in their approach, include a study of the family (Lynda Boose), of sight imagery and theme (Frances Teague), of structure (James Hirsh), and of archetypes (Ann Imbrie). Michael Warren describes the two texts of the play, and David Krantz, John Harcourt, and J. L. Styan discuss methods of engaging student participation in the staging/reading of particular scenes.

1473. RIEBETANZ, JOHN. *The Lear World: A Study of "King Lear" in Its Dramatic Context.* Toronto: University of Toronto Press, 1977, 142 pp.

King Lear

Insists that only by examining *Lear* within its Jacobean context will its full power be revealed. The grotesque world of love tests and wicked sisters lends a peculiar expositional quality unlike that of any previous Shakespearean tragedy. Like contemporary tragedies it abandons the Elizabethan concern for narrative continuity in favor of a structural unity based on scenic emphasis. Instead, the action, leaping from one scene to another and focusing upon the evil natures of Goneril, Regan, and Edmund along with the mounting suffering of Lear and Gloucester, emphasizes the evolving anarchy at both the political and domestic level. Emblematic design and costuming reinforce this pattern of action.

1474. ROSENBERG, JOHN. "King Lear and His Comforters." *Essays in Criticism* 16 (1966):135–46.

Argues that readings of *King Lear* as Christian allegory lead us away from the searing tragic center of the play. Furthermore, the more the critics attempt to justify the existence and the action of the gods, the more appalling the gods become. By doubling the agony and perversion through the use of the Gloucester subplot, Shakespeare almost makes cosmic malevolence a character in the play. The catastrophe is absolutely open-ended; a world of grace—or utter nothingness—may exist beyond the mortal's death.

1475. ROZETT, MARTHA TUCK. "Tragedies Within Tragedies: Kent's Unmasking in *King Lear*." *Renaissance Drama* , n.s. 18 (1987):237–58.

Maintains that Kent's failure to be recognized by the king to whom he has dedicated all his life "constitutes a self-contained tragic moment that contributes to the all-encompassing tragic atmosphere of the last scene" (p. 238). The full power of this tragedy within a tragedy results from Shakespeare's ability to manipulate an essentially comic convention to achieve an unexpectedly tragic effect. The scene is also the more striking in that both the *Leir* source play and Tate's Restoration adaptation make full use of the moment of recognition between king and loyal lord. Kent, by contrast, stands powerless to prevent the developing tragedy of the friend he loves.

1476. SEWALL, RICHARD B. *The Vision of Tragedy*. New Haven: Yale University Press, 1959, 178 pp.

Observes that *King Lear* combines Greek, pagan, or humanistic values with Christian values to produce "a world of alternatives, terrible in its inconclusiveness" (p. 68). Whatever is Christian about the play is psychological, not eschatological. Lear must win his redemption through his own efforts, and even then Cordelia's death must follow the moment of spiritual bliss. All one can ultimately say is that "human nature, in some of its manifestations has transcended the destructive element and made notable salvage" (p. 78).

1477. SHICKMAN, ALLEN R. "The Fool's Mirror in *King Lear.*" *English Language Renaissance* 21 (1991): 75–86.

Claims that the fool is intended to carry a mirror on stage to mimic emblems of folly, prudence, and self-knowledge. Various passages in the play take on added significance if one assumes the actual presence of such a prop. Especially poignant is Lear's probable use of the fool's cracked mirror in the final scene to determine whether Cordelia is breathing.

1478. STAMPFER, JUDAH. "The Catharsis of *King Lear.*" *Shakespeare Survey* 13 (1960):1–10.

Views the conclusion, with its tragic events and the massive intrusion of Christian elements, as the central problem of *King Lear*. Neither Lamb's assertion that Lear's death was a "fair dismissal" from life in light of his great suffering nor Bradley's claim that Lear experiences a transfiguration of joy is supported by the full text. The true catharsis is the revelation of an imbecilic universe. The tragic hero "dies unreconciled and indifferent to society" (p. 7). Penance is proved to be impossible in a world without God—without charity, resilience, or harmony.

1479. STERN, JEFFREY. "*King Lear*: The Transference of the Kingdom." *Shakespeare Quarterly* 41 (1990):299–308.

Maintains that Lear's division of the kingdom is a means by which he can prevent Cordelia's departure. By giving her her portion while he is still alive, "he will block her passage across the sea with a husband and keep her in Britain with him to rule" (p. 299). Lear's claim on her allegiance will thus remain paramount. He finds love on her terms intolerable when she insists that, at the point of her marriage, half of her affection will go to her husband. Psychologically what Lear wants from Cordelia is maternal. The transference of the kingdom has reawakened powerful infantile feelings and attitudes.

1480. STRIER, RICHARD. "Faithful Servants: Shakespeare's Praise of Disobedience." In *The Historical Renaissance: New Essays on Tudor and Stuart Literature and Culture*. Edited by Heather Dubrow and Richard Strier. Chicago and London: University of Chicago Press, 1988, pp. 104–33.

Argues that Shakespeare in this play establishes a meditation on the occasion when resistance to legally constituted authority becomes a moral necessity, when neutrality is not a viable possibility. Lear is dealing with a genuine crisis in dividing the kingdom among his daughters, and his decision to disinherit Cordelia produces a familial and political situation of unprecedented disaster. Oswald stands for the disreputable ideal of the servant who obeys without moral qualms. The good servant who disobeys immoral commands is reflected in Kent, the second servant of Cornwall, and above all Gloucester.

1481. TAYLER, EDWARD W. *"King Lear* and Negation." *English Literary Renaissance* 20 (1990):17–39.

Observes that Shakespeare repeats the word "nothing" early in the drama and plays upon the verbal equivocation in "no" and "know" to prepare us for what we see and hear at the end of the tragedy. In Shakespeare's art negation may produce knowledge, and negation leads to anagnorisis. Even though the play seems to move toward a happy ending, we are forewarned and prepared for the ultimate disaster. Lear's apocalypse is to learn that the world will wear out to naught, and his experience with Cordelia unfolds the deepest and most final of truths.

1482. WITTREICH, JOSEPH. *"Image of That Horror"*: History, Prophecy, and Apocalypse in "King Lear." San Marino: Huntington Library, 1984, 185 pp.

Treats *King Lear* both within its historical context in relation to the political ideology of King James and within poetry's highest order, that of prophecy of the tragedy of human history. The play mirrors in its dialectic conflicting systems and contending attitudes toward the cosmos, but it also demands that some choices be made. If it is an encounter with inconclusiveness, it is not itself altogether inconclusive. Most important, it draws upon apocalyptic prophecy in the Book of Revelation; in the literal action it is a "mind-transforming event that culminates in a king's redemption" (p. 22).

1483. ZAK, WILLIAM F. *Sovereign Shame: A Study of "King Lear."* Cranbury: Rutgers University Press, 1982, 208 pp.

Moves beyond the critical impasse of Lear as redeemed or absurd by arguing that he suffers desperately from an ontological anxiety, a fear of personal worthlessness and doubt about deserving love. This unacknowledged shame drives him from the absurdity of the love-action to the extreme distraction of his own madness and Cordelia's death. The man beneath Lear's outraged masks, then, is a king in disgrace; his tragedy is his inability to perceive what impels him to such desperate acts.

1484. ZIMBARDO, ROSE. "The King and the Fool: *King Lear* as Self-Deconstructing Text." *Criticism* 32 (1990):1–30.

Suggests that there is a strong quality of "unconsciously-held consciousness of its age" about *King Lear* in large part because, while it was composed "in the light of an unconscious consciousness formed and dominated by Medieval/Renaissance artistic representation," critical understanding of the play has been articulated in "a quite different unconscious consciousness, an Enlightenment, or modern consciousness" (p. 2). In such a fashion Shakespeare's emblematic characters have been turned into realistic, novelistic ones. Above all, this critical practice obscures the emblematic manner in which the king and the fool interact or "cross over, in a chiasmic reversal, their properties, nature, and customs" (p. 8).

Stage History

1485. ROSENBERG, MARVIN. *The Masks of "King Lear."* Berkeley: University of California Press, 1972, 431 pp.

Seeks an answer to the meaning of *King Lear* through the interpretations of American and European actors, directors, and critics. Sources include books, essays, periodical reports, memoirs, and acting versions. Additionally the author himself followed a production of *Lear* through two months of rehearsal. A firm artistic control gives to the ambiguities and paradoxes of the play a "system of reciprocating tensions" (p. 5). While the role of Lear, for example, can be performed in various ways, the actor must move generally from the pains of civilization with its robed furs to the austere position in which he can voice compassion for "unaccommodated man."

MACBETH

Reference Works

1486. TANNENBAUM, SAMUEL A., and TANNENBAUM, DOROTHY R., comps. *William Shakespeare: "Macbeth."* Elizabethan Bibliographies, 9. New York: Privately printed, 1939, 165 pp.

Includes 3,153 unannotated entries covering major scholarship on *Macbeth* from the beginnings to 1937. The material is divided by the following categories and is arranged alphabetically by section—editions, translations; burlesques, satires, parodies; music, songs, operas, dances; commentary on music; illustrations; *Macbeth* in the theater; commentary on *Macbeth*; book titles. The majority of the entries (1,936 items) are loosely classified under commentary on the play.

1487. WHEELER, THOMAS, *comp. "Macbeth": An Annotated Bibliography*. Garland Reference Library of the Humanities, 522: Garland Shakespeare Bibliographies, 22. New York and London: Garland Publishing, 1990, 1009 pp.

Contains 2,692 items, representing virtually all publications on the play between 1940 and 1988, along with significant items prior to 1940. The categories, each arranged chronologically, include criticism, sources and background, textual studies, bibliographies, editions, translations, stage history, major productions, films, music, television, teaching aids, and adaptations and synopses. A brief introductory essay traces the history of recent criticism and research.

Editions

1488. BROOKE, NICHOLAS, ed. *Macbeth*. The Oxford Shakespeare. Oxford and New York: Oxford University Press, 1990, 232 pp.

Includes an introductory essay addressing issues of illusion, language, baroque drama, staging, text (lineation, the brevity), Middleton and the revision of the play, dates (original version, revised version), and sources (chronicles, Stuart politics, classical ladies, Weird Sisters, devil porters). Extensive notes on each page of the text address problems of language and provide background material.

1489. MUIR, KENNETH, ed. *Macbeth*. The Arden Shakespeare. London: Methuen; Cambridge, Mass.: Harvard University Press, 1951, 201 pp.

Includes discussion of the text, date, interpolations, sources, stage history, and critical interpretations, as well as appendixes featuring selections from Holinshed's *Chronicles* and William Stewart's *Book of the Chronicles of Scotland*. The text is based on the First Folio, for which the copy was probably a transcript of the promptbook. *Macbeth* in many ways is Shakespeare's most profound vision of evil; its theme of damnation focuses on a struggle between creation and destruction and Macbeth's loss of soul. Any attempt to read fatalism into the work, however, is reductionistic.

1490. WILSON, JOHN DOVER, ed. *Macbeth*. Cambridge: Cambridge University Press, 1947, 186 pp.

Provides extensive textual notes, a critical introduction, a discussion of the copy text, a section on stage history, and a glossary. This edition is based on the First Folio, for which the copy was probably a bookkeeper's transcript. Additions and alterations by Middleton are likely. Shakespeare's most striking departure from his source is the alteration of Banquo's character, a move that serves both his art and his design to compliment James I. The extant text probably represents Shakespeare's own revision and compression in 1606.

Criticism

1491. ALLEN, MICHAEL. "Macbeth's Genial Porter." *English Literary Renaissance* 4 (1974):326–36.

Argues that the porter scene possesses a structural and thematic significance as a consequence of the etymology and the semantic variants of the words *porter* and *genius* and of the occult associations the Elizabethans attached to them. The porter's language about heaven, hell gates, and devil porter reinforce such associations, and his sudden appearance suggests the presence of Macbeth's evil familiar. Moreover, the characters mentioned by the porter signify the stages of Macbeth's degeneration. Finally, when the porter opens the gate, he lets in Macbeth's executioner who eventually sends his soul to hell.

1492. ASP, CAROLYN. " 'Be Bloody, Bold and Resolute': Tragic Action and Sexual Stereotyping in *Macbeth*." *Studies in Philology* 78 (1981):153–69.

Argues that sexual stereotyping plays a central role in *Macbeth*. Lady Macbeth perceives that in her society femininity is equated with weakness. Consciously rejecting her femininity to adapt a masculine role, she pits herself against nature and loses. Similarly, Macbeth by stretching courage and boldness beyond normal proportions pits himself against nature and loses. By attempting to alter their fundamental nature, both Macbeth and Lady Macbeth become inhuman symbols of sexual sterility. The tension results from the conflict of the sexual roles they believe they must play in order to achieve their ambitions in moving beyond the limits imposed by nature and society.

1493. BERGER, HARRY J. "The Early Scenes of *Macbeth*: Preface to a New Interpretation." *ELH* 47 (1980):1–31.

Argues that Scotland in the play suffers from instability, conflict, sedition, murder, a general evil that moves beyond the wickedness of one or two individuals. As a society that sanctions violence and in which ferocity inspires, Scotland must praise its heroes while suffering concern at the same time that such actions will split the fabric of civil order. Duncan's uneasiness is signaled in his rewards to Macbeth. Macbeth himself is not so much the villain as is Scottish society that in its very nature makes such regicide likely.

1494. BOOTH, WAYNE. "Macbeth as Tragic Hero." *Journal of General Education* 6 (1951):17–25.

Views Shakespeare's principal difficulty in *Macbeth* as maintaining the spectators' sympathy for the protagonist and at the same time depicting a credible path of moral degeneration. Shakespeare succeeds by emphasizing the genuine goodness of Macbeth at the beginning of the play, by portraying his mental anguish and self-torture immediately after each of his three murders, by endowing him with a highly poetic gift, and by indicating that his tragic error was provoked in part by outside forces (the witches, Lady Macbeth) and that he failed to comprehend the effects of such action on his own character.

1495. BROOKS, CLEANTH. "The Naked Babe and the Cloak of Manliness." In *The Well–Wrought Urn*. New York: Harcourt Brace Javanovich, 1947, pp. 22–49.

Observes that two principal chains of imagery in *Macbeth* involve old clothes and babes. Banquo's comparison of Macbeth's "new honors" to "strange garments" in 1.3 and Macbeth's reference four scenes later to Duncan's conscience as like a "naked newborn babe" establish ideas that reverberate throughout the play. Ultimately, clothing represents the inhumane savagery with which Macbeth attempts to cover his humanity, and the babe symbolizes the future that Macbeth is unable to control.

1496. CALDERWOOD, JAMES L. *If It Were Done: "Macbeth" and Tragic Action.* Amherst: University of Massachusetts Press, 1986, 156 pp.

Features three disparate interpretations of the tragedy, one sociological, one psychological, and one historical. The first uses the text of Hamlet as a gloss for that of *Macbeth*. The latter is a kind of "counter-*Hamlet*," counterpoising Macbeth's "initiative" mode of action with Hamlet's "reactive" mode. Both plays in different ways resist closure. The "deed without a name" is charged with oedipal suggestions of parricide and incest. The third reading investigates the nature of evil, finding its source in the Scot's validation of warfare as a ceremony of violence. Malcolm's victory renews the creed of violence when he, like Duncan earlier, rewards the subversives.

1497. CHEUNG, KING-KOK. "Shakespeare and Kierkegaard: 'Dread' in *Macbeth*." *Shakespeare Quarterly* 35 (1984):430–39.

Attempts to explain our ambiguous response to Macbeth by examining his decision to murder Duncan in the light of Kierkegaard's concept of dread, the possibility of "being able" that produces sin in the state between possibility and reality, the desire to do what one fears that precedes one's leap into evil. Dread informs the very atmosphere of *Macbeth*; the witches, in creating the apprehension or dread of Macbeth's being king, create his fatal enticement to sin; and the spectators, too, under the spell of Shakespeare's poetry are caught in a shuddering complicity.

1498. CODDEN, KARIN S. " 'Unreal Mockery': Unreason and the Problems of Spectacle in *Macbeth*." *English Literary Renaissance* 56 (1989):485–501.

Observes that the spectacle of punishment following the Gunpowder Plot was, as a strategy of containment, equivocal, that some traitors were penitent while others were defiant. *Macbeth* is framed by the death of two traitors at the beginning (Cawdor and Macdonwald) and one at the end (Macbeth). The play, however, rather than endorsing the ideological efficacy of the performance of punishment, seems to focus on the spectacle itself with radically ambiguous effects. The efficacy of symbolic closure "at once enables and unsettles theatrical representation" (p. 499).

1499. CUNNINGHAM, DOLORA G. "Macbeth: The Tragedy of the Hardened Heart." *Shakespeare Quarterly* 14 (1963):39–46.

Argues that Macbeth through choice becomes a slave to evil, which feeds upon itself unto destruction. At the outset a good and sensitive man, he falls through error and goading to commit murder; then, overcome by guilt and resentment, he murders Banquo. At this point he determines to harden his heart against all reminders of his former self. His decision to murder Macduff's family indicates his confirmation in his new identity. The logical extreme of the hardened heart is insanity, enacted literally by Lady Macbeth and figuratively by Macbeth's courage and desperation.

1500. CURRY, WALTER CLYDE. *Shakespeare's Philosophic Patterns*. Baton Rouge: Louisiana State University Press, 1937, 244 pp.

Notes that evil in Shakespeare's day was considered not only as a subjective force but also as an objective power "in a metaphysical world whose existence depended in no degree upon the activities of the human mind" (p. 58). Shakespeare probably chose witches to convey this

Macbeth

demonic power to avoid the comic associations that had developed with stage devils. No such demonic force can of itself actually penetrate the substance of the soul, but Macbeth's liberty of choice is progressively diminished by his increasing inclination toward evil; in this sense fate compels him to certain destruction. Lady Macbeth, to the contrary, is literally and willingly possessed of demons.

1501. Dyson, J. P. "The Structural Function of the Banquet Scene in *Macbeth*." *Shakespeare Quarterly* 14 (1963):369–78.

Describes the banquet scene as important structurally because it presents analogously the entire movement of the play, from order to chaos, from good to evil. Traditionally a symbol of harmony, fellowship, order, and hierarchy, the banquet scene is also the moment when Macbeth realizes that his world has turned upside down, that he has moved from the martlet world to the raven world. The ghost of Banquo is the catalyst of insight, the messenger from another world who forces Macbeth to realize that he has penetrated to a level of existence where nothingness has come to life.

1502. FERGUSSON, FRANCIS. "*Macbeth* as the Imitation of an Action." In *English Institute Essays 1951*. Edited by Alan S. Downer. New York: Columbia University Press, 1952, pp. 31–43.

Argues that the action of *Macbeth* demonstrates Aristotle's definition of Aristotle's term *praxis*, by which he means not so much the outward deed as the motive. When he speaks of tragedy as the imitation of an action, he refers to the motive that governs the psyche's life for a period of time. Plot, character, and diction all spring from this dominating thought. *Macbeth*, in each of these aspects, imitates action based on vaulting ambition that overthrows reason.

1503. FOSTER, DONALD W. "Macbeth's War on Time." *English Literary Renaissance* 16 (1986):319–42.

Questions the critics' virtually unanimous assumption that bliss and political harmony will follow Malcolm's ascent to the Scottish throne at the end of the play. That the play follows a narrative curve from order to chaos and back again is a fictive vision of "a neatly contained world without causality or transience" (p. 322). When the grisly cycle of atrocities culminates in Macduff's decapitation of one king and holding that head before the face of another, the scene serves as a mirror indicating that Malcolm's succession to the throne is not a redemption but merely a repetition.

1504. FRENCH, WILLIAM W. " 'What May Become a Man': Image and Structure in *Macbeth*." *College Literature* 12 (1985):191–201.

Observes that, despite the straightforward folio stage direction that Macduff in the final lines enters with Macbeth's head, there has been a general tendency in theatrical practice from the Restoration to the present day to omit that scene. Display of the severed head, however, is a fitting conclusion to the tragedy. For one thing, it is a grisly reminder of the wages of crime, one that resonates at the inmost and most ancient core of our being. For another, it reiterates the violent punishment of violence, and for yet another it depicts Macbeth's ultimate fragmentation in a fusion of poetry and spectacle that excites an audience to emotional participation.

1505. FREUD, SIGMUND. "These Wrecked by Success." In *The Complete Psychological Works of Sigmund Freud*. Edited and translated by James Strachey. Vol. 4. London: Hogarth Press and the Institute of Psycho-Analysis, 1957, pp. 318–24.

Cites Lady Macbeth as an example of one who strives for success with a single-minded energy and then collapses after achieving it. Prior to victory there is no sign whatsoever of an internal struggle, either in the knocking at the door or at the banquet scene. It is ultimately impossible to know whether she cracks from frustration or from same deeper motivation. Not impossibly her mental deterioration is due to her childlessness, and her crime (her unsexing of herself) has robbed Macbeth of the better part of his fruits.

1506. FRYE, ROLAND M. "Theological and Non-Theological Structure in Tragedy." *Shakespeare Studies* 4 (1969):132–48.

Distinguishes between plays dramatically structured on theological doctrines (for example, *Dr. Faustus*, *Samson Agonistes*) and plays that are not (for example, *Macbeth* and *Antony and Cleopatra*). While both Faustus and Macbeth succumb to demonic temptation and are referred to as damned, Faustus's temptation is specifically linked with the doctrine of original sin; he signs a pact with the devil, and Lucifer himself appears to carry away his soul. In *Macbeth* the references are symbolic, and we are left to ponder Macbeth's fate; his tragedy has been in the horror and wasted potential of his life.

1507. HEILMAN, ROBERT B. "The Criminal as Tragic Hero." *Shakespeare Survey* 19 (1966):12–24.

Notes the critical indecisiveness about whether we are to view Macbeth at the end of the play as splendidly bold in desperate valor or as monstrously evil. Clearly Shakespeare forces us to identify with Macbeth early in the play by drawing us within his psychic struggle. Even as his villainy deepens, his suffering makes him more than a murderer in our eyes. At every point at which our sympathy might end (for example, the Macduff murders), we are drawn back (by his sickness of heart, his wife's death, his role as underdog). To acknowledge our sympathy for Macbeth is not to deny our sympathy as well for Malcolm and the conquering party.

1508. HUNTLEY, FRANK L. "*Macbeth* and the Background of Jesuitical Equivocation." *PMLA* 79 (1964):390–400.
   Discusses the doctrine of equivocation developed in the seventeenth century by the Society of Jesus and clearly defined at the trial of Father Garnett, superior of the Jesuits in England, on 28 March 1606. The doctrine was much in the minds of Shakespeare's spectators at the initial presentation of *Macbeth* shortly after the Gunpowder Plot and again at its revival in 1611 shortly after Henri IV had died in a Jesuit plot. The drunken porter refers to equivocators, but the theme is much more pervasive. Macbeth, originally brave and true, falls because he embraces the doctrine.

1509. JAARSMA, RICHARD. "The Tragedy of Banquo." *Literature and Psychology* 17 (1967):87–94.
   Rejects the idea that Banquo is a static character who never succumbs to the evil in the play. While Banquo does resist temptation and serves as a foil early in the play, he changes after entering Macbeth's castle. He tells Macbeth of his own dream of the Weird Sisters, revealing inner suspicions and imaginings, suspecting Macbeth's intentions, suggesting after Duncan's murder that they remain silent until they put on clothes (and thus symbolically hide their true natures). Banquo, in a word, becomes Macbeth's silent accomplice.

1510. JACK, JANE H. "*Macbeth*, King James, and the Bible." *ELH* 22 (1955):173–93.
   Claims that the fact that *Macbeth* was composed with direct connections to King James proved to be an artistic asset rather than a liability. The works of James, more specifically, are part of the background of the tragedy, particularly in the strong theological bias of James's mind and his constant references to certain passages in the Old and New Testaments. James's overmastering theme is that the kingdom of evil lies very close to that of Christianity; he saw life as a war between grace and the Devil. The scriptural imagery supporting this argument provided Shakespeare a means of organizing the play.

1511. JAECH, SHARON L. JANSEN. "Political Prophecy and Macbeth's 'Sweet Bodements.'" *Shakespeare Quarterly* 34 (1983):290–97.

Examines the meaning of the three mysterious apparitions that appear to Macbeth when he demands further information from the witches in light of their relationship to the long tradition of political prophecy in England. Each of the apparitions had a host of associated meanings in contemporary prophecy. While not necessarily indicating a single specific thing, these apparitions would have been recognized as powerful and ambiguous prophetic symbols, and the audience would immediately perceive the folly and danger of Macbeth's interpreting them according to his own desires.

1512. JORGENSEN, PAUL A. *Our Naked Frailties: Sensational Art and Meaning in "Macbeth."* Berkeley: University of California Press, 1971, 234 pp.

Considers the most powerful and distinctive feature of the play to be the painfully dark atmosphere created by unparalleled sensational artistry—whether verbal ambivalence of fair and foul, the hints of metaphysical disarray, the haggish witches with their intent set on Macbeth, the brutal slaughter of Macduff's wife and children, the illusionary dagger of Macbeth, or the hideously real ghost. This constant emphasis on stark sensation renders Macbeth most ironically pitiable in his ultimate loss of all feeling.

1513. KLEIN, JOAN L. "Lady Macbeth: 'Infirm of Purpose.' " In *The Woman's Part: Feminist Criticism of Shakespeare.* Edited by Carolyn Ruth Swift Lenz, Gayle Greene, and Carol Thomas Neely. Urbana: University of Illinois Press, 1980, pp. 240–55.

Observes that, whatever her claim to the contrary, Lady Macbeth is firmly bound by the Renaissance concept of the married woman characterized by passivity and kindness in the role of wife, helpmate, and hostess. Once she violates this premise, she destroys the basis for her own existence. Caught up in a world that becomes increasingly male dominated in a struggle for power, with her husband no longer counseling with her in his plans concerning Banquo, and without friend or confidante, she becomes morbidly obsessed with the memory of a lost past and the horrors of the murder.

1514. KNIGHTS, L. C. "Macbeth." In *Some Shakespearean Themes.* Stanford: Stanford University Press; London: Chatto & Windus, 1959, pp. 110–32.

Maintains that the essential structure of *Macbeth* (and many other tragedies) is found in the poetry. Lady Macbeth's reference to dashing out the brains of a child to whom she has given suck, for example, is an image of unnatural violence that reverberates with others throughout the play. This interaction demands a liveliness of attention that forces

the spectator to respond fully through his active imagination as meanings below the level of plot and character take form as a living structure.
Macbeth's lust for power is defined through a series of such externally
and internally destructive patterns.

1515. LAWLOR, JOHN J. "Mind and Hand: Some Reflections on the Study of
Shakespeare's Imagery." *Shakespeare Quarterly* 8 (1957):179–93.
Suggests that attention to imagery aids in one's sharing the authentic Shakespearean experience. It helps one to perceive that Macbeth, for example, is incapable of distinguishing bad acting from good,
that he senses life as circular and meaningless. The most powerful images are set, not in word alone, but in the interplay of character and
stage effect as well. Duncan's comment about Macbeth's castle as a
"pleasant seat" and the imagery concerned with Banquo's response
about the martlet broaden the spectators' apprehension concerning
Banquo's fate and the unnaturalness of Macbeth's desiring.

1516. LEVIN, RICHARD. "The New Refutation of Shakespeare." *Modern Philology* 83 (1985):123–41.
Attacks what he calls the new ironic or revisionist readings of
Shakespeare, for instance Harry Berger's discussion of *Macbeth* as having an apparent level at which Malcolm and Macduff are to be taken as
admirable but also an ironic level at which they are reprehensible, with
the argument turning on their perverted conception of manliness and
their scapegoating of women. The argument is that Shakespeare constructed his apparent level to satisfy the vulgar customers, reserving his
ironic level for the knowledgeable few who could perceive the subtle
undermining of such an attitude. Such a reading is circularly absurd;
presumably it would endlessly preach to the converted, since only they
would have the sensibilities to perceive the "real" meaning.

1517. LISTON, WILLIAM T. " 'Male and Female Created He Them': Sex and
Gender in *Macbeth*." *College Literature* 16 (1989):232–39.
Insists that no play of Shakespeare is so explicit as *Macbeth* in
demarcating man from woman and that, despite its narrative of regicide
and kingship, its primary focus is domestic. The norms against which
the Macbeths' tragedies develop are that a man should be "valorous,
firm, commanding, humane, and limited" and that a woman should be
"soft, maternal, nourishing, a help meet to her husband, humane, and
limited" (p. 238). The assertion of the full and complex values of peace,
family, and humanity are dramatized most positively in the Macduffs.

1518. MCGEE, ARTHUR R. "*Macbeth* and the Furies." *Shakespeare Survey* 19
(1966):55–67.

Examines the Elizabethan beliefs concerning the supernatural background of the play and Shakespeare's relation to it. The concept of witchcraft, on the one hand, had classical associations with mythological creatures from Greece and Rome like the furies, Medusa, and the Harpies. It involved also the fairy world of trolls, genii, and satyrs. In their powers of operative magic, demon-furies, witches, and fairies were virtually interchangeable. They could prompt madness or diabolic possession; they could torture a man's conscience and inflict supernatural punishment upon the guilty. Our modern psychological approach falls far short of the horror that the spectators and Macbeth would have experienced concerning the witches.

1519. MULLANEY, STEVEN. "Lying like the Truth: Riddle, Representation and Treason in Renaissance England." *ELH* 47 (1980):32–47.
Concerns the language and representation of treason during the Renaissance, an age when society viewed traitors as treading a thin line between human and demonic, rational and possessed. *Macbeth* is the fullest literary representation of treason's amphibology, the use of double or doubtful language to confuse and deceive. The porter's use of equivocation has reference to Father Garnett's comments at his trial for complicity in the Gunpowder Plot. Macbeth gives himself up to amphibology in the course of the play; his head in the final scene is a kind of gruesome visual representation of a verbal pun.

1520. MURRAY, W. A. "Why Was Duncan's Blood Golden?" *Shakespeare Survey* 19 (1966):34–44.
Focuses on the line in which Macbeth refers to Duncan as lying with his "silver skin lac'd with his golden blood." The associative matrix of words from Paracelsus's *De Sanguine Ultra Mortem* (About the blood beyond death) would appear to provide the meaning that would have been clear to Shakespeare's audience. In Macbeth's imagination Duncan's blood assumes an alchemical tincture transforming the dross body into the spiritual; it is already in the hand of God.

1521. PAUL, HENRY N. *The Royal Play of "Macbeth": When, Why, and How It Was Written by Shakespeare.* New York: Macmillan, 1948, 438 pp.
Argues that *Macbeth* was written especially for performance before King James I, the occasion being the state visit of his brother-in-law King Christian of Denmark in 1606, and that the site was Hampton Court on 7 August. Inconsistencies are the result of haste in readying the material for this performance. James's delight at the presentation of *Tres Sibyllae* at Oxford in 1603 prompted Shakespeare to consider whether the prophecy of Banquo could be set to stage. In doing so,

Macbeth

Shakespeare used selections from Holinshed in combination with material from the King's *Basilikon Doron* and *Daemonology*.

1522. POLLARD, DAVID L. " 'O Scotland, Scotland': The Anti-Heroic Play of *Macbeth*." *Upstart Crow* 8 (1988):69–76.

Poses the kingdom of Scotland as the true subject of *Macbeth*, a kind of *Mirror for Magistrates* in dramatic form. The political crisis occurs when the proper defender of the land becomes instead its predator. The decidedly lesser figures of Malcolm and Macduff with the help of the Scottish citizenry rescue the bleeding country. The emphasis at the conclusion is not on individual figures but on the commonwealth preserved and the tyrant defeated.

1523. RAMSEY, JAROLD. "The Perversion of Manliness in *Macbeth*." *Studies in English Literature 1500–1900* 13 (1973):285–300.

Describes the concept of manliness as one of the principal themes in the play, specifically the disjunction of aggressive manliness from humanness. At the outset Macbeth's manly actions are not devoid of kindness. His moral degeneracy is reflected in his progressive repudiation of all humane considerations, culminating in the savage slaying of Lady Macduff and her children. In the final moments Macbeth regains a vestige of human quality in his desire to avoid Macduff, who "cows" his reckless courage and rekindles a spark of remorse.

1524. REID, B. L. "*Macbeth* and the Play of Absolutes." *Sewanee Review* 58 (1965):19–46.

Considers Macbeth's attempt to disrupt the formal and orderly movement of time to be the action that leads to the emptiness and futility of his life and produces his ultimate damnation. Both Macbeth and Lady Macbeth pervert time, transport themselves past the "ignorant present," and base their vision on actions yet to be committed. Macbeth in 1.7 is in normal time, his moral outlook clear; but Lady Macbeth spurs him to commandeer time and misuse the moral order. Following Duncan's murder he wanders in a limbo devoid of time; and by the end time—and life itself—have lost all meaning.

1525. RIEBLING, BARBARA. "Virtue's Sacrifice: A Machiavellian Reading of *Macbeth*." *Studies in English Literature 1500–1900* 31 (1991):273–86.

Suggests for the political context of the play a discourse of civic humanism that reflects standards of conduct far more Machiavellian than Christian. Duncan's faith and trust, for example, cost him his life; Malcolm learns the art of survival through negotiation with Macduff and the rebels against Macbeth. Macbeth's greatest weakness is the inability to commit himself fully to the course of wrongdoing his position as usurping prince has made essential.

1526. SINFIELD, ALAN. "*Macbeth*: History, Ideology and Intellectuals." *Critical Quarterly* 28 (1986):63–77.

Promotes an oppositional reading of the play that interrogates rather than promotes state ideologies. The conversation between Macduff and Malcolm reveals considerable overlap between tyrant and true king; here Macduff acknowledges that the illusion of power is insufficient and that numerous acts of moral and political depravity can be tolerated. Moreover, any reading that Macbeth's overthrow reestablishes the healthy state is disturbed by the fact that Malcolm (as king-maker on whom monarchy depends) stands in the same relationship to Malcolm as had Macbeth to Duncan.

1527. TAYLOR, MARK. "Letters and Readers in *Macbeth*, *King Lear*, and *Twelfth Night*." *Philological Quarterly* 69 (1990):31–55.

Comments on the significance of letters in all three plays (that which tells Lady Macbeth about Macbeth's prophesied kingship, that which wrongly informs Gloucester of Edgar's villainy, that which goads Malvolio into wooing Olivia) but also notes that, since the spectators are aware of the contents in each case, their real purpose is to reveal the motivations and proclivities of those who read them. Lady Macbeth, for example, is more interested in the nature of the letter's author and whether her husband will have the nerve to spur the prophecy into actuality. Gloucester accepts the lies against Edgar because he already harbors suspicions about his son; Malvolio does the same because he suffers under the delusion that Olivia is romantically interested in him.

1528. TETZELI VON ROSADOR, KURT. "Supernatural Soliciting: Temptation and Imagination in *Doctor Faustus* and *Macbeth*." In *Shakespeare and His Contemporaries*. Edited by E. A. J. Honigmann. Manchester: Manchester University Press, 1986, pp. 42–59.

Observes that *Faustus* and *Macbeth* stage the dynamics and experience of temptation. In both protagonists the agent of temptation (whether the devil or the witches) operates on the level of what the Elizabethan would perceive as his fantasy or imagination. The vehicle for tempting Macbeth is the prophecy, a verbal image, while for Faustus it is an imagination weakened and corrupted by a love for magic. The cost for both is uncompromising and pitiful. Macbeth moves from a display of creative potential to the barren futility of a life without imagination and without the possibility of alternatives. Faustus moves from the unbounded exhilaration of knowledge to imaginative atrophy and self-consuming license.

Macbeth

1529. TRUBOWITZ, RACHEL. " 'The Single State of Man': Androgyny in *Macbeth* and *Paradise Lost*." *Papers on Language and Literature* 26 (1990):305–33.

Points out the shared focus on the ideal of androgyny in *Macbeth* and *Paradise Lost*. Whereas Shakespeare accommodates the spiritual ideal of sexual wholeness to the imperial and masculinist ideology of the play, Milton revises the concept in his vision of the microcosmic heaven Adam experiences within himself as he leaves the physical paradise. Macbeth, more precisely, is forced to choose between the truly androgynous Duncan and the fiendish hermaphrodite Lady Macbeth. The figurations of androgyny underscore the ideological structure of Shakespeare's text.

1530. WALKER, ROY. *The Time Is Free: A Study of "Macbeth."* London: Andrew Dakers, 1949, 234 pp.

Investigates *Macbeth* through the pattern of its poetic symbolism, focusing on Shakespeare's vision to much of which our changing world makes us strangers. The opening scene is apocalyptic, with meanings convoluted and distorted, in short, with an elemental convulsion. The fair-foul dichotomy establishes a poetic theme that reverberates throughout the play. Darkness also pervades the play both figuratively and literally; the sun apparently shines only twice in the entire play. The daybreak at the end is a new dawn signaling the mutual workings of the ardor of nature and the army of heaven.

1531. WILLSON, ROBERT F., Jr. "Macbeth the Player King: The Banquet Scene as Frustrated Play within the Play." *Shakespeare Jahrbuch* 114 (1978):107–14.

Describes the banquet scene as a play that goes wrong, revealing the process of change by which Macbeth hardens into villainy and suffers the psychological consequences and by which Lady Macbeth loses control of him. Banquo, whose ghost sits in Macbeth's seat, reasserts his right both as king and host. As Macbeth's birth into kingship the wine serves as a link between birth and death, representing not only the water of a baptismal celebration but also the blood of Christ-like victims. He is born into a world of death of his own creation.

1532. WINTLE, SARAH, and WEIS, RENÉ. "Macbeth and the Barren Sceptre." *Essays in Criticism* 41 (1991):128–46.

Asserts that in its own way *Macbeth* testifies as eloquently as any of the comedies or romances to the human centrality of the process of generation. Above all, *Macbeth* is a tragedy in which for the protagonist the most poignant agony is the inability to transfer his power to the next generation, the "barren sceptre" for which he has murdered. Macbeth's childlessness renders his manhood suspect, and this "unnatural quality" reverberates in connection with his willingness to slaughter other people's children—the little Macduffs and Fleance.

Stage History

1533. BARTHOLOMEUSZ, DENNIS. *Macbeth and the Players*. Cambridge: Cambridge University Press, 1969, 302 pp.

Reconstructs and evaluates players' interpretations of Macbeth and Lady Macbeth, in terms of both thematic analysis and the concrete realities of speech, costume, gesture, and expression. The discussion focuses on major figures such as Burbage, Betterton, Garrick, Kemble, Macready, and Irving. The closing chapters stress the return to Elizabethan stage techniques in the twentieth century and in that regard the importance of the work of Harley Granville-Barker. Olivier's production in Stratford in 1955 is described as the most successful in this century.

1534. ROSENBERG, MARVIN. *The Masks of "Macbeth."* Berkeley and Los Angeles: University of California Press, 1978, 802 pp.

Surveys important critical and theatrical interpretations of *Macbeth* from Europe, America, Asia, Africa, and Australia. By attempting to reexperience the conflicting emotions that ravage Macbeth's soul while at the same time being conscious of his outer mask by which he hides them, we can come to appreciate something of Shakespeare's art in characterization. The play's visual imagery and spectacle combine many multiple signals. This study moves through the play scene by scene, interweaving the author's own interpretation with numerous references to critics and actors.

OTHELLO

Reference Works

1535. MIKESELL, MARGARET LAEL, and VAUGHAN, VIRGINIA MASON, eds. *"Othello": An Annotated Bibliography*. Garland Reference Library of the

Humanities, 964: Garland Shakespeare Bibliographies, 20. New York and London: Garland Publishing, 1990, 979 pp.

Contains 2,427 items, representing virtually all publications on the play from 1940 to 1988, along with most significant items prior to 1940. Material is categorized under such divisions as criticism, editions, textual studies, dating, sources and background, stage productions, and bibliographies. A brief essay traces the history of recent criticism and research.

1536. TANNENBAUM, SAMUELL A., and TANNENBAUM, DOROTHY R., comps. *William Shakespeare: "Othello."* Elizabethan Bibliographies, 28. New York: Privately printed, 1943, 132 pp.

Includes 3,100 unannotated entries covering major scholarship on *Othello* from the beginnings to 1941. The material is divided by the following categories and is arranged alphabetically by section—English editions, adaptations, abstracts; translations; travesties, parodies, imitations, continuations; bibliography; sources; songs for *Othello*; incidental music; Verdi's *Otello*; Rossini's *Otello*; electric and mechanical recordings; commentary on *Othello* music; theatrical history; Othello, Iago, Desdemona; commentary on the play; illustrations, costumes; book titles; addenda. The majority of the material (1,205 items) is loosely classified under commentary on the play.

Editions

1537. RIDLEY, M. R., ed. *Othello*. The Arden Shakespeare. London: Methuen; Cambridge, Mass.: Harvard University Press; 1958, 246 pp.

Includes discussion of the text, date, sources, the "double time" scheme, and critical interpretations, as well as appendixes on Cinthio's narrative and on various textual problems. The text is based on the first quarto (1622), for which the copy was probably a transcript of Shakespeare's foul papers. *Othello* may well be Shakespeare's greatest theatrical production. Through the soliloquies of both Othello and Iago Shakespeare forces the spectators to become involved in the action.

1538. SANDERS, NORMAN, ed. *Othello*. The New Cambridge Shakespeare. Cambridge: Cambridge University Press, 1984, 209 pp.

Features an introductory essay on date, sources, Othello's race, the plot and its inconsistencies, the play and its critics, the language, stage history, and the copy text. Explanatory notes appear on individual pages of the text, and supplementary notes, a textual analysis, and a reading list are appended. Illustrations depict four black Othellos (Edmund Kean, Paul Robeson, Frederick Valk, Laurence Olivier) and four Arab Othellos (Spranger Barry, Tommaso Salvini, Johnston Forbes-Robertson, Godfrey Tearle).

Criticism

1539. ADAMSON, JANE. *"Othello" as Tragedy: Some Problems of Judgment and Feeling*. Cambridge: Cambridge University Press, 1980, 301 pp.

Insists that critical appreciation for *Othello* has been crippled between arguments that the protagonist is noble and arguments that he is a creature of monstrous ego. The play is tragic in the fullest sense of the word, the supposed limitations reflecting the readers' restricting moral and artistic preconceptions. The play, more specifically, focuses powerfully on each character's perception of reality so that we tend painfully to identify with a partial view of truth instead of recognizing the fallibility that links us with the other characters as well and universalizes the tragedy.

1540. BABCOCK, WESTON. "Iago—An Extraordinary Honest Man." *Shakespeare Quarterly* 16 (1965):297–301.

Observes that "honest" and "honesty" are applied to Iago ten times in *Othello*. These references, however, have a pejorative connotation; they are used in a patronizing way to an inferior and serve to intensify Iago's hatred and his determination to strike back at those who subtly denigrate him. The use of "thee" and "thou" (55 times) and "fellow" function similarly in the play. Such social snobbery exacerbates his emotions, combining with his native shrewdness and intelligence to form a notable villain.

1541. BAYLEY, JOHN. "Love and Identity: *Othello*." In *The Characters of Love: A Study in the Literature of Personality*. London: Constable, 1960, pp. 125–201.

Notes that *Othello* focuses intensely on problems of domesticity and daily living with something of the familiarity of a novel or a newspaper. Reflecting the many sides of love, it is above all highly personal, culminating in a total loneliness of spirit that leaves the spectators with a similar sense of solitude. The spectators are made to see both with the eye of love and without it, sympathetically and judgmentally. At the end Othello assures us that suicide will cut him off from the last hope of mercy, and in that act his love endures, if not triumphs.

1542. BEEHLER, SHARON. " 'An Enemy in Their Mouths': The Closure of Language in *Othello*." *Upstart Crow* 10 (1990):69–85.

Comments on the "slipperiness" of language in the play, with words in dialogue often shifting in meaning with or without the speaker's intentions. Such a problem of interpretation forms the basis for Iago's practice upon Othello, eventually altering the Moor's very understanding of the way language works. Ultimately, the authorial voice is uncertain, the communicative act a collaborative task of creation; and Iago's skill in aborting that process is the source of his power.

1543. BERRY, EDWARD. "Othello's Alienation." *Studies in English Literature 1500–1900* 30 (1990):315–34.

Suggests that Shakespeare in *Othello* attempts to create a realistic portrait of a Moor, set apart from Venetian society in virtually every aspect, and that his tragedy results not from what innately he is but from how he is perceived. Those tainted by racism in the play are Iago, Brabantio, and Emilia, while Desdemona is attracted to the erotic in his personality. For Othello the most devastating consequence of his racial alienation is not the hostility of the Venetians but his own acceptance of the framework or mental construct within which they define him.

1544. BERRY, RALPH. "Pattern in *Othello*." *Shakespeare Quarterly* 23 (1972):3–19.

Asserts that an overly rigid symbolic interpretation of *Othello* destroys vitality and plausibility by smothering the naturalistic and psychological human qualities. These qualities are apparent in the pattern of interaction Shakespeare sets up among individuals. Brabantio, for example, moves from calm assurance to shock and outrage under the careful guidance of Iago, and the pattern is repeated in Othello. Iago's methods and motives are revealed through his relationship with Roderigo. Shakespeare through the surrounding characters refuses to offer an absolute judgment of Othello's character.

1545. BETHELL, S. L. "Shakespeare's Imagery: The Diabolical Imagery in *Othello*." *Shakespeare Survey* 5 (1951):62–80.

Observes that functional imagery assists in clarifying the meaning of a passage, possibly helping to develop character or theme. *Othello*, more specifically, is built on a theological structure, and pervasive diabolic imagery reinforces the spiritual struggle for the Moor's soul. Interestingly, these images apply only to Iago in the early acts, but they attach themselves to Othello in 4.5. His sin is that of Adam in that passion usurps reason. Since he is a Christian, his suicide seals his fate.

1546. BODKIN, MAUD. "The Image of the Devil, of the Hero, and of God." In *Archetypal Patterns in Poetry*. Oxford: Oxford University Press, 1934, pp. 217–70.

Views Iago as an archetype of the devil concentrating on hunting in order to destroy his hero, the destined prey. Once Othello wrenches himself free of Iago's power, his sense of the villain's deviltry is overwhelming. Othello, a romantic symbol of faith in human values of love and war, and Desdemona, not so much an individual woman as a symbol of the female divinity of love, are also archetypal conceptions. Iago is a limitless, negative denial of all romantic values whose only pleasure is to destroy.

1547. BOOSE, LYNDA E. "Othello's Handkerchief: The Recognition and Pledge of Love." *English Literary Renaissance* 5 (1975):360–74.

Focuses on the strawberry-red fruit embroidered on Desdemona's handkerchief and its symbolic significance as the virgin blood of her consummated marriage. When she is unable to produce the handkerchief, Othello's passion mounts steadily to the point of his murdering her for what he assumes to be whoredom. By using the handkerchief as the visual symbol of Desdemona's fidelity, Shakespeare emphasizes for the spectator the significance in the play of concepts and misconcepts of vision.

1548. BRAXTON, PHYLLIS NATALIE. "Othello: The Moor and the Metaphor." *South Atlantic Review* 55, n.s. 4 (1990):1–18.

Suggests that color, not ethnic background, is the significant feature in the depiction of Othello and discusses the dramaturgical purposes of that feature. Specifically, the controlling metaphor of the play is that of a fly caught and destroyed within the web of a spider, a metaphor established through Iago's references to Cassio as a fly (2.1.168) and his "net / That shall enmesh them all" (2.3.361–62). Othello's blackness in such a pattern is needed to reinforce the metaphor; the fly is normally black, and it (the alien) has wandered into the spider's territory. Racism is the fatal poison Iago injects, gloating as he lets his "medicine" work.

1549. BURGESS, C. F. "Othello's Occupation." *Shakespeare Quarterly* 26 (1975):208–13.

Observes that Othello's military code, under which he has prospered, fails to educate him to double-dealing. Unprepared for the subtleties of the Venetian world, he cannot accept ambiguity or equivocation. Even in his final moments his demeanor is military as he reminds the audience of the services he has rendered and then kills himself. Traditional among the military is the belief that one has a right to kill himself before being killed. His greatest military flaw is his breaking of the code of ethics in discussing Cassio with Iago, a subordinate.

1550. CALDERWOOD, JAMES. *The Properties of "Othello."* Amherst: University of Massachusetts Press, 1989, 159 pp.

Relates the tensions of the play to those generated by property. Since property, for example, defines selfhood and one is identified by what one owns, Desdemona emerges as the symbol or representation of Othello's worth. For him both Desdemona and Cyprus are properties; to the one he is ally and defender while to the other he is thief and owner. Iago is described as the repressed biases of the Venetian society grown to a destructive point at which they can no longer be ignored, as indicated in the play by comments that at first could be spoken only in Iago's soliloquies moving into the open dialogue of the play.

1551. CAMDEN, CARROLL. "Iago on Women." *Journal of English and Germanic Philology* 48 (1949):57–71.

Traces the main points of antifeminism through the period and describes Iago's conversation with Desdemona as they await Othello's arrival at Cyprus as in the main current of this tradition, reflecting many Elizabethan conceptions. Since Shakespeare is at such pains to depict Desdemona as an example of the ideal wife, Iago's words have sharply ironic force, just as her precise wifely devotion in the bedchamber scene adds horrible poignancy to the murder.

1552. DOEBLER, BETTIE ANNE. "Othello's Angels: The *Ars Moriendi*." *ELH* 34 (1967):156–72.

Asserts that Shakespeare evokes the *ars moriendi* tradition in 5.2, following Desdemona's murder, in Gratiano's reference to Brabantio's death. This tradition, which views the death-bed scene as a climactic struggle between the forces of evil and good for the possession of man's soul, is used to signal Othello's struggle with the temptation to despair. The juxtaposition of the art of dying well with Othello's actual death suggests Othello's damnation, but the suffering resulting from recognition and admission of his guilt also generates intense dramatic sympathy for the hero.

1553. ELIOT, T. S. "Shakespeare and the Stoicism of Seneca." In *Selected Essays of T. S. Eliot*. New York: Harcourt, Brace, 1932, pp. 107–20.

Argues that Othello, and to a lesser degree Coriolanus and Antony, in their final moments adopt a stoic attitude of self-dramatization in order not to have to admit failure. Othello's words express, not the greatness in defeat of a noble, erring nature, but a determination to envision himself against his environment. He is "cheering himself up," adopting an aesthetic rather than moral posture in an endeavor to escape reality.

1554. ELLIOTT, MARTIN. *Shakespeare's Invention of Othello: A Study in Early Modern England.* New York: St. Martin's Press, 1988, 284 pp.

Provides a lexical and syntactic study of Othello's major speeches. The tragedy of the Moor originates in his own mind and that mind can be analyzed through his diction. His words manifest his habit of "self-publication" or self-fashioning, his need to fix his figure in the world and to secure his reputation. This anxiety about his identity prompts him time and again to flee from doubt rather than examine it. And this obsession with "good name (something associated with male heroic militarism" (p. 180) makes him oblivious to Desdemona's view of marriage as a union of souls and compels him to the destruction of the Turk within himself.

1555. EMPSON, WILLIAM. "Honest in *Othello*." In *The Structure of Complex Words.* London: Chatto & Windus, 1957, pp. 218–49.

Explores the interplay of meaning with the word *honest* as a key to understanding the relationship of Othello and Iago. The word appears fifty-two times in the play, used divergently by the main characters in a kind of symbolic charade. Other characters use the word to describe Iago, but with Othello it becomes an obsession. All elements of Iago's character are represented in its range of meanings as is the range of moral values that an audience would experience about him.

1556. EVANS, K. W. "The Racial Factor in *Othello*." *Shakespeare Studies* 5 (1969):124–40.

Regards the racial factor as the fatal point of *Othello* and as the source of much of its philosophic significance. Blacks on the Elizabethan stage traditionally play upon social and religious prejudices, as well as satisfying a taste for the strange and exotic. Through the opening comments of Iago and Brabantio the spectators are conditioned to expect a fierce and violent individual, but Othello's appearance is just the opposite. In acts 3–5, however, the hero degenerates from nobility to the condition prejudicially associated with the race. His tragic nobility arises from the fact that, true to his Moorish nature, his judgment upon himself is as harsh as it had been upon Desdemona.

Othello

1557. FLATTER, RICHARD. *The Moor of Venice*. London: William Heinemann, 1950, 225 pp.

Maintains that to view Othello as a caged animal without the nobility and intelligence to be a match for the conniving Iago is totally to miss Shakespeare's intention. Othello, to be sure, is trusting, nobly so; and as such he is relatively easy prey for Iago. The complexity of the protagonist, though, is evident in the final act. Confident that he is a minister of justice, he falls to despair when he learns of Desdemona's innocence; but, when he learns further of Iago's machinations, he emerges from despair to a new sense of self-esteem and of love for his wife. When he "dies upon a kiss," he is joyously welcoming death as a reunion, combining the frenzy of death with the rapture of love.

1558. GARDNER, HELEN. "The Noble Moor." *Proceedings of the British Academy* 41 (1955):189–205.

Asserts that *Othello* has a supreme beauty, sensuous, intellectual, and moral, qualities arising from the nature of the hero. The living personality defeats any effort at allegorizing, and scatological concerns bow to attraction for human passion. As a drama of passion and love, however it fails to sustain such heights. Iago is monstrous, motivated by a detestation of superiority. The theme involves Othello's loss of faith at a sexual level where body meets spirit. His assassination of Desdemona is heroic in its absoluteness, committed to save her from herself. The godlike is mingled with the brutal.

1559. GERARD, A. " 'Egregiously an Ass': The Dark Side of the Moor: A View of Othello's Mind." *Shakespeare Survey* 10 (1957):98–106.

Suggests that a new look at Shakespeare's transmutation of Cinthio's material might provide insight into the playwright's intentions. As a study in the relationships between the moral and the intellectual, *Othello* depicts the ultimate responsibility for the fateful developments as resting with the Moor. The fundamental tragic flaw is a shortcoming in his intellect in that he fails to distinguish between the ideal and the actual. In his anagnorisis he recognizes this flaw and sees himself for what he is, a fool. Yet he remains barbarian to the end in condemning his soul to hell.

1560. GONZALEZ, ALEXANDER G. "The Infection and Spread of Evil: Some Major Patterns of Imagery and Language in *Othello*." *South Atlantic Review* 50 (1985):35–49.

Identifies five major patterns that act as "indicators or gauges for the spread of evil from Iago to most of the important characters in the play, and especially to Othello" (p. 35). The imagistic pattern of corruption, disease, and illness, initiated by Iago in the opening act, is first caught by intellectually weaker characters like Roderigo and Brabantio but then blossoms in act 3. Similar patterns are at work in the juxtaposition of light/dark, in religious language, in demonic language, and in cannibal imagery. In each case Iago "sets his plan in motion and then practically retires to let his infected victims finish things for him, even as they act and speak like him" (p. 45).

1561. GREENBLATT, STEPHEN. "The Improvisation of Power." In *Renaissance Self-Fashioning: From More to Shakespeare*. Chicago and London: University of Chicago Press, 1980, pp. 222–54.

Describes the key to Iago's power as improvisation, "the ability both to capitalize on the unforeseen and to transform given materials into one's own scenario" (p. 227). He is able to play upon Othello's subliminal perception of his relationship with Desdemona as adulterous. In doing so, he is forced into role-playing, whether to Othello, to Roderigo, to Desdemona, or even to Cassio and Lodovico. Othello has succeeded in self-fashioning himself in an alien culture, and Iago realizes that any such construct can be undone and rewritten into a different narrative.

1562. GRENNAN, EAMON. "The Women's Voices in *Othello*: Speech, Song, Silence." *Shakespeare Quarterly* 38 (1987):275–92.

Insists that the speech of the women plays a pivotal role in the spectators' understanding of the play's moral experience. A key scene is 4.3, in which the shifting tonality in the conversation between Emilia and Desdemona—the intimacy, the lyric beauty of the song, the strident quality of Emilia's defense of wives, the dying fall of Desdemona's concluding prayer—"composes both a 'theatrical' and a 'dramatic' interlude suggesting peace and freedom, within the clamorous procession of violent acts and urgent voices" (p. 277). Bianca's voice, though minor, is also significant; silenced in her honest statements and led off to be tortured, she underlines the female abuse at the heart of the play.

1563. HEILMAN, ROBERT B. *Magic in the Web: Action and Language in "Othello."* Lexington: University of Kentucky Press, 1956, 298 pp.

Observes that in *Othello* verbal drama (poetic language) and actional drama (the narrative line) combine to form a harmonious structure of meaning. Iago operates primarily by manipulating appearances through insinuation, thus inducing a kind of blindness, and his major imagistic mode is one of light-darkness. He also repeatedly expresses his views in terms of bodily functions, dehumanizing love by treating it as mechanical animality. Othello's breakdown in 3.3 is a consequence of his loss of position and of a sense of being loved. His plurality of motives consistently reflects both the noble Moor bent on justice and a loathsome monster of self-deception.

1564. HIBBARD, GEORGE R. "*Othello* and the Pattern of Shakespearian Tragedy." *Shakespeare Survey* 21 (1968):39–46.

Argues the atypicality of *Othello* as Shakespearean tragedy in that there is no public eulogy, little comment about his successor and the disposal of his estate, and no close interconnection of the public and the private. The play's action seems to contract rather than expand. Othello's painful and private loss emphasizes a sense of wanton waste; he suffers brutal degradation at the hands of an outside force and so privately has he become the focus of his tragedy that he alone is able to speak his own valediction.

1565. HUBLER, EDWARD. "The Damnation of Othello: Some Limitations on the Christian View of the Play." *Shakespeare Quarterly* 9 (1958):295–300.

Concerns the danger of utilizing selected points of Christianity as a handle upon which to hang clusters of images or symbols and then claiming to have perceived Shakespeare's deepest dramatic intentions. Whether Othello's soul goes to heaven or hell is peripheral to the play. Shakespeare's audience was diverse, living in a time of rapid change and doubt. It is foolish to insist on any kind of doctrinaire consistency; a hallmark of Shakespeare was the ability to see the many-sidedness of things.

1566. HYMAN, STANLEY EDGAR. *Iago: Some Approaches to the Illusion of His Motivation.* New York: Atheneum, 1970, 181 pp.

Displays the pluralism of literary analysis through five schools of interpretation of Iago—genre criticism, Iago as a stage villain descended from the Vice character; theological criticism, Iago as Satan with Desdemona having Christological overtones; symbolic criticism, with Iago as a partial portrait of the artist; psychoanalytic criticism, with Iago as a latent homosexual; and historical criticism, with Iago as a Machiavel. Any single view is reductive and partial; only taken together do they produce a full understanding of the complex imaginative creation.

1567. JORGENSEN, PAUL A. "Honesty in *Othello*." *Studies in Philology* 47 (1950):557–67.

Explores the connotation of "honest" that relates language to theme in *Othello*, specifically the mystery of how to distinguish an honest man from a knave. The study traces this theme through several morality and early Elizabethan plays. Iago is active in his surface role as the honest man, most skillful in creating the appearance that Desdemona and Cassio are but "seeming honest." His pose is complex, that of a knave posing as a hunter of knaves.

1568. KAY, CAROL McGINNIS. "Othello's Need for Mirrors." *Shakespeare Quarterly* 34 (1983):261–70.
Points out that Othello's suicide is staged as a public event. Both his first (interrupted) attempt that he has called Gratiano to witness and his second (successful) attempt involve his recalling his military accomplishments, his blaming the events on external forces, and his claims of honorable but misdirected intentions. Reaction to the deed is horror and regret, as Othello would have wished. Whatever his ability, bravery, and eloquence, this hero here and throughout the play is characterized by an immature ego.

1569. KING, ROSALIND. " 'The Murder's Out of Tune': The Music and Structure of *Othello*." *Shakespeare Survey* 39 (1987):149–58.
Observes that Shakespeare makes more use of music and musical references in this play than in any other tragedy. One such reference is Iago's comment: "O, you are well-tuned now, / But I'll set down the pegs that make this music." The dramatist sets forth his actions "as part of an extensive pattern of musical images and effects" (p. 149). One of many examples is Desdemona's "Willow Song," which speaks directly to the hearts and minds of the audience about the absolute truth of what she represents even as duplicity and misconception are closing in from every side. Another is Othello's comment that murder is out of tune moments after he has smothered his wife.

1570. KIRSCHBAUM, LEO. "The Modern Othello." *ELH* 11 (1944):283–96.
Disagrees with modern criticism that places the central cause of Othello's collapse in Iago. Instead, Othello like Shakespeare's other protagonists is nobly tragic in part because he is very much the maker of his own destiny. A romantic idealist who overidealizes both himself and Desdemona, he also readily shifts to suspicion at the least provocation. His refusal to face his crime squarely in act 5 and to see himself as ordinarily human is what makes him psychologically consistent. Iago succeeds with Othello because the Moor is tragically and nobly susceptible, not because Iago is a Devil-man against whom one is doomed to failure.

1571. LEAVIS, F. R. "Diabolic Intellect and the Noble Hero." In *The Common Pursuit*. London: Chatto & Windus, 1952, pp. 136–59.

Othello

Claims that, even though it is the simplest of Shakespeare's tragedies, *Othello* suffers from an essential and denaturing falsification. Bradley's mistaken notion of the play as the undoing of a noble Moor is largely responsible. Othello, instead, is the supreme egotist given from first to last to self-approving self-dramatization. His own mind, not Iago's, undoes him. "Self-pride becomes stupidity, ferocious stupidity, an insane and self-deceiving passion" (pp. 146–47). At the end there is no tragic self-discovery, only the *coup de théâtre* of Othello's contemplating the spectacle of himself.

1572. LERNER, LAURENCE. "The Machiavel and the Moor." *Essays in Criticism* 9 (1959):339–60.

Describes Iago as a mixture of the subhuman metaphor of evil from the medieval morality plays and the super-subtle human Machiavel who calculates and conceals behind his honest facade. This mixture of the symbolic and the naturalistic was a phenomenon of characterization, a transitional stage, in the literature of Shakespeare's day. Similarly, there are two Othellos, the stylized noble Moor of the first half and the realistic passionate Moor of the last half. Othello at the end has reverted to nobility.

1573. LEVITSKY, RUTH M. "All-in-All Sufficiency in Othello." *Shakespeare Studies* 6 (1972):209–21.

Analyzes Othello's weakness in terms of the Pelagianism inherent in Iago's comments on will and reason. Specifically, *Othello* is more about the weakness of the mind and the understanding than of the body. Faulty reason, not drunkenness and adultery, wreaks the havoc in the play. Othello is a character of self-sufficiency, but as such his stoicism sacrifices a part of his humanity and requires a subjugation of human emotions. He murders his wife according to his belief in strict justice, never humbling himself before man or God, more antique Roman than Christian.

1574. LOOMBA, ANIA. *Gender, Race, Renaissance Drama*. Manchester: Manchester University Press; New York: St. Martin's Press, 1989, 178 pp.

Views Othello as a colonized subject marginalized and alienated by the white Venetian society. By the end of the play he is a near-schizophrenic hero whose lost speech portrays him as "simultaneously the Christian and the Infidel, the Venetian and the Turk, the keeper of the state and its opponent" (p. 48). At the center of the play is the threat to a white racist state by both a black man and a white woman. In *Antony and Cleopatra* Cleopatra, like Elizabeth, evokes fears of female government. Roman patriarchy demonizes her world by defining it as female (robbing Antony of his manhood) and as barbaric (Antony as a slave of gypsies).

1575. MERCER, PETER. *"Othello* and the Form of Heroic Tragedy." *Critical Quarterly* 11 (1969):45–61.

Complains that Leavis, in locating the reason for Othello's collapse in the Moor himself, has reduced the play to a rather arbitrary intrigue against a self-deceiving egotist. Likewise, to view Othello in his final words as merely cheering himself up, as Eliot does, is to neglect the nature of heroic tragedy in favor of psychological peculiarities. Instead, Othello's progress is "from heroic certainty to total unbearable uncertainty" (p. 50), with the play turning upon distinctions between linguistic and existential worlds and a general movement toward rhetorical reassertion.

1576. NEILL, MICHAEL. "Unpopular Beds: Race, Adultery, and the Hideous in *Othello*." *Shakespeare Quarterly* 40 (1989):384–412.

Observes that the scene of the violated marriage bed triggers deeply felt racial fears and repulsions in the spectators, so much so that it was traditional to play it behind a screen during the Victorian period. In the final act the bed becomes insistently the place on which the action is centered, and Iago's insinuations eventually make it appear that what has happened there is an assault on the natural order of things, whether the challenge to patriarchal authority or the flagrant transgression of alleged boundaries of nature itself. "The object that 'poisons sight' is nothing less than a mirror for the obscene desires and fears that *Othello* arouses in its audiences" (p. 412).

1577. NEWMAN, KAREN. " 'And Wash the Ethiop White': Femininity and the Monstrous in *Othello*." In *Shakespeare Reproduced: The Text in History and Ideology*. Edited by Jean Howard and Marion F. O'Connor. New York and London: Methuen, 1987, pp. 143–62.

Argues that Shakespeare uses issues of racism to drive the plot of the play, whether the assumption that the marriage is considered unthinkable by others or Othello's own prejudices against his blackness. Miscegenation is also an issue of language in that black-white oppositions characterize the play's discourse. "As the object of Desdemona's illegitimate passion, Othello both figures monstrosity and at the same time represents the white male norms the play encodes through Iago" (p. 153).

1578. NORRIS, CHRISTOPHER. "Post-structuralist Shakespeare: Text and Ideology." In *Alternative Shakespeares*. Edited by John Drakakis. London and New York: Methuen, 1985, pp. 47–66.

Othello

Raises questions about the practice and traditions of Shakespearean criticism involving textual scholarship and problems of interpretation as well as the processing and maintaining of Shakespeare (as a textual phenomenon) within particular political and social constraints. *Othello*, as a case in point, has been subjected to comment as diverse as that of Johnson and Leavis, and yet the upshot has been to cast doubt on the power of criticism to distinguish between the interpretive and the textual. Poststructuralism aims to free Shakespeare's plays from the powerful bias of imposing meanings and values as conceived by the dominant ideology.

1579. NOWOTTNY, WINIFRED M. T. "Justice and Love in *Othello*." *University of Toronto Quarterly* 21 (1951–52):330–44.

Maintains that the play turns upon a conflict between justice and love, hence the significance of Othello's claim in act 5 that he is a minister of justice. His agony results from the simultaneous growing intensity in his realization of continued love for Desdemona and his growing compulsiveness to enact the sanctions of justice. His tragic error is that, in applying judgment to love, he attempts to join two concepts incompatible in their essential natures. In that he accepts justice as life's supreme value, it is wholly consistent that ultimately he executes himself.

1580. ORKIN, MARTIN. "Othello and the Plain Face of Racism." *Shakespeare Quarterly* 38 (1987):166–88.

Argues that racist mythology inscribes critical responses to the play and that in South Africa silence about these racist tendencies actually supports racist doctrine and practice. The play itself opposes racism both by implanting racist comments into the mouths of those who consciously use it in an attempt to control others for their own ends (Iago, Roderigo, Brabantio) and by even reversing the normal color associations, depicting the white Iago as amoral, unchristian, and savage. Nonetheless, this strategy of racism utilizes the law to shatter the lives of two people in love; within its own context, "racism and the abuse of the legal process play a terrible part" (p. 188).

1581. PARKER, PATRICIA. "Shakespeare and Rhetoric: 'Dilation and Delation' in *Othello*." In *Shakespeare and the Question of Theory*. Edited by Patricia Parker and Geoffrey Hartman. New York and London: Methuen, 1985, pp. 54–74.

Suggests that Othello's assumption during the temptation scene that Iago's insinuations about Desdemona are "close dilations, working from the heart"—resonates with multiple meanings which serve to enrich the spectators' response. *Dilation*, itself, can mean either an expansion and enumeration or a delay or dilatoriness. Moreover, as Samuel Johnson first suggested, the word could be read as *delations*, occult and secret accusations. Iago's plot involves all three—an unfolding of accusations just so far as to suggest more and the dilatory time for Othello's suspicions to grow.

1582. REESE, JOAN. "*Othello* as a Key Play." *Review of English Studies*, n.s. 41 (1990):185–90.

Views *Othello* as a central play, locking together crucial Shakespearean themes and preoccupations. For example, the theme that a character must come to know his identity through confirmation from the outside is pervasive in Shakespeare. Here Iago seeks such confirmation following Othello's failure to promote him. For Othello, Desdemona's love is the supreme ratification of what he is and what he has done; when doubt enters his mind, his identity dissolves into chaos. The play, in a word, "gathers together recurrent themes of trust and betrayal . . . on which the late romances will provide a final commentary" (p. 190).

1583. RICE, JULIAN C. "Desdemona Unpinned: Universal Guilt in *Othello*." *Shakespeare Studies* 7 (1974):209–26.

Rebuts the traditional view of Desdemona as a Christ-like innocent victim and points to a significant flaw of psychological dishonesty. Her Neoplatonic view of Othello in 1.3, for example, denies a sexual basis for their relationship; she later needs reassurance from Iago of her virtue; she is blind to her own pride in her ready willingness to help Cassio regain office; and she is naive in her response to Othello's charges of infidelity. In the unpinning scene (4.3) Shakespeare uses the conventional *topos* of clothing to symbolize Desdemona's psychological exposure.

1584. SIEGEL, PAUL N. "The Damnation of Othello." *PMLA* 68 (1953):1068–78.

Draws an analogy between *Othello* and the fall of man, with Desdemona reminiscent of Christ in her purity and Iago of Satan in his destructiveness. Othello must choose between Christian love and Satanic hate and vengefulness. As his passion takes control, Othello assumes Faustian qualities, and Iago like Satan is conveniently on hand to spur the Moor to his final act of damnation. Iago is sentenced to unnatural earthly torments as a prelude to his future suffering in hell, while Othello attempts to execute poetic justice on himself and brings perdition to his soul.

Othello

1585. SMITH, DANNY. *"To Be Once in Doubt": Certainty and the Marriage of Minds in "Othello."* American University Studies, Series, 4: English Language and Literature, 90. New York: Lang, 1989, 205 pp.

Describes the character interaction in *Othello* as a "triumvirate of pride, naivete, and cynicism" (p. 117). Othello, Desdemona, and Iago are locked into particular mind-sets, and the result is disastrous for all three. Iago is overbearingly certain of his low estimation of others, their motives, and their qualities. Desdemona cannot bring herself to question her own image of the perfect husband. Othello refuses to question his self-sufficiency. When suspicions arise, rather than confront them rationally, he elevates his jealousy to a kind of divine wrath that demands righteous vengeance; even after discovering his error, he justifies his action as honorable by blaming fate and the devil.

1586. STEMPEL, DANIEL. "The Silence of Iago." *PMLA* 84 (1969):252–63.

Envisions Iago as a "Jesuitical Machiavel," Shakespeare's capitalizing on a combination of the Elizabethan concept of Machiavelli and of the Jesuit priest. Seventeenth-century religious and political sources speak of an "Ignatian Matchivell" who justified his villainy by an appeal to faith and piety. Specifically, Iago symbolizes the doctrine of the autonomous will, a doctrine advocated by the Spanish Jesuit Luis de Molina and denounced by Protestantism and Catholicism alike. Iago's silence is reflective of the obdurate resistance of imprisoned Jesuits.

1587. VAUGHAN, VIRGINIA MASON, and CARTWRIGHT, KENT, eds. *"Othello": New Perspectives.* Rutherford: Fairleigh Dickinson University Press; London and Toronto: Associated University Presses, 1991, 280 pp.

Features essays by Thomas Berger, Joe Porter, Michael Mooney, James Hirsh, Barbara Hodgdon, and Martha Rozett, among others, utilizing a wide diversity of critical methodologies—deconstructionism, feminism, performance theory, speech act theory, and cultural poetics. An introductory essay relates each of these contemporary perspectives to traditional viewpoints of earlier twentieth-century critics.

1588. WEINSINGER, HERBERT. "Iago's Iago." *University Review* 20 (1954):83–90.

Observes that the main confusion about Iago's character is a consequence of his stated motivations—frustrated ambitions, revenge for cuckoldry, unrequited love for Desdemona—not fully justifying the depths and passion of his villainy. Iago has been a man of faith, but his faith has been shattered before the play begins; and he now turns his fierce intellect to the development of a materialistic and individualistic philosophy. Both Iago and Othello are incomplete men; the intellect of the one united with the passion of the other would result in a humane individual.

Stage History

1589. ROSENBERG, MARVIN. *The Masks of "Othello."* Berkeley: University of California Press, 1961, 313 pp.

Provides a stage history of *Othello*. Described as a play ripe for the era of sexual promiscuity in James's Court, *Othello* also warmly accommodated the appearance of women on stage in the Restoration but suffered from the censors and charges of indecorum in the eighteenth century. Major nineteenth-century Othellos are discussed in some detail—Kean, Macready, Fechter, Irving, Booth, Forrest, Salvini. Desdemona during this period steadily gained in courage, dignity, and tenderness. While the present century has produced no great interpretations, those particularly notable in the role of the Moor have been Laurence Olivier, Godfrey Tearle, Wilifred Walter, and Paul Robeson.

ROMEO AND JULIET

Reference Works

1590. MARDER, LOUIS, comp. *"Romeo and Juliet": A Supplementary Bibliography 1871–1964.* The New Variorum Shakespeare. New York: American Scholar Publications, 1965, 20 pp.

Includes representative scholarship on *Romeo and Juliet* from 1871 through 1964 and is intended to supplement H. H. Furness's Variorum edition of 1871. The material is categorized under folio facsimiles, quarto facsimiles, editions of the play in chronological order, and critical studies (alphabetically arranged). While not exhaustive, the material represents every major category of scholarship and criticism.

1591. TANNENBAUM, SAMUEL A., and TANNENBAUM, DOROTHY R., comps. *William Shakespeare: "Romeo and Juliet."* Elizabethan Bibliographies, 41. New York: Privately printed, 1940, 107 pp.

Includes 2,354 unannotated entries covering major scholarship

Romeo and Juliet

from the beginnings to 1938. The material is divided by the following categories and is arranged alphabetically by section—editions, adaptations; translations; selections; sources; theatrical history; music; recordings; ballet; travesties, burlesques; Juliet, Romeo; commentary. The majority of the material (1,225 items) is loosely classified under commentary.

Editions

1592. EVANS, G. BLAKEMORE, ed. *Romeo and Juliet*. The New Cambridge Shakespeare. Cambridge: Cambridge University Press, 1984, 249 pp.

Features an introductory essay on the date, sources and structure, the tragic pattern, language and style, characters, and stage history. A textual analysis addresses both the nature of the first quarto (a bad quarto) and the manner in which the second quarto (set from Shakespeare's foul papers and the copy text for this edition) is tainted by the first. Supplementary notes and excerpts from Arthur Brooke's *The Tragical History of Romeus and Juliet* are also included.

1593. GIBBONS, BRIAN, ed. *Romeo and Juliet*. The Arden Shakespeare. London: Methuen; Cambridge, Mass.: Harvard University Press, 1980, 280 pp.

Includes discussion of the text, the date, sources, and critical interpretations, as well as appendixes on the Queen Mab speech in the first quarto and a selection from Arthur Brooke's *Romeus and Juliet*. The text is based on the second quarto, for which the copy was probably Shakespeare's foul papers. The first quarto is clearly a memorial reconstruction.

Textual Studies

1594. BAINS, YASHDIP SINGH. "The Bad Quarto of Shakespeare's *Romeo and Juliet* and the Theory of Memorial Reconstruction." *Shakespeare Jahrbuch* 126 (1990):164–73.

Argues that the two quartos of the play represent different versions that Shakespeare wrote for the stage and that the second is superior to the first because it represents a revision with careful attention to speeches, scenes, and characters. The folio version probably represents yet another stage of revision. Through these revisions the plot is lengthened considerably, and the character of Romeo is made fuller and more complex. Shakespeare and his fellow playwrights did not produce "a stable and authoritative single text for each play" (p. 173); instead, they completed their work in stages, and the three extant versions of *Romeo and Juliet* illuminate their method of composition.

1595. HOPPE, HARRY R. *The Bad Quarto of "Romeo and Juliet": A Biblio-graphical and Textual Study.* Ithaca: Cornell University Press, 1948, 230 pp.

Argues that the first quarto (1597) is a memorial reconstruction of a version represented in substantially correct form in the second quarto (1599). External evidence includes the nature of the stage directions, errors in versification, omitted scenes, wordy passages, and attributions of speeches to the wrong characters, while internal evidence includes shifting of words, lines, or passages to another part of the play, appro-priations from other plays, and anticipations of words and phrases. Probably the text was reconstructed by Gabriel Spencer and William Bird, who deserted the Chamberlain's Company for Pembroke's in 1597.

Criticism

1596. ADAMS, BARRY. "The Prudence of Prince Escalus." *ELH* 35 (1968):32–50.

Deals with the dramatic function of Escalus and how his action, to some extent, leads to the tragedy of the play. The prince's first appear-ance establishes him as a mediator between the play world and the audience. His second appearance follows Tybalt's death, and his final appearance follows the suicides of Romeo and Juliet. In each case he brings order to prevailing confusion. But Escalus, like all men lacking sufficient understanding of the past to make completely reliable infer-ences about the future, is forced to make key decisions that play into the hand of evil fortune.

1597. BLACK, JAMES. "The Visual Artistry of *Romeo and Juliet*." *Studies in English Literature 1500–1900* 15 (1975):245–56.

Views *Romeo and Juliet* as an exercise suiting action to words in such a manner as to produce special intensity. Scenes, for example, are repeated for visual effect and striking contrasts. The first balcony scene is marked by delight and sweet anticipation, ending in "sweet sorrow"; the second is altered by Romeo's banishment and his engagement in

Romeo and Juliet

bloodshed, ending in desperation. In the friar's cell scenes, the first finds Romeo seeking advice for love while the second finds Juliet seeking a remedy for it. Other examples are the framing scenes with Prince Escalus. These scenes stand on opposing sides of Mercutio's death.

1598. BOWLING, LAWRENCE E. "The Thematic Framework of *Romeo and Juliet*." *PMLA* 64 (1949):208–20.

Disagrees with the view that *Romeo and Juliet* as a work of Shakespeare's adolescence lacks a central theme. To the contrary, the unifying motif is that character after character must come to the realization of the complexity of things, the mixture of good and evil. Such paradoxicality is signaled in the prologue in Friar Lawrence's soliloquy, Juliet's "dove-feather raven" speech, Capulet's festival-funeral speech, Romeo's "loving hate" speech, and his speech about gold as a cordial poison. Both Romeo and Juliet mature in the course of the action through the acceptance of this duality, as to a lesser extent do their parents.

1599. BRENNER, GERRY. "Shakespeare's Politically Ambitious Friar." *Shakespeare Studies* 13 (1980):47–58.

Argues that, in marrying Romeo and Juliet without parental consent, failing to acquaint Prince Escalus with his plan, and using a sleeping potion when removing Juliet to Mantua would be far simpler, Friar Lawrence acts from self-aggrandizing political ambitions. He views Romeo and Juliet as political tools by which to "assert his superiority over domestic and civil authorities" (p. 52). In doing so, he oversteps the bounds of religious responsibilities. His flight from the tomb results from "fear of social exposure lest he be punished" (p. 55).

1600. BRYANT, J. C. "The Problematic Friar in *Romeo and Juliet*." *English Studies* 55 (1974):340–50.

Argues that, in light of Friar Lawrence's questionable conduct in the drama, one must judge him as an ecclesiastic, the stereotype of comical friars derived from medieval fabliaux and *commedia erudita*. The friar becomes comic and problematic at the very points at which he deviates from his spiritual functions. In having Lawrence disregard the canon law forbidding clandestine marriage, marry minors without parental consent, and counsel Juliet to engage in deliberate lying, Shakespeare strips him of priestly dignity and ultimately leaves him little more than a coward.

1601. CARROLL, WILLIAM C. " 'We Were Born to Die': *Romeo and Juliet*." *Comparative Drama* 15 (1981):54–71.

Notes that the ending of the play represents what the action has pointed to from the outset, the consummation of the love of Romeo and Juliet in the tomb. Romeo and Juliet appear alone on stage on only three occasions, at the beginning of their love, at its consummation, and at their death. All three scenes are nocturnal, and each represents their extreme sense of isolation while suggesting the three ages of man in passing from life to death. Not only does the play include several allusions to journeys and pilgrims; image clusters of wombs and tombs, sex and death, also link the idea of the beginning to the end.

1602. EVANS, BERTRAND. "The Brevity of Friar Lawrence." *PMLA* 65 (1950):841–65.

Describes *Romeo and Juliet* as more than any other of Shakespeare's plays a tragedy of unawareness. The full force of fate as the operative agent in the play comes in Friar Lawrence's final speech, filled with dramatic irony since the spectators know the full range of events and no one of the characters is aware of all the details. Most stand in awe at the unexplained carnage. Friar Lawrence can explain much, but Balthazar must relate why Romeo was in the tomb and a page tells why Paris was there. Only as the events unfold do the characters become aware of their individual actions that make a part of the fatalistic design.

1603. EVANS, ROBERT. *The Osier Cage*. Lexington: University of Kentucky Press, 1966, 108 pp.

Offers a rhetorical analysis of *Romeo and Juliet* with specific attention to the dramatic function of Friar Lawrence and of Mercutio's Queen Mab speech. The oxymoron, in particular, allows Shakespeare to weave together the inexorably bound motifs of the tragedy—the combination of love and violence, the imagery of darkness and light, and the ambiguous relationship of reality and appearance, of passion and rationality. Even in this highly rhetorical play, Shakespeare seldom utilized ornament for its own sake. Mercutio's speech, for example, totally preoccupied with rhetoric, both points forward to the dramatic action and also illustrates the fullness of Mercutio's character.

1604. EVERETT, BARBARA. *"Romeo and Juliet*: The Nurse's Story." *Critical Quarterly* 14 (1972):129–39.

Suggests that the nurse's story in 1.3 involving her memory of her husband and her own daughter is significant in that it provides both a framework and a leitmotif on death for the tragic events of the play. Acting almost as a choric commentary, in close conjunction with the chorus's remarks in the prologue, the nurse concentrates attention on Juliet's age, her weaning, and her fall.

Romeo and Juliet

1605. FABER, M. D. "The Adolescent Suicide of Romeo and Juliet." *Psycho-analytic Review* 59 (1972):169–82.

Maintains that the suicide of Romeo and Juliet is caused by the thwarting of an adolescent's attempt to transfer his libidinal energies to a nonincestuous object, thereby achieving the successful separation of the sexually mature child from the parent. The Montague-Capulet feud is narcissistic and restrictive, blocking the attempt of Romeo and Juliet to unite in a healthy complementary relationship. Romeo in taking his life desires both to unite with Juliet and to take out his aggression against the world and against his parents' association with the feud.

1606. FARRELL, KIRBY. "Love, Death, and Patriarchy in *Romeo and Juliet*." In *Shakespeare's Personality*. Edited by Norman N. Holland, Sidney Homan, and Bernard J. Paris. Berkeley and London: University of California Press, 1989, pp. 86–102.

Sees a major conflict between patriarchy and romantic love as symbols through which individuals validate self and imagine they can transcend death. Hero-worship, the symbol of personal male vitality in ancient systems of social order, merged with the Christian concept of the victorious Father/Son to create the core of patriarchy; for this institution marriage is a key factor because it is the means of parental control of the transference of power. Romeo and Juliet defy this system, substituting an apotheosis in each other, "an equivocal vision of redemptive destruction that resists any ready evaluation" (p. 92).

1607. HOLMER, JOAN OZARK. " 'Myself Condemned and Myself Excus'd': Tragic Effects in *Romeo and Juliet*." *Studies in Philology* 88 (1991):345–62.

Maintains that the play provokes complex intellectual and emotional responses not unlike those of the major tragedies. The key to such responses is the manner in which Shakespeare "complicates much of what is straightforward in his literary sources" (p. 346). An example is the role of Mercutio in spreading the contagion of the feud through his quarrelsome temper early in Act 3. Romeo tragically assumes that his friend has been fighting in his behalf and thus thrusts himself into the duel against Tybalt. The spectator, however, realizes that Mercutio was motivated primarily by his own hot-blooded nature.

1608. LEVIN, HARRY. "Form and Formality in *Romeo and Juliet*." *Shakespeare Quarterly* 11 (1960):1–11.

Calls the mutuality of the love of Romeo and Juliet the one organic relationship in the midst of highly stylized expressions and attitudes. Romeo at the outset is the traditional Petrarchan lover, doting on

Rosaline, and even his first encounter with Juliet is set within the literary restrictions of the sonnet form. The quarrel at the opening is highly stylized with servants, young members of the feuding families, the heads, and finally the prince entering in seriatim fashion. Romeo's violation of tradition by overhearing Juliet's soliloquy signals the naturalness of their love; after their death their private world disappears, and the social ambience closes around them.

1609. McArthur, Herbert. "Romeo's Loquacious Friend." *Shakespeare Quarterly* 10 (1959):35–44.

Describes earlier criticism of Mercutio as focusing on his bawdiness or his inconsistency and, thus, on Shakespeare's deficiency in developing a tragic tone as long as Mercutio is on stage. To the contrary, his function as a foil to Romeo is critical to the structure of the play. In his attempt to dislodge Romeo's melancholy in the Queen Mab speech, he prompts his friend out of his role as a fashionable lover, and Romeo catches a somber and prophetic glimpse of the future. Romeo's own destruction is prefigured in the vulgarization and death of Mercutio.

1610. Moore, Olin H. "Shakespeare's Deviations from *Romeo and Juliet*." *PMLA* 52 (1937):68–74.

Notes that, whereas the general assumption is that Shakespeare altered his source for *Romeo and Juliet* only in terms of the minor characters, there are four significant modifications in the roles of the major characters—in Romeo's object in attending the Capulet's ball, in Romeo's motivation for killing Tybalt, in Juliet's attending her wedding without the nurse, and in the balcony scene in which Romeo and Juliet first exchange their love vows. Apparently Shakespeare had direct access to the story as treated in Italian by Luigi da Porta.

1611. Nevo, Ruth. "Tragic Form in *Romeo and Juliet*." *Studies in English Literature 1500–1900* 9 (1969):241–58.

Observes that, as a drama stressing the accidental, *Romeo and Juliet* could have failed either through the excessively melodramatic or the excessively didactic. The network of ironies and the paradoxical effects of coincidences prevent the former, while Romeo's initial effort to avoid a confrontation with Tybalt combined with his engagement only to avenge a friend prevents the latter. The friar's Christian counsel of moderation is tragically useless in the face of Romeo and Juliet's conviction that love fulfills the needs of both flesh and spirit.

1612. Nosworthy, J. M. "Two Angry Families of Verona." *Shakespeare Quarterly* 3 (1952):219–26.

Romeo and Juliet

Argues that *Romeo and Juliet* was influenced by Henry Porter's farce *The Two Angry Women of Abingdon* and that this influence is responsible for the lack of tragic tone and substance in Shakespeare's play. Parallels of tone and style are far more significant than parallels in language. Specifically, Romeo and Juliet never develop as characters, the feud is more comic than tragic, fate and tragic necessity are not blended, the divergent styles are incongruous, and the surrounding action is so filled with the frivolous and the trivial that no tragedy can carry it.

1613. PETTET, E. C. "The Imagery of *Romeo and Juliet.*" *English* 8 (1950):121–26.

Observes that the note of fate or premonition affects every character and development in the narrative of *Romeo and Juliet*, for example, Romeo's sudden misgiving mind in act 1, Juliet's chilling comment about having no joy of her newfound love in act 2, or Friar Lawrence's admonition against haste. With such emphasis on fate Shakespeare not surprisingly makes frequent use of star imagery; also, the pilot image recurs at three key points—when Romeo decides to attend Capulet's ball, when he first gains Juliet's love, and when he defies the stars in act 5. The imagery of darkness also appears at significant moments throughout the action.

1614. PORTER, JOSEPH A. "Mercutio's Brother." *South Atlantic Review* 49 (1984):31–41.

Investigates the ghost character of Valentine, who is described in Capulet's guest list as brother of Mercutio, but who never appears in the play. While Shakespeare's source Arthur Brooke is of no direct help, he does indirectly provide the answer, for Brooke's Romeus is the source of minor incidents for Shakespeare's Valentine. Romeo and Valentine were paired in Shakespeare's mind; and in transforming Mercutio to a fuller character, the playwright added Valentine to enhance the character's quality of brotherly affection.

1615. ———. *Shakespeare's Mercutio: His History and Drama.* Chapel Hill: University of North Carolina Press, 1988, 288 pp.

Argues, while examining the history of the character before, with, and after Shakespeare, that Mercutio is "the hero of the play [who] keeps it alive" (p. 192). In name, manner, and cultural meaning Mercutio is an avatar of Mercury—with his youthfulness, eloquence, dreams, death, and misogyny—but, more important, with his brutal maleness, his homosexual fascination, and his prominent phallus. In Mercutio Shakespeare affirms bonds among men against the incursions of women. By killing off the character, Shakespeare silences the major spokesman against heterosexual love. He also, perhaps, lays to rest his anxiety concerning his dramatic and commercial rival, Christopher Marlowe.

1616. ROZETT, MARTHA TUCK. "The Comic Structure of Tragic Endings: The Suicide Scenes of *Romeo and Juliet* and *Antony and Cleopatra*." *Shakespeare Quarterly* 36 (1985):152–64.

Notes that the tragic sequence at the end of both *Romeo and Juliet* and *Antony and Cleopatra* consists of the feigned death of the heroine, the suicide of the lover, the "resurrection" of the heroine, and her suicide. Each in turn is afforded the status of protagonist, dying in expiation for the death she or he has provoked. Conventions traditional to comedy make up the core of the plot—the need to overcome the social and political situation, blocking figures, a pattern of misunderstanding and confusion leading to clarification and reunion. Tonal emphasis at the end of one play is on the sense of loss and guilt shared by the survivors, in the other on the sense of joy, apotheosis, and victory.

1617. RYAN, KIERNAN. "*Romeo and Juliet*: The Language of Tragedy." In *The Taming of the Text: Explorations in Language, Literature, and Culture*. Edited by Willie Van Peer. London and New York: Routledge, 1988, pp. 106–21.

Argues that *Romeo and Juliet* underscores the struggle for sexual and social liberation. The source of the play's power is its vision of love free of social and ideological constraints. Romeo at the outset is trapped in the discourse of the Petrarchan lover as is Juliet in the discourse of subordination to the husband. They woo through the love sonnet and fall in love before they know the names that signify feudal opposition. After they meet, they are willing to defy patriarchal traditions of language, to speak in freer terms, and to die for their commitment.

1618. SIEGEL, PAUL N. "Christianity and the Religion of Love in *Romeo and Juliet*." *Shakespeare Quarterly* 12 (1961):371–92.

Asserts that Shakespeare in *Romeo and Juliet* employs the Renaissance concept that sexual love is a manifestation of divine love to fuse the doctrine of the religion of love and the Christian concept of love into a complex unified pattern. At the conclusion of the play it is the lovers' paradise of the religion of love rather than the Christian afterlife (with its associated judgment on despair and suicide) that is envisioned. Romeo's suicide, more specifically, is depicted as an act of meditative deliberation in which love triumphs over death and hate, uniting Romeo and his enemies in general reconciliation.

Romeo and Juliet

1619. SMITH, WARREN D. "Romeo's Final Dream." *Modern Language Review* 62 (1967):579–83.

Asserts that the key to the resolution in *Romeo and Juliet* is found in Romeo's dream in 5.1, in which he joyously recounts that his lady found him dead and breathed life into him, making him an emperor. These lines are not tragically ironic, as they are usually regarded, but are symbolically true. Romeo in spirit is revived by Juliet's kiss and becomes an emperor by the side of his dead bride. In death and timeless bliss, they need no golden statues as mortal mementos.

1620. SNOW, EDWARD. "Language and Sexual Difference in *Romeo and Juliet*." In *Shakespeare's "Rough Magic": Renaissance Essays in Honor of C. L. Barber*. Edited by Peter Erickson and Coppélia Kahn. Newark: University of Delaware Press; London and Toronto: Associated University Presses, 1985, pp. 168–92.

Views the play of language as a constitutive force in the tragedy of the young lovers. In their first meeting their languages join to form a sonnet, "a medium in which their relationship takes form" (p. 169). Thereafter, however, their languages bifurcate along sexual lines. Romeo conceives of love as a moment of satisfaction against a backdrop of loss, as a force with veiled "threats of impotence, emasculation, and effeminacy" (p. 186). Juliet, to the contrary, views love as a process of growth; her images visualize love as a force with "inwardness and depth" (p. 173) and with a power to transform and reshape reality.

1621. SNYDER, SUSAN. "*Romeo and Juliet*: Comedy into Tragedy." *Essays in Criticism* 20 (1970):391–402.

Claims that *Romeo and Juliet* contains a generic transformation from comedy to tragedy. Mercutio's death marks the turning point from the comic game of the sexes to a sacrifice with the lovers as its marked victims. The play has dramatic unity, despite the tonal shifts, in that the spectators are aware that premonitions of disaster precede Mercutio's death and hopes for avoiding disaster persist until the conclusion. The friar's attempt to adjust the situation to serve the course of love is the final hope for comedy.

1622. STAMM, RUDOLPH. "The First Meeting of the Lovers in *Romeo and Juliet*." *English Studies* 67 (1986):1–13.

Acknowledges the signal importance of the first encounter between Romeo and Juliet, unarguably the turning point of the play, and finds the real power in the close connection of the sonnet with the gestic events of the meeting scene. The bewildered and passionate Romeo resorts to Petrarchan cliches in the first quatrain, describing his lips as two blushing pilgrims. In the second quatrain Juliet distributes the roles properly, naming him, not his lips, as the pilgrim and acknowledging her own role as personal saint. The wit combat of the sestet culminates in their first kiss, and the additional quatrain "signals a possibly ominous excess in their love" (p. 13).

1623. UTTERBACK, RAYMOND. "The Death of Mercutio." *Shakespeare Quarterly* 24 (1973):105–16.

Views Mercutio's death as structurally significant in that it establishes a chain of events culminating in the final catastrophe. Specifically, his death (the tragic consequence) occurs because of a threatening situation, a provocation that actualizes the threat, the response to the provocation, the tragic consequence, and a blurring of the sense of responsibility. The same pattern occurs in three different instances—the death of Juliet, the death of Romeo, and the actions of Friar Lawrence. The force of destiny and the force of moral choice are balanced throughout these patterns.

1624. WALLACE, NATHANIEL. "Cultural Typology in *Romeo and Juliet*." *Studies in Philology* 88 (1991):329–44.

Observes that Romeo and Juliet cannot extricate themselves from the determinations of their culture, one that is experiencing a transition from feudalism to a stage of civic prosperity. Rhetorically, metonymy and metaphor "serve to categorize a diverse array of relations and transpositions" (p. 330) in the city of Verona, with the former reflecting traditional values and the latter reflecting the principle of change, dissolution, and the lovers' independence. The chaotic play of language shadows the ruptured social matrix.

TIMON OF ATHENS

Reference Works

1625. ELTON, W. R., and RAUCHET, E. A., comps. *A Selective Annotated Bibliography of Shakespeare's "Timon of Athens."* Lewiston, N.Y.: Edwin Mellen Press, 1991, 84 pp.

Contains briefly annotated items arranged under editions, attributions and completeness of text, text, date, criticism, commentary, sources, stage history, and music. This selective bibliography comprises items of scholarly or critical interest through 1989. Entries within each category are arranged alphabetically by authors, except for the editions, which are chronological. An author-editor index is included.

1626. RUSZKIEWIEZ, JOHN J., comp. *"Timon of Athens": An Annotated Bibliography*. Garland Reference Library of the Humanities, 388: Garland Shakespeare Bibliographies, 10. New York and London: Garland Publishing, 1986, 274 pp.

Contains 794 items, representing virtually all publications on the play between 1940 and 1984, along with significant items prior to 1940. The categories, each arranged chronologically, include criticism, sources, authorship, dating, text, bibliographies, editions, staging and stage history, and adaptations and influences. A brief introductory essay traces the history of recent criticism and research.

Editions

1627. MAXWELL, J. C., ed. *Timon of Athens*. Cambridge: Cambridge University Press, 1957, 189 pp.

Provides extensive textual notes, a critical introduction, a discussion of the copy text, a section on stage history, and a glossary. This edition is based on the First Folio, for which the copy was probably Shakespeare's incomplete draft. In technique the play mixes the quality of the moral and the realistic, and the result is, albeit imperfectly, to provoke the spectator's judgment, but not in Jonson's satiric spirit.

1628. OLIVER, H. J., ed. *Timon of Athens*. The Arden Shakespeare. London: Methuen; Cambridge, Mass.: Harvard University Press, 1969, 155 pp.

Includes discussion of the text, theories of authorship, the unfinished state of the play, sources, the date, and critical interpretations, as well as appendixes covering the stage history and selections from North's *Life of Marcus Antonius* and *Life of Alcibiades* and from Lucian's dialogue *Timon the Misantrope*. The text is based on the First Folio, for which the copy was a combination of Shakespeare's foul papers and Ralph Crane's transcript of them. Inconsistencies in major figures and in the verse have long prompted the observation that *Timon* is an unfinished play; presumably it was inserted in the folio only when printers thought they would be unable to include *Troilus and Cressida*.

Criticism

1629. BRADBROOK, MURIEL C. *"The Comedy of Timon*: A Reveling Play of the Inner Temple." *Renaissance Drama* 9 (1966):83–103.

Suggests that the anonymous play *The Comedy of Timon* is a law students' burlesque of *Timon of Athens*, probably presented at a Christmas revel at the Inner Temple. In order to create this reaction Shakespeare's play must obviously have been staged. *Timon of Athens* is a novel experiment, a spectacular pageant or show presented as a series of tableaux rather than a drama. *The Comedy*, probably presented in 1611, burlesques Shakespeare in the presentation of the excesses of the student cast as Christmas Lord.

1630. ———. *The Tragic Pageant of Timon*. Cambridge: Cambridge University Press, 1966, 38 pp.

Suggests that *Timon of Athens* is perhaps not a full play at all, that it represents in its pageantic qualities Shakespeare's response to the challenge of moving to the new indoor theater at Blackfriars in 1609. This rough draft experiments with various possibilities concerning the indoor lighted stage. Much is made of the scenic contrast between the city and the woods, and there are no battle scenes or mobs. The role of Timon offered Burbage in the succession of moods the opportunity for a virtuoso performance.

1631. BUTLER, FRANCELIA. *The Strange Critical Fortunes of "Timon of Athens."* Ames: Iowa State University Press, 1966, 188 pp.

Traces the history of diametrically opposed critical opinions of *Timon of Athens* concerning structure, characterization, meaning, whether Shakespeare left the play unfinished, whether Shakespeare wrote the play, and whether the play is a success. Structural critics have adjudged the work clumsy, unfinished, perhaps a collaboration. Thematic critics, to the contrary, either disregard the structure or praise it as experimental, shaped to contain the thought. Through the structural diptych and the starkly drawn characterization, Shakespeare was perhaps attempting to force the spectator to participate actively in resolving the question of how the idealist fits into society.

1632. COOK, DAVID. *"Timon of Athens." Shakespeare Survey* 16 (1963):83–94.

Asserts that *Timon of Athens* handles the theme of pride more objectively and offers less resolution of the issues raised than any other Shakespearean play. Timon's polar extremes prevent his gaining self-knowledge. He is in both halves of the play a study in human aberrations provoked by subtle pride. From playing the role of the god of men, he moves to the role of animal; in neither case will he accept man's real condition. The resolution comes not in Timon but in Alcibiades, who acts on having learned to accept and love the human condition for what it is.

1633. ELLIS-FERMOR, UNA. *"Timon of Athens*: An Unfinished Play." *Review of English Studies* 18 (1942):270–83.

Argues that *Timon of Athens* is either Shakespeare's reworking of an older play, his unfinished play completed by someone else, an incredibly cut and corrupted folio text, or his unfinished work. Most likely it is the last, roughed out, worked over in part, and then abandoned. Such a theory accommodates the fact that the power of Shakespeare is felt throughout but that there are undeniable fragments and loose ends— primarily in the character of Timon, who is inadequate to the theme, and in the action, which does not integrate his fate and that of the other characters.

1634. GOMME, ANDOR. *"Timon of Athens."* *Essays in Criticism* 9 (1959):107– 25.

Admits that *Timon of Athens* with its mood of cynicism that informs the whole movement of the verse seems to represent Shakespeare writing in a genre he did not find wholly congenial. The problem, in part, is our constant attempt to sentimentalize Shakespeare's tragic heroes and to sympathize with them; this we find difficult with Timon because his personality is unattractive. His failure to come to terms with his society is at once intellectual and moral. Timon and his society, in a word, appear too decadent for Shakespeare's purpose.

1635. HONIGMANN, E. A. J. *"Timon of Athens."* *Shakespeare Quarterly* 12 (1961):3–20.

Observes that two Timon traditions meet in Shakespeare's tragedy—Plutarch's account of his misanthropy and Lucian's description of his prodigality reduced to poverty. *Timon* also mirrors details from Plutarch's accounts of both Antony and Coriolanus, reducing the possibility of a lost source for the play. Supposed structural weaknesses, if examined carefully, prove fragmentary—the unsympathetic character of Timon, the episodic structure, the intellectual quality of the play. Quite probably Shakespeare was striving for a new kind of tragic effect for a coterie audience.

1636. KAHN, COPPÉLIA. " 'Magic of Bounty': *Timon of Athens*, Jacobean Patronage, and Maternal Power." *Shakespeare Quarterly* 38 (1987):34– 57.

Believes that a deeply felt fantasy of women and power drives the play and provides a paradigm for the curiously bifurcated action. Shakespeare draws upon the cultural forms that constituted patronage in the Elizabethan-Jacobean period—gift giving and credit finance. Timon is a man, like many an Elizabethan courtier, who gives and spends far beyond his means. The core fantasy is that Timon is a child of the female Fortuna, whom he sees as crassly abandoning him. Such a psychological concept helps to explain the degree of his bitterness and his misanthropy in the last acts and thus credibly joins the two halves of the action.

1637. KERNAN, ALVIN. *The Cankered Muse: Satire of the English Renaissance.* New Haven: Yale University Press, 1959, 261 pp.

Describes Thersites (*Troilus and Cressida*) as the most intense image of the satiric character in English literature. Composed only of the fundamental energy that drives the satirist, he is developed unchecked to a point of loathing for all other characters. In *Timon* the satirist occupies center stage; a mutation from a creature of love, he is a penetrating analysis of the satiric sense of life. The grandeur of his titanic loathing is emphasized through the contrast with two lesser satiric figures, the poet and Apemantus. Since Timon cannot obliterate the world, he turns upon himself in suicide.

1638. MERCHANT, W. MOELWYN. "*Timon of Athens* and the Conceit of Art." *Shakespeare Quarterly* 6 (1955):249–57.

Claims that the poet and the painter in their discussion and rivalry have an integral relationship to the major themes of *Timon of Athens*. In this technical flyting in which two professionals argue the mystery of their crafts by stating the case for the status of their arts in society's intellectual economy, Shakespeare may echo da Vinci's argument that painting is a liberal art and that it provides an insight into reality not unlike philosophy and poetry. Timon in his generosity commends these artists for their ability; but, when he turns misanthropist, he claims that neither is capable of depicting corruption that lies beneath the surface.

1639. PARROTT, THOMAS MARC. *The Problem of "Timon of Athens."* Oxford: Oxford University Press, 1923, 34 pp.

Describes *Timon of Athens* as, at once, fascinating, perplexing, and disappointing. It must forever remain a play for the study rather than the stage because it lacks sufficient creative power. Shakespeare probably started work on the play just after *Lear* in 1606, writing Timon's monologues in the last acts and sketching out the early acts. He then put it aside and moved on to *Macbeth*. After Shakespeare left the company Chapman was perhaps assigned to complete the play. Later the company had to overhaul it yet again. The resultant folio text is almost unintelligible.

1640. SCOTT, WILLIAM O. "The Paradox of Timon's Self-Cursing." *Shakespeare Quarterly* 35 (1984):290–304.

Examines Timon's curses as an undoing of the verbal form he purports to observe. His effusions in prosperity invite being turned back on themselves, and he in a sense creates the shock of his friends' infidelity during his time of need. His anger quickly turns to bitterness, but he is ineffectual in buying with gold the enactment of his curse of a general destruction. His curses include himself in all mankind as well as the audience. Even in death he denounces mankind in his epitaph, but he invites the continued curses of others as well.

1641. SOELLNER, ROLF. *"Timon of Athens": Shakespeare's Pessimistic Tragedy.* Columbus: Ohio State University Press, 1979, 245 pp.

Attempts to demonstrate that *Timon of Athens* is artistically deserving of its recent popularity as a play that speaks directly to our times. It is a tragedy set in the Renaissance context of the *contemptus mundi* of Christian humanism, a context best seen in works like Pierre Boaistuau's *Theatrum Mundi* and Richard Barkley's *A Discourse on the Felicity of Man*. Timon's rejection of the world represents not merely the obverse of his flawed idealism but an awakening to the evil in rapacious and exploitative society. The tragedy lies in his failure to recognize his own overreactions, his inability to live with this knowledge without developing a misanthropy that is both microcosmic and macrocosmic.

1642. WATERS, D. DOUGLAS. "Shakespeare's *Timon of Athens* and Catharsis." *Upstart Crow* 8 (1988):93–105.

Focuses on catharsis as meaning a clarification of human experience, specifically in *Timon of Athens* the spectators' recognition that the central figure destroys himself through a tragic flaw of excess feelings, that Timon's anger is tragic because it springs from shattered idealism. Part of the catharsis as intellectual and emotional clarification is the spectators' recognition of the loss and destructiveness in Timon's severing all ties with human association. If the catharsis works for the viewer, we need not express moral disdain for Timon's misanthropy.

1643. WRIGHT, ERNEST HUNTER. *The Authorship of "Timon of Athens."* New York: Columbia University Press, 1910, 104 pp.

Views *Timon of Athens* as one of Shakespeare's most perplexing plays in its corrupt text, its indeterminate date, its questions of authorship, its relationship to Shakespeare's other work, its stage history, its wide variations in style, and its eccentric form. Evidence suggests divided authorship with someone of limited talent reworking Shakespeare's original and unfinished material. The alien hand is far more visible in 1–3 than 4–5, with spurious additions accounting for approximately one-third of the play.

TITUS ANDRONICUS

Editions

1644. ADAMS, JOSEPH QUINCY, ed. *Shakespeare's "Titus Andronicus": The First Quarto, 1594*. New York and London: Charles Scribner's Sons, 1936, 122 pp.

Reproduces in facsimile the unique copy in the Folger Shakespeare Library. The copy was discovered in 1904 in Sweden and was purchased by Henry Clay Folger. Ownership of the volume can be traced from the seller, Petrus Johannes Krafft, back through three generations to Charles Robson (d. 1794), who came to Sweden from Scotland. The quarto text is now able to correct emended lines in the last three leaves of the previously published second quarto (1600). Also discussed are the date, the Longleat manuscript with the sketch of Alarbus, and the newly discovered source—a chapbook entitled *The History of Titus Andronicus*.

1645. MAXWELL, J. C., ed. *Titus Andronicus*. The Arden Shakespeare. London: Methuen; Cambridge, Mass.: Harvard University Press, 1953, 132 pp.

Includes discussion of the text, date, authorship, source, and literary interpretations. The text is based on the first quarto, for which the copy was probably Shakespeare's foul papers. The Longleat manuscript contains a drawing representing Tamora and her two sons on their knees pleading with Titus. No source survives in a form that we know to have been available to Shakespeare, but a mid-eighteenth century chapbook (*The History of Titus Andronicus*) may reflect a pre-Shakespearean version of the story.

1646. WAITH, EUGENE, ed. *Titus Andronicus*. The Oxford Shakespeare. Oxford and New York: Oxford University Press, 1984, 226 pp.

Titus Andronicus

Includes an introductory essay addressing matters of date, authorship, sources, and text. More extensive consideration is devoted to the play in performance, notably Peter Brook's production with Laurence Olivier. A section on reception and interpretation examines the play in its historical context, identifies salient issues of theme, characterization, and imagery, and traces the varying critical fortunes of the play.

1647. WILSON, JOHN DOVER, ed. *Titus Andronicus*. Cambridge: Cambridge University Press, 1948, 173 pp.

Provides extensive textual notes, a critical introduction, a discussion of the copy text, a section on stage history, and a glossary. This edition is based on the first quarto, for which the copy was probably Shakespeare's foul papers. *Titus Andronicus* is a tragedy of blood, a kind of crude melodrama that grew in the hands of Shakespeare and Webster to tragedy of the highest order. While there are human touches such as Aaron's protective instincts for his black child and Lavinia's pleas to Tamora for mercy, much of the action seems to represent a burlesquing of melodramatic form.

Criticism

1648. BAKER, HOWARD. *Induction to Tragedy: A Study in the Development of Form in "Gorboduc," "The Spanish Tragedy," and "Titus Andronicus."* Baton Rouge: Louisiana State University Press, 1939, 247 pp.

Describes *Titus Andronicus* as an Elizabethan transformation of the Philomela story, the transformation occurring through additions of plot fragments from the stories of Virginia, Lucrece, and Coriolanus. Rhetorical flourishes are derived from Virgil, and Aaron stems from the Vice of the morality plays. The flaw is that the treatment of character is superficial, with Titus largely impotent before Aaron's wickedness. The claim for extensive Senecan influence is seriously questioned; the pyramidal *de casibus* structure of medieval drama is clearly exemplified in the play.

1649. BOLTON, JOSEPH H. G. *"Titus Andronicus*: Shakespeare at Thirty." *Studies in Philology* 30 (1933):208–24.

Argues that Shakespeare in *Titus Andronicus* was carefully and systematically revising the work of another writer, that four acts of the play (1–4) reflect his artistic ability on the eve of his thirtieth birthday. The original was probably written for Pembroke's Men and, sold to Henslowe in 1593, was revised by Shakespeare. Acted by Sussex's Men early in 1594, it was then submitted to John Danter for publication. While critics have attacked crudities of action, they have failed to appreciate the careful and complex plotting of a young playwright in an age of general immaturity in drama.

1650. BROUDE, RONALD. "Four Forms of Vengeance in *Titus Andronicus*." *Journal of English and Germanic Philology* 78 (1979):494–507.

Asserts that the play is an anatomy of revenge exemplifying four forms of vengeance—human sacrifice to placate ghosts of the slain, the vendetta of blood revenge to avenge past injury, state justice or a civic response to transgression to maintain civil order, and divine vengeance by heavenly intervention. The general movement in the play is away from the self-government whose tenets underlie the first two to the principles of state justice that Lucius proclaims at the end, made possible by the actions of Titus that he perceives as divinely ordered.

1651. BRYANT, JOSEPH A., Jr. "Aaron and the Pattern of Shakespeare's Villains." *Renaissance Papers* (1984):29–36.

Claims that the creation of Aaron is one of the uniquely Shakespearean things about the play, with no counterpart in Kyd, and that this figure gives us an important insight into the playwright's subsequent presentation of evil. In a sense, he is closer to Shylock than to an apotheosis of the Vice. As the alien, the outsider, he confronts constant social hatred; we must see him as sinned against by the same society he attempts to wound. All spectators can appreciate his concern to protect his child. Like all Shakespeare's antagonists, he is made, not born, a villain.

1652. CUTTS, JOHN P. "Shadow and Substance: Structural Unity in *Titus Andronicus*." *Comparative Drama* 2 (1968):161–72.

Suggests that the unifying dramatic pattern in *Titus Andronicus* is based on the Renaissance *topos* frequently found in iconography: *the mistaking of the shadow for the substance*. Titus, in making mistake after mistake, is unaware that his comprehension is faulty. In allowing Alarbus to be butchered, for example, he in fact is attempting to appease the shadow of his own ambitions. When Tamora, disguised as Revenge, speaks to him, he fails to recognize the shadow of his own vengeful heart.

1653. ETTIN, ANDREW V. "Shakespeare's First Roman Tragedy." *ELH* 37 (1970):325–41.

Views *Titus Andronicus* as both an acceptance and a testing of the literary tradition of Rome as representative of the values of civilization, especially those concerning law, justice, and political order. While embodying these concepts in the opening scenes describing Rome as conqueror of a warring tribe and in Tamora and Aaron's bestial revenge against Titus, Shakespeare also utilizes Ovidian and Senecan allusions to signify darkness and barbarism in Rome as well. The Roman characters progressively come to hide human passion behind Senecan stoicism and Ovidian rhetoric.

1654. GREEN, DOUGLAS E. " 'Interpreting Her Martyr'd Signs': Gender and Tragedy in *Titus Andronicus.*" *Shakespeare Quarterly* 40 (1989):317–26.

Suggests that it is largely through and on the female figures that Shakespeare constructs the dominant characterization of Titus in the play. Tamora is positioned as one pole on the female scale, marking his strength by her being victim and his goodness by her cruelty and evil. Lavinia is the other pole; her mutilated body articulates Titus's own suffering and victimization, and her muteness symbolizes his powerlessness.

1655. HAMILTON, A. C. "*Titus Andronicus*: The Form of Shakespearean Tragedy." *Shakespeare Quarterly* 14 (1963):201–13.

Finds thematic unity in the development of Titus as a tragic figure. Honored as a conquering hero in act 1, he overreaches himself in his godlike decision to allow the sacrifice of Alarbus. Following a period of fury and grief, he recognizes his responsibility for placing the tyrant on the throne and seeks justice. He is pitied by both the messenger who brings his hand and his sons' heads and by Lucius and his grandson at the end of the play. In sketchy terms, Titus is humanized in the play.

1656. HILES, JOAN. "A Margin for Error: Rhetorical Context in *Titus Andronicus.*" *Style* 21 (1987):62–75.

Observes that the play turns on a series of rhetorical implorations—Tamora's plea for Alarbus's life, Lavinia's plea for mercy, Titus's plea for his sons' lives—and that none of these succeeds because the speaker fails to define the context. Tamora's address, for example, is inserted into the political debate over Rome's next ruler and thus fatally mixes deliberations of mercy with those of state. Similarly, her ploy to present her sons to Titus as Rape and Revenge later in the play fails because she does not recognize a submerged context, Titus's awareness of her subterfuge. The tragedy illustrates that language achieves power through the context that defines and gives it meaning.

1657. HUFFMAN, CLIFFORD CHALMERS. "*Titus Andronicus*: Metamorphosis and Renewal." *Modern Language Review* 67 (1972):730–41.

Considers the resolution of *Titus Andronicus* to consist of Rome's returning from an Iron Age of injustice and violence to a Golden Age of justice and peace. Barbarous Roman justice against Alarbus at the outset sets in motion a chain of atrocities, and Lucius pointedly pursues the initial act of cruelty. When he returns as leader of an army of the Goths in act 5, he brings not warfare but a restoration of order. He has no direct association with Titus's vindictive actions and thus stands untainted at the end of the play as a spokesman for the new day in Rome.

1658. HUNT, MAURICE. "Compelling Art in *Titus Andronicus*." *Studies in English Literature 1500–1900* 28 (1988):197–218.

Suggests that the characters' use of Ovidian myth may represent their attempt to comprehend or order their individual experiences through self-conscious reversion to literary models. Chiron and Demetrius, for example, verbalize the rape and mutilation of Lavinia as a reenactment of Ovid's story, Marcus comments on the same myth when he discovers her, and Lavinia uses the book of the legend when she identifies the nature of her violation. Titus's decision to use the art of myth when he gains vengeance may stem from his perception that the gods themselves have used such art in revealing the truth. The use of Ovid in the play moves far beyond naive imitation on Shakespeare's part.

1659. HUNTER, G. K. "Shakespeare's Earliest Tragedies: *Titus Andronicus* and *Romeo and Juliet*." *Shakespeare Survey* 27 (1974):1–9.

Views *Titus Andronicus* and *Romeo and Juliet* as experiments in which Shakespeare marks out the opposite poles of his tragic boundaries, with *Titus* reflecting Senecan influence and *Romeo* the influence of the Italian novella. The structure of the plays is similar in several ways. Both open with a scene of discord into which an authority figure enters (Titus, Prince Escalus); both involve families in conflict; and in both a tomb is a central physical and symbolic prop.

1660. MOWAT, BARBARA A. "Lavinia's Message: Shakespeare and Myth." *Renaissance Papers* (1981):55–69.

Sees the scene in which Lavinia turns the pages of Ovid to the tale of Philomela as Shakespeare's calling attention to the deliberate parallels in that account and his play. Since the incident occurs halfway through the action, it encourages the spectators to anticipate events that will follow and to attribute to Titus and Lavinia the anguish and desperation of Procne and Philomela as they move toward their revenge. It is

Titus Andronicus

the most obvious of Shakespeare's many uses of myth for structural purposes. *The Merchant of Venice* is also considered in some detail.

1661. PARKER, DOUGLAS H. "Shakespeare's Use of Comic Conventions in *Titus Andronicus*." *University of Toronto Quarterly* 56 (1987):486–97.
    Insists that formal comic convention used repeatedly in the play works to enhance the tragedy through creating a trenchant tone of irony. More specifically, Shakespeare periodically utilizes the traditional comic pattern of discord followed by resolution and reconciliation. The rural environment used in romantic comedy as a haven of peace and tranquility for beleaguered lovers here becomes a place for effecting diabolic goals. The birth motif, a symbol of new life in the comedies and romances, is used instead to suggest death and destruction. Finally, the banquet, in comedy a symbol of renewed harmony, serves to encapsulate the horrible murders.

1662. REESE, JACK E. "The Formalization of Horror in *Titus Andronicus*." *Shakespeare Quarterly* 21 (1970):77–84.
    Suggests that Shakespeare deliberately utilizes several methods of formalization to abate the impact of wanton bloodshed and horror in *Titus Andronicus*. The characters, for example, are highly stylized as good or evil; also there is a careful and consistent system of balances in the plot, both in the elements of the action and in the symmetry of stage scenes. Repetition of word, phrase, scene, and image functions as a form of stylization.

1663. SAMS, ERIC. *Shakespeare's Lost Play: "Edmund Ironside."* New York: St. Martin's Press, 1985, 383 pp.
    Resurrects E. B. Everitt's thesis (1954) that Shakespeare is the author of this chronicle play and defiantly hurls his claim into the teeth of the scholars who serve as "self-appointed guardians of the gateway" (p. 9). The planning and plotting of the action are firm, the prose "suitably sinewy," the verse "vigorous" (pp. 50–51); and similarities between *Edmund Ironside* and *Titus Andronicus* are so great that one must have served as a source for the other. The explanation is that *Ironside* was suppressed in 1594 and that Shakespeare responded with *Titus Andronicus*.

1664. SARGENT, RALPH M. "The Source of *Titus Andronicus*." *Studies in Philology* 46 (1949):167–83.
    Examines the prose history, *The History of Titus Andronicus*, extant in an eighteenth-century chapbook, as the source for Shakespeare's

play. Most probably the chapbook is a reprint of the actual prose history and ballad that existed in the sixteenth century. Clearly its origin is independent of the play. A careful consideration of the work strengthens the supposition that Shakespeare worked from it, although he alters the political significance, making the dominant motif the injustices suffered by the loyal Andronici at the hands of a wicked queen and her lover.

1665. SOMMERS, ALAN. " 'Wilderness of Tigers': Structure and Symbolism in *Titus Andronicus*." *Essays in Criticism* 10 (1960):275–89.

Views the conflict in *Titus Andronicus* as a struggle between Rome (civilization) and primitive nature (barbarism). Titus, by committing errors, releases the conflict, and chaos ensues in his mind and in Rome. Tamora and Aaron, agents of barbarism, are triumphant; but eventually order is restored through Titus's revenge—the sacrifice of Lavinia and the death ritual of the feast. Lavinia's mutilation symbolizes the frustration of self-conscious virtue; Tamora's meal symbolizes self-devouring appetite.

1666. WAITH, EUGENE M. "The Metamorphosis of Violence in *Titus Andronicus*." *Shakespeare Survey* 10 (1957):34–49.

Asserts that Shakespeare's extreme use of violence and the excessive adornment of language in *Titus Andronicus* is the consequence of Shakespeare's attempting, with only partial success, to adapt Ovidian narrative techniques to the stage. The tales in the *Metamorphoses* describe the power of intense emotional states to transform individuals beyond their normal selves. Similarly, Shakespeare in Titus and Lavinia depicts the dehumanizing effects of passion produced by extreme outrage, a movement toward a metamorphosis of character that transcends individuality and becomes a phenomenon of nature or personified emotion.

Stage History

1667. METZ, G. HAROLD. "The Stage History of *Titus Andronicus*." *Shakespeare Quarterly* 27 (1976): 154–69.

Notes that, while *Titus Andronicus* has been among the least frequently produced of Shakespeare's plays, there have been four periods of relative popularity—in the years around the turn of the seventeenth century by Sussex's, Chamberlain's, and the King's Men, in the Resto-

Titus Andronicus

ration period as revised by Edward Ravenscroft, in the 1840s as revised by the black actor Ira Aldridge, and in the twentieth century, especially the last thirty years. Among the most significant productions are those directed by Peter Brook in 1955 by the Royal Shakespeare Company (with Laurence Olivier and Vivien Leigh) and by Joseph Papp in 1967 by the New York Shakespeare Festival Theater.

VI.
The Romances

GENERAL STUDIES

1668. BERGERON, DAVID M. "Reading and Writing in Shakespeare's Romances." *Criticism* 33 (1991):91–114.

Observes that the romances, more so than the earlier plays, depend upon the authority of the written word for closure—Gower's narrative, Apollo's oracle, Jupiter's tablet, and Prospero's book. Both literacy and book production increased dramatically during Shakespeare's lifetime. He writes at a time when questions of interpretation abound in print, along with their political consequences. The romances embody an image both of the power of writing and of the necessity of interpretation, thus celebrating "the restorative nature of reading and writing" (p. 111).

1669. ———. *Shakespeare's Romances and the Royal Family*. Lawrence: University Press of Kansas, 1985, 256 pp.

Claims that the family of King James constitutes a text that Shakespeare incorporated into the plots of his final plays. Shakespeare's contemporary audiences would have seen an immediate political and social reality in these dramas, whether in Pericles's quest for a wife in Antioch, Florizel's elopement with Perdita, or Ferdinand's betrothal to Miranda. In each play the salient political issue is dynastic—the need for an heir, and the establishment of a clear line of succession.

1670. CUTTS, JOHN P. *Rich and Strange: A Study of Shakespeare's Last Plays*. Pullman: Washington State University Press, 1968, 106 pp.

General Studies

Views the final plays as an extension of the experience of the major tragedies in that they utilize dream texture, mirror techniques, and visions heightened by masque, song, and dance—in a word, the framework of a romance—to heighten man's vision of himself. This juxtaposition of style and rhetoric, of fanciful elegance and vulgar grotesqueness, dramatizes man's desire to hide his true nature behind a mask of putative innocence. Pericles, Cymbeline, Posthumous, Leontes, and Prospero are all flawed; they suffer a sea change that permits them to accept life for the paradoxical mixture of good and evil that it is.

1671. FELPERIN, HOWARD. *Shakespearean Romance.* Princeton: Princeton University Press, 1972, 319 pp.

Explores the poetics and problematics of Shakespeare's romances. Part 1 deals with the specific definition and delineation of the form, part 2 with the relationship to the remainder of the canon. Three modes of romance converge in Shakespeare—the classical Greek romance of the third century, the chivalric romance of the Middle Ages, and the romance of medieval religious drama. Basically Shakespeare's romances involve stories in which characters overcome difficulties against enormous odds; near or at the center are figures resembling the morality hero. Salvation or reconciliation and sexual union are inevitably accompanied by family reunion and international alliance.

1672. FRYE, NORTHROP. *A Natural Perspective: The Development of Shakespearean Comedy and Romance.* New York: Columbia University Press, 1965, 159 pp.

Focuses on the recurring images and structural devices of Shakespeare's romances, the genuine culmination of Shakespeare's dramatic achievement. Frye observes that Shakespearean comedy is highly stylized, nondidactic, and consciously primitive in its origins both dramatically and psychologically. The internal structure is consistent with its logic, utilizing the rhythms of atonement, saturnalia, and festivity. In the romances the dramatic conventions are descended from myths—all moving from anticomic to comic, from loss to discovery of identity— and all involving a movement through the green world toward the "rebirth and renewal of the powers of nature." (p. 119).

1673. GESNER, CAROL. *Shakespeare and the Greek Romance: A Study of Origins.* Lexington: University Press of Kentucky, 1970, 216 pp.

Examines the Greek romance tradition in Boccaccio and Cervantes and then relates Shakespeare to the overall tradition. This material is a major strand of Renaissance narrative prose and drama; many of the motifs and patterns of marvelously adventurous story, especially those calculated to produce horror or some spectacular effect, derive from the Greek romances. Shakespeare's romances, unified in tone, theme, and incident, all make direct use of the tradition, *Pericles,* for example, adapting the narrative of *Apollonius of Tyre; Cymbeline,* a mixture of several; *The Winter's Tale,* Heliodorus's *Aethiopica* (from Greene's *Pandosto*); and *The Tempest, Daphnis and Chloe* along with pastoral motifs from Longus.

1674. HARTWIG, JOAN. *Shakespeare's Tragicomic Vision.* Baton Rouge: Louisiana State University Press, 1972, 196 pp.

Stresses the artifice in the romances and the ambivalence of response provoked by these plays. Each contains similar narrative characteristics—a lost child, sea journeys, characters miraculously resurrected, a reconciliation through the agency of young people, the fulfillment of aspirations in a manner that leaves characters and spectators amazed. Elements of comedy and tragedy are mixed to produce a kind of emotional dislocation. The dramatic logic is that conventional modes of representation are inadequate for the values of these plays. The stylized theatrical fiction becomes a metaphor for examining genuine emotional issues of familial and marital relationships.

1675. HUNT, MAURICE. *Shakespeare's Romance of the Word.* Cranbury: Bucknell University Press; London and Toronto: Associated University Presses, 1990, 184 pp.

Focuses on the destructive potentialities and the redemptive workings of language in Shakespeare's last plays. More specifically, rare acts of expression and perception that occur in the medium of literary pastoral supersede and rectify earlier disasters of speech and understanding. In *Pericles,* for example, the destructive language of Antiochus's riddle plays against the repeated salvatory word delivered by Gower in a manner reminiscent of the providential utterances of the biblical Jonah. In *Cymbeline* the providential word is provided by Jupiter, interpreted by the soothsayer; in *The Winter's Tale,* by Apollo's oracle; in *The Tempest,* by Prospero's and Ariel's epiphanic pronouncements.

1676. LONG, JOHN H. *Shakespeare's Use of Music: The Final Comedies.* Gainesville: University of Florida Press, 1961, 159 pp.

Observes that Shakespeare uses music in the comedies to underscore climactic or crucial scenes, to render supernatural effects more sharply, and to symbolize abstract or psychological ideas. All three uses converge in the romances, dealing with a character's recognition of a truth concerning divine providence. Pericles's perception of divine in-

General Studies

tercession, for example, is signaled by the music of the spheres; so, too, music in *Cymbeline* occurs when members of Posthumous's family importune Jupiter's intercession. Music throughout the romances is used to indicate harmony within oneself, between men, or between men and the gods.

1677. McFarland, Thomas. *Shakespeare's Pastoral Comedy*. Chapel Hill: University of North Carolina Press, 1972, 218 pp.

Argues that the pastoral element is not merely superimposed on comedy by Shakespeare but is fused with it to create a stronger and deeper vision of life uniquely capable of artistically depicting a paradise. In Shakespeare's pastoral comedies the common thematic thread is that characters must come to terms with the reciprocity of social and religious concerns. The stuff of tragedy at the outset of *As You Like It*, transferred to Arden, is softened to deviance and resolved by marriage. In *The Tempest* the ambience of the isle provides a favorable setting for transforming crimes to faults subject to correction by tempered punishment.

1678. Marshall, Cynthia. *Last Things and Last Plays: Shakespeare's Eschatology*. Carbondale: Southern Illinois University Press, 1991, 142 pp.

Maintains that Shakespeare's age was deeply involved with issues of apocalypticism, the anticipation of revelation and the expectation of imminent cosmic cataclysm in which the forces of evil will be overthrown. Such concerns are evident in Shakespeare's plays, especially in the romances, which pass through and beyond tragedy to a view of a purged and enlightened society. *Pericles, Cymbeline, The Winter's Tale,* and *The Tempest* are examined concerning questions of death, judgment, and afterlife.

1679. Mowat, Barbara A. *The Dramaturgy of Shakespeare's Romances*. Athens: University of Georgia Press, 1976, 163 pp.

Views Shakespeare's romances as a conscious blend of representational and presentational modes, creating "open form" drama with special theatrical experiences. Comic devices confront tragic passions; the realistic or mimetic action, the artificial or spectacular; the dramatic, the narrative. Generically, stylistically, dramaturgically, the romances combine the joy and vivacity of romantic comedy with the passion and power of the tragedies. Individual chapters are devoted to *Cymbeline, The Winter's Tale,* and *The Tempest*.

1680. Nevo, Ruth. *Shakespeare's Other Language*. New York and London: Methuen, 1988, 170 pp.

Finds the most striking aspect of the romances to be their assault upon our credulity coupled with the incomparable realism of the characterization. Individual chapters are included on *Pericles, Cymbeline, The Winter's Tale,* and *The Tempest.* Freud's study of dreams provides the point of analysis for *The Winter's Tale,* yielding a structural model with which to address the two halves or interrelated plots of the play (one a terror ineluctably realized, the other a restitutive wish fulfillment). *The Tempest* is viewed as Shakespeare's most indissolubly tragicomic drama, depicting "the pain both of renunciation itself and of the knowledge of the dark backward and abysm of love" (p. 152).

1681. PETERSON, DOUGLAS L. *Time, Tide, and Tempest: A Study of Shakespeare's Romances.* San Marino: Huntington Library, 1973, 259 pp.

Argues that Shakespeare in the romances was not following the style of Beaumont and Fletcher or retreating into the happy comedy of his youth but instead was seeking for an effective manner of dealing with metaphysical and epistemological problems broached by the tragedies. The result, a radically new form of tragicomedy, by appropriating the improbable fictions of romance to plots depicting genuinely destructive evil celebrates the restorative power of human love in the vision of a morally coherent universe that defies growing Jacobean skepticism.

1682. SMITH, HALLETT. *Shakespeare's Romances: A Study of Some Ways of the Imagination.* San Marino: Huntington Library, 1972, 244 pp.

Views the romances as a natural outgrowth of Shakespeare's experience in writing comedy and tragedy. Full of theatrical spectacle and elaborate devices, these plays were written with an eye for the court and the private stage as well as for the Globe. Particular attention is also directed to the heroine, her symbolic names, the relationship between her innocence and pastoralism, and to the romantic tradition in general. In the tragedies and problem comedies, the sacrifice of the younger generation leads to redemption and salvation. In the romances, in which the appearance is evil but the reality is good, the younger generation is the full recipient of the cathartic wisdom and joy of the older.

1683. THORNDIKE, ASHLEY H. *The Influence of Beaumont and Fletcher upon Shakespeare.* Worcester: Wood, 1901, 176 pp.

Maintains that the romances written by Beaumont and Fletcher and by Shakespeare were not the end results of the development of current forms or of manifest dramatic tendencies, but were an altogether new artistic form. An examination of the order of composition of the plays and especially of the influence of *Philaster* on *Cymbeline* reveals that Beaumont and Fletcher initiated this movement and that Shakespeare was their debtor. Shakespeare, writing with a keen eye for theatrical success, was willing to adapt his work to follow current fashions, and this fashion under his genius produced *The Winter's Tale* and *The Tempest*.

1684. Tillyard, E. M. W. *Shakespeare's Last Plays*. London: Chatto & Windus, 1938, 85 pp.

Views Shakespeare's purpose in the romances as to supplement tragedy, a process begun in *Antony and Cleopatra* and *Coriolanus*. This concentration on the regenerative process in tragedy involves a destruction of the old order and the reshaping into a new. Specifically, the pattern in each romance moves from prosperity to destruction to recreation. The motifs of repentance and regeneration lend a tone of religious mystery.

1685. TRAVERSI, DEREK A. *Shakespeare: The Last Phase*. New York: Harcourt, Brace, 1954, 272 pp.

Stresses the significance in the romances of poetic drama, a movement away from realism and toward a subsuming of character and action in a symbolic unity or expanded image. The dominant pattern is a movement from loss to reconciliation, involving the "divisions created in love and friendship by the passage of time and the action of 'blood' and of the final healing of these divisions" (p. 107). Characters and the situation in *The Tempest*, the logical consumption of Shakespeare's art, are clearly symbolic with tragedy of human passion followed by trial issuing in redemption.

1686. UPHAUS, ROBERT W. *Beyond Tragedy: Structure and Experience in Shakespeare's Romances*. Lexington: University Press of Kentucky, 1981, 150 pp.

Argues that Shakespeare's romances develop a concept of life beyond tragedy by placing a greater value upon the process of the life cycle than upon individual life. Inherent to this continuing cycle is a sense in which time is reversible and characters are offered a means of expiation short of death. *Pericles* is a skeletal romance, utilizing all of the features but without counterpoint or complication. *Cymbeline* parodies the very conventions upon which it is constructed. *The Winter's Tale* invests the elements of romance with a profound human significance by directly juxtaposing the tragic perspective of acts 1–3 with the providential view of act 5 and developing the pastoral comedy of act 4 as a means of transition between the two. *The Tempest* enacts the imaginative descent of the experience of romance into areas more accessible to reason.

1687. WARREN, ROGER. *Staging Shakespeare's Late Plays.* Oxford: Clarendon Press, 1990, 264 pp.

Focuses on rehearsals of *Pericles, Cymbeline,* and *The Winter's Tale* in 1986 at the Shakespeare Festival in Stratford, Ontario, those in 1987 of *Cymbeline, The Winter's Tale,* and *The Tempest* at the National Theatre in London, and those of *Pericles* in 1989 at the Royal Shakespeare Company in Stratford, England. The common link that emerged was that all of those late plays build on the technique of combining a highly fictive, overtly theatrical quality with "point-blank" projection of emotional reality to dramatize a spiritual journey in the character. Also, an unusually realistic emphasis on suffering and affliction demonstrated that in these works the comedy is defined by tragedy.

1688. YATES, FRANCES A. *Shakespeare's Last Phase: A New Approach.* London: Routledge & Kegan Paul, 1975, 140 pp.

Theorizes that the imagery of the last plays directly relates them to a conscious and nostalgic revival of Elizabethanism centered on Prince Henry and Elizabeth, children of James I. *Cymbeline,* for example, is seen symbolically as a reenactment of the Tudor mythology, and the analysis of *Henry VIII* focuses on imperial reform. The mystical atmosphere of the romances suggests the influence of the Rosicrucian movement in Germany, and in Prospero one sees a renewed respect for the magus figure.

CYMBELINE

Reference Work

1689. JACOBS, HENRY E., COMP. *Cymbeline.* Garland Reference Library of the Humanities, Garland Shakespeare Bibliographies, 3. New York and London: Garland Publishing, 1982, 591 pp.

Contains 1,379 annotated entries, representing virtually all publications on the play from 1940 through 1980, along with the most significant items of scholarship prior to 1940. The categories, each arranged chronologically, are criticism, sources, dating, textual studies, bibliographies, editions, productions, and translations. A brief introductory essay traces the history of recent criticism and research.

Editions

1690. FURNESS, HENRY HOWARD, ed. *The Tragedie of Cymbeline*. A New
Variorum Edition of Shakespeare. Philadelphia: J. B. Lippincott, 1913,
523 pp.
Uses the First Folio as the copy text. On each page, for that
portion of the text, are provided variant readings, textual notes, and
general critical commentary. Following the text are sections on the date
of composition, the sources, the text of Durfey's version, and criticisms.

1691. MAXWELL, J. C., ed. *Cymbeline*. Cambridge: Cambridge University
Press, 1960, 246 pp.
Provides extensive textual notes, a critical introduction (covering
matters of date and authenticity, sources, and the play itself), a discussion of the copy text, a section on stage history, and a glossary. This
edition is based on the First Folio, for which the copy was probably a
transcript of the promptbook. The term *tragicomedy* effectively describes
the play's unusual combination of elements; the serious matter is undercut by the comic and pastoral. It is concerned with loss and recovery,
reconciliation and rebirth, a sense of the deeper rhythms of life.

1692. NOSWORTHY, J. M., ed. *Cymbeline*. The Arden Shakespeare. London:
Methuen; Cambridge, Mass.: Harvard University Press, 1955, 216 pp.
Includes discussion of the text, sources, authenticity, the experimental quality, style, imagery, significance, the relationship to *Philaster,*
and literary interpretations, as well as appendixes featuring information
on the stage history and the songs and selections from Holinshed and
other sources. The text is based on the First Folio, for which the copy
was probably a scribe's transcript of foul papers which had preceded the
promptbook and were difficult to read. Shakespeare, in fashioning
a straightforward romantic plot, apparently worked from a variety
of sources without a reputable model, one that influenced Fletcher's
Philaster.

Criticism

1693. BROCKBANK, J. P. "History and Histrionics in *Cymbeline.*" *Shakespeare
Survey* 11 (1958):42–49.
Argues that *Cymbeline* should be regarded primarily as a historical
romance in that it attempts to express certain truth about the processes

that have shaped Britain's past. *Cymbeline,* more particularly, describes a brazen world transmuted to golden by the agency of miraculous providence. Along with *Henry VIII* it is the last chronicle fruits of Shakespeare's art. Cloten and the queen represent a range of views threatening the integrity of the court. Imogen represents all innocence that must pass through animal barbarism (Cloten) and duplicity (Posthumous); the agreement to pay tribute to Rome signals the approach of the Golden Age.

1694. BRUSTER, DOUGLAS. *"Cymbeline* and the Sudden Blow." *Upstart Crow* 10 (1990):101–12.
  Observes that in this play the inconsistencies of plot are insistently obtrusive, especially in the final act, so much so that the effect upon the spectators is often overtly humorous. In such scenes as that in which Imogen assumes the headless body of Cloten to be Posthumous (4.2) and that in which Posthumous mistakenly assaults Imogen (5.5), the playwright employs "self-conscious irony and its corollary, the spectator's cruel ridicule, as a means of foregrounding for the audience its cultural capacity for violence" (p. 103). In such a way, this melodrama of pre-Christian England projects a critical focus on the social consciousness of its Jacobean audiences.

1695. HIEATT, A. KENT. *"Cymbeline* and the Intrusion of Lyric into Romance Narrative: Sonnets, 'A Lover's Complaint,' Spenser's *Ruins of Rome."* In *Unfolded Tales: Essays on Renaissance Romance.* Edited by George M. Logan and Gordon Tesky. Ithaca and London: Cornell University Press, 1989, pp. 98–118.
  Considers the influence of the lyric on the tone and quality of *Cymbeline,* with its "romance patterns of figured calamity surmounted by transfigured fulfillment" (p. 117). Possibly the enforced inactivity of plague years (like those of 1592–94) and his concern with the publication of his most important nondramatic work (the sonnets in 1609), led Shakespeare to a preoccupation with the lyric at the time he was writing *Cymbeline* (1609–10). In the play he envisions Rome achieving a kind of external pacification, a perpetuation of the Roman concept of order and universalism. But the path to such achievement is not the heroic but the softer qualities of conciliation and rapprochement.

1696. HOENIGER, F. DAVID. "Irony and Romance in *Cymbeline." Studies in English Literature 1500–1900* 2 (1962):219–28.
  Argues that the pervasively ironic perspective in *Cymbeline* affects the play's characterization and tone, its structure, and its vision. Dramatic irony may be comforting and amusing in matters such as the

Cymbeline

spectators' knowledge of the true identity of the king's sons, but it is something else again when it provokes Imogen's despair over the headless body of what she presumes to be Posthumous but we know to be Cloten or when it underscores the vulnerability of honest women in the bedchamber scene. Only at the end does mockery yield to vision, appearance to reality and joy, as irony dissolves into romance.

1697. JONES, EMRYS. "Stuart *Cymbeline.*" *Essays in Criticism* 11 (1961):84–99.

Acknowledges that *Cymbeline* appears to abound in wild incongruities and apparent absurdities. For Shakespeare's audience, however, the play had special meaning. Not only does the action of the play, moving from division and war to harmony and peace, prepare historically for the universal time of peace at Christ's birth; it also pays topical tribute to James's strenuous peacemaking policy. The arrival of James was a fulfillment of prophecy; a second Arthur, uniting England and Scotland, James delighted in also being called a second Augustus, the pacific emperor under whom Christ was born.

1698. KIRSCH, ARTHUR C. "*Cymbeline* and Coterie Dramaturgy." *ELH* 34 (1967):285–306.

Maintains that the characteristics of *Cymbeline* and other romances are determined in part through the developing pattern of drama in the private theater. Central to such drama is the principle of discontinuity, a sensationally mingled tone creating both empathy and critical detachment. *Cymbeline* is experimental, exploring the techniques and implications of self-conscious dramaturgy in Posthumous's sudden change and counterchange, the arrant villainy of Iachimo, the melodramatic exploitation of Imogen's distress, and the bewildering montage of events.

1699. LAWRENCE, JUDIANA. "Natural Bonds and Artistic Coherence in the Ending of *Cymbeline.*" *Shakespeare Quarterly* 35 (1984):440–60.

Considers the concluding scenes of *Cymbeline* to be neither straight romance nor parody, but an examination of the means and ends of fiction. Balancing on the edge between solemnity and farce, these scenes hold in delicate suspense a response of affirmation and skepticism, a tension between engagement and detachment that informs all of Shakespeare's work and much of the literary output of the Renaissance. The play's ironic and elusive tone constitutes through its constant emphasis on chance and changed perceptions an artistic triumph over both the unreality of the mode and the rigidity of its form.

1700. LEWIS, CYNTHIA. " 'With Simular Proof Enough': Modes of Misperception in *Cymbeline.*" *Studies in English Literature 1500–1900* 31 (1991):343–64.

Argues that the play in the opening scene broaches a theme of misperception that it reiterates throughout the plot. Before the conclusion, nearly every character has been duped at least once, as has the spectator. Despite this complex interweaving of blindness and revenge, however, Shakespeare "decidedly settles on faith as the only viable means to living harmonious spiritual and social lives"; by blinding us at every turn, *Cymbeline* "fools us into seeing anew" (p. 361).

1701. MARSH, D. R. C. *The Recurring Miracle: A Study of "Cymbeline" and the Last Plays.* Pietermaritzburg: University of Natal Press, 1962, 197 pp.

Argues that *Cymbeline* is an affirmation of life, revealing death to be an illusion primarily through the influence of Imogen as the active agent of truth and her role in the restoration of the younger generation. Neither botched work as a trial run for later drama nor the effects of boredom, *Cymbeline,* like all the romances, is a stylized examination of love as self-denial and self-discipline that produces a miraculous sense of renewal.

1702. PARKER, PATRICIA. "Romance and Empire: Anachronistic *Cymbeline.*" In *Unfolded Tales: Essays on Renaissance Romance.* Edited by George M. Logan and Gordon Tesky. Ithaca and London: Cornell University Press, 1989, pp. 189–206.

Insists that the anachronism involved in Iachimo as both a contemporary Italian "jay" and a nobleman of ancient Rome is central to the play's meaning. Throughout the plot Posthumous is linked to Virgil's Aeneas, and he moves through a dizzying series of exchanges of national identity, as does Imogen in her service as a page in the employment of Rome. By the end of the play the strident British nationalism of Cloten and the queen has been eliminated. Cymbeline, though victorious in battle, pays tribute to Rome, but at the same time Iachimo bows in submission to Posthumous. Thus, the anachronism embodies both Rome's victory in history but also the later passing of true Roman virtue to England.

1703. SIMONDS, PEGGY MUÑOZ. "The Marriage Topos in *Cymbeline:* Shakespeare's Variations on a Classical Theme." *English Literary Renaissance* 19 (1989):94–117.

Insists that a knowledge of Renaissance emblem literature clarifies the significance of Posthumous's line to Imogen, "Hang thou like fruit my soul, / Till the tree die" (5.5.263–64), and the loving embrace that follows. The lines derive from the marriage topos of the elm and the vine. But the fact that Imogen, as bride, is still dressed as a boy suggests, as well, the need for friendship between man and wife as social equals. Drawing on additional emblems, Shakespeare depicts her as no longer merely the clinging vine embraced by her husband but as one who "is finally accepted in public as a human and living symbol of divine friendship and of Posthumous's own immortal soul" (p. 115).

1704. SMITH, WARREN D. "Cloten with Caius Lucius." *Studies in Philology* 49 (1952):185–94.

Argues that Cloten is not inconsistent as a despicable lout who suddenly assumes political prudence in refusing to pay tribute to Rome, that in defying Rome and advocating war he is acting contrary to the desires of Cymbeline. His attitude toward Lucius, moreover, directly opposes the traditional courtesy afforded visiting dignitaries, and all of his speeches fall far below the ideal of modesty. This behavior is totally consistent with his villainous character elsewhere in the play.

1705. SOLWAY, DAVID. "Intoxicated Words: Language in Shakespeare's Late Romances." *Sewanee Review* 95 (1987):619–25.

Suggests that the worlds evoked in the romances are essentially prelapsarian and that we view them at that critical moment of disjuncture when the serpent of reality effects its entry. From that moment, too, language is corrupted, its purpose now being to possess a throne or a woman, to extort obedience, to experience revenge, to acquire riches. The sickness that Camillo tells Polixenes of is diseased language; it is Paulina with "words as medicinal as true" who acts as the agent of reconciliation.

1706. THORNE, WILLIAM BARRY. "*Cymbeline*: 'Lopp'd Branches' and the Concept of Regeneration." *Shakespeare Quarterly* 20 (1960):143–59.

Views *Cymbeline* as a sophisticated extension of themes from the early comedies interweaving a serious element in that, with its folk materials and national orientation, it is deliberately holding up a glass to Elizabethan culture. It is "a patriotic affirmation of national unity and a sentimental extolling of established social mores" (p. 144). Concerned with the restoration of both the king and his realm, the action is not unlike that of a mummers' play with its mock ritualistic death. Impulses toward regeneration and reconciliation in the young transcend the evil forces within and without and revitalize the whole kingdom.

PERICLES

Reference Work

1708. MICHAEL, NANCY J. *"Pericles": An Annotated Bibliography*. Garland Reference Library of the Humanities, 424: Garland Shakespeare Bibliographies, 13. New York and London: Garland Publishing, 1987, 289 pp.

Contains 816 items, representing virtually all publications on the play from 1940 to 1985, along with the most significant items prior to 1940. The categories, each arranged chronologically, include criticism, sources and analogues and background, dating, authorship, textual studies, bibliographies and concordances, editions, stage history and recorded performances, and adaptations (influences, synopses, excerpts). A brief introductory essay traces the history of recent criticism and research.

Editions

1708. HOENIGER, F. DAVID, ed. *Pericles*. The Arden Shakespeare. London: Methuen; Cambridge, Mass.: Harvard University Press, 1963, 188 pp.

Includes discussion of the text, sources, authorship, stage history, and literary interpretations, as well as appendixes featuring material from Lawrence Twine, evidence for collaboration with John Day, conjectural reconstructions of episodes, and conjectural rearrangements of verse. The text is based on the first quarto (1609), from which the third folio is derived. Since the quarto text is seriously corrupt, Hoeniger has adopted emendations whenever a reading can be attributed convincingly to compositor's error. The majority of contemporary critics believe Shakespeare had little or nothing to do with acts 1–2 but that he wrote either completely or in large part acts 3–4.

1709. MAXWELL, J. C., ed. *Pericles*. Cambridge: Cambridge University Press, 1956, 211 pp.

Provides extensive textual notes, a critical introduction (covering the story, the problem of authorship, Shakespeare's contribution), a discussion of the copy text, a section on stage history, and a glossary. This edition is based on the first quarto, for which the copy was probably a bad quarto resulting from memorial reconstruction. George Wilkins's novel *The Painfull Adventures of Pericles Prince of Tyre* (1608) was most likely based on the same version of the play that the quarto reports.

Criticism

1710. ARTHOS, JOHN. *"Pericles, Prince of Tyre:* A Study in the Dramatic Use of Romantic Narrative." *Shakespeare Quarterly* 4 (1953):257–70.

Advocates approaching *Pericles* as a structurally sound plot in order to focus on how Shakespeare was turning romantic narrative material to dramatic use. The play explores a wide world stocked with mysteries and riddles, and its fundamental wisdom rests in Pericles's trials testing his patience to the utmost. It explores, also, a world of miracles and visions that resonate with something beyond the immediacy of our flawed existence. Gower's choruses lend a fictive distance, placing the story far in the past and triggering our willing suspension of disbelief.

1711. BARBER, C. L. " 'Thou That Beget'st Him That Did Beget': Transformation in *Pericles* and *The Winter's Tale.*" *Shakespeare Survey* 22 (1969):59–67.

Notes that, whereas the festive comedies stress freeing the younger generation from the blockage of the older, the romances involve reconciliation of the two. In both *Pericles* and *The Winter's Tale* the recovery of a daughter precipitates the discovery of a wife. In the process Marina and Perdita temporarily become objects of wonder to a father, and the relationship prepares the father for a penitent reunion and reconciliation with his family.

1712. CRAIG, HARDIN. *"Pericles* and *The Painfull Adventures.*" *Studies in Philology* 45 (1948):600–605.

Calls recent neglect of *Pericles* surprising, considering that a novel exists by George Wilkins based on the play. Wilkins apparently worked from notes based on a theatrical performance. The notable difference in the handling of the brothel scenes suggests that the play was revised after Wilkins wrote his account. These revised sections are universally attributed to Shakespeare. Probably the extant text of *Pericles* is not a bad quarto, but a "painstaking and successful revision." (p. 604).

1713. CUTTS, JOHN P. "Pericles' 'Downright Violence.' " *Shakespeare Studies* 4 (1968):275–93.

Asserts that Pericles is not an innocent Job-like plaything of fortune but instead is flawed with impetuosity, rashness, and infatuation. Imagistically, from the first of the play until his reunion with Marina at which time he hears the music of the spheres, he destroys musical harmony. The five knights who vie with him at Antiochus's tournament emblematically suggest the stages through which he has passed. Only Marina's song triggers his sympathy for another and prompts him to stop boasting of his great endurance. Impurities are purged at Diana's temple, and his acknowledged infirmities glorify the blessed gods.

1714. DICKEY, STEPHEN. "Language and Role in *Pericles.*" *English Literary Renaissance* 16 (1986):550–56.

Maintains that the characterization of Gower and Pericles illuminates the "romance aura of improbability and glimmers of psychological motivation and self-conscious action" (p. 550). Gower, for example, pointedly calls attention to the personal cost involved in his story. Moreover, his moral certitude and feigned humility are registered as well in the character of Pericles. Both view themselves as long-suffering and virtuous (patient, generous, self-sacrificial); both are tinged with a degree of condescension, Gower to the spectators, Pericles to his fellow characters.

1715. FELPERIN, HOWARD. "Shakespeare's Miracle Play." *Shakespeare Quarterly* 18 (1967):363–74.

Focuses on the marked dramaturgic changes that occur in *Pericles* and set the scene for the other romances. Projecting a beneficent supernature that presides over the natural world of action, *Pericles* is a kind of idealized *Everyman*, reflecting in Pericles's personal experiences the universal condition of mankind. Here, however, the salvation is translated into an earthly destiny, the fruit of faith, charity, chastity, and patience. Each of the late plays fuses elements of allegorical-religious drama with elements of naturalistic-secular drama.

1716. GLAZOV-CORRIGAN, ELENA. "The New Function of Language in Shakespeare's *Pericles:* Oath versus 'Holy Word.'" *Shakespeare Survey* 43 (1990):131–40.

Observes that Shakespeare in this play reexamines the power of language. Facing stark misfortunes, Pericles refuses to speak; when he does speak again, it is a language of "amazement, suspense, and celebration" (p. 131). A spate of oaths by Pericles, Cleon, and Leonine suggests an important and sentimental anger against the gods. It is only after the protagonist has been tutored by Marina that he learns that the real power of language to restore comes from a nurture of the inner self,

Pericles

a reawakening of trust in the capacity of language to elicit a mutual response from another.

1717. GREENFIELD, THELMA N. "A Re-Examination of the 'Patient' Pericles." *Shakespeare Studies* 3 (1967):51–61.
Notes that, whereas recent critics have focused on Pericles's patience, the more salient feature is his wisdom, his ability to survive as a solver of riddles and a master of escape. Like Odysseus and Oedipus, Pericles travels and learns to use his wits. Marina reenacts this role through her dangerous adventures and, sharing his virtue, is the true heir to the father. To overstress Pericles's patience is to minimize his courage and wisdom that help him to endure his tribulations.

1718. HILLMAN, RICHARD. "Shakespeare's Gower and Gower's Shakespeare: The Larger Debt of *Pericles.*" *Shakespeare Quarterly* 36 (1985):427–37.
Describes the role of Gower as the most sustained literary allusion to be found in Shakespeare. We warm to him as a character in part because he is a moment of living tradition in English poetry. More significantly, the *Confessio Amantis* furnishes Shakespeare a paradigmatic source in its use of love themes to explore larger issues of human spirituality and self-realization, namely, the "distinction between vain and selfish *amor,* bound up with self-delusion, and the *caritas* through which the sufferer finally becomes reconciled to himself and reintegrated into the human condition" (p. 428).

1719. HOENIGER, F. DAVID. "Gower and Shakespeare in *Pericles.*" *Shakespeare Quarterly* 33 (1982):461–79.
Argues that the immense popularity of *Pericles* in Shakespeare's day and the strikingly successful productions of the past thirty years must make us question the academic quibbling about the character and the action. The effect of Gower as chorus is one of enchantment, and the sense of illusion remains strong even after he calls actors upon the stage. With him on stage on six subsequent occasions, the action seems to be a series of adventures or spectacles, a show of colorful episodes. Shakespeare in recreating an old tale turned, in large part, to imitating the very manner of early storytelling.

1720. SOKOL, B. J. "William Shakespeare: Sole Author of *Pericles.*" *English Studies.* 71 (1990):230–43.
Maintains that Shakespeare is the author of the entire play. The essay is built on the evidence that the imagery and theme present a coherent whole that argues a single hand, that the disputed first half of the play contains too many echoes of earlier and later Shakespeare for

it to be by any other author, that the versification of the first half shares undisputable Shakespearean elements, and that demonstrably the much-debated question of sources and earlier versions can be resolved with Gower and Twine as source and Shakespeare as author.

1721. THOMPKINS, J. M. S. "Why *Pericles?" Review of English Studies,* n.s. 3 (1952):315–24.
   Questions why Shakespeare chose to write *Pericles* immediately after his most profound tragedies. The admitted financial success, its popularity, its affinity with the romances to come—nothing explains why he opted to develop this old-fashioned play with its chronological sequence of disconnected adventures and its virtually static protagonist. Perhaps in working up Coriolanus and Alcibiades from Plutarch he took note of the two patient men (Pericles and Fabius Maximus) who were juxtaposed with the impatient and determined to dramatize in *Pericles* the patience that saves.

THE TEMPEST

Reference Work

1722. MARDER, LOUIS, COMP. *"The Tempest": A Supplementary Bibliography 1892–1965.* The New Variorum Shakespeare. New York: American Scholar Publications, 1965, 23 pp.
   Includes representative scholarship on *The Tempest* from 1892 to 1965 and is intended to supplement H. H. Furness's Variorum edition of 1892. The material is categorized under reproductions of original folio editions, bibliographical sources, modern editions, and critical studies (arranged alphabetically). While not exhaustive, the material represents every major category of scholarship and criticism.

Editions

1723. KERMODE, FRANK, ed. *The Tempest.* The Arden Shakespeare. London: Methuen; Cambridge, Mass.: Harvard University Press, 1954, 173 pp.
   Includes discussion of the text, date, themes of the play, the concept of the New World, of nature, of art, pastoral tragicomedy, anal-

ogous literature, structure, verse, and critical interpretations; appendixes on Ariel, Montaigne, music, lineation, and critical interpretations; and selections from Strachey, Jourdain, and Ovid (Golding's translation). The text is based on the First Folio, for which the copy was probably a transcript by Ralph Crane of Shakespeare's foul papers. The New World stimulated interest in nature; the events of 1609 (the voyage of the Virginia Company) seem to embrace the whole situation.

1724. ORGEL, STEPHEN, ed. *The Tempest*. The Oxford Shakespeare. Oxford and New York: Oxford University Press, 1987, 248 pp.

Includes an introductory essay addressing first appearances, the genre, readings and interpretations, wives and mothers, magic, Caliban, suitors and rapist, the Renaissance political context (political marriages, Utopia and the New World, authority), epic and history (Italy and Carthage, Jacobean court spectacles, the masque as image and symbol, renunciation and resolution), the text, the date, and the play on the stage. Extensive notes on each page of the text address specific problems of language and interpretation and provide background information.

1725. QUILLER-COUCH, ARTHUR, AND WILSON, JOHN DOVER, eds. *The Tempest*. Cambridge: Cambridge University Press, 1921, 116 pp.

Provides extensive textual notes, a critical introduction, and a glossary. This edition is based on the First Folio, for which the copy was Shakespeare's foul papers that had served as a promptbook. An additional general introduction offers a historical sketch of criticism and an analysis of the state of textual research.

Criticism

1726. ABRAMS, RICHARD. "*The Tempest* and the Concept of the Machiavellian Playwright." *English Literary Renaissance* 8 (1978):43–66.

Compares the playwright to a Machiavellian politician, capable through role casting of manipulating artistic time just as history is subject to manipulation. Prospero, who identifies himself with the author through references to "my project" in the epilogue, is a powerful protagonist, standing behind the action as a supernatural force and prime mover. Manipulating the action against Antonio, who himself has seized his dukedom through Machiavellian means, Prospero acts as a benevolent despot; but like the playwright he realizes that he can sustain the dreamworld for only a short time.

1727. BARKER, FRANCIS, AND HULME, PETER. "Nymphs and Reapers Heavily Vanish: The Discursive Con-Texts of *The Tempest.*" In *Alternative Shakespeares*. Edited by John Drakakis. London and New York: Methuen, 1985, pp. 191–205.

Views English colonialism as the play's dominant discursive con-texts ("the precondition of the play's historical and political significa-tion" [p. 195]). Prospero's protasis establishes his rule, dependent upon Caliban's enslavement to supply food and water. The plot attempts to set forth the legitimacy of this action by displacing a series of actual or attempted usurpations of authority. Prospero's peculiar irritation over Caliban's conspiracy signals perhaps an "unconscious anxiety concern-ing the grounding of his legitimacy" (p. 202), bringing to the surface the repressed contradiction between his role as usurped and usurper.

1728. BELTON, ELLEN R. " 'When No Man Was His Own': Magic and Self-Discovery in *The Tempest.*" *University of Toronto Quarterly* 55 (1985):127–40.

Observes that Prospero succeeds in manipulating nature through magic but has little success in provoking genuine repentance in the surrounding figures. Prospero's real aim, however, is through a series of trances (a world of imagination, of spiritual wholeness, of visionary reality) to free the self from the conventional restraints of rationality and ignorance of its own condition and "to give each character a chance to recognize and to affirm or change his own nature" (p. 135). Pros-pero himself through the incantatory quality of his final speeches also undergoes an experience that will generate his forgiveness of others.

1729. BERGER, KAROL. "Prospero's Art." *Shakespeare Studies* 10 (1977):211–39.

Compares Prospero's art to Ficino's theories of music in that it centers on man's imagination through the instrument of the spirit, utilizing the imagery of both words and music to transmit its influ-ences. The garment, staff, and book are also characteristic of Ficinian magic. While Prospero could easily have avenged himself through his power, his "political wisdom" is his recognition of the necessity of forgiveness and of leading the surrounding figures (Alonso, Miranda) to similar action.

1730. BLACK, JAMES. "The Latter End of Prospero's Commonwealth." *Shake-speare Survey* 43 (1990):29–41.

Suggests that Prospero's intention from the beginning is to de-velop for Miranda a marriage plot anchored in realism. Prospero creates the opportunity for her to be alone with Ferdinand where her defiance of her father in pitying the young man is part of her growth toward independence. He ultimately will give up his book in exchange for the Neapolitan royal house, of which Miranda will be a part. Realist enough not to believe in myths of renewal, he knows little has changed in Sebastian and Antonio, but that Miranda's future must be secured. Wrongs must be forgiven and forgotten; "the end of his commonwealth must forget the beginning" (p. 41).

1731. BRIGHT, CURT. " 'Treason Doth Never Prosper': *The Tempest* and the Discourse of Treason." *Shakespeare Quarterly* 41 (1990):1–28.

Reads the play as a "politically radical intervention in a dominant contemporary . . . discourse of treason that became an increasingly central response to difficult social problems in late Elizabethan and early Jacobean London" (p. 1). The English government practiced domination based on coercion, and *The Tempest,* while on the surface seeming to embrace official discourse by depicting treason as never prospering, in reality forces the spectators to observe the blatant manipulation of people and events to effect their containment. Prospero stage-manages the series of conspiracies "to produce a bunch of Calibans" (p. 19). The humiliated lower-class conspirators serve as a grim object lesson for Prospero's upper-class enemies.

1732. BROCKBANK, PHILIP. *"The Tempest:* Conventions in Art and Empire." In *Later Shakespeare.* Edited by John Russell Brown and Bernard Harris. Stratford-upon-Avon Studies, 8. London: Edward Arnold, 1966, pp. 183–202.

Views *The Tempest* as complex allegory dealing simultaneously with the social and moral nature of man, with providential design, and with the aims and methods of art itself. Moral growth is envisioned as a seasonal process requiring strange mutations and interventions of magical nature imposed by a figure who is at once godlike and theatrical. Harmony in the world can be achieved only by allowing to providence and to Prospero the powers of a playwright skilled in masque. Beyond the play Antonio and Sebastian will return to their hard nature in Milan and Prospero will return to human vulnerability.

1733. BROWER, REUBEN A. "The Heresy of Plot." In *English Institute Essays 1951.* Edited by Alan S. Downer. New York: Columbia University Press, 1952, pp. 44–69.

Describes the heresy of plot as the Aristotelian tendency to discuss elements of drama in abstract terms, in isolation from the other structures that exist in the play. *The Tempest,* 5.1, effectively illustrates how words and action combine to achieve the effect of dramatic fact and metaphorical qualification. Prospero describes the behavior of the king and his courtiers as they are released from the magic spell. The metaphoric sea change is fully experienced only in the atmosphere of music and songs and dissolving storm. While the Aristotelian sense directs us to technical movements, the modern sense of "poetic" directs us to a perception of the close interactions of meaning at various levels.

1734. BROWN, PAUL. " 'This Thing of Darkness I Acknowledge Mine': *The Tempest* and the Discourse of Colonialism." In *Political Shakespeare: New Essays in Cultural Materialism*. Edited by Jonathan Dollimore and Alan Sinfield. Ithaca and London: Cornell University Press, 1985, pp. 48–71.

Charges that the play serves as a "limit text" of colonial discourse reflecting exploitation, beleaguerment, and radical ambivalence. In the accounts of colonial expansion of British interests, groups as divergent as the Negro, the Amerindians, and the Irish are often considered bestial, marginal, and irreformable; such discourse transformed savage killing into the triumph of civility. *The Tempest* opens with the disruption of social deference and elementary harmony that will be settled by the operation of Prospero's power and his division of the inhabitants into the malleable and the irreformable.

1735. CARTELLI, THOMAS. "Prospero in Africa: *The Tempest* as Colonialist Text and Pretext." In *Shakespeare Reproduced: The Text in History and Ideology*. Edited by Jean Howard and Marion F. O'Connor. New York and London: Methuen, 1987, pp. 99–115.

Notes that *The Tempest* has made seminal contributions to the development of colonialist ideology in the literature of newly independent nations of Africa and the West Indies. Kenyan and West Indian writers draw from the play to depict Shakespeare as a purveyor of an ideology of white paternalism basic to the material aims of Western imperialism. It is still an essentially uneducable, bestial Caliban who survives modern adjustments in Western racial prejudices; it is still a blindly self-righteous, authoritarian Prospero who remains in Third World redactions.

1736. CHEYFITZ, ERIC. *The Poetics of Imperialism: Translation and Colonization from "The Tempest" to "Tarzan."* New York and Oxford: Oxford University Press, 1991, 202 pp.

Calls *The Tempest* a prologue for a significant body of literature that "represents, among other things, the violent history of imperialism in the Americas, a history of crimes from which the United States has yet to disentangle itself" (p. 23). The play, more specifically, conceives of power as eloquence, the power of class and literacy. The driving force of usurpation is seen as a displacement from domestic to foreign shores. The claim of property in Caliban figures Prospero's dependence on the slave for services that set his life-style apart from such work.

1737. CORFIELD, COSMO. "Why Does Prospero Abjure His 'Rough Magic'?" *Shakespeare Quarterly* 36 (1985):31–48.

Suggests that Prospero at the end of the play is an old man and spent mage who is morally required to return to the fold of humanity but whose magic has failed him and left him infinitely humiliated. As a magus Prospero must lead a strictly pure life to retain his powers. His original intention to exact vengeance on his enemies destroys that purity and debases his power, a diminution directly noticeable when the figures of the masque vanish. His decision to forgive his enemies represents his realization and admission that his impurities have destroyed his magic and that he must return to human society.

1738. DOBRÉE, BONAMY. *"The Tempest." Essays and Studies,* n.s. 5 (1952):13–25.

Admits that the romances must be considered as a group and that the general theme is the necessity of forgiveness as the rarer virtue. *The Tempest,* however, moves beyond this theme. Repentance and forgiveness seem to be fossils rather than active principles in the play. *The Tempest,* in a word, while grouped with the other plays, is not infused with the same sentiment about life. It is composed of the impulses of love and forgiveness, of fear of destiny and the immortality of our existence and the brutality of matter—all brought into a harmony that belies contradiction.

1739. EAGEN, ROBERT. " 'This Rough Magic': Perspectives of Art and Morality in *The Tempest." Shakespeare Quarterly* 23 (1972):171–82.

Argues that Prospero's mistake, as protagonist-magician-dramatist, is to uphold his warped view of morality by which he in his self-righteousness would purify Caliban, Antonio, Alonso, Sebastian, and even Ferdinand. Until Ariel forces him to relent, he is vengeful and vindictive. In drowning his book he drowns his idealism and joins the world of humanity. Yet, Prospero's and Shakespeare's project remains unfinished unless the spectators accept Prospero's vision of love as an act of love on their own part. Prospero, Shakespeare, and the spectators join at the end in a celebration of shared humanity.

1740. GILBERT, ALLAN. *"The Tempest:* Parallelism in Characters and Situations." *Journal of English and Germanic Philology* 14 (1915):63–74.

Calls attention to Shakespeare's doubling of action and character in *The Tempest* to reinforce by contrast or by similarity. Both Prospero and Gonzalo are virtuous men from the court, for example, but one for neglect of his duty in favor of retired study has brought evil on himself and others. Prospero and Sycorax exercise magical powers in diametrically different manners. Caliban and Ariel are contrasted as creatures beyond the human. The two conspiracies (Stephano, Trinculo, and Caliban against Prospero; Antonio and Sebastian against Alonso) emphasize one another even in details. The main theme is that people are good or bad by virtue of that which is within.

1741. GILLIES, JOHN. "Shakespeare's Virginian Masque." *ELH* 53 (1986):673–707.

Insists that, in its emphasis on self-discipline, its assumption that savagery must be contained through strict constraint, and its endorsement of power as a means to civilized prosperity, *The Tempest* mirrors both specific events of 1609 and also the mood which gave them significance. Raleigh's choice of the name Virginia, in effect, created a myth, "suggesting an attractive combination of innocence, docility, and quasi-erotic availability" (p. 678). The masque of Ceres posits a land of temperance and fruitfulness, but it is interrupted by Caliban, the inassimilable force of strangeness and mystery.

1742. GILMAN, ERNEST B. " 'All Eyes': Prospero's Inverted Masque." *Renaissance Quarterly* 33 (1980):214–30.

Suggests that the nuptial masque presented by Prospero for Ferdinand and Miranda shapes our response to the play as a whole, especially in the crucial factor of its sudden collapse and dissolution. The sequence of the disrupted masque followed by the reappearance of evil in Caliban constitutes an exact reversal of the contemporary court masque. This deliberate reversal of masque-antimasque motifs reflects the play's coherent structure by pointing us to the thematic center of the play—"that the cure for distemper lies not in withdrawing from time's sometimes violent jars but in tempering oneself to them" (p. 223).

1743. GRUDIN, ROBERT. "Prospero's Masque and the Structure of *The Tempest*." *South Atlantic Quarterly* 71 (1972):401–09.

Focuses on the masque in 4.1, in its language and its configuration of goddesses, as a mirror of Prospero's perspective in the first three acts and as an axis shifting his view to a more realistic one. Venus and Caliban, representing disruptive cosmic and human forces, are banished from the masque, a vision of nature purified by knowledge and art.

The Tempest

Following the masque, however, Prospero realizes social order requires that knowledge and art coexist with human baseness.

1744. HENZE, RICHARD. "*The Tempest:* Rejection of a Vanity." *Shakespeare Quarterly* 23 (1972):420–34.
Envisions a growth in Prospero that leads him to reject the masque as a vanity of his art in particular and the concept of a passive life that attempts to live apart from the world in general. He is able to make the island, a physical and symbolic representation of his ducal deficiencies, a place for blessed recognition; he returns to his dukedom a different man because he has learned patience, control of the flesh, and the necessary balance between learning and public responsibility.

1745. HILLMAN, RICHARD. "Chaucer's Franklin's Magician and *The Tempest*: An Influence beyond Appearances." *Shakespeare Quarterly* 34 (1983): 426–32.
Examines the relationship between Chaucer's "The Franklin's Tale" and *The Tempest*, both of which concern the role of generosity and compassion in ideal relationships and both of which include a scene of magical illusion with essentially the same words. The main magical event in Chaucer—an illusion of protection from shipwreck—virtually mirrors Prospero's trick. Both illusions of destruction become means of redemption in that each provokes a generous response from the magician himself. In both cases the magician is the agent of forgiveness as he releases his control; in both his role has providential overtones.

1746. HUNT, JOHN D. *A Critical Commentary on Shakespeare's "The Tempest."* London: Macmillan, 1968, 76 pp.
Observes that the ideal comprehension of a work of art mediates between a sense of the details and a retrospective view of the whole. *The Tempest* summarizes and recapitulates much of Shakespeare's vision of the world. The controlling theme of the play is art, both that of civil order and that of providence; it translates delight into instruction and philosophic speculation into entertainment.

1747. JAMES, DAVID GWILYM. *The Dream of Prospero.* Oxford: Clarendon Press, 1967, 174 pp.
Considers *The Tempest* Shakespeare's mature philosophic response to the dark vision of life expressed in *King Lear,* depicting in Prospero the tension between the love of the inner life and the desperate need of a culture for a spiritual basis. Chastened by his exile, Prospero will return to Europe and his political responsibilities, not because evil has been destroyed but because it will continue to exist and must be coun-

tered in the best manner possible by humane individuals willing to be involved in the public life. *The Tempest* does not negate the horror of *King Lear;* it asserts that man's answer must be conscientious constructive efforts and prayer rather than despair.

1748. JOHNSON, W. STACY. "The Genesis of Ariel." *Shakespeare Quarterly* 2 (1951):205–10.

Considers the Elizabethan belief that spirits are either affiliated in some way with God or Satan (medieval Christianity) or with a wise man ascending toward spiritual unity with the divine (Neoplatonism). Ariel's function is benevolent rather than diabolic. The name is that of an angelic epithet and, whatever its direct source, is appropriate for this creature of air. The spirit is primarily elemental, associated with the spirit-operated world of Neoplatonism, but Shakespeare endows him with the personality of a familiar and thus makes him more than merely inhuman.

1749. KNOX, BERNARD. *"The Tempest* and the Ancient Comic Tradition." In *English Institute Essays 1954.* Edited by W. K. Wimsatt, Jr. New York: Columbia University Press, 1955, pp. 52–73.

Observes that in *The Tempest* the fantasy and originality of the setting are counterbalanced by close adherence to tradition in character and plot. While the play projects the most fantastic of all Shakespeare's settings in its geographically unlocatable nameless isle, the pattern of action and character is a virtual paradigm of classical comedy. The old man with a marriageable daughter controls the other principals. Caliban and Ariel are variations of the clever servant. The action culminates in release, reconciliation, and marriage.

1750. MAGNUSSON, A. LYNNE. "Interruption in *The Tempest." Shakespeare Quarterly* 37 (1986):52–65.

Notes the recurrence of interruptions in the action, rifts in the plot, and suggests that Shakespeare employs this interruptive strategy to upset the fundamental expectation of the theater audience that a narrative form is being fulfilled. One such interruption occurs when Antonio and Sebastian deconstruct Gonzago's vision of the Golden Age. That pattern, in turn, reflects what happens in Prospero's relations with those on the island. He has hoped to create the idealized world that Gonzago describes. What he achieves through compromise falls far short of that since it is subject to destruction by the ill will of Antonio and Sebastian or the inexperience of Miranda and Ferdinand.

1751. MEBANE, JOHN S. "Magic as Love and Faith: Shakespeare's *The Tempest."* In *Renaissance Magic and the Return of the Golden Age: The Occult*

Tradition in Marlowe, Jonson, and Shakespeare. Lincoln: University of Nebraska Press, 1989, pp. 174–99.

Notes that in Prospero Shakespeare confirms the belief of the Renaissance magician that human art can become a vehicle of divine power. Prospero has obtained power to command the forces of nature through self-discipline, and in the course of the play he uses his power to move others to that same self-knowledge. His art renews the bonds uniting the human community by bringing "nature into conformity with the rational and spiritual planes of reality and thus with Providence" (p. 196). At the same time Prospero symbolizes the limitations of art; if humankind possess an indeterminate creative potential, it is not ultimately within the power of magic to effect proper human relationships.

1752. NUTTALL, ANTHONY DAVID. *Two Concepts of Allegory: A Study of Shakespeare's "The Tempest" and the Logic of Allegorical Expression*. London: Routledge & Kegan Paul; New York: Barnes & Noble, 1967, 175 pp.

Reviews and rejects nineteenth-century attempts to make *The Tempest* allegorical in the sense that a system of specified metaphysical significancies is consistently adumbrated in the text. Instead, the peculiar wedding of the marvelous and the circumstantial creates a "pre-allegorical" (p. 159) quality in which paradisiacal intuitions are undermined by a doubt about reality. The vision of Prospero may transcend objective facts, but it does not obliterate them. Shakespeare throughout the play fleshes out allegorical inclinations with a perceptive skepticism.

1753. ORGEL, STEPHEN. "Prospero's Wife." In *Rewriting the Renaissance: The Discourses of Sexual Difference in Early Modern Europe*. Edited by Margaret N. Ferguson, Maureen Quilligan, and Nancy J. Vickers. Chicago: University of Chicago Press, 1986, pp. 50–64.

Describes the absence of Prospero's wife as reflective of a larger subject, the absent and the unspoken in *The Tempest*. Prospero fills the space of the absent female with a series of surrogates—the witch Sycorax, the good child/wife Miranda, the obedient Ariel, the violently libidinized adolescent Ferdinand. In what appear to be acts of renunciation (his giving his daughter in marriage and his leaving the island), he actually increases his power through recouping his throne and through confirming and legitimizing the political alliance with Naples.

1754. PARIS, BERNARD J. "*The Tempest*: Shakespeare's Ideal Solution." In *Shakespeare's Personality*. Edited by Norman N. Holland, Sidney

Homan, and Bernard J. Paris. Berkeley and London: University of California Press, 1989, pp. 206–25.

Provides a Horneyan psychological reading of Prospero as, like Shakespeare, a man torn between a vengeful, aggressive, power-hungry side (masculine) and a forgiving, submissive, idealistic side (feminine). *The Tempest* embodies Shakespeare's ideal solution "because Prospero's magical powers permit him to satisfy his sadistic and vindictive impulses without sacrificing his moral nobility" (p. 210). He can enjoy the terror of his victims since he has not physically harmed them. When he gives up his magic, he assumes a self-effacing, conciliatory posture, a part of which is his forgiveness of the unrepentant Antonio and Sebastian.

1755. SEMON, KENNETH. "Shakespeare's Tempest: Beyond a Common Joy." *ELH* 40 (1973):24–43.

Describes the sense of wonder that infuses the play as a consequence of Prospero's magic and the sense of wonder experienced by the spectators when he gives over his magic at the end of the play to return to the ambiguities of a fully human life. The spectators enjoy with Prospero the therapeutic amazement he visits upon the European travelers during the storm, upon Ferdinand when he first meets Miranda, and upon Alonso when he discovers his son alive. Because of the shared level of perception throughout the play, the spectators also share his sense of mystery and apprehension for what awaits him beyond his art.

1756. SISSON, C. J. "The Magic of Prospero." *Shakespeare Survey* 11 (1958):70–77.

Describes the terrifyingly real quality of magic to Shakespeare and his contemporaries. Whereas Sycorax as a witch represents the world of black magic and the power of Satan, Prospero works in white magic, its power emanating from a study of the liberal arts. *The Tempest* is a companion play to *Measure for Measure,* in which a duke also dispenses justice by opposing wrongs by mysterious means. Both may have been designed to flatter King James through the image of the powerful and benevolent ruler.

1757. SKURA, MEREDITH ANNE. "Discourse and the Individual: The Case of Colonialism in *The Tempest.*" *Shakespeare Quarterly* 40 (1989):42–69.

Takes issue with new historicists who claim that English colonialism provides the discursive context for the play, that the drama served the political purpose of mystifying or justifying Prospero's power over Caliban. It seems not to matter that Caliban is nothing like the native American as described in travel reports, or that the play is *anticolonialist* to the degree it qualifies Prospero's scorn by showing Caliban's virtues. The greatest flaw, however, is that these critics falsify historical specificity by surrounding the play with a critical aura of what colonialism was like in 1625 or 1911, not 1611, when settlers did not possess enough power to euphemize and were concerned only with survival.

1758. STOLL, ELMER EDGAR. "The Tempest." *PMLA* 47 (1932):699–726.
    Denies the presence of allegorical intent in *The Tempest*. Ariel, sprung out of popular superstition, is simply an Elizabethan sprite, Caliban but a creature of earth, Prospero but a man with knowledge of magic, *The Tempest* but a play for stage enjoyment. Nor is the play serene, Shakespeare's harmonious farewell to his art. Critics who fail to perceive the ugly and the monstrous in the last plays are "not reading but reading in" (p. 723). A tendency to enjoy a mood of reverie has indeed grown upon the poet, and there is something less than vital, less than clear-cut.

1759. TRAISTER, BARBARA HOWARD. *The Magician in English Renaissance Drama.* Columbia: University of Missouri Press, 1984, 196 pp.
    Views Prospero as the most extensively drawn dramatic stage magus and the most vital to the themes and structure of the play. Indeed, the core of *The Tempest* is a series of five shows that Prospero produces ranging from the opening storm to the closing chess match between Ferdinand and Miranda. Having learned much about control and balance during his eleven years on the island, he utilizes the magic spectacles for didactic purposes, ultimately choosing to "remain human, despite all the weakness and danger human beings are subject to" (p. 142).

1760. TRAVERSI, DEREK A. "The Tempest." *Scrutiny* 16 (1949):127–57.
    Asserts that *The Tempest* represents a logical development in Shakespeare's symbolic technique in the last plays. While *The Winter's Tale* delineates characters in the process of an experience that will lead them to assume symbolic values, *The Tempest* begins after such an experience has already occurred, and the characters exist entirely in their symbolic function. Alonso, like Lear, becomes penitent, and Prospero declares that it is time for the past to be set aside for a harmony all the richer for their experience. Gonzalo as the voice of destiny proclaims a newborn vision of humanity, a second, redeemed, and reasonable life.

1761. VAUGHAN, ALDEN T. "Caliban in the 'Third World': Shakespeare's Savage as Sociopolitical Symbol." *Massachusetts Review* 29 (1988):289–313.

Explores the metaphoric use of Caliban in Latin American and African literature to reflect nationalistic reactions to Western imperialism. Depictions range from exploiter to exploited, from an image of all that is gross in a domineering nation to a victim of colonization, a rebellious and resilient survivor. A Latin-American example of the first is the Caliban of Jose Enrique Eodo, of the second, that of Anibal Ponce. African examples include Leonard Barnes and Mannoni. It is Shakespeare's quality of imprecision in the text that makes his island native so malleable to ideological and sociopolitical interpretation.

1762. ———. "Shakespeare's Indian: The Americanization of Caliban." *Shakespeare Quarterly* 39 (1988):137–53.

Traces the development of the idea that Caliban "reflects early Stuart England's perceptions of American natives and their complex interaction with European colonists" (p. 137) and how that concept has varied with changing sociopolitical climates. Sidney Lee in 1898 was the first unequivocally to claim the connection of Caliban and "the aboriginal savage of the New World," stating also that Bermuda is Prospero's island. Caliban as exploited native emerged in Leo Marx and Leslie Fiedler out of the sociopolitical upheavals of the 1960s and 1970s. In the last decade new historicists have viewed Caliban as a discursive matrix within which to see conceptions of the "Other" or alien.

1763. VAUGHAN, VIRGINIA. " 'Something Rich and Strange': Caliban's Theatrical Metamorphoses." *Shakespeare Quarterly* 36 (1985):390–405.

Traces the evolution of the characterization of Caliban from drunken beast to noble savage and missing link, to Third World victim of oppression. Representing changing Anglo-American conceptions of primitive man, Shakespeare's island native "once represented bestial vices that must be eliminated; now he personifies noble rebels who symbolize the exploitation of European imperialism" (p. 390). Caliban, in a word, represents society's "Other," a thing of darkness we must acknowledge as our own.

1764. WICKHAM, GLYNNE. "Masque and Anti-Masque in *The Tempest*." *Essays and Studies*, n.s. 28 (1975):1–14.

Argues that *The Tempest* operates on three levels—theatrical romance, political commentary, and metaphysical allusion. The phantom banquet of act 3 serves as antimasque, the heavenly vision of act 4 as the masque. Prospero controls both, haunting Alonso and Antonio in the one and rewarding Miranda and Ferdinand in the other. On the political level, alluded to in the prologue and the epilogue, reference is to the wedding and prosperity of Scotland and England through King James and to the hope for the future in the younger generation of Henry, Prince of Wales, and Elizabeth.

1765. WILLIAM, DAVID. "*The Tempest* on the Stage." In *Jacobean Theatre*. Edited by John Russell Brown and Bernard Harris. Stratford-upon-Avon Studies, 1. London: Edward Arnold, 1960, pp. 133–57.

Notes that no other Shakespearean play so tempts a director to such exaggerated emphasis on scenery, spectacle, and costume. The danger lies in blurring the play's major focus on Prospero, whose moral decision to renounce vengeance provides the resolution of the action. An effective production must reveal the tension between his rational desire to tell the story objectively and the passion that both his recollections and the contemporary action sporadically generate. All elements must cohesively yield a primary dramatic interest in Prospero and the impact of past and present events on his decision concerning Alonso and Antonio.

1766. WILLIS, DEBORAH. "Shakespeare's *Tempest* and the Discourse of Colonialism." *Studies in English Literature 1500–1900* 29 (1989):277–89.

Sees the play as the celebration of an ideal ruler, one who can contain a tendency toward oligarchy and division, and identifies Antonio (not Caliban) as the threatening "Other." Antonio is fashioned out of Shakespeare's culture's anxieties "about factious and rebellious aristocrats and by aggressions unmodulated by a sense of familial or communal bonds" (p. 286). His earlier actions against Prospero, along with his excitement of Sebastian to usurpation and murder, suggest a kind of pathological addiction to treason and fratricide. What makes him more sinister is his inability to bond with any kind of normal affection.

1767. WILSON, JOHN DOVER. *The Meaning of "The Tempest."* Newcastle upon Tyne: Literary and Philosophical Society, 1936, 23 pp.

Locates the meaning of *The Tempest* in its spiritual mood, a mood all the more significant because Shakespeare's mind has already experienced *Hamlet* and *King Lear*. There can be little doubt that the play is Shakespeare's valedictory; that he himself probably played the role of Prospero at a court performance lends added poignancy to the epilogue. While each of the romances develops the theme of reconciliation and forgiveness, *The Tempest* has an especially powerful atmosphere of serenity and peace. Shakespeare's tragic vision of life in act 1 is confronted with his new vision in the resolution.

1768. ZIMBARDO, ROSE. "Form and Disorder in *The Tempest*." *Shakespeare Quarterly* 14 (1963):49–56.

Does not consider *The Tempest* a part of the last plays dealing with the theme of regeneration. The play focuses, instead, on the continuous conflict between order and chaos, specifically on the limited ability of art to impose form on that which is chaotic. Prospero is a very human artist, irascible at times in his confrontation with evil he cannot control. He is able to subject the travelers to the ordering influence of his art; but it is at best temporary, and Caliban, the "incarnation of chaos," defies even that degree of order.

Stage History

1769. SUMMERS, MONTAGUE, ed. *Shakespeare's Adaptations: "The Tempest," "The Mock Tempest," and "King Lear."* London: J. Cape, 1922, 282 pp.
Includes William Davenant and John Dryden's *The Tempest, or the Enchanted Island* (1670) and Thomas Duffet's *The Mock Tempest: or the Enchanted Castle* (1675), and Nahum Tate's *The History of King Lear* (1681). The preface describes the nature of the three texts, and the extensive introduction traces the popularity of Shakespeare's plays in the Restoration and the general manner in which they were modified. While it is proper to condemn alterations in Shakespeare's texts, we must remember that it is still frequently done today. Generally, the Restoration adaptations were the works of "playwrights of practical knowledge and no inconsiderable talent" (p. cviii).

THE WINTER'S TALE

Reference Work

1770. MARDER, LOUIS, COMP. *"The Winter's Tale": A Supplementary Bibliography 1898–1965.* The New Shakespeare Variorum. New York: American Scholar Publications, 1965, 17 pp.
Includes representative scholarship on *The Winter's Tale* from 1898 to 1965 and is intended to supplement H. H. Furness's Variorum edition of 1898. The material is categorized under reproductions of original folio editions, bibliographical sources, modern editions, and critical studies (arranged alphabetically). While not exhaustive, the material represents every major category of scholarship and criticism.

Editions

1771. PAFFORD, J. H. F., ed. *The Winter's Tale*. The Arden Shakespeare. London: Methuen; Cambridge, Mass.: Harvard University Press, 1963, 225 pp.

Includes discussion of the text, date and authorship, sources, and critical interpretations, as well as appendixes covering music and the songs, the stage history, and a selection from Greene's *Pandosto*. The text is based on the First Folio, for which the copy was probably an edited transcript made by the scrivener Ralph Crane possibly from Shakespeare's foul papers. For *The Winter's Tale*, which shares common characteristics with *Pericles*, *Cymbeline*, and *The Tempest*, the keynote is that it is experimental, directed to the new tastes for the court masque or for the private theater or for variations of the theme of reconciliation.

1772. QUILLER-COUCH, ARTHUR, AND WILSON, JOHN DOVER, eds. *The Winter's Tale*. Cambridge: Cambridge University Press, 1931, 206 pp.

Provides extensive textual notes, a discussion of the copy text, a critical introduction, a section on stage history, and a glossary. This edition is based on the First Folio, for which the copy was probably an assembled text prepared from individual parts by the scrivener Ralph Crane. Shakespeare's alterations from Greene's *Pandosto* are discussed at length—for example, the acceleration of Leontes's jealousy, the interchange of kingdoms, the removal of Leontes's incestuous desire, the "resurrection" of Hermione. Generally the play reflects Shakespeare's declining dramatic powers, but the beauty of the setting, the language, and the theme of reconciliation amply redeem it.

Criticism

1773. BETHELL, S. L. *"The Winter's Tale": A Study*. New York and London: Staples Press, 1947, 128 pp.

Describes *The Winter's Tale*, with its synthesis of natural and supernatural and its elevation of the natural to a genuine and universal symbolism, as "the supreme literary example of the Baroque" (p. 110). In it the medieval and the classical coexist in both form and matter. The Hellenic-medieval romance (Florizel-Perdita) has been fused with the otherworldliness of orthodox medieval religion (Leontes-Hermione). The natural virtue of Florizel and Perdita restores family and kingdom, but that virtue has been earned by Hermione's submission and Leontes's penitence.

1774. BIGGINS, DENNIS. " 'Exit Pursued by a Bear': A Problem in *The Winter's Tale.*" *Shakespeare Quarterly* 13 (1962):3–13.

Argues that Shakespeare's audience would have reacted seriously to the bear scene in *The Winter's Tale*. Indeed, the scene has a tonal, symbolic, and structural function. It focuses on Leontes's brutality and false suspicion of Antigonus and dramatically destroys those qualities, symbolically purging the tragic world. Antigonus in his own words has reduced himself to a level of wild beasts in agreeing to carry out Leontes's tyrannical command, and it is ironically appropriate that he should be killed by such a beast. Occurring in a storm that reflects an angry providence, this action both spares the innocent child and destroys the corrupt agent of tyranny.

1775. BLISSETT, WILLIAM. "This Wide Gap of Time: *The Winter's Tale.*" *English Literary Renaissance* 1 (1971):52–70.

Concentrates on the contrast between the tragic and comic halves of the play with Leontes offending and Polixenes in a state of innocence in the first and Polixenes offending and Leontes in a state of penitence in the second. Time's gesture of turning the hourglass marks the division between the two. Destructive time characterizes acts 1–3; redeeming time, acts 4–5. Leontes's final words about the "wide gap" of sixteen years refer to the redemption involved in his penitential process but echo as well Ovid's reference to time as an engulfing mouth of destruction.

1776. BONJOUR, ADRIEN. "Polixenes and the Winter of His Discontent." *English Studies* 50 (1969):206–12.

Focuses on the parallel outbursts of temper by Leontes in act 1 and by Polixenes in act 4 of *The Winter's Tale*. Previous critics have erred in stressing the similarities rather than the differences. Whereas Leontes is in dead earnest in his threats against Polixenes and his wife and we fear for the life of the newborn infant, Polixenes's threats are but shadows. Since the spectators know Florizel's decision to be true to Perdita and the real identity of Perdita, their attitudes and feelings are controlled in a manner totally unlike the situation in act 1.

1777. BRISTOL, MICHAEL D. "In Search of the Bear: Spatiotemporal Form and the Heterogeneity of Economies in *The Winter's Tale.*" *Shakespeare Quarterly* 42 (1991):145–67.

The Winter's Tale

Suggests that *The Winter's Tale* is situated between two "narrative space-times," that the first half of the play deals with Winter Festival or Christmastide and the last half with the post-Lenten season of Pentecost. The first is characterized by the ethos of gift, hospitality, and expenditure (reflected in Leontes's fierce battle with Polixenes for honor and prestige in his role as host), the latter in the agricultural and market activities of the sheepshearing scene. The point of demarcation between the two seasons was in England the appearance of the straw bear on Plough Monday, and it is in that context that the bear assumes a significance within the rhythmic pattern of the play.

1778. BRYANT, JERRY H. "*The Winter's Tale* and the Pastoral Tradition." *Shakespeare Quarterly* 14 (1963):387–98.

Asserts that Shakespeare transcends the Greek, Roman, and Italian pastoral tradition in *The Winter's Tale* by transforming its conventions into a subtle commentary on the nature of truth, specifically the dangers of assuming appearance to be reality. Both Florizel's ability to see truth through pastoral disguise and Autolycus's recognition of himself as a knave serve as a foil to Leontes's blindness and delusions. The pastoral episode in act 4 prepares the cure for Leontes's infected mind in act 5.

1779. BRYANT, JOSEPH A., Jr. "Shakespeare's Allegory: *The Winter's Tale*." *Sewanee Review* 63 (1955):202–22.

Views *The Winter's Tale* as a parable of sin and redemption, a Pauline pattern for salvation, with Hermione symbolizing St. Paul's Christ who saves by grace, Leontes the Jew, Mamillius the Jewish church in his death, and Perdita the true church. The play thus participates in an action which is "Christian, divine, and eternal." In act 4 Shakespeare uses the same metaphor of grafting regarding the relationship of Florizel and Perdita that Paul used to refer to the union of the Gentile and the church.

1780. COX, LEE SHERIDAN. "The Role of Autolycus in *The Winter's Tale*." *Studies in English Literature 1500–1900* 9 (1969):283–301.

Perceives Autolycus, a tale-teller and singer, rogue agent of providence, man of masks and busy clothes-changer, as furnishing an important counterpart to the story of Leontes and as serving to advance the theme of appearance versus reality. Since it is by his interference that Perdita's revelation occurs, he can be seen as an agent of a superior power for good. His first appearance—as a victim robbed by Autolycus—parallels the self-destructive nature of Leontes's wrongdoing.

1781. EWBANK, INGA-STINA. "From Narrative to Dramatic Language: *The Winter's Tale* and Its Source." In *Shakespeare and The Sense of Perfor-*

mance: Essays in the Tradition of Performance Criticism in Honor of Bernard Beckerman. Edited by Marvin Thompson and Ruth Thompson. Newark: University of Delaware Press; London and Toronto: Associated University Presses, 1989, pp. 29–47.

Observes that, whereas Greene's language is general and his characters broadly drawn, Shakespeare's language renders experience and his characters are drawn vividly within the moment. Greene, for example, has the king's jealousy develop slowly and credibly over a long period of time. Shakespeare's Leontes, to the contrary, dramatizes an explosion with terrifyingly precise language. Recent productions tend to depend on visual symbolism for language and emblems for words and thus run the risk of minimizing the effects of Shakespeare's magic and realism.

1782. FELPERIN, HOWARD. "Tongue-Tied Our Queen?: The Deconstruction of Presence in *The Winter's Tale.*" In *Shakespeare and the Question of Theory*. Edited by Patricia Parker and Geoffrey Hartman. New York and London: Methuen, 1985, pp. 3–18.

Questions the definitiveness of the oracular pronouncement as the basis for the critics' happy consensus that Hermione is chaste. Once cut off from their divine origin, the words enter the realm of "the human, the fallible, the ambiguous, in sum, the interpretable" (p. 8). Many of Hermione's words to Polixenes, for example, may be considered either inside or outside the bounds of royal hospitality and wifely decorum. The words lack ontological stability, a situation parodied in the "certified truth" of Autolycus's ballads. In *The Winter's Tale* the "backgrounding of the divine referee . . . becomes the condition for a new and extraordinary realism" (p. 16).

1783. FREY, CHARLES. *Shakespeare's Vast Romance: A Study of "The Winter's Tale."* Columbia and London: University of Missouri Press, 1980, 174 pp.

Consists of three major sections—a selective history of critical responses to the play, a discussion of the play in the context of Shakespeare's development and of his use of Greene's *Pandosto* as a source, and an analysis of the play itself. *The Winter's Tale*, quite the opposite of a philosophic play, is a drama of sudden, spontaneous, and manifold action demanding both aesthetic and intellectual assent. The vastness of its design forces us to realize that, if it is a work of delight, it also radically shocks in its vision of regeneration and redemption.

1784. FRYE, NORTHROP. "Recognition in *The Winter's Tale.*" In *Essays on Shakespeare and Elizabethan Drama in Honor of Hardin Craig*. Edited by

The Winter's Tale

Richard Hosley. Columbia: University of Missouri Press, 1962, pp. 235–46.

Observes that the two halves of *The Winter's Tale* form a diptych of parallel or contrasting actions. The first deals with age, jealousy, winter, and death; the other with youth, summer, love, and life. Symbolically central to the action is the natural cycle of seasons from winter to summer and the human cycle of the passage of sixteen years. The play ends with a double recognition—that of Perdita's parentage and that of the awakened statue of Hermione and her reunion with daughter and husband. Leontes and the spectators share in a sense of participation in the redeeming and relative power of nature.

1785. GARNER, STANTON B. "Time and Presence in *The Winter's Tale*." *Modern Language Quarterly* 46 (1985):347–67.

Notes that the play in its diptych presents the experience of time in terms of a paradoxical duality. On the one hand, man lives so fully in the immediacy of the moment that he seems to escape time. On the other hand, the stage presence of Leontes and Polixenes is a vivid reminder of passing time and its fleeting present moment. The second half of the play forces the characters to come to terms with time's changes and the consequences. Shakespeare builds such rhythms into the play's dramaturgy and stagecraft so pervasively that the audience, too, must come to terms with the fundamental duality.

1786. GRANTLEY, DARRYLL. "*The Winter's Tale* and Early Religious Drama." *Comparative Drama* 20 (1986–87):17–37.

Investigates *The Winter's Tale* as a drama of redemption, noting that the tragic loss of Mamillius and Antigonus figures the serious result of sinful action against which the process of redemption works. Leontes and to some extent Polixenes resemble the Mankind figures of moral interludes; similarly, the females are constructed in terms of moral forces. Pauline, for example, both in her monitory role and subsequently as moral mentor during Leontes's penitence, resembles Conscience. Hermione's role conflates aspects of both Christ and the Virgin Mary. Shakespeare is drawing on the rich religious traditions of earlier drama.

1787. GURR, ANDREW. "The Bear, the Statue, and Hysteria in *The Winter's Tale*." *Shakespeare Quarterly* 34 (1983):420–25.

Focuses on the significance of the bear and statue episodes as matching counterparts that conclude respectively the tragic and comic halves of the play. Both events blatantly challenge credulity and transform tragedy into comedy through the exploitation of theatrical illusion. In the first half passions prevail at court; in the last half art prevails in the natural world of the shepherds. This art used to disguise nature is comically symbolized by Autolycus, who on three occasions deceives the same audience with disguises.

1788. KETTERER, ROBERT C. "Machines for the Suppression of Time: Statues in *Suor Angelica, The Winter's Tale,* and *Alcestis.*" *Comparative Drama* 24 (1990–91):3–23.

Examines three narratives based on a pattern of error, repentance, death, and resurrection, all employing the motif of the statue-come-to-life that drives their final scenes. In each case the statue seems to suppress time by erasing its effects in a moment of wondrous resurrection. Yet, equally important, the ends are implicit in their beginnings. The title of Shakespeare's play in itself suggests a story of wonder and surprise. Moreover, the plot is governed by the cycle of the seasons. Of the three works, only *The Winter's Tale* successfully incorporates the problematic passage of time with its suppression—the principals are wrinkled; years are wasted; no miracle of resurrection erases that fact.

1789. KURLAND, STUART M. " 'We Need No More of Your Advice'; Political Realism in *The Winter's Tale.*" *Studies in English Literature 1500–1900* 31 (1991):365–86.

Believes that Shakespeare in this play consciously foregrounds the significance of courtly counsel between a king and his advisers, an issue of particular concern at the time of composition. Camillo, for example, unsuccessfully attempts to advise Leontes on the limits of royal prerogative, as did a book (Cowell's *Interpreter*) that James suppressed by proclamation in 1610. In matters of royal advice and succession, *The Winter's Tale* is genuinely engaged with political issues of considerable contemporary importance.

1790. LANDE, MAYDEE G. "*The Winter's Tale:* A Question of Motive." *American Imago* 43 (1986):51–67.

Insists that Leontes's jealous rage is caused, not by repressed homosexual desire or by an oedipal desire for fusion with a maternal object, but by what he perceives as an "all-inclusive attack upon his power to rule, to order experience, to control, to demand submission" (p. 59). Unable to control his wife or his subjects, he comes increasingly to believe he is an object of scorn to all around him. His desperate attempt to reorder his life collapses when—through the oracle—he is unable, as well, to control his god. The decisive clues to understanding his jealousy and despondency are his words, not psychoanalytic theory.

The Winter's Tale

1791. LAWLOR, JOHN J. "*Pandosto* and the Nature of Dramatic Providence."
Philological Quarterly 41 (1962):96–113.

Explores the major differences between Greene's *Pandosto* and *The
Winter's Tale* as an aid to addressing the characteristics of romance as a
dramatic form. Shakespeare's major changes involve the development in
Leontes of jealous passion followed by lengthy repentance, the omission of crude low comedy, the use of the sheepshearing festival as a
meeting place for the young and old. Most important, he invests
Greene's subtitle "The Triumph of Time" with new meaning in preserving Hermione and allowing Leontes to be reconciled with her and
his daughter. Both the story of Leontes and Hermione and that of
Perdita and Florizel gain richest meaning in the complex manner in
which they are interwoven.

1792. McDONALD, RUSS. "Poetry and Plot in *The Winter's Tale*." *Shakespeare
Quarterly* 36 (1985):315–29.

Demonstrates that the style of the play is a microcosm of its tragicomic structure. In tragicomedy the shape and meaning of events become apparent only in the final moments; events build in a convoluted
manner toward apparent disaster only to explode at the end into benign
resolution and clarity. The sentences do the same thing. Convoluted
sentences or difficult speeches become coherent only in the final clause
or movement; sentences gain momentum through grammatical obfuscation or suspension and then "discharge powerfully or unexpectedly"
(p. 316). In *The Winter's Tale* and other romances poetry and syntax
become an extension of the plot.

1793. MAGNUSSON, A. LYNNE. "Finding Place for a Faultless Lyric: Verbal
Virtuosity in *The Winter's Tale*." *Upstart Crow* 9 (1989):96–106.

Focuses on Florizel's love lyric to Perdita, "What you do, / Still
betters what is done." Traditionally, the love lyric, of all literary genres,
was most closely tied to elaborate comparison of the woman with
external objects. Florizel's lyric, to the contrary, sets its gaze intently on
Perdita itself, finding her queenliness in her everyday activities and in
dramatic context responding to her reluctance to play-act at being a
goddess by urging her merely to be herself. The idea of the lyric is also
the idea of the play—the ideal for Leontes is Hermione with wrinkles.

1794. MIKO, STEPHEN J. "Winter's Tale." *Studies in English Literature 1500–
1900* 29 (1989):259–75.

Insists that Shakespeare in the last plays was engaged in a kind of
playful experimentation, especially with those literary conventions intended to control the spectators' response to death, obsession, extreme

or contrary emotions, and the desire for a fixed world in a teleological system. The bear scene, for example, is calculatingly comic and thus jolting. Similarly, an oblique response is generated by Leontes's burst of jealousy in the opening act. We can react to Hermione's "resurrection" either as a humanized act of divine grace or a clever joke on Paulina's part. In a word, we can consciously watch the play in the making and "cast our lots with one set of conventions over another" (p. 273).

1795. Morse, William R. "Metacriticism and Materiality: The Case of Shakespeare's *The Winter's Tale.*" *ELH* 58 (1991):283–304.

Maintains that the play interrogates not only the dominance of the court ideology but also that of analytico-referential discourse. Actively assuming the typicality of the royal family and its psychic drama, it "suggests that the emergent ideology is already achieving cultural dominance" (p. 289). Leontes's characterization embodies the modern essentialist conception of an autonomous independent consciousness, a rationalist ideology. At the same time, however, through its stylization that play draws attention to the artifice of human action, thus creating an "epistemic rupture . . . of two discourses" (p. 296).

1796. Pafford, J. H. F. "Music, and the Songs in *The Winter's Tale.*" *Shakespeare Quarterly* 10 (1950):161–75.

Notes that the chief musical element in *The Winter's Tale* is in the singing roles of Autolycus, Dorcas, and Mopsa. The songs in the text, the numerous references to songs and ballads, and the dances constitute a variety of musical styles from the period. The music, moreover, is integral to the play, contributing much to the spirit of the sheepshearing scene and much to the personality of the clown. Seventeenth-century musical texts exist for "Whoop do me no harm good man," "Jog on," and "Lawn as white as driven snow." The songs, in Shakespeare's late style, help to date the play.

1797. Pyle, Fitzroy. *"The Winter's Tale": A Commentary on the Structure.* London: Routledge & Kegan Paul; New York: Barnes & Noble, 1969, 195 pp.

Offers a scene-by-scene analysis of *The Winter's Tale* as a transmutation of the source, Robert Greene's *Pandosto.* The highly unified play combines courtly and popular elements in a setting of pastoral romance. By keeping Leontes alive, restoring Hermione to life, and linking Hermione's return with the discovery of Perdita, Shakespeare gives organic character to Greene's welter of events. Hermione's apparent resurrection from the dead, a shock of amazement to Leontes and to the spectators as well, characterizes the power of the human spirit to achieve the miraculous.

1798. RANDALL, DALE B. J. " 'This Is the Chase': Or, The Further Pursuit of the Bear." *Shakespeare Jahrbuch* 121 (1985):89–95.

Observes that the bear scene is equidistant between the exploration of Leontes's jealousy and the resurrection of Hermione's statue and that it serves as a fulcrum for Shakespeare on which the tragic and comic halves are counterpoised. Each half ends with a highly fictive *coup de théâtre,* but the bear and statue episode are different in virtually every respect. The one is played against a roar leading to death, the other against hushed silence leading to new life. Possibly, also, in the bear scene Shakespeare is making a wry comment on theatrical taste through an allusion to Horace's observation that the rabble delights in bears.

1799. RONK, MARTHA. "Recasting Jealousy: A Reading of *The Winter's Tale.*" *Literature and Psychology* 36 (1990):50–78.

Suggests that Leontes's retreat into a potential silence in 3.3 signals as well a retreat into the imagination and recreation of the past and provides—in juxtaposition to the images of procreation, pregnancy, and fertility in act 4—a psychological basis for his spiritual transformation. We understand his withdrawal into himself and the phases of his penitence by what occurs onstage. The storm scene symbolizes that what is occurring within him is painful and discomforting. In the final act he is witness to "that which is more wondrous and powerful than even he could have dreamed possible" (p. 74).

1800. SCHANZER, ERNEST. "The Structural Pattern of *The Winter's Tale.*" *Review of English Literature* 5 (1964):72–82.

Claims that *Pericles* provides a model for *The Winter's Tale* in structure, plot, and imagery. In both cases acts 1–3 focus on a royal father; act 4, following a great lapse of time, is devoted to the daughter; and act 5 fuses the two elements through a double reunion. In both cases the first half is basically destructive and the second half constructive. In both a harmonious relationship is shattered, and the early acts are marked by images of uprooting, blight, and infection. "Great creating nature" becomes virtually a character in itself in the final acts.

1801. SCHWARTZ, MURRAY M. "Leontes's Jealousy in *The Winter's Tale.*" *American Imago* 30 (1974):250–73.

Claims that Leontes's sudden jealousy in act 1 is a result of a repressed homosexual interest in Polixenes that precipitates the development of paranoia. This paranoia is a form of psychic imprisonment that perverts the mutuality and innocence of their boyhood friendship. Leontes tries desperately to exclude himself from the fantasies he projects onto both Hermione and Polixenes. The focus of the final act is on the process of recovery.

1802. TAYLOR, JOHN. "The Patience of *The Winter's Tale.*" *Essays in Criticism* 23 (1973):333–56.

Describes the structure of the play as a series of four emotional peaks (Leontes's jealousy, Polixenes's rage against his son, Perdita's sudden acceptance of her role as mistress of the sheepshearing feast, and Leontes's outburst of love before the living Hermione), all the result of a long passage of time and of something beyond human design. The great lesson of these events is the virtue of patience. The spectators, too, gain patience as the play progresses, almost expecting a miracle in act 5 by which the resolution will be effected.

1803. WARD, DAVID. "Affection, Intention, and Dreams in *The Winter's Tale.*" *Modern Language Review* 82 (1987):545–54.

Argues that Leontes, in the oft-discussed passage beginning with his "Can thy dam?—may't be?— / Affection! thy intention stabs the centre" (1.2.137–38) is attempting in a positive spirit to diagnose his own psychological condition. The lines mean "Could your mother [really commit adultery, or] may it be affection? which" by intensifying every passion in me "wounds and disables the centre [of my being, the soul]?" (pp. 549–50). Standing back momentarily from the disease, Leontes tries to assess it for what it is. His next speech to Polixenes is not ironic or a cover for his inward hatred, but a genuine attempt to regain composure.

1804. WILLIAMS, JOHN A. *The Natural Work of Art: The Experience of Romance in Shakespeare's "The Winter's Tale."* Cambridge, Mass.: Harvard University Press, 1967, 47 pp.

Describes Shakespearean romance as a poetic solution to the metaphysical problem of mutability in human life. Shakespeare in *The Winter's Tale* replaces Leontes's experience of pain with that of wonder, guiding him to a new perception of man at the center of a beneficent creation. Nature in this vision of art becomes the means by which hope and happiness are sustained even in the midst of pain and death, namely in the multiple generations of life. The transformation of Hermione's statue caps Leontes's realization of the necessity of patience in attuning oneself to natural order.

1805. WILSON, HAROLD S. " 'Nature and Art' in *The Winter's Tale.*" *Shakespeare Association Bulletin* 18 (1943):114–20.

The Winter's Tale

Describes the passage in which Perdita and Polixenes discuss the merits of artificial flowers (4.4.79ff.), a variation of the relative merits of nature and art, as commonplace both in antiquity and in the Renaissance. Examples are cited from Plato, Aristotle, Cicero, Petrarch, Daniello, Peletier, Sidney, and Daniel. A particular passage is quoted at length from George Puttenham's *Art of English Poetry* as the probable source for Shakespeare's dialogue. Drawn from agriculture, it describes art as an alterer and surmounter of nature's skill.

1806. ZIEGLER, GEORGIANA. "Parents, Daughters, and 'That Rare Italian Master': A New Source for *The Winter's Tale*." *Shakespeare Quarterly* 36 (1985):204–12.

Suggests that Shakespeare's reference to Julio Romano may have been derived from the English translation of a book of instruction for young women by Giovanni Bruto that mentions the Italian artist by name. The book was printed in 1598 by Adam Islip, and it is likely that Shakespeare would have known the work since he made use of other translations by Islip. Moreover, there are suggestive similarities between Bruto's volume and *The Winter's Tale*. Both fathers are separated from their daughters, both have lost their wives, and both raise questions about the proper nurture of a daughter.

Stage History

1807. BARTHOLOMEUSZ, DENNIS. *"The Winter's Tale" in Performance in England and America 1611–1976*. Cambridge: Cambridge University Press, 1982, 279 pp.

Traces major performances of *The Winter's Tale* from Jacobean England through the mid-twentieth century. Particular attention is directed to productions by John Philip Kemble, William Charles Macready, Samuel Phelps, Charles Kean, Lawrence Barrett, Herbert Beerbohm Tree, Trevor Nunn, and Peter Brook. Analysis of textual cuts, costuming, set designs, and music reflects the various stage interpretations and the shifting impact of the play's theme. A table of performances and theaters is included.

Index

Note: References are to entry numbers; italic numbers in listings for play titles indicate entries specifically on that play.